Global Economic Issues and Policies

Third edition

This introduction to all aspects of international economics, public policy, business, and finance is the clearest guide available to the economics of the world we inhabit. Written in a highly engaging style, packed full of up-to-date, real-world case studies, and pitched at an introductory level, the book does an expert job of drawing in students, and will equip them with a comprehensive toolkit of methods and essential facts. Covering the wide range of economic issues and policies generated by globalization, the text provides an introduction to the topic that emphasizes facts as well as theories, presenting economic concepts clearly and in detail.

This third edition reflects continuing developments in the world economy and in the analysis of international economics. Chapter introductions, pedagogy, and data have all been thoroughly updated, and key topics for expansion and revision include:

- Free trade versus fair trade
- Bilateral and multilateral treaties
- International outsourcing
- Public perceptions of international trade
- The trilemma issue
- Business-cycle synchronization
- Central bank emergency tools
- Sovereign-debt problems

This text is suitable for any introductory module in international economics, public policy, and business, whether taught as part of an economics, public policy, business, or international studies program. It is also the ideal MBA-level introduction to the global economy.

Joseph P. Daniels is Professor and Chair of Economics at Marquette University, USA.

David D. VanHoose is Professor of Economics and Herman W. Lay Professor of Private Enterprise at the Hankamer School of Business at Baylor University, Texas, USA.

Global Economic Issues and Policies

Third edition

**Joseph P. Daniels and
David D. VanHoose**

Routledge
Taylor & Francis Group

LONDON AND NEW YORK

First edition published 2004,
Second edition published 2011,
Third edition published 2014
by Routledge
2 Park Square, Milton Park, Abingdon, Oxon OX14 4RN

and by Routledge
711 Third Avenue, New York, NY 10017

Routledge is an imprint of the Taylor & Francis Group, an informa business

British Library Cataloguing in Publication Data
A catalogue record for this book is available from the British Library

Library of Congress Cataloging-in-Publication Data
Daniels, Joseph P.
Global economic issues and policies / Joseph P. Daniels and David VanHoose.
– 3rd edition.
pages cm
1. Economics. 2. Economic policy. 3. Globalization–Economic aspects.
4. International economic relations. 5. International trade. 6. International finance.
I. VanHoose, David D. II. Title.
HB171.5.D164 2014
337–dc23   2013038836

ISBN: 978-0-415-71020-6 (hbk)
ISBN: 978-0-415-71019-0 (pbk)
ISBN: 978-1-315-79674-1 (ebk)

Typeset in Perpetua and Bell Gothic
by Sunrise Setting Ltd, Paignton, UK

Printed and bound in the United States of America by Edwards Brothers Malloy, Inc.

Dedications

To Cindy—J.D.
To Carol—D.V.

Contents

List of illustrations

TABLES

Preface

Identifying accessible yet high-quality textbooks addressing the complete set of topics appropriate for a survey course covering global economic issues and policies is often a challenging task for instructors. Of course, instructors can readily find numerous good texts on international economics. The bulk of these books, however, presume a relatively sophisticated audience, made up of students who have completed courses in principles of economics or, in many cases, even intermediate economics. In the past, this presumption was sensible because most of the students interested in taking courses in international economics were economics students.

Nevertheless, a growing number of students in business and public policy programs have become excited about studying the economic issues confronting the global economy. Consequently, students enrolling in a global economics course today have much more diverse academic backgrounds than in years past. Fewer students are interested in being immersed in economic theory. Our key objective in writing *Global Economic Issues and Policies* has been to develop a book suitable for this group of students. We have aimed to write a book accomplishing the following:

- Covering the wide range of economic issues and policies generated by globalization
- Emphasizing *facts*, as well as theories
- Providing a general student with only the *essential* theoretical concepts required to understand the various economic issues associated with globalization
- Relying only on *principles* of economics to acquaint students with the fundamentals of issues and policies in international trade and finance
- Communicating key economic concepts *verbally* and using diagrams only as an additional—and optional—means of reinforcing student understanding

In an effort to achieve these goals, this text has the following features:

- The text addresses a full set of topics relating to globalization:

    - Why nations trade
    - How governments regulate international trade
    - Regionalism and multilateralism in trade policies
    - The role of foreign exchange markets and exchange-rate arrangements

- Public policy issues in international money and finance
- Effects of globalization on both the developed nations and emerging economies
- Industrial and public sector policies in the global economy
- Economic development
- Policies regarding financial crises and the international financial architecture

■ All chapters emphasize factual information about the global economy
■ Every new economic concept is introduced and explained within the text, without requiring an instructor to rely on economic diagrams to teach the material
■ All topics are discussed at a principles level, so that even students who have not taken a course in economic principles can develop the tools they require to understand how to apply economic concepts to global economic issues and policies
■ All theoretical diagrams appear alongside self-contained "Visualizing global economic issues" features. These features are designed to reinforce economic concepts, which are introduced and explained within the text without reliance on the diagrams. Thus, an instructor can choose to cover all, some, or none of the theoretical diagrams
■ A range of supplements to the text are available on the Website: www.routledge.com/cw/daniels.

FEATURES THAT TEACH AND REINFORCE

To further motivate student learning, we have included examples drawn from nations throughout the world. In addition, four types of application feature are incorporated throughout the text.

Policy notebook

Events relating to global economic policymaking dominate the news. Hence, features covering a wide range of important policy issues appear at appropriate locations. Topics covered include:

■ Gains from international trade in nineteenth-century Japan
■ Indian transportation gridlock hinders international trade flows
■ Many African nations have finally progressed beyond "paper" regional trade agreements
■ Trade-creation outcomes for APEC member nations
■ Germany—and perhaps Texas—wants gold deposits back from the Federal Reserve
■ As the Egyptian pound gets pounded, the nation's foreign exchange reserves disappear
■ Could new U.S. exports to China cause mint tea to taste like coal?
■ Euros are all the same everywhere except in Cyprus

Management notebook

To acquaint students with the variety of issues faced by business managers in a globalized economy, we have included features on topics such as the following:

- Explaining the two most recent globalization waves
- Using ice-class shipping to reduce the opportunity cost of the international distribution of natural gas
- U.S. taxpayers subsidize foreign buyers of U.S. exports—and foreign rivals of U.S. firms
- Covered interest-parity breakdowns during the financial crisis—developed versus emerging economies
- The European Monetary Union's tribulations create uncertainties for firms operating within African currency unions
- China's steel industry sneezes, and employment at many U.S. coal mines suffers a near-death experience
- The mysteriously growing importance of distance in international trade
- U.S. airlines make room for Canadian air travelers—who pay more U.S. taxes and fewer Canadian taxes

Online globalization

The Internet has emerged as an important factor in international trade and finance. Students can learn more about the role of global electronic commerce in features such as the following:

- Why the international spread of Internet hosts is a globalization indicator
- Iceland discovers a comparative advantage in operating data centers
- French booksellers confront an e-book threat to a quota's protection from foreign book imports
- Will regional trade agreements break a multilateral logjam on global e-commerce?
- A threatened ban on credit cards could curtail consumer currency trading
- In Iran, the unofficial quantity of circulating money includes a Web currency
- A rise in online purchases of imported goods raises employment of motorbike delivery drivers in Nigeria
- A global exporter of consumer goods differentiates its product

Visualizing global economic issues

Economic diagrams often help students gain a deeper understanding of how economists apply essential concepts and theories to better understand global economic issues and policies. Topics covered in features relating to diagrammatic explanations of key issues include the following:

- The demand and supply curves
- Production possibilities frontiers and comparative advantage

- The factor price equalization theorem
- A tariff in a small-country setting
- Trade creation versus trade diversion in a three-country world
- The dollar demand-euro supply relationship
- Why covered interest parity is often satisfied
- The wage and employment effects of increased competition from abroad
- International trade and economies of scale
- Foreign monopoly and dumping in a domestic market—who gains, and who loses?

Critical thinking exercises

Critical thinking is an important aspect of every college student's education. We make sure that students are introduced to critical-thinking activities by ending each applications feature with critical-thinking questions called "For critical analysis." The suggested answers to these critical-thinking questions are included in the Instructor's Manual.

CONNECTING TO GLOBAL ECONOMIC ISSUES AND POLICIES ON THE WEB

Today, students around the world know how to use the Internet. We provide two very useful features for them:

- Margin URL: A feature entitled "On the Web" appears in the margins throughout the text. At appropriate locations relative to text discussions, a URL is presented that relates to the topic at hand.
- Online Application: Each chapter concludes with an extensive Internet exercise, which guides the student to a particular URL and provides application questions. Each Online Application concludes with a group exercise called "For group study and analysis."

SPECIAL NOTE ON THE GRAPHS

This textbook contains more than 80 charts and graphs. All lines and curves are shaded in a consistent manner to assist students in understanding the relationships depicted in the figures. In addition, full explanations are provided in the captions.

KEY PEDAGOGY

Student learning must be an active process. We have included an ample number of pedagogical devices to help students master the material.

Fundamental issues and answers

A key feature of *Global Economic Issues and Policies* is the inclusion of five to seven fundamental issues at the opening of each chapter. At appropriate locations within the chapter, these fundamental issues are repeated, and appropriate answers are provided.

This allows students to see clearly the relationship between the text materials and the fundamental issues while reading the chapter.

Vocabulary is emphasized

Vocabulary is often a stumbling block in economics courses, and this can be a particular difficulty for students in a course on international economics. Consequently, important vocabulary terms within the text appear in bold type and are defined in the margin. They are further defined in a Glossary at the end of the book.

Chapter summary

Each chapter contains a numbered summary that corresponds to the Fundamental Issues listed at the start of the chapter, further reinforcing the circular nature of the learning process for each chapter.

Questions and problems

Each chapter ends with several questions and problems. Suggested answers are provided in the Instructor's Manual.

References and recommended readings

Appropriate references for materials in the chapter are given in this section.

WEB-BASED SUPPLEMENTS

Global Economic Issues and Policies is supported by a full set of supplementary materials, available at www.routledge.com/cw/daniels.

Study guide

The online study guide includes a chapter overview, key terms and concepts, and true/false and multiple choice questions to aid students in their study.

Lecture slides

Instructors can download PowerPoint lecture slides for use in enhancing lectures and incorporating technology into the classroom, at www.routledge.com/cw/daniels.

Instructor's Manual/Test Bank

The Instructor's Manual/Test Bank is designed to simplify the teaching tasks faced by instructors of courses in international money and finance. It includes an outline of each chapter, possible response(s) to the critical thinking questions that conclude the pedagogical features, and answers to the end-of-chapter questions.

Acknowledgments

This third edition of *Global Economic Issues and Policies* benefited from very energetic and diligent reviewers. They were tough and critical, but the rewrites of the manuscript improved accordingly. To the following reviewers, we express our heartfelt appreciation for the constructive tone of your comments, which helped make this an improved text.

- Mikhail Melnik, Southern Polytechnic State University, USA.
- Bing Anderson, California Polytechnic State University, USA.

A textbook project is never completed solely by the authors. We are grateful to Commissioning Editor Emily Kindleysides for her direction, and to Editorial Assistant Laura Johnson for her hard work to keep everything on schedule. Additionally, thanks are due to Donald Watt, who did a good job of copy editing the manuscript, and to Eliza Wright for her careful proof-reading. Thank you to Senior Production Editor Emma Hart for her efforts in moving the book from manuscript to its final physical and electronic forms.

We are looking forward to continuing to revise this text as the global economy evolves during the coming years. Thus, we welcome comments and criticism from both students and instructors.

J.P.D.
D.D.V.

Unit I
Introduction to the global economy

Chapter 1

Understanding the global economy

FUNDAMENTAL ISSUES

1. Why study global economic issues and policies?
2. How important are global markets for goods and services?
3. How important are the international monetary and financial markets?
4. What are market supply and demand?
5. What are consumer surplus and producer surplus?
6. How are market prices determined?

In early 2013, an assessment of the global economic downturn that began in 2008 revealed the full extent of the setbacks experienced by the residents of many of the world's nations. For instance, the overall annual inflation-adjusted income of Germany's residents had experienced a 4-year setback, to its 2009 level. The aggregate annual inflation-adjusted earnings loss experienced by residents of France was 7 years, to a level previously observed in 2006. The number of years of setbacks were even greater in several other nations—9 years in Italy; 10 years in Spain, the United Kingdom, and Hungary; 11 years in Ireland, Portugal, and the United States; and 12 years in Iceland and Greece.

At the same time as the global income assessment was conducted, however, the annual inflation-adjusted volume of trade of goods and services among the world's nations had almost fully returned to the pre-downturn level. To be sure, between 2008 and 2009, the total amount of international trade fell by nearly 10 percent, and four full years passed before the volume of global trade returned to its 2008 level. Nevertheless, international trade among the world's nations recovered much more speedily than overall economic activity within many of those countries. Indeed, many economists credited the quick recovery of global trade flows for generating export earnings that helped prevent steeper income drops from taking place in a number of nations. Without international trade, they concluded, the income setbacks around the globe would have been even more pronounced.

What is globalization? What is the extent of global trade in goods and services? How important are the international capital markets? What concepts do economists use to examine international economic issues and policies? In this chapter you will begin your investigation of international economic issues and policies by addressing these questions.

GLOBAL ECONOMIC POLICY AND ISSUES

Globalization:

The increasing interconnectedness of peoples and societies and the interdependence of economies, governments, and environments.

The process of globalization and its impact on societies and peoples everywhere are topics of great importance today. In general, **globalization** is defined as the increasing interconnectedness of people and societies and the increasing interdependence of economies, governments, and environments. Despite all the attention paid to globalization, there is no clear-cut method for measuring its extent. Researchers have employed a number of measures, including the total duration of all international phone calls; the number of international travelers; the volume of trade in goods, services, and capital; co-movements of prices and interest rates; and the number of Internet servers per person. (To consider why economists have been paying closer attention to the last of these measures, see *Online Globalization: Why the international spread of Internet hosts is a globalization indicator*.)

ONLINE GLOBALIZATION

Why the international spread of Internet hosts is a globalization indicator

Since the early 1990s, the global number of Internet hosts has increased from only a few million to nearly 700 million. During the past decade, the number of Internet hosts in North America has more than doubled, and as a consequence North America has experienced the *least* growth of any of the world's continents. Over the same span, the number of Internet hosts in Europe has tripled and the number in Asia has more than quadrupled. In South America, the Middle East, and Africa, the number of hosts has risen by more than tenfold. The rapid growth of Internet hosts outside North America has been reflected by a redistribution of the world's online population. Today, only 15 percent of the world's people who are regularly online reside in North America. About 25 percent are in Europe, 40 percent in Asia, 10 percent in South America, and 5 percent in Africa.

Most people tend to buy online from firms located within their own continent. But continents contain multiple countries, so a share of the online purchases within those regions typically takes place across national borders. In this way, the spread of Internet access across the world's continents is translating into growth in the volume of global trade.

For critical analysis: Why do you suppose that people who buy items online from firms located in other nations tend to purchase most of those items from firms based in neighboring countries?

The most globalized nations

The KOF Swiss Economic Institute combines economic, political, and social measures in an attempt to measure the degree of globalization worldwide and to rank individual nations according to their degree of globalization. Table 1.1 shows the ranking of the ten most globalized nations and the ten least globalized. As the table indicates, it is the smaller advanced economies with relatively unrestricted financial markets that occupy the top positions. Though, in general, the industrialized nations tend to be the most globalized, the economies of South-Central Asia and Eastern Europe made the greatest advances in the globalization index.

Additional research on various measures of globalization attempts to determine if globalization is associated with civil liberties, political rights, levels of perceived corruption, and income patterns. There appears to be a clear direct relationship among greater civil liberties, more political rights, lower levels of corruption, and the level of globalization, but there is no clear pattern between the inequality of income patterns and globalization. Based on this information, it appears that increasing globalization brings real benefits to the citizens of globalizing nations. Nevertheless, as you will learn in later chapters, globalization can be a contentious topic.

ON THE WEB:

For timely articles on international issues and policies, visit Foreign Policy's home page at www.foreignpolicy.com.

Important issues advanced in this text

In this text you will consider many of the issues underlying globalization and assess the policies intended to manage global commerce. The next two sections of this chapter narrow the scope of analysis to focus on the economic components of globalization. We will concentrate on **economic integration**, which refers to the

Economic integration: *The extent and strength of real sector and financial sector linkages among national economies.*

Table 1.1 *The ten most and ten least globalized nations. Using several measures of global integration, economists at the KOF Swiss Economic Institute ranked the top ten most globalized nations and least globalized nations. The smaller advanced economies tend to be the most globalized countries.*

Rank	Nation	Rank	Nation
1	Belgium	178	Afghanistan
2	Ireland	179	Comoros
3	Netherlands	180	Liberia
4	Austria	181	Bhutan
5	Singapore	182	Eritrea
6	Denmark	183	Solomon Islands
7	Sweden	184	Equatorial Guinea
8	Portugal	185	Solomon Islands
9	Hungary	186	Kiribati
10	Switzerland	187	Timor-Leste

Source: globalization.kof.ethz.ch.

extent and strength of commercial linkages—international transactions in goods and services and exchanges of financial assets—among national economies.

Economic integration is arguably the most important—and the most contentious—element of globalization. So the economic aspects of globalization represent a dynamic and interesting area of study. Your study of international economic issues and policies will lead you to consider these topics:

- The benefits and costs of international trade in goods and services, and the global exchange of national currencies and financial assets
- The efficiency gains from increased trade in goods and services and unrestricted capital flows
- The distribution of gains and losses stemming from economic integration, and the regulation of international commerce
- The advantages and disadvantages of joining regional trade blocs that establish common rules governing the international trade of member nations
- The extent to which globalization benefits workers of developing and industrialized nations
- The implications of increased trade and capital flows for the world's environment
- The effects of globalization on the ability of national governments to finance public expenditures and social service programs
- The pros and cons of the international coordination of economic policies
- Whether international organizations rob nations of policy sovereignty, and the role of international organizations in expanding and managing world trade and global capital flows

Fundamental Issue #1: Why study global economic issues and policies? The process of economic integration is shaping political and social institutions, affecting the way that nations approach policymaking and changing the incomes and purchasing patterns of households. With its far-reaching impact, economic integration is one of the most hotly contested issues today. So a thorough understanding of global economic issues and policies is important to students of all academic disciplines.

Real sector:
A designation for the portion of the economy engaged in the production and sale of goods and services.

Financial sector:
A designation for the portion of the economy in which people trade financial assets.

GLOBAL MARKETS FOR GOODS AND SERVICES

In order to measure domestic and international economic activity, economists typically separate the production of goods and services from the exchange of financial assets. This is not to say that these two types of activity are independent. Indeed, they are not. Nonetheless, these activities are distinct.

The real sector

The **real sector** of an economy refers to the domestic and international production and exchange of goods and services. The **financial sector** refers to domestic and international transactions of financial assets. The most common measures of economic integration focus on three aspects:

1. The volume of international trade in the real sector
2. Global markets for goods and services
3. The volume of trade in the international monetary and financial markets

After the end of World War II, global markets for goods and services experienced reductions in trade barriers, advances in telecommunications, and declines in transportation costs. As a result, global trade in goods and services steadily increased until a sharp 2009 drop associated with the world economic slump. The inflation-adjusted volume of trade since has returned to its prior level. (To consider the importance of reduced barriers to trade for globalization, see *Management Notebook: Explaining the two most recent globalization waves.*)

MANAGEMENT NOTEBOOK

Explaining the two most recent globalization waves

There have been several great waves of globalization throughout human history. The most recent of these occurred between 1870 and 1913 and between 1950 and 2000. To better understand these globalization periods, David Jacks of Simon Fraser University, Christopher Meissner of the University of California-Davis, and Dennis Novy of the University of Warwick have examined data on trade flows involving pairings of 27 different nations since 1870. Jacks, Meissner, and Novy find evidence that a crucial determinant of flows of international trade was trade costs—the expenses incurred in shipping, transferring ownership, and completing exchanges of goods and services. They estimate that between 1870 and 1913, the average decline in trade costs between pairs of nations was 33 percent. Between 1950 and 2000, the average decrease in trade costs was less dramatic but still substantial, at 16 percent.

Volumes of international trade fell considerably during the 1913–1950 interval between these two globalization waves—that is, between the years just preceding World War I and following the conclusion of World War II. Jacks, Meissner, and Novy find trade costs also were a key factor explaining the "de-globalization" that took place during this period. Trade costs increased by an average of 18 percent during the period, which undermined incentives for people to buy and sell goods and services across national borders.

For critical analysis: Recent estimates by economists at the International Monetary Fund have indicated that average global trade costs probably have risen slightly since 2008. If an upward trend in trade costs is in progress, what does the study by Jacks, Meissner, and Novy suggest will happen to future globalization trends?

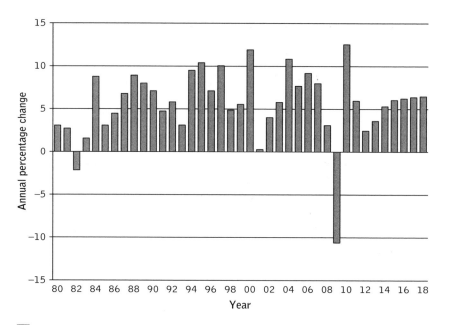

Figure 1.1 *Growth of global trade in goods and services*

World trade in goods and services has increased at an average annual rate of more than 5 percent since 1980. In spite of the 2009 plunge in world trade, the cumulative effect of global trade growth since the 1970s has been a nearly sixfold increase in the volume of world trade.

Source: International Monetary Fund, *World Economic Outlook Database,* IMF forecasts begin in 2014.

Figure 1.1 displays the annual percentage change in the global trade in goods and services since 1980. World trade of goods and services expanded in all but two of those years. For the entire period shown in the figure, the growth of world trade increased at an average annual rate of more than 5.5 percent. Even though there was a precipitous drop in trade growth following the recent global recession, the cumulative effect of annual growth since 1980 resulted in nearly a thirteenfold increase in the volume of world trade.

The importance of global trade

Global markets for goods and services have become increasingly important for most nations. To measure the importance of global trade to individual countries, economists typically divide the volume of a nation's global trade—that is, its exports plus its imports—by the total volume of its domestic output. The resulting measure estimates the nation's global trade as a share of the total amount of economic activity in its real sector.

Figure 1.2 on page 9 displays this measure of global trade for 1980 and 2011 for ten nations. As the figure demonstrates, among the selected nations the importance of global trade in goods and services increased significantly for all countries. Generally, the economies of larger nations, such as the United States and Japan, tend to

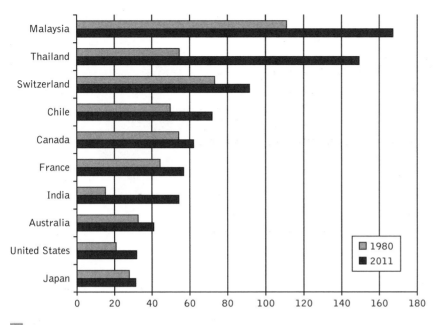

Figure 1.2 *Selected individual nations' trade in goods and services*

Global markets for goods and services have become increasingly important for individual nations. The figure plots the sum of each nation's exports and imports as a percentage of the nation's volume of economic output for the years 1980 and 2011. This percentage measures the nation's trade as a share of the total economic activity in its real sector. This percentage increased for every nation listed since 1980.

Source: World Bank, *World Development Indicators.*

depend less on global markets for goods and services and more on their domestic markets. The economies of smaller nations, such as Thailand and Malaysia, rely much more on global markets for goods and services. Regardless, all the nations graphed in Figure 1.2 experienced increases in the share of international trade, by amounts ranging from 12 percent to more than 200 percent. (Growth in trade flows between Asian and non-Asian nations have exhibited particularly significant growth, as evidenced by shifts in volumes of trade between the United States and Asian nations; see *Management Notebook: An increase in Asia's share of U.S. trade flows*.)

MANAGEMENT NOTEBOOK

An increase in Asia's share of U.S. trade flows

In the early 1960s, Europe was the destination of more than 70 percent of U.S. firms' exports and the source of almost 75 percent of U.S. imports. Only about 20 percent of U.S. exports of goods and services produced by U.S. firms went to Asian nations, and a slightly smaller percentage of U.S. imports originated in countries located in Asia.

During the following five decades, the distributions of U.S. trade flows have shifted away from Europe and in favor of Asian nations. Although about 65 percent of the exports of U.S. firms continue to flow to European countries, Asian nations are now the destination of about 30 percent of U.S. exports of goods and services. European nations' share of U.S. imports has dropped to just over 50 percent, while Asia's share of U.S. imports has increased to nearly 40 percent.

For critical analysis: Even though Europe's shares of U.S. trade flows have decreased during recent decades, the absolute levels of annual inflation-adjusted U.S. trade flows with Europe have increased. What do the rising shares of U.S. trade with Asia imply about growth in absolute Asian trade flows?

Fundamental Issue #2: How important are global markets for goods and services? Since the 1980s, the volume of global trade in goods and services has grown at an average annual rate of more than 5.5 percent per year. The cumulative effect of this growth has been nearly a thirteenfold expansion of global markets for goods and services. As measured by the trade in goods and services as a share of domestic output, global markets for goods and services have become more important for the world's nations.

THE INTERNATIONAL MONETARY AND FINANCIAL MARKETS

Although the growth of global markets for goods and services has been remarkable, it pales in comparison with developments in the international monetary and financial markets.

The foreign exchange markets

Foreign exchange market: *A system of private banks, foreign exchange brokers, and central banks through which households, firms, and governments buy and sell national currencies.*

Table 1.2 on the following page displays estimates of the annual turnover in **foreign exchange markets**—that is, the markets for national currencies—and the growth of world exports. The first column of the table provides estimates of the turnover, or value of transactions, of foreign currencies. The second column displays the volume of world exports of goods. Using this table, we can calculate that overall, the value of world exports has increased by more than 800 percent since 1979. The first column, however, shows that turnover in the foreign exchange markets increased by more than 5,000 percent over this same period. The final value in the first column reveals that the *annual* turnover in the foreign exchange markets is estimated at $955 trillion. This means that the *daily* turnover in the foreign exchange markets is nearly $4 trillion.

The third column of Table 1.2 provides the ratio of the turnover in foreign exchange instruments to the volume of world exports, which is a measure of the value of foreign exchange transactions to world exports. The computed ratios show

Table 1.2 *Annual turnover in foreign exchange markets. Overall, world exports have grown at an impressive rate since 1979. The turnover of foreign exchange has increased even more, however, from 12 times the volume of world exports of goods to a maximum of 70 times.*

Year	Foreign exchange turnover ($ trillion)	World exports of goods ($ trillion)	Ratio
1979	17.5	1.5	12:1
1986	75.0	2.0	38:1
1989	190.0	3.1	61:1
1992	252.0	4.7	54:1
1995	297.5	5.0	60:1
1998	372.5	5.4	69:1
2001	300.0	6.6	45:1
2004	475.0	9.1	52:1
2007	797.8	13.9	57:1
2010	955.4	14.2	67:1
2013	1,351.0	19.3	70:1

Sources: Held et al. (1999), p. 209; Bank for International Settlements, *Central Bank Survey of Foreign Exchange and Derivatives Market Activity,* various issues; International Monetary Fund, *World Economic Outlook,* various issues; 2013 IMF estimates.

ON THE WEB:

For definitions and data relating to foreign direct investment, visit the home page of the United Nations Conference on Trade and Development at www.unctad.org.

that foreign exchange turnover has grown from approximately 12 times the value of world exports to 69 times the value of world exports in 1998 before declining to 45 times the value of world exports in 2001. The decline in 2001 is attributed to both the introduction of the euro and a temporary decline in global trade. Since 2001, the ratio has begun to rise again.

Foreign direct investment

A second significant trend in the international monetary and financial markets is the growth of foreign direct investment (FDI). **Foreign direct investment** is an investment that involves a long-term relationship and represents a controlling interest in an enterprise located in another economy. Since the 1970s, there has been a gradual deregulation of long-term capital markets and a harmonization of national tax policies and accounting rules. Table 1.3 shows the remarkable increase in FDI flows that resulted. After a worldwide recession and a debt crisis in the Latin American economies during the early 1980s, the rates of growth of FDI easily surpassed the growth rates of world exports, up to the decline associated with the global economic downturn of the late 2000s.

Foreign direct investment: *The acquisition of assets that involves a long-term relationship and controlling interest of 10 percent or greater in an enterprise located in another economy.*

Capital flows to emerging economies

A recent development concerning the international monetary and financial markets is the sizable increase in private (non-governmental) capital flows to the emerging economies. Figure 1.3 on the next page illustrates the most recent data on these flows. The figure separates capital flows into FDI and shorter-term portfolio capital. As

Table 1.3 *Global foreign direct investment flows. A gradual deregulation of long-term capital markets and a harmonization of tax policies has led to remarkable increases in FDI flows. In spite of a worldwide recession in the early 1980s, the rates of growth of FDI flows surpassed the rates of change in world exports, and the pace of growth continued throughout the 1990s. In the 2000s, FDI flows were negatively impacted by a drop in global activity following the terrorist attacks of September 11, 2001 and the financial crisis and global recession of 2008 and 2009. There was a temporary rebound in 2010 and 2011 and another decline in 2012.*

Years	FDI inflows (percent change)	FDI outflows (percent change)	World exports (percent change)
1971–1975	19.8	17.3	24.0
1976–1980	18.5	17.4	18.1
1981–1985	2.1	2.4	−0.6
1986–1990	24.0	27.6	14.5
1991–1995	20.0	15.7	8.3
1996–2000	31.9	27.0	8.0
2001–2005	−2.4	−3.3	5.4
2006–2012	−1.4	−2.2	3.1

Sources: UNCTAD, *World Investment Report;* International Monetary Fund, *World Economic Outlook*, various issues; authors' estimates.

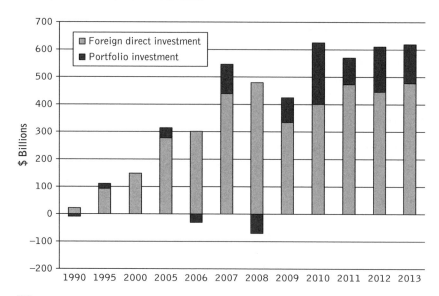

Figure 1.3 *Private capital flows to the developing and emerging economies*

Private capital flows to the developing and emerging economies have grown at an impressive rate since 1990. Despite the 1994 Mexican financial crisis and the East Asian crises of 1997 and 1998, FDI and portfolio investment continued to flow to the emerging economies through 2007. Portfolio investment flows were significantly and negatively affected by the financial crisis and global recession of 2008 and 2009.

Source: International Monetary Fund, *World Economic Outlook Database*.

shown in the figure, total private capital flows have averaged $190 billion annually since 1990. Although there was a decline in private capital flows following the 1997–1998 financial crises in East Asia and Russia, long-term private capital flows continued with some strength until the global economic downturn of the late 2000s.

As you can see, during the past few decades global markets for goods and services have grown considerably. Nonetheless, the rates of growth of the international monetary and financial markets dwarf those of global markets for goods and services. Now that you know about the real and financial sectors and their global expansions, you will embark on a more detailed study of each sector. The remainder of this chapter develops the conceptual framework that is employed in a substantial portion of this text.

Fundamental Issue #3: How important are the international monetary and financial markets? The international monetary and financial markets have experienced substantial growth, greatly surpassing the volume of trade in goods and services. Foreign exchange turnover has grown to more than 60 times the volume of exports of goods and services. Foreign direct investment continues to expand, in spite of worldwide recessions and debt crises. Foreign direct investment flows rebounded from both the 1997–1998 financial crises and the global economic downturn in 2001–2002. There was significant drop in international capital flows following the financial crisis and global recession of the late 2000s. Nonetheless, private capital continues to flow to developed and emerging economies.

UNDERSTANDING GLOBAL MARKETS: SUPPLY AND DEMAND

For the remainder of this chapter, you will consider a framework of basic economic concepts that may be used to quantify and evaluate the impact of global issues and policies. You will learn about the concepts of supply, demand, consumer surplus, and producer surplus, and you will develop an understanding of how to apply these tools to a number of domestic and international examples.

Demand and supply

How much are consumers willing and able to pay for given quantities of a product or service? That is, what is the demand for the product or service?

Demand

Economists define **demand** as the relation displaying the prices that consumers are willing and able to pay for various quantities demanded during a specified time period, holding all other things constant. The relation between price and quantity demanded follows an economic law. This **law of demand** states that there is an inverse, or negative, relationship between price and quantity demanded. As the price rises, an individual's quantity demanded declines.

Demand: *The relationship between the prices that consumers are willing and able to pay for various quantities of a good or service for a given time period, all other things being constant.*

Law of demand: *An economic law that states that there is an inverse, or negative, relationship between the price that consumers are willing and able to pay and the quantities that they desire to purchase.*

13

Table 1.4 *An individual consumer's demand schedule. A demand schedule tabulates possible prices and the quantities that a consumer demands of a good or service at those prices. Quantity demanded and price are negatively related. As the price of gasoline falls, quantity demanded rises.*

Per-unit price ($)	Quantity (gallons)
3.95	1
3.90	2
3.85	3
3.80	4
3.75	5

The demand schedule

An individual's demand schedule tabulates the price the consumer is willing and able to pay for various quantities of a good or service during a specified period, all other things held constant. Table 1.4 displays an individual consumer's demand schedule for gasoline. As the table shows, the demand schedule lists possible prices and the quantities demanded at each of these prices. At a price of $3.90 per gallon, for example, the consumer's quantity demanded is 2 gallons per week, while at a price of $3.85 per gallon, the quantity demanded is 3 gallons per week. As you can see, the demand schedule displays a negative relationship between price and quantity demanded: as the price of gasoline falls, quantity demanded rises.

Supply: *The relationship between the prices of a good or service and the quantities supplied to the market by producers within a given time period, all other things being constant.*

Law of supply: *An economic law that states that there is a positive or direct relationship between the prices producers receive and the quantities that they are willing to supply to the market.*

Supply

Economists define **supply** as the relation displaying the prices that a producer is willing to accept for various quantities supplied during a given time period, holding all other things constant. This relation between price and quantity supplied follows an economic law. The **law of supply** states that price and quantity supplied are positively related. When price rises, for example, the higher price induces a greater quantity supplied.

The supply schedule

A supply schedule tabulates the minimum price a supplier is willing to accept for various quantities supplied of a good or service. Table 1.5 on the next page displays an individual firm's weekly supply of transportation gasoline. The supply schedule depicts possible prices and the weekly quantity supplied by the firm at each of the possible prices. At a price of $3.90 per gallon, for example, the quantity supplied by the firm is 200 gallons per week. At a price of $3.85 per gallon, however, the quantity supplied falls to 150 gallons per week. As you can see, the supply schedule displays a positive relationship between price and quantity supplied: as the price falls, the quantity supplied declines. (To observe how to depict the demand and supply curves in graphs, see *Visualizing Global Economic Issues: Demand and supply curves*.)

Table 1.5 *An individual firm's supply schedule. A supply schedule tabulates possible prices and the quantities that a producer supplies of a good or service at those prices. Quantity supplied and price are positively related. As the price of gasoline falls, quantity supplied declines.*

Price per unit ($)	Quantity (gallons)
3.95	250
3.90	200
3.85	150
3.80	100
3.75	50

VISUALIZING GLOBAL ECONOMIC ISSUES

Demand and supply curves

To see how to graph demand and supply schedules, consider the demand schedule for transportation gasoline in Table 1.4, and the individual producer's supply schedule in Table 1.5. The demand curve labeled *D* in panel (a) of Figure 1.4 plots the weekly quantities of gasoline demanded by the individual at various prices. The curve slopes downward, illustrating the law of demand, or a negative relationship between price and quantity demanded.

The supply curve labeled *S* in panel (b) of Figure 1.4 plots the weekly quantities supplied by the individual firm at various prices. The supply curve is upward sloping, or has a positive slope, because of the positive relation between price and quantity supplied.

When using graphs of demand and supply, it is very important to differentiate between demand and quantity demanded and between supply and quantity supplied. As already stated, the demand curve is the overall relationship between price and quantity demanded. The demand for gasoline is represented by the position of the entire demand curve in the graph. Quantity demanded is represented by an individual point on the demand curve, such as the point labeled A in panel (a) of Figure 1.4, which indicates that at a price of $3.90 per gallon, the quantity demanded is 2 gallons.

Likewise, the supply of gasoline is the overall relationship between price and quantity supplied. The entire supply curve and its position in the graph represents supply, whereas an individual point on the supply curve, such as point A in panel (b) of Figure 1.4, represents the quantity supplied.

To further consider the difference between demand and quantity demanded and between supply and quantity supplied, consider a change in the price of gasoline. Suppose that the price of gasoline falls from $3.90 to $3.85 per gallon. As shown in panel (a) of Figure 1.4, as the price declines from $3.90 to $3.85 per gallon, there is a movement down and along the demand curve as quantity demanded rises from 2 to 3 gallons. In panel (b), this price drop causes a movement down and along the supply curve as quantity supplied falls from 200 gallons of gasoline to 150 gallons. A movement along the demand curve, therefore, is a change in *quantity demanded* induced by a price change, while a movement along the supply curve is a change in *quantity supplied*. The demand and supply curves remained in their original position, so demand and supply have not changed.

For critical analysis: What might cause a change in the demand for gasoline? What might cause a change in the supply of gasoline? Can you think of a single event that might shift both the demand curve and the supply curve?

Changes in demand and supply

As shown in the previous section, quantity demanded and quantity supplied depend on the price of the good or service. The demand for and supply of a particular good or service depend on a number of other factors, however. Because these factors are elements other than the price of the item, we refer to them as *factors that influence demand and supply*.

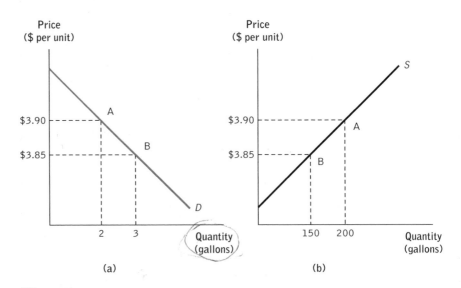

Figure 1.4 *The demand for and supply of gasoline*

Panel (a) illustrates an individual consumer's weekly demand curve for transportation gasoline. Each point on the demand curve represents the maximum price the consumer is willing and able to pay for a specific quantity of gasoline. Panel (b) illustrates an individual firm's weekly supply curve for transportation gasoline. Each point on the supply curve represents the quantity the producer is willing to offer for a specific price.

Table 1.6 *Factors influencing demand. A number of factors influence demand. Economists typically group these factors into categories. The most important categories of factors influencing demand are tastes and preferences, changes in income, changes in the price of related goods, and changes in the number of consumers in the market.*

Factor	How it affects demand
Changes in consumer preferences	An increase in consumer tastes or preferences for an item increases the demand for that item. A decrease in consumer tastes or preferences for an item decreases the demand for that item.
Changes in income	An increase (decrease) in a consumer's income increases (decreases) the consumer's demand for *normal goods* and decreases (increases) the consumer's demand for *inferior goods*.
Changes in the prices of related goods	An increase (decrease) in the price of a *complement good* decreases (increases) a consumer's demand for a related good. An increase (decrease) in the price of a *substitute good* increases (decreases) a consumer's demand for a related good.
Changes in the number of consumers	An increase (decrease) in the number of consumers in a market increases (decreases) the demand for a good or service.

Factors influencing demand

We say that demand increases when there is a greater quantity demanded at any given price. Demand decreases when there is a lower quantity demanded at any given price.

Although there are numerous factors that affect demand, we can group them into a small number of general categories, summarized in Table 1.6.

Consumer tastes and preferences are perhaps the most important factors influencing demand. For example, when European scientists discovered that bovine spongiform encephalopathy—mad-cow disease—could be transmitted to humans as new variant Creutzfeldt–Jakob disease, there was an immediate drop in the demand for beef and an increase in demand for substitute food items such as veggie burgers. At any given price of beef, therefore, the quantity of beef demanded decreased. At any given price of veggie burgers, there was an increase in the quantity of veggie burgers demanded.

As incomes change, consumers' ability to purchase an item changes. If an increase in income results in a decrease in the demand for a particular good, that good is considered an *inferior good*. A *normal good*, on the other hand, is a good for which consumer demand rises with an increase in income. Most goods are normal goods, so that when incomes increase, people demand a larger quantity at any given price.

Consumers purchase a broad range of goods and services. When the price of one good changes, consumers must reallocate their budgets. They may increase their purchases of some goods while decreasing purchases of others. Goods that are consumed together, such as coffee and cream, are called *complement goods*. Goods that substitute for each other, such as coffee and tea, are called *substitute goods*.

Factors influencing supply

As with demand, supply depends on a number of factors other than the price of the particular good or service supplied. These are factors influencing supply. That is, the quantity of the good supplied changes at any given price. When there is an increase in supply, the quantity supplied at each of the various prices increases. When there is a decrease in supply, the quantity supplied at each of the various prices declines.

There are many factors that affect supply, summarized in Table 1.7 and grouped into a small number of categories.

A change in the cost and availability of inputs or resources is perhaps the most important factor influencing supply. When inputs become less expensive, production costs fall and producers are willing to offer a larger quantity of the good or service at a given price. Hence, supply increases when input costs decrease.

A change in technology affects supply in the same way as a change in the price of inputs. A technological advance allows a firm to produce more units of a good or service with the same amount of resources. A technological advance, therefore, results in an increase in supply. At any given price, the firm can produce more units than it could previously.

A change in the price of related goods may also affect supply. An increase in the price of a *substitute good in production*—a good that substitutes for another good in the production process—results in a decrease in the supply of the other good. An increase

Table 1.7 *Factors influencing supply. A number of factors influence supply. Economists typically group these factors into categories. The most important categories of factors influencing supply are the cost and availability of inputs, changes in technology, changes in the prices of related goods or services, taxes and producer subsidies, and the number of producers in the market.*

Factor	How it affects supply
Changes in the cost and availability of inputs	Supply increases when input costs fall. Supply decreases when input cost rise.
Advances in technology	An advance in technology allows a firm to produce more units of a good or service with the same amount of resources. Hence, at any given price, the firm can produce more units than it could previously.
Changes in the prices of related goods or services	An increase (decrease) in the price of a *substitute good in production* results in a decrease (increase) in the supply of the related good. An increase (decrease) in the price of a *complement good in production* results in an increase (decrease) in the supply of the related good.
Taxes and producer subsidies	A production tax causes supply to decrease, while a production subsidy causes supply to increase.
Change in the number of producers	An increase (decrease) in the number of producers in a market increases (decreases) the supply of a good or service.

in the price of a _complement good in production_—a good that is produced in conjunction with another good—results in an increase in the supply of the other good.

Taxes and producer subsidies are also factors that influence supply. Taxes and subsidies affect the prices that producers are willing to receive for a particular quantity of a good and, therefore, change supply. Taxes and subsidies are covered in greater detail in later chapters.

We shall consider other factors that influence demand and supply later in this chapter. These additional categories, however, are best understood after considering the _market demand_ and _market supply_, as opposed to an individual's demand or supply.

Market demand and supply

Now that you understand individual demand and supply, let's consider _market_ demand and supply.

Market demand is the sum of the quantities demanded by _all_ consumers at various prices during a specific time period, all other things being constant. From this point onward, when we refer to demand in this text, we shall be speaking of market demand unless otherwise specified.

To better understand market demand, suppose that in a particular market there are 1,000 identical consumers, each having the same demand schedule for gasoline as that given in Table 1.4 on page 14. At each price, therefore, there is 1,000 times the quantity demanded in the individual consumer's demand schedule.

Now consider an additional factor affecting a change in demand: the number of consumers in the market. As just explained, market demand is the sum of all consumers' quantity demanded at various prices. Hence, if there is an increase in the number of consumers, the total quantity demanded at each of the various prices is greater. Conversely, if the number of consumers decreases, demand declines.

Market supply is the sum of the quantities supplied by all producers at various prices during a specific time period, all other things being constant. When we refer to supply in this text, we shall be speaking of market supply unless otherwise indicated.

Suppose that, in a particular market, there are 20 identical producers, each having the same supply schedule of gasoline as that given in Table 1.5 on page 15. At each price, therefore, there is 20 times the quantity supplied by the individual producer.

Now we can consider another factor influencing supply: the number of producers. As explained above, market supply is the sum of all producers' quantity supplied at various prices. If there is an increase in the number of producers, the total quantity supplied at each of the various prices is greater. Consequently, supply increases. By way of comparison, if the number of producers decreases, supply declines.

Market demand:
A curve illustrating the prices consumers are willing and able to pay for various quantities of a good or service for a given time period, all other things being constant. Because of the negative relationship between price and quantity demanded, the demand curve slopes downward.

Market supply:
A curve illustrating the prices producers are willing to accept for various quantities of a good or service they supply to the market for a given time period, all other things being constant. Because of the positive relationship between price and quantity supplied, the supply curve slopes upward.

Fundamental Issue #4: What are market supply and demand? Demand is the relationship between prices and the quantities consumers are willing and able to purchase, while supply is the relationship between prices and the quantities producers are willing and able to supply.

CONSUMER AND PRODUCER SURPLUS

The previous section introduced you to the concepts of supply and demand. Next we will build on these concepts by considering consumer surplus and producer surplus. Consumer and producer surplus are two important tools that we will apply in this text to gauge the impact of domestic and international events and policies on the welfare of consumers, producers, taxpayers, and governments.

Consumer surplus

Market price: *The price determined by the interactions of all consumers and producers in the marketplace.*

Consumer surplus: *The benefit that consumers receive from the existence of a market price. Consumer surplus is measured as the difference between what consumers are willing and able to pay for a good or service, and the market price.*

Producer surplus: *The benefit that producers receive from the existence of a market price. Producer surplus is measured as the difference between the price that producers are willing to accept to supply a particular quantity, and the market price.*

As described above, demand is the relationship between prices and the quantities that consumers are willing and able to purchase. Table 1.4 on page 14, which displays an individual consumer's demand schedule for gasoline, showed that the consumer is willing and able to pay $3.95 for one gallon of gasoline. It follows that the value of the first gallon to this consumer is $3.95 per gallon.

What if, however, the **market price** of gasoline, the price determined by the interaction of *all* consumers and producers in the market, is only $3.85 per gallon? Because consumers can purchase a gallon of gasoline for the market price of $3.85 per gallon, and yet each consumer values the first gallon of gasoline at a price of $3.95 per gallon, each consumer receives a benefit, or surplus. The difference between what consumers are willing to pay for a particular quantity of a good or service and the market price they must pay to purchase that quantity of the good or services is called **consumer surplus**.

Producer surplus

As discussed above, supply is the relationship between prices and the quantities that producers are willing to provide. Table 1.5 on page 15 displays an individual firm's supply schedule of gasoline. The table shows that at a price of $3.80 per gallon, the producer is willing to supply 100 gallons. It follows that the producer must receive $3.80 per gallon to be motivated to offer the first 100 gallons for sale.

What if the market price for gasoline is $3.85 per gallon? The producer can sell 150 gallons of gasoline at the market price, even though it is willing to accept $3.80 per gallon for the first 100 gallons of gasoline. Hence, producers receive a benefit, or surplus. **Producer surplus** is the difference between the market price that producers can charge for a particular quantity of a good or service and the minimum price they are willing to receive for that quantity. (To gain a further understanding of consumer and producer surplus, see on the next page *Visualizing Global Economic Issues: Measuring consumer and producer surplus*.)

Fundamental Issue #5: What are consumer surplus and producer surplus? Consumer and producer surplus are concepts that economists use to gauge the benefits that consumers and producers receive from the existence of a market price.

Consumer surplus is the difference between what consumers are willing to pay for a given quantity and the price they must pay. Producer surplus is the difference between what producers are willing to accept for a given quantity and the price they are able to receive for that quantity.

HOW MARKET PRICES ARE DETERMINED

How is the market price, introduced in the previous section, determined? To answer this question we bring together the concepts of supply and demand.

Together, the laws of supply and demand demonstrate the different price perspectives of producers and consumers. On one hand, as the price of a good or service rises, the quantity supplied rises. On the other hand, as the price rises, the quantity demanded falls. These different price perspectives are resolved through a market process in which the quantity demanded and the quantities supplied eventually are equalized.

VISUALIZING GLOBAL ECONOMIC ISSUES

Measuring consumer and producer surplus

To visualize consumer and producer surplus, let's consider the market demand and supply curves discussed above. Panel (a) of Figure 1.5 (p. 23) depicts the demand curve that results if there are a thousand identical consumers, each with the same demand as that illustrated in panel (a) of Figure 1.4 (p. 14). Likewise, panel (b) of Figure 1.5 illustrates the supply curve that results if there are 20 identical producers, each with the same supply of gasoline as that shown in panel (b) of Figure 1.4.

The demand curve in panel (a) of Figure 1.5 shows that consumers value the first gallon of gasoline at a price of $3.95 per gallon, but the market price is only $3.85 per gallon. Consumers, therefore, receive a surplus. This surplus is the difference between the price that consumers are willing and able to pay and the market price—in our example, $0.10 per gallon. Likewise, for the second 1,000 gallons of gasoline, consumers are willing and able to pay $3.90 per gallon. For the third 1,000 gallons of gasoline, the market price is equal to what consumers are willing and able to pay. Hence, there is no additional surplus associated with the third 1,000 gallons of gasoline.

As with other goods and services, gasoline can be bought in much smaller units than thousand gallons. If we were to consider all the possible quantities in the figure that consumers are willing and able to purchase at a price of $3.85 per gallon, consumer surplus equals the triangle formed by points A, B, and C in panel (a) of Figure 1.5. Hence, we can say that consumer surplus is the area below the demand curve and above the market price.

We can quantify consumer surplus by simply calculating the area of the triangle in panel (a) in Figure 1.5. Recall that the area of a triangle is the value of the base multiplied by the height, divided by two. In this example, therefore, consumer surplus is $300:

consumer surplus = [($4.05 − $3.85) × 3,000]/2 = $300

We can determine producer surplus in a similar manner. Panel (b) of Figure 1.5 shows that producers are willing to accept no less than $3.75 per gallon for the first 1,000 gallons of gasoline, yet the market price is $3.85 per gallon. Likewise, producers are willing to accept $3.80 per gallon for the second 1,000 gallons of gasoline. For the third 1,000 gallons of gasoline, producers are willing to accept a price of $3.85 per gallon, which equals the market price. Hence, there is no additional surplus associated with the third 1, 000 gallons.

If we consider all the possible quantities in panel (b) of Figure 1.5 that producers are willing and able to supply at a price of $3.85 per gallon, then producer surplus is given by the triangle formed by points A, B, and C. Hence, we can say that producer surplus is the area below price and above the supply curve. We can quantify producer surplus by calculating the area of triangle ABC in panel (b) of Figure 1.5. In this example, producer surplus is $225:

producer surplus = [($3.85 − $3.70) × 3,000]/2 = $225

For critical analysis: OPEC, the Organization of Petroleum Exporting Countries, seeks to protect the interests of its members. Explain, using the concepts of consumer and producer surplus, how OPEC might achieve this objective.

Excess quantity supplied and excess quantity demanded

Excess quantity supplied: *The amount by which quantity supplied exceeds quantity demanded at a given price.*

Consider, for example, what happens if, at a given market price, the quantity supplied is greater than the quantity demanded. At this price, there is an **excess quantity supplied**, which is the amount by which quantity supplied exceeds quantity demanded at a specific price. Because of the excess quantity supplied, there is downward pressure on the market price, as producers will want to eliminate their excess inventories. Hence, the market price will fall, spurring an increase in quantity demanded and a decrease in quantity supplied. The price will continue to fall until an excess quantity supplied no longer exists, or until the quantity demanded equals the quantity supplied.

Excess quantity demanded: *The amount by which quantity demanded exceeds quantity supplied at a given price.*

Next, consider what happens if the market price is at a level where quantity demanded is greater than quantity supplied. At this price, there is an **excess quantity demanded**, which is the amount by which quantity demanded exceeds quantity

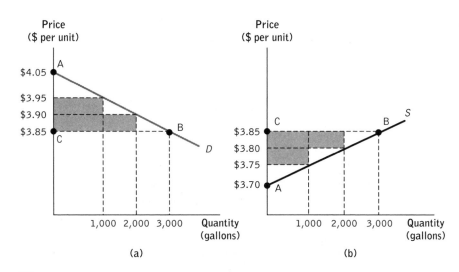

Figure 1.5 *Consumer and producer surplus*

Panel (a) illustrates the weekly demand curve for transportation gasoline for 1,000 identical consumers. In this figure, the market price is $3.85 per gallon. The quantities demanded at the prices given are taken from Table 1.4 (p. 14)(e.g., at $3.95 per gallon, 1,000 identical consumers would buy a total of 1,000 gallons). Consumer surplus is illustrated by the triangle denoted by points A, B, and C—the area above the market price and below the demand curve. Panel (b) illustrates a weekly supply curve for 20 identical producers. Price and quantity supplied are taken from Table 1.5 (p. 15). At the market price of $3.85 per gallon, producer surplus is illustrated by the triangle formed by points A, B, and C—the area below the market price and above the supply curve.

supplied. Because of the excess quantity demanded, there is pressure for the market price to rise. In turn, the price increase spurs an increase in the quantity supplied and a decrease in the quantity demanded. The price will continue to rise until the excess quantity demanded is eliminated, or when the quantity demanded equals the quantity supplied.

Equilibrium market price

When quantity demanded and quantity supplied are equal, there is neither an excess quantity demanded nor an excess quantity supplied, and the market is said to have *cleared*. The price at which quantity demanded equals quantity supplied is called the **equilibrium market price**. Because there is neither an excess quantity demanded nor an excess quantity supplied, there is no pressure on price to change. All other things being constant, the good or service will continue to be exchanged at the market-clearing price. (To understand the equilibrium market price and how changes in supply and demand effect the equilibrium market price, see *Visualizing Global Economic Issues: The equilibrium market price*.)

Equilibrium market price: *The price at which quantity supplied equals quantity demanded. At the equilibrium market price, there is neither an excess quantity demanded nor an excess quantity supplied.*

23

VISUALIZING GLOBAL ECONOMIC ISSUES

The equilibrium market price

To visualize the determination of the equilibrium market price, view panel (a) of Figure 1.6, which combines the supply and demand curves of Figure 1.5. Using the data in Figure 1.5 (p. 23), consider what happens if the price of transportation gasoline is $3.90 per gallon. At this price, the quantity supplied is 4,000 gallons, while the quantity demanded is 2,000 gallons. Hence, there is an excess quantity of gasoline supplied. Producers will offer to supply gasoline at a lower price to induce greater sales, and the price will begin to fall in the marketplace.

Next, consider what happens if the market price is $3.80 per gallon. At this price, quantity demanded is 4,000 gallons while the quantity supplied is 2,000 gallons. Hence, there is an excess quantity demanded. Consumers will offer to purchase gasoline at a higher price, and the price will begin to rise in the marketplace.

At a price of $3.85 per gallon, quantity supplied equals quantity demanded, and there is neither an excess quantity supplied nor an excess quantity demanded. Hence, $3.85 per gallon is the equilibrium market price.

Now let's consider what happens if there is a change in the price of crude oil. In the late 2000s, for example, the price of crude oil rose considerably. Because gasoline is refined from crude oil, the price of an essential input increased. This caused a decrease in supply, illustrated by a leftward shift of the supply curve to S' in panel (b) of Figure 1.6.

At a price of $3.85 per gallon, there is now an excess quantity of gasoline demanded. Quantity demanded exceeds quantity supplied by 2,000 gallons. Because of the excess quantity demanded, the market price rises, generating an increase in the quantity supplied and a decrease in the quantity demanded. The price of gasoline will continue to rise until it reaches $3.90 per gallon, where quantity supplied equals quantity demanded. All other things being constant, 2,000 gallons of gasoline will continue to be exchanged at the equilibrium market price of $3.90 per gallon.

For critical analysis: Suppose that, as the supply of gasoline falls, consumers turn to more fuel-efficient automobiles. How would these two events together affect the equilibrium price of gasoline and the quantity transacted in the market?

A global market

The market supply and demand framework can be extended to consider a global market for goods and services. What is required is to bring together the forces of supply and demand of all participants in the global market. As noted previously, the equilibrium market price is the price at which quantity demanded equals quantity supplied. This also remains true in a global setting. Excess quantities supplied and

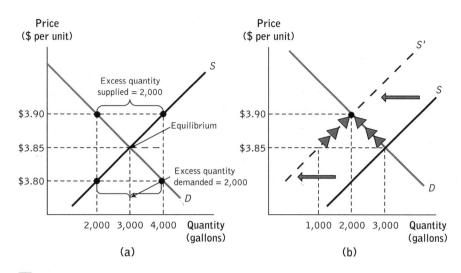

Figure 1.6 *The equilibrium market price*

Panel (a) illustrates the weekly demand curve for, and weekly supply curve of, transportation gasoline. A price of $3.85 per gallon is the equilibrium market price because at this price there is neither an excess quantity demanded nor an excess quantity supplied. Panel (b) shows that a decrease in supply, illustrated by a leftward shift of the supply curve, results in a higher equilibrium market price and a lower quantity transacted.

excess quantities demanded, however, take on a special significance in a global market framework.

Exports

Suppose that the global equilibrium market price of personal computers is higher than the equilibrium market price that would prevail in the domestic economy if international trade did not take place. If the domestic nation's government was to open the country's borders to international trade, the price of personal computers would rise, spurring an increase in the quantity supplied and a decrease in the quantity demanded. At the global price, therefore, the domestic nation experiences an excess quantity supplied of computers.

Residents of the domestic nation could use the excess quantity supplied of personal computers to purchase, or import, other goods and services not available to it prior to international trade. That is, domestic residents could export the personal computers so as to import other items. In this way, an excess quantity supplied is equivalent to a nation's exports of the good or service.

Imports

In contrast, suppose that the global price of personal computers is below the equilibrium market price that would prevail in the domestic economy if international trade did not take place. If the domestic nation's government was to open the country's borders to international trade, the price of personal computers would fall, spurring a decrease in the quantity supplied and an increase in the quantity demanded. At the global price, therefore, the domestic nation experiences an excess quantity demanded of computers. Residents of the domestic nation could satisfy the excess quantity demanded of personal computers by purchasing them on the global market, or importing computers. In this way, an excess quantity demanded is equivalent to a nation's imports of the good or service.

The equilibrium global market price is the price at which all excess quantities demanded equal all excess quantities supplied. In other words, equilibrium is reached when the quantity of exports supplied equals the quantity of imports demanded.

An example: the global coffee market

As an example of a global market process, let's examine the international supply of and demand for coffee. The coffee producers of Latin American nations such as Brazil and Colombia account for a large share of the supply of coffee in the international market. Other nations, such as the United States and Canada, are large importers of raw coffee beans and major producers of processed coffee.

Suppose the international price of unprocessed coffee is $1.65 a pound, and that 3 million metric tons are sold each year. Consider what happens if an unexpected frost occurs in Brazil, damaging a large portion of the coffee crop. Undoubtedly, the frost would cause a precipitous drop in the supply of coffee.

At a price of $1.65, the quantity demanded of coffee by residents of importing nations would now exceed the quantity supplied by producers in exporting nations. In other words, the excess quantity demanded by residents of importing nations will not be met by the excess quantity supplied of producers of exporting nations. As a result, the global price of coffee will rise. In turn, the price increase induces an increase in the quantity supplied and a decrease in the quantity demanded. The price of coffee continues to rise until the market eventually clears.

Consumer and producer surplus and the global market

You have learned that when a nation opens its borders to international trade, it might face prices different from those that would prevail in the domestic economy if trade did not take place. When prices change, consumer and producer surplus also change. Recall that the area below the demand curve and above price measures consumer surplus, while the area above the supply curve and below price measures producer surplus. Hence, when the price increases, all other things being constant, consumer surplus falls and producer surplus rises. In a more general sense, some groups are better off and some are not. (To better understand the determination of the global equilibrium market price and change in consumer and producer surplus, see *Visualizing Global Economic Issues: A global coffee market*.)

As you can see, the change in consumer and producer surplus gives us insight into the groups who may benefit from trade and those who may suffer. In the following

ON THE WEB:

For information on the global market for coffee and tea, access the Tea & Coffee Trade Journal at www.teaandcoffee.net.

chapters, you will learn about the sources of nations' global price advantages and disadvantages. You will also contemplate the distribution of gains and losses of international trade and international policies.

Fundamental Issue #6: How are market prices determined? The forces of supply and demand determine the market price. For an individual nation, equilibrium market price occurs when there is neither an excess quantity demanded nor an excess quantity supplied. If nations engage in international trade, however, the *global* equilibrium market price arises when excess quantities demanded, or imports, equal excess quantities supplied, or exports.

VISUALIZING GLOBAL ECONOMIC ISSUES

A global coffee market

To visualize the determination of the global equilibrium market price and the effects of trade on consumer and producer surplus, consider the supply of, and demand for, coffee for two hypothetical nations, Coffeeland and Creamerland. Panel (a) of Figure 1.7 (p. 28) shows the supply and demand conditions for Coffeeland, which has land well suited to growing coffee, while panel (b) of Figure 1.7 shows the supply and demand conditions for Creamerland, which does not have land well suited for growing coffee. Creamerland, consequently, has only a small domestic coffee industry.

As illustrated in Figure 1.7, if the two countries do not trade, the equilibrium market price of coffee in Coffeeland is $1.35 per pound. The equilibrium market price of coffee is $2.00 per pound in Creamerland. Consumer surplus in each nation is given by the triangle formed by the points *A*, *B*, and *C*. Producer surplus is given by the triangle formed by the points *C*, *B*, and *D*.

Now suppose the two nations begin to trade. At a price of $2.00, there is an excess quantity supplied of 20 tons of coffee in Coffeeland, whose producers would seek to export this amount. Residents of Coffeeland would not be able to export any coffee, however, because Creamerland has neither an excess quantity supplied nor an excess quantity demanded. Hence, the price of coffee would fall below $2.00 per pound. At a coffee price of $1.35, however, there is an excess quantity of coffee demanded in Creamerland, whose residents would seek to import 20 tons of coffee. Creamerland would be unable to import coffee, however, as Coffeeland has neither an excess quantity demanded nor an excess quantity supplied. Hence, the price of coffee would rise above $1.35 per pound.

What is the global equilibrium market price? This price arises when the excess quantity demanded, or imports, of coffee by Creamerland residents exactly matches the excess quantity supplied, or exports, of coffee by Coffeeland producers.

The equilibrium market price in this example is $1.65. Exports of Coffeeland, 10 tons, equal coffee imports of Creamerland.

We can also see what happens to consumer and producer surplus when there is international trade. Before the two nations were opened to trade, consumer surplus was equal to the triangle formed by points A, B, and C, while producer surplus was equal to the triangle shaped by points C, B, and D. After trade, consumer surplus in Coffeeland equals the triangle A, F, and E in panel (a), and consumer surplus in Creamerland equals the triangle A, G, and E in panel (b). After trade, producer surplus in Coffeeland equals the triangle shaped by points E, G, and D in panel (a), and producer surplus in Creamerland equals the triangle formed by points E, F, and D in panel (b).

For critical analysis: Suppose that a frost damages a major portion of Coffeeland's crop. Show what would happen to the global price of coffee, and to consumer and producer surplus, in both nations.

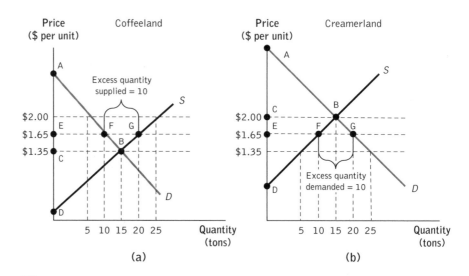

Figure 1.7 *The global coffee market*

Panel (a) illustrates the supply of and demand for coffee in Coffeeland. Panel (b) illustrates the supply of and demand for coffee in Creamerland. At a price of $1.65 per pound, producers in Coffeeland supply 20 tons of coffee and consumers demand 10 tons of coffee. Hence, Coffeeland has an excess quantity supplied of 10 tons. At a price of $1.65 per pound, producers in Creamerland supply 10 tons of coffee and consumers demand 20 tons of coffee. Creamerland, therefore, has an excess quantity demanded of 10 tons. Under free trade, the global equilibrium market price is $1.65 because, at this price, Coffeeland's excess quantity supplied equals Creamerland's excess quantity demanded.

CHAPTER SUMMARY

1. **Why the study of global economic issues and policies is important:** Global economic integration affects many aspects of our day-to-day lives, as well as important business and government policy decisions. In turn, business and government policy decisions affect the pace and breadth of the process of economic integration. Global economic issues and policies, therefore, have become an important area of study for all disciplines.

2. **The importance of global markets for goods and services:** Overall, in spite of a recent drop, global trade in goods and services has increased dramatically during recent decades. Accumulated growth in global trade has resulted in nearly a thirteenfold expansion of the global market for goods and services since 1980. As measured by the sum of exports and imports as a share of overall economic activity, global trade in goods and services today is more important for nearly all nations relative to a few decades ago.

3. **The importance of the international monetary and financial markets:** Although the growth of global trade in goods and services is impressive, it is greatly surpassed by the growth of the international monetary and financial markets. The value of all transactions in the foreign exchange markets grew from 12 times the volume of global exports in 1979 to more than 70 times the value of global exports. Foreign direct investment among the leading industrialized nations and private capital flows to emerging and developed nations have continued to grow in spite of worldwide recessions and sudden and severe financial crises.

4. **Market supply and demand:** Demand is the relationship between prices that consumers are willing and able to pay for various quantities of a good or service during a given time period. The law of demand states that there is a negative relationship between price and the quantity demanded. A demand schedule tabulates possible prices and the quantities demanded at the possible prices. Supply is the relationship between prices that producers are willing to accept for various quantities supplied during a given time period. The law of supply states that there is a positive relationship between price and quantity supplied. A supply schedule tabulates possible prices and the quantities supplied at those prices.

5. **Consumer and producer surplus:** Consumer and producer surplus are concepts that economists find useful in evaluating the welfare effects of global issues and policies. Consumer surplus is the difference between what consumers are willing to pay for a given quantity of a good or service and the market price. Producer surplus is the difference between the price that producers are willing to receive to supply a particular quantity and the market price.

6. **How market prices are determined:** The forces of supply and demand determine market prices. For an individual nation, the equilibrium market price arises when the quantity demanded equals the quantity supplied. The equilibrium market in a global market arises when excess quantity demanded, or imports, equals excess quantities supplied, or exports. An increase in demand results in a higher equilibrium market price. An increase in supply results in a lower equilibrium market price.

QUESTIONS AND PROBLEMS

1. Economists often use the sum of a nation's exports and imports divided by its overall economic activity as a measure of the nation's degree of *openness*. Explain why a large value for this measure may not always be a good indicator of openness.

2. Some researchers use the number of Internet sites per person in a given nation as a measure of that nation's degree of globalization. Explain why this may or may not be a good measure of globalization.

3. Suppose that advances in genetically modified crop technology enable farmers to produce greater amounts of agricultural products on the same amount of land. Explain how this event would affect demand, supply, price, quantity demanded, and quantity supplied in the global market.

4. Suppose that consumers in a region where residents import large quantities of agricultural products become fearful about the health consequences associated with consuming genetically modified agricultural produce. Explain how this event would affect demand, supply, price, quantity demanded, and quantity supplied in the global market.

5. Suppose the events described in questions 3 and 4 above occur simultaneously. Explain the effects on demand, supply, price, quantity demanded, and quantity supplied in the global market.

6. Suppose U.S. government officials are concerned about importing beef that might be contaminated with hoof-and-mouth disease, and they react by restricting imported beef from Argentina. Explain the impact of this action on price, quantity, consumer surplus, and producer surplus in both the United States and Argentina.

7. Consider Figure 1.7 on page 28. Calculate the value of consumer surplus in both nations. Calculate the value of producer surplus in both nations when residents of the two nations do not trade.

8. Consider Figure 1.7 on page 28 once more. Calculate the value of consumer surplus and producer surplus for both nations after the nations engage in trade. How has consumer surplus changed in both nations? How has producer surplus changed in both nations?

9. Suppose that the government of a nation whose producers export coffee burns one-third of all the coffee fields before they can be harvested. Explain the impact of this action on the global price and quantity of coffee.

10. Consider the event described in question 9. Can you explain, in economic terms, why the government would be motivated to do such a thing?

ONLINE APPLICATION

URL: www.imd.org/wcc

Title: World Competitiveness Center

Navigation: To obtain national competitiveness rankings, go to the home page of the Institute for International Management Development (www.imd.org). Then click on "Research and Knowledge" and "World Competitiveness Center." Finally, click on

"News and Results." Click on either the "Watch the video" link or "Learn more," and download the PDF version of the rankings.

Application: Based on either the video or the PDF report, answer the following questions.

1. Compare the top ten nations that appear in the competitiveness ranking and the top ten nations in the globalization ranking of Table 1.5. How many of the top ten nations in Table 1.1 appear in the top ten of the competitiveness ranking?

2. What do the nations in the top ten of both rankings have in common? What is different about them?

3. Why do you think these nations appear in each list? In other words, does the extent of a nation's globalization have an effect on its competitiveness, or does its competitiveness have an effect on its degree of globalization?

For group study and analysis: Assign this exercise to different groups, giving them specific nations that appear on the competitiveness list. Have them independently come up with answers to the questions above. Discuss and debate the different hypotheses that are put forward.

REFERENCES AND RECOMMENDED READINGS

Bhagwati, Jagdish. *In Defense of Globalization.* New York: Oxford University Press, 2004.

Bradford, Scott C., and Robert Z. Lawrence. *Has Globalization Gone Far Enough? The Costs of Fragmented Markets.* Washington, DC: Institute for International Economics, 2004.

Davis, John B., and Joseph P. Daniels. "Corporations and Structural Linkages in World Commerce." In Alan Rugman and Gavin Boyd, eds., *The World Trade Organization in the New Global Economy.* Cheltenham, U.K.: Edward Elgar Publishing, 2001, pp. 70–94.

Davis, John B., and Joseph P. Daniels. "US Corporations in Globalization." In Stephan S. Cohen and Gavin Boyd, eds., *Corporate Governance and Globalization: Long Range Planning Issues.* Cheltenham, U.K.: Edward Elgar Publishing, 2000, pp. 190–215.

Dreher, Axel. "Does Globalization Affect Growth? Evidence from a New Index of Globalization." *Applied Economics* 38(10) (2006): 1091–1110.

Dreher, Axel, Noel Gaston, and Pim Martens. *Measuring Globalisation – Gauging its Consequences.* New York: Springer, 2008.

Held, David, Anthony McGrew, David Goldblatt, and Jonathan Perraton. *Global Transformations.* Palo Alto, CA: Stanford University Press, 1999.

Jacks, David, Christopher Meissner, and Dennis Novy. "Trade Booms, Trade Busts, and Trade Costs." *Journal of International Economics* 83(2) (2011): 185–201.

Keidel, Albert. "China's Economic Rise – Fact and Fiction," Policy Brief 61. Washington, DC: Carnegie Endowment for International Peace, July 2008.

Lewis, Howard III, and J. David Richardson. *Why Global Commitment Really Matters.* Washington, DC: Institute for International Economics, 2001.

Rivoli, Pietra. *The Travels of a T-Shirt in the Global Economy*. Hoboken, NJ: John Wiley and Sons, 2005.

Rodrick, Dani. "How Far Will International Economic Integration Go?" *Journal of Economic Perspectives* 14(1) (Winter 2000): 177–186.

Rugman, Alan M. "Regional Multinationals and Regional Trade Policy: The End of Multilateralism." In Michele Fratianni, Paolo Savona, and John J. Kirton, eds., *Corporate, Public and Global Governance: The G8 Contribution*. Burlington, VT: Ashgate Publishing, 2007, pp. 77–86.

Schaeffer, Robert K., *Understanding Globalization*. Oxford, U.K.: Rowman & Littlefield, 2004.

Steger, Manfred B., ed. *Rethinking Globalism*. New York: Rowman & Littlefield, 2004.

Chapter 2

Comparative advantage — how nations can gain from international trade

FUNDAMENTAL ISSUES

1. What are a nation's production possibilities, and what do they tell us about the costs of producing goods and services within that nation?
2. What is absolute advantage, and how can it help explain why nations engage in international trade?
3. Why is absolute advantage alone insufficient to account for trade among nations?
4. What is comparative advantage, and how does it allow countries to experience gains from trade?
5. Why, in spite of its benefits, does international trade ebb and flow and create so much controversy within the world's nations?

During the 2012 Olympic games, a U.S. senator learned that the U.S. team had attended the opening ceremony wearing uniforms made in China. "I'm so upset," the senator said. "Take all of the uniforms, put them in a big pile, and burn them. We have people in the textile industry who are desperate for jobs."

When asked in a later interview to comment on the senator's statement, Art Carden, a U.S. economist, responded, "One could argue that the American uniforms were not manufactured in China, but grown in soybean fields in Iowa. We export soybeans to China. Because we're incredibly productive in the soybean market [while people in China are more productive in the uniform market], we get more uniforms... and the Chinese get more soybeans."

Not surprisingly, the U.S. senator's comments reflect the sentiments of many voters who perceive that international trade can lead to fewer employment opportunities for some U.S. residents. The economist's arguments, however, reflect a broader perspective regarding the factors that motivate trade in the first place. People do not engage in international trade out of a desire to eliminate jobs. Instead, they trade across borders with an aim to generate mutually agreeable benefits. When you have read this chapter, you will understand why international trade can offer substantial benefits to the world's nations.

THE ECONOMICS OF "GOING IT ALONE"

To think about why residents of rich nations with large economies might wish to trade with residents of poor nations that have small economies—and *vice versa*—let's begin by thinking about a country that does not trade with any other nations.

Production possibilities

The residents of any nation normally produce and consume a number of different goods and services. To keep things simple so that we can emphasize fundamental concepts, however, let's imagine a situation in which a country produces only two goods.

A nation's production possibilities

Let's consider a particular nation called Northland, which engages in no international trade. Furthermore, let's suppose that Northland's residents currently produce and consume food and computers. Given its current technology and resources—people, machines, and so on—Northland has a fixed capability to produce food and computers. Its overall production capabilities for a given year, which economists call a nation's **production possibilities**, are displayed in Table 2.1.

Production possibilities: *All possible combinations of total output of goods and services that residents of a nation can produce, given currently available technology and resources.*

The maximum amount of food, measured in baskets (which might include a certain amount of drinks, fruit, pasta, and so on) that the people of Northland can produce within the year, is 700,000 baskets. To produce this amount of food, Northland's residents must devote all of their resources to food production, which means that the nation cannot produce any computers during that year.

If Northland's residents are willing to forgo all food production during the year, however, they can produce 1,000,000 (1 million) computers. Nevertheless, producing this quantity of computers entails devoting all of the nation's resources to computer

Table 2.1 Northland's production possibilities

Thousands of computers	Thousands of baskets of food
0	700
400	600
500	550
600	490
700	410
800	310
900	220
1,000	0

production, so this is the maximum number of computers that Northland's residents can produce, given its current technology and resources.

Table 2.1 illustrates a fundamental economic rule: With a given technology and fixed amounts of fully employed resources, increasing production of one good requires reducing production of another good. That is, a nation faces a *production possibilities trade-off*. In the case of Northland, Table 2.1 indicates that if Northland's residents initially were producing nothing but 700,000 baskets of food, but then decided to develop a completely "high-tech" economy producing 1 million computers per year, then they would have to halt all food production.

Production possibilities and opportunity cost

A fundamental economic concept is **opportunity cost**, which is the highest-valued, next-best alternative that must be sacrificed to obtain an item. For Northland, any production decision entails an opportunity cost. As already noted, Northland's residents must give up producing 700,000 baskets of food to produce 1 million computers instead. This means that in Northland, the opportunity cost of producing 1 million computers is the 700,000 baskets of food that it could have otherwise produced with its current technology and all its resources.

Opportunity cost: *The highest-valued, next-best alternative that must be sacrificed to obtain an item.*

Let's suppose that Northland has chosen not to be purely a food producer or a computer producer. Currently, it produces 400,000 computers. Table 2.1 indicates that, given current production possibilities, this means that Northland also produces 600,000 baskets of food. If Northland's residents decide to become a little more high-tech-oriented by producing 100,000 more computers, thereby yielding a total of 500,000 new computers this year, then they must reallocate to computer production tasks some of the resources that they previously had devoted to food production. This means that they must cut back on food production. According to Table 2.1, Northland's residents can raise their computer production from 400,000 to 500,000 only if they reduce food production from 600,000 baskets to 550,000 baskets. Thus, producing 100,000 more computers entails incurring an opportunity cost equal to 50,000 baskets of food.

Now suppose that Northland's residents decide to aim for an even more high-tech production mix by raising their computer production by 100,000 more units, to 600,000 computers. This requires reducing food production from 550,000 baskets to 490,000 baskets. Consequently, producing another 100,000 computers requires Northland's residents to incur an opportunity cost equal to 60,000 baskets of food.

If Northland's residents raise computer production by yet another 100,000-unit increment, from 600,000 to 700,000 computers, then Table 2.1 indicates that food production must decline from 490,000 to 410,000 baskets. The opportunity cost of producing the next 100,000 computers, therefore, is 80,000 baskets of food.

Note that each 100,000-unit increase in computer production requires a successively larger—50,000, then 60,000, and then 80,000—reduction in the quantity of baskets of food that Northland can produce. This illustrates a fundamental characteristic of the production possibilities tradeoffs that countries normally face: The opportunity cost of producing additional units of a particular good increases as more of that good is produced.

If you think about this for a minute, it will become clear to you that it makes a lot of sense. If the residents of a country such as Northland start transferring resources from food production to computer production, initially they will transfer over those people who are best at designing and manufacturing microprocessors, modems, DVD drives, operating systems, and so on. Initially they will also shift resources that are best suited to computer production—silicon, precious metals, materials useful for making plastics, and the like. As they continue to increase their production of computers, however, Northland's residents will discover that fewer resources readily

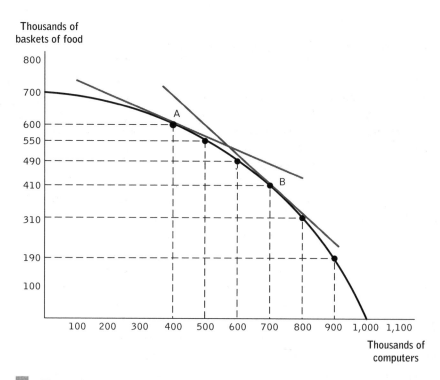

Figure 2.1 *Northland's production possibilities frontier*

This diagram displays the combinations of food and computer production listed in Table 2.1 on page 34, which together with all other feasible combinations of production of goods and services is Northland's production possibilities frontier. Given technology and available resources, Northland's residents can produce combinations of food or computers that lie on or inside this frontier but cannot produce combinations that lie beyond the frontier. To increase production of computers from 400,000 at point A to 700,000 at point B, Northland's residents must reduce their food production from 600,000 to 410,000 baskets, so the opportunity cost of 300,000 computers is 190,000 baskets of food. At point A the opportunity cost of producing one additional computer is the slope of the line tangent to point A. Likewise, at point B the opportunity cost of producing one more computer is the slope of the line tangent to that point. The absolute slope of the tangent line at point B is greater than the absolute slope of the tangent line at point A, which indicates that increasing total computer production generates a rise in the opportunity cost of producing computers.

lend themselves to producing computers. Some people transferred from food production to computer production may know a lot about botany, farming, or agricultural machinery, but relatively little about computer manufacturing or programming. Iron, steel, and other resources that are useful for farming will also be less readily applied to computer production. Thus, each successive 100,000-unit increase in production of computers requires transferring successively larger numbers of resources away from food production. The result is a successively larger reduction in production of food due to each incremental increase in computer production, and hence a higher opportunity cost of producing computers. (To see how to examine opportunity costs on a graph of Northland's production possibilities, see *Visualizing Global Economic Issues: The production possibilities frontier.*)

VISUALIZING GLOBAL ECONOMIC ISSUES

The production possibilities frontier

The production possibilities for Northland can be displayed on a diagram, as shown in Figure 2.1. This figure plots the combinations of food and computer production from Table 2.1 on page 34, with the amount of food measured along the vertical axis and the amount of computers measured along the horizontal axis. These production combinations, plus all other feasible combinations of production of goods and services given technology and available resources, lie along a curve that economists call the production possibilities frontier. Northland's residents can produce combinations of food or computers that lie on or inside the frontier, but they cannot produce combinations that lie beyond the frontier.

Point A in Figure 2.1 corresponds to the second line of Table 2.1, and at this point Northland's residents can produce 400,000 computers and 600,000 baskets of food in a year. Point B corresponds to the fifth line of Table 2.1, which indicates that Northland's residents are able to raise their computer production to 700,000 computers if they reduce their production of food to 410,000 baskets.

Thus, we can calculate the opportunity cost of moving from one point to another along the production possibilities frontier. Let's consider a different question, however. What is the opportunity cost of increasing computer production by a *single unit* if Northland's residents currently are producing at point A? We can determine the answer by looking at the *slope* of a line tangent to the production possibilities frontier at point A. Recall that the slope of a line is the "rise" divided by the "run." A one-unit increase in computer production is a one-unit horizontal movement, or *run*, along the line. The accompanying vertical movement back down along the line is the *rise*, which is negative because it tells us the opportunity cost of the one-unit increase in computer production, which is measured in baskets of food.

Likewise, we can find the opportunity cost of a one-unit increase in computer production at point B by considering the slope of the line tangent to the production possibilities frontier at that point. Note that the *rise* accompanying a one-unit run along this tangent line is a larger negative amount. Thus, the opportunity cost of computer production is higher at point B than at point A. That is, when more resources are already devoted to computer production, shifting sufficient resources from food production to computer production to achieve a one-unit increase in computer production entails a higher opportunity cost measured in baskets of food.

For critical analysis: If the opportunity cost of producing one additional computer was always the same, no matter how many computers Northland produced, what would be the shape of its production possibilities frontier?

Consumption possibilities and choices

By assumption, residents of Northland engage in no international trade. Hence, whatever combination of food and computers that Northland's residents produce stays within the nation's borders for domestic consumption.

Consumption possibilities: *All possible combinations of goods and services that a nation's residents can consume.*

This means that Northland's **consumption possibilities**, or the amounts of goods and services that its residents are able to consume, are exactly the same as its production possibilities. The production possibilities depicted in Table 2.1 (p. 34), therefore, are also Northland's consumption possibilities.

How much will the residents of Northland choose to produce and consume? This will depend on their preferences. If they have a taste for baskets of food, then they will choose a combination toward the upper part of Table 2.1. By way of contrast, if they enjoy playing computer games and surfing the Internet, then they will choose a production mix toward the lower part of Table 2.1.

Fundamental Issue #1: What are a nation's production possibilities, and what do they tell us about the costs of producing goods and services within that nation? The production possibilities of a nation are combinations of goods and services that its residents are capable of producing, given currently available technology and resources. When the nation's residents raise their production of one item, they must forgo producing some amount of another good or service, thereby incurring an opportunity cost. This opportunity cost increases as the nation's residents produce more of the particular item.

ABSOLUTE ADVANTAGE—DO BIG COUNTRIES HAVE AN UPPER HAND?

As noted at the beginning of this chapter, it is not uncommon for residents of countries with relatively high productive capabilities to engage in trade with people residing in nations with relatively low production capabilities. To many people, such trade flows seem counterintuitive. Indeed, some observers of trade flows between large countries and small countries jump to the conclusion that such flows imply exploitation of the small country (say, Nepal) by the large country (say, the United States)—and possibly some of the workers in the large country.

Before you can begin to think through why trade might be beneficial for both types of country, you must first understand the concept of absolute advantage. As you will see, this concept can help explain why international trade takes place, but it cannot provide a complete justification for real-world trade patterns.

ON THE WEB:

For data on U.S. trade with all other nations of the world, go to www.census. gov/foreign-trade/ balance/index.html.

Absolute advantage as a rationale for trade

For a variety of reasons, such as differing terrains, climates, and technologies, countries of the world differ in their ability to produce various goods. At one time, international trade was thought to arise from the ability of some countries to produce goods or services at a lower production cost, in terms of units of labor or other resource inputs required to produce each unit of a good or service.

Absolute advantage

Because of this emphasis on production costs, early thinking about why countries trade focused on the possibility that one country might have an **absolute advantage** arising from its ability to produce more output, as compared with other nations, from given inputs of resources. As an example, consider Table 2.2. If a representative set of 100 workers from Northland is assigned to manufacture computers, given a fixed set of additional productive resources, then in a week's time they can produce 30 computers. Alternatively, if a set of 100 Northland residents is put to work producing food, the result is 50 baskets of output in a week's time. By way of contrast, in a neighboring country called Westcoast, during a given week and using an identical set of additional resources, one set of 100 workers can produce 40 computers, while another group of 100 workers can produce 25 baskets of food. Thus, if the two countries engage in no trade, the combined weekly output by the 200 workers is 70 computers and 75 baskets of food.

Because 100 workers in Northland can produce more baskets of food than the same number of workers can produce each week in Westcoast, we can conclude that Northland has an absolute advantage in producing food. Westcoast, however, has an absolute advantage in computer production, because 100 workers in that nation can produce more computers than the same number of workers in Northland are able to produce during a given week.

Absolute advantage: *The ability of a nation's residents to produce a good or service at lower cost, measured in resources required to produce the good or service, or, alternatively, the ability to produce more output from given inputs of resources, as compared with other nations.*

Absolute advantage as a basis for trade

Absolute advantage can provide a rationale for cross-border trade between Northland and Westcoast. The reason is that, in principle, both countries can gain from specializing in producing the goods for which they have an absolute advantage. To see

Table 2.2 *Weekly production in Northland and Westcoast without specialization*

Product	Northland		Westcoast		Combined weekly output
	Workers	Weekly output	Workers	Weekly output	
Computers	100	30	100	40	70
Food	100	50	100	25	75

Table 2.3 *Weekly production in Northland and Westcoast with specialization*

Product	Northland		Westcoast		Combined weekly output
	Workers	Weekly output	Workers	Weekly output	
Computers	0	0	200	80	80
Food	200	100	0	0	100

why this is so, take a look at Table 2.3. Northland has an absolute advantage in producing food, and if both groups of workers in Northland produce food, then the 200 workers together can produce 100 baskets of food each week. At the same time, if the 200 workers in Westcoast manufacture computers—the good that Westcoast has an absolute advantage in producing—then their weekly output is 80 computers.

If you look back at Table 2.2, you will see that specialization increases the total output of both nations. The 100 baskets of food that the 200 workers in Northland can produce each week exceeds the 75 baskets that the same number of workers in both nations can produce when the countries do not specialize. Likewise, the 80 computers that the 200 workers in Westcoast are able to manufacture in one week is greater than the 70 computers that a total of 200 laborers in both countries can make without specialization.

This means that both countries have an incentive to specialize in production and engage in trade. To see why, suppose that the countries' residents agree to trade one basket of food for one computer. Suppose, further, that the residents of Northland exchange 35 baskets of food for 35 of Westcoast's computers each week. From Table 2.3, you can see that Northland's residents will still have 65 baskets of food available for domestic consumption each week, which is more than the 50 baskets that Table 2.2 indicates they would have been able to consume without specialization and trade.

At the same time, the 35 baskets of food that Westcoast's residents are able to obtain through specialization and trade exceed the 25 baskets that they could consume in the absence of trade. Furthermore, the 35 computers that residents of Northland can obtain via trade exceeds the 30 that Table 2.2 indicates that they could have produced on their own, while the 45 computers that Westcoast residents can retain after trading away 35 each week to Northland exceeds the 40 that they would have available for domestic use in the absence of specialization and trade.

> *Fundamental Issue #2: What is absolute advantage, and how can it help explain why nations engage in international trade?* A nation has an absolute advantage in producing an item if its residents can produce more of that good or service with a given amount of resources, as compared with other nations. This can give the nation's residents an incentive to specialize in producing goods and services for which their nation has an absolute advantage, and to trade those goods and services for items produced in nations that have an absolute advantage in producing those items.

What absolute advantage implies—and what it doesn't

The previous example shows that absolute advantage can provide a rationale for trade among nations. By specializing in producing goods or services for which they have an absolute advantage in production, and then trading these goods and services, countries potentially can consume more goods and services than they could otherwise.

Production possibilities and absolute advantage

Another way to illustrate how countries can gain from specialization and trade is by examining their overall production possibilities. Take a look at Table 2.4 overleaf, which displays Northland's production possibilities from Table 2.1 alongside the overall production possibilities available to Westcoast.

Table 2.4 indicates that Northland has an absolute advantage over Westcoast in producing food, in the sense that if the residents of both countries produce nothing but food, Northland can produce 700,000 baskets, whereas Westcoast can produce only 600,000. Westcoast has an absolute advantage in producing computers, because if residents of both Northland and Westcoast produce only computers, those in Westcoast can produce 1.25 million computers, as compared with the 1 million computers that residents of Northland can manufacture.

It is not obvious from the table, however, that this absolute advantage will necessarily induce the two countries to trade. For instance, each country might happen to produce 500,000 computers and 550,000 baskets of food (see the third line of Table 2.4). If both countries choose this identical production mix, it is unclear why they might want to trade—at least from the standpoint of any argument based on the idea of absolute advantage.

Absolute advantage cannot fully explain international trade

In general, it turns out that absolute advantage has limited usefulness in helping us to understand why many countries trade. Consider, for instance, the weekly computer and food production capabilities of two groups of 100 residents in Northland versus two other groups of 100 residents in Southsea, a neighboring island archipelago

Table 2.4 Production possibilities in Northland and Westcoast

Northland		Westcoast	
Thousands of computers	Thousands of baskets of food	Thousands of computers	Thousands of baskets of food
0	700	0	600
400	600	350	585
500	550	500	550
600	490	650	495
700	410	800	425
800	310	950	335
900	220	1,100	120
1,000	0	1,250	0

Table 2.5 Weekly production in Northland and Southsea without specialization

Product	Northland		Southsea		Combined weekly output
	Workers	Weekly output	Workers	Weekly output	
Computers	100	30	100	15	45
Food	100	50	100	10	60

nation. As you can see from Table 2.5, Northland has an absolute advantage over Southsea in producing *both* goods. From the perspective of absolute advantage, therefore, Northland has no incentive to specialize and engage in trade with Southsea.

Nevertheless, there are good reasons to think that both countries would gain from trading. Table 2.5 indicates that, to produce 30 more computers in a given day, Northland must reallocate 100 workers from food production and give up 50 baskets of food. Thus, the opportunity cost of a computer in Northland is 50 baskets of food divided by 30 computers, or 5/3 baskets of food per computer. In Southsea, producing 15 more computers would require giving up only 10 baskets of food, so the opportunity cost of a computer in Southsea is 10 baskets of food divided by 15 computers, or 2/3 basket of food per computer. Even though Northland has an absolute advantage in producing computers, the opportunity cost of producing computers is lower in Southsea.

Table 2.5 also indicates that to produce 50 more baskets of food on a given day, Northland's residents must give up 30 computers, so that the opportunity cost of producing food in Northland is 30 computers divided by 50 baskets of food, or 3/5 computer per basket of food. In Southsea, producing 10 more baskets of food on a given day requires forgoing the production of 15 computers. Consequently, the opportunity cost of producing a basket of food in Southsea is 15 computers divided by 10 baskets of food, or 1.5 computers per basket of food. Hence, the opportunity cost of producing a basket of food is lower in Northland than in Southsea.

Now, for the sake of argument, let's suppose that residents of Northland and Southsea are willing to exchange one basket of food for one computer, and *vice versa*. Trading goods at this rate of exchange is beneficial for Northland residents, because giving up one basket of food to Southsea residents in exchange for a computer is a better deal than sacrificing 5/3 baskets of food to obtain a computer within its own borders. Likewise, giving one computer for one basket of food from Northland is advantageous for residents of Southsea, because this is a better deal than giving up 1.5 computers to obtain a basket of food within its own borders.

Clearly, absolute advantage alone cannot fully explain why many countries engage in international trade. Differences in internal opportunity costs are likely to be fundamental determinants of whether countries can gain from trading goods and services with other nations. We turn next to this fundamental explanation for why countries trade with one another.

> *Fundamental Issue #3: Why is absolute advantage alone insufficient to account for trade among nations?* Absolute advantage by itself cannot fully explain why countries trade, because residents of a nation can benefit from trade with another country even when their nation has an absolute advantage in producing all goods and services. The reason is that the opportunity cost of producing an item within their nation may exceed the amount of goods and services required to obtain that item from residents of another country.

COMPARATIVE ADVANTAGE—WHY TRADE BENEFITS NEARLY EVERYONE

As the previous example indicates, two countries may have an incentive to trade goods or services even if one has an absolute advantage over the other in producing the goods or services. The reason is that *opportunity costs* of producing goods and services vary from country to country. If the opportunity cost of producing a good or service in even a very small country with meager production of goods and services is low, relative to the opportunity cost of producing the same good or service in a large nation capable of producing massive quantities of output, trade may still take place.

Comparative advantage

When residents of a country are able to produce a good or service at a lower opportunity cost compared with other nations, then that country is said to have a **comparative advantage**. Even if a country is at an absolute disadvantage in producing goods or services, that country may still have a comparative advantage in producing one or more goods or services, which can induce other nations to engage in trade with that country. (As discussed in more detail below, opportunity cost-motivated trade implies more efficient resource allocations that enable nations to expand their production and consumption of goods and services; to consider how a lower

Comparative advantage: *The ability of a nation's residents to produce an additional unit of a good or service at a lower opportunity cost relative to other nations.*

opportunity cost of *distributing* items can motivate trade, see *Management Notebook: Using ice-class shipping to reduce the opportunity cost of the international distribution of natural gas*.)

MANAGEMENT NOTEBOOK

Using ice-class shipping to reduce the opportunity cost of the international distribution of natural gas

The tanker ship *Ob River* is carrying deep-chilled liquefied natural gas from Norway to Japan. Chilling, liquefying, and shipping natural gas between nations is not a new idea. What is novel about this international shipment is the *Ob River*'s route. In years past, a ship would have carried the gas through the Mediterranean Sea, the Suez Canal, and around Asia. The *Ob River* is instead traveling from Norway through the Artic Ocean north of Russia. This route will enable the ship to deliver its load of natural gas 3 weeks faster than any other ship that would have charted a course along the usual Mediterranean Sea–Suez Canal route.

The *Ob River* is one of a small group of ice-class tanker ships capable of making the iceberg-infested journey across the Arctic Ocean. The 3 weeks that the *Ob River* is shaving off of the normal shipping time by braving the icy Arctic waters is significantly reducing a key opportunity cost of international trade in natural gas: the time ships spend at sea on dedicated trips transporting natural gas over long distances. The 3 weeks of time gained by the *Ob River*'s route will now be freed up to for shipments of additional gas, substantially reducing the overall expense of moving large volumes of gas between nations.

Residents of Norway and other natural gas-producing nations possessing Arctic ports are watching the *Ob River*'s progress closely. Firms in these countries already have developed new techniques for producing natural gas at a much lower opportunity cost, measured in terms of forgone output of other goods and services, than in years past. The potential further reduction in the opportunity cost of distributing natural gas made possible by ice-class tanker ships promises to strengthen further the growing comparative advantage that residents of Arctic-bordering nations have developed in the international trade of natural gas.

For critical analysis: Why do you suppose some economists have suggested that melting of some polar ice, caused by potential climate change, could strengthen the comparative advantage in natural gas trade for nations possessing Arctic ports?

(handwritten margin note: Faster, more efficient route)

Production possibilities and comparative advantage

For another perspective on why comparative advantage is such a crucial factor influencing international trade, consider Table 2.6, which gives overall production possibilities for Northland and Southsea. The feasible combinations of food and

Table 2.6 Production possibilities in Northland and Southsea

Northland		Southsea	
Thousands of computers	Thousands of baskets of food	Thousands of computers	Thousands of baskets of food
0	700	0	300
400	600	100	295
500	550	150	285
600	490	200	270
700	410	250	240
800	310	300	200
900	220	350	150
1,000	0	400	0

computer production for Northland are again the same as in Table 2.1 on page 34. Note that Southsea is capable of producing both fewer computers and fewer baskets of food than Northland. Thus, Northland has an *absolute advantage* in producing both goods.

Now suppose that, in the absence of trade, both nations choose to produce combinations of computers and food listed in the fifth row of Table 2.6. Hence, Northland currently produces 700,000 computers and 410,000 baskets of food during the year, while Southsea produces 250,000 computers and 240,000 baskets of food. The table indicates that, if Northland were to increase its production of computers by 100,000, to 800,000, it would have to give up 100,000 baskets of food, which implies an *average* opportunity cost of one basket of food per computer. In Southsea, however, increasing computer production by 100,000 units, to 350,000 computers, would entail reducing the amount of food production to 150,000 baskets (by 90,000 baskets). This means that the *average* opportunity cost of increasing computer production in Southsea is 0.9 basket of food per computer. Over these ranges along the two nations' production possibilities, therefore, Southsea has a comparative advantage in producing computers.

Over the same ranges, however, Northland has a comparative advantage in producing food. Increasing food production from 310,000 to 410,000 baskets in Northland requires giving up producing 100,000 computers, or an *average* opportunity cost of one computer per basket of food. In Southsea, however, raising food production from 150,000 to 240,000 baskets (by 90,000 baskets) entails forgoing the production of 100,000 computers, which implies an *average* opportunity cost of approximately 1.11 computers per basket of food (100,000 computers divided by 90,000 baskets of food). Thus, the opportunity cost of producing food over these ranges of production possibilities is lower in Northland, so that Northland has a comparative advantage in food production over these ranges of production possibilities. (Iceland is a "small nation" compared with the United States, yet U.S. e-commerce firms have begun importing data-center services from Iceland; see *Online Globalization: Iceland discovers a comparative advantage in operating data centers*.)

ONLINE GLOBALIZATION

Iceland discovers a comparative advantage in operating data centers

With a population of fewer than 325,000 people, Iceland is a very small nation that has an absolute disadvantage relative to most other nations in producing many items, including the services of data centers. Nevertheless, residents of Iceland are utilizing more than $40 billion worth of facilities containing computer servers to provide data-center services to e-commerce companies in other nations.

Because Iceland possesses both a volcanic geology and a normally chilly atmospheric temperature, its residents are able to utilize geothermal energy to power computer facilities, and to funnel cool outside air to keep servers and other sensitive equipment air-conditioned. These features have enabed Iceland to operate data centers at a much lower opportunity cost than is feasible in the United States and Europe. As a consequence of this comparative advantage, Icelandic data centers are already exporting their services to many U.S. and European companies.

For critical analysis: How would a general wage increase for Icelandic data-center workers relative to U.S. and European counterparts affect Iceland's comparative advantage in providing data-center services?

Production possibilities and trade

We have determined that Northland has a comparative advantage in food production while producing 700,000 computers and 410,000 baskets of food and that Southsea has a comparative advantage in computer production while producing 250,000 computers and 240,000 baskets of food. Does this mean there may be an incentive for Northland's residents to specialize in producing food to trade for computers that Southsea's residents specialize in producing?

To answer this question, note that based on our calculations, if Northland's residents wish to obtain more computers than the 700,000 they currently produce, on average it would cost one basket of food to obtain each computer. This means that Northland's residents will be willing to obtain more computers through trade with Southsea's residents if Southsea's residents will be willing to accept less than one basket of food in exchange.

At the same time, if Southsea's residents desire to consume more than the 240,000 baskets of food they currently produce, then on average it would cost 1.11 computers to obtain each basket of food. Southsea's residents, therefore, will be willing to offer to trade their computers for food produced in Northland as long as they can trade fewer than 1.11 computers for each basket of Northland's food. A rate of exchange of 1.11 computers per basket of food is the same as a rate of exchange of 0.9 basket of food per computer. Thus, as long as the rate of exchange of food for computers is higher than 0.9 basket of food per computer, Southsea residents will be willing to trade their computers for food produced in Northland.

We can conclude that, in this example, as long as the rate of exchange of food for computers is between 0.9 basket of food per computer and one basket of food per computer, Northland's residents are willing to consider trading some of their food for Southsea's computers, and Southsea's residents are willing to consider trading some of their computers for Northland's food. The reason is that as long as the food–computer exchange rate is within this range, both can come out ahead if they can agree about how many baskets of food and computers to trade. (To see how to examine comparative advantage and incentives to trade on a diagram, see the box: "Visualizing global economic issues: Production possibilities frontiers and comparative advantage.")

ON THE WEB:

View the most recent overall trade statistics for the United States at www.census. gov/indicator/www/ ustrade.html.

Gains from trade

Let's suppose that residents of Northland and Southsea agree to exchange food and computers at a rate of exchange of 0.95 basket of food per computer (which is

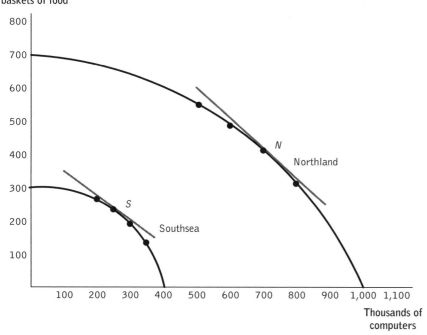

Figure 2.2 *Production possibilities frontiers for Northland and Southsea*

This graph uses the data from Table 2.6 on p. 45 to display the production possibilities frontiers for Northland and Southsea. Northland has an absolute advantage in producing both food and computers. Consequently, Southsea's production possibilities frontier lies inside Northland's production possibilities frontier, and absolute advantage cannot explain trade between the nations. The residents of the countries currently produce at points S and N. Because the line tangent to point S is slightly less steeply sloped than the line tangent to point N, Southsea presently produces an additional computer at lower cost. At the same time, Northland produces an additional basket of food at lower cost. Hence, there is an incentive for both nations to consider trading.

approximately the same as 1.053 computer per basket of food). Let's further suppose that, at this exchange rate, Northland trades 100,000 baskets of food to Southsea in exchange for 105,300 computers.

Gains from trade: *Additional goods and services that a nation's residents can consume, over and above the amounts that they could have produced within their own borders, as a consequence of trade with residents of other nations.*

We can use Table 2.6 to determine that each country will experience **gains from trade**, or additional goods and services over and above the amounts it could have produced on its own, as a result of this transaction. According to Table 2.6, if Northland's residents had given up 100,000 computers, they could have increased their own production of computers by 100,000. Hence, the trade with Southsea entails a gain from trade equal to 5,300 computers for Northland.

For Southsea, recall that the average opportunity cost of food was equal to 1.11 computers per basket of food. Hence, obtaining 100,000 baskets of food (at least, in the production possibilities range that we considered) would have cost Southsea residents about 110,000 computers if they had produced them on their own. Because they are able to trade only 105,300 computers for 100,000 baskets of Northland's food production, however, Southsea's residents experience a gain from trade equal to 4,700 computers.

VISUALIZING GLOBAL ECONOMIC ISSUES

Production possibilities frontiers and comparative advantage

Figure 2.2 shows the production possibilities frontiers for Northland and Southsea, based on the information in Table 2.6 (p. 45). Because Northland has an absolute advantage in producing both food and computers, the production possibilities frontier for Southsea lies completely inside Northland's production possibilities frontier. Hence, absolute advantage cannot provide a rationale for trade between Northland and Southsea.

In our example, we examined *average* opportunity costs for Northland and Southsea in a range containing the fifth row of Table 2.6, where initially Northland produces 700,000 computers and 410,000 baskets of food, and Southsea produces 250,000 computers and 240,000 baskets of food. These are denoted as points *N* and *S* in the figure.

Recall that the opportunity cost of increasing computer production by a single unit is equal to the slope of the production possibilities frontier at the current production combination. Consequently, the exact opportunity cost of higher computer production in Northland equals the slope of the line tangent to point *N*. Likewise, the exact opportunity cost of higher computer production in Southsea equals the slope of the line tangent to point *S*. The line tangent to point *S* is slightly less steeply sloped than the line tangent to point *N*, thereby indicating that at point *S* Southsea can produce an additional computer at less cost than Northland can produce at point *N*. As long as the rate of exchange of food for computers is between the values of these two slopes, there is an incentive for both nations to consider engaging in trade.

For critical analysis: Would the incentives for residents of Northland and Southsea change if points N and S were in different locations along the nations' production possibilities frontiers?

Finally, note that this trade adds to Northland's trade balance in food while subtracting from its trade balance in computers, and it adds to Southsea's trade balance in computers while subtracting from its trade balance in food. If these two nations have similar comparative advantages *vis-à-vis* other countries, then Northland is likely to have an overall trade surplus in food and an overall trade deficit in computers, and Southsea is likely to have an overall trade deficit in food and an overall trade surplus in computers. Hence, a nation's trade balances in categories for specific goods or services are likely to be related in large part to comparative advantage. (Only rarely can economists observe gains from trade that occur when a nation engages in international trade after previously experiencing no trade. A recently studied exception is Japan before and after the 1860s; see *Policy Notebook: Gains from international trade in nineteenth-century Japan*.)

POLICY NOTEBOOK

Gains from international trade in nineteenth-century Japan

For almost two centuries preceding the 1860s, government restraints prevented residents of Japan from engaging in international trade and thereby prohibited them from experiencing gains from trade. In 1859, however, Japan's government committed the nation to a new policy of trade openness that began after 1864.

Daniel Bernhofen and John Brown of the University of Nottingham have used data on production employment of factors of production in Japan before and after 1865 to estimate the gains that the nation experienced during its first dozen years of international trade. Measured in terms of arable lands effectively freed up by trade for alternative uses, Bernhofen and Brown find that opening Japan to trade provided a gain during this period equal to 3.9 percent of these lands. Measured in terms of additional labor resources effectively made available for other uses, they estimate gains equal to 3.3 percent of Japan's male labor force and 5.5 percent of its female labor force. Thus, the Japanese government's decision to open the nation to international trade in the nineteenth century generated significant gains from trade.

For critical analysis: Why did the expansion of Japan's resources available to produce additional goods and services permitted by international trade translate into consumption gains for the country's residents? Explain your reasoning.

Fundamental Issue #4: What is comparative advantage, and how does it allow countries to experience gains from trade? A nation has a comparative advantage when its residents can produce additional units of a good or service at a lower cost than in other countries. This gives to residents of a country with higher costs of producing additional units of the good or service an incentive to trade with the nation that has a comparative advantage. Residents of the country with higher opportunity costs can reap gains from trade because, through trade, they can obtain more units of the good or service at a lower cost than the domestic cost of producing it.

WHY TRADE IS NOT A CLEAR-CUT ISSUE

You have learned that absolute advantage gives nations an incentive to specialize in production and engage in international trade. Furthermore, *comparative advantage* promises gains from trade, even in situations when *absolute advantage* fails to provide a motivation for trade.

Why, then, do the volumes of trade among nations tend to ebb and flow over time? In addition, why does international trade often generate so much controversy and debate within nations around the world? Let's consider each of these questions in turn.

Gains from trade can be fleeting

Until the mid-twentieth century, many Nepalese village blacksmiths were able to export handcrafted copper containers to residents of other nations. During the rest of the century, cross-border trade in their wares dried up. Then the flow of trade recovered again at the beginning of this century. Undoubtedly, the ability to market their wares over the Internet helped Nepalese artisans establish a new foothold in the international marketplace for handcrafted goods. Nevertheless, changing opportunity costs likely played a role as well, as evidenced by the fact that other nations developed a comparative advantage in producing close substitutes for copper containers that tended to crowd out trade in Nepalese handicrafts during several decades of the twentieth century.

In our examples, we were careful to emphasize two key assumptions underlying our examinations of production possibilities and opportunity costs: (1) a *given* technology, and (2) a *fixed* set of available resources. Of course, these assumptions apply only to a short-run time horizon. Countries' production possibilities do not remain unchanged over time. Technological improvements expand a nation's production possibilities, and the amounts of resources, such as labor, can increase over time. Furthermore, technological change and growth in available resources sometimes favor the production of one good over another.

This means that a nation's absolute advantage in producing a particular item often can dissipate with the passage of time as other countries develop greater capabilities to produce the same good or service. In addition, opportunity costs of producing particular goods or services can change as technological innovations and changes in resources tend to make one good or service less expensive to produce relative to another. As a result, a nation that once had a comparative advantage in, say, crafting copper containers may discover within a few years that this advantage has evaporated following changes in the opportunity costs of production in other nations.

In short, gains from trade can evaporate for one item for a time, but then gradually reappear years later. Sometimes changes in nations' production possibilities can even result in reversing gains from trade, so that a country that once was a net exporter of a good for which it had a comparative advantage ultimately becomes a net importer when other nations develop a comparative advantage in producing that good.

The redistributive effects of trade

For Nepalese blacksmiths, change was painful. Before the mid-twentieth century, artisans of Nepal had a comparative advantage in producing inexpensive bowls, jars, and jugs, and they were able to earn a modest living producing these goods. When alternatives that could be produced at lower opportunity cost arrived on the scene, many felt obliged to move to India to find gainful employment producing goods or services in which that nation had an absolute or comparative advantage. When conditions changed a few years ago because of improved marketing opportunities, changed consumer preferences, and altered opportunity costs outside Nepal, good times returned for Nepalese blacksmiths as consumers in the United States and elsewhere began to buy their copper containers.

This boom-and-bust story of Nepalese copperware is just a small example of the sweeping *internal* changes that individual countries can witness as a result of ebbs and flows in absolute or comparative advantages among nations. Such changes illustrate the **redistributive effects of trade**, which are internal rearrangements of income flows among a nation's residents arising from variations in flows of international trade. Through such redistributive effects, technological change, and other factors that affect nations' production possibilities and alter global absolute and comparative advantages, have domestic as well as international impacts. Naturally, redistributive effects of trade have implications for domestic politics within each of the world's nations. More importantly, however, they affect the well being of people around the globe. We shall revisit this theme throughout the following chapters.

Redistributive effects of trade: *Altered allocations of incomes among a nation's residents as a result of changes in international trade flows.*

Fundamental Issue #5: Why, in spite of its benefits, does international trade ebb and flow, and create so much controversy within the world's nations? The potential for gains from specialization and trade arising from absolute and comparative advantage varies over time as changes in technology and available resources alter opportunity costs of production within nations. As a result, nations can develop or lose absolute and comparative advantages over time, and domestic income redistributions can thereby take place.

CHAPTER SUMMARY

1. Production possibilities and what they indicate about a nation's costs of producing goods and services: A nation's production possibilities are combinations of goods

and services that its residents can feasibly produce using currently available technology and fixed amounts of productive resources. Increasing production of one item entails reducing production of some amount of another good or service, which implies that the nation's residents must incur an opportunity cost. The opportunity cost of producing an item rises as the nation's residents produce more of that item.

2. **Absolute advantage and how it can help explain why nations engage in international trade:** A country has an absolute advantage in producing a good or service if those residing in that country can produce more of the item than residents of another nation. This can give the nation's residents an incentive to specialize in producing goods and services for which their nation has an absolute advantage. They can then trade these items for goods and services produced in countries with an absolute advantage in producing those items.

3. **Why absolute advantage alone is insufficient to account for trade among nations:** By itself, absolute advantage is unable to explain completely why countries trade. Residents of a country can benefit from trading with another nation even though their nation may have an absolute advantage, because the opportunity cost of producing an item within their country may exceed the amount of goods and services required to obtain that item from residents of another nation.

4. **Comparative advantage and how it enables countries to experience gains from trade:** A country has a comparative advantage when residents of that country can produce additional units of an item at a lower opportunity cost compared with other nations. Residents of another nation with a higher cost of producing that item thereby have an incentive to engage in trade with the nation that has a comparative advantage. Residents of the country with higher costs of producing the item can reap gains from trade. By trading, they can obtain more units of the item at a lower cost relative to the cost of producing the item domestically.

5. **Why, in spite of its benefits, international trade ebbs and flows and creates controversy within nations of the world:** Technological innovations and changes in the availability of resources within nations alter the extent to which countries experience absolute and comparative advantage by affecting relative opportunity costs of production across countries. As a result, the potential for gains from specialization and trade changes over time, and countries can develop or lose absolute and comparative advantages as time passes, resulting in redistributions of income within countries.

QUESTIONS AND PROBLEMS

1. Consider the following production possibilities for a country that produces computer modems and DVD drives, and then answer the questions that follow, assuming that currently residents of this nation produce 500,000 modems and 570,000 DVD drives.

Thousands of DVD drives	Thousands of modems
800	0
700	300
640	400
570	500
490	600
400	700
250	800
0	900

(a) What is the opportunity cost of producing 200,000 more modems?

(b) What is the opportunity cost of producing 70,000 more DVD drives?

(c) What is the opportunity cost of completely specializing in the production of modems? Why might residents of this nation consider specializing in modem production?

2. Consider the following table, which shows unspecialized productive capabilities of sets of workers in Northland and neighboring Eastshore, when answering the questions that follow.

Product	Northland		Eastshore		Combined
	Workers	Output	Workers	Output	Output
Modems	50	25	50	45	70
DVD drives	50	50	50	15	65

(a) Which country has an absolute advantage in producing modems? DVD drives?

(b) Which country has a comparative advantage in producing modems? DVD drives?

(c) Abstracting from any other factors, what is the range for rates of exchange of modems for DVD drives that will induce Northland and Eastshore to trade modems and DVD drives? If trade occurs, which country exports modems and imports DVD drives?

3. Refer to the table below when answering the following questions.

Northland		Eastshore	
Thousands of modems	Thousands of DVD drives	Thousands of modems	Thousands of DVD drives
0	800	0	500
300	700	100	485
400	640	150	455
500	570	200	400
600	490	250	330
700	400	300	250
800	250	350	160
900	0	400	0

53

(a) Which, if either, country has an absolute advantage in producing modems? DVD drives?

(b) Currently, both nations produce the combinations displayed in the fourth line of the table. Based on the average opportunity costs that each nation would face if it were to produce 100,000 additional modems, is it possible that Northland could gain from trading with Eastshore if it desires to obtain more computer modems? Explain.

4. The following table displays the labor input requirements to produce identical quantities of two goods in two different nations, holding all other inputs unchanged. Use this information to answer the following questions.

Country	Cheese	Wine
Denmark	8	4
Portugal	10	4

(a) Which, if either, country has an absolute advantage in producing cheese? Wine?

(b) Which, if either, country has a comparative advantage in producing cheese? Wine?

(c) If Denmark imports one additional unit of its import good, how much labor does it save?

(d) If Portugal imports one additional unit of its import good, how much labor does it save?

(e) Explain why Denmark and Portugal can realize gains from trade if they import the good in which the other nation has a comparative advantage.

5. The following table displays the labor input requirements to produce identical quantities of three goods in two nations, holding all other inputs unchanged. Use this information to answer the following questions.

Country	Grains	Wine	Clothing
Nepal	3	4	3
India	4	3	1

(a) Arrange the goods in order of Nepal's comparative advantage, from greatest advantage to lowest advantage (or disadvantage).

(b) Which good or goods could Nepal gain from exporting to India? From importing from India?

6. Take a look back at the table in question 2, which applied to Northland and Eastshore 10 years ago. After technological change has taken place in each nation, the following table now applies in the absence of specialization and trade.

Product	Northland		Eastshore		Combined
	Workers	Output	Workers	Output	Output
Modems	50	50	50	150	200
DVD drives	50	100	50	75	175

(a) Which country now has an absolute advantage in producing modems? DVD drives?

(b) Which country now has a comparative advantage in producing modems? DVD drives?

(c) Abstracting from any other factors, what is the range for rates of exchange of modems for DVD drives that will now induce Northland and Eastshore to trade modems and DVD drives? If trade occurs, which country currently exports modems and imports DVD drives?

ONLINE APPLICATION

URL: www.census.gov/foreign-trade/data/index.html

Title: U.S. international trade in goods and services

Navigation: Go to the home page of the U.S. Census Bureau (www.census.gov).Scroll to the bottom of the page and under "Business and Industry," click on "Foreign Trade." Click on the "Data" tab and then select the "Latest U.S. International Trade in Goods and Services Report."

Application: Perform the indicated operations, and answer the accompanying questions.

1. Scroll down and click on "Exhibit 15: Goods by Principal SITC Commodities" and examine the data. During the most recent months displayed in the report, what are some examples of goods for which the United States experienced a trade surplus? A trade deficit? Are there any patterns among types of goods within surplus and deficit categories? If so, do these patterns provide any indication of whether the United States may have either an absolute or a comparative advantage?

2. Back up and click on "Exhibits 3: Services Exports" and "Exhibits 4: Services Imports,"and examine the data in each exhibit. Does the United States tend to experience trade surpluses or deficits in services? Does this provide any indication of whether the United States may have either an absolute or a comparative advantage in services?

For group study and analysis: Divide the class into groups, and assign different product and service categories to each group. Ask each group to identify goods or services for which the United States appears to have an absolute or comparative advantage. For each category, discuss whether trade likely arises because the United States has an absolute or a comparative advantage.

REFERENCES AND RECOMMENDED READINGS

Bernhofen, Daniel, and John Brown. "A Factor Augmentation Formulation of the Value of International Trade," University of Nottingham Research Paper No. 2015/05, 2012.

Blonigen, Bruce A. "Revisiting the Evidence on Trade Policy Preferences." *Journal of International Economics* 85 (September 2011): 129–135.

Caves, Richard, Jeffrey Frankel, and Ronald Jones. *World Trade and Payments*, 11th edn. New York: Addison-Wesley, 2006.

Feenstra, Robert, and Alan Taylor. *International Economics*. New York: Worth, 2008.

Harford, Tim. *The Undercover Economist: Exposing Why the Rich are Rich, the Poor are Poor – and Why You Can Never Buy a Decent Used Car!* New York: Oxford University Press, 2006.

Mayda, Anna Maria, and Dani Rodrik. "Why are Some People (and Countries) More Protectionist than Others?" *European Economic Review* 49 (2005): 1393–1430.

Rivoli, Pietra. *The Travels of a T-Shirt in the Global Economy*. Hoboken, NJ: John Wiley and Sons, 2005.

Rodrick, Dani. "Symposium on Globalization in Perspective: An Introduction." *Journal of Economic Perspectives* 12(4) (1998): 3–8.

Samuelson, Paul A. "Where Ricardo and Mill Rebut and Confirm Arguments of Mainstream Economists Supporting Globalization." *Journal of Economic Perspectives* 18(3) (2004): 135–146.

Unit II
International trade: enduring issues

Chapter 3

Sources of comparative advantage

Madagascar, the island nation off the African coast, has substantial labor resources and ready proximity to high-quality cotton produce. Yet exporters commonly experience expensive delays in moving textile products to and beyond the nation's borders. Because of the nation's weak transportation infrastructure and aging fleet of vehicles, moving finished textile goods the roughly 300 miles from mills to shipping ports typically requires about 14 hours. Furthermore, Madagascar's port facilities lack modern capital equipment, which further slows the conveyance of goods toward their ultimate destinations abroad. Many observers have concluded that, unless the nation's companies undertake substantially greater capital investments, Madagascar will be unable to establish a comparative advantage in the global textile market.

In the previous chapter you found that a key basis of trade is comparative advantage. What are the sources of a nation's comparative advantage, which sometimes can hinge on the relative availability of specific factor resources? In this chapter you will learn about the factor proportions explanation of comparative advantage. You will also develop an understanding of how to relate the factor proportions approach to issues such as factor prices, free trade's winners and losers, outsourcing, and economic growth.

THE FACTOR PROPORTIONS EXPLANATION OF INTERNATIONAL TRADE

As discussed in Chapter 2, the concept of comparative advantage can explain why residents of different nations trade. That is, by producing those goods in which a nation has a comparative advantage and trading them for goods in which it has a comparative disadvantage, the nation's residents may reap gains from trade. In this way, there are mutual benefits from trade. In this chapter we shall explore the basic theory that economists use to explain the *source* of a nation's comparative advantage.

The factor proportions approach

ON THE WEB:

To find information on the Nobel laureates in economics, see the Bank of Sweden's Nobel e-museum at www.nobel.se/ economics/laureates.

Factors of production: *The resources firms utilize to produce goods and services.*

Capital: *The physical equipment and buildings used to produce goods and services.*

The basic theory of comparative advantage that you studied in Chapter 2 represents the main framework that economists used to discuss and analyze trade patterns for nearly 100 years. In the early 1900s, however, two Swedish economists, Eli Heckscher and Nobel laureate Bertil Ohlin, developed a more general approach to explaining trade patterns, known as the Heckscher–Ohlin theorem.

In the mid-twentieth century, the work of Heckscher and Ohlin was expanded and articulated by another Nobel laureate, Paul Samuelson of MIT. Samuelson's contribution to this economic theory was so significant that it is often called the Heckscher–Ohlin–Samuelson model. As you will soon understand, this model highlights a nation's endowment of the various **factors of production**—the resources that firms utilize to produce goods and services—as a source of comparative advantage. Hence, we shall refer to the simple version of the model used here as the *factor proportions* model.

The basic factor proportions approach examines two nations that produce two identical goods using two identical factors of production, or inputs, and the same production technology. The two inputs, **capital**—the physical equipment and buildings used to produce goods and services—and labor, can move freely from industry to industry, but cannot move from one nation to another. There are no restrictions on trade and no transportation costs, so the two goods move freely across nations. The residents of the two nations have identical tastes for each of the two goods.

Factor endowments

As you can see, there is nothing at this point to distinguish one nation from the other. Where the nations differ is in the *quantities* of the two factors they possess. The two goods differ as well, because their relative requirements of the two inputs in the production process are distinct.

To understand the difference in factor endowments, let's use once again the example of the nation of Northland, introduced in Chapter 2. Suppose that residents of Northland consider trade with residents of Eastisle, who have the same tastes and preferences for computers and food, the two goods in question, as the residents of Northland. Firms in these two nations combine labor and capital using the most current and identical technology to produce food and computers. Suppose that the residents of Northland have 800 units of labor and 1,000 units of capital, while the residents of Eastisle have 1,000 units of labor and 800 units of capital.

Using these figures for the factor endowments of both nations, we can calculate their respective labor-to-capital ratios. The labor-to-capital ratio for Eastisle is $1{,}000/800 = 1.25$, while the ratio for Northland is $800/1{,}000 = 0.80$. The labor-to-capital ratios show that Eastisle is the **relatively labor–abundant nation** because it is endowed with more labor units per capital unit than is Northland.

If we invert the labor-to-capital ratios calculated above, we can determine the capital-to-labor ratio and, therefore, the **relatively capital-abundant nation**. Doing so, we find that Eastisle's capital-to-labor ratio is 0.80 $(800/100 = 0.80)$, while the capital-to-labor ratio for Northland is 1.25 $(1{,}000/800 = 1.25)$. Hence, Northland is the relatively capital-abundant nation because it is endowed with more capital units per labor unit than is Eastisle. (The Indian sub-continent is endowed with fertile and mineral-rich land and substantial labor resources, but firms seeking to move traded products to and across India's borders confront costly barriers; see *Policy Notebook: Indian transportation gridlock hinders international trade flows*.)

Relatively labor-abundant nation: *In a two-country setting, the nation endowed with more labor units per capital unit than the other nation.*

Relatively capital-abundant nation: *In a two-country setting, the nation endowed with more capital units per labor unit than the other nation.*

POLICY NOTEBOOK

Indian transportation gridlock hinders international trade flows

Moving imported items or goods intended for export by truck across the 1,300 miles between the Indian port city of Chennai and Delhi in the nation's interior typically requires at least a full week at an average speed of less than 10 miles per hour. This sluggish transportation speed is slower than that of a good long-distance runner. The lower miles per gallon of fuel at lower speeds and additional payroll hours for drivers drive up importers' and exporters' costs.

Also driving up trade transportation expenses and contributing to slow truck traffic are the 177 tax and permit checkpoints along Indian highways. These checkpoints are operated by the nation's 28 states and its national government to ensure collection of 15 different transportation taxes.

The government-provided system of roads is also insufficient to handle large volumes of truck traffic. Furthermore, the government hinders efforts for the private sector to make capital investments in toll roads and bridges that would help reduce traffic pressures. Taken together, all of these bottlenecks on goods transportation constitute significant barriers to flows of traded goods to and from India.

For critical analysis: Why does a longer required period for transport of merchandise automatically boost costs of engaging in international trade?

Insufficient Transportation Costs

Factor intensities

Now let's consider the factor intensities, or input requirements to produce food and computers. Suppose that the current production technology for food always requires,

Relatively labor-intensive good: *In a two-good setting, the good with a production process requiring more labor per capital unit than the other good.*

in fixed proportions, more labor per capital unit than the labor-per-capital requirement for producing computers. Or, equivalently, the production technology for computers always requires more capital per labor unit than the capital-per-labor requirement of food. Hence, food is the **relatively labor–intensive good**, because production of food uses more labor units per capital unit than does the production process for computers. Likewise, we can say that computers are **relatively capital-intensive goods**, because production of computers requires more capital units per labor unit than does the production of food.

Relatively capital-intensive good: *In a two-good setting, the good with a production process requiring more capital per labor unit than the other good.*

Both countries employ the same production technology. Hence, the relative factor endowments of the two nations and the relative factor requirements of the two goods determine where comparative advantages lie. (To consider and compare the production possibilities of both nations, see *Visualizing Global Economic Issues: Factor endowments and the production possibilities frontier.*)

VISUALIZING GLOBAL ECONOMIC ISSUES

Factor endowments and the production possibilities frontier

To see how factor endowments affect the production possibilities frontier (PPF), consider the two PPFs in Figure 3.1. The figure illustrates the PPF for Northland, the relatively capital-abundant nation, and for Eastisle, the relatively labor-abundant nation. Next consider the relative factor intensities. Computers are relatively capital intensive in their production process, while food is relatively labor intensive in its production process.

Because Northland is the relatively capital-abundant nation and computers are the relatively capital-intensive good, residents of Northland have a greater relative capacity to produce computers than do residents of Eastisle. Hence, Northland's PPF is skewed toward computers, as compared with the shape of Eastisle's PPF. Likewise, because Eastisle is the relatively labor-abundant nation and food is the relatively labor-intensive good, residents of Eastisle have a greater relative capacity to produce food than do residents of Northland. Hence, Eastisle's PPF is skewed toward food, as compared with the shape of Northland's PPF.

As explained in Chapter 2, the slope of a line tangent line to the PPF reflects the opportunity cost of production at that particular bundle of goods. With this in mind, suppose that in *autarky*, or a no-trade situation, both nations produce and consume at point A. At this point, the absolute slope of the line tangent to Eastisle's PPF is much larger than that of Northland. Hence, residents of Northland have a lower opportunity cost in the production of computers than do residents of Eastisle. It is in this way that the relative factor endowments and relative factor intensities affect a nation's PPF.

For critical analysis: Suppose Eastisle has many fewer residents and resources than Northland. Do any of the points made above change?

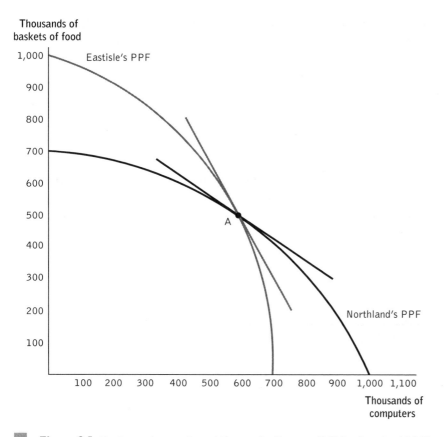

Figure 3.1 *Factor endowments and the production possibilities frontier (PPF)*

Because Northland is relatively capital abundant, its PPF is skewed toward computers. Because Eastisle is relatively labor abundant, its PPF is skewed toward food. Suppose both nations produce and consume the bundle indicated by point A. Because Northland has a lower opportunity cost of producing more computers at this point, the slope of the line tangent to Northland's PPF is shallower than the slope of the line tangent to Eastisle's PPF.

Fundamental Issue #1: What is the factor proportions explanation of comparative advantage? According to the factor proportions approach, the relative factor endowments of two nations and the relative factor requirements of two goods that their residents trade determine where comparative advantage lies. The factor proportions model is a two-country, two-factor, two-good model that focuses on relative factor endowments of nations and relative factor intensities of goods. This model can be used to prove the factor proportions explanation of comparative advantage.

The Heckscher–Ohlin theorem and international trade

Using the factor proportions model, Heckscher and Ohlin developed one of the most fundamental, and perhaps one of the most tested, ideas in economics,

Heckscher–Ohlin theorem: *A theorem stating that a relatively labor-abundant nation will export a relatively labor-intensive good, while a relatively capital-abundant nation will export a relatively capital-intensive good.*

known as the **Heckscher–Ohlin theorem**. According to this theorem, residents of a nation that is relatively labor abundant will export the relatively labor-intensive good, while residents of a nation that is relatively capital abundant will export the relatively capital-intensive good.

The Heckscher–Ohlin explanation of trade

We can restate the Heckscher-Ohlin theorem in another way:

> **The nation that is relatively labor abundant will have a comparative advantage in the production of the relatively labor-intensive good, while the nation that is relatively capital abundant will have a comparative advantage in the production of the relatively capital-intensive good.**

Using the example of Northland and Eastisle, we can determine the trade pattern that results when residents of these two nations trade. Because Northland is the relatively capital-abundant nation, its residents will export computers, the relatively capital-intensive good, and will import food, the relatively labor-intensive good. Residents of Eastisle, the relatively labor-abundant nation, will export food, the relatively labor-intensive good, and will import computers, the relatively capital-intensive good. (To view the application of the theorem to the example of Northland and Eastisle, see *Visualizing Global Economic Issues: The Heckscher–Ohlin theorem*.)

VISUALIZING GLOBAL ECONOMIC ISSUES

The Heckscher–Ohlin theorem

To see an application of the Heckscher–Ohlin theorem, let's return to the earlier example of Eastisle and Northland. Consider Figure 3.2 (p. 66), which builds on Figure 3.1.

Suppose that, under autarky, residents of Eastisle and Northland produce and consume a bundle of computers and food indicated by point A on their PPFs. As shown in Figure 3.2, at this combination of food and computers, of Northland residents face the lower opportunity cost of producing additional computers—equivalent to its domestic price ratio—given by the tangent line labeled P_A^N, while residents of Eastisle face the higher opportunity cost, given by the tangent line labeled P_A^E.

Now suppose that the residents of the two nations decide to engage in trade. Further, for the sake of simplicity, let's suppose that the residents of Eastisle and Northland are willing to exchange the two goods at a price ratio of 1.1 baskets of food for each computer. (Recall from Chapter 2 that there are constraints on the value of the rate of exchange if trade is to be mutually beneficial.) This price ratio is illustrated in the figure as a line tangent to both PPFs and labeled P_T. The absolute value of P_T equals 1.1. We calculate this slope using the points of tangency, P_T^E and P_T^N. Over this segment of the tangent line, the absolute value of the rise equals 440,000 baskets of food and the run equals 400,000 computers. Hence, the absolute value of the line is 440/400 = 1.1.

You can see that when the residents of the two nations trade at price P_T, their production bundles adjust. Northland residents adjust their production bundles in response to the new and greater relative price for computers by moving down and along the PPF, producing more computers and less food. Residents of Eastisle adjust their production bundles in response to the new and lower relative price for computers by moving up and along its PPF, producing more food and fewer computers.

Finally, let's assume that residents of both nations consume the combination of food and computers given by point C. Note that point C lies beyond each nation's PPF, so that residents of both nations can now produce and consume more of both goods. This illustrates the benefits of specializing in the production of the good in which the nation has the comparative advantage, as discussed in Chapter 2.

Because Eastisle's residents now consume 600,000 computers but produce only 400,000, they must be importing 200,000 computers from residents of Northland. Likewise, because Eastisle's residents produce 750,000 baskets of food but consume only 530,000 baskets, they must be exporting 220,000 baskets to residents of Northland. In the same manner, because Northland's residents consume 530,000 baskets of food but produce only 310,000 baskets, they must be importing 220,000 baskets from residents of Eastisle. Because Northland's residents produce 800,000 computers but consume only 600,000 computers, they must be exporting 200,000 computers to residents of Eastisle.

Note that in this two-country example, exports of the residents of Eastisle are equivalent to imports of the residents of Northland, and exports of the residents of Northland are equivalent to imports of the residents of Eastisle. Further note that the 220,000 baskets of food traded exchange for 200,000 computers—at a ratio of 1.1 baskets of food per computer.

As you can see, under free trade, residents of Eastisle, the relatively labor-abundant nation, export the relatively labor-intensive good. Residents of Northland, the relatively capital-abundant nation, export the relatively capital-intensive good.

For critical analysis: Why, in Figure 3.2, do residents of Northland and Eastisle consume identical baskets of food and computers?

A general application of the Heckscher–Ohlin theorem

We can apply the Heckscher–Ohlin theorem to the real world and attempt to derive some conclusions about trade patterns among different nations if trade is truly free. Advanced economies tend to be relatively capital-abundant nations, whereas emerging and developing economies tend to be relatively labor-abundant. Based on these assumptions, the Heckscher–Ohlin theorem implies that the advanced economies

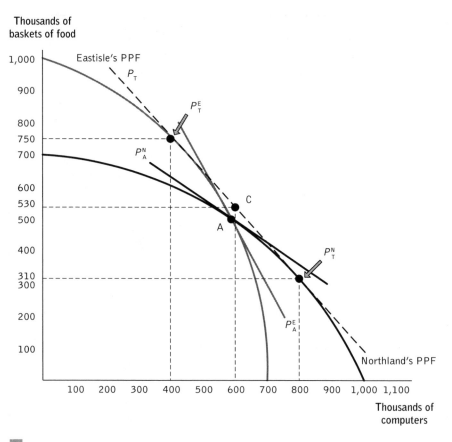

Figure 3.2 *Illustrating the Heckscher–Ohlin theorem*

Suppose the residents of Northland and Eastisle are willing to trade at a rate of exchange of 1.1 baskets of food for each computer. Also suppose that, at this rate of exchange, the residents of each country consume 530,000 baskets of food and 600,000 computers, illustrated by point C. At this rate of exchange, the residents of Northland export 200,000 computers and import 220,000 baskets of food, and the residents of Eastisle export 220,000 baskets of food and import 200,000 computers.

will be net exporters of relatively capital-intensive goods such as chemicals, electrical equipment, and precision instruments, while the emerging and developing economies will be net exporters of labor-intensive goods such as clothing, toys, and sporting goods. (We would also expect the advanced economies to be net exporters of business services, a topic covered later in this chapter.)

Nations with large landmass are relatively abundant in land and natural resources. Based on the Heckscher–Ohlin theorem, we would expect large-landmass nations to be net exporters of agricultural and food products, and minerals.

Do our general conclusions correspond to the evidence on trade in goods? Table 3.1 shows the international trade of goods and services for selected nations during 2012. It presents exports, imports, and trade balances for nine categories. Using this information, we can draw some general conclusions.

Table 3.1 *Trade in goods and services of selected nations*

Country	Classification	Exports ($)	Imports ($)	Balance ($)
Argentina	All food items	43,571,764	2,117,898	41,453,865
	Agricultural raw materials	863,802	823,726	40,076
	Ores and metals	3,052,128	1,920,866	1,131,262
	Fuels	7,033,844	6,231,052	802,792
	Labor-intensive and resource-based manufactures	2,403,297	5,628,440	−3,225,143
	Manufactures with low skill and technology intensity	2,675,351	4,412,156	−1,736,805
	Manufactures with medium skill and technology intensity	11,427,980	24,353,916	−12,925,936
	Manufactures with high skill and technology intensity	8,198,364	22,153,764	−13,955,400
	Services	14,602,000	18,022,000	−3,420,000
Canada	All food items	46,329,388	33,357,236	12,972,152
	Agricultural raw materials	16,504,772	4,552,031	11,952,741
	Ores and metals	32,998,598	13,430,772	19,567,826
	Fuels	115,897,361	51,366,447	64,530,914
	Labor-intensive and resource-based manufactures	22,536,053	41,274,340	−18,738,286
	Manufactures with low skill and technology intensity	15,822,713	34,457,553	−18,634,840
	Manufactures with medium skill and technology intensity	104,417,463	155,751,860	−51,334,397
	Manufactures with high skill and technology intensity	63,068,429	99,181,929	−36,113,500
	Services	79,181,000	106,384,000	−27,203,000
China	All food items	64,399,954	96,476,435	−32,076,481
	Agricultural raw materials	10,055,608	72,283,233	−62,227,624
	Ores and metals	28,403,258	258,005,960	−229,602,702
	Fuels	43,501,645	350,256,693	−306,755,048
	Labor-intensive and resource-based manufactures	509,662,595	50,817,924	458,844,671
	Manufactures with low skill and technology intensity	212,839,309	58,777,771	154,061,538
	Manufactures with medium skill and technology intensity	395,930,705	309,333,500	86,597,205
	Manufactures with high skill and technology intensity	730,159,872	600,382,587	129,777,285
	Services	190,939,000	282,098,000	−91,159,000
Germany	All food items	76,995,884	86,271,166	−9,275,283
	Agricultural raw materials	11,765,726	17,092,099	−5,326,373
	Ores and metals	42,421,033	53,690,508	−11,269,475
	Fuels	38,361,769	173,144,968	−134,783,199
	Labor-intensive and resource-based manufactures	98,564,571	107,617,282	−9,052,711
	Manufactures with low skill and technology intensity	101,412,463	78,560,256	22,852,206

67

Table 3.1 *continued*

Country	Classification	Exports ($)	Imports ($)	Balance ($)
	Manufactures with medium skill and technology intensity	568,145,148	269,283,257	298,861,891
	Manufactures with high skill and technology intensity	368,018,116	290,126,138	77,891,979
	Services	258,860,000	286,290,000	−27,430,000
South Korea	All food items	6,645,669	25,552,431	−18,906,762
	Agricultural raw materials	5,797,843	8,207,413	−2,409,570
	Ores and metals	12,226,638	36,691,080	−24,464,442
	Fuels	54,759,112	183,672,282	−128,913,169
	Labor-intensive and resource-based manufactures	25,228,493	26,887,056	−1,658,563
	Manufactures with low skill and technology intensity	80,971,699	36,229,932	44,741,767
	Manufactures with medium skill and technology intensity	147,511,076	76,074,591	71,436,485
	Manufactures with high skill and technology intensity	205,652,809	119,332,466	86,320,342
	Services	110,319,000	106,254,000	4,065,000
United Kingdom	All food items	29,422,198	60,229,540	−30,807,342
	Agricultural raw materials	3,371,233	6,640,584	−3,269,351
	Ores and metals	18,359,612	27,548,897	−9,189,286
	Fuels	65,792,294	95,388,920	−29,596,626
	Labor-intensive and resource-based manufactures	23,963,575	70,866,480	−46,902,906
	Manufactures with low skill and technology intensity	20,081,061	28,271,616	−8,190,555
	Manufactures with medium skill and technology intensity	128,953,564	146,017,701	−17,064,137
	Manufactures with high skill and technology intensity	114,317,263	142,022,710	−27,705,446
	Services	282,072,000	181,882,000	100,190,000
United States	All food items	138,252,221	117,140,746	21,111,474
	Agricultural raw materials	33,880,269	24,711,597	9,168,672
	Ores and metals	50,010,601	52,650,606	−2,640,005
	Fuels	137,339,549	433,222,382	−295,882,832
	Labor-intensive and resource-based manufactures	65,897,638	260,964,223	−195,066,585
	Manufactures with low skill and technology intensity	65,248,075	112,970,279	−47,722,204
	Manufactures with medium skill and technology intensity	392,808,454	586,872,917	−194,064,463
	Manufactures with high skill and technology intensity	426,207,632	589,322,868	−163,115,236
	Services	633,028,000	436,459,000	196,569,000

Source: Data from UNCTAD, *Handbook of Statistics,* 2012.

As you can see, countries such as Argentina, Canada, and the United States, which are endowed with a great deal of farmable land, show a trade surplus in food items, and those with mineral-rich land show surpluses in fuels, ores, and metals. Nations with a relatively large labor force, such as China, display surpluses in manufactures across skill levels, but with considerable specialization in labour-intensive and resource-based manufactures. Countries with higher-skilled manufacturing workers, such as Germany and Korea, show larger surpluses in manufactures with medium and high-skill technology. The United States and the United Kingdom are endowed with populations that are highly educated, and they run surpluses in services. Hence, a casual look at the data on global trade indicates that the Heckscher–Ohlin theorem does provide some insight on trade patterns. In the next section you will go beyond a casual look at trade data and consider the empirical evidence on the factor proportions approach in explaining trade patterns. (Accumulation of expertise in assembling self-directed capital has helped U.S. firms develop a comparative advantage in a number of markets—see *Management Notebook: A high relative intensity of robotic capital pays off for U.S. companies.*)

MANAGEMENT NOTEBOOK

A high relative intensity of robotic capital pays off for U.S. companies

Media reports about the shrinkage in the relative size of the U.S. manufacturing production, from nearly 25 percent of annual national output in 1970 to less than 13 percent today, ignore a broader story: Manufacturing output accounts for a decreasing share of output elsewhere as well. In 1970, world manufacturing production accounted for about 28 percent of global output. Today, manufacturing production's share of total world output per year is only about 18 percent.

During the course of this contraction in the relative size of the manufacturing sector of the global economy, producers of durable goods have engaged in considerable quality competition that has led to a proliferation of automated product features. Refrigerators and freezers that self-adjust their internal temperature to variations in external room temperature have aided U.S.-based Maytag and Whirlpool's efforts to boost their export sales. Self-propelled wheelchairs with a growing array of auto-safety features have enabled U.S. firms such as ActiveCare Medical and C.T.M. Homecare to penetrate the global market as well. U.S. plumbing products manufacturer Kohler has generated considerable export sales by marketing a robotic toilet that uses motion detectors and remote control devices to open and close its seat and to flush. These are just a few of many examples of U.S. manufacturing firms that have carved out a comparative advantage in trade through accumulation of greater relative intensity of robotic capital, as compared with firms in most other nations.

For critical analysis: Why do you suppose that a nation's comparative advantage based on a higher relative capital intensity may not necessarily last for many years? (Hint: Capital goods are themselves manufactured resources.)

Fundamental Issue #2: What is the Heckscher–Ohlin theory of trade? Using the factor proportions model, Eli Heckscher and Bertil Ohlin developed the Heckscher–Ohlin theorem. This theorem asserts that a nation's residents will export goods and services that use the nation's relatively abundant factor relatively intensively. Likewise, the theorem claims that a nation's residents will import goods and services that use the nation's relatively scarce factor relatively intensively. The predictions of the Heckscher–Ohlin theorem relate, in an informal manner, to trade patterns in basic commodities and manufactured goods.

HOW WELL DOES THE FACTOR PROPORTIONS APPROACH EXPLAIN TRADE?

Does the factor proportions approach explain a nation's trade? Do countries relatively well endowed with a particular resource export goods that use that resource relatively intensively in their production? Several decades passed before economists were able to rigorously evaluate the merits of the Heckscher–Ohlin theorem and the factor proportions approach explanations of trade.

The Leontief paradox

In 1954, Wassily Leontief completed the first empirical examination of the factor proportions approach. Leontief pioneered an approach that tracked the resources used to produce a good from its first step of production until the good is in its final form. This approach, called *input–output analysis*, allowed him to determine the amount of capital and labor used in the production of various goods. The U.S. Bureau of Economic Analysis continues to use input–output analysis to track U.S. production.

Leontief's approach

At the time when Leontief conducted his research, it was widely accepted that the United States was a relatively capital-abundant nation. The factor proportions approach, therefore, implies that U.S. residents would be net exporters of relatively capital-intensive goods and net importers of relatively labor-intensive goods. Using data on U.S. trade for 1947, Leontief tested this hypothesis.

Leontief's study was limited in a number of ways. First, his input-output analysis was confined to U.S. industries. This meant that the value of capital used per worker in each U.S. industry—the capital-to-labor ratio—was used to infer the capital-to-labor ratio of industries in other countries. In other words, he used the capital-to-labor ratio of U.S. automobile manufacturers, for example, to infer the capital-to-labor ratios of German and Japanese automobile manufacturers. Second, because he used U.S. production data, Leontief had to exclude industries in which there was no domestic production. Coffee, for example, is an industry in which the residents of the United

ON THE WEB:

To see U.S. input–output production data, visit the Website of the Bureau of Economic Analysis at the U.S. Department of Commerce: www.bea.gov.

States import substantial quantities but produce very little. Nonetheless, he was able to examine the production and trade data for approximately 200 industries.

Leontief's paradox

Leontief determined that the annual expenditures on capital per labor unit for industries in which U.S. residents were net exporters was more than $24,864 (in 2002 dollars). That is, annual expenditures on capital totaled more than $24,864 per worker. In net-import industries, by way of contrast, this value was slightly more than $31,968. Hence, Leontief's results indicated that the *imports* of residents of the United States were relatively *more capital intensive* than their exports. In other words, the results were in direct contradiction to the factor proportions approach explanation of international trade. Because of this contradiction, Leontief's result became known as the **Leontief paradox**.

Leontief's research was controversial, because it directly contradicted a fundamental theory of trade, the Heckscher–Ohlin theorem. Hence, Leontief's work met with a great deal of criticism. One complaint was the period Leontief chose to examine. Many economists argued that 1947, being so close to the end of World War II, did not represent a "typical" trade year for the United States. In response, Leontief repeated his test using data for 1951. His general conclusion, that the net imports of residents of the United States are relatively more capital intensive than their net exports, still held true. This sparked a number of empirical studies, and the factor proportions approach is now one of the most tested propositions in the field of economics.

Leontief paradox: *A finding by Wassily Leontief that contradicted the Heckscher–Ohlin theorem, in that it indicated that imports of the United States, a relatively capital-abundant nation, were relatively more capital intensive than exports of the United States.*

More recent tests of the factor proportions approach

Much of the research conducted during the 30 years following Leontief's path-breaking study confirmed his general results. The paradoxical result forced economists to consider generalizations of the factor proportions approach.

Generalizations of the factor proportions approach

One such generalization is to allow for the residents of differing nations to have different tastes for goods and services. Residents of the United States, for example, may have much stronger preferences for relatively capital-intensive goods than the residents of other nations. If this is the case, it may explain why U.S. imports tend to be more capital intensive.

Another important generalization is to disaggregate labor and capital into more specific categories, thereby increasing the number of factors considered. Workers, for example, may be separated into the categories of *skilled* and *non-skilled* labor, based on their level of **human capital**—the amount of knowledge and skill that workers possess.

Yet another generalization is to allow that some factors (e.g., skilled labor) move from one nation to another. Other factors, however, may be unable to move from one industry to another within the domestic economy.

Human capital: *The knowledge and skills that workers possess.*

Performance of a more generalized approach

Adrian Wood of Sussex University provides one example of recent studies that use a generalized factor proportions approach. Wood argues that capital moves freely internationally and, therefore, does not explain trade patterns. He assumes that labor is heterogeneous—separating workers into skilled groups and unskilled groups—and does not move from one nation to another.

Allowing for these generalizations, Wood finds that the Heckscher–Ohlin theory explains trade in manufactured goods between residents of developed nations and residents of developing nations. Wood found that the developed nations are relatively well endowed with skilled workers, while developing nations are relatively well endowed with unskilled workers. Consistent with the factor proportions approach, residents of developed economies tend to export relatively skilled-labor-intensive goods and import relatively unskilled-labor-intensive goods from residents of the developing economies.

What years of studies show is that the traditional factor proportions approach is rather weak at explaining the direction of trade flows. A more generalized approach, however, does yield useful insights for particular types of trade flow, such as primary commodities and manufactured goods. (A nation that has persistently preserved an advantage in trade of goods produced with skilled labor is Germany; see *Management Notebook: How Germany's export industries maintain a comparative advantage in skilled-labor-intensive goods.*)

MANAGEMENT NOTEBOOK

How Germany's export industries maintain a comparative advantage in skilled-labor-intensive goods

For many years, Germany has upheld a comparative advantage in production and trade in a variety of global vehicle, machinery, and chemical markets. The linchpin for sustaining the nation's trade advantage for these and other goods typically produced using highly skilled labor resources has been its export industries' continuing success in training workers.

Many German firms utilize apprenticeship programs for workers. Under these programs, firms offer their own vocational programs to provide background education on their products to newly hired workers. Following completion of their vocational studies, these employees gradually gain hands-on experience in operating sophisticated machinery under the watchful eyes of experienced workers. Only after 3–5 years of training do companies finalize an employee's status as a fully prepared worker. Even then, many employees typically must update their certification status by obtaining additional education or on-the-job training and practice. In this way, German firms maintain a substantial, highly trained labor force capable of manufacturing the world's most skilled-labor-intensive export products.

For critical analysis: Why do you suppose that a number of U.S. manufacturing firms, such as the heavy-equipment maker Caterpillar and the bearings manufacturer Timken, have established apprenticeship programs following the German model?

Fundamental Issue #3: How well does the factor proportions approach explain trade patterns? For several decades following the development of the Heckscher–Ohlin theorem, economists were unable to test the factor proportions approach to trade rigorously. In the mid-1950s, using input–output analysis, Wassily Leontief examined U.S. trade data and found that U.S. imports were relatively more capital intensive in their production than U.S. exports. This contradiction to the factor proportions approach sparked substantial research on the approach and its predictions. Most subsequent studies show that the factor proportions approach is rather weak at explaining a nation's trade pattern. As a result, a more generalized factor proportions approach emerged. Generalized approaches do predict trade patterns for particular sectors, such as primary commodities and manufacturing.

TRADE, FACTOR PRICES, AND REAL INCOME

As discussed in Chapter 2, international trade can result in redistributive effects, or changes in income flows among residents *within* a nation. Redistributive effects of international trade may also occur *between* nations. The size of these effects is often at the center of debates on international trade and globalization.

On one hand, opponents claim that trade has caused a gap in earnings, with upper-income groups within most nations getting richer and lower income groups becoming poorer. Likewise opponents claim that trade has caused a gap between nations, with the richer advanced economies becoming wealthier and the poorer developing economies becoming poorer. On the other hand, proponents of trade and globalization contend that international trade is the best hope to improve conditions and incomes in the poorest nations.

The relationship between trade, prices, and incomes, therefore, is an important issue. What insight does the factor proportions approach offer in this regard?

Factor price equalization

Two important theorems on international trade, wages, and income resulted from the factor proportions model. The first, the **factor price equalization theorem**, asserts that, given the assumptions of the factor proportions model, uninterrupted trade will lead to the global equalization of all factor prices, such as wages paid to resource owners for their labor, interest paid to resource owners for use of their

Factor price equalization theorem: *A theorem indicating that, under the assumptions of the factor proportions model, uninterrupted trade will bring about equalization of goods prices and factor prices across nations.*

73

capital—also called the *rental rate of capital*—and rental payments to resource owners for the use of their land, across nations.

Role of the global market for goods and services

Recall that the factor proportions approach assumes that factors of production cannot move freely from one nation to another. Hence, there is no *global* market for factors of production, and no supply-and-demand mechanism to equilibrate factor prices. Factor price equalization, therefore, results through the price adjustment that occurs in the global market for *goods and services*. In other words, the global market for goods and services provides the equilibrating mechanism for factor price adjustment.

The equalization process

To understand how the factor price equalization process occurs, consider the example of Northland and Eastisle once again. Recall that Northland is the relatively capital-abundant nation and Eastisle is the relatively labor-abundant nation. In autarky, therefore, we would expect the wage rate relative to the rental rate of capital to be higher in Northland than in Eastisle.

The Heckscher–Ohlin theorem tells us that, under free trade, residents of Northland will export computers, the relatively capital-intensive good, and import food, the relatively labor-intensive good. Because Northland has a comparative advantage in computers and a comparative disadvantage in food, the free-trade relative price of computers is higher than Northland's domestic relative price under autarky. The free-trade relative price of food is lower than Northland's domestic relative price of food under autarky.

As discussed earlier, under free trade, residents of Northland will adjust their level of production, producing more computers and less food. When they reduce the production of food, the residents of Northland free up more labor relative to the capital that they release. Hence, the supply of labor relative to the supply of capital increases. When Northland's residents increase the production of computers, they must hire more capital relative to labor, so the demand for labor declines relative to the demand for capital. Thus, the adjustment process increases the relative supply of labor and decreases the relative demand for labor, which lowers the value of the wage rate relative to the value of the rental rate of capital.

The residents of Eastisle, in a similar manner, adjust their production pattern, producing more food and fewer computers. As Eastisle's residents produce fewer computers, they reduce their utilization of capital relative to labor. As they produce more food, however, they require more labor relative to capital. Hence, the adjustment process in Eastisle bids up the wage rate relative to the rental rate of capital.

This process continues until prices are equal across both nations and there are no further gains from specialization. Or, in other words, the process continues until the wage rate relative to the rental rate of capital is the same in both nations. (For additional insight on the factor price adjustment process, see *Visualizing Global Economic Issues: The factor price equalization theorem*.)

VISUALIZING GLOBAL ECONOMIC ISSUES

The factor price equalization theorem

To visualize the factor price adjustment process under free trade, consider again the example of Northland and Eastisle. Figure 3.3 overleaf, plots the price of food, P_F, relative to the price of computers, P_C, on the vertical axis, labeled P_F/P_C. The figure relates P_F/P_C to the wage rate, W, relative to the rental rate of capital, R, which is plotted on the horizontal axis. Recall that Eastisle is the relatively labor-abundant nation, while Northland is the relatively labor-scarce nation. Hence, under autarky, the wage rate relative to the rental rate of capital in Northland, $(W/R)_N$, is greater than the wage rate relative to the rental rate of capital in Eastisle, $(W/R)_E$.

Also, recall that, according to the Heckscher–Ohlin theorem, Northland has a comparative advantage in computers and Eastisle has a comparative advantage in food. Hence, under autarky, the price of food relative to the price of computers in Northland, $(P_F/P_C)_N$, is greater than the price of food relative to the price of computers in Eastisle, $(P_F/P_C)_E$.

The adjustment process in Northland

Suppose that the combination of (P_F/P_C) and (W/R) under autarky is given by point N for Northland and by point E for Eastisle, as in Figure 3.3. Next, consider what happens as the residents of the two nations begin to trade. As the residents of Northland reduce their production of food, they free up more labor relative to the capital they release. Hence, the supply of labor relative to the supply of capital increases. When the residents of Northland increase their production of computers, they must hire more capital relative to labor, so the demand for capital rises relative to the demand for labor. This adjustment process bids up the rental rate of capital relative to the wage rate, or a decline in $(W/R)_N$. As the residents of Northland begin to export computers and import food, the price of food relative to the price of computers declines. The change in goods prices and factor prices is shown by the movement down and along the dotted line, as indicated by the arrows.

The adjustment process in Eastisle

As the residents of Eastisle reduce their production of computers, they free up more capital relative to the labor they release. Hence, the supply of labor relative to the supply of capital decreases. When the residents of Eastisle increase their production of food, they must hire more labor relative to capital, so the demand for labor rises relative to the demand for capital. This adjustment process bids up the wage rate relative to the rental rate of capital, or an increase in $(W/R)_E$. As the residents of Eastisle begin to export food and import computers, the price of food relative to the price of computers rises. The movement up and along the dashed line indicated by the arrows shows the change in goods prices and factor prices.

The equalization process

As you can see in Figure 3.3, the wage rate relative to the rental rate of capital in Eastisle and Northland becomes more equal. According to the factor price equalization theorem, if free trade continues to take place, factor prices eventually equalize.

For critical analysis: Suppose both nations open their borders to trade but retain polices that constrain trade to a level lower than under free-trade conditions. How would this affect the adjustment of factor prices, and how would you illustrate this situation in Figure 3.3?

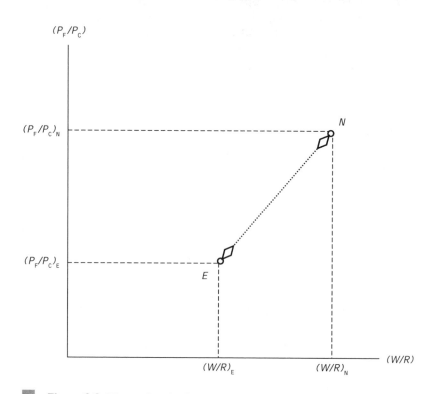

Figure 3.3 *Illustrating the factor price equalization theorem*

As the residents of Northland increase their production of computers and decrease their production of food, their demand for labor falls relative to their demand for capital, and the supply of labor relative to the supply of capital rises. The change in production causes the wage rate relative to the rental rate of capital and the price of food relative to computers to decline, shown by the movement down and along the dashed line. As the residents of Eastisle increase their production of food and decrease their production of computers, their demand for labor rises relative to their demand for capital, and the supply of labor relative to the supply of capital falls. The change in production causes the wage rate relative to the rental rate of capital and the price of food relative to computers to rise, shown by the movement up and along the dashed line. The movement along the dashed line illustrates that factor prices become more equal.

Evidence on factor price convergence

Now that you understand the theory of factor price convergence, let's consider the evidence. Recall that the factor price equalization theorem asserts that unhindered trade will cause a convergence of commodity prices. As commodity prices converge, so will factor prices. In regard to the real-world evidence, factor price equalization is perhaps the most controversial theorem among economists.

Chapter 8 explains that trade has yet to cause a complete convergence of commodity prices. Hence, we should not expect a complete convergence of factor prices. Nonetheless, trade may be causing factor prices to become *more equal*, even though they have yet to equalize.

The process of factor price equalization should be recognized as a very long-run process. With this in mind, Jeffrey Williamson of Harvard University examined the behavior of wage rates relative to the rental rates of capital over a very long time period. Williamson considered three different periods, 1830 through 1853, 1854 through 1913, and post-World War II. For the early period, Williamson found no evidence of factor price convergence among the Atlantic economies of Brazil, France, Great Britain, Ireland, the Netherlands, Spain, Sweden, and the United States. The evidence is explained by the fact that this early period was one of restrictions on international trade and labor migration, and was marked by an underdeveloped capital market.

The second period, however, is one of extensive relative wage convergence. Although much of the convergence can be explained by the mass migration that occurred during this period, the evidence also shows that wage convergence is greater among the most open economies and lower among the most closed economies. The post-World War data shows relative wage convergence along the lines of the previous period. Post-war restrictions on labor mobility, however, slowed the pace of wage convergence relative to that of the previous period.

> *Fundamental Issue #4: What is the relationship between trade and factor prices?*
> The factor proportions approach spurred the development of two very important ideas about factor prices and international trade. The factor price equalization theorem contends that unhindered trade brings about an equalization of goods prices and, therefore, an equalization of factor prices across nations. This equalization process results through the price adjustment that occurs in the global market for goods and services. Real-world evidence indicates that trade may be causing factor prices to become more equal, but they have yet to equalize.

Trade and real income

The factor price equalization theorem is helpful for us to understand how factor prices might adjust across nations. But how does trade affect earnings of workers and owners of capital within nations? Arguably all major economic changes result in winners and losers. Who are the winners and losers when a nation engages in international trade?

Stolper–Samuelson theorem: *Theory that, in the context of the factor proportions model, free trade raises the earnings of the nation's relatively abundant factors and lowers the earnings of the relatively scarce factors.*

The Stolper–Samuelson theorem

The **Stolper–Samuelson theorem**, contributed by Wolfgang Stolper and Paul Samuelson in the early 1940s, is another important theorem resulting from the factor proportions model. The Stolper–Samuelson theorem asserts that, in the context of the factor proportions model, free trade raises the earnings of the nation's relatively abundant factor and lowers the earnings of the relatively scarce factor.

Returning to our previous example, the Stolper–Samuelson theorem implies that as residents of Northland, the relatively capital-abundant nation, begin to trade with residents of Eastisle, the wage rate will fall and the rental rate of capital will rise. This occurs because as Northland opens its borders to trade, the price of computers will rise and the price of food will fall.

The magnification principle

Magnification principle: *A position of the Stolper–Samuelson theorem which implies that the change in the price of a factor is greater than the change in the price of the good that uses the factor relatively intensively in its production process.*

A key proposition of the Stolper–Samuelson theorem is the **magnification principle**, which implies that the change in the price of a factor is greater than the change in the price of the good that uses the factor relatively intensively in its production process. Suppose that as the residents of Northland begin to trade, the price of computers rises by 5 percent and the price of food falls by 2 percent. According to the magnification principle, the rental rate of capital must rise by more than 5 percent, and the wage rate must fall by more than 2 percent. Hence, if the rental rate of capital rises by 7 percent, owners of capital are better off, because their ability to consume computers and food, that is, the *real income* of the owners of capital, is enhanced. Workers, however, because their ability to consume the two goods is reduced—the real income of workers—are worse off. Hence, in Northland, owners of capital are clearly better off with free trade, while workers are worse off.

Implications of the Stolper–Samuelson theorem

ON THE WEB:

For data on wages in a large number of nations, visit the Website of the International Labour Organization at www.ilo.org.

The Stolper–Samuelson theorem has very important policy implications. It shows that even though free trade may bring overall gains to a nation, there are winners and losers. Free trade, therefore, will certainly have supporters and detractors. The theorem also implies that those who support free trade are likely to be the owners of the nation's relatively abundant factors, whereas those who oppose free trade are the owners of the nation's relatively scarce factors. We might expect that in the advanced economies, which tend to be relatively capital abundant, owners of capital will support free trade, and workers will oppose free trade.

Fundamental Issue #5: What is the relationship between trade and real income? The Stolper–Samuelson theorem is another important development of the factor proportions approach. This theorem asserts that free trade benefits owners of the nation's relatively abundant factor by increasing their real income, and harms owners of the nation's relatively scarce factor by decreasing their real income. An important implication is that the owners of the relatively abundant factor are likely to support free trade, whereas the owners of the relatively scarce factor are likely to oppose free trade.

INTERNATIONAL PRODUCTION AND COMPARATIVE ADVANTAGE

The production of a good involves many stages. Each stage involves combining resources and technology to produce a given output. Hence, the entire production process entails many separate activities. Take, for example, the computers that the residents of Northland and Eastisle produce. Each stage of production requires different components, different combinations of skilled and unskilled labor, and different types of capital. Suppose that the production of a computer can be broken down into four stages: manufacturing components, assembly of the computer, marketing the computer, and delivering the computer to the final user. It might be that Northland has a comparative advantage in some of the stages of production, for example, manufacturing components and assembly of the computer, while Eastisle has a comparative advantage in marketing and delivery.

The internationalization of production

As described in Chapter 1, economic integration, the reduction of transportation costs, and advances in communications have generated remarkable gains in trade. At the same time, these advances change the way that firms approach the production of goods and services. Firms can now focus on the stage of production in which they have the greatest comparative advantage.

Outsourcing

At each stage of production, a firm adds resources and technology, creating additional value. Economists refer to the difference between the value of a good or service and the cost of intermediate goods as the **value added** for that particular stage of production. Lower transportation costs and advances in communications allow firms to break down the production process and concentrate on the stages of production in which the firm has the greatest profit. The firm can then **outsource**, or hire other firms to complete other stages of production. Economists refer to this strategy as the *internationalization of production*. (We shall revisit and learn more about outsourcing in Chapter 10.)

Value added: *The revenue received by a producer less the cost of the intermediate good it purchased.*

Outsourcing: *A strategy in which one organization hires another organization to complete a particular stage of the production process.*

Internationalizing and outsourcing Barbie

Robert Feenstra of the University of California-Davis and the National Bureau of Economic Research offers the Barbie doll as an example of outsourcing and the internationalization of production processes. The raw materials for Barbie are plastic and high-tech hair, purchased from Taiwan and Japan, and cotton cloth, purchased from China. The molds for the doll, and some paints used to decorate the doll, come from the United States. Assembly occurs in Indonesia, Malaysia, and China. The dolls are shipped from Hong Kong to the United States. The export cost of each doll is roughly $2.00. Of this $2.00 value added, $0.35 derives from Chinese labor, $0.65 from material, and the remaining $1.00 goes to transportation and overhead. When the Barbie doll is sold in the United States, it retails for about $10.00. Mattel Corporation earns about $1.00 of this. The rest covers transportation, advertising, wholesaling, and retailing within the United States. Most of the value added occurs through activity within the United States that takes place after the doll is actually manufactured. According to sales data for 1995, two Barbie dolls are purchased every second, totaling $1.4 billion in annual sales for Mattel Corporation.

Kaleidoscopic comparative advantage

The fact that firms engage in internationalized production and specialize in specific stages of production reflects the competitive nature of the global marketplace. Increased competition forces firms to produce in the most efficient manner, which entails concentrating on their expertise or comparative advantage.

Intense competition and rivalry push firms to produce at the highest value-added stages of production in pursuit of maximum profits. This makes it difficult for firms to hold an edge in a particular stage of production. As we concluded in Chapter 2, comparative advantage can be fleeting.

As a firm internationalizes its production process and outsources various stages of production, specializing in but a part of the overall production process, it can gain or lose a competitive advantage very quickly. Jagdish Bhagwati and Vivek Dehejia of Columbia University have called the propensity for comparative advantage to shift suddenly from one country to another as *kaleidoscopic comparative advantage*. In an environment of kaleidoscopic comparative advantage, firms must be very concerned with the actions of their competitors. Rapid changes in comparative advantage can also cause workers to lose their jobs very quickly in one industry, while bringing about a shortage of workers in another industry. Both effects lead to greater pressure on policymakers to enact barriers to trade, a subject of later chapters.

Fundamental Issue #6: Is international production consistent with the concept of comparative advantage? Economic integration and reduced transportation and communication costs allow firms to specialize in certain stages of production and outsource other stages to firms in other nations. This process of internationalized production is consistent with the concept of comparative advantage as applied to the specific stages of production, such as the design, marketing, and manufacturing of a good. As a firm internationalizes its production process and outsources various stages of production, it can gain or lose a comparative advantage very quickly. This property for comparative advantage to shift suddenly from one country to another is known as kaleidoscopic comparative advantage.

ECONOMIC GROWTH AND INTERNATIONAL TRADE

So far in this chapter, you have learned about three of the fundamental theorems on trade: the Heckscher–Ohlin theorem, the factor price equalization theorem, and the Stolper–Samuelson theorem. There is one remaining theorem, which deals with economic growth and a nation's trade pattern: the Rybczynski theorem. Together, these theorems represent the basic foundation of analysis employed by economists who study international trade.

Economic growth

As discussed in Chapter 2, a nation's production possibilities are the various combinations of goods and services that it can produce, given its limited resources and fixed technology. **Economic growth** occurs when there is an increase in available resources or a technological advance, so that the nation's production possibilities expand.

Economic growth:
Occurs when a nation experiences an increase in available resources or a technological advance and the nation's production possibilities expand.

How economic growth occurs

When there is an increase in a nation's endowment of resources, the new resources can be put to use in production and can increase the nation's set of production possibilities. Technological advance is similar to an increase in available resources. One view of technological advance is that it is resource saving. That is, with the same amount of resources, the nation can generate higher levels of output. Technological advance, therefore, has the same effect as an increase in the nation's endowment of resources. Economic growth, whether it is an increase in resources or a technological advance, expands a nation's set of production possibilities.

Industry-specific effects

In the framework of factor proportions, economic growth may well have different effects on two industries. To see why this is so, reconsider the earlier examples of food, a relatively labor-intensive good, and computers, a relatively capital-intensive good. Suppose that the residents of Northland, because of past savings, experience an increase in their capital endowments. Because of the increase in capital, Northland's residents could increase their production of either food or computers. The gains that occur in either industry would not be the same, however. Northland's residents could not increase the production of food as easily as computers, because food requires a larger amount of labor per capital unit than does the production of computers. Thus, even though an increase in the endowment of a particular factor causes Northland's production possibilities to expand, the expansion favors the good that uses the growing factor intensively in its production process.

Technological advance could generate differential effects as well. If the advance occurs in both industries and saves the same amount of each factor, then production possibilities proportionately expand the same amount for each good. If technological advance occurs in only one industry, then that industry will experience the greatest growth. If technological advance occurs in both industries, but saves on capital, then the capital-intensive industry, in this case the computer industry, will experience the greatest growth.

Regardless of how economic growth occurs, the nation effectively experiences an increase in its endowment of resources. As you learned earlier, in the factor proportions framework a nation's trade pattern is determined by factor endowments and factor intensities. Economic growth, therefore, will affect a nation's exports and imports.

The Rybczynski theorem

Rybczynski theorem: *The theory that if a nation experiences an increase in the amount of a resource, it will produce more of the good that uses the resource relatively intensively in its production process, and will produce less of the other good.*

The **Rybczynski theorem**, developed by T. M. Rybczynski, addresses the way that economic growth affects a nation's trade. The theorem maintains that an expansion of a nation's endowment of a particular factor of production will, in the context of the factor proportions approach, and at a given opportunity cost, lead to an increase in the production of the good that uses that factor intensively in its production process and a decrease in the production of the other good.

If the residents of Northland, for example, were to experience an increase in their endowments of capital, then their output of computers would rise while their output of food would decline. (For an illustration of the Rybczynski theorem, see *Visualizing Global Economic Issues: The Rybczynski theorem.*)

VISUALIZING GLOBAL ECONOMIC ISSUES

The Rybczynski theorem

To visualize the Rybczynski theorem, consider Northland's PPF in Figure 3.4. Suppose that, prior to economic growth the residents of Northland produce F_1 baskets of food and C_1 computers, as indicated by point P in the figure. As discussed in Chapter 2, the slope of the line tangent to point P, labeled OC, indicates the opportunity cost of producing this combination of goods.

Now consider the effects of an increase in Northland's residents' capital endowments. Because computers are relatively capital intensive and food is relatively labor intensive, the increase in capital disproportionately affects the production of computers. The increase in capital causes the PPF to rotate outward as it shifts, reflecting the disproportional effect on the computer industry.

The Rybczynski theorem assumes that opportunity costs remain the same after economic growth occurs. To reflect this assumption, the line OC shifts outward, maintaining the same slope, until it is tangent to the new PPF at point P'. Point P' indicates that the residents of Northland now produce F_2 food and C_2 computers.

Note that the production of computers, the relatively capital-intensive good, increased from C_1 to C_2 computers while the production of food fell from F_1 to F_2

---

baskets. This outcome illustrates the Rybczynski theorem, an increase in capital leads to an increase in the production of the capital-intensive good, computers, and to a decrease in the production of the labor-intensive good, food.

For critical analysis: Does the increase in capital make Northland's residents more or less likely to trade? What if labor were to increase instead of capital?

Growth and trade

The Rybczynski theorem helps us understand how a nation's production bundle changes. Now let's consider how a change in the production bundle resulting from economic growth affects the nation's trade pattern.

Consider the result of Northland's economic growth just described. An increase in capital led to an increase in the production of computers and a decrease in the

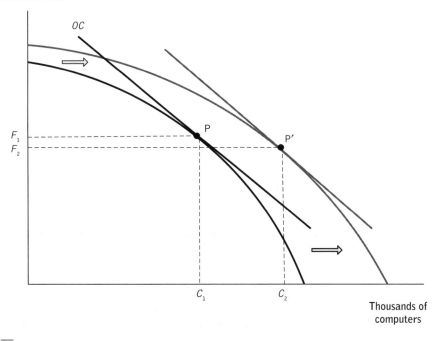

Figure 3.4 *Illustrating the Rybczynski theorem*

If the residents of Northland experience an increase in their endowments of capital, Northland's PPF rotates outward. At constant opportunity costs, this type of economic growth leads the residents of Northland to increase their production of the good that uses capital intensively, computers, from C_1 to C_2, and decrease their production of the good that uses labor intensively, food, from F_1 to F_2.

83

production of food. Prior to economic growth, Northland's residents exported computers and imported food. Economic growth led residents of Northland to increase their production of the export good, computers, and decrease their production of the import good, food. This change in production will lead Northland's residents to increase both their imports and their exports. In other words, this particular type of economic growth had a pro-trade effect.

Not all production changes are pro-trade, however. Consider what happens if Northland's residents experience an increase in their relatively scarce factor, labor. According to the Rybczynski theorem, an increase in labor leads Northland's residents to produce more food and fewer computers. In other words, residents of Northland will increase their production of the import good and decrease the production of the export good. This change in the production bundle leads Northland's residents to engage less in trade. Thus, this type of economic growth had an anti-trade effect.

As you can see, the Rybczynski theorem is very useful in determining how economic growth might affect a nation's trade. In Chapter 1, you learned that the United States continues to experience very high levels of capital inflows. Based on the Rybczynski theorem, we would expect the United States to continue to expand in high-technology areas, while its labor-intensive industries contract further.

Fundamental Issue #7: How does economic growth affect trade patterns? The Rybczynski theorem asserts that an increase in the endowment of a particular factor will, with prices constant, lead to an increase in the production of the good that uses the factor relatively intensively in the production process, and to a decrease in the production of the other good. The change in production that results from economic growth can generate more trade, or less trade. An increase in the nation's relatively abundant factor will lead the nation's residents to produce more of the export good and less of the import good, spurring additional trade. An increase in the nation's relatively scarce factor will induce residents to trade less.

CHAPTER SUMMARY

1. **The factor proportions explanation of comparative advantage:** The factor proportions approach focuses on the relative factor endowments of nations and the relative factor intensities of goods and services as explanations of comparative advantage. The factor proportions model is a two-country, two-factor, two-good model. Relative factor endowments and relative factor intensities are the central features of this model. The factor proportions model is often used to test the factor proportions explanation of comparative advantage.

2. **The Heckscher–Ohlin theory of trade:** The Heckscher–Ohlin theorem resulted from the factor proportions approach. This theory maintains that a nation's residents will

export goods and services that use the relatively abundant factor intensively. Likewise, the nation's residents will import goods and services that use the relatively scarce factor intensively.

3. **Evidence on the factor proportions explanation of trade patterns:** In 1954, Wassily Leontief conducted the first rigorous examination of the factor proportions approach. Leontief found that U.S. trade data contradicted the predictions of the factor proportions approach. Economists refer to his findings as the Leontief paradox. His results sparked a great deal of research into the factor proportions approach. As a result, a more generalized factor proportions approach emerged.

4. **The relationship between trade and factor prices:** The factor price equalization theorem asserts that unhindered international trade will bring about an equalization of factor prices among trading nations. The equalization process occurs through the price adjustments that take place in the global market for goods and services.

5. **The relationship between trade and real income:** The Stolper–Samuelson theorem indicates that free trade increases the real income of a nation's relatively abundant factor and reduces the real income of a nation's relatively scarce factor. In other words, international trade benefits a nation's relatively abundant factor and harms a nation's relatively scarce factor. An important implication of this theory is that the owners of a nation's relatively abundant factor are likely to support free-trade policies, while the owners of a nation's relatively scarce factor are likely to oppose free-trade policies.

6. **International production and comparative advantage:** In the current global environment of increased economic integration and lower transportation and communication costs, firms often engage in internationalized production. Internationalized production occurs when firms specialize in particular stages of production and outsource other stages to firms in other countries. As firms internationalize their production process, they can gain or lose their comparative advantage very quickly. This property of comparative advantages shifting suddenly from one nation to another is known as kaleidoscopic comparative advantage.

7. **Economic growth and trade patterns:** The Rybczynski theorem indicates that an increase in a particular endowment will, with opportunity costs constant, lead a nation's residents to produce a greater quantity of the good that uses that factor intensively and to produce less of the other good. The change in production that results from economic growth may induce a nation's residents to trade more or less. An increase in the relatively abundant factor leads a nation's residents to produce more of the export good and less of the import good, which generates greater levels of trade. An increase in the nation's relatively scarce factor leads it to trade less as the production of the export good falls and the production of the import good rises.

QUESTIONS AND PROBLEMS

1. Utopia's residents are endowed with 100 labor units and 75 capital units. Idealand's residents are endowed with 75 labor units and 50 capital units. Which nation is relatively labor abundant and which is relatively capital abundant?

2. Suppose that, at the current level of production, sandwiches require 1 labor unit and 0.5 capital units to produce, while bicycles require 0.9 labor units and 0.9 capital units. Based on this information, which of the two goods is relatively capital intensive in its production process, and which is relatively labor intensive?

3. Answer the following using your answers to questions 1 and 2. Suppose Utopia's and Idealand's residents begin to trade. Which good will Utopia's residents export, and which good will Utopia's residents import? Explain your answer in the context of the Heckscher–Ohlin theorem.

4. Based on your answer to question 3, under autarky, will Utopia or Idealand have the higher price of sandwiches relative to bicycles? Which has the higher price of bicycles relative to sandwiches? Under autarky, which nation has the higher wage rate relative to the rental rate of capital? Explain how the wage rate relative to the rental rate of capital adjusts when the residents of the two nations begin to trade.

5. Based on your answer to question 3, explain how free trade between the residents of Utopia and Idealand benefits or harms workers and the capital holders in the two nations.

6. Consider Figure 3.2 (p. 66). If the residents of the two nations, Northland and Eastisle, are able to expand their consumption possibilities by specializing in the production of the good in which they have their respective comparative advantage, why did they not specialize completely? In other words, why did they stop specializing at the points labeled P_T^N and P_T^E?

7. Suppose that the manufacturing process for personal computers involves five stages: design, manufacturing of components, assembly, marketing, and delivery. Consider a computer company, such as U.S.-based Hewlett-Packard (HP). For which stages of production do you think HP has a comparative advantage relative to a firm in a developing economy? In other words, if HP were to restructure, what are the stages of production in which it has the greatest comparative advantage?

8. Emerging nations in East Asia experienced considerable inflows of capital during the late 1990s and 2000s. According to the Rybczynski theorem, how would an increase in East Asia's residents' capital endowments affect their patterns of trade?

9. Consider your answer to question 8. Do you think the economic growth that took place in East Asia during the 2000s made the residents of East Asian nations more or less likely to engage in trade with residents of other regions?

10. Explain how the migration of labor from Central America to the United States might affect production in the United States.

ONLINE APPLICATION

URL: www.wto.org

Title: World Trade Organization

Navigation: Begin at the home page of the World Trade Organization (WTO). Click on "Documents and resources," and in the drop-down menu, click on "Statistics." Next, click "Trade in Merchandise and Services." Then scroll down and click on

"International Trade Statistics." Scroll to the right and select the option "Download the complete International Trade statistics in pdf format" and open the PDF file for the most recent trade statistics.

Application: Perform the following operations, and answer the following questions.

1. Before reviewing the statistics in the file you opened, answer the following questions.
   (a) Which regions do you think the residents of the NAFTA nations (Canada, Mexico, and the United States) collectively trade with the most: North America, Asia, Europe, South and Central America, the Middle East, Africa, or the CIS nations (Commonwealth of Independent States)? Rank these regions from highest to lowest.
   (b) Which of the product groups (agricultural products, fuels and mining products, and manufactures) do you think are *net* exports of the residents of the NAFTA countries? Which of the product groups do you think are *net* imports of the residents of the NAFTA countries?

2. Return to the document you opened. Move down to the tables titled "Bilateral trade of leading traders." Based on the information you see there, answer question 1(a) again. Advance in the document to "Regional trade agreements." Answer question 1(b) again.

For group study and analysis: Assign questions 1 and 2 to three different groups, assigning to each group one of the three NAFTA countries. Have each group present its findings and explain how they compare with the Heckscher–Ohlin theorem.

REFERENCES AND RECOMMENDED READINGS

Anderson, James E., and Eric Van Wincoop. "Trade Costs." *Journal of Economic Literature* XLII (September 2004): 691–751.

Baldwin, Robert. *The Development and Testing of Heckscher–Ohlin Trade Models.* Cambridge, MA: MIT Press, 2008.

Bhagwati, Jagdish, and Vivek H. Dehejia. "Freer Trade and Wages of the Unskilled—Is Marx Striking Again?" In Jagdish Bhagwati and Marvin H. Kosters, eds., *Trade and Wages: Leveling Wages Down?* Washington, DC: American Enterprise Institute, 1994.

Bhagwati, Jagdish, and Marvin H. Kosters, eds. *Trade and Wages: Leveling Wages Down?* Washington, DC: American Enterprise Institute, 1994.

Borjas, George J. "The Internationalization of the U.S. Labor Market and the Wage Structure." *Federal Reserve Bank of New York Economic Policy Review* (January 1995), pp. 3–8.

Chipman, John S. *The Theory of International Trade: Volume 1.* Northampton, MA: Elgar, 2008.

Davis, John. "Is Trade Liberalization an Important Cause of Increasing U.S. Wage Inequality? The Interaction of Theory and Policy." *Review of Social Economy* LVII(4) (1999): 488–506.

Deardorff, Alan V. "A Trade Theorist's Take on Skilled-Labor Outsourcing." *International Review of Economics and Finance* 14(3) (2005): 259–271.

Feenstra, Robert C. "Integration of Trade and Disintegration of Production in the Global Economy." *Journal of Economic Perspectives* 12(4) (1998): 31–50.

Hummels, David. "Transportation Costs and International Trade in the Second Era of Globalization." *Journal of Economic Perspectives* 21(3) (2007): 131–154.

Kemp, Murray C. *International Trade Theory: A Critical Review.* London: Taylor & Francis/ Routledge, 2008.

Kemp, Murray C., and Binh Tran-Nam. "On Trade Gains and International Disparities in Factor Proportions." In K. Shimomura, ed., *International Trade and Economic Dynamics.* Berlin: Springer, 2009, pp. 13–18.

Markusen, James R., and Anthony J. Venables. "Interacting Factor Endowments and Trade Costs: A Multi-Country, Multi-Good Approach to Trade Theory." *Journal of International Economics* 73(2) (November 2007): 333–354.

Morrow, Peter. "Ricardian–Heckscher–Ohlin Comparative Advantage: Theory and Evidence." *Journal of International Economics* 82(2) (November 2010): 137–151.

Opp, Marcus M., Hugo F. Sonnenschein, and Christis G. Tombazos. "Rybczynski's Theorem in the Heckscher–Ohlin World – Anything Goes." *Journal of International Economics* 79(1) (September 2009): 137–142.

Rassekh, Farhad, and Henry Thompson. "Factor Price Equalization: Theory and Evidence." *Journal of Economic Integration* 8(1) (1993): 1–32.

Romalis, John. "Factor Proportions and the Structure of Commodity Trade." *American Economic Review* 94(1) (2004): 67–97.

Samuelson, Paul A. "International Factor–Price Equalisation Once again." In E. Leamer, ed., *International Economics*, Worth Series in Outstanding Contributions. New York: Worth, 2001 [1949], pp. 19–32.

Thompson, Henry. "Definitions of Factor Abundance and the Factor Content of Trade." *Open Economies Review* 10(4) (October 1999): 385–393.

Trefler, Daniel. "The Case of the Missing Trade and Other Mysteries." *American Economic Review* 85(5) (December 1995): 1029–1046.

Williamson, Jeffrey G. "Globalization, Labor Markets and Policy Backlash in the Past." *Journal of Economic Literature* 12(4) (1998): 51–72.

Wood, Adrian. "Give Heckscher and Ohlin a Chance!" *Weltwirtschaftliches Archiv* 130(1) (1994): 20–49.

Vane, Howard R., and Chris Mulhearn, eds. *Wassily W. Leontief, Leonid V. Kantorovich, Tjalling C. Koopmans and J. Richard N. Stone. Pioneering Papers of the Nobel Memorial Laureates in Economics, Vol. 4.* Northampton, MA: Elgar Reference Collection, 2009.

Chapter 4

Regulating international trade—trade policies and their effects

---

FUNDAMENTAL ISSUES

1. How do taxes affect the market price, and what are the redistributive effects of taxes?
2. What are the economic effects of tariff barriers?
3. What are quotas, and how do they represent a direct approach to restricting trade?
4. What are voluntary export restraints?
5. What are the effects of export subsidies, and how do policymakers typically react to export promotion policies?
6. What are the advantages and disadvantages of trade barriers?

Argentina and India are separated by thousands of miles, but their governments share a common international trade policy: Industries in other nations desiring to sell exported items to their nation's residents are prohibited unless the industries produce at least one product within their nation's borders. Argentina's government prohibits its residents from importing iPhones because no U.S. manufacturers of smartphones produce any of their products in Argentina. Based on the same reasoning, India's government prevents the importation of a wide range of U.S.-produced information technology products, including laptop computers, wi-fi digital devices, and computer-networking equipment.

The shared perspective of the Argentine and Indian governments is that the unwillingness of U.S. firms to operate within their nation hinders residents' job opportunities, thereby justifying the import restrictions. Apparently the two nations' governments also are willing to accept a fundamental trade-off associated with such trade restraints: higher prices that their consumers must pay for the products of domestic firms that the import restrictions protect from foreign competition.

Imposing quantity restrictions on imports of goods and services—quotas—is just one way in which governments can choose to regulate international trade. In this chapter, you will learn why trade restrictions such as the trade quotas imposed by Argentina and India, typically lead to higher domestic prices.

Quotas usually lead to higher domestic prices.

TAXES AND THEIR DIRECT EFFECT ON PRICE

Policymakers can use a wide variety of instruments to restrict or alter trade flows. To begin our examination of these tools, we shall start with one of the most commonly used international policy instruments, which is a **tariff** barrier. A tariff is a tax on an imported good or service. To understand how a tariff works, you must first understand how a tax affects the market for a good or service.

Tariff: *A tax on imported goods and services.*

Taxes as a factor influencing supply

As discussed in Chapter 1, taxes are among the various categories of factors that influence supply. Let's now evaluate how a tax influences supply and, in turn, how a tax influences market outcomes.

The effect on the supply schedule

Consider the monthly supply schedule for a running shoe manufacturer, given in Table 4.1. As the table shows, at a market price of $75.00 per pair, the manufacturer is willing to produce and offer for sale 1,000 pairs of a particular running shoe.

Now consider the effects of a tax on running shoes. (To make our example easy to track, we shall assume the manufacturer sells its shoes directly to the customer over the Internet.) Suppose the government imposes a tax of $5.00 on each pair of running shoes the manufacturer sells, and that the government requires the manufacturer to remit the tax to a designated tax agency.

Table 4.2 shows the original, pre-tax, supply schedule, and the new combinations of price and quantity after tax—the post-tax supply schedule. After the government

Table 4.1 *The supply schedule of a running shoe manufacturer. The supply schedule tabulates the quantity supplied at various prices.*

Price per pair ($)	Quantity of pairs
72.50	750
75.00	1,000
77.50	1,250
80.00	1,500

Table 4.2 *The after-tax supply schedule. The imposition of a tax causes a decline in the quantity supplied at each of the various prices.*

Price per pair ($)	Pre-tax quantity	Post-tax quantity
72.50	750	250
75.00	1,000	500
77.50	1,250	750
80.00	1,500	1,000

imposes the tax, the manufacturer now requires $80.00 for each pair of running shoes to be willing to manufacture and offer for sale 1,000 pairs of shoes a month. When the customer pays $80.00 per pair, the manufacturer collects $80.00, remits $5.00 to the government, and keeps $75.00. (We are ignoring any costs associated with recording sales and taxes, and reporting the taxes to the government. These "red tape" costs, however, may be quite sizable.) In a similar manner, the manufacturer now requires $75.00 to supply 500 pairs of shoes and $77.50 to supply 750 pairs. Thus, the price the manufacturer requires at each quantity rises by the amount of the tax.

There is another way we can view the difference between the pre-tax supply schedule and the post-tax supply schedule. Note that at each of the various prices the quantity supplied is lower after the imposition of the tax. Hence, the *supply* of running shoes decreases.

The effect on price

As discussed in Chapter 1, because the supply of running shoes decreases, there is upward pressure on the market price. Does this mean that the market price of running shoes rises by $5.00 per pair? According to the law of demand, when price rises, quantity demanded falls. At a price of $80.00, therefore, fewer running shoes are sold. As a result of this relationship between price and quantity demanded, imposing a tax causes the market price to rise, but not by the full amount of the tax.

Who really pays a tax?

Because a tax influences market outcomes, it has redistributive effects, meaning that it transfers purchasing power among consumers, producers, and the government. A tax is **forward shifted** if the consumer must pay the tax in the form of a higher price per unit. A tax is **backward shifted** if the producer must pay the tax in the form of lower revenue per unit.

As just discussed, imposing a tax typically causes an increase in the market price that is less than the full amount of the tax. This means that part of the tax is forward shifted and part of the tax is backward shifted. By definition, the amount of the tax that is forward shifted and the amount that is backward shifted is the amount the government receives in tax revenue.

To see how taxes are typically forward and backward shifted, suppose that after the tax is imposed, the market price of a pair of running shoes rises to $77.50, and the equilibrium quantity falls to 750 pairs. At the new equilibrium, the producer receives $77.50 per pair of running shoes sold to the consumer, pays $5.00 to the government, and keeps $72.50 per pair. The tax revenue that the government receives is $5.00 × 750 = $3,750.00. The portion of the tax that is forward shifted onto consumers—the portion of the $3,750.00 paid by consumers in the form of a higher price—is ($77.50 − $75.00) × 750 = $1,875.00. The portion of the tax that is backward shifted—the portion of the $3,750.00 paid by the producer in the form of revenue per unit—is ($75.00 − $72.50) × 750 = $1,875.00.

If part of the tax is backward shifted and part is forward shifted, then both the consumer and the producer share in paying the tax. The degrees to which a tax is

Forward shifted:
The portion of a tax that consumers pay in the form of a higher price per unit.

Backward shifted:
The amount of a tax that producers pay in the form of lower revenue per unit.

forward shifted and backward shifted depend on the responsiveness of consumers and producers to changes in price. (To further consider the redistributive effects of a tax, see the box: "Visualizing global economic issues: The effects of a tax.") We reach the following conclusion:

Typically, imposing a tax causes the market price to rise, but not by the full amount of the tax. Forward shifting of a tax is the amount of the tax that the consumer pays in the form of a higher price. Backward shifting of a tax is the amount of the tax that is paid by the producer in the form of lower prices. Because the price typically does not rise by the full amount of the tax in most situations, part of the tax is forward shifted and part is backward shifted.

VISUALIZING GLOBAL ECONOMIC ISSUES

The effects of a tax

To see how a tax alters market outcomes, consider Figure 4.1. As shown in the figure, the market for running shoes is initially in equilibrium at point A, with a market price of $75.00 per pair of shoes and an equilibrium quantity of 1,000 pairs.

Now suppose the government imposes a $5.00 tax on each pair of shoes sold. The quantity supplied declines at each of the various prices, so the tax causes a decrease in supply. The decrease in supply is shown by the leftward and upward shift of the supply curve to S'. Note that at each of the various quantities, the supply curve shifts vertically by the amount of the tax.

Because of the decrease in supply, there is upward pressure on the price of running shoes. Consumers are resistant to this price increase and reduce their quantity demanded, as shown by a movement up and along the demand curve. A new equilibrium is reached at point B, at a price of $77.50 per shoe and a quantity of 750 pairs. As you can see in the figure, the tax causes the market price to rise above its initial level of $75.00, but not by the full amount of the tax.

In this example, the government's tax revenue equals $5.00 × 750 = $3,750. The total tax revenue is illustrated in Figure 4.1 by the rectangle formed by areas C and P. The base of this rectangle equals the equilibrium quantity sold, 750 units, and the height equals the per-unit tax, $77.50 − $72.50 = $5.00. Hence, the area of the rectangle formed by areas C and P is equal to the tax revenue.

Figure 4.1 also illustrates the portion of the tax that is forward shifted and the portion that is backward shifted. The amount of the tax that is forward shifted, which is shown by the rectangle labeled C, is $1,875 [($77.50 − $75.00) × 750]. The base of this rectangle is equal to the equilibrium quantity sold, and the height is equal to the difference between the equilibrium price after the tax and the equilibrium price before the tax, $77.25 − $75.00 = $2.50. Thus the area of rectangle C equals the total amount of the tax forward shifted onto consumers.

The amount of the tax that is backward shifted, which is depicted by the rectangle labeled *P*, is $1,875 [($77.50 − $75.00) × 750]. The base of this rectangle is equal to the quantity transacted, and the height is equal to the difference between the equilibrium price before the tax and the price the producer keeps after paying the tax to the government tax agency, $75.00 − $72.50 = $2.50. The area of rectangle *P*, therefore, equals the total amount of the tax backward shifted onto shoe producers.

For critical analysis: Suppose the tax was 5 percent of the price, as opposed to a fixed amount per unit. How would Figure 4.1 be different?

Fundamental Issue #1: How do taxes affect the market price, and what are the redistributive effects of taxes? The imposition of a tax causes the supply of the particular good or service to decrease. Although the decrease in supply generates an increase in the market price, it typically does not rise by the full amount of the tax in most situations. Because a tax influences market outcomes, it has redistributive effects. A tax is forward shifted if the consumer must pay the tax in the form of a higher price per unit. A tax is backward shifted if the producer must pay the tax in the form of lower revenue per unit.

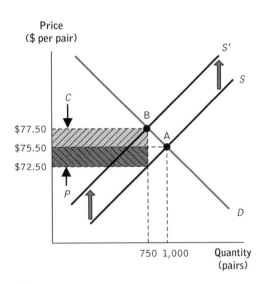

Figure 4.1 *The effects of a tax*

The imposition of a tax causes the supply curve to shift vertically by an amount equal to the tax. The decrease in supply generates an increase in the market price. Although the market price rises, it typically does not rise by the full amount of the tax. The entire amount of tax revenue is given by the sum of areas C and P. Area C is the portion of the tax forward shifted onto consumers and area P is the amount of the tax backward shifted onto producers.

THE ECONOMIC EFFECTS OF A TARIFF

ON THE WEB:

Obtain information on U.S. tariff rates from the International Trade Administration at the U.S. Department of Commerce at www. ita.doc.gov.

As discussed earlier, a tariff is a tax on imported goods or services. A tariff, therefore, has many of the same effects on price and quantity as in the example of a tax on running shoes. There is, however, an important difference. A tariff is a tax on imported goods and services and does not apply to the output of domestic producers. This means that the backward shifting of a tariff is different from the backward shifting of a tax on domestic output. Another aspect to consider is that a tariff has the potential to affect the global price by affecting the global supply, as discussed in Chapter 1. Before you can begin to analyze the economic effects of a tariff, you must first understand the basic types of tariff and their strengths and weaknesses. Then we will consider economic effects in two possible environments: a *small-country* setting and a *large-country* setting.

Types of tariff

Specific tariff: *A tariff specified as an amount of money per unit of the good sold.*

Ad valorem tariff: *A tariff calculated as a percentage of the value of the good or service.*

Combination tariff: *A tariff that combines an ad valorem tariff and a specific tariff.*

There are three basic kinds of tariff. A **specific tariff** is a fixed tariff amount per unit imported. An **ad valorem** tariff is calculated as a percent of the value of the good or service imported. A **combination tariff** is a blend of a specific tariff and an *ad valorem* tariff. Table 4.3 lists tariff rates applied by the United States on selected items. Grass shears, for example, are subject to a combination tariff consisting of a 5.1 percent *ad valorem* tariff and a $0.02 specific tariff.

Benefits and weaknesses of specific tariffs

There are advantages and disadvantages of using specific tariffs and *ad valorem* tariffs. A specific tariff is easy to calculate, but it does not adjust to price changes. Consider, for example, a $1,000 specific tariff applied to Swedish automobiles. The tariff is easy to calculate, because the trade authorities must simply count the number of

Table 4.3 *Selected U.S. tariff rates*

Item	Ad valorem tariff (percent)	Specific tariff ($ per unit)
Grass shears and parts thereof	5.1	0.02
Carpets and other textile floor coverings of wool or fine animal hair	0	0
Floor coverings of coconut fibers	0	1.29
Capers	8.0	0
Mushrooms	20.0	0.22
Cigars	4.7	1.89
Cigarettes	0.9	0.417
Pre-shave, shaving, or after-shave preparations	4.9	0
Lawn-tennis rackets, strung	5.3	0
Bicycles	11.0	0

Source: Harmonized tariff schedule of the United States, www.usitc.gov.

automobiles brought into the country and then multiply this number by $1,000. Suppose that the imported auto wholesales for $20,000, so that the $1,000 specific tariff represents 5 percent of the value of the automobile. The Swedish auto manufacturer, however, can export a more expensive model valued at $25,000. Then the $1,000 tariff represents only 4 percent of the value of the auto. The relative size of the tariff—as a percent of the value of the automobile—declines when the manufacturer simply substitutes a more expensive automobile.

Benefits and weaknesses of ad valorem tariffs

The benefit of an *ad valorem* tariff is that it always amounts to the same percentage of the value of the good or service. A 5 percent *ad valorem* tariff, for example, remains 5 percent of the value of the automobile, regardless of the model the Swedish automobile manufacturer exports. The tariff amount generated by an *ad valorem* tariff, therefore, rises as the price of the good increases. An *ad valorem* tariff, however, is more difficult to calculate. The trade authorities can no longer simply count the number of autos. They must first determine the numbers of each type of imported auto and tabulate the market prices of all models.

As you can see, specific tariffs and *ad valorem* tariffs have their own strengths and weaknesses. To take advantage of the strengths of each type of tariff, trade authorities often find combination tariffs useful.

Effects of a tariff in a small-country setting

A **small country** is one in which the consumption and production decisions of its domestic residents do not affect the international price in a particular market, so that the residents of a small country take the international price in that market as a given. Hence, in the small-country setting, the imposition of a tariff causes the domestic price of the good or service to change, but it does not affect the international price.

Small country: *A country so small its consumption and production decisions do not affect the international price, so that its residents take the international price as a given.*

The price effect of a tariff in a small-country setting

In any environment, the domestic price that consumers must pay equals the global price plus the amount of the tariff. In a small-country setting, however, the decisions of domestic producers and domestic consumers do not affect the global price. Consequently, the domestic price paid by domestic consumers and the revenue received by domestic producers rises by the full amount of a tariff. The increase in domestic price causes quantity demanded to decline and induces domestic producers to increase their quantity supplied.

Foreign producers must remit the tariff to the domestic government. The per-unit revenue they receive after the tariff, therefore, is still equal to the international price. Nonetheless, because quantity demanded declines and quantity supplied by domestic producers increases, the tariff causes the quantity of imports to shrink. (Sometimes foreign producers based in countries targeted by tariffs seek to shift production to other nations not subjected to the tariffs, but typically the outcomes are still a reduction in total domestic supply and a higher domestic market price; see *Policy Notebook: U.S. tariffs on solar panels imported from China yield more U.S. imports of Chinese-produced panels assembled in other countries.*)

POLICY NOTEBOOK

U.S. tariffs on solar panels imported from China yield more U.S. imports of Chinese-produced panels assembled in other countries

In the late 1970s, the U.S. price of electricity generated by solar panels was, in 2013 dollars, about $50 per watt. By 2013, the price had dropped to nearly $0.80 per watt. Naturally, many U.S. residents responded to this substantial price reduction by purchasing and installing more solar panels. At the beginning of the twenty-first century, U.S. residents purchased more than 20 percent of solar panels from U.S. producers. By 2008, however, the percentage of U.S.-produced solar panels bought by U.S. consumers had dropped to 7 percent. Today, fewer than 3 percent of solar panels purchased in the United States are sold by domestic manufacturers.

The top foreign sources of solar panels purchased in the U.S. market are producers based in China. U.S. imports of Chinese-produced solar panels doubled between 2008 and 2010, and then doubled again between 2010 and 2012, when U.S. consumers spent more than $3 billion on solar panels imported from China.

The rate of growth of U.S. imports of Chinese solar panels has dropped considerably since 2012, when the U.S. government imposed *ad valorem* tariff rates ranging from 24 percent to 36 percent on U.S. imports of solar panels from China. One reason for the decline in solar panel imports from China was, naturally, that a resulting increase in the post-tariff U.S. market price of solar panels initially induced a slight decline in purchases of solar panels by U.S. consumers. Another reason for the decline in imports from China was that many Chinese manufacturers responded by shipping components from China to newly established assembly plants in Taiwan and South Korea. The Chinese firms then assembled and exported solar panels to the United States from these nations. In this way, most Chinese manufacturers ultimately escaped paying the U.S. solar panel tariff. Nevertheless, rearranging their production facilities and incurring additional shipping expenses pushed up Chinese manufacturers' costs, so the market supply of solar panels in the United States still declined as a result of the tariff. As a consequence, the market price of solar panels rose slightly.

For critical analysis: Why do you suppose that the U.S. government collected fewer Chinese solar panel tariff revenues than it originally had anticipated collecting?

Forward and backward shifting of the tariff in a small-country setting

The forward- and backward-shifting aspects of a tariff are straightforward in a small-country setting. The revenue per unit that domestic producers receive increases, so none of the tariff is backward shifted to domestic producers. The revenue per unit that foreign producers receive after paying the tariff remains the same, so none of the tariff is backward shifted to foreign producers. Because the domestic price rises by the full amount of the tariff, all of the tariff revenue is forward shifted. Domestic consumers pay the entire tariff in the form of higher prices of foreign products they purchase.

Redistributive effects of a tariff in a small-country setting

Now that you understand the forward and backward shifting of a tariff in a small-country setting, let's consider the redistributive effects of a tariff using the concepts of consumer and producer surplus. Recall from Chapter 1 that consumer surplus is the difference between what consumers are willing to pay for a particular quantity and the market price they must pay. Producer surplus is the difference between the market price that producers receive and the price needed to persuade them to supply a particular quantity. Consumer and producer surplus, therefore, are affected by a change in price, which, in turn, changes when a government imposes a tariff.

In the case of the tariff in the small-country setting, there is an increase in both the price that consumers must pay and the revenue per unit that domestic producers receive. Consumer surplus, therefore, falls, and the surplus of domestic producers rises. Because the revenue per unit that foreign producers receive remains unchanged, foreign producer surplus remains unchanged.

Part of the loss of consumer surplus, the forward-shifted tariff revenue, is transferred to the domestic government as tariff revenue. Another part of the loss of consumer surplus is transferred to domestic producers as an increase in domestic producer surplus. Finally, part of the loss of consumer surplus is not transferred to any other party. Losses of consumer or producer surplus not transferred to any other party, or **deadweight losses**, result from a loss of economic efficiency. **Economic efficiency** requires that resources be allocated in the most cost-efficient manner. Because a tariff distorts the domestic price, scarce domestic resources are shifted into the tariff-protected industry and away from other, more efficient industries, resulting in a loss of economic efficiency.

A tariff, therefore, redistributes consumer surplus to domestic producers and the domestic government. The loss of consumer surplus exceeds the amount transferred to domestic producers and the domestic government. Hence, a tariff in a small-country setting leads to a net welfare loss for domestic residents. (To further evaluate the effects of a tariff in a small country, see *Visualizing Global Economic Issues: A tariff in a small-country setting*.)

Deadweight loss: *A loss of consumer or producer surplus that is not transferred to any other party and that represents a decline in economy efficiency.*

Economic efficiency: *A condition when scarce resources are allocated in a most productive, least-cost pattern.*

VISUALIZING GLOBAL ECONOMIC ISSUES

A tariff in a small-country setting

To visualize the impact of a tariff in a small-country setting, consider the market for steel depicted in Figure 4.2 (p. 99). In the figure, the demand curve labeled *D* is the domestic demand, and the curve labeled S_{dom} is the supply of domestic steel producers. The global price is $800, and residents of the small country can purchase as much steel as they desire at the global price of $800 without driving up the global price. Hence, *from the perspective of the residents of the small country*, the global supply curve — representing the supply curve of all foreign producers — is horizontal at the global price.

At the global price of $800, domestic producers supply 75 tons of steel to the domestic market and the total quantity demanded is 150 tons of steel. Steel imports, or the difference between domestic quantity demanded and the quantity supplied by domestic producers, equal 75 tons.

Suppose that the domestic government imposes a specific tariff of $50 per ton. Because the tariff is on imported steel only, the global supply curve faced by domestic residents shifts upward by $50 to S'_{Global}, while the domestic supply curve remains at its original position. As shown in Figure 4.2, the domestic price of steel rises by the full amount of the tariff, to a new equilibrium price of $850 per ton. As the domestic price of steel rises, the quantity supplied by domestic producers rises from 75 tons to 85 tons. Domestic quantity demanded, however, falls to 135 tons, and imports shrink to 50 tons.

Redistributive effects of the tariff

Because the domestic price rises by the full amount of the tariff, the entire tariff is forward shifted onto the consumer. The areas labeled *C*, *E*, *F*, and *G* in Figure 4.2 represent the total loss of consumer surplus. Of this total, the rectangle labeled *C* illustrates the amount of the tariff revenue and, therefore, the amount that is forward shifted onto steel consumers. The base of this rectangle equals the quantity imported, 50 tons, and the height equals the amount of the tariff, $50. Hence, the area *C*, $50 \times \$50 = \$250$, equals the tariff revenue.

The area *E* represents a loss of consumer surplus that is transferred to domestic producers in the form of higher revenue per ton of steel sold in the domestic market. In other words, domestic producers' surplus rises as the revenue per unit increases. The value of this transfer is determined by calculating the area of the rectangle and the triangle that together form the area *E*, or $(75 \times \$50) + [(10 \times \$50)/2] = \$4,000$.

Deadweight losses

As shown in Figure 4.2, the loss of consumer surplus exceeds the amounts transferred to the domestic government and to domestic producers. Hence, there are deadweight losses resulting from the tariff. The two triangles labeled *F* and *G* represent the tariff deadweight losses. The triangle *F*, which has an area equal to $(10 \times \$50)/2 = \$250$, represents a loss of economic efficiency that results when domestic producers shift scarce resources from unprotected, more efficient industries to domestic production within the protected industry. The triangle G, which has an area equal to $(15 \times \$50)/2 = \$375$, represents a loss of steel consumers' satisfaction that results when they shift consumption from steel to less-desired substitutes. The total deadweight loss generated by the tariff equals $\$250 + \$375 = \$625$.

For critical analysis: Suppose the domestic government imposed a 6.25 percent ad valorem *tariff as opposed to a specific tariff. Would the graphical analysis differ from that shown in Figure 4.2?*

Effects of a tariff in a large-country setting

The effects of a tariff in a **large-country** setting differ from those arising in a small-country setting in an important regard. A large country's market share is sufficiently large that the production and consumption decisions of domestic consumers and producers affect the global prices of goods and services. A tariff applied in a large-country setting distorts the domestic price and induces changes in the domestic quantities demanded and supplied, thereby altering the global price.

Large country *A large country's market share is sufficiently large that the production and consumption decisions of its residents affect the global prices of goods and services.*

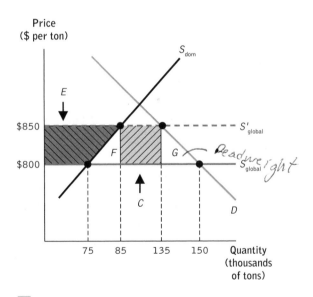

Figure 4.2 The small-country tariff

The imposition of a tariff by the government in a small country causes the market price in the small country to rise by the full amount of the tariff. The entire amount of the tariff is forward shifted onto consumers. The loss of consumer surplus equals the sum of areas E, F, C, and G. Area E is transferred to domestic producers as an increase in producer surplus. Area C is transferred to the small-country government as tariff revenue. Areas F and G are deadweight losses.

The price effect of a tariff in a large-country setting

Consider the following example to understand the price effect of the imposition of a tariff in a large country. Suppose that at a global price of $800, U.S. manufacturers import 50 million tons of steel per month from Japanese steel producers, and suppose the respective market shares of Japan and the United States are sufficiently large to affect the global price of steel. Consider what happens when the U.S. government imposes a specific tariff of $50 per ton. Imposing the tariff causes the U.S. price of steel to rise, which reduces the domestic quantity demanded and increases the domestic quantity supplied, thereby reducing U.S. imports of steel from Japan.

If the global price of steel remains at $800, Japanese steel producers continue to supply 50 million tons of steel in the global market. Thus, an excess quantity supplied results in the global market. As explained in Chapter 1, an excess quantity supplied causes the price to fall until the quantity demanded equals the quantity supplied and a new equilibrium is reached. Hence, the global price of steel declines until the quantity supplied to the global market by Japanese steel producers equals the quantity demanded by U.S. steel consumers.

There are two prices that we must keep track of in this example: the U.S. price of steel (the global price of steel plus the $50 tariff), and the global price of steel. Let's suppose that after the U.S. government applies the tariff, the excess quantity of steel supplied in the global markets causes the global price of steel to decline to $780 per ton. The price of steel in the United States rises from the global price of $800 to $830 ($780 + $50).

Forward and backward shifting of a tariff in a large-country setting

As you can see in this example, applying the tariff causes the price of steel in the United States to rise, but not by the full $50 per ton. We can conclude that in a large-country setting, part, but not all, of a tariff is forward shifted to domestic consumers. The remaining portion of the tariff is backward shifted. But to whom is the tariff backward shifted?

The higher price of steel in the United States causes the surplus of U.S. steel producers to increase, so the tariff is not backward shifted to domestic producers. At the same time, the surplus of Japanese steel producers falls because of the decline in the global price of steel. Consequently, part of the tariff is backward shifted to Japanese steel producers.

Backward shifting a portion of the tariff results in a gain for the country applying the tariff because the domestic government captures foreign producer surplus as tariff revenue. This constitutes a loss for foreign producers. Economists call a tariff applied by a large country a **beggar-thy-neighbor policy**: it benefits agents in one nation at the expense of agents in another nation.

Beggar-thy-neighbor policy: *A policy action that benefits one nation's economy but worsens economic performance in another nation.*

Redistributive effects of a tariff in a large-country setting

Like a tariff in a small-country setting, a tariff in a large-country setting has redistributive effects. The increase in the domestic price generates a loss of consumer surplus.

Part of this loss is transferred to domestic producers as higher revenue and a corresponding increase in producer surplus. Another part of the loss of consumer surplus is transferred to the domestic government as tariff revenue. As in the small-country setting, the loss of consumer surplus exceeds the amount of surplus transferred to other parties. Thus, deadweight losses arise from the same types of inefficiencies created by a tariff in a small-country setting.

As explained earlier, there is also a loss of foreign producer surplus. Part of this loss is transferred to the domestic government in the form of tariff revenue. The entire loss of foreign producer surplus caused by the tariff, however, exceeds the total amount transferred to other parties in either the domestic economy or the foreign economy. Hence, in contrast to the case of a small country, a tariff in the large-country setting results in deadweight losses in the foreign economy as well as in the domestic economy. (To further understand the redistributive effects of a tariff in a large-country setting, see *Visualizing Global Economic Issues: The effects of a tariff in a large-country setting*.)

VISUALIZING GLOBAL ECONOMIC ISSUES

The effects of a tariff in a large-country setting

A tariff applied by the government of a large country can affect the global price. To see the effects of a tariff in a large-country setting, consider a simplified example of related steel markets in only two nations, the United States and Japan.

U.S. and Japan

Panel (a) in Figure 4.3 (p. 103) shows the U.S. market for steel, and panel (b) depicts the Japanese market for steel. The initial global price of steel is $800. Figure 4.3 shows that, at this price, Japanese steel producers export 50,000 tons of steel to the United States.

Now suppose the United States government imposes a specific tariff on steel imports equal to $50 per ton. As shown in Figure 4.3, the tariff causes the U.S. price of steel to rise to $830 per ton. The higher U.S. steel price spurs a decrease in the quantity demanded by U.S. residents to 135,000 tons and an increase in the quantity supplied by U.S. producers to 115,000 tons. Hence, U.S. imports of steel from Japan fall to 20,000 tons.

At the initial global price of $800, the decline in U.S. steel imports from Japan results in an excess quantity supplied of 30,000 tons of steel in the Japanese steel market. This excess quantity supplied causes the global price of steel to decline to $780 per ton. At this price, exports of Japanese steel producers equal the imports of U.S. steel consumers.

Redistributive effects of the tariff

The tariff applied to U.S. steel imports generates tariff revenue for the U.S. government totaling (20,000 × $50) = $1 million. The areas labeled *C* and *E* in panel (a) of Figure 4.3 illustrate the amount of the tariff revenue. Area C, which equals $(20,000 \times \$30) = \$600,000$, depicts the amount forward shifted to U.S. steel consumers. Area E, which equals $(20,000 \times \$20) = \$400,000$, shows the amount of the tariff backward shifted to Japanese steel producers.

The increase in the U.S. price of steel results in a loss of U.S. consumer surplus shown by the areas labeled A, B, C, and D in panel (a). Area A is a loss of consumer surplus that is transferred to U.S. steel producers in the form of higher revenue per ton of steel. This increase in U.S. producer surplus equals $(100,000 \times \$30) + [(15,000 \times \$30)/2] = \$3,225,000$. Areas B and D indicate the deadweight losses, and both areas equal $(15,000 \times \$30)/2 = \$225,000$. Hence, the total loss of U.S. consumer surplus is $\$3,225,000 + \$225,000 + \$600,000 + \$225,000 = \$4,275,000$.

The areas labeled F, G, H, and I in panel (b) illustrate the loss of producer surplus for Japanese steel producers. Area F illustrates the transfer of producer surplus to Japanese steel consumers in the form of a lower price per ton of steel. This increase in Japanese steel consumer surplus equals $(75,000 \times \$20) + [(15,000 \times \$20)/2] = \$1,650,000$. The area labeled H represents the transfer of Japanese steel producer surplus to the U.S. government in the form of tariff revenue. [Note that area E in panel (a) equals area H of panel (b): $\$400,000$.] Areas G and I illustrate the deadweight losses, and both equal $(15,000 \times \$20)/2 = \$150,000$. Thus, the total decline in Japanese producer surplus equals $\$2,350,000$.

Deadweight losses

As you can now see, the U.S. tariff results in deadweight losses for both economies. The reason is that economic inefficiencies are created as U.S. steel producers shift scarce resources into the U.S. steel industry and away from more efficient industries, and as U.S. steel consumers reduce their quantity demanded of steel and switch to less desirable substitutes. At the same time, Japanese producers move scarce resources out of the Japanese steel industry, and Japanese steel consumers increase their quantity demanded and reduce their consumption of more desirable substitutes.

For critical analysis: In Figure 4.3, the tariff transferred surplus away from Japanese steel producers to the U.S. government. On net is the U.S. economy better off because of the tariff?

Can residents of a large country benefit from the imposition of a tariff?

Because a tariff in a large-country setting results in deadweight losses in the domestic economy and a transfer of surplus from foreign producers to the domestic government, the amount of foreign producer surplus transferred to the domestic government could be greater than the amount of deadweight losses in the domestic economy. If so, domestic residents could, on net, *benefit* from the application of a tariff.

Although a tariff in the large-country setting may lead to a net gain for domestic residents, the loss of producer surplus incurred by foreign producers is likely to spur retaliatory actions by the foreign government. The foreign government could apply tariffs or other types of trade barrier to goods imported from the domestic country. In this case, the action of the domestic government and reaction of the foreign government most likely would lead to net losses for both economies.

Fundamental Issue #2: What are the economic effects of tariff barriers? The redistributive effects of a tariff differ in a small-country setting compared with a large-country setting. Because a tariff in a small-country setting does not affect the global price, the entire amount of the tariff is forward shifted to domestic consumers. The imposition of a tariff in a large country causes the global price to decline. Thus, part of the tariff is forward shifted to domestic consumers and part is backward shifted to foreign producers. A tariff always results in deadweight losses for both small and large countries.

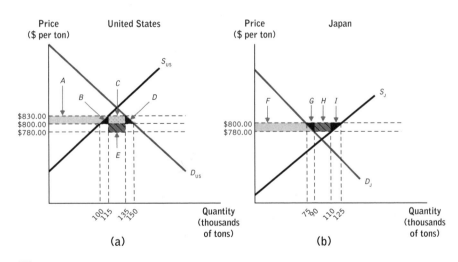

Figure 4.3 *The effects of a tariff in a large-country setting*

The imposition of a tariff by the government of a large country, such as the United States, results in an increase in the market price of steel in the United States and a decrease in the market price of steel in the global market. The loss of U.S. consumers' surplus due to the higher price of steel in the United States equals the sum of areas A, B, C, and D. Area A is transferred to U.S. steel producers; area C is transferred to the U.S. government as tariff revenue; and areas B and D are deadweight losses. The loss of Japanese steel producers' surplus due to the lower global price of steel equals the sum of areas F, G, H, and I. Area F is transferred to Japanese steel consumers; area H, which equals area E, is transferred to the U.S. government as tariff revenue; and areas G and I are deadweight losses.

Non-tariff barriers:
Instruments other than import tariffs that restrict international trade.

Import quota: *A policy that restricts the quantity of imports.*

Absolute quota:
A quantitative restriction that limits the amount of a product that can enter a country during a specified time period.

Tariff-rate quota: *A quota that allows a specified quantity of a good to enter the country at a reduced tariff rate. Any quantity above that amount is subject to a higher tariff rate.*

QUOTAS: A DIRECT APPROACH TO RESTRICTING TRADE

There are a number of policy instruments other than tariffs, called **non-tariff barriers**, which policymakers can use to restrict global trade. Policymakers often use an **import quota**, which restricts the physical quantity of a product that can be imported. An **absolute quota** is a quantitative amount that may enter the country during a specified time period. A **tariff-rate quota** allows entry of a specified quantity at a reduced tariff rate. Quantities above the specified amount are subject to a higher tariff.

Table 4.4 provides information on quotas applied by the U.S. International Trade Administration on beef for selected countries.

Economic effects of a quota

Because an import quota limits the amount of a product that can be imported, it has a *direct* effect on the quantity sold in the domestic market. A tariff, by way of contrast, directly influences the price of an imported good, and thereby *indirectly* affects the quantity sold in the domestic market. Nevertheless, in spite of this difference between tariffs and quotas, their price, quantity, and redistributive effects are comparable. Because of the similarities, we shall restrict our analysis of quotas to an absolute quota in a small-country setting, and then generalize the results to a large-country setting.

A quota's effect on quantity and price

An absolute quota affects the quantity of a product consumed and sold by restricting the amount that may enter the country. To understand the effects of a quota on the price of a product, consider an example. Suppose that at the global price of $30 a blouse, domestic consumers in a small country import 1 million women's cotton blouses over the course of a year and purchase an additional 500,000 from domestic manufacturers. In addition, suppose that domestic policymakers succumb to pressure applied by domestic garment manufacturers and enact a quota that limits the quantity of imported cotton blouses to 500,000 units a year.

ON THE WEB:

For information on U.S. quotas visit the home page of U.S. Customs and Border Protection at www. cbp.gov. For information on U.S. textile programs and tariff-rate quotas on textiles, visit the U.S. International Trade Administration's Office of Textiles and Apparel at www. otexa.ita.doc.gov. For information on U.S. tariff-rate quotas and tariffs on dairy and sugar products, visit the home page of the U.S. Department of Agriculture's Foreign Agricultural Service at www.fas.usda.gov.

Table 4.4 *Selected U.S. import quotas. The table provides 2012 U.S. quotas for beef in selected countries.*

Country	Quota (kg)
Argentina	20,000,000
Australia	378,214,000
Canada	No limit
Japan	200,000
Mexico	No limit
New Zealand	213,402,000
Uruguay	64,805,000
Other countries	64,805,000

At the current domestic price of $30, the quantity of cotton blouses demanded remains at 1.5 million blouses, while the quantity supplied falls to 1 million blouses (500,000 by domestic producers and 500,000 imported under the quota), so the quota creates an excess quantity demanded. This excess quantity demanded causes the domestic price of blouses to rise above the global price. Thus, a quota directly affects the quantity of imports and indirectly affects the domestic price.

Price of Blouses ↑

As the domestic price rises, the quantity demanded by domestic consumers declines, and the quantity supplied by domestic producers rises. At a new equilibrium, the quantity demanded by domestic consumers exactly equals the total quantity of cotton blouses supplied by domestic producers plus the quota-restricted quantity supplied by foreign producers.

Let's suppose that, after the quota is in place, the new equilibrium price is $35, at which the quantity of cotton blouses demanded is 1.2 million blouses and the quantity of cotton blouses supplied by domestic producers is 700,000. Hence, the quantity supplied by foreign producers, 500,000, and the quantity supplied by domestic producers, 700,000, exactly equals the quantity demanded. By restricting imports, the quota increases the domestic price and expands the market share of domestic producers.

Redistributive effects of a quota

This example shows that the price and quantity effects of a quota are similar to the price and quantity effects of a tariff. The redistributive effects differ because the domestic government does not receive tariff revenue, however.

Like a tariff, a quota causes the domestic price to rise and thereby generates a decline in consumer surplus. Part of this loss of consumer surplus is transferred to domestic producers in the form of higher revenues. Another part of this loss of consumer surplus is transferred to the foreign producers who fill the quota and receive a higher price per unit. In addition, the increase in price generates a rise in domestic quantity supplied and a decline in domestic quantity demanded. These changes in price and quantity result in the same type of deadweight losses that tariffs create, as domestic producers shift scarce resources away from production in more efficient industries into the quota-protected industry, and consumers substitute away from the quota-protected good to less desirable substitutes. (The competitive protections that a quota accords a French industry are in danger of being undone by an influx of an imperfect substitute for the industry's product; see *Online Globalization: French booksellers confront an e-book threat to a quota's protection from foreign book imports*.)

ONLINE GLOBALIZATION

French booksellers confront an e-book threat to a quota's protection from foreign book imports

Since the 1980s, French legislation limiting imported "printed volumes" has protected the nation's independent bookstores from competition from large foreign booksellers. This law has effectively placed a quota on imports of physical books. The quota has reduced the market supply of books, which has generated higher book prices for domestic bookstores. This fact helps to explain how 3,000 independent bookstores have been able to operate profitably in France, with a population of 65 million. By way of comparison, in the United States, where no printed-volumes quota exists, there are 2,000 independent bookstores serving a population exceeding 300 million.

Now owners of independent bookstores face a new competitive threat: low-priced e-books not covered by the printed-volumes quota on imports of physical books. In an effort to head off the threat of imported e-books with prices averaging at least 25 percent less than prices of physical books, independent booksellers are pressing for passage of a new law covering imported e-books. The proposed law would prohibit the sale of e-books in France at prices below those established by book publishers, which in turn have a profit motive to keep e-book prices very close to the prices of physical books. In effect, the law would assure that overall book prices would remain at nearly the current level generated by the quota on imports of physical books.

For critical analysis: If the independent booksellers' lobbying efforts succeed in producing the law that they desire, why might these firms still experience reduced sales if some French readers develop a preference for reading e-books on digital devices instead of reading physical books?

Quota rent

In our example of a quota on women's blouses, domestic consumers pay $5 more for each imported blouse after the quota is in place. With the imposition of a tariff, this higher price per unit on imported blouses would be transferred to the domestic government as tariff revenue. With a quota, however, this amount is transferred to another party, such as foreign producers, as an increase in surplus.

Calculating the quota rent

Quota rent: *A portion of the loss of consumer surplus caused by an import quota that is transferred to the foreign supplier as additional profits.*

Economists call this transfer of consumer surplus a **quota rent**. A quota rent is calculated by multiplying the number of units of the product imported under the quota by the higher price per unit generated by the quota. In our example, the quota rent is $(500,000 \times \$5) = \$2.5$ million. If the government imposed a tariff that generated a $5 increase in price, the tariff revenue would exactly equal the quota rent.

Allocating the quota rent

Because governments can determine which foreign firms may fill the quota, they also have the ability to determine who receives, or has the rights to, the quota rent.

Government has the ability to decide who receives the quota rent

The way in which an agency allocates the right to supply imports up to the quota limit determines the allocation of the quota rent. One way a government could allow the quota to be filled is on a first-come basis. In this case, the quota revenue is allocated to those firms that get their goods and services to the nation's customs agency first.

A second way the government can allocate the quota rent is to allow the quota to be filled by the firms of nations receiving preferential treatment. A developed nation, for example, might let the firms in a developing nation fill the quota and receive the quota rent.

A third way to allocate the quota rent is for the domestic government to charge for licenses that authorize foreign firms to fill the quota. By charging for a license, the government receives some or all of the quota rent as revenue, in a manner similar to a tariff. If the government charges a per-unit license fee that is exactly equal to the per-unit quota rent, then all of the quota rent is transferred to the domestic government as revenue. In this case, the redistributive effects of the quota are identical to a tariff. (To further analyze the effects of a quota, see *Visualizing Global Economic Issues: The effects of an import quota*.)

VISUALIZING GLOBAL ECONOMIC ISSUES

The effects of an import quota

To understand in greater detail the effects of an import quota, consider the market for women's cotton blouses illustrated in Figure 4.4 (p. 109). At a global price of $30, the quantity of cotton blouses demanded by domestic consumers equals 1.5 million, and the quantity of cotton blouses supplied by domestic producers is 500,000. Imports, therefore, equal 1 million units.

Suppose the domestic government establishes an import quota that restricts the quantity of cotton blouses imported each year to 500,000 units. At the global price of $30, the quantity demanded is 1.5 million blouses and the total quantity supplied by domestic and foreign producers is 1 millions, so the quota creates an excess quantity demanded.

The effects on price and quantity

To evaluate the resulting price increase, we add the amount of the quota, 500,000 units, to the quantity supplied by domestic producers at each of the various prices above the global price of $30. This results in a new supply curve, labeled $S_{dom+quota}$, which lies 500,000 units to the right of the supply curve of domestic producers at each of the various prices.

As you can see, the figure indicates that the import quota results in a new domestic equilibrium at a price of $35 per blouse. Moreover, you will note that the equilibrium price is no longer equal to the global market price because of the quota restricting the quantity of imports. The increase in the domestic price generates a decrease in quantity demanded to 1.2 million units, and an increase in domestic quantity supplied to 700,000 units. Hence, the total quantity of cotton blouses supplied by domestic and foreign producers again equals the quantity demanded.

The redistributive effects of the quota

Because the domestic price of blouses increases, there is a decline in domestic consumer surplus. The sum of the areas labeled A, B, C, and D depicts the total loss of consumer surplus. Area A represents a transfer of $(500,000 \times \$5) + [(200,000 \times \$5)/2] = \$3$ million from domestic consumers to domestic producers. Area B, which equals $(200,000 \times \$5)/2 = \$500,000$, is a deadweight loss arising when domestic producers shift scarce resources out of more productive industries to increase production within the less-efficient quota-protected industry. Area D, which equals $(300,000 \times \$5)/2 = \$750,000$, is a deadweight loss that results when domestic consumers switch away from the quota-protected good to less desirable substitutes.

Area C, which equals $(500,000 \times \$5) = \$2.5$ million, is a quota rent that is transferred from domestic consumers to another party designated by the domestic government. The domestic government can allocate the quota rent to foreign firms or sell licenses to supply the import good and capture some or all of the quota rent as government quota revenue.

For critical analysis: In which industries do you suppose policymakers are more likely to impose import quotas, goods, or services? Why?

Effects of a quota in a large country

As you can now see, other than the allocation of the quota rent, tariffs and quotas have similar effects on the market. Earlier, you learned that a tariff in a large-country setting can influence the global price of a good or service. A quota applied by the government of a large country can also affect the global price of a product.

At the global price, a quota levied by a large country, like a tariff, creates an excess quantity supplied of a product in the global market. This excess quantity supplied causes the global price of the good or service to decline. As a result, producer surplus of foreign firms falls. Some of the loss of foreign producer surplus is transferred to foreign consumers due to a decline in the price per unit that they must pay.

A quota rent is another portion of the loss of foreign producer surplus. Foreign producers may be able to recapture this, depending on how the government of the large country allocates the rights to sell under the quota. The remainder of the loss of foreign producer surplus represents the deadweight losses created by a large-country government's imposition of the quota.

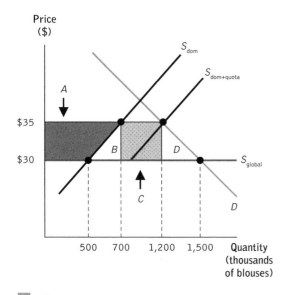

Figure 4.4 *The effects of an import quota*

The imposition of an import quota results in an excess quantity demanded, thereby generating an increase in the market price. Because of the increase in the market price, consumer surplus falls by an amount equal to the sum of the areas A, B, C, and D. Area A is transferred to domestic producers as an increase in producer surplus. Area C is a quota rent, whose distribution is determined by the government imposing the import quota. Areas B and D are deadweight losses.

Fundamental Issue #3: What are quotas, and how do they represent a direct approach to restricting trade? An import quota is a restriction on the amount of a particular good or service that domestic residents can import during a specific time period. A quota directly affects the quantity of imports, whereas a tariff indirectly influences quantity by altering the product price. A domestic government may allocate the quota rent to foreign firms, or charge for licenses that authorize foreign firms to fill the quota. Hence, the welfare effects of a quota and a tariff may differ, depending on how the quota rent is distributed.

VOLUNTARY EXPORT RESTRAINTS

Voluntary export restraints are another type of non-tariff barrier. They have become more popular among policymakers during the past few decades. A **voluntary export restraint (VER)** is an informal agreement between policymakers in one nation and policymakers and producers in another nation to restrict exports within a particular sector of the economy.

Voluntary export restraint (VER): *An agreement between policymakers and producers in two nations to restrict the exports at a good from one nation to the other.*

The appeal of VERs

Because a VER restricts the quantity of imports, it is, in effect, an absolute quota. Why, then, would policymakers in either nation choose to enact a VER as opposed to a formal import quota? One reason is that formal trade legislation can take a long time finally to pass through the necessary government channels. As a result, by the time trade legislation is enacted, it is often much broader than originally intended. In addition, once governments enact formal trade barriers, such barriers are often difficult to repeal. Hence, exporters may find it preferable to restrict their activities on their own, instead of submitting themselves to the whims of foreign policymakers. Perhaps the most important motivating factor behind the increased use of VERs is that these agreements are voluntary. Consequently, VERs do not come under the jurisdiction of regulatory bodies that monitor the types of regional and multilateral trade agreement you will learn about in Chapter 5.

U.S. automobiles and Japanese VERs

Because of its large consumer market, the United States is the destination of many nations' exports. U.S. policymakers often leverage the size of its lucrative consumer market to pressure foreign governments and exporters to agree to implement VERs.

VER as a bilateral agreement

In the early 1980s, U.S. automobile producers faced both stiff competition from imported Japanese-made economy cars and a downturn in the demand for larger and less fuel-efficient U.S.-produced autos. U.S. automobile producers and labor representatives of U.S. automobile workers responded by lobbying the U.S. government for protection.

U.S. and Japanese policymakers, and Japanese automobile manufacturers, reacted by negotiating a VER on Japanese autos. The agreement called for a physical limit to the number of automobiles that Japanese manufacturers would export to the United States. The VER did not limit, however, automobiles manufactured in *other* nations for export to the United States or by Japanese producers operating within the United States.

VERs and prices

A VER, like an import quota, causes the domestic price to rise. Hence, a VER is a bilateral agreement that only indirectly affects imports from producers in another nation through its effect on price. An unintended consequence of the Japanese VER with the United States is that it helped European automobile manufacturers that exported automobiles to the United States.

In the case of the Japanese automobile manufacturers, the price effect of the VER had a significant effect on the *type* of car exported. Because there was an agreement on quantity, but not on price, Japanese automobile manufacturers switched from exporting economy cars to more luxurious automobiles, which proved to be lucrative. In the late 1980s, the U.S. government ended its request for export restraints. Because Japanese automobile manufacturers were experiencing higher revenues producing luxury cars for export to the United States, they were slow to increase their exports of ordinary automobiles.

Effects of VERs

A VER establishes an informal quota on exports, so its economic effects are similar to the effects of a quota. Because the domestic price rises, there is a loss of domestic consumer surplus. Part of this surplus is transferred to domestic producers in the form of higher revenue per unit. Deadweight losses are another portion of the loss of consumer surplus. A rent, similar to a quota rent, is also part of the loss of domestic consumer surplus. Unlike a quota, however, the rent accrues to the foreign producers that agree to the VER.

Because VERs are a bilateral agreement, third-country effects are an important difference between a VER and a quota. By agreeing to restrict automobile exports to the United States, for example, the Japanese VER offered protection to automobile manufacturers in other nations that exported their autos to the United States. Hence, part of the loss of domestic consumer surplus was transferred to third-country automobile manufacturers in the form of higher revenues on automobiles exported to the U.S. market.

Fundamental Issue #4: What are voluntary export restraints? Voluntary export restraints (VERs) are informal agreements between policymakers in an importing country and policymakers and producers in another country to restrict the quantity of a product exported for a specified time period. VERs are similar to quotas in the way they affect price and quantity, and their redistributive effects. One important difference, however, is that the quota rent is always transferred to foreign producers. Because they are voluntary agreements, VERs typically do not come under the jurisdiction of regional and multilateral trade regulators.

EXPORT SUBSIDIES AND COUNTERVAILING DUTIES

Domestic industry and worker advocacy groups often argue to policymakers that they face "unfair" competition from abroad. Frequently, they claim that foreign governments subsidize firms, enabling foreign firms to sell their products abroad at lower prices than they do in their own markets, or below the cost of production.

An **export subsidy** is a payment by a domestic government to a domestic firm for exporting goods or services. A government can provide an export subsidy either as a specific amount per unit exported, or as a percent of the value of the exported goods or services. Governments specifically design export subsidies to promote exports and increase revenues of domestic firms.

Export subsidy: *A payment by a government to a domestic firm for exporting its goods or services.*

111

Effects of an export subsidy

As with a tariff, a quota, and a VER, an export subsidy influences the market price and the quantity consumed. Because of this influence on price and quantity, an export subsidy also has redistributive effects.

Price and quantity effects of a subsidy

For ease of analysis, let's consider a two-country setting in which the foreign government provides an export subsidy to firms in the foreign country. Foreign firms receive a payment for every unit exported, which induces them to increase the amount they export, thereby increasing the supply of the product in the global market. Because global supply increases, the global market price declines. The price that residents in the domestic nation must pay for imports of the product declines as well. As the domestic price falls, the quantity demanded by domestic consumers rises and the quantity supplied by domestic firms falls. Hence, the imposition of the subsidy by the foreign government generates an increase in the amount imported by domestic residents.

Redistributive effects of a subsidy

The redistributive effects of an export subsidy also mirror those of a tariff. Suppose that, in our two-country setting, the foreign government subsidizes steel exports. Because the foreign subsidy causes the domestic price of steel to fall, domestic consumer surplus increases. Domestic manufacturers, for example, can now purchase steel at a lower price, reducing their overall costs of production. The decline in the domestic price of steel, however, reduces domestic steel producers' surplus. (Sometimes governments offer subsidies to foreign customers of their nations' exporting firms; see *Management Notebook: U.S. taxpayers subsidize foreign buyers of U.S. exports—and foreign rivals of U.S. firms.*)

MANAGEMENT NOTEBOOK

U.S. taxpayers subsidize foreign buyers of U.S. exports—and foreign rivals of U.S. firms

Each year, the U.S. Export-Import Bank provides about $100 billion of subsidized loans to foreign buyers of the products of U.S. firms, including U.S. manufacturers of items such as aircraft, construction equipment, and haircare products. The rationale for the Export-Import Bank's lending to foreign customers of U.S. companies is that the availability of subsidized—and hence low-cost—credit to these customers provides them with incentives to purchase larger quantities of U.S. export goods.

Among the U.S. exporters particularly enthused about the Export-Import Bank's activities is Boeing, the aircraft manufacturer. Boeing contends that the loan subsidies are required to enable the firm to compete with foreign competitors such as Airbus, the European aircraft manufacturer that is the recipient of analogous assistance from European governments. According to Boeing, the Export-Import Bank is "vital to helping level the playing field" for the company in the global aircraft market.

In spite of the enthusiasm expressed by Boeing and echoed by other U.S. aircraft exporters, the U.S. commercial airline company Delta is displeased with the Export-Import Bank's activities. Delta is especially unhappy about loans that the bank has provided to Air India, which enabled that Indian firm to purchase commercial jets from Boeing at below-market interest rates. According to Delta, the result is that Air India was provided a cost advantage—courtesy of U.S. taxpayers—over Delta on the route between New York City and Mumbai. As a consequence, Delta alleges, Air India was able to offer ticket prices so low that Delta could not continue to fly its planes profitably on that route. Other U.S. airlines likewise contend that the Export-Import Bank is subsidizing their foreign competitors, and they have sued the bank in an effort to halt its low-cost lending to airlines in other nations.

For critical analysis: Why do you suppose U.S. firms that build facilities are unhappy about subsidized loans that the Export-Import Bank provides to foreign competitors to assist them in purchasing U.S. firms' exports construction equipment?

Dumping

By promoting exports, the subsidy induces foreign firms to place more attention on exporting their output as opposed to selling it in their home market. Dumping can be defined two ways. The definition used most often by economists is that **dumping** occurs when a firm charges foreign consumers a price that is lower than the price it charges its domestic consumers. The second is that dumping occurs when a firm prices its exports below their cost of production.

Dumping: *A situation in which a firm sells its output to foreign consumers at a price less than what the firm charges its domestic consumers, or when a foreign firm prices its exports below their cost of product.*

Is dumping harmful to domestic firms?

As you will learn in more detail in Chapter 11, domestic firms typically claim that dumping by foreign firms costs domestic firms revenues they would otherwise earn if global trade were "fair." The lost revenues, they claim, are a combination of the decline in the revenue per unit on quantities that domestic firms continue to sell to domestic consumers, and the previous domestic price multiplied by the reduction in the quantity they sell. Note, however, that firms that use the *dumped* good as an input in their production process receive a benefit. Foreign governments, in effect, subsidize production for these domestic firms.

113

Countervailing duties

Sometimes domestic workers and firms in an industry are successful in arguing that, through the use of production subsidies, foreign governments support foreign firms and harm the domestic industry. If the domestic government is able to determine that the foreign industry is subsidized by its government, and that it inflicted harm on domestic producers, then by the rules of most regional and multilateral trade arrangements (described in more detail in Chapters 5 and 11), the domestic government is allowed to impose a countervailing duty.

Countervailing duty (CVD): *A tax on imported goods and services designed to offset the domestic price effect of foreign export policies.*

A **countervailing duty (CVD)** is a tax on imported goods—a tariff—designed to offset the domestic price effect of foreign export subsidies. By taxing imports and raising the domestic price, domestic producers' revenue per unit rises and domestic producer surplus increases. If the CVD is equal to the subsidy, the gain in surplus that domestic consumers previously experienced from the foreign subsidy is lost.

Each year, the U.S. government and U.S. firms initiate dozens of investigations of foreign subsidies to industries, which most typically involve the steel industry. Other industries in which claims of foreign subsidies and subsequent dumping are being investigated include chemicals and plastics, mechanical appliances, textiles, food and agricultural products, and paper and wood.

As you can imagine, foreign subsidies, dumping investigations, and retaliatory duties result in considerable losses of economic efficiency. As you will learn in the next section, the costs of protection can be very high.

> *Fundamental Issue #5: What are the effects of export subsidies, and how do policymakers typically react to export promotion policies?* An export subsidy is a payment to firms for selling abroad. Providing an export subsidy increases global supply, and drives down the global price and the price in the domestic market. The lower price per unit reduces domestic producer surplus and increases domestic consumer surplus. Governments often react to the claims of dumping and unfair trade by firms and labor groups by imposing a countervailing duty (CVD). A CVD is designed to offset the effect the subsidy has on the domestic price.

TRADE BARRIERS AND THEIR COSTS

In this chapter you have learned that tariff and non-tariff trade barriers have redistributive effects and, in most cases, cause a net loss of welfare. Why, then, do policymakers continue to use these instruments?

One common explanation is that those who benefit from trade barriers—firms and workers in protected industries—share a common objective, are relatively few in number (thereby benefiting considerably from protection), and therefore are easy to organize. Those who pay the costs of protection—domestic consumers, in particular—do not share a common view on trade, are relatively large in number (thereby the individual costs of protection are rather small), and are therefore not easily organized. Hence, those who benefit from protection are able to lobby policy-makers much more effectively than those who pay the costs.

Many other arguments for trade barriers are covered in later chapters. What we are concerned with here is whether trade barriers are the "best" policy approach.

First- and second-best policies

To gauge the appropriateness of a particular policy, economists often consider whether the policy is a first- or second-best response. A **first-best trade policy** is a policy that deals directly with the problem that the policy is designed to remedy. A **second-best trade policy** is a policy that attempts to remedy a problem through indirect means.

Suppose, for example, that firms and workers in a particular industry seek protection from foreign competition because foreign producers are more efficient and able to produce at a lower cost. A first-best policy deals directly with the inefficiency of the domestic industry. A trade barrier is a second-best policy because it deals indirectly with the problem of less-efficient domestic firms by raising the domestic price of the good or service to compensate for the inefficiency.

First-best trade policy: *A trade policy that deals directly with a problem that policymakers seek to remedy.*

Second-best trade policy: *A trade policy that deals indirectly with a problem that policymakers seek to remedy.*

The costs of protection

Because trade barriers are second-best policy responses, they create additional economic inefficiencies. These deadweight losses make trade protection a very costly policy action.

During the past few years, the Peterson Institute for International Economics in Washington, DC has commissioned several studies in an attempt to measure the costs of protection in various nations. The authors of these studies examined protected sectors and determined the benefits to consumers, costs to domestic producers, and gains in economic efficiencies that would result from removing existing trade barriers. The authors also considered the cost of protecting a job in the domestic industry.

Table 4.5 illustrates these costs for four nations: China, Japan, Korea, and the United States. (Note that some of the figures are in U.S. dollars and others are not; some data for European industries are provided in Chapter 5.) Column 1 identifies the nations and the particular industry. Column 2 provides the increase in consumer surplus that would result from removing the barriers, column 3 provides the decrease in producer surplus, and column 4 the deadweight loss that would be transferred back to domestic consumers. Columns 5 and 6 show the costs of protecting the average job in the industry in terms of consumer costs and losses of economic efficiency.

As you can see in the table, the costs of protecting these domestic industries are very high. More importantly, the loss of economic efficiency makes the cost of preserving a single domestic job very expensive—more expensive than the income that each worker would typically receive. In the United States, for example, the annual cost to consumers of preserving a job in the women's handbag industry is nearly $200,000, which is considerably more than what the average worker receives in the industry.

Table 4.5 The costs of protection

Product	Change in consumer surplus	Change in producer surplus	Deadweight loss	Cost of preserving job	
				To consumers	In loss of efficiency
China	($ millions)			($)	
Sugar	1,497	543	285	5,059	964
Plywood	685	104	58	23,338	1,968
Motorcycles	1,746	635	137	56,721	4,460
Color televisions	227	139	4	15,859	305
Europe	(€ millions)			(€ thousands)	
Fertilizers	641.6	86.0	78.5	182.6	22.3
Hardboard	739.1	112.8	99.6	611.1	194.9
Photocopiers	313.5	4.8	66.4	3,483.3	737.8
Sugar	4,268.3	979.5	2,306.1	146.5	79.2
Japan	(¥ billions)			(¥ millions)	
Clothing	878.9	221.6	234.9	63.7	17.0
Pharmaceuticals	182.9	151.0	0.9	153.5	0.8
Cosmetics	500.6	102.1	351.0	213.3	149.5
Semiconductor devices	1,046.6	538.3	332.4	44.9	13.9
Korea	(won billions)			(won billions)	
Beef	771	453	82	30	5
Milled rice	3,469	3,102	367	15	3
Dairy products	1,289	1,066	94	241	49
Cosmetics	29	24	1	139	24
United States	($ millions)			($ thousands)	
Women's handbags	148	16	13	191.5	16.8
Canned tuna	73	31	4	187.2	25.6
Sugar	1,357	776	185	600.2	257.0
Peanuts	54	32	22	136.0	55.4

Sources: Data from Messerlin (2001); Shuguang et al. (1998); Sazanami et al. (1995); Kim (1996); Hufbauer and Elliott (1994).

In the case of the United States, the study found that the average annual cost to consumers of preserving a job across all industries was $170,000. It would actually be cheaper to buy the imported goods and pay idle workers their salaries than to protect the domestic industry.

Fundamental Issue #6: What are the advantages and disadvantages of trade barriers? There are many explanations for why policymakers resort to trade barriers. One commonly held view is that domestic firms and workers who benefit from trade protection are better organized than the consumers who pay the costs of protection. Because they are well organized, firms and workers can lobby policymakers more effectively. A first-best policy is a policy that deals directly with the problem the policy is designed to remedy. Trade barriers are second-best policies because they deal only indirectly with the problems that policymakers seek to remedy. As second-best policies, trade barriers are costly to domestic consumers and entail considerable losses of economic efficiency.

CHAPTER SUMMARY

1. **The effect of taxes on domestic price, and the redistributive effects of taxes**: The imposition of a tax causes the supply of a good or service to decrease. This decline in supply generates an increase in the market price. Although the market price rises, it typically does not rise by the full amount of the tax. Because the tax influences market outcomes, it has redistributive effects. A tax is forward shifted if consumers must pay the tax in the form of a higher price per unit. A tax is backward shifted if producers must pay the tax in the form of a lower price per unit.

2. **Economic effects of tariff barriers**: A specific tariff is calculated as a fixed tariff amount per unit, whereas an *ad valorem* tariff is calculated as a percent of the value of the good or service. A combination tariff consists of a specific tariff component and an *ad valorem* component. A tariff imposed by policymakers in a small country does not affect the global price. As a result, the domestic price rises by the full amount of the tariff, and the entire tariff is forward shifted to domestic consumers. A tariff imposed by policymakers in a large country may cause the global price to decline. In this setting, part of the tariff is forward shifted to domestic consumers, and part is backward shifted to foreign producers. It is in this sense that a large-country tariff is a beggar-thy-neighbor policy. For both small and large countries, a tariff results in net welfare losses, either at home or abroad.

3. **Quotas as a direct approach to restricting trade**: An import quota is a policy limiting the amount of a good or service that can enter a country during a specified time period. A quota directly affects the quantity of imports, whereas a tariff indirectly affects the quantity of imports by first affecting the price. An absolute quota establishes a quantitative limit. A tariff-rate quota allows a specific quantity to enter the country at a reduced tariff rate. If the government collects the quota rent in the form of an import license, then a quota and an equivalent tariff have identical redistributive effects.

4. **Voluntary export restraints**: A VER is an informal agreement between policymakers and producers in two nations to restrict the quantity of a product exported from one nation to the other. Because they are voluntary agreements, VERs typically do not come under the scrutiny of regional and multilateral trade agreements. The price, quantity, and distributive effects of VERs are similar to those of a quota. One important difference between a quota and a VER is that the quota rent is always transferred to foreign producers.

5. **Effects of an export subsidy, and the reaction of policymakers to export promotion policies:** An export subsidy is a payment to a firm for exporting their output as opposed to selling it in the domestic market. Governments design export subsidies to increase the revenue of domestic firms. From the perspective of firms and consumers in the importing country, export subsidies have effects similar to the removal of a tariff, because they increase supply in the global market and drive down the domestic price. The decrease in domestic price results in an increase in domestic consumer surplus and a decrease in domestic producer surplus. Often policymakers will answer the claims of dumping and unfair trade by domestic industry and labor groups by imposing a countervailing duty (CVD). A CVD is intended to offset the effect that an export subsidy has on domestic price.

6. **Advantages and disadvantages of trade barriers:** One explanation for why policymakers continue to use trade barriers in spite of their high costs is that the groups that benefit from trade protection are highly organized, while those that pay the costs of protection are not. Because they are highly organized, firms and labor groups can effectively lobby for protection. A first-best policy deals directly with the problem the policy is designed to remedy. Trade barriers are second-best policies that deal indirectly with the problem that policymakers seek to remedy. Hence, trade barriers entail greater economic inefficiencies and are costly. Recent studies of the costs of protection show that, on average, the cost of preserving a job in a protected industry typically is much greater than the income received by the worker whose job is saved.

QUESTIONS AND PROBLEMS

1. Suppose that policymakers *eliminate* tariffs on imported pharmaceuticals. For a specific drug, the tariff originally was $0.60 per unit, and the domestic price with the tariff in place was $2.90. Now, under free trade, the domestic price is $2.50. With the tariff, the domestic quantity demanded was 14 million units, and domestic quantity supplied was 6 million. Now, under free trade, the domestic quantity demanded is 20 million, and the domestic quantity supplied is 4 million.
   (a) Is the country in question a large country or a small country? Explain your answer.
   (b) Illustrate this example in a supply-and-demand framework for the home country *and* the international market.

2. Using the diagram you constructed for question 1, answer the following questions.
   (a) What is the value of the gain to the domestic consumers due to the removal of the tariff?
   (b) What is the value of the loss to the domestic producers due to the removal of the tariff?
   (c) What is the value of the loss of tariff revenue due to the removal of the tariff?

3. In questions 1 and 2, does the home country experience a net welfare gain or loss from the removal of the tariff?

4. Is the statement "A tariff on imports *always* leads to a reduction of domestic welfare" true, false, or uncertain? Explain your answer.

5. Consider the following situation for a nation in a small-country setting that has an import quota on men's shirts.

	With quota	Free trade
Price	$45	$30
Quantity purchased	1 million	1.2 million
Domestic quantity supplied	400,000	300,000
Quota	600,000	None

(a) Illustrate the effects of the quota in a supply-and-demand framework.
(b) Indicate in your diagram, and calculate:
   (i)   the loss of consumer surplus
   (ii) the gain in domestic producer surplus
   (iii) the deadweight losses
   (iv) the quota rent.

6. Suppose that policymakers in the nation depicted in question 5 would like to switch from a quota to a tariff. What is the equivalent tariff rate for a specific tariff? For an *ad valorem* tariff? What benefits would there be to switching from a quota to a tariff?

7. Suppose that, to protect domestic producers from "unfair" competition, policymakers impose a countervailing duty on imported automobiles. Should domestic automakers receive the duty? Why, or why not?

8. Suppose that, under free trade, the global price of automobiles is $20,000. At this price, the quantity supplied in a small country, country 1, is 750,000. Producers in country 2 supply 500,000 autos to consumers in country 1, and producers in country 3 supply 2.25 million autos to consumers in country 1. Now suppose that policymakers in country 1 and country 3 agree to a VER that restricts the quantity of automobiles exported from country 3 to country 1 to 1 million. Because of the VER, the price in country 1 rises to $25,000, the quantity supplied by producers in country 1 rises to 1.25 million, and the quantity supplied by producers in country 2 rises to 550,000.
(a) Diagram the situation described above in a supply-and-demand framework for country 1.
(b) Who benefits from the VER? Who is harmed?

9. Each year, consumers in a small country purchase 1 million pounds of sugar at the global price of $1.50 per pound. Domestic firms produce 500,000 pounds and domestic consumers import the remainder. Policymakers of the world's major supplier of sugar begin an export-subsidy program that rewards firms for exporting sugar. This program causes the global price of sugar to drop to $1 per pound. The domestic quantity demanded in the small country climbs to 1.3 million pounds, and the domestic quantity supplied falls to 300,000 pounds.
(a) Draw a diagram of the small-country market for sugar under free trade, and with the export subsidy in place.
(b) Calculate the loss of domestic producer surplus, and the increase in domestic consumer surplus.

(c) What is the total value of the subsidy in the small-country market?

(d) Can you identify any deadweight losses?

10. Based on the information in question 9, what is the *ad valorem* countervailing duty rate that would restore the domestic price in the small country to its free trade level? Who do you think is entitled to the revenue generated by the countervailing duty?

ONLINE APPLICATION

URL: www.cbp.gov

Title: U.S. Customs and Border Protection

Navigation: Start at the home page for the U.S. Customs and Border Protection (www. cbp.gov). Note the search box with the word "SEARCH."

Application: Explore different types of quota used by the United States. Perform the following operations, and answer the following questions.

1. At the top of the page, click on "Trade." At the left of the page click on "Trade Programs." Scroll down and click on "Textiles and Quotas." Scroll down again and click on "Quota Frequently Asked Questions." Scroll down and click on "II Types of Quotas." Read the information provided.

2. Write a short definition of an *absolute quota*.

3. Explain how *tariff-rate quotas* and *tariff preference levels* differ from an absolute quota.

For group study and analysis: Using Figure 4.2 on page 99, suppose that the first 20,000 tons of imported steel can enter the small country tariff-free. After that, all imported steel is subject to the $50 specific tariff. How do the redistributive effects differ in this case of a tariff-rate quota?

REFERENCES AND RECOMMENDED READINGS

Baier, Scott L., and Jeffrey H. Bergstrand. "The Growth of World Trade: Tariffs, Transport Costs, and Income Similarity." *Journal of International Economics* 53(1) (February 2001): 1–27.

Batra, Ravi. "Are Tariffs Inflationary?" *Review of International Economics* 9(3) (August 2001): 378–382.

Blonigen, Bruce, Benjamin Liebman, Justin Pierce, and Wesley Wilson. "Are All Trade Protection Policies Created Equal? Empirical Evidence for Nonequivalent Market Power Effects of Tariffs and Quotas." *Journal of International Economics* 89(2) (March 2013): 369–378.

Bussière, Matthieu, Emilia Pérez, Roland Straub, and Daria Tagolini. "Protectionist Responses to the Crisis: Global Trends and Implications." European Central Bank, Occasional Paper Series, Number 110, May 2010.

Cipollina, Maria, and Luca Salatici. "Measuring Protection: Mission Impossible." *Journal of Economic Surveys* 22(3) (July 2008): 577–616.

Collie, David R. "A Rationale for the WTO Prohibition of Export Subsidies: Strategic Export Subsidies and World Welfare." *Open Economics Review* 11(3) (July 2000): 229–249.

Daly, Michael, and Sergios Stamnas. "Tariff and Non-tariff Barriers to Trade in Korea." *Journal of Economic Integration* 16(4) (December 2001): 500–525.

Ethier, Wilfred J. "Unilateralism in a Multilateral World." *Economic Journal* 112(479) (April 2002): 266–292.

Harrigan, James, and Geoffrey Barrows. "Testing the Theory of Trade Policy: Evidence from the Abrupt End of the Multifiber Arrangement." *Review of Economics and Statistics* 91(2) (May 2009): 282–294.

Hickson, Charles. "The WTO, the IMF, and the Impact of Their Free-Trade Policies on Developing Nations." *Global Business and Economics Review* 3(2) (December 2001): 175–185.

Hufbauer, Gary Clyde, and Kimberly Ann Elliott. *Measuring the Costs of Protection in the United States*. Washington, DC: Institute for International Economics, 1994.

Kerr, William, and James Gaisford, eds. *Handbook on International Trade Policy*. Cheltenham, U.K.: Edward Elgar, 2007.

Kim, Namdoo. *Measuring the Costs of Visible Protection in Korea*. Washington, DC: Institute for International Economics, 1996.

Lahiri, Sajal et al. "Optimal Foreign Aid and Tariffs." *Journal of Development Economics* 67(1) (February 2002): 79–99.

Magee, Christopher. "Why Are Trade Barriers So Low?" *Economic Affairs* 31(3) (October 2011): 12–17.

Messerlin, Patrick. *Measuring the Costs of Protection in Europe*. Washington, DC: Institute for International Economics, 2001.

Pandit, Ram. "US Trade Barriers and Import Price of Canadian Softwood Lumber." *International Trade Journal* 23(4) (October–December 2009): 399–421.

Sazanami, Yoko, Shujiro Urato, and Kawai Hiroki. *Measuring the Costs of Protection in Japan*. Washington, DC: Institute for International Economics, 1995.

Shuguang, Zhang, Zhang Yansheng, and Wan Zhongxin. *Measuring the Costs of Protection in China*. Washington, DC: Institute for International Economics, 1998.

Watts, Julie R. *Immigration Policy and the Challenge of Globalization: Unions and Employers in Unlikely Alliance*. Ithaca and London: Cornell University, ILR Press, 2002.

Chapter 5

Regionalism and multilateralism

FUNDAMENTAL ISSUES

1. What are the main types of regional trade agreement, and how do economists measure trade within regional trading groups?
2. How is a free trade area such as the North American Free Trade Agreement different from other types of preferential trade arrangements?
3. What distinguishes customs unions such as the European Economic Community of the 1970s and the current Andean Community from common markets such as today's European Union and Mercosur?
4. How can regional trading arrangements lead to both trade creation and trade diversion?
5. What is trade deflection, and how do rules of origin help to limit the extent to which trade deflection occurs?
6. How do multilateral trade agreements contrast with regional trading arrangements?

The first modern regional trade agreement—a system of rules through which a group of nations called a "regional trade bloc" grants trade preferences to all nations within the group—came into existence in 1958 with the formation of the European Community. The success of this regional trade agreement, which ultimately developed into today's European Union, motivated other groups of nations to establish their own agreements.

Between 1959 and 1980, the number of regional trade agreements worldwide increased to about 50. There was little change in the number of outstanding agreements through to 1990. Since then, however, there has been an upsurge in the number of regional trade agreements as many nations have opted to participate in multiple regional trade blocs. As a consequence, the total number of regional trade agreements has increased to about 575 of which at least 350 are still functionally active agreements promoting trade among their member nations.

How do nations experience gains from participating in regional trade agreements? To evaluate this question, you must first understand the issues raised by such agreements. As you will learn, in theory the establishment of these trading arrangements can potentially either encourage or discourage international trade.

REGIONAL TRADE BLOCS

During recent years, there has been a proliferation of special trade deals among nations granting trade preferences in the form of reduced or eliminated tariffs, duties, or quotas. There are currently hundreds of regional trade agreements in force or under negotiation around the globe. Figure 5.1 indicates that of the roughly 200 most significant regional trade agreements, just below three-quarters involve merchandise trade, and the remainder relate to trade in services. Less than one-quarter of the agreements are among developed nations only. More than one-third of them involve only developing nations, and the remainder have memberships including both developed and developing countries.

Regional trade agreements

Nearly half of the current regional trade agreements were adopted after 1990, and a number of these establish *regional trade blocs*, or countries that have granted preferential trade status to one or more nations.

There are five basic types of regional trade agreement.

1. The least restrictive sort of regional trade agreement is a **preferential trade arrangement**, under which a nation grants partial trade preferences to a set of trading partners. Often a preferential trade arrangement is one-sided. In some cases, however, nations can form *reciprocal* arrangements. These entail the establishment of equal trade preferences among two or more trading partners.
2. One type of reciprocal trade arrangement is a regional trade agreement that establishes a **free trade area**. Within a free trade area, participating nations agree to remove all trade barriers. Each nation, however, retains its own barriers to trade with countries outside the free trade area.

Preferential trade arrangement: *A trading arrangement in which a nation grants partial trade preferences to one or more trading partners.*

Free trade area: *A trading arrangement that removes all barriers to trade among participating nations, but that allows each nation to retain its own restrictions on trade with countries outside the free trade area.*

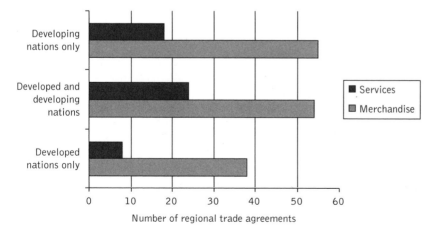

Figure 5.1 *The distribution of regional trade agreements*

A large share of regional trade agreements, which include as members both developed and developing nations, cover trade in physical merchandise, and the rest cover trade in services.

Source: Fiorentino et al. (2009).

Customs union: *A trading arrangement that entails eliminating barriers to trade among participating nations and common barriers to trade with other countries outside the group.*

Common market: *A trading arrangement under which member nations remove all barriers to trade among their group, erect common barriers to trade with other countries outside the group, and permit unhindered movements of factors of production within the group.*

Economic union: *A trading arrangement that commits participating nations to remove all barriers to trade among their group, to abide by common restrictions on trade with other countries outside the group, to allow unhindered movements of factors of production within the group, and to closely coordinate all economic policies with other participants.*

Regionalism: *Establishment of trading agreements among geographic groupings of nations.*

3. When nations participating in a regional trade agreement go beyond removing trade barriers among themselves, and adopt common barriers to trade with other countries, then they have established a **customs union**. To ensure equivalent trade policies, members of a customs union must establish elaborate coordination schemes. In principle, therefore, a customs union entails a more significant commitment than a free trade area.

4. Preferential trade arrangements, free trade areas, and customs unions establish rules breaking down barriers to cross-border trade in goods and services. When countries also agree to remove barriers to free movement of factors of production, they have created a **common market**. Thus, nations that form a common market agree to open cross-border flows of both final outputs of goods and services, and inputs used in production.

5. The next step beyond freeing up cross-border flows of goods, services, and factors of production is to coordinate uniform national economic policies. Countries that take this next step have established an **economic union**. Political union is not technically a prerequisite to economic union, but successful implementation often requires considerable political coordination among participating nations.

Economists are divided about whether this trend toward **regionalism**—the formation of trading agreements among geographic groupings of countries—promotes or discourages trade. Before you can understand why this is an issue, you must first understand how economists measure trade among regional trade blocs. You must also have a broader background on how the various types of regional trading groups function. (Although there are about 550 regional trade agreements, nearly 200 of these are "paper" agreements that nations no longer honor and that thereby serve no true economic function; see *Policy Notebook: Many African nations have finally progressed beyond 'paper' regional trade agreements*.)

POLICY NOTEBOOK

Many African nations have finally progressed beyond "paper" regional trade agreements

The oldest customs union in the world, formally established in 1910, is the Southern African Customs Union (SACU). The SACU currently has 14 members, including nations such as Angola, Botswana, South Africa, and Zimbabwe, which permit free movement of many non-agricultural products and most labor and other resources.

For more than seven decades, however, the SACU was one of the few regional trade-bloc success stories in Africa. Beginning in the early 1960s, most nations of Africa sought to jumpstart economic development efforts through the establishment of regional trade agreements. Nevertheless, a number of these, such as the Organization for African Union (later the African Union), the Economic Community of the Countries of the Great Lakes, the East African Community, and the

Economic Community of Central African States, eventually fell into inactivity and became "paper" agreements that are economically irrelevant.

In recent decades, however, African regional trade agreements have experienced a functional resurgence. Key agreements established since the 1970s that blossomed into fruition during and following the 1990s include the Common Market for Eastern and Southern Africa (COMESA), which includes 19 nations including Burundi, Egypt, Kenya, and Rwanda; and the Economic Community Of West African States (ECOWAS), which includes 15 countries including Benin, Gambia, Nigeria, and Sierra Leone. The still-functioning SACU, COMESA, and ECOWAS, which together contain more than 500 million people, form the core set of regional trade blocs on the African continent that have achieved notable reductions in barriers to international trade among their member nations.

For critical analysis: Why do you think that warfare among some African nations that had previously joined regional trade blocs has transformed some of these blocs' trade agreements into "paper" arrangements that are economically meaningless?

Measuring how much regionalism matters for trade

How much trade takes place among members of regional trading groups? Trying to answer this question first requires considering how to measure the extent of a nation's trade with the rest of the world.

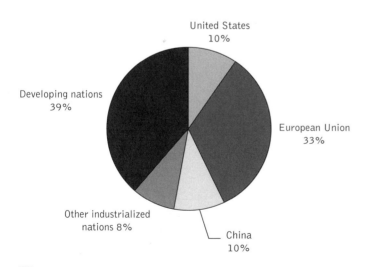

Figure 5.2 *World trade shares*

Industrialized countries account for about two-thirds of total international trade. Together, the United States and the European Union account for more than 40 percent of cross-border trade flows.

Source: International Monetary Fund, *Direction of Trade Statistics,* various issues.

Shares of trade

The most commonly used measure of international trade is the total flow of trade across national borders, which is simply the sum of export and import flows within a given interval. Economists make nations' trade flows comparable by measuring all countries' exports and imports in terms of a common currency, such as the U.S. dollar. Then they often consider **trade shares**, which are a nation's trade flow as percentage of regional or world trade totals.

Trade share: *One nation's flow of international trade as a percentage of a regional or global trade total.*

Figure 5.2 displays trade shares for the European Union, the United States, Japan, other industrialized nations, and developing nations. These shares are U.S. dollar measures of nations' cross-border trade flows as percentages of the total dollar value of world trade. As the figure indicates, trade crossing the borders of industrialized countries accounts for about two-thirds of total world trade. International trade flowing across EU and U.S. borders alone accounts for more than half of global flows of international trade.

One way to try to determine how much nations within regional trading groups engage in trade with countries inside and outside their trading groups is to examine their shares of regional and world trade. Table 5.1 shows trade shares for nations within the North American Free Trade Agreement (NAFTA), Mercosur (the Southern Common Market), the Andean Community, the Association of Southeast Asian Nations (ASEAN), and the European Union. Note that each EU nation conducts at least half of its trade with other countries within the European Union. Furthermore, Canada and Mexico conduct at least three-quarters of their trade with their other NAFTA partner, the United States.

Figure 5.3 (p. 128) displays the aggregate shares of world trade for each of the regional trading groups from Table 5.1. Based on trade-share data, the European

Table 5.1 *Regional and world trade shares of nations in selected regional trading blocs*

Regional trading bloc/country	Share of trade with regional trading bloc (percent)	Share of world trade (percent)
NAFTA		
United States	28.41	9.63
Canada	65.01	2.50
Mexico	67.01	1.94
Mercosur		
Argentina	27.82	0.44
Brazil	9.81	1.33
Paraguay	25.88	0.05
Uruguay	86.75	0.02
Andean Community		
Bolivia	9.17	0.04
Colombia	5.13	0.31

Table 5.1 continued

Regional trading bloc/country	Share of trade with regional trading bloc (percent)	Share of world trade (percent)
Ecuador	11.15	0.12
Peru	7.65	0.20
ASEAN		
Brunei	21.30	0.05
Cambodia	40.54	0.05
Indonesia	22.39	1.16
Laos	57.61	0.01
Malaysia	22.64	1.15
Myanmar	33.28	0.08
Philippines	21.37	0.30
Singapore	32.82	2.15
Thailand	20.06	1.24
Vietnam	16.72	0.55
European Union		
Austria	75.49	1.00
Belgium	71.30	2.56
Bulgaria	61.44	0.17
Cyprus	66.99	0.03
Czech Republic	79.27	0.87
Denmark	69.38	0.56
Estonia	77.74	0.09
Finland	50.00	0.53
France	65.70	3.55
Germany	63.47	7.28
Greece	63.57	0.25
Hungary	74.33	0.58
Ireland	62.81	0.52
Italy	56.66	2.88
Latvia	73.36	0.08
Lithuania	59.66	0.16
Luxembourg	81.41	0.14
Malta	67.02	0.03
Netherlands	63.23	3.45
Poland	76.49	1.06
Portugal	73.43	0.38
Romania	72.69	0.36
Slovak Republic	82.38	0.43
Slovenia	69.37	0.19
Spain	61.43	1.85
Sweden	64.09	0.97
United Kingdom	51.38	3.05

Source: International Monetary Fund, *Direction of Trade Statistics,* 2012.

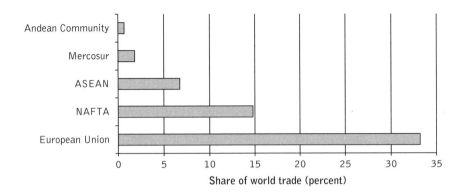

Figure 5.3 *Trade shares of selected regional trade blocs*

The European Union and NAFTA together account for nearly 60 percent of global trade. World trade shares of ASEAN, the Andean Community, and Mercosur are much smaller.

Source: International Monetary Fund, *Direction of Trade Statistics,* 2012.

Union and NAFTA clearly emerge as important regional trading groups. ASEAN and the two South American blocs—the Andean Community and Mercosur—appear to be much less significant regional trading arrangements.

The pitfall of using trade shares to measure regional trade

Trade-share statistics must be interpreted with caution, however. It is hardly surprising that the European Union and NAFTA are regional trading groups with large shares of global trade, because nations within those groups engage in the bulk of the world's international trade. Nations within these regional blocs are among the most powerful players in global trade.

Looking back at Table 5.1 indicates that even the smallest EU nation, Luxembourg, engages in almost three times as much international trade as Mercosur's Paraguay. Does being a member of the European Union necessarily make it more likely that Luxembourg will engage in trade with other EU members than that Paraguay will do so with other nations in Mercosur? It is conceivable that the answer is yes. Because Luxembourg already comprises a relatively larger share of the world economy than Paraguay, however, it is inevitable that Luxembourg trades more with EU nations than Paraguay does with nations within Mercosur.

Luxembourg is, of course, a relatively small country. More dramatically, NAFTA's largest member, the United States, engages in about 31 times more international trade than Colombia, which conducts more international trade than any other member of the Andean Community. Canada conducts more than eight times as much international trade as Colombia, and even Mexico engages in about six times as much trade as Colombia. Hence, the size of NAFTA's share of world trade as compared with the trade share of the Andean Community at least partly reflects the relatively large trade volumes of NAFTA's members.

Determining how a regional trade arrangement affects trade patterns requires taking into account absolute size differences of nations within the regional trading group. That is, we must use a measure of the relative *intensity* of trade *within* the group. Trade-share measures are useful for indicating whether members of regional trade blocs are powerful players on the world scene, but they fail to indicate just how intensively international trade is concentrated within regional trading groups themselves.

Trade concentration ratios

To measure the intensity of trade within trading groups, economists have developed a trade measure called the **trade concentration ratio**, which equals the sum of bilateral trade shares within a regional trading bloc divided by the region's share of world trade. For instance, to calculate the trade concentration ratio for NAFTA, we first add together the tradeflows between the United States and Canada, between the United States and Mexico, and between Canada and Mexico. Then we divide this sum by the combined trade flow of NAFTA to determine the portion of all three NAFTA members' trade that takes place with other NAFTA members. Finally, we divide this NAFTA trade share by NAFTA's total share of world trade to obtain the NAFTA trade concentration ratio. If NAFTA bilateral trade patterns are simply proportionate to the distribution of its member nations' overall trade with other nations of the world, then the NAFTA trade concentration ratio will equal 1.0. If the trade flows of NAFTA nations tend to be more concentrated within NAFTA, however, then the ratio will exceed 1.0. Hence, a relatively larger trade concentration ratio indicates a relatively greater intensity of trade within a regional trade bloc.

> **Trade concentration ratio:** *The sum of bilateral trade shares within a regional trading bloc divided by the region's share of world trade.*

Table 5.2 (overleaf) depicts an example involving a fictitious "world" of five nations—Central Republic, East Isle, Northland, Southsea, and West Coast. The table displays total annual bilateral trade flows—that is, the sum of annual exports and imports, in billions of dollars—for each possible pairing of the five nations. The total annual world trade flow sums to $100 billion. Suppose that Northland and West Coast form a regional trade bloc called the NorthWest Trade Area (NWTA). Trade of Northland and West Coast with respect to all other nations, including other NWTA members—the country names associated with trade flows involving these two NWTA member nations are in bold type in Table 5.2—sums to $60 billion per year. Trade by these three nations that involves *only* other NWTA members, however, totals $45 billion per year. Consequently, the portion of the two NWTA members' trade involving only other NWTA members is $45 billion/$60 billion = 0.75, or 75 percent. NWTA's combined trade share with respect to *all* of this fictitious world's nations, *including* Central Republic, East Isle, and Southsea, is $60 billion/$100 billion = 0.60, or 60 percent. Thus, the trade concentration ratio for the NorthWest Trade Area is 75 percent/60 percent = 1.25. The fact that NWTA's trade concentration value exceeds 1.0 indicates that trade flows of the NWTA nations

Table 5.2 *Annual trade flows in a fictitious five-country world*

Bilateral trade flow	$ billions
Northland and West Coast	45
Northland and *Southsea*	1
West Coast and *Southsea*	1
East Isle and West Coast	1
East Isle and Northland	10
East Isle and *Southsea*	10
Central Republic and West Coast	1
Central Republic and *Southsea*	15
Central Republic and *East Isle*	15
Central Republic and Northland	1
Total world trade flow	100

within their trade bloc are more than proportionate to the nations' trade with the entire "world" considered in this example. We may conclude that, in our example, the NWTA nations' trade is relatively concentrated within their trade bloc.

Now suppose that Southsea and East Isle decide to form another regional trade bloc called the SouthEast Trade Area (SETA). Summing these nations' total annual trade flows with respect to the rest of this fictitious world, including between these two nations within SETA, yields $53 billion (the country names associated with trade flows involving these two SETA member nations are in bold, italic type in Table 5.2). This implies that the portion of the two SETA members' trade involving *only* other SETA members is $10 billion/$53 billion = 0.189, or 18.9 percent. The SETA's combined trade share with respect to *all* of this fictitious world's nations, *including* Central Republic, Northland, and West Coast, is $53 billion/$100 billion = 0.53, or 53 percent. Thus, the trade concentration ratio for the SouthEast Trade Area is 18.9 percent/53 percent = 0.36. The fact that the SETA trade-concentration value is less than 1.0 indicates that intra-SETA trade flows of Southsea and East Isle are less than proportionate to the distribution of the two nations' overall trade with respect to the example's five-nation "world." We may conclude that, in this example, the SETA nations' trade is not particularly concentrated within their trade bloc.

Figure 5.4 displays actual trade concentration ratios for the Andean Community, Mercosur, ASEAN, the European Union, and NAFTA. If you compare Figure 5.4 with Figure 5.3, you can readily see how important it is to take into account countries' relative importance in world trade. The NAFTA trade concentration ratio of nearly 1.8 certainly indicates that the United States, Canada, and Mexico trade somewhat more intensively with one another than they do with other countries. Nevertheless, the Andean Community's trade concentration ratio, exceeding 5.8, is more than three times greater than NAFTA's trade concentration ratio. Colombia

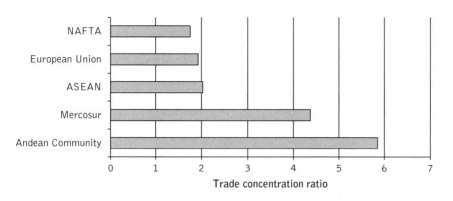

Figure 5.4 *Trade concentration ratios for selected regional trade blocs*

Even though NAFTA and the European Union have greater shares of world trade, trade concentration ratios, or sums of bilateral trade shares within each regional trading bloc divided by the region's share of world trade, reveal that the intensity of trade is greater within Mercosur and the Andean Community.

Source: International Monetary Fund, *Direction of Trade Statistics,* 2012.

and the rest of the Andean Community account for less than 1 percent of global trade, compared with the just over 14 percent trade share of NAFTA. The much higher trade concentration ratio for the Andean Community reflects a significantly greater concentration of Andean Community members' relatively smaller trade volumes within their trade area.

ASEAN's trade concentration ratio of about 2.0 implies that intra-ASEAN trade flows are more important to Singapore and other ASEAN members than intra-NAFTA flows are to the United States, Canada, and Mexico. Nevertheless, the value of Mercosur's trade concentration ratio near 4.4 indicates that more than twice the trade intensity exists among Paraguay and other Mercosur members relative to nations within ASEAN.

Fundamental Issue #1: What are the main types of regional trade agreement, and how do economists measure trade within regional trading groups? The major forms of regional trade agreement are preferential trade arrangements, free trade areas, customs unions, common markets, and economic unions. Economists often measure the extent of trade—the sum of exports and imports—within regional trading groups using trade shares, which are percentages of a nation's trade flows relative to a regional or world total. A country's absolute importance in world trade can distort simple trade share measures, however. Thus, economists measure the intensity of trade within a group of nations using trade concentration ratios, which equal the sum of bilateral trade shares of nations within a regional trading group divided by the region's share of world trade.

PREFERENTIAL TRADE ARRANGEMENTS AND FREE TRADE AREAS

What factors determine whether being part of a regional trading group causes trade with others in that group to increase mildly or dramatically? Before we can address this question, you must first understand in greater detail how each type of regional trade arrangement functions. Let's begin with the weakest trade arrangements, which are preferential trade arrangements and free trade areas.

Preferential trade arrangements

Hollywood has produced innumerable movies called romantic comedies. Some romantic relationships that Hollywood depicts on the big screen start off very one-sided: One person becomes romantically attracted to another and tries to get him or her to pay attention. Some preferential trade arrangements have mirrored this storyline. A country may, for instance, unilaterally lower trade barriers to inflows of goods or services from another nation. This has happened, for instance, when countries facing famine have sought to obtain lower prices on imports of grains and other foodstuffs by eliminating tariffs or duties.

There is also a standard romantic-comedy plot in which an attractive, outgoing, and popular young man or woman takes pity on an especially withdrawn, bashful, and neglected individual. The normal happy ending to such a tale entails two outcomes. First, the popular individual becomes less smug about his or her status. Second, the neglected person experiences a personality transformation and becomes attractive, outgoing, and popular.

A preferential trade arrangement usually is intended to achieve this sort of happy ending for specially selected nations. A good example is the *Caribbean Basin Initiative*. This is a preferential trade arrangement under which the United States gives numerous trade preferences, though only to a specific set of goods, to less developed Caribbean nations. The United States grants these preferences partly so that its residents can aid their neighbors. It also does so in the hope that greater trade with the United States will enhance growth and development of Caribbean nations, thereby making them better neighbors.

Not all preferential trade arrangements are one-sided affairs. In principle, a group of countries can form a *preferential trade area*, in which they grant reciprocal, partial trade concessions to each member nation. When the concessions entail full elimination of tariffs, duties, and import restrictions, then the countries have established a free trade area.

Free trade areas

Most romantic comedies released by Hollywood chronicle complications faced by pairs of fictional characters who meet and then proceed, in fits and starts, in the direction of perhaps ultimately "tying the knot." Typically, one of the individuals has trouble going beyond just having a relatively informal but steady relationship. A basis for a typical movie plot hinges on the difficulties arising from the willingness of a person to "go steady," but his or her inability to "make a commitment."

"Going steady"

A marriage between two people is more than just a publicly announced commitment. Marriage is also a legal arrangement that links the financial status of a couple. In the eyes of governments, therefore, a marriage is a legally binding union of two people. In a way, when two nations form a free trade area, it can be analogous to a couple "going steady": Both parties seek certain benefits of a relationship without entering into a formal union that neither feels certain is in its long-term interest. By granting reciprocal trade preferences, nations may seek to jumpstart trade flows that both feel will yield significant gains from trade. Alternatively, they may have in mind deriving benefits from a longer-term relationship—as when some couples choose to live together without a formal marriage—but wish to avoid political entanglements that might arise if they were to enter into a broader and deeper commitment.

The Andean Community and ASEAN are examples of free trade areas. So is the European Free Trade Association (EFTA), which is composed of Iceland, Liechtenstein, Norway, and Switzerland. The EFTA has also worked out preferential trade arrangements with more than 20 countries, including the European Union.

Australia and New Zealand also constitute a free trade area. There have even been efforts to establish an all-encompassing Western Hemisphere free trade area, tentatively called the Free Trade Area of the Americas. In addition, 21 nations, including Japan and the United States, make up the Asia-Pacific Economic Cooperation (APEC) forum, which commits them to establishing a broad free trade area by no later than 2020. (Several nations that are members of APEC are progressing toward this free-trade goal; see *Policy Notebook: Concluding negotiations for a trans-Pacific partnership*.)

ON THE WEB:

Visit the APEC home page at www.apecsec.org.

POLICY NOTEBOOK

Concluding negotiations for a trans-Pacific partnership

In November 2011, a subset of APEC nations—Australia, Brunei, Canada, Chile, Malaysia, Mexico, New Zealand, Peru, Singapore, Vietnam, and the United States—announced a proposed regional trade agreement. In March 2013, Japan also indicated an interest in being a member. The proposed Trans-Pacific Partnership (TPP) among these nations has the stated aim of freeing up international trade in nearly all goods and services. Indeed, current proposals call for eliminating virtually all tariff and non-tariff barriers to trade and investment among participating members. The TPP nations' governments have indicated that they hope the proposed agreement will provide a framework that trade agreements binding other Asia-Pacific nations may seek to emulate. In this way, trade across the Pacific region may become more liberalized.

One complication to concluding formalization of a final agreement for the TPP is that a U.S. legal framework called trade promotion authority (TPA), granting the U.S. president authority to negotiate an agreement such as TPP, expired in 2007.

U.S. negotiators informally followed TPA procedures in developing the proposed TPP agreement. Nevertheless, it remains to be seen whether the U.S. Congress ultimately will authorize formal membership for the United States under the range of liberalization terms that U.S. government officials have negotiated.

For critical analysis: Given that every nation has its own legal process for approving a regional trade agreement, why do you think typically a number of years are required to attain formal commitments to such an agreement by all member nations?

Experience with the North American Free Trade Agreement

The NAFTA is a good example of nations "going steady" while avoiding a commitment to broader forms of trade liberalization. Before NAFTA's establishment in 1994, there was considerable controversy within the United States concerning its entry

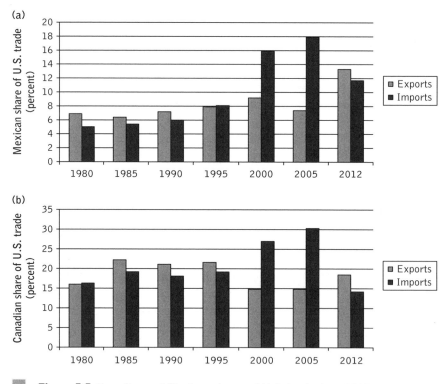

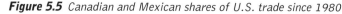

Figure 5.5 *Canadian and Mexican shares of U.S. trade since 1980*

Panel (a) shows that the 1994 establishment of NAFTA initially appeared to be associated with a noticeable increase in the Mexican import share of U.S. trade. Panel (b) indicates that it did not have a significant effect on the combined Canadian shares of U.S. trade.

Source: International Monetary Fund, *Direction of Trade Statistics and authors' estimates.*

into the regional trading group. A major worry was that a number of U.S. producers might respond, possibly for some reasons we shall discuss, by shifting operations to Mexico. The result, U.S. NAFTA critics claimed, would be the loss of many U.S. jobs and an increase in U.S. imports from Mexico that would not be accompanied by a rise in U.S. exports to Mexico.

In fact, the U.S. employment picture brightened from the early 1990s, when many producers began developing more trading connections in anticipation of NAFTA's formation, through to the beginning of the first decade of the twenty-first century, before worsening again later in that decade. As panel (a) in Figure 5.5 indicates, the Mexican share of U.S. imports did increase substantially between 1990 and 2005, from 6 percent to nearly 18 percent, before dropping in recent years as U.S. trade with China and other Asian nations has increased. The share of exports to Mexico initially rose from about 7 percent in 1990 to more than 9 percent in 2000. During the 2000s, however, Mexico's share of U.S. exports then fell back somewhat, before recovering to nearly 14 percent by 2012.

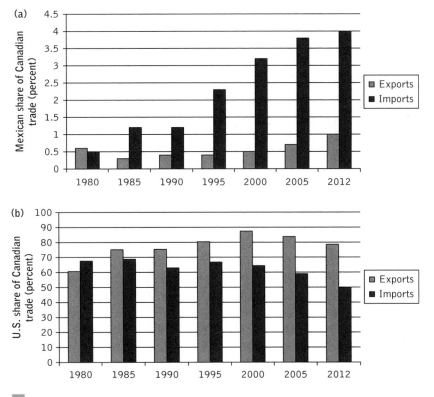

Figure 5.6 *Mexican and U.S. shares of Canadian trade since 1980*

Panel (a) indicates that Mexico's share of Canadian trade jumped following the 1994 establishment of NAFTA. Panel (b) shows that NAFTA did not appear to result in a significant change in the U.S. share of Canadian trade.

Source: International Monetary Fund, *Direction of Trade Statistics and authors' estimates.*

NAFTA critics voiced fewer concerns about possible adverse effects of U.S. links with Canada, perhaps because the two countries had already successfully implemented a bilateral free-trade agreement years earlier. Panel (b) shows that, in fact, the formation of NAFTA had little effect on *total* U.S. trade shares with Canada. Nevertheless, the distribution of Canadian shares of U.S. exports and imports did change. Reflecting the widening U.S. trade gap with most nations, Canadian shares of U.S. exports decreased during the early 2000s before recovering by 2012. Canadian shares of U.S. imports increased considerably before dropping off noticeably.

Canadian worries about the Mexican connection created by NAFTA were more subdued. Most Canadian residents concluded that the potential gains from free trade with the United States would more than offset any complications created by increased trade with Mexico. As panel (a) of Figure 5.6 shows, Mexico's shares of Canadian exports and imports have increased since 1990. Nevertheless, they remain relatively small. As shown in panel (b), Canada's U.S. trade shares have remained relatively

ON THE WEB:

Visit the home page of NAFTA at www. nafta-sec-alena.org.

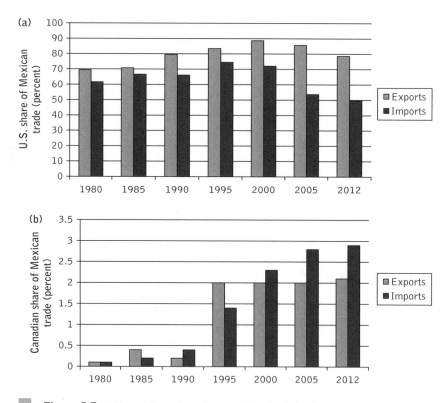

Figure 5.7 *U.S. and Canadian shares of Mexico's trade since 1980*

Panel (a) indicates that the U.S. share of Mexico's trade actually dropped slightly with the 1994 establishment of NAFTA, but panel (b) indicates that the Canadian share of Mexico's trade rose significantly.

Source: International Monetary Fund, *Direction of Trade Statistics and authors' estimates.*

stable, though they have slackened slightly recently, again undoubtedly reflecting in part an increase in U.S. trade with China and other Asian nations.

Figure 5.7 displays U.S. and Canadian shares of Mexican trade. Mexico has expanded its trade with several nations, so the U.S. share of Mexican trade has not increased much since 1990. Consistent with the jump in the Mexican share of U.S. exports shown in panel (a) of Figure 5.5 (p. 134), there has been an increase in Mexican imports from the United States.

Panel (b) shows that from Mexico's perspective, NAFTA opened a new horizon in its trade relationship with Canada. Canadian exports and imports were minuscule shares of Mexican trade before the early 1990s. Now Canada is a more important export market for Mexican producers, as reflected by a Canadian export share nearing 2.5 percent. There has also been a noticeable increase in Mexican imports from Canada.

On net, therefore, the formation of NAFTA initially had somewhat more significant effects on Canadian and Mexican trade than it has exerted on U.S. trade patterns. The United States engages in much larger volumes of international trade—in recent years particularly with China and other Asian countries. The relatively mixed changes in trade patterns within NAFTA explain why the NAFTA trade concentration ratio (see Figure 5.3 on page 128) is relatively low.

Fundamental Issue #2: How is a free trade area such as the North American Free Trade Agreement different from other types of preferential trade arrangement? A preferential trade arrangement establishes trade preferences that apply to specific goods. In addition, it may be one-sided, so that only one nation or group of nations within the preferential trading arrangement benefits. By way of contrast, nations within a free trade area such as NAFTA establish reciprocal trade preferences that apply to all members of the regional trading group. Since the establishment of NAFTA, U.S. exports to Mexico, and Mexican trade with Canada, have increased notably, but U.S. imports from Mexico and Canadian trade with the United States have not changed dramatically.

CUSTOMS UNIONS AND COMMON MARKETS

Some nations have been able to make a firmer commitment to longer-term, coordinated trade relationships. A few have formed customs unions, and some have taken a bigger step beyond just "going steady" by establishing common markets.

Customs unions: Treating outsiders equally

As we discussed earlier, a customs union differs from a free trade area in one fundamental way. Besides agreeing to treat themselves preferentially in trade, nations that are members of a customs union also commit themselves to adopting identical trade policies with respect to nations outside the customs union.

The Treaty of Rome and the European Economic Community

The most important customs union of the twentieth century existed in Europe from 1957 to 1968. It was important for two reasons. First, the major trading countries of Western Europe were members. Second, it blossomed into the European Economic Community, which established a common market and then a fledgling economic union.

On March 25, 1957, the governments of Belgium, France, then-West Germany, Italy, Luxembourg, and the Netherlands signed the Treaty of Rome. The road leading up to establishing a customs union composed of these nations was not a smooth one. Naturally, these nations had to overcome considerable political complications held over from the massive conflict of World War II.

These nations' economic objectives also were not always in complete harmony. For instance, on the one hand, West Germany was anxious to increase trade flows with all nations to help stimulate an economy that had been devastated by the war. On the other hand, France was anxious to maintain restrictions on trade with countries outside Europe. Ultimately, the nations that signed the Treaty of Rome agreed to a compromise that entailed a gradual movement toward free trade among their group, but imposed common restrictions on trade with other countries.

By 1969, trade among nations within the European customs union and between these countries and nations outside the customs union had expanded considerably. This induced other countries, most notably the United Kingdom, to consider joining the regional group, which became the European Economic Community. Negotiations during the early 1970s ultimately culminated with admittance of the United Kingdom and transformation of the customs union into a common market.

The Andean Community

At the same time as the European Common Market was launched, Bolivia, Chile, Colombia, Ecuador, and Peru were in the process of working out and signing the Cartagena Agreement establishing reciprocal trade preferences. Between 1973 and 1976, Chile withdrew from the agreement and was replaced by Venezuela. During the next two decades, this collection of South American nations gradually developed a free trade area, the Andean Community, which went into operation in January 1993. Peru gained full admittance to the group in 1997.

ON THE WEB:

Find out how the Andean Community is pursuing further trade integration at www. comunidadandina.org.

As the trade concentration ratio in Figure 5.4 on page 131 indicates, there is considerable intensity of trade within the Andean Community. In addition, since 1998 the Andean Community has negotiated trade agreements with other countries, such as the United States and Canada, as a single entity. Thus, the Andean Community has become a customs union within just a few years. Currently negotiations are underway to transform the Andean Community into a common market.

Common markets: Freeing up resource flows

The step from a free trade area to a customs union is a big one. When countries truly become serious about breaking down economic barriers, however, they typically reach the conclusion that they must take an even larger step by forming a common market. As we noted earlier, when a group of nations establish a common market, they remove most or even all barriers to cross-border flows of labor, capital, and other resources.

Mixed messages from the European Union

In 1969, the European Economic Community became a common market. Since 1986, it has also styled itself as an economic union with highly coordinated policies regarding trade and resource flows.

Refer back to the concentration ratios depicted in Figure 5.4 on page 131, however, and you will see that concentration ratios indicate that trade among EU members is less intensive than trade within Mercosur and the Andean Community.

Economists disagree about exactly why free trade areas such as Mercosur experience more intensive regional trade than the European Union. One likely reason is that many EU nations historically had developed very broad trading relationships. After formation of the European Union, exporters and importers in these countries maintained these relationships. As we discuss later, it is also possible that countries in other regional trading blocs have adopted policies that do more to discourage trade from outside their own group. That is, it is possible that trade increases within some regional blocs at the expense of trade between their members and nations outside the blocs. From this perspective, one might interpret the continuing trade between EU nations and other non-EU countries as indicative of a general movement toward freer trade—or, at least, no further movement toward protectionism—within the European Union.

Mercosur: Success and strains

Argentina, Brazil, Paraguay, and Uruguay began moving toward a common market in 1991, when they initiated a *trade liberalization program* of gradual tariff reductions to zero for many goods and resources, beginning in 1995. The establishment of Mercosur was a major development in a region where nations have not always had harmonious relationships.

This may help to explain why trade liberalization within Mercosur has taken place in fits and starts. Between Mercosur's founding and the end of 1998, trade between Argentina and Brazil expanded by 400 percent. Then, in early 1999, Brazil reduced the value of its currency and then allowed its value to vary in foreign exchange markets, while Argentina kept its currency equal to the U.S. dollar, as it had done since 1991. Many multinational companies responded to the nearly 30 percent drop in the cost of doing business in Brazil by shifting production from Argentina to Brazil, to which Argentina responded by slowing integration into Mercosur. Additional tensions arose within Mercosur when Argentina abandoned its explicit ties to the U.S. dollar in early 2002. Nevertheless, the common market survived these episodes. A key reason, most economists agree, is that these neighboring nations have consistently concluded that their close proximity to one another yields gains from trade that adherence to the Mercosur agreement promotes.

ON THE WEB:

Learn more about Mercosur at http:// actrav.itcilo.org/ actrav-english/telearn/ global/ilo/blokit/ mercosur.htm.

139

Fundamental Issue #3: What distinguishes customs unions such as the European Economic Community of the 1970s and the current Andean Community from common markets such as today's European Union and Mercosur? Customs unions like the old European Economic Community and the Andean Community operate as free trade areas for their members, and also establish common restrictions on trade with countries outside the customs union. Nevertheless, nations within a customs union often retain barriers to flows of factors of production, such as labor and capital. Within a common market such as the European Union and Mercosur, participating countries also remove restraints on the flows of factors of production.

TRADE CREATION, DIVERSION, OR DEFLECTION?

The rise of regional trade agreements has altered the landscape of the world trading system. As we noted earlier, there is some evidence that they have encouraged trade within regional trading groups. Economists who favor unhindered trade, however, are divided about whether the net effect of regional trade agreements is to enhance or to reduce *overall* international trade around the globe.

Trade creation versus trade diversion

Trade creation:
An additional amount of international trade resulting from trade preferences that a nation grants to a trading partner.

Trade diversion: *A shift in international trade caused by one nation giving trade preferences to another, which can cause trade with a third country to decline.*

Figure 5.4 on page 131 shows that the intensity of trade, as revealed by trade concentration ratios, is greater within the Andean Community and Mercosur than within NAFTA and the European Union. There are two ways that one might interpret relatively high trade intensity within a regional trading bloc. On the one hand, intensive trade among members of a regional trading group could indicate that their regional trade agreement has contributed to **trade creation**, or a trade enhancement relative to the trade flows that would have taken place without the agreement. On the other hand, intensive trade within a regional trading bloc might imply that a trade agreement among its members has induced **trade diversion**. Trade diversion occurs when an increase in a nation's imports from members of its regional trading group displace imports that otherwise would have come from non-member countries. (A recent study of the trade effects of membership in the Asia-Pacific Economic Cooperation forum found evidence consistent with trade creation; see *Policy Notebook: Trade-creation outcomes for APEC member nations.*)

POLICY NOTEBOOK

Trade-creation outcomes for APEC member nations

Hyun-Hoon Lee of the APEC Policy Support Unit and Jung Hur of Sogang University recently assessed the extent of international trade by its member nations. They find that since APEC's 1989 inception, export linkages among nations within

APEC have strengthened for 19 of the trade bloc's 21 members, and that linkages involving other APEC nations have strengthened for 16 members. As a consequence, today an APEC member nation exports nearly three times more to other APEC nations than to non-APEC countries, and imports nearly twice as much from other APEC nations than from non-APEC countries.

Lee and Hur also find evidence that member nations have experienced overall growth in trade exceeding that of non-member nations, consistent with a trade-creation effect for APEC. The average annual rate of growth of APEC nations' total exports to nations throughout the world was 0.6 percentage point per year higher than the average growth rate for non-APEC countries. The average annual rate of growth of APEC nations' total imports was 0.2 percentage point higher. The implication of these growth differentials is that, since APEC's founding, APEC nations have experienced 12 percent more overall export expansion and 4 percent more overall import expansion than non-APEC countries.

For critical analysis: APEC is not a free-trade area, but the Trans-Pacific Partnership (TPP) that several APEC members are negotiating would be. Is it possible that countries in the proposed TPP might face a greater potential for trade diversion than currently is the case for APEC member nations?

Why the net effect matters

If regional trading blocs encourage trade creation, then on net the formation of these regional trading groups will contribute to larger volumes of *global* trade. As discussed in Chapter 3, the likely effect of trade creation will be that more nations will recognize existing absolute or comparative advantages. As a result, more of the world's people will experience gains from trade.

If the net effect of the widespread establishment of regional trade blocs is trade diversion, however, then global trade flows will not necessarily increase as a result of regional trade agreements. Equal-sized substitutions of regional trading partners' imports for the imports of countries outside regional trading groups will leave global trade flows unchanged. Furthermore, if members of regional trade blocs establish sufficiently protectionist policies against non-member countries, it is possible that international trade flows could actually *decline*. For instance, consider what would happen if Mercosur were to place high tariffs on imports of digital devices, such as tablet computers and smartphones, from countries outside Mercosur. Naturally, imports of digital devices into Mercosur nations from the United States and other digital device-exporting countries would decline. Undoubtedly, this would also cause a net decline in overall Mercosur trade in digital devices, however, because there are few manufacturers of these products in Argentina, Brazil, Paraguay, or Uruguay that could offer a full range of substitute digital devices. Hence, trade diversion likely would lead to incomplete substitution of members' imports for the imports of non-members. (To see why both trade creation and trade diversion typically occur when members of regional trade blocs grant fellow members trade preferences, see *Visualizing Global Economic Issues: Trade creation versus trade diversion in a three-country world.*)

VISUALIZING GLOBAL ECONOMIC ISSUES

Trade creation versus trade diversion in a three-country world

Let's apply basic demand–supply analysis to explain why it is that regional trading preferences typically produce *both* trade creation *and* trade diversion. Take a look at Figure 5.8. Panel (a) shows a nation's demand and supply curves for tablet devices (or "tablets") manufactured domestically. Panel (b) shows the curves for tablets produced in another country that becomes a fellow member of a regional trade bloc. Panel (c) shows the nation's demand and supply for tablets made in another nation that is not a member of the regional trading group. The initial equilibrium dollar price of tablet devices in the home nation is $350.

Suppose that the initial foreign supply curves in panels (b) and (c) reflect a tariff on the nation's imports of tablets. After the country depicted in panel (b) joins the nation's regional trading group, however, the domestic country cuts the tariff on tablets imported from this new regional partner. Thus, as shown in panel (b), the supply of tablets from the regional partner increases. As the price of tablet devices imported from the regional partner declines toward $250, domestic residents substitute away from purchases of *both* domestically manufactured tablets *and* tablets manufactured in the nation that is not in the regional trading group and that still face a tariff. Hence, the demand curves shift leftward in panels (a) and (c). The new equilibrium dollar price of tablet devices in this nation is equal to $250.

Notice what happens to this nation's trade in tablet devices. To some extent, domestic residents shift some of their domestic purchases of tablets abroad, as illustrated by the decline in domestic purchases in panel (a) and the increase in purchases from the regional trading partner in panel (b). Thus, *trade creation* results from extending trade preferences to the new regional partner, as domestic purchases decline in favor of purchases from the member of the regional trading bloc. As panel (c) indicates, however, purchases of tablets from the foreign country that is not a member of the regional trade bloc decline. Thus, *trade diversion* also takes place.

For critical analysis: In this example, would trade diversion occur if digital-device producers in both foreign nations were exempted from tariffs?

Limiting regional trade diversion

In light of the proliferation of regional trade blocs, economists who favor free trade have sought to determine how regional trading groups might limit tendencies to divert trade instead of fostering an environment of more open trade with all nations. Some have advanced a proposal that, on its surface, seems inconsistent with

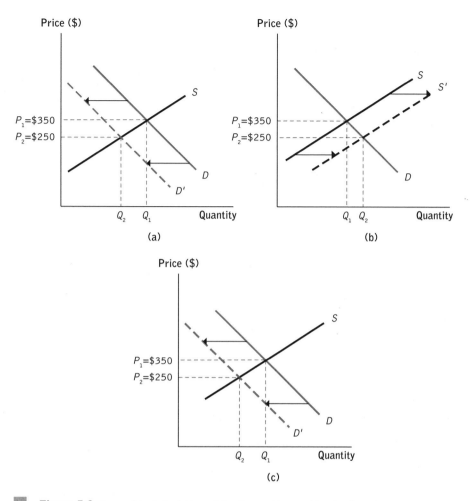

Figure 5.8 *A graphical depiction of trade creation and trade diversion*

Panel (a) shows a nation's demand and supply curves for tablet devices manufactured domestically, and panel (b) displays the domestic demand for and supply of tablet devices produced in another country that becomes a fellow member of a regional trade bloc. Panel (c) depicts the domestic demand and supply curves for tablets manufactured in another nation that is not a member of the regional trading group. The initial equilibrium U.S. dollar price of all tablets is $350. After the country depicted in panel (b) joins the nation's regional trading group, the domestic country cuts the tariff on tablets imported from this new regional partner, causing the supply of tablets from the regional partner to increase in panel (b). The decline in the price of tablets imported from the regional partner induces domestic residents to substitute its tablets for both domestically manufactured tablets and tablets manufactured in the nation outside the regional trading group that continues to still face a tariff, resulting in the declines in demands shown in panels (a) and (b). Trade creation occurs as domestic residents shift some of their domestic purchases of tablets abroad, as shown by the fall in domestic purchases in panel (a) and the rise in purchases from the regional trading partner in panel (b). At the same time, however, panel (c) shows that trade diversion occurs as domestic residents reduce their purchases of tablets from the foreign country that is not a member of the regional trade bloc.

143

a free-trade philosophy: granting partial instead of complete reductions of trade barriers within a regional trade agreement. One basis of this argument is that complete removal of trade restrictions within a regional trade bloc that otherwise maintains restraints on trade with other nations provides a strong incentive for trade diversion. Another is that complete removal of tariffs that generate revenues for governments of nations in a regional trading group gives the governments an incentive to raise tariffs on countries outside the group, further increasing the incentive to divert trade.

Naturally, free-trade-oriented economists propose keeping all trade restrictions to a minimum. If regional trading groups insist on maintaining higher barriers for non-members than for members, then these economists promote keeping the differentials among tariffs, duties, and other barriers as low as possible.

Nearly all economists agree that a key way to encourage trade creation through regional trade agreements is to keep membership in such arrangements open to all. They argue that rules that effectively limit membership in more than one regional trading group at a time, such as EU rules preventing the United Kingdom from, say, belonging to the European Union and NAFTA simultaneously, can do little but drive wedges among regional trade blocs that contribute to trade diversion.

> *Fundamental Issue #4: How can regional trading arrangements lead to both trade creation and trade diversion?* When one nation reduces trade restrictions previously imposed on another, there are two effects. One is a trade creation effect. The nation's residents substitute purchases of domestic goods with purchases of goods produced by the nation with which trade barriers have been reduced. In addition, however, they tend to reduce their purchases of goods from countries with which their nation retains barriers to trade, so there is also trade diversion.

Trade deflection:

The movement of goods or components of goods from a country outside a trading arrangement to one within such an arrangement so that the seller can benefit from trading preferences within the arrangement.

Trade deflection

Another complication that arises when assessing the overall trade effects of regional trade agreements is **trade deflection**. This takes place when a company located in a nation outside a regional trade bloc finds a way to move goods that are not quite fully assembled into a member country, complete assembly, and then export them to countries offering the trade preferences. A common way to engage in trade deflection is for a company to move a portion of its production facilities to nations participating in a regional trade agreement.

Rules of origin:

Regulations governing conditions under which products are eligible for trading preferences under trade agreements.

Rules of origin

To try to reduce the extent to which trade deflection occurs, most regional trading agreements include **rules of origin**. These are regulations that carefully define categories of products that are eligible for trading preferences under the agreements.

Some rules of origin require any products trading freely among members of a regional trading group to be composed entirely of materials produced within a member nation. For instance, if Mercosur applied such a stringent rule of origin, then an automobile assembled in, say, Argentina that contained a single component manufactured in a Mexican auto parts plant would not be eligible for free trade to Brazil.

Rules of origin typically are not so stringent, however. Most rules of origin instead mandate that goods eligible for preferred trade must have a certain percentage of value added by manufacturing within a country that is a member of the regional trading group.

Trade deflection and gains from trade

Some economists favoring free trade applaud successful trade deflection. They argue that successful trade deflection circumvents trade restrictions and thereby allows residents of nations within regional trade blocs to experience gains from trade.

Other free-trade-oriented economists, however, worry that trade deflection can lead to welfare losses for residents of nations that fail to receive imports that are deflected when trading partners pursue favorable trade preferences offered by special regional trade agreements. For instance, Mexican auto parts that are used as components in Argentine-manufactured automobiles to take advantage of Mercosur trade preferences might help prop up relatively inefficient Argentine auto producers that might be less able to compete with, say, Mexican producers in a truly open trading environment.

According to this second view, therefore, trade preferences established by regional trade agreements can introduce fundamental distortions into international trading patterns. As a consequence, regional trade agreements potentially can make residents of both member and non-member nations worse off. In short, increased regionalism will not necessarily make the world's people better off. It is even possible that greater regionalism could make them worse off. This conclusion leads many economists to favor wider trade initiatives that encompass many nations, irrespective of their location on the globe.

Fundamental Issue #5: What is trade deflection, and how do rules of origin help to limit the extent to which trade deflection occurs? When a nation extends trade preferences to one or more countries, producers located in a nation not eligible for these preferences have an incentive to move goods that are not in completely finished form into one of those countries, in an effort to benefit from the preferences. The producer might, for instance, move a portion of its facilities to nations eligible for preferences. If the producer is successful, then it engages in trade deflection. To combat trade deflection, countries that establish preferential trade arrangements enforce rules of origin categorizing products that are eligible for preferential trade.

MULTILATERAL APPROACHES AND BENEFITS

Multilateralism:
An approach to achieving freer international trade via a wide interplay among many of the world's nations, with an aim toward inducing each country to treat others equally in trading arrangements.

Generally speaking, economists favoring free and open international trade look askance on regional trade agreements. They tend to favor a more broadly based global approach—**multilateralism**. This approach to international trade emphasizes a broad interaction among nations, with each country treating others equally to the greatest possible extent.

Most favored nation status

Most favored nation (MFN): *A country that receives reductions in trade barriers to promote open international trade.*

Many countries, including the United States, have implemented a multilateral approach by abiding by a rule known as the *unconditional most favored nation principle*. Under this rule, reductions in trade barriers that a country extends to a trading partner classified as a **most favored nation (MFN)** are automatically extended to other trading partners with MFN status. (In the United States, however, MFN status is referred to as "normal trade relations status.")

The motivation behind the MFN principle is that, if a number of countries follow the principle, discrimination in international trade arrangements will become less common. Of course, the United States and other countries already discriminate through their membership in NAFTA and other regional trade blocs. Nevertheless, the overall hope of the nations that abide by the MFN principle is that if more and more countries abide by the principle, discriminatory trade arrangements will gradually die out.

To become a most favored nation, a country must show that it can credibly commit to patterns of conduct in international trade that other nations have also adopted. This raises an important question, however: Who is to decide whether a country has established a credible commitment to "acceptable" conduct? The answer that most of the world's nations have developed is to establish global trade agreements. More recently, nations have also agreed to have their trade conduct monitored by international organizations.

General Agreement on Tariffs and Trade (GATT): *An international agreement among more than 140 nations about rules governing cross-border trade in goods.*

Multilateral trade regulation

From 1947 until 1993, nations accounting for more than 85 percent of global international trade flows signed the **General Agreement on Tariffs and Trade (GATT)**. Under the terms of this agreement, participating nations began to meet periodically to iron out disagreements about trade policies.

World Trade Organization (WTO): *The multinational organization that oversees multilateral trade negotiations and adjudicates trade disputes that arise under multilateral trade agreements formed under the GATT and the GATS.*

"Rounds" of GATT negotiations were named according to most clearly identified locations or individuals. The 1993 Uruguay Round of GATT, which 117 nations ratified, established the **World Trade Organization (WTO)**. The WTO commenced formal operations on January 1, 1995, and today it has grown to encompass more than 150 member nations. A key factor contributing to the WTO's growth has been the growing importance of its functions as a global arbiter of trade rules and enforcement. Even nations that have had spotty records for "playing by the rules" in international trade have sought to join this multinational trade group.

Functions of the World Trade Organization

The WTO has several basic functions. It serves as a global forum for all multinational negotiations concerning international trade. It oversees rounds of trade negotiations and monitors compliance with trade agreements. In addition, it conducts periodic assessment of national trade policies and assists countries in developing these policies.

The WTO, which is based in Geneva, Switzerland, also administers the **General Agreement on Trade in Services (GATS)**, another agreement reached in the Uruguay Round. This agreement covers most international service transactions and generally requires national treatment for services on the same terms as trade in goods. Nevertheless, services receive somewhat different treatment under the GATS than goods do under the GATT.

General Agreement on Trade in Services (GATS): *An international agreement among more than 130 nations about rules under which services are traded internationally.*

Addressing allegations of unfair trading practices

Another fundamental role of the WTO is to settle and adjudicate trade disputes. Under the terms of the WTO *Agreement on Subsidies and Countervailing Measures*, for example, the WTO has the power to discipline the use of subsidies that any country's government transmits to domestic firms to give them a trade advantage over firms located in other nations (see Chapter 4). A nation that feels it has been harmed by such subsidies can use the WTO's dispute-settlement procedure to press for the WTO to force a country that provides trade subsidies to withdraw them; or the nation experiencing the harm can seek WTO sanction to charge a countervailing duty. In recent years a key subject of WTO investigation of trade subsidies has been national tax laws, because to make their subsidies less overt, many nations offer exporting firms tax breaks instead of direct payments.

Not all trade subsidies are unlawful under current WTO rules, and the WTO does not fully extend its powers to oversee countervailing duties. Until 2003, the WTO exempted most developing nations from restraints on trade subsidies, and it continues to extend exemptions to the least-developed nations of the world, which it defines to be those with per capita incomes of less than $1,000 per year. A number of developing nations also receive preferential treatment from the WTO in its enforcement of rules governing countervailing duties.

As noted in Chapter 4 (and see Chapter 12 for further discussion), when a firm sells a product in a nation at a price lower than it charges in its home country, it is said to be *dumping* the product. The WTO determines whether nations that claim to be recipients of dumped products can respond with anti-dumping policies, such as subsidies to companies affected by dumping, or countervailing duties on the products of offending firms.

Will regionalism ultimately evolve into multilateralism?

The WTO has had to perform a careful balancing act to promote multilateralism and lower trade restrictions as regional trade agreements have proliferated. Economists continue to debate whether regionalism will add to, or subtract from, efforts to enhance free-trade efforts around the world.

Some indications from trade shares

In an exhaustive study of world trade from the 1960s to the early 1990s, Jeffrey Frankel of Harvard University sought to address whether regionalism has improved or worsened prospects for freer trade. His conclusions generally favored a positive outlook for world trade as a result of regional trading agreements. Specifically, Frankel found that ASEAN and other parts of East Asia have become highly open to trade. So has the EU portion of Europe (but not the rest of Europe) and the Mercosur portion of South America. In addition, Frankel concluded that the degree of trade openness of NAFTA countries, and in particular the United States, has tended to increase over time.

Frankel's study indicated that most countries with the greatest increase in openness to trade had also joined regional trade arrangements. These included Argentina, Brazil, and Paraguay of Mercosur, and Malaysia and Thailand of ASEAN. Frankel suggests that when countries go to the trouble to develop a political consensus favoring trade concessions to regional trading partners, it may become a shorter step to open borders to trade with other nations as well. Consequently, trade creation generally outweighs trade diversion within regional trade blocs. If Frankel is correct, regional trade arrangements may indeed act as a bridge to broader multilateral efforts to promote freer trade among the world's nations.

A gradual overlapping of regional trade arrangements

One development that offers some support for Frankel's interpretation is that a number of regional trade agreements are beginning to overlap. For instance, the budding APEC forum includes countries that are members of NAFTA, ASEAN, Mercosur, and the Andean Community. Furthermore, these and other regional trade blocs have negotiated partial reciprocal trade preferences across their trading groups.

The European Free Trade Association has also developed into an overlapping set of reciprocal trade arrangements. Certainly, the EU remains a clearly separate bloc. Nevertheless, trade agreements linking EU and other EFTA nations to individual countries inside and outside Europe have blurred many of the trade borders that previously surrounded the European Union.

At present, therefore, at least some economists believe that regionalism has not necessarily emerged as a *substitute* for multilateralism. There is some indication, however, that regionalism has been *complementary* to multilateral efforts to enhance more open trade among nations. (Efforts to reach multilateral agreement on rules governing international electronic commerce may be boosted by regional agreements on Web-based trade; see *Online Globalization: Will regional trade agreements break a multilateral logjam on global e-commerce?*.)

ONLINE GLOBALIZATION

Will regional trade agreements break a multilateral logjam on global e-commerce?

In a number of countries, governments impede free flows of information on the Internet. In some countries, such activities are rationalized by concerns over Web privacy and cyber security. In other nations, political motivations induce government officials to block certain online data flows.

The desires of various governments to regulate Internet information flows have complicated efforts within the WTO to establish rules governing international trade conducted via electronic commerce. Indeed, the WTO has experienced difficulties in simply finding multilateral agreement on defining permissible private e-commerce trading activities. As a result, efforts to establish a framework of rules for online international exchange of goods, services, and assets have been gridlocked for nearly a decade.

In contrast, more than 10 percent of all regional trade agreements now include agreed-upon definitions of private e-commerce trade activities covered by the agreements. Nations participating in these agreements have also hammered out rules governing flows of information that governments must permit private individuals and firms to transmit and share via the Internet so that e-commerce exchanges can occur. Currently, a number of regional trade blocs are working toward integrating these agreements' rules for e-commerce trade into their own rulebooks as well. Indeed, a number of observers have suggested that WTO-based multilateral progress on e-commerce will occur only after most regional trade blocs have developed relatively standardized guidelines for global online trade.

For critical analysis: Why might it be easier for the members of a regional trade bloc to negotiate agreements covering e-commerce than for all of the WTO members to do so?

Fundamental Issue #6: How do multilateral trade agreements contrast with regional trading arrangements? Whereas regional trading arrangements establish trade agreements among limited sets of countries, multilateral trade agreements seek to involve most of the world's nations in efforts to free up flows of international trade. The fundamental multilateral trade agreements among more than 150 nations are the General Agreement on Tariffs and Trade (GATT) and the General Agreement on Trade in Services (GATS). Since 1995, the World Trade Organization has been responsible for monitoring compliance with these agreements. Recent evidence indicates that the proliferation, and gradual overlapping, of regional trade agreements has reinforced multilateral trade arrangements.

CHAPTER SUMMARY

1. **The main types of regional trade agreement, and how economists measure trade within regional trading groups:** The most important types of regional trade agreement are preferential trade arrangements, free trade areas, customs unions, common markets, and economic unions. Trade shares, or percentage of a country's flows of trade (the sum of its exports and imports) relative to a regional or world total, are commonly used to measure the extent of a country's trade. Because a country's absolute importance in world trade can distort simple trade shares, economists measure the intensity of trade within a group of nations using a trade concentration ratio. This equals the sum of bilateral trade shares of nations within a regional trading group, divided by the region's share of world trade.

2. **How a free trade area such as the North American Free Trade Agreement differs from other types of preferential trade arrangement:** Preferential trade arrangements often create trade preferences for specific goods, and they are often one-sided agreements that benefit only one nation or group of nations. By way of contrast, countries within a free trade area such as NAFTA set up reciprocal trade preferences for all nations within the regional trading bloc. The establishment of NAFTA has so far led to rises in U.S. exports to Mexico, and in Mexican trade with Canada, but U.S. imports from Mexico and Canadian trade with the United States have not changed notably.

3. **How customs unions such as the European Economic Community of the 1970s and the current Andean Community are distinguished from common markets such as the European Union and Mercosur:** The European Economic Community and the Andean Community are examples of customs unions that function as free trade areas, but also impose identical rules governing trade with countries outside the regional trading bloc. Today's European Union and Mercosur are common markets that additionally remove restraints on the flows of factors of production such as labor and capital.

4. **How regional trading arrangements can lead to simultaneous trade creation and trade diversion:** Reduction or elimination of trade barriers that a domestic nation had previously imposed on another induces the domestic nation's residents to reduce purchases of domestic goods in favor of buying goods produced by the country with which trade restrictions have been relaxed. This trade creation effect, however, is at least partly countered by a trade diversion effect. This second effect arises because the nation's residents also have an incentive to reduce their purchases of goods from countries with which their nation maintains barriers to trade.

5. **Trade deflection and how rules of origin limit its occurrence:** The establishment of preferential trade agreements or regional trading arrangements gives companies located in countries not covered by the trade preferences an incentive to move incompletely assembled goods into nations that are eligible. The companies can then complete production and take advantage of the trade preferences, thereby engaging in trade deflection. Nations often seek to reduce the extent of trade deflection by establishing and enforcing rules of origin regulating the eligibility of products for trade preferences.

6. **How multilateral trade agreements differ from regional trading arrangements:** In contrast to regional trading arrangements that link relatively small groups of nations,

the two main multilateral trade agreements, the General Agreement on Tariffs and Trade (GATT) and the General Agreement on Trade in Services (GATS), encompass more than 140 countries. Under the auspices of these agreements, the World Trade Organization monitors compliance and adjudicates disputes. There is some evidence that the growing number of regional trade agreements that are now beginning to overlap complements a multilateral approach to freeing up trade among the world's nations.

QUESTIONS AND PROBLEMS

1. Consider the following data on flows of exports and imports among three nations, and suppose that the "world" is composed solely of these countries:

    country A exports to country B: $35 million
    country A exports to country C: $25 million
    country B exports to country A: $30 million
    country B exports to country C: $25 million
    country C exports to country A: $20 million
    country C exports to country B: $40 million

Calculate the following as a share of total world trade. Express your answers as percentages, and round to the nearest tenth of a percent.
(a) Country A's trade with country B
(b) Country A's trade with country C
(c) Country B's trade with country C

2. Based on the information in question 1, which nation(s) has an overall trade deficit? Which has an overall trade surplus? Is world trade balanced?

3. Use the information in question 1 to calculate the following, and express your answers as percentages rounded to the nearest tenth of a percent.
(a) Country A's total share of world trade
(b) Country B's total share of world trade
(c) Country C's total share of world trade

4. Suppose that country A and country B in question 1 together constitute a regional trade bloc known as the A–B Trade Area. Use your answers to questions 1 and 2 to calculate the trade concentration ratio of this regional trade bloc.

5. In principle, why is the trade concentration ratio you calculated in question 4 a better measure of the intensiveness of trade within the A–B Trade Area than simply the combined share of world trade of countries A and B? Give a verbal answer.

6. Suppose that a year passes, and the trade concentration ratio of the A–B Trade Area increases significantly. Does this observation necessarily imply that formation of the A–B Trade Area has enhanced overall world trade?

7. Another year passes, and the A–B Trade Area changes its name by inserting the word "Free" before "Trade Area." Under the agreement the two nations have reached, country A will remove all remaining restrictions on trade with country B this year. Both agree that another year will pass, however, before country B will reciprocate by removing all remaining barriers to trade with country A. Draw diagrams to illustrate,

from country A's perspective, how this year's action by country A is likely to generate both trade creation and trade diversion during the current year. Be sure to take into account country A's trade with country C as well.

8. It is now a year later, and country B removes all remaining restraints on trade with country A. Draw diagrams to show, from country B's perspective, how this action is likely to generate both trade creation and trade diversion during the current year. Be sure to take into account country B's trade with country C as well.

9. One more year passes, and the A–B Free Trade Area negotiates a partial reduction in barriers to their trade with country C. Without drawing any additional diagrams, is this action more likely on net to generate trade creation or trade diversion? Explain your reasoning.

10. Suppose that all three nations agree to remove remaining barriers to trade among the entire set, so that the "world" becomes a free trade area. Country C is twice as far from both country A and country B as country A and country B are from each other. In addition, country A and country B are of equal size, but country C is half as large. Are trade flows likely to be unequal even with unhindered trade? If so, how?

ONLINE APPLICATION

URL: http://ec.europa.eu/trade/

Title: The European Commission – EU Trade

Navigation: Begin at the above Web page, and click on "Policy." In the left-hand panel, click on "Transatlantic Trade and Investment Partnership (TTIP)."

Application: Perform the indicated operations, and answer the questions that follow.

1. Give an explanation of the proposed "Transatlantic Trade and Investment Partnership (TTIP)."

2. How important is trade between the European Union and the United States? Qualify and quantify this relationship.

3. In addition to reducing tariff barriers, how would the formation of the TTIP promote trade between European Union member nations and the United States?

For group study and analysis: Divide into four groups. Assign each group an economy, the European Union or the United States. Have one of the EU groups support and the other oppose the TTIP. Likewise, have one of the US groups support and the other oppose the TTIP. Each group should give two arguments to frame their position.

REFERENCES AND RECOMMENDED READINGS

Aaronson, Susan Ariel, with Miles Townes. "Can Trade Policy Set Information Free?" Policy Brief, Elliot School of International Affairs, George Washington University, November 30, 2012.

Baier, Scott, and Jeffrey Bergstrand. "Do Free Trade Agreements Actually Increase Members' International Trade?" *Journal of International Economics* 71 (2007): 72–95.

Baldwin, Richard. "The Euro's Trade Effects." European Central Bank Working Paper No. 594, March 2006.

Baldwin, Richard, and Patrick Low, ed. *Multilateralizing Regionalism: Challenges for the Global Trading System*. Cambridge, U.K.: Cambridge University Press, 2009.

Fergusson, Ian, William Cooper, Remy Jurenas, and Brock Williams. "The Trans-Pacific Partnership Negotiations and Issues for Congress." Congressional Research Service Report for Congress, March 19, 2013.

Fiorentino, Roberto, Jo-Ann Crawford, and Christelle Toqueboeuf. "The Landscape of Regional Trade Agreements and WTO Surveillance." In Richard Baldwin and Patrick Low, eds., *Multilateralizing Regionalism: Challenges for the Global Trading System*. Cambridge, U.K.: Cambridge University Press, 2009, pp. 28–76.

Frankel, Jeffrey. *Regional Trade Blocs*. Washington, DC: Institute for International Economics, 1997.

Freund, Caroline, and Emanuel Ornelas. "Regional Trade Agreements." Policy Research Working Paper 5314, World Bank Development Research Group, May 2010.

Herman, Lior. "Multilateralising Regionalism: The Case of E-Commerce." OECD Trade Policy Paper No. 99, Organization for Economic Cooperation and Development, June 2010.

Lee, Hyun-Hoon, and Jung Hur. "Trade Creation in the APEC Region: Measurement of the Magnitude of and Changes in Intra-Regional Trade since APEC's Inception." Asia-Pacific Economic Cooperation Policy Support Unit Report, October 2009.

Lynch, David. *Trade and Globalization: An Introduction to Regional Trade Agreements*. Plymouth, U.K.: Rowman & Littlefield, 2010.

Rose, Andrew. "One Money, One Market: The Effect of Common Currencies on Trade." *Economic Policy* 30 (April 2000): 9–33.

World Bank. *Trade Blocs*. Oxford, U.K.: Oxford University Press, 2000.

Unit III
International finance: enduring issues

Chapter 6

Balance of payments and foreign exchange markets

FUNDAMENTAL ISSUES

1. What is a country's balance of payments, and what does it measure?
2. What is the role of foreign exchange markets in the global marketplace?
3. What is the spot foreign exchange market?
4. What is foreign exchange risk, and what is the role of forward foreign exchange markets?
5. What determines the value of a currency?
6. How are the spot and forward markets related?
7. What other foreign exchange instruments are commonly traded?

In the spring of 2012, only about £0.62 was required in exchange for $1.00 in markets for foreign currencies. Exactly one year later, however, almost £0.67 had to be given up in exchange for $1.00. Thus, the British pound depreciated by approximately 8 percent in relation to the dollar.

A number of factors accounted for this depreciation. Perhaps the most important factors were that between 2012 and 2013, economic activity in the United Kingdom decreased, several British financial and non-financial firms experienced low profitability levels, and tax revenues collected by the British government shrank. As a consequence, savers worldwide became less confident that households, firms, and the government in the United Kingdom would be able to repay their debts fully and in a timely manner. Thus, savers opted to cut back on their holdings of British bonds in favor of holding more U.S. bonds. This switch in preferences for bond holdings generated a pound depreciation—and thus a dollar appreciation—by reducing the demand for pounds and increasing the demand for dollars.

To understand fully how relative changes in British pound and U.S. dollar demands influenced the pound–dollar exchange rate between 2012 and 2013, you must first contemplate how economists measure flows of international transactions, and then learn about the determinants of the demand for, and supply of, foreign currencies. These are key topics of this chapter.

Balance of payments:

A system of accounts that measures transaction of goods, services, income, and financial assets between domestic residents, businesses, and governments, and the rest of the world, during a specific time period.

BALANCE OF PAYMENTS

The **balance of payments** is a complete tabulation of the total market value of goods services, and financial assets that domestic residents, firms, and governments exchange with residents of other nations during a given period. A nation's balance of payments is a system that accounts for flows of income and expenditures and the flow of financial assets. Table 6.1 provides a summary statement of the U.S. balance of

Table 6.1 *Summary statement of the U.S. balance of payments (credits +, debits −)*

Line	2013	$ million	Line	2013	$ million
	Current account			Capital and financial account	
1	Exports of goods, services, and income receipts	751,962	13	U.S.-owned assets abroad, net [increase/ financial inflow (−)]	−218,757
2	Goods	390,974	14	U.S. official reserve assets	−876
3	Services	166,222	15	U.S. government assets, other than official reserve assets	826
4	Income receipts	196,896	16	U.S. private assets abroad	−218,707
5	Imports of goods, services, and income payments	−823,644	17	Foreign-owned assets in the U.S., net [increase/ financial inflow (+)]	295,540
6	Goods	−570,112	18	Foreign Official Assets in the United States	84,768
7	Services	−112,564	19	Other Foreign Assets in the United States	210,772
8	Income payments	−140,968	20	Capital account transactions, net	−1
9	Unilateral current transfers, net	−34,463	21	Financial derivatives, net	3,888
10	Balance on merchandise trade (lines 2 and 6)	−179,138	22	Balance on private capital and financial account (lines 16, 19, 20 and 21)	−4,048
11	Balance on goods, services, and income (lines 1 and 5)	−71,682	23	Balance on capital and financial account (lines 13, 17, 20, and 21)	80,670
12	Balance on current account (lines 1, 5, and 9)	−106,145	24	Statistical discrepancy (lines 12 and 23 with sign reversed)	25,745

Source: Bureau of Economic Analysis, International Accounts Data, U.S. Department of Commerce, Q1, 2013.

payments system that we shall refer to throughout the next several sections of this chapter.

Balance of payments as a double-entry bookkeeping system

A *double-entry bookkeeping system* records both sides of any two-party transaction with two separate and offsetting entries: a debit entry and a credit entry. The result is that the sum of all the debit entries, in absolute value, is equal to the sum of all the credit entries. The balance-of-payments system is like a typical double-entry accounting system in that every transaction results in two entries being made in the balance-of-payments accounts. A **debit entry** records a transaction that results in a domestic resident making a payment abroad. A debit entry has a negative value in the balance-of-payments account. A **credit entry** records a transaction that results in a domestic resident receiving a payment from abroad. A credit entry has a positive value in the balance-of-payments account.

In the balance-of-payments accounts, an international transaction that results in a credit entry also generates an offsetting debit entry, and an international transaction that results in a debit entry also generates an offsetting credit entry. In the balance-of-payments accounts, therefore, the sum of all the credit entries is equal in absolute value to the sum of all the debit entries.

To illustrate the double-entry nature of the balance-of-payments system, consider the following example. Suppose a U.S. manufacturer exports a shipment of computers to a Canadian firm in exchange for a payment of $2,000. Table 6.2 shows the transaction's effects on the U.S. balance-of-payments accounts. The export of the computers is a $2,000 credit, because it results in a $2,000 payment being made to the U.S. firm from the Canadian firm. Because of the double-entry nature of the system, there is an offsetting $2,000 debit entry made. Note that the sum of the debits in absolute value, $2,000, is equal to the sum of the credits, $2,000.

Debit entry: *A negative entry in the balance of payments that records a transaction resulting in a payment abroad by a domestic resident.*

Credit entry: *A positive entry in the balance of payments that records a transaction resulting in a payment to a domestic resident from abroad.*

ON THE WEB:

Get current data on U.S. international transactions on the Bureau of Economic Analysis Website: www.bea.gov.

Balance-of-payments accounts

Countries exchange a vast array of goods, services, and financial assets. Economists group these transactions by type. There are different categories for each type of transaction, with various categories combined together to form accounts. Therefore, the balance-of-payments system consists of a number of different accounts. For most nations, the number of accounts can be quite large. We can easily understand the balance-of-payments system, however, by focusing on just three accounts: the current account, the private capital account, and the official settlements balance.

Table 6.2 *Recording a U.S. firm's export in the balance-of-payments accounts*

Transaction	Offsetting entries	Credit ($)	Debit ($)
Computer export	$2,000 computer exported by the U.S. firm	2,000	
	$2,000 payment received by the U.S. firm		−2,000

Current account:
Measures the flow of goods, services, income, and transfers or gifts between domestic residents, businesses, and governments, and the rest of the world.

The current account

The **current account** measures the flow of goods, services, and income across national borders. It also includes transfers or gifts from the domestic government and residents to foreign residents and governments, and foreign transfers to the domestic country. The four basic categories within the current account are goods, services, income, and unilateral transfers. Table 6.1 on page 158 shows the exports and imports of goods, services, and income for the United States on lines 1 through 8. Line 9 is for the unilateral transfers category. Let's examine each of these four categories of the current account.

Goods

The goods category measures the imports and exports of tangible goods. This category includes trade in foods, industrial materials, capital goods (such as machinery), autos, and consumer goods. An export of any of these items is a credit in the goods category, because this would result in a payment from abroad. An import of any of these items is a debit in the goods category, because this would result in a payment made abroad.

Most economists consider the goods category to be the most accurately measured balance-of-payments category, because it measures the trade of tangible items that, in many countries, must be registered with customs agents.

Services

The services category measures the imports and exports of services, tourism and travel, and military transactions. Payments, royalties, or fees received from abroad for providing consulting, insurance, banking, or accounting services, for example, are recorded as credits in the service category. Likewise, payments, royalties, or fees sent abroad for the import of these services is a debit in the service category. The service category also includes the import and export of military equipment, services, and aid.

To understand how travel and tourism services appear in the balance of payments, consider a domestic college student who traveled abroad during a semester break. Expenditures by this student on items such as a rail pass and hotel accommodations are imports, or debits, in the service category because these services are, in a sense, imported by the student.

The imports and exports of services are much more difficult to measure than exports and imports of goods. Because a tangible item is not registered at a customs point, it can be very difficult to estimate the amount of services provided internationally. Hence economists refer to services as *invisibles*.

Income

The income category tabulates interest and dividend payments to foreign residents and governments who hold domestic financial assets and payments received by domestic residents, and governments who hold financial assets abroad. It also includes the compensation of employees who are temporarily (one year or less) living abroad.

To illustrate how investment income appears in the balance of payments, suppose a U.K. resident receives an interest payment on a German treasury bill that she holds. The interest payment is an export, or credit, in the income category of the U.K. balance of payments because there is a receipt of a payment from abroad. Therefore, income payments received by domestic residents who hold financial assets abroad are credits, or exports, whereas income payments made to foreign residents who hold domestic financial assets are debits, or imports.

It is important to note that economists do not record the *purchase* of a financial asset in the service category. Only the income earned on the financial asset is included in the current account, because income earned on assets can be used for current consumption.

Unilateral transfers

The unilateral transfers category measures international transfers, or gifts, between individuals, charitable organizations, and governments. This category, therefore, records the offsetting entries of exports or imports for which nothing except *goodwill* is expected in return. To illustrate how a gift appears in the unilateral transfers category, suppose the U.S. government sends $500,000 worth of rice as humanitarian aid to a country that had just experienced a flood. The export of the rice appears in the goods category as a credit. However, the U.S. government expects no payment for this export. A debit entry appears in the unilateral transfers category, indicating that the United States effectively has imported a $500,000 payment of goodwill from the foreign country. (For the United States and other countries that are sources of unilateral transfers, these amounts typically account for small portions of their current accounts, but for some recipient nations the transfers can be very important; see *Management Notebook: For a few nations, the "remittance business" generates a substantial portion of total income.*)

MANAGEMENT NOTEBOOK

For a few nations, the "remittance business" generates a substantial portion of total income

When people who move from their home nation to another country to work and earn income, they usually do not forget about family members and friends back home. These people often send portions of their earnings back to families and friends in their nation of origin.

For a country within which such an individual is residing while working, the funds that the individual sends home constitute a unilateral transfer in the current account. For the nation in which the recipients of the transfer reside, the funds are income receipts in its current account. Economists commonly refer to such receipts as "remittances" from abroad.

In some nations, remittances are so substantial that the associated incomes exceed those that residents derive from any of the nations' largest businesses.

Hence, the receipt of remittances from abroad constitutes these nations' largest income-producing "business." Figure 6.1 indicates the 10 nations that receive the largest share of their total national income from cross-border transfers, with the primary remittance-source countries indicated parenthetically. For these 10 nations, cross-border remittances account for at least $9 out of every $100 of total income received by their residents.

For critical analysis: In the current accounts of the source countries indicated in parentheses in Figure 6.1, are the remittances flowing to the 10 nations recorded as credits or debits? Explain.

Capital and financial account:
A tabulation of the flows of financial assets between domestic private residents and businesses and foreign private residents and businesses.

The capital and financial account

The private **capital and financial account** measures the outflow of domestic assets abroad and the inflow of foreign assets into the domestic country that result from transactions involving private (non-governmental) individuals and companies. The private capital and financial account includes transactions of private domestic financial assets and foreign financial assets. These financial assets include physical assets and financial assets such as bonds, bills, stocks, deposits, and currencies.

The private capital and financial account also includes net capital account transactions and net financial derivatives. The net financial derivatives account records cross-border transaction in financial derivatives. The private net capital account transactions consist primarily of two major categories. The first category records purchases and sales of "non-produced and non-financial assets." This includes the sale or purchases of items such as mineral rights or oil-drilling rights, and items such as copyrights and trademarks. The second category of net capital account transactions

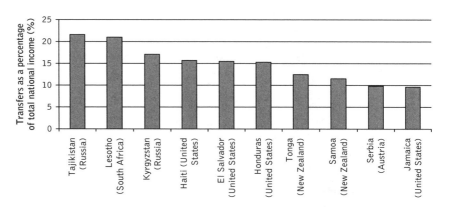

Figure 6.1 Nations with largest shares of total national income received from unilateral transfers

For these 10 nations, unilateral transfers from other countries (main sources indicated in parentheses) account for more than 9 percent of total national income receipts.

Source: World Bank.

records "capital transfers." These transfers consist of items such as large insurance payments for catastrophic loss, such as that caused by Hurricane Katrina in 2005.

The private capital and financial account tabulates two types of asset *flow*: investment flows, and changes in banks' and brokers' cash deposits that arise from foreign transactions. Investment flows include the following:

- Purchases of foreign securities by domestic residents and purchases of domestic securities by foreign residents
- Lending to foreign residents by domestic residents and borrowing by domestic residents from foreign residents
- Investment by domestic firms in their foreign affiliates and investment by foreign firms in their domestic affiliates

A debit entry in the private capital and financial account, for example, records the purchase of a foreign financial asset by a domestic private resident, because this transaction results in a payment made abroad. Likewise, a credit entry records the purchase of a domestic financial asset by a foreign private resident, as this transaction generates a payment from abroad.

Table 6.1 (page 158) shows the categories of the private capital and financial account for the first quarter of 2013 on lines 16, 19, 20, and 21. These categories tabulate primarily private transactions of domestic assets and foreign assets. Changes in private U.S. assets abroad reflect an increase or decrease in private ownership of foreign assets. A net capital outflow means that the net purchases of foreign assets by domestic residents exceed the net purchases of domestic assets by private foreign residents. Changes in foreign assets in the United States reflect an increase or decrease in private foreign ownership of domestic assets. A net financial inflow means that the net purchases of domestic assets by private foreign residents exceeds the net purchases of foreign assets by domestic private residents. (Financial flows between China and Germany have recently experienced an upswing; see *Management Notebook: Residents of China invest in German engineering*.)

MANAGEMENT NOTEBOOK

Residents of China invest in German engineering

Some firms in Germany are called *Mittelstand companies*. They are a collection of small, traditionally family-owned engineering businesses—including firms operating within diverse industries such as automotive parts manufacturing, machine building, and solar power—that typically employ fewer than 500 people. Many of these firms have been operating as independent businesses for decades.

During this decade, however, residents of China have acquired ownership of the assets of dozens of the Mittelstand companies that continue to operate in Germany. Each year that such acquisitions have occurred, hundreds of billions of yuan have flowed out of China as financial investments in Germany and thereby have generated debits in China's capital and financial account. Simultaneously, hundreds of billions of euros have flowed into Germany and consequently have generated credits in Germany's capital and financial account.

For critical analysis: As the Mittelstand companies that are now Chinese-owned but continue to produce in Germany have generated annual profits for their owners, are these profits credits or debits in China's balance of payments—and in which of China's accounts? What about for Germany?

The official settlements balance

Official settlements balance: *A balance-of-payments account that tabulates transactions of reserve assets by official government agencies.*

The third and final account, the **official settlements balance**, measures the transactions of financial assets and deposits by official government agencies. Typically, the central banks and finance ministries, or treasuries, of national governments conduct these types of official transaction.

It is common for foreign central banks and government agencies to keep deposit accounts with other central banks. If, for example, the U.S. Treasury or Federal Reserve were to make a deposit with the Bank of England, the deposit appears as a capital outflow, or *debit*, in the U.S. balance of payments. If the Bank of England were to make a deposit with the Federal Reserve, however, the deposit is a capital inflow, or *credit*, in the U.S. balance of payments. In Table 6.1 (p. 158), line 14 shows the U.S. official assets, including gold and foreign currencies and special drawing rights, a composite currency at the International Monetary Fund, discussed in greater detail in Chapter 14. Line 15 shows other U.S. government assets. Foreign official assets in the United States are shown on line 18 of Table 6.1. The official settlements balance is the sum of lines 14 and 18.

Deficits and surpluses in the balance of payments

If we sum all of the debits and credits that appear in the current account, private capital and financial account, and official settlements balance, the total should be zero. However, this seldom happens in practice. A number of transactions are missed in the accounting process or hidden from the process intentionally. For example, illegal transactions are hidden from government agencies, and some legal transactions may be hidden from government agencies, such as customs officials, to avoid taxes. Furthermore, government statisticians make errors in their tabulation of credits and debits.

If the sum of the credits and debits in the current account, private capital account, and official settlements is not zero, then an offsetting entry appears in the balance of payments. Economists call this offsetting entry the *statistical discrepancy*. The statistical discrepancy can be very large. Line 24 of Table 6.1 shows that the statistical discrepancy for the United States for the first quarter of 2013 was more than $25 billion.

The *overall balance of payments* is the sum of the credits and debits in the current account, private capital and financial account, official settlements, and the statistical discrepancy. Because debit entries offset each and every credit entry, and the statistical discrepancy offsets any errors, the overall balance of payments necessarily is equal to zero.

It is common, and somewhat confusing, when economists and the media refer to balance-of-payments deficits or surpluses. As explained above, ignoring the statistical discrepancy, the overall balance of payments must sum to zero. Therefore, what economists and the media refer to is something other than the overall balance of payments.

A *balance-of-payments deficit* refers to a situation in which the official settlements balance is positive. Ignoring a statistical discrepancy, if the sum of the credits and debits in the current account, government assets other than official reserves assets, and the private capital and financial account is negative, private payments made to foreigners exceeds private payments received from foreigners. In this case, the official settlements balance must be positive, and is called a balance-of-payments deficit. A situation where the sum of the debits and credits in the current account, government assets other than official reserve assets, and private capital and financial account is positive means that private payments received from foreigners exceed private payments made to foreigners. In this case, the official settlements balance is negative, and is called a *balance-of-payments surplus*. A *balance-of-payments equilibrium* refers to a situation where the sum of the debits and credits in the current account and the private capital account is zero, and thus the official settlements balance is zero. Therefore, we can conclude the following:

A balance of payments equilibrium, ignoring a statistical discrepancy, arises when the sum of the debits and credits in the current account, government assets other than official reserve assets, and the private capital and financial account equal zero, so that the official settlements balance is zero. A balance-of-payments deficit corresponds to a positive official settlements balance, and a balance-of-payments surplus corresponds to a negative official settlements balance.

Other deficit and surplus measures

Economists use other deficit and surplus measures that are part of the balance-of-payments system. The *balance on merchandise trade* is the sum of the debit and credit entries in the merchandise or goods category. If the sum of the debit entries in this category exceeds the sum of the credit entries, then the balance on merchandise trade is negative, and there is a deficit in merchandise trade. If the sum of the debit entries is less than the sum of the credit entries, then the balance on merchandise trade is positive, and there is a merchandise trade surplus. Table 6.1 (page 158) lists merchandise or goods credits on line 2, and debits on line 6. The sum of the two amounts is the balance on merchandise trade, and this balance appears on line 10 of Table 6.1. Because the debits, or merchandise imports, exceed the credits, or merchandise exports, the total is a negative amount representing a merchandise deficit on line 10. (Recently, Japan joined the United States on the list of nations experiencing merchandise trade deficits; see *Policy Notebook: Japan enters a new trade era.*)

POLICY NOTEBOOK

Japan enters a new trade era

For nearly every year between 1948 and 2012, Japan's economy operated with surpluses in its merchandise trade balance. In 2012, however, Japan experienced its first annual merchandise trade deficit since 1980.

Most economists forecast that 2012 is unlikely to join 1980 as an isolated trade-deficit year, but instead is more likely to be the first of many such years to come. The key factor contributing to Japan's shift to a status as net importer of physical goods is that other countries, such as China and South Korea, have developed comparative advantages in producing an array of manufactured products, such as toys, electronics, and autos. As Japanese residents' comparative advantage in producing such products has disappeared, its exports of these items have decreased, and the nation's merchandise trade balance has swung to a deficit.

For critical analysis: What do you suppose has happened to the merchandise trade balances of China and South Korea in recent years?

The *balance on goods, services, and income* is the sum of the debit and credit entries that appear in the merchandise, service, and income categories. If the total of the debit entries, or imports, exceeds the sum of the credit entries, or exports, then there is a deficit in goods, services, and income. If the total of the debit entries, or imports, is less than the sum of the credit entries, or exports, then there is a surplus in goods, services, and income. Table 6.1 provides the balance on goods, services, and income on line 11. This amount is negative, indicating that the United States experienced a negative balance, or deficit, on goods, services, and income in 2013.

As explained earlier, the current account includes the categories of goods, services, income, and unilateral transfers. Thus the *balance on the current account* is the sum of all the debit and credit entries in these categories. The current account balance is the most reported balance-of-payments measure. If the sum of the debit entries exceeds the sum of the credit entries, then there is a current account deficit. If the sum of the debit entries is less than the sum of the credit entries, then there is a current account surplus. Table 6.1 provides the balance on the current account on line 12. This balance is also negative, indicating that the United States experienced a negative balance, or deficit, on the current account for 2013.

The *balance on the private capital and financial account* reflects some non-financial transfers and the net flow of financial assets purchased by private individuals. As explained earlier, purchases of foreign financial assets by private domestic residents represent a capital outflow, and appear as a debit. Purchases of domestic financial assets by private foreign residents represent a capital inflow, and appear as a credit. The balance on the capital and financial account reflects the net inflow or outflow of capital. If the debit entries exceed the credit entries, there is a net capital outflow. If the debit entries are less than the credit entries, there is a net capital inflow. This balance appears on line 22 of Table 6.1. This negative balance indicates that private inflows of financial assets in United States exceeded private outflows of financial assets in the first quarter of 2013.

> *Fundamental Issue #1: What is a country's balance of payments, and what does it measure?* The balance of payments is an accounting system used to tabulate a nation's international transactions. The balance-of-payments system measures transactions of goods, services, income, unilateral transfers, private transactions of financial assets, and official reserves.

THE ROLE OF FOREIGN EXCHANGE MARKETS IN THE GLOBAL MARKETPLACE

In a sense, the *markets for foreign exchange* are the financial plumbing that facilitates the flow of goods and services. As you learned in Chapter 1, the *foreign exchange market* is a system of private banks, foreign exchange brokers, and central banks through which households, firms and governments buy and sell the currencies of other nations, or foreign exchange. Providing an arrangement for valuing transactions and delivering payments, the foreign exchange markets promote the flow of goods, services, and assets among nations. **Exchange rates**, which are the market prices of foreign exchange, are a critical element of this system.

Exchange rate:
Expresses the value of one currency relative to another currency as the number of units of one currency required to purchase one unit of the other currency.

How foreign exchange rates and foreign exchange markets facilitate global transactions

As an example of the role of exchange rates, suppose you decide to purchase a new smartphone. You select a smartphone manufactured by a South Korean company with a dollar price of $300. Your decision to purchase this particular piece of equipment depends largely on its price. Conveniently, the price is denominated in your own currency, the currency you have in your billfold or handbag, or in your bank account. Your payment to the appliance store for the smartphone is therefore a simple, straightforward transaction.

The South Korean residents who own the South Korean digital-device company, however, must pay the company's workers and suppliers in units of the South Korean currency, the won. South Korean residents do not want to receive dollars. Therefore, after they receive a dollar-denominated bank deposit as payment from the U.S. digital-device retailer for orders of additional smartphones, South Korean residents who own the digital device-manufacturing company deposit the payment with their bank, which converts the proceeds into won. They can now make payments to their workers and suppliers from a won-denominated bank account.

The role of the exchange rate

How many won is each dollar worth? That is, what is the value of the dollar relative to the won? This is what an exchange rate tells us. An exchange rate expresses the value of one currency relative to another. It expresses the number of units of one currency required to purchase one unit of another currency, and thereby converts the value of this transaction into local currency terms.

The role of the foreign exchange market

What role does the foreign exchange market perform in the previous example involving the South Korean firm? The notion of a foreign exchange market may invoke the image of frantic traders in shirtsleeves and visors hustling money on a cluttered trading floor, with their actions determining the quotations for currencies that we see in daily newspapers such as the *Wall Street Journal* and the *Financial Times*. In our example, however, a foreign exchange market is not prominent. The South Korean company uses the services of its bank, not the foreign exchange market. Further, dollars and won never crossed international borders. Only the smartphones did.

Foreign-currency-denominated financial instrument: *A financial asset, such as a bond, a stock, or a bank deposit, whose value is denominated in the currency of another nation.*

Indeed, the actual flow of currencies across national borders is an insignificant element of the foreign exchange market. The bulk of foreign exchange transactions occur in cyberspace via digital devices and computers. Hard currency flows usually arise only as a result of activities such as tourism or illegal transactions. The financial assets that are typically traded in foreign exchange markets are **foreign-currency-denominated financial instruments**, which are financial assets such as bonds, stocks, and especially bank deposits denominated (valued) in terms of another nation's currency.

How a foreign exchange transaction is conducted

Let's return to the previous example, and consider how a foreign exchange transaction might have been conducted. Suppose you purchased your smartphone from the retailer Best Buy. After selling a number of smartphones, the managers of Best Buy decide to purchase more equipment from Samsung, a South Korean digital-device firm. As shown in Figure 6.2, Best Buy presents a $1 million payment to Samsung, which, in turn, presents the payment to its bank, Industrial Bank of Korea, for deposit.

As stated earlier, Samsung must pay its workers and suppliers in won. Hence, it prefers its deposit to be denominated in won. Industrial Bank of Korea, acting on behalf of Samsung, must exchange the $1 million payment for won. Typically, Industrial Bank of Korea has two options. The first is to contact another large bank, say Citigroup, and negotiate an exchange of dollars for won.

The second option is to contact a *foreign exchange broker*. A foreign exchange broker brings together buyers and sellers of currencies in return for a commission. Foreign exchange brokers constantly survey market participants to determine who is willing to buy or sell various currencies and at what exchange rates those parties are willing to trade. Because brokers collect and centralize this information, they typically have superior exchange rate information. On the one hand, the primary benefit of working with a broker is to reduce information costs that may result in a lower price for a particular currency. On the other hand, dealing directly with another bank eliminates the commission that a broker charges.

As shown in the figure, the foreign exchange broker may exchange information with Deutsche Bank, Bank of America, UBS, and Kwangju Bank. Let's suppose that Industrial Bank of Korea works with the broker, who has determined that UBS has the lowest price for won. When the broker receives its commission, it connects an agent of Industrial Bank of Korea with an agent at UBS, who then completes an electronic transfer of U.S. dollars for won at the agreed rate of exchange.

What is the foreign exchange market?

The foreign exchange market is the oldest and largest financial market in the world. As discussed in Chapter 1, the average daily turnover in this market is more than $4 trillion. To make this number more relevant, consider that in past years, the average daily turnover in the foreign exchange market is nearly five times the size of the market for U.S. government securities—the world's second largest financial market— and more than 25 times the combined volume of the world's 10 largest stock markets.

A global market

Unlike stock or commodity markets, the foreign exchange market has no central trading floor where buyers and sellers meet. Foreign exchange traders conduct most foreign exchange trades by telephone or computer, so the foreign exchange market has evolved into a truly global market with transactions throughout the world. Nonetheless, most transactions are concentrated in a few major trading centers. The largest foreign exchange trading centers are, in rank order, the United Kingdom, the United States, Japan, Singapore, Germany, France, Hong Kong, and Switzerland.

A 24-hour market

The foreign exchange market is open 24 hours a day, except for short gaps on weekends. Starting at the international dateline, trading first opens in Asian-Pacific markets. Before these markets close, trading opens in the Middle East and then in Europe. In the middle of the trading day in Europe, trading opens in New York. It then begins in the Western United States. Before North American markets close, trading begins once again in Asian-Pacific markets.

Market participants and instruments

Figure 6.2 on page 170 illustrates a hypothetical foreign exchange transaction in which the primary options for Industrial Bank of Korea are to trade with another large bank

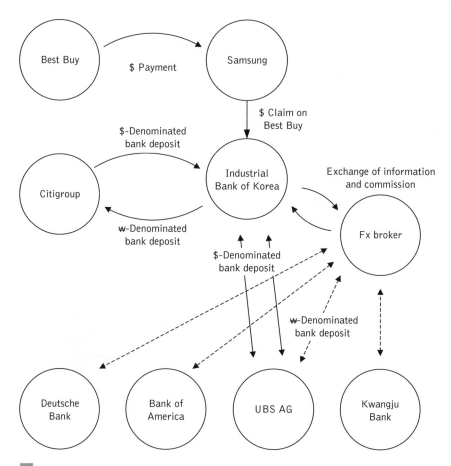

Figure 6.2 *How a foreign exchange transaction is conducted*

Samsung receives a dollar-denominated payment ($) from Best Buy. Samsung presents the payment to Industrial Bank of Korea. This South Korean bank, acting on behalf of Samsung, must exchange the dollar-denominated payment for won (₩). Industrial Bank of Korea typically has two options. The first option is to contact another large bank, such as Citigroup, and negotiate an exchange of dollars for won. The second option is to contact a foreign exchange broker. The foreign exchange broker connects an agent of Industrial Bank of Korea with an agent at Union Bank of Switzerland (UBS), who then completes an electronic transfer of U.S. dollars for won at an agreed rate of exchange.

or with a foreign exchange broker. These two types of financial institution make up nearly 85 percent of all foreign exchange market transactions. Global banks account for approximately two-thirds of the market volume, while foreign exchange brokers and dealers account for approximately 20 percent. The remainder of foreign exchange volume involves non-financial businesses. This latter group has grown and become more diverse as more businesses and individuals have found easier modes of access to the foreign exchange markets via so-called *retail* foreign-currency trading. Today, retail trades contribute more than $380 billion per day to the aggregate quantity of currency exchanges, or almost 10 percent of total global trading volume.

As you will discover in the remainder of this chapter, a wide array of financial instruments are traded on the foreign exchange market. It is not uncommon for the values of individual trades in these foreign exchange instruments to exceed $250 million. Studies show that foreign exchange market volumes are so large that transactions of this magnitude have little if any effect on currency values. In addition, quoted prices on instruments traded in the foreign exchange market change quickly, often more than 20 times per minute.

> *Fundamental Issue #2: What is the role of foreign exchange markets in the global marketplace?* The foreign exchange market is a system of private banks, brokers, and central banks through which households, firms, and governments buy and sell foreign exchange. These institutions develop market mechanisms for valuing transactions and delivering payments, thereby promoting the flows of goods and services among nations. The foreign exchange market is the oldest and largest financial market in the world. This market is truly a global market that is, for all practical purposes, open 24 hours a day.

THE SPOT MARKET FOR FOREIGN EXCHANGE

In the previous example, we assumed that the managers at Fuji Bank wanted to convert its dollar holdings into yen immediately. The market in this example is the **spot market** for foreign exchange, which is a market for immediate purchase and delivery of currencies. Delivery in the spot market for foreign exchange usually occurs within 2–3 days. The media publish spot rates that pertain to the trading of foreign currency-denominated deposits among major banks for $1,000,000 or more. You will examine other important foreign exchange markets and instruments later in this chapter.

Spot market: *A market for immediate purchase and delivery of currencies.*

Spot exchange rates are the market prices of foreign exchange in the spot market. Table 6.3 overleaf, displays spot exchange rates published on the Web sites or news outlets of business media such as the *Wall Street Journal* or the *Financial Times*.

The spot exchange rates in Table 6.3 are for foreign exchange transactions undertaken in the London market, and they represent the rate that a currency sold for at the close of the market. Notice in the text at the top of the Table 6.3 that the rates apply to trading among banks in amounts of $1 million and more. This means that the quoted spot rates pertain to very large transactions. Smaller spot transactions, such as those involving individuals and small- to medium-sized businesses, incur less favorable exchange rates. Table 6.3 displays two versions of the spot rate: *U.S. dollar per currency* and *currency per U.S. dollar*. In the next section, we shall explain these two versions of the spot rate. In later sections you will find out about various ways in which economists use spot rates to construct other useful measures of a currency's value.

Exchange rates as relative prices

Because an exchange rate relates the values of two currencies, it is a relative price economists call a *bilateral exchange rate* (bilateral means "two sides"). Table 6.3 displays

Table 6.3 *Spot rates for currency exchange. Values below are derived from data for the London closing rates and pertain to transactions among banks in the amount of $1 million or more.*

Country (currency)	U.S. dollar per currency[1]	Previous close	Currency per U.S. dollar[1]	Previous close	Bank of England Index[2]
Argentina (peso)	0.1850	0.1853	5.4063	5.3958	
Australia (Australian $)	0.9065	0.9176	1.1031	1.0898	101.89
Brazil (real)	0.4414	0.4416	2.2653	2.2647	
Canada (Canadian $)	0.9445	0.9514	1.0588	1.0511	110.05
Denmark (Danish krone)	0.1721	0.1731	5.8117	5.7768	107.64
Euro (€)	1.2894	1.2730	0.7756	0.7855	95.39
Hong Kong (HK$)	0.1290	0.1290	7.7547	7.7540	
Japan (yen)	0.0099	0.0100	100.9050	100.0250	143.78
Malaysia (ringgit)	0.3136	0.3142	3.1885	3.1827	
Mexico (Mexican peso)	0.0765	0.0776	13.0721	12.8815	
Thailand (baht)	0.0321	0.0333	31.1300	30.0265	
United Kingdom (£)	1.4883	1.5066	0.6719	0.6637	79.93
United States ($)	–	–	–	–	87.15

[1] Closing midpoint value.

[2] Bank of England nominal effective exchange rate index (January 2005 = 100).

Sources: www.ft.com; www.bankofengland.co.uk.

two columns for spot exchange rates. The first is the *U.S. dollar per currency*, or how many U.S. dollars it takes to purchase one unit of a foreign currency. For example, in Table 6.3 the exchange rate for the U.S. dollar relative to the British pound (£) is 1.4883 $/£, meaning that a trader must give 1.4883 U.S. dollars in exchange for one British pound.

The exchange rate also expresses how many foreign currency units it takes to purchase one dollar, or *currency per U.S. dollar*. This is the reciprocal of the U.S.-dollar-per-currency rate. Hence, the rate of exchange of the British pound for the U.S. dollar is 1/(1.4883 $/£), or 0.6719 £/$, so a trader must provide 0.6719 pounds in exchange for one U.S. dollar. Because there are two different ways to express an exchange rate, it is important to be sure whether an exchange rate is a U.S.-dollar-per-currency rate, or a currency-per-U.S.-dollar rate.

Currency appreciation and depreciation

As you can see in Table 6.3, the U.S.-dollar-per-currency rate for the British pound in Table 6.3 changed from 1.5066 $/£ to 1.4883 $/£. This means that the dollar *appreciated* against the pound, because the number of dollars required to purchase one pound decreased. In other words, the dollar price of the pound fell. Hence, we say that the pound *depreciated* relative to the dollar. Likewise, the currency-per-U.S.-dollar rate changed from 0.6637 £/$ to 0.6719 £/$, indicating that the number of pounds required to purchase one dollar increased, so that the pound price of the dollar rose.

We can determine the rate of appreciation or depreciation by calculating the percentage change in the exchange rate. We calculate the percentage change of an exchange rate by subtracting the previous value of the exchange rate from the new value, dividing this difference by the previous value, and multiplying by 100. Using the U.S.-dollar-per-currency rates in Table 6.3, the percentage change in the spot exchange rate is $[(1.4883 - 1.5066)/1.5066] \times 100 = -1.22$ percent. In words, the pound depreciated relative to the dollar by 1.22 percent. Using the currency-per-U.S.-dollar rate, the percentage change is $[(0.6719 - 0.6637)/0.6637] \times 100 = +1.24$ percent.

The first percentage change calculation is negative, because the number of dollars required to purchase a pound decreased. The second percentage change calculation is positive, because the number of pounds required to purchase a dollar increased. As you can see, in order to determine whether a positive change or a negative change indicates an appreciation or depreciation, we must know whether the exchange rate is expressed as a U.S.-dollar-per-currency rate or as a currency-per-U.S.-dollar rate.

Cross rates

Table 6.3 indicates that, on this particular day, the U.S.-dollar-per-currency and currency-per-U.S.-dollar exchange rates for the euro (€) were equal to 1.2894 $/€ and 0.7756 €/$, respectively. Suppose, however, that our interest is in the rate of exchange between the British pound and the euro, not the rate of exchange between the dollar and the euro. To determine this rate of exchange, we can compute a *cross rate*, which is another bilateral exchange rate that we calculate from two bilateral rates.

In Table 6.3, the U.S.-dollar-per-currency rate for the British pound is 1.4883 $/€, and the U.S.-dollar-equivalent rate for the euro is 1.2894 $/€. Using these two bilateral rates, it is straightforward to calculate either the British-pound-per-euro exchange rate or the euro-per-British-pound exchange rate.

To calculate the British-pound-per-euro cross rate, we divide the dollar rate of exchange for the euro by the dollar exchange rate for the British pound. Thus, the pound-euro cross rate equals

$$(1.2894 \ \$/€) / (1.4883 \ \$/£)$$

Dividing by a fraction is the same as multiplying by the reciprocal of the fraction. Therefore, we can express the cross rate as

$$1.2894/1.4883 \times \$/€ \times £/\$$$

Notice in the calculation above, the dollar cancels out because it appears in the numerator of one fraction and the denominator of another. This yields the British-pound-per-euro cross rate, which is 0.8664 £/€.

If we wish to determine the euro-per-British-pound cross rate, we invert the British-pound-per-euro cross rate, which yields

$$1/(0.8664 \ £/€) = 1.1543 \ €/£$$

173

Using the U.S.-dollar-per-currency rates for the British pound and the euro, we have calculated a cross rate of exchange between the British pound and the euro.

The foreign exchange sections of major newspapers provide cross rates for many high-volume currencies in a *cross-rate table*. Table 6.4 is an example. This cross-rate table lists the currencies across the top row and the left-hand column. The cross rates in the table are the exchange rates between the currencies of the countries listed on the corresponding row and column. When the same country appears on both the row and the column, the entry is either blank or 1. The first column provides the U.S.-dollar-per-currency rate for each currency listed on the corresponding row. Therefore, the first row provides the currency-per-U.S.-dollar exchange rates.

Real exchange rates

So far we have discussed **nominal exchange rates**. These are exchange rates that do not reflect changes in nations' price levels. By measuring rates of depreciation and appreciation, the nominal exchange rate gauges changes in the market value of our own currency in exchange for a foreign currency.

What if we are interested in the amount of foreign *goods and services* that we can buy with our domestic currency, rather than how many units of the foreign currency we can purchase? The **real exchange rate** adjusts the nominal exchange rate for changes in both nations' price levels, and thereby measures the *purchasing power of domestic goods and services in exchange for foreign goods and services*. Consequently, appraising how much of another country's goods and services individuals and firms can obtain by trading their own nation's goods and services, using their own currency as a medium of exchange in the transaction, requires knowing the value of the real exchange rate.

Nominal exchange rate changes

To see why the real exchange rate matters, consider the bilateral exchange relationship between the United States and China between July 2005 and July 2012. This period provides an excellent example because of the appreciation of the yuan, the currency of China, relative to the dollar. In July 2005, the U.S. dollar-per-yuan spot

ON THE WEB:

For daily exchange rates, a currency converter for 164 currencies, and cross rates, visit the homepage of Oanda at www.Oanda.com.

Nominal exchange rate: *A bilateral exchange rate that is unadjusted for changes in the two nations' price levels.*

Real exchange rate: *A bilateral exchange rate that has been adjusted for price changes that occurred in the two nations.*

Table 6.4 *Cross-rate table based on rates in Table 6.3. The values are cross-rates of exchange between the currency listed in the row relative to the currency listed in the column. The first value listed in the column below the dollar, for example, is the U.S.-dollar-per-Canadian-dollar cross rate.*

Currency	U.S. dollar	Canadian dollar	Euro	British pound
U.S. dollar	–	1.0588	0.7756	0.6719
Canadian dollar	0.9445	–	0.7325	0.6346
Euro	1.2894	1.3652	–	0.8663
British pound	1.4883	1.5758	1.1543	–

rate was 0.1220 $/yuan. By 2012, the yuan's value had risen, and the exchange rate had climbed to 0.1584 $/yuan.

Based on the values of these nominal exchange rates, the rate of appreciation of the yuan relative to the dollar between 2005 and 2012 was equal to $[(0.1584 - 0.1220)/0.1220] \times 100 = 29.84$ percent. This means that in 2012 it required 29.8 percent more dollars to buy a yuan in the foreign exchange market than was necessary in 2005.

Measuring price changes: consumer price indexes

To measure the purchasing power of a nation's currency, economists require measures of overall levels of prices. International economists typically find that a particularly useful measure of a nation's price level is the country's **consumer price index (CPI)**, which is a measure of the economy-wide price level. Economists calculate a CPI by selecting fixed sets of domestic and foreign goods and services, and tracking the prices of these specific goods and services from year to year.

To illustrate a CPI, let's make up a simple example. Let's call our example the "college consumer price index." Suppose that the "typical" college student spends a quarter of his or her available resources on tuition, a quarter on housing, a quarter on domestically manufactured food, clothing, and supplies, and a quarter on foreign-manufactured food, clothing and supplies. We could then collect information on the average prices of each of these components of the typical college consumer's expenses. Then we could multiply each one by a quarter. Summing the results would then yield a numerical value for our college consumer price index.

Consumer price index (CPI):
A weighted sum of prices of goods and services that a typical consumer purchases each year.

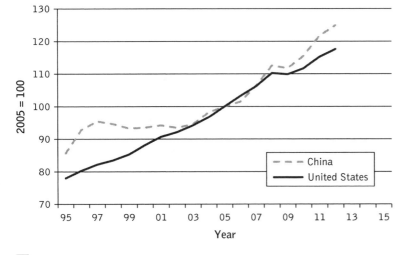

Figure 6.3 *Consumer price indexes in the United States and China*

The consumer price index (CPI) is a weighted average of prices of a fixed group of goods and services. The base year for both nations' consumer price indexes is 2005 and, therefore, equals 100 in that year.

Source: World Bank, *World Development Indicators.*

175

Government agencies of the United States, nations in the Economic and Monetary Union (EMU), and other countries compute the overall consumer price index in the same basic manner as in our fictitious example. The actual computation of an economy-wide CPI is much more complex than in our example, because it is a weighted sum of prices of a full set of goods and services that governments determine that their typical consumers purchase each year. Figure 6.3 displays the U.S. and Chinese consumer price indexes since 1995. Economists express the CPI in *index number* form, where a value of 100 applies to the *base year* for the index. This is a year selected to serve as a foundation for comparing changes in the aggregate price level over time. In the figure, the base year for both nations' consumer price indexes is 2005.

The real exchange rate and real currency appreciation or depreciation

The immediate effects of the increase in the value of the yuan relative to the dollar were that Chinese goods and services effectively became more expensive for U.S. consumers to purchase, and that U.S. goods and services became cheaper from the perspective of Chinese consumers. Something else that also happened between 2005 and 2012, however, was that China had a higher inflation rate than the United States.

In China, the CPI for 2005 (the base year for the CPI) was 100, while the CPI for 2012 was 124.90. Economists use the percentage change in CPI as a measure of the rate of consumer price inflation over a given time interval. Using these figures for China, the rate of consumer price inflation from 2005 to 2012 was $[(124.90 - 100)/100] \times 100 = 24.90$ percent. In the United States, the CPI for 2005 was 100 and for 2012, 117.56. This means that the rate of consumer price inflation in the United States over the same time period was $[(117.56 - 100)/100] \times 100 = 17.56$ percent.

These relative inflation differences matter because changes in the prices of goods and services alter the effective prices that Chinese residents pay for U.S. goods and services and that U.S. residents pay for Chinese goods and services. To see how the inflation differences matter, let's measure the real exchange rates for 2005 and 2012.

To measure the real exchange rate between China and the United States in 2005, we multiply the nominal exchange rate at that time, 0.1220 $/€, by the ratio of the Chinese consumer price index to the U.S. price index, 100/100, to get 0.1220.

To calculate the real exchange rate for 2012, we multiply the nominal exchange rate at the end of that year, 0.1584 $/€, by the ratio of the Chinese consumer price index to the U.S. price index, 124.90/117.56, which yields 0.1683. Using these two real exchange rates implies that the *real rate of appreciation* for the yuan was equal to $[(0.1683 - 0.1220)/0.1220] \times 100 = 37.95$ percent. This calculated real rate of yuan appreciation was slightly higher for the 2005–2012 period than the nominal appreciation rate of 29.84 percent.

The relatively lower rate of consumer inflation in the U.S.—or relatively higher rate of consumer inflation in China—implied that U.S. consumers' purchasing power of Chinese goods and services decreased relative to their purchasing power of U.S. goods and services. Hence, the relatively higher consumer price inflation in China amplified the nominal appreciation in the yuan's value to produce a slightly larger real appreciation in the yuan's value relative to the dollar.

Measuring the overall strength or weakness of a currency: effective exchange rates

Bilateral exchange rates measure the value of a currency relative to *one* other currency. On any given day, a currency will strengthen, or appreciate, against some currencies and weaken, or depreciate, against others. On a given day, the dollar's value may have fallen against the British pound, Japanese yen, and Canadian dollar. Its value may have risen, however, against the euro, Swiss franc, and Mexican peso. So, some bilateral-rates would have fallen and some would have risen. But overall is the dollar "stronger" or "weaker?" To answer this question, economists use an **effective exchange rate**, which is a weighted-average measure of the value of a currency relative to two or more other currencies.

Effective exchange rate: *A weighted-average measure of the value of a currency relative to two or more currencies.*

How economists construct effective exchange rates

It is not practical to measure the value of a currency against every other currency in the world. Thus, in constructing an effective exchange rate, economists include only the currencies that they judge to be most important. What constitutes "important" currencies depends on the particular application. If a businessperson wants to know how changes in the value of the dollar affect U.S. imports and exports, then the individual will include the bilateral exchange rates of the largest trading partners of the United States. If a portfolio manager wants to know how changes in the value of the dollar affect the return on a portfolio of international assets, then the manager will want to include the bilateral exchange rates of the currencies that represent the largest shares of the portfolio. The currencies selected compose what economists call the currency basket.

Like the consumer price index, an effective exchange rate is expressed in an index number form, where a value of 100 applies to the base year, which serves as a reference point in time. Economists then measure changes in the value of the effective exchange rate from this base year. For example, if 2013 is the base year, then the value of the effective exchange rate for 2013 is 100. If the effective exchange rate is 125 for 2014, then we know there was a percentage increase in the effective exchange rate from 2013 to 2014 equal to $[(125 - 100)/100] \times 100 = 25$ percent.

Finally, because an effective exchange rate is a weighted average of bilateral exchange rates, economists select *weights* that place greater emphasis on the more important currencies in the currency basket, and place smaller emphasis on the less important currencies in the currency basket. Economists use these weights to calculate the weighted-average value of the currency relative to all of the currencies in the basket.

What an effective exchange rate tells us

What does an effective exchange rate tell us? On any given day, a currency may depreciate against some currencies and appreciate against others. The weighted-average value of the effective exchange rate tells us what happened, overall, to the value of the currency on that day.

A number of effective exchange rates are available from leading exchange rate sources. The Bank of England publishes effective exchange rates for several currencies, and Figure 6.4 illustrates these rates for the U.S. dollar, the euro, and the Japanese yen. The International Monetary Fund also publishes effective exchange rates in its monthly bulletin *International Financial Statistics*. The Federal Reserve Board publishes several different effective exchange rates for the U.S. dollar in the *Federal Reserve Bulletin*. The *Financial Times* and the *Wall Street Journal* report the J.P. Morgan effective exchange rate index. Figure 6.4 displays effective exchange rates for the U.S. dollar, the U.K. pound, and the Japanese yen since 1980.

The figure shows that there was a dramatic increase in the average value of the dollar over the period 1980 through 1985 and a subsequent decline from 1985

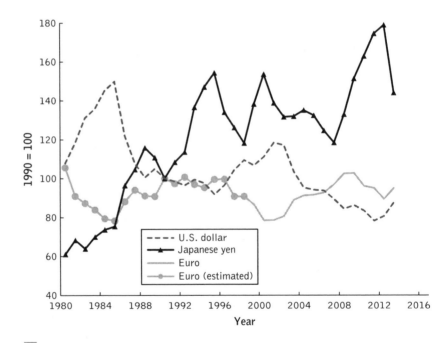

Figure 6.4 *Effective exchange rates since 1980*

Between 1985 and 1995, the average value of the U.S. dollar declined. The average value of the dollar then increased from 1996 through 2001, and declined through 2011 before rising slightly. The average value of the yen generally has increased over time, but sharp declines occurred in the mid-1990s and early 2000s. The average value of the Japanese yen increased considerably from 2008 through 2012 until actions by the Bank of Japan reversed the appreciation. The euro was introduced in 1999. The euro's average value declined until 2002, increased from 2002 through 2006, and then diminished until 2012 before rising slightly. The average values of all three currencies were affected by the global recession that began in 2008 and the debt crisis involving Greece, Cyprus, and other euro-member countries in 2010.

Source: www.bankofengland.co.uk.

through 1988. Following 1988, there was a steady, general decline in the average value of the dollar until 1995, when the dollar began to gain value again. This trend continued until 2001 and, in general, the dollar has declined in value since 2001. The figure shows that for the euro, there was a decline in the average value since its introduction in 1999 through the period until 2002. Since 2002, there has been a steady rise in the average value of the euro.

The Japanese yen rose from an index value of 60 in 1985 to an index value of 150 in 1995, which implied a 150 percent appreciation over the period. Between 1995 and 1998, however, the yen lost more than 13 percent of its overall value, appreciated again the following 2 years, before settling into a general trend downward until 2008. The weighted-average values of all three currencies were affected by the global financial crises. More recently, the weighted-average value of the euro declined with the onset of the debt crisis. During the same period, the average value of the yen increased considerably until the Bank of Japan altered monetary policy, reversing the rise in value.

Real effective exchange rates

Earlier in this chapter, you discovered that it is the real exchange rate that indicates changes in international purchasing power. It is possible to construct a *real effective exchange rate*, which is an effective exchange rate based on real exchange rates instead of nominal exchange rates. A real effective exchange rate is calculated in much the same way as a nominal effective exchange rate. In contrast to calculating effective nominal exchange rates, however, we use real exchange rates in computing the real effective exchange rate. Thus, constructing a real effective exchange rate also requires obtaining CPI data for all countries in the index, converting each nominal exchange rate to a real rate, and completing the remaining calculations as described earlier for nominal effective exchange rates.

> *Fundamental Issue #3: What is the spot foreign exchange market?* The spot market for foreign exchange is the market for contracts requiring immediate delivery of currencies. The spot market for foreign exchange is dominated by large-value transactions among commercial banks and foreign exchange brokers. Spot exchange rates are the prices of currency transactions that occur in this market. Economists use spot exchange rates to measure the appreciation and depreciation of currencies and to construct cross rates, real exchange rates, and effective exchange rates.

FOREIGN EXCHANGE RISK AND THE FORWARD MARKET FOR FOREIGN EXCHANGE

Exchange rates vary over time. Changes in exchange rates expose households, firms, and others who engage in international transactions to potential risk.

Foreign exchange risk

Let's consider an example of how an international transaction may expose a firm to risk from exchange rate changes. Suppose you work for an international property developer based in the United States, and your firm has an interest in commercial real estate in the United Kingdom. The property agents will consider "substantial offers" on the property for a period of 3 months, at which time they will arrange sale of the property to the party submitting the highest offer. It will take approximately three more months for your employer to conclude the transaction and to assume possession of the property.

Based on an estimate of the property's income potential, your managers instruct you to submit a bid of £15 million. Suppose that the exchange rate is currently $1.4883 per pound, so from your firm's perspective, the current price of the bid that you are submitting is $22,324,500, or the dollar price of the offer (£15 million × 1.4883 $/£ = $22,324,500). Your managers have indicated that they value the property at $22,324,500.

Foreign exchange risk: *The risk that the value of a future receipt or obligation will change due to variations in foreign exchange rates.*

Suppose the sellers of the property accept your offer to pay £15 million 6 months from now. Your firm has a foreign currency-denominated obligation that spans time and, therefore, creates a *foreign-exchange-risk exposure*. **Foreign exchange risk** is the prospect that the value of a foreign currency-denominated liability or asset will change because of a variation in the exchange rate.

Suppose that during the next 6 months the pound appreciates against the dollar by 5 percent, to 1.5627 dollars per pound. The British pound price of the commercial estate is still £15 million. The dollar price, however, changes because of the change in the spot exchange rate. The dollar price of the property rises to $23,440,500 (£15 million × 1.5627 $/£ = $23,440,500). Because of the change in the exchange rate, the dollar price of the property increases by $1,116,000, or by 5 percent. By agreeing to the future foreign currency-denominated transaction, your firm incurs a 5 percent increase in their dollar costs from foreign-exchange-risk exposure.

Transaction exposure: *The risk that the revenues or costs associated with a transaction expressed in terms of the domestic currency may change due to variations in exchange rates.*

Types of foreign exchange risk exposure

There are three different ways in which individuals or firms may expose themselves to foreign exchange risk. The first type of foreign exchange exposure, which the previous example illustrates, is **transaction exposure**, which is the risk that the revenues or costs of a transaction may change in terms of the domestic currency. A transaction exposure results when a firm agrees to complete a foreign currency-denominated exchange some time in the future.

Translation exposure: *Foreign exchange risk resulting from the conversion of a firm's foreign currency-denominated assets and liabilities into the domestic currency value.*

The second type of foreign exchange risk is **translation exposure**, which arises when converting the values of foreign currency-denominated assets and liabilities into a single currency value. It is easier to understand translation exposure by considering the balance sheet of a multinational corporation. The assets and liabilities of, say, a Swiss multinational corporation may be denominated in many different currencies. At the end of the year, the accountants at the Swiss corporation tabulate its balance sheet and value all its assets and liabilities in a common currency, the Swiss franc. As the exchange value of the Swiss franc changes, so does the value of assets and liabilities denominated in foreign currencies. The net worth of the company reported in the balance sheet also changes.

The final type of foreign exchange risk is **economic exposure**, which is the effect that exchange rate changes have on a firm's current valuation of future income streams. Economic exposure affects the ability of a firm to compete in a particular market over an extended period. Some economists believe that at least a portion of the foreign direct investment flows described in Chapter 1 results from firms' efforts to avoid economic exposure. Owning a plant or office in a foreign location of operation may help a firm avoid some of the foreign exchange risk that it would have incurred if all its plants and offices were in domestic locations only. (Recently, the fast-food firm McDonald's addressed a significant economic exposure to foreign exchange risk; see *Management Notebook: Why hamburgers are harder to find in Iceland*.)

Economic exposure: *The risk that changes in exchange values might alter today's value of a firm's future income streams.*

MANAGEMENT NOTEBOOK

Why hamburgers are harder to find in Iceland

In the wake of the global financial meltdown of the late 2000s, the multinational seller of fast food McDonald's found itself experiencing losses resulting from a significant economic risk exposure in Iceland. McDonald's imported from Germany the bulk of the ingredients that the company utilized to produce fast food in Iceland. As a consequence of the long-term collapse in the value of the krona, Iceland's currency, the firm's costs of operating in the small nation rose by 100 percent.

McDonald's determined that, in light of this substantial cost increase, it would be unable to compete in the Icelandic fast-food market. To eliminate this economic exposure to continuing losses in Iceland, the company closed its restaurants in that country. The firm indicated that it had no plans to return.

For critical analysis: Why do you think that firms typically regard their transaction and translation exposures to foreign exchange risk to be more of more immediate, sometimes day-to-day concern than their economic exposure to foreign exchange risk?

Hedging foreign exchange risk

When considering foreign exchange risk, it is important to understand that a change in the exchange rate may be positive or negative from the perspective of an individual or firm. Nonetheless, the possibility that the exchange rate may change introduces uncertainty that can make planning difficult. Individuals or firms can attempt to

Hedging: *The act of offsetting or eliminating risk exposure.*

Covered exposure: *A foreign exchange risk that has been completely eliminated with a hedging instrument.*

reduce or eliminate this uncertainty by cutting or removing the foreign exchange risk. **Hedging** is the act of offsetting exposure to risk. An exposure is **covered** if the hedging activity eliminates *all* of the exposure to risk.

There are a number of financial instruments available to offset foreign exchange risk. One such instrument is a *forward contract* for foreign exchange. Later in this chapter you will consider other instruments, *derivative instruments*, used to offset foreign exchange risk.

The forward market for foreign exchange

Let's assume again that you work for the U.S. property developer that has offered to buy a U.K. property. It is highly unlikely that your firm would want to purchase the British pound at the time of notification of acceptance of your company's offer. By immediately purchasing the pound, the firm would have more than $15 million of funds tied up in a foreign currency for 6 months. Your firm, therefore, desires the future delivery of the British pound.

Forward exchange market: *A market for contracts that ensures the future delivery of and payment for a foreign currency at a specified exchange rate.*

The **forward exchange market** is a market for contracts ensuring the future delivery of a currency at a specified exchange rate. Most forward exchange trades are in the amount of $1 million or more, and occur between large commercial banks. Forward exchange rates, which are the prices of contracts traded in the forward exchange market, are quoted in the foreign exchange tables of many business and financial publications. These publications typically provide prices for 1-month, 3-month, 6-month, and 1-year forward contracts.

Covering a transaction with a forward contract

Because a forward contract guarantees a rate of exchange at a future date, it can eliminate foreign exchange risk, or *cover* an exposure. Following acceptance of the firm's offer on the commercial property, it has a *short position* in the pound, which is a future obligation denominated in a foreign currency, the pound. As explained earlier, the firm now has a foreign exchange risk exposure.

You could suggest to your superiors that the firm arrange a 6-month forward contract on the pound, which would cover the transaction. Suppose that at the time the owner of the property accepts your firm's offer, the 6-month forward rate on the pound is 1.5255 $/£. A 6-month forward contract for £15 million guarantees that your firm can purchase the £15 million 6 months from now at an exchange rate of 1.5255. Entering into a forward contract thereby ensures that the final price of the commercial property will, 6 months from now, be $22,882,500 (£15 million × 1.5255 $/£ = $22,882,500). There is no uncertainty about the price of the property, so the transaction is covered.

A firm also can experience transaction exposures resulting from foreign currency-denominated payments that it will receive in the future. In such a situation, a firm has a *long position* because it will receive future amounts denominated in foreign currencies. In this case, the firm can arrange a forward contract enabling it to sell foreign currencies at guaranteed exchange rates. The forward sell contracts will eliminate all of its foreign exchange risks and thus cover its receipts.

In both these examples, firms eliminate positions with foreign exchange risk by entering into forward contracts that ensure the purchase or sale of a foreign currency at a guaranteed price. By assuming equal and offsetting positions in the forward market, firms can eliminate transaction risk and cover their risk positions. The elimination of uncertainty about the future value of foreign currency-denominated assets and liabilities via forward exchange markets can generate additional international transactions of goods, services, and financial instruments.

> *Fundamental Issue #4: What is foreign exchange risk, and what is the role of forward foreign exchange markets?* Foreign exchange risk is the prospect that the values of foreign currency-denominated transactions change because of variations in the exchange rate. There are three types of foreign exchange risk exposure: transaction exposure, translation exposure, and economic exposure. The forward exchange market is a market for contracts ensuring the future delivery of a currency at a specified exchange rate. By guaranteeing a price for the future delivery of a currency, firms can cover their foreign exchange risk, thereby promoting greater flows of goods, services, and financial instruments across nations.

DEMAND FOR AND SUPPLY OF CURRENCIES

So far our discussion has focused on descriptions of the spot and forward exchange markets and the prices or exchange rates in these markets. Now let's consider the factors that determine the value of a nation's currency, using the concepts of supply and demand discussed in Chapter 1. In applying these concepts, we shall assume that there are no obstructions or controls on foreign exchange transactions. In addition, we shall assume that governments do not buy or sell currencies in order to manipulate their value. Under these assumptions, market forces of supply and demand determine the value of a currency.

Demand for a currency

The primary function of a currency is to facilitate transactions. Thus, the demand for a currency is a *derived demand*, meaning that the demand for a currency arises from the demand for the goods, services, and assets that people use the currency to purchase. The demand for the euro, for instance, stems from U.S. residents' demand for European goods, services, and euro-denominated assets. If U.S. consumers' demand for European goods were to increase, then, indirectly, there would be a rise in the demand for the euro to purchase the European goods. (For more analysis of the demand for a currency and changes in the demand for a currency, see *Visualizing Global Economic Issues: The demand for the euro.*)

183

VISUALIZING GLOBAL ECONOMIC ISSUES

The demand for the euro

Figure 6.5 illustrates a hypothetical demand curve for the euro. Notice in panel (a) that the "price" on the vertical axis is the U.S. dollar-per-euro exchange rate ($/€). Because the exchange rate between the dollar and the euro can be expressed as either the dollar-price of the euro ($/€) or the euro-price of the dollar (€/$), it is extremely important to keep in mind that the proper rate, the dollar price of the euro, appears on this vertical axis.

The downward sloping demand curve in panel (a) also illustrates the negative relationship between the exchange rate and the quantity of euros demanded. Suppose that the initial spot exchange rate is S_A, at which the quantity of euros demanded is Q_A. Now suppose that the dollar appreciates relative to the euro to S_B. At this new exchange rate, European goods are relatively less expensive to U.S. consumers. As a result, U.S. consumers would desire to purchase more European goods and require a greater amount of euros to do so. Hence, the quantity demanded of euros rises to Q_B, illustrated by a movement down and along the demand curve from point A to point B.

Now suppose that at the exchange rate S_A, illustrated in panel (b) of Figure 6.5, U.S. consumer tastes for European goods increases. In order to purchase a greater amount of European goods, U.S. consumers desire a greater quantity of euros at the given exchange rate. Hence, there is an increase in the demand for the euro, illustrated by a rightward shift of the demand curve from $D_€$ to $D'_€$ in panel (b) of Figure 6.4.

For critical analysis: Would an appreciation of the dollar relative to the euro always result in a greater quantity demanded of euros? What role does the slope of the demand curve play in determining the answer to this question?

Quantity demanded and the exchange rate

As with goods and services, the demand for a currency satisfies the law of demand. The intuition behind this relationship between the exchange rate and the quantity is that, as the dollar appreciates relative to the euro, and the dollar price of the euro falls, European goods become relatively less expensive to U.S. consumers. As a result, U.S. consumers desire to purchase more European goods and require a greater amount of euros to facilitate these additional transactions. Consequently, there is a negative relationship between the price of the currency and the quantity demanded: a rise in the exchange rate causes a fall in the *quantity demanded* of a currency.

Changes in currency demand

Let's suppose that, at a given exchange rate, U.S. consumers' tastes and preferences for European goods increase. In this case, U.S. consumers desire a larger quantity of

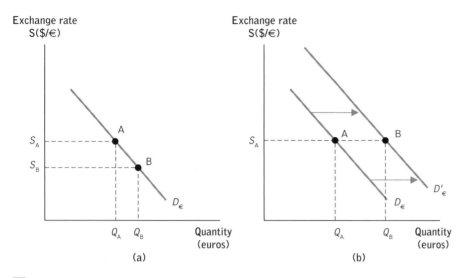

Figure 6.5 *The demand for the euro*

Panel (a) illustrates the demand curve for the euro. A decrease in the exchange rate from S_A to S_B indicates that the U.S. dollar has appreciated relative to the euro. This makes European goods relatively less expensive to U.S. consumers. As a result, U.S. consumers increase their quantity of euros demanded to buy more European goods and services. An increase in U.S. consumers' demand for European goods and services leads to an increase in the demand for the euro. Panel (b) illustrates the increase in demand for the euro by a rightward shift of the demand curve from D_ϵ to D'_ϵ.

euros at the given exchange rate to purchase additional European goods. This is a *change in the demand* for the euro. Because the demand for a currency is a derived demand, the various factors that cause a change in the demand for a currency are all of the factors that cause a change in the foreign demand for that country's goods, services, and assets, such as a change in foreign residents' tastes and preferences for the nation's goods, services, and financial assets.

Supply of a currency

The supply of a currency is also derived from the demand for goods, services, and financial assets. The supply of a currency, however, is derived from *domestic* residents' demand for another nation's goods, services, and financial assets.

Quantity supplied and the exchange rate

To understand the supply of a currency, consider a European consumer's demand for U.S. goods, services, and financial assets and, in turn, for the U.S. dollar. When the European consumer purchases U.S. dollars in order to buy U.S. goods, services, or financial assets, the European consumer exchanges euros for dollars. As a result, there is an increase in the quantity of euros supplied in the foreign exchange market.

Thus, the European demand for the dollar also represents the supply of euros. It is in this way that the supply of the euro is derived from the demand for U.S. goods, services, and financial assets. (To understand how to derive the euro supply curve, see *Visualizing Global Economic Issues: The dollar demand-euro supply relationship*.)

VISUALIZING GLOBAL ECONOMIC ISSUES

The dollar demand-euro supply relationship

To see how the supply of a currency is derived from the demand of a nation's residents for another nation's goods, services, and financial assets, first consider European consumers' demand for the U.S. dollar. Panel (a) of Figure 6.6 illustrates the demand for the dollar. At an initial exchange rate of S_1^*, the quantity demanded of dollars equals Q_A^*. If the dollar were to depreciate—a decline in the €/$ exchange rate—U.S. goods become relatively cheaper to European consumers. As a result, European consumers desire more U.S. goods and, therefore, a greater amount of U.S. dollars to make these additional purchases. Hence, there is a movement down and along the demand curve from point A to point B, and the quantity demanded rises from Q_A^* to Q_B^*.

Panel (b) of Figure 6.6 shows an equivalent way of expressing this relationship. Note that panel (b) plots the quantity of euros on the horizontal and the dollar price of the euro ($/€) on the vertical axis. When the euro appreciates, the $/€ exchange rate rises from S_A to S_B. As European consumers purchase more dollars, they exchange euros for dollars. Hence, there is an increase in the quantity of euros supplied, shown by a movement up and along the supply curve from point A to point B. Thus, there is a positive relationship between the exchange rate and the supply of the euro, as depicted by the upward-sloping supply curve in panel (b).

For critical analysis: How would you derive the supply curve for the U.S. dollar? What factors would influence the demand for the U.S. dollar?

Changes in currency supply

If, at a given exchange rate, there is an increase in the demand for U.S. goods by European consumers, there is an increased demand for the dollar. As European consumers purchase dollars to facilitate additional purchases of U.S. goods, they exchange euros for dollars, increasing the quantity supplied of euros in the foreign exchange market, at the given rate. This is a *change in the supply* of euros. As you can now see, the various factors that cause a change in the supply of a currency are all of the factors that cause a change in the domestic demand for another nation's goods, services, and financial assets.

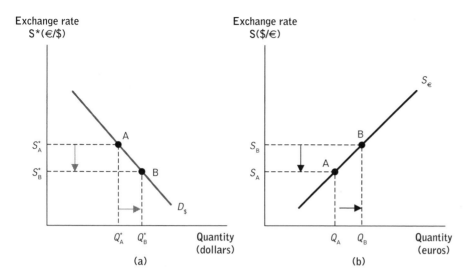

Figure 6.6 *The dollar demand-euro supply relationship*

Panel (a) depicts the demand for the U.S. dollar. A decrease in the euro-per-dollar exchange rate leads to an increase in the quantity of dollars demanded. The quantity of euros supplied in the foreign exchange market increases as more U.S. dollars are purchased with the euro. Panel (b) illustrates the relationship between the dollar-per-euro exchange rate and the quantity of euros supplied. As the dollar-per-euro exchange rate rises, the quantity of euros supplied increases. The supply curve, S_{ϵ}, illustrates the positive relationship between the dollar-per-euro exchange rate and the quantity of euros supplied.

The equilibrium exchange rate

If currencies can flow freely across nations' borders, and governments do not buy or sell currencies in order to manipulate their values, the forces of demand and supply determine equilibrium, or market-clearing, exchange rates. The equilibrium exchange rate is the exchange rate at which the quantity of a currency demanded is equal to the quantity supplied. At the equilibrium exchange rate, the market *clears*, meaning that the quantity demanded of a currency is exactly equal to the quantity supplied. (To understand how the forces of supply and demand determine the equilibrium exchange rate in the supply-and-demand framework, see *Visualizing Global Economic Issues: The equilibrium exchange rate*.)

VISUALIZING GLOBAL ECONOMIC ISSUES

The equilibrium exchange rate

To illustrate the determination of the equilibrium exchange rate, Figure 6.7 on page 188 combines the demand and supply curves for the Japanese yen. Initially,

S_A is the equilibrium dollar-per-yen exchange rate ($/¥). At this exchange rate, the quantity demanded of the yen exactly equals the quantity supplied, so there is neither an excess quantity demanded of the yen nor an excess quantity supplied.

Suppose that at exchange rate S_A, there is an increase in U.S. consumers' demand for Japanese electronic equipment. In order to purchase greater amounts of these Japanese goods, U.S. consumers wish to obtain a larger quantity of yen to facilitate their transactions. In other words, the demand for the yen rises, as shown by a shift of the demand curve from $D_¥$ to $D_¥'$.

At the initial exchange rate S_A, the increase in the demand for the yen results in an excess quantity demanded, which is the difference between quantity Q' and the initial quantity Q_A. The excess quantity of yen demanded generates upward pressure on the $/¥ exchange rate, indicating an appreciation of the yen relative to the dollar. As the exchange rate rises, there is a movement up and along the demand curve from point A' to point B. The yen continues to appreciate until the excess quantity demanded is eliminated and the market clears. A new equilibrium occurs at point B and spot exchange rate S_B.

For critical analysis: What would happen to the equilibrium exchange rate of the yen if the demand for the yen and the supply of the yen were to increase simultaneously?

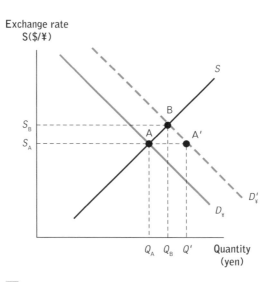

 **Figure 6.7** *The equilibrium exchange rate*

At the equilibrium exchange rate S_A, the quantity of yen demanded equals the quantity of yen supplied. An increase in U.S. consumers' demand for Japanese goods results in an increase in demand for the yen. The shift in the demand curve from $D_¥$ to $D_¥'$ illustrates the increase in the demand for yen.

A change in demand

Let's return to the first example of this chapter dealing with U.S. imports of Japanese electronics equipment. Suppose that there is an increase in U.S. consumers' demand for these types of Japanese-manufactured product. As U.S. consumers increase their purchases of these products, they desire a greater amount of yen to facilitate the additional transactions. Hence, the demand for yen rises. At the initial exchange rate, the increase in demand for the yen results in an excess quantity demanded of yen. As discussed in Chapter 1, an excess quantity demanded generates upward pressure on price. Hence, the dollar-per-yen exchange rate ($/¥) rises, indicating an appreciation of the yen relative to the dollar.

A change in supply

Now consider the effects of a change in Japanese residents' demand for U.S. financial instruments. Suppose that the returns on typical U.S. financial instruments rise above the returns on similar Japanese financial instruments, which causes Japanese residents to shift funds from Japan to the United States. In order to purchase the U.S. financial instruments, Japanese savers must obtain a larger amount of U.S. dollars. In doing so, Japanese residents exchange yen for dollars, thereby increasing the supply of yen. At the initial exchange rate, the increase in the supply of yen results in an excess quantity supplied of yen. An excess quantity supplied puts downward pressure on price. Hence, the excess quantity supplied of yen causes the dollar-per-yen exchange rate to decline and depreciates the yen relative to the dollar.

> **Fundamental Issue #5: What determines the value of a currency?** The interaction between the demand for a currency and the supply of the currency determines the equilibrium exchange rate. If the exchange rate is free to change, then it adjusts to its equilibrium value through a market-clearing process. The equilibrium exchange rate is the exchange rate at which the quantity of the currency demanded equals the quantity of the currency supplied in the market.

RELATIONSHIP BETWEEN THE SPOT MARKET AND THE FORWARD MARKET

You learned earlier that the forward exchange market is a market for contracts that ensure the future delivery of foreign exchange at a specified exchange rate, the *forward* rate. If exchange rates are free to adjust, the forces of supply and demand in the forward market for foreign exchange determine the forward exchange rate. Because the forward exchange rate reflects the supply and demand for a currency for future delivery, it is possible that the forward exchange rate provides information about the future spot exchange rate. That is, the forward exchange rate may be useful in forming expectations about future values of the spot rate. To begin to assess the relationship between the forward rate and the future spot rate, let's first explore the relationship between the forward rate and the *current* spot rate.

The forward premium and discount

Forward premium or discount: *The difference between the forward exchange rate and the spot exchange rate expressed as a percentage of the spot exchange rate.*

Suppose that the 6-month forward rate on the British pound is 1.5255 dollars per pound, and that the spot rate is 1.4883 dollars per pound. Because the dollar price of the pound in the forward market—that is, the forward exchange rate of the pound—is more than the dollar price of the pound in the spot market, the pound is said to trade at a **forward premium**. In a similar manner, if the forward exchange rate of a currency is less than the spot exchange rate, in contrast, the currency is said to trade at a **forward discount**.

The standard forward premium

Economists usually state the forward premium or discount in a standardized manner by calculating the *standard forward premium or discount* as a percentage, and expressing it in annual terms. To do this, they use the following formula:

$$\text{standard forward premium/discount} = (F_N - S)/S \times 12/N \times 100$$

where F_N is the forward rate, S is the spot rate, and N is the number of months of the forward contract.

This formula has three parts. The first part is the forward premium, which is the difference between the forward exchange rate and the spot exchange rate relative to the spot rate, $(F_N - S)/S$. The second part annualizes the forward premium by dividing by the number of months of the contract, expressing the forward premium on a monthly basis, and then multiplying by 12 to express the forward premium on an annual basis. The third part multiplies the annual forward premium by 100 to express it as a percentage. In our example, the standard forward premium is:

$$(F_N - S)/S \times 12/N \times 100 = (1.5255 - 1.4883)/1.4883 \times 12/6 \times 100 = 5.0$$

Hence, the standard forward premium is 5 percent.

The forward rate and the expected future spot rate

Now let's suppose that a foreign currency trader believes that the pound will appreciate against the dollar by 0.5 percent over the next 6 months (or 1 percent on an annual basis). The trader's expectation of future appreciation of the pound is different from the forward premium of the pound. Consequently, the trader may be able to profit from engaging in a forward currency transaction.

Suppose that the trader exchanges £1 million for dollars in the forward market at a forward exchange rate of $1.5225 per pound. In the assumed absence of transaction costs, 6 months from now the trader will pay £1 million to buy $1,525,500 forward [(£1 million × 1.5255 $/£) = $1,525,500]. Next, let's suppose that the trader's expectations are correct and the pound appreciates by 0.5 percent, from a rate of 1.4883 $/£ to 1.4957 $/£. The trader may use the proceeds from the forward contract to purchase the pound on the spot market. The $1,525,500 obtained with the forward contract exchanges for £1,019,924 on the spot market ($1,525,500/ 1.4957 $/£ = £1,019,924), yielding a profit of £19,924.

If other traders share the same expectation as this trader, then there is an increase in the total supply of pounds on the forward market. (Likewise, we could say that there is an increase in the total demand for dollars on the forward market.) Using what we now know about the interaction of the forces of supply and demand, an increase in the supply of pounds on the forward market places downward pressure on the forward exchange rate. This reduces the amount of the forward premium and eliminates the difference between the forward premium and the expected rate of appreciation. Thus, the actions of savvy traders, such as the one in our example, eventually eliminate the opportunity to systematically profit from differences between the forward premium and actual changes in the spot rate. Hence, the following equilibrium condition must hold, on average:

$$(F_N - S)/S = (S_N^e - S)/S$$

where S_N^e is the spot exchange rate expected to prevail N months from now. This condition states that, in equilibrium, the forward premium must equal the expected appreciation of the currency, and the forward discount must equal the expected depreciation of the currency.

The condition can be simplified to yield

$$F_N = S_N^e$$

This simplified version of the equilibrium condition implies that the forward exchange rate on a contract in N months must equal the spot exchange rate expected to prevail N months from now. If the forward rate differs systematically from the expected spot rate, then, as in our previous example, a profit opportunity exists. If a profit opportunity exists, we can expect traders to take advantage of it. The actions of traders, in theory, generate changes in expected future spot exchange rates and forward exchange rates, eliminating the difference between the two. Based on this equilibrium condition, we might expect a close relationship between the forward exchange rate and the realized future spot exchange rate. This is the reason that we might also expect the forward exchange rate to have some useful information for forecasting the future spot rate. Many empirical studies indicate that there is some co-movement between the forward exchange rate and the actual future spot exchange rate. The forward exchange rate sometimes overestimates the future spot exchange rate and sometimes underestimates it, however. Most economists conclude, therefore, that the forward premium has limited ability in forecasting the future spot exchange rate. In Chapter 8 you will explore the theories relating the spot rate, forward rate, and other economic variables.

Fundamental Issue #6: How are the spot and forward markets related? If exchange rates are free to adjust, the forces of supply and demand determine the forward exchange rate. A currency is said to trade at a forward premium if the forward exchange rate is greater than the spot exchange rate. If the forward exchange rate is less than the spot exchange rate, a currency is said to trade at a discount. The standard forward premium expresses the forward premium on an annual percentage basis. If the forward exchange rate differs systematically from the expected future spot rate, a profit opportunity exists. Thus, in theory, the actions of currency traders should eliminate this difference. Economists have studied the relationship between the forward rate and the spot rate quite extensively. The evidence indicates that the forward rate is limited in its use as a guide to future spot rate values.

OTHER FOREIGN EXCHANGE INSTRUMENTS

Forward exchange contracts are just one type of foreign exchange instrument that currency traders use to hedge against foreign exchange risk. During the past two decades, traders developed other *foreign exchange derivative instruments*, or *foreign exchange derivatives*.

Foreign exchange derivatives

Foreign exchange derivative instruments:
Currency instruments with a return that is linked to, or derived from, the returns of other financial instruments.

Foreign exchange derivative instruments are currency instruments with a return linked to, or derived from, the returns of other financial instruments. Forward exchange contracts fit the description of a derivative security because their payoff to traders depends upon spot exchange rates.

Hedging and speculating with foreign exchange derivatives

Earlier you learned how a forward contract was used to hedge a short position in the pound. The forward exchange contract allowed a property developer to cover a foreign-exchange exposure and remove all uncertainty about the cost to complete a pound-denominated transaction in the future. By locking in a rate of exchange for the pound, the firm relieves itself of the risk that the dollar cost of the property will rise above that guaranteed by the forward contract.

Although traders can use foreign exchange derivatives to protect against risks of loss, this does not mean that they do not use foreign exchange derivatives for purposes of risky speculation in the pursuit of profits. To see how foreign exchange derivatives may increase overall risk, let's slightly change the condition of the previous example. Suppose that a currency trader thinks that the spot exchange rate of the pound will not change during the next 6 months. His belief, however, is not consistent with the widespread views of other exchange market participants, who generally expect that the pound will appreciate. Nevertheless, the trader is so sure his expectation will turn out to be correct that he is willing to enter into a forward exchange contract with the managers of the U.S. property developer.

Recall that the current spot exchange rate between the dollar and the pound is 1.4883 $/£, and that the 6-month forward rate is 1.5255 $/£. Let's suppose that the currency trader and the managers of the property development firm settle on a forward contract that calls for the currency trader to exchange £15 million for U.S. dollars with the managers, at a forward rate of 1.5255 $/£. In other words, the managers exchange $22,882,500 for £15 million with the trader.

Let's suppose that the currency trader plans to buy the pound at the market rate that prevails in 6 months. If the trader's expectations hold true, his cost of purchasing the pound in the spot market 6 months from today is $22,324,500 [(£15 million × 1.4883 $/£) = $22,324,500]. The trader then exchanges the £15 million with the managers of the property development firm for $22,882,500, netting a profit of $558,000. If the widespread expectation of a pound appreciation holds true, however, the trader's dollar cost of fulfilling the contract rises above what the trader currency *speculates* that it will be. Thus, to the extent that the consensus forecast of a pound appreciation indicates a strong likelihood that this actually will occur, the currency trader would have negotiated a speculative contract and added to his overall risk.

This example indicates that, while foreign exchange market participants can use foreign exchange derivatives to hedge against risks, they also can use them to engage in speculative activities. Worldwide use of foreign exchange derivatives has increased dramatically since the early 1980s, as financial managers found ways to use derivatives in hedging strategies. At the same time, however, many traders determined that they could earn significant profits by speculating with foreign exchange derivatives.

Unfortunately, several traders found out that foreign exchange derivatives speculations can turn out badly. The results were sizable financial losses for a number of firms and individuals. The most notable losses resulting from foreign currency derivatives speculations were Volkswagen's $260 million loss, Procter & Gamble's $157 million loss, and PacifiCorp's $65 million loss in the 1990s. What is important to understand, however, is that for each loser in a derivatives speculation there is a winner. In the case of the three companies above, this means that these firms lost money because their managers' speculations about market outcomes were wrong, but that the losses resulted in profits for other firms and traders whose market expectations were correct.

Common foreign exchange derivatives

There are many types of foreign exchange derivatives, yet they all share the same characteristic that their returns depend on prices of other financial instruments. In addition, traders may use foreign exchange derivatives in hedging strategies or in speculative strategies.

The most common types of foreign exchange derivative instrument, in addition to forward exchange contracts, are *currency futures*, *currency options*, and *currency swaps*. Table 6.5 summarizes the characteristics of these instruments. Let's consider each instrument in some detail.

Table 6.5 *Basic foreign exchange derivative instruments. Foreign exchange derivatives are currency instruments whose return is linked to the returns of other financial instruments. The most common foreign exchange derivatives are forward exchange contracts, currency futures, currency options, and currency swaps.*

Forward exchange contract	A contract that ensures the delivery of a foreign currency at a specified exchange rate
Currency futures contract	An agreement to deliver to another party a standardized quantity of a specific nation's currency at a designated future date
Currency option contract	A contract granting the right to buy or sell a given amount of a nation's currency at a certain price within a specific time period
Currency swap	A contract entailing an exchange of different payment flows denominated in different currencies

Currency futures

One type of foreign exchange derivative instrument that has grown in popularity among traders is a **currency futures** contract, which is an agreement by one party to deliver to another party a quantity of a national currency at a specific future date in exchange for a specified amount of another currency. In contrast to forward exchange contracts, currency futures contracts specify in advance *standardized* quantities of currencies and narrow guidelines for transactions. Because futures contracts are standardized, parties do not have to spend time negotiating contract terms. The world's largest currency futures market is the International Monetary Market of the Chicago Mercantile Exchange (CME), in which traders conduct futures transactions in a large number of currencies.

Holders of currency futures experience profits or losses on the contracts at any time before the contract expires. This is because futures contracts require daily cash-flow settlements. That is, profits or losses are settled daily. By way of contrast, profits or losses occur only at the expiration date of a forward contract, which requires settlements only at maturity. As a result, the market prices of currency futures contracts and forward exchange contracts usually differ.

Currency futures typically involve smaller currency denominations, as compared with forward exchange contracts. Large banking institutions and corporations that transmit large volumes of foreign currencies in their normal business operations are the primary users of forward contracts. Individuals and smaller firms that wish to undertake hedging or speculative strategies typically trade currency futures instead. (Concerns about speculative currency futures trading fueled by borrowed funds may lead to a new regulation that could shrink retail foreign exchange trading considerably; see *Online Globalization: A threatened ban on credit cards could curtail consumer currency trading*.)

Currency futures:
An agreement to deliver to another party a standardized quantity of a specific nation's currency at a designated future date.

ON THE WEB:

Learn more about the Chicago Mercantile Exchange and currency futures at www.cmegroup.com.

ONLINE GLOBALIZATION

A threatened ban on credit cards could curtail consumer currency trading

A number of companies offer online retail currency-trading accounts to individual traders around the globe. Gain Capital's customers, for instance, reside in nearly 150 countries and use its Internet-based system to exchange more than $4 billion in currencies per day. Other companies offering online currency-trading systems include FXCM, Oanda, CitiFX Pro, and FXDD. These and other Web-based companies generate a substantial fraction of retail currency transactions.

To simplify the process through which individual traders provide funds to exchange, online currency-trading firms typically allow individuals to charge trades to credit cards. Nevertheless, this also means that people aiming to engage in speculative trading sometimes borrow against their credit-card accounts to finance their potentially— and sometimes actually—risky activities. Recently, the National Futures Association (NFA), the self-regulatory body for most of the U.S. futures industry, announced that it was considering phasing in a ban on the use of credit cards to fund futures trades. Most industry observers anticipate that if the NFA adopts the credit-card ban for its members, the U.S. government's Commodity Futures Trading Commission would likely impose the restriction on non-NFA futures-trading firms as well.

If individuals were unable to use credit cards to fund online foreign currency trades, they would have to switch to more cumbersome and costly methods, such as arranging wire transfers to, or mailing physical checks to, brokers. Some online trading firms have concluded that imposition of a credit-card ban ultimately would reduce the volume of foreign exchange trading via the Internet by approximately 60 percent.

For critical analysis: Who would stand to benefit if a credit-card ban for online foreign exchange trading brings about a substantial shrinkage of retail currency-trading volumes?

Currency options

Another type of foreign exchange derivative instrument is a **currency option**, which is a contract providing the holder the right to purchase or sell an amount of a national currency at a given price. This right does not require the holder to buy or sell. It gives the holder the *option* to do so. The given price at which the holder can exercise the right to purchase or sell an amount of currency is the option's **exercise price**, which traders also call the *strike price*.

Call options are options that allow the holder to *purchase* an amount of a currency at the exercise price. **Put options** are options that allow the buyer to *sell* an amount of a currency at the exercise price. Traders refer to an option granting the holder the right to exercise the right of purchase or sale at any time before or

Currency option:
A contract granting the right to buy or sell a given amount of a nation's currency at a certain price within a given period or on a specific date.

Exercise price:
The price at which the holder of an option has the right to buy or sell a financial instrument; also known as the strike price.

Call option: *An options contract giving the owner the right to purchase an amount of a currency at a specific rate of exchange.*

Put option: *An options contract giving the owner the right to sell an amount of a currency at a specific rate of exchange.*

American option:
An option in which the holder may buy or sell an amount of a currency any time before or including the date at which the contract expires.

European option:
An option in which the holder may buy or sell an amount of a currency only on the day that the contract expires.

Currency swap:
An exchange of payment flows denominated in different currencies.

including the date the contract expires as an **American option**. They call an option that allows the holder to exercise the right of purchase or sale *only* on the date the contract expires a **European option**.

Multinational corporations can purchase currency options directly from banks via *over-the-counter* contracts, but they can also purchase them in organized exchanges. One of the largest options markets is the Philadelphia Stock Exchange.

Currency swaps

A fourth type of foreign exchange derivative is a **currency swap**, which is an exchange of payment flows denominated in different currencies. Figure 6.8 illustrates a sample currency swap, in which we suppose that International Business Machines (IBM) Corporation earns a flow of yen-denominated revenues from computer sales in Japan, while Toshiba Corporation earns dollar revenues from selling computers in the United States. IBM pays dollar dividends and interest to its owners and bondholders, and Toshiba pays yen-denominated dividends and interest to its owners and bondholders. Therefore, IBM and Toshiba could, in principle, use

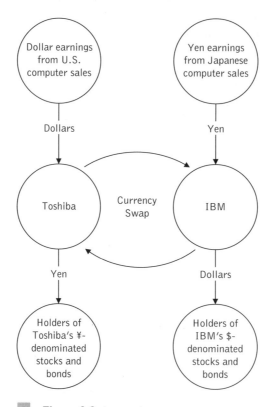

Figure 6.8 *A sample currency swap*

IBM receives yen earnings from selling computers in Japan, and Toshiba receives dollar earnings from selling computers in the United States. The two companies could use a currency swap contract to trade their yen and dollar earnings to make payments to holders of the stocks and bonds.

a currency swap as a mechanism for trading their yen and dollar earnings for the purpose of paying income streams to their stockholders and bondholders.

In addition, firms often use currency swaps to lock in the domestic currency value of a debt payment or a future receipt. Sometimes swap partners are easier to find than counterparties to forward contracts, because swaps directly match traders that require flows denominated in currencies held by one another.

Fundamental Issue #7: What other foreign exchange instruments are commonly traded? In addition to foreign exchange forward contracts, other commonly traded foreign exchange instruments include currency futures, currency options, and currency swaps. Currency futures are an agreement to deliver to another party a standardized quantity of a specific nation's currency at a designated future date. Currency futures differ from forward contracts because traders exchange them in standardized quantities in organized markets in which flows of profits or losses take place daily, rather than only at maturity. A currency option is a contract granting the right to buy or sell an amount of a nation's currency at a certain rate of exchange within a specific period of time. A currency swap is an exchange of payment flows denominated in different currencies.

CHAPTER SUMMARY

1. **What the balance of payments measures:** The balance of payments is a system of accounts used to record the international transactions of a nation. This system measures trade in goods, services, income, unilateral transfers, private transactions of financial assets, and official reserves. The current account comprises the goods, services, income, and unilateral transfers categories.

2. **The role of the foreign exchange markets in the global marketplace:** The foreign exchange market—a system of banks, brokers and central banks through which households, firms, and governments buy and sell foreign exchange—is the oldest and largest financial market in the world. The foreign exchange market is a global arrangement for valuing transactions and delivering payments, thereby facilitating the flow of goods and services among nations. The foreign exchange market functions 24 hours a day. There is a wide array of financial instruments traded in the foreign exchange market, in which exchange rates can change as often as 20 times a minute.

3. **The spot foreign exchange market:** The spot market for foreign exchange is the market for contracts that require the immediate delivery of foreign currencies. Large transactions of foreign currency-denominated deposits of $1 million or more among commercial banks dominate this market. Economists use spot exchange rates to gauge an appreciation and depreciation of a currency, and to construct cross rates, real exchange rates, and effective exchange rates.

4. **Foreign exchange risk and the role of the forward foreign exchange markets:** Foreign exchange risk is the effect that uncertain future values of the exchange rate

may have on the value of a foreign currency-denominated obligation, receipt, asset, or liability. There are three types of exposure to foreign exchange risk: transaction exposure, translation exposure, and economic exposure. In principle, an individual or firm can use a forward exchange contract, which is a contract that obliges the future delivery of a foreign currency at a specified rate of exchange, to offset, or hedge, some or all of the exposure to foreign exchange risk. By eliminating uncertainty about the future value of a foreign currency-denominated transaction, forward contracts spur additional international transactions of goods, services, and financial instruments.

5. **Determining the value of a currency:** The interaction between the demand for a currency and the supply of a currency determines the currency's market value. If the exchange rate is free to change, then a currency's value adjusts to its market equilibrium through a market-clearing process. The equilibrium exchange rate is the value at which the quantity of a currency supplied equals the quantity of the currency demanded.

6. **The relationship between the spot and forward markets:** If exchange rates are free to adjust, the forces of supply and demand determine the forward exchange rate. The forward premium or discount is the difference between the forward exchange rate and the spot exchange rate, expressed as a percentage of the spot exchange rate. A currency is said to be trading at a premium if the forward exchange rate is greater than the spot exchange rate. A currency is said to be trading at discount if the forward exchange rate is less than the spot exchange rate. The standard forward premium expresses the forward premium on an annual basis.

7. **Other commonly traded foreign exchange instruments:** In addition to forward exchange contracts, commonly traded foreign exchange derivative instruments, which are foreign exchange instruments whose returns are linked to the returns of other financial instruments, include currency futures, currency options, and currency swaps. A currency future is an agreement to deliver to another party a standardized quantity of a specific nation's currency at a designated date. A currency option is a contract guaranteeing the right to buy or sell a given amount of a nation's currency at a certain price within a specific time period. A currency swap is an exchange of payment flows denominated in different currencies.

QUESTIONS AND PROBLEMS

1. Using the following data (billions of dollars) for a given year, calculate the balance on merchandise trade; the balance on goods, services and income; and the current account balance. Indicate whether these balances are deficits or surpluses.

Exports of merchandise	106	Imports of services	28
Exports of services	34	Capital inflow	6
Net unilateral transfers	8	Imports of merchandise	119
Statistical discrepancy	0	Capital outflow	29
Official settlements balance	22		

2. Suppose the US dollar-per-euro exchange rate ($/€) was 1.3245 on Thursday and 1.3221 on the following Friday. Did the euro depreciate or appreciate relative to the dollar? How much was the appreciation or depreciation (in percentage change terms)?

3. Complete the following cross-rate table. (*Hint*: The first exchange rate is the £/$ exchange rate.)

	U.S. $	U.K. £	Canadian $	Euro €
U.S. $	–	0.6621	1.0409	0.7664
U.K. £		–		
Canadian $			–	
Euro €				–

4. In January 2012 the spot exchange rate for the euro was 1.40$/€, the eurowide CPI was 107.0, and the U.S. CPI was 108.1. In July 2013, the spot exchange rate for the euro was 1.31$/€, the euro-wide CPI was 110.1, and the U.S. CPI was 111.8.

   (a) Based on this information, in nominal terms did the euro appreciate or depreciate against the dollar? What was the rate of appreciation or depreciation of the euro relative to the dollar?

   (b) What were the rates of consumer price inflation in the United States and in the EMU?

5. Based on this information, did the euro experience a real appreciation or a real depreciation against the dollar? What was the rate of real appreciation or depreciation?

6. An effective exchange rate for the euro was 91.62 in January 2005 and 94.44 in January 2013. At the same time, an effective exchange rate for the Japanese yen was 132.41 in January 2005 and 144.12 in January 2013. Overall, did the euro and the yen appreciate or depreciate between January 2005 and January 2013?

7. Based on the information in question 6, can you surmise whether the euro appreciated or depreciated against the yen from 2005 to 2013?

8. On a particular day, the spot exchange rate for the Thai baht was 31.80 (Bt/$). On the same day, the 3-month forward exchange rate for the baht was 32.50. Was the Thai baht trading at a premium or discount? Given this information, what is the standard forward premium or discount for the Thai baht?

9. For each of the following events, illustrate the demand for, and supply of, the Canadian dollar. Show how each event would affect the euro-per-Canadian-dollar (€/C$) equilibrium exchange rate.

   (a) European savers desire to shift funds from euro-denominated financial assets to Canadian-dollar-denominated financial assets.

   (b) European firms switch from buying minerals from Canadian firms to purchasing them from Russian firms.

10. Suppose that the two events described in question 8(a,b) occur at the same time. Illustrate the effect on the supply of, and demand for, the Canadian dollar, and on the equilibrium exchange rate.

11. On Monday, the spot exchange rate for the Philippine peso was 43.20 P/$. On the same day, the 1-year forward rate was 44.29 P/$. What would you expect the rate of appreciation or depreciation for the peso to be over the course of the year?

ONLINE APPLICATION

URL: www.Oanda.com

Title: Forex Trading Basics

Navigation: Go to the home page of Oanda at the above URL. Click on "Forex Trading."
Click on "Learn" and then scroll down to "Learn the Basics" and click on "Intro-
duction to Currency Trading." Scroll down and click on "Lesson 3: Currency Trading
Conventions – What You Need to Know before Trading."

Application: Read Topics 1–5 and answer the following questions.

1. Explain the settlement of a "spot" trade.
2. What is the "bid" price?
3. What is the "ask" price?
4. What is the "spread?"
5. What is a "pip?"
6. Explain how you would close your position if you are long 500,000 Swiss francs.

For group study and analysis: Divide into two groups. One group is to speculate that the
U.S. dollar will depreciate relative to the euro, while the other group is to speculate that
the U.S. dollar will appreciate relative to the euro. Based on Topic 3, each group is to
describe how it would undertake a currency transaction to profit on movements of the
dollar–euro spot exchange rate. Both groups should explain how hypothetical profits or
losses are calculated.

REFERENCES AND RECOMMENDED READINGS

Bach, Christopher L. "A Guide to the U.S. International Transactions Accounts and
the U.S. International Investment Position Accounts." *Survey of Current Business*
(February 2010): 33–51.

Bergsten, C. Fred, ed., *The Long-Term International Economic Position of the United
States*, Special Report 20. Washington, DC: Peterson Institute for International
Economics, May 2009.

Bodnar, Gordon, Gregory Hart, and Richard Marston. "Wharton Survey of Derivative
Usage by U.S. Non-Financial Firms." *Financial Management* 24(2) (Summer 1995):
104–114.

Catão, Luis. "Why Real Exchange Rates?" International Monetary Fund *Finance and
Development* 44(3) (September 2007): 46–47.

Cherny, Kent, and Ben R. Craig. "Reforming the Over-the-Counter Derivatives Market:
What's to Be Gained?" Federal Reserve Bank of Cleveland Economic Commentary,
Number 2010-6, July 2010.

Fouquin, Michel. "The Impact of Fluctuation of the Dollar on European Industry." *CEPII
News Letter* 12 (Winter 1999–2000): 3–4.

Hellerstein, Rebecca, and Cédric Tille. "The Changing Nature of the U.S. Balance of Payments." Federal Reserve Bank of New York, *Current Issues in Economics and Finance* 14(4), June 2008.

Higgins, Matthew, and Thomas Klitgaard. "Financial Globalization and the U.S. Current Account Deficit." Federal Reserve Bank of New York, *Current Issues in Economics and Finance* 13(11), December 2007.

Kraus, James. "Forex Trading Sites May Erode Bank Revenue." *American Banker* (May 4, 2000).

Walmsley, Julian. *The Foreign Exchange and Money Market Guide*. New York: John Wiley and Sons, 2000.

Chapter 7

Exchange-rate systems, past to present

FUNDAMENTAL ISSUES

1. What is an exchange-rate system?
2. How does a gold standard constitute an exchange-rate system?
3. What was the Bretton Woods system of "pegged" exchange rates?
4. What post-Bretton Woods system of "flexible" exchange rates prevails today?
5. What are crawling-peg and basket-peg exchange-rate systems?
6. What is a currency board, and what is dollarization?
7. Which is best: a fixed or flexible exchange-rate system?

Between 2008 and 2012, both the United States and the European Monetary Union experienced financial crises that induced many individuals and firms around the world to reduce their holdings of dollars and euros. As a consequence, the values of the dollar and the euro dropped in relation to other world currencies. One currency that appreciated rapidly relative to the dollar and the euro was the Swiss franc (SFr), as savers sought to hold francs in an effort to preserve the value of their stocks of wealth. The Swiss National Bank, Switzerland's central bank, halted the surge in the franc's value by committing to do whatever might be required. Ultimately, the Swiss National Bank embarked on a policy of creating Swiss francs in sufficient amounts to buy large enough quantities of euros to prevent the franc-per-euro exchange rate from falling below 1.20 SFr/€.

Another currency that appreciated considerably as the values of the dollar and euro sank was the Japanese yen. In an effort to assure that the Japanese central bank, the Bank of Japan, would follow the Swiss example and create sufficient yen to halt the yen's rapid appreciation, the Japanese government took a dramatic step: It removed nearly all of the Bank of Japan's top officials and replaced them with people who had agreed that they would not permit the yen to appreciate further.

The determination of the international value of a nation's currency is a very important issue. Together with the way in which a nation conducts its macroeconomic policies, an *exchange-rate system* may promote a stable economic environment that promotes trade and investment, or an unstable environment that puts its industries at a competitive disadvantage. The history of exchange-rate management shows us that, even if adopted with the best intentions, few exchange-rate systems can avoid speculative and political pressures forever.

EXCHANGE-RATE SYSTEMS

Before we can begin to understand the institutional framework that governs the value of a nation's currency, we must first understand a nation's **monetary order**—a set of laws and regulations that establishes the framework within which individuals conduct and settle transactions.

One decision a nation must make is whether its national money will be commodity money, commodity-backed money, or fiat money. *Commodity money* is a tangible good that individuals use as means of payment, or a medium of exchange, such as gold or silver coins. *Commodity-backed money* is a monetary unit that has a value relating to a specific commodity or commodities, such as silver or gold, and that national authorities will accept in exchange for the commodity. *Fiat money*, which is our money today, is a monetary unit not backed by any commodity. Its value is determined solely by the worth that people attach to it as a medium of exchange.

A nation's monetary order also sets forth the rules that form the nation's exchange-rate system, and, either formally or informally, the nation's participation in an exchange-rate system. An **exchange-rate system** is the set of rules governing the value of an individual nation's currency relative to other foreign currencies.

To better explain the relationships among a monetary order and an exchange-rate system, we will examine the history of three important exchange-rate systems: The gold standard, the Bretton Woods system, and the post-Bretton Woods floating-rate system.

Monetary order: *A set of laws and regulations that establishes the framework within which individuals conduct and settle transactions.*

Exchange-rate system: *A set of rules that determine the international value of a currency.*

> *Fundamental Issue #1: What is an exchange-rate system?* An exchange-rate system is the set of rules established by a nation to govern the value of its currency relative to foreign currencies. The exchange-rate system evolves from the nation's monetary order, which is the set of laws and rules that establishes the monetary framework within which transactions are conducted.

THE GOLD STANDARD

By the mid-1870s, the major economies of the world had adopted a commodity-backed monetary order for their national currencies. Gold served as the underlying commodity, and the period until 1914 became known as the *gold standard era*. Under this framework, a nation would fix an official price of gold in terms of the national currency, known as the mint parity, and establish convertibility at that rate. **Convertibility** is the ability to freely exchange a currency for a commodity or another currency at a given rate of exchange. For example, between 1837 to 1933 (except for the suspension of convertibility during the Civil War), the U.S. mint parity of one fine ounce of gold was $20.646, with the dollar convertible at that rate.

Convertibility: *The ability to freely exchange a currency for a reserve commodity or reserve currency.*

To maintain the mint parity, or the exchange value between gold and the national currency, a nation must condition its money stock on the level of its gold reserves.

The gold standard as an exchange-rate system

Other industrialized nations had adopted a commodity-backed order before or shortly after the same time as the United States reinstated convertibility following the Civil War, which ended in 1865. These decisions, though adopted unilaterally, also established each nation's exchange-rate system and led informally to an exchange-rate system among the nations. The gold standard established an exchange-rate system because it meant that people could exchange the dollar, both domestically and internationally, at the mint parity rate. Thus, the exchange value between gold and the dollar determined the international value of the dollar.

This also established an exchange-rate system among the countries that had adopted a gold standard. Because each country valued its currency relative to gold, this indirectly established an exchange value between the domestic currency and the currencies of all other countries on a gold standard.

As an example, under the gold standard, Britain's gold parity rate was £4.252 per fine ounce (Figure 7.1). Using the gold parity rates of the U.S. dollar and the British pound, we can determine the rate of exchange that existed between the two currencies. The mint parity rate of the United States was $20.646 and the mint parity rate of the British pound was £4.252. As shown in Figure 7.1, the U.S.-dollar-per-currency rate of the British pound, $/£, was, therefore, $20.646/£4.252, or 4.856 $/£.

If the exchange rate deviated from this amount, ignoring transportation costs of gold, then an opportunity to profit from buying and selling the two currencies and gold would have existed. For example, suppose that, at the mint parity rates just given, the exchange rate between the U.S. dollar and the British pound was 5 $/£. One would have been able to take $20.646 and exchange it for one ounce of gold. The gold could then have been exported to Britain and exchanged for £4.252.

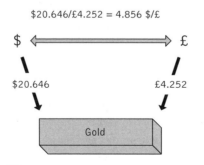

$20.646/£4.252 = 4.856 $/£

Figure 7.1 *The gold standard as an exchange-rate system*

Countries adopting a gold standard valued their currencies relative to gold. The gold parity rate for the British pound was £4.252 per troy ounce of gold, and for the U.S. dollar $20.646 per troy ounce. The gold parity rates determined the rate of exchange between the two currencies.

The £4.252 would have exchanged on the foreign exchange market for £4.252 × 5 $/£, or $21.26, earning a profit of $0.614. If we consider the transportation costs of gold, the exchange rate between two currencies would remain in a range or band centered on the ratio of the mint parity values. These transportation and transaction costs of gold determine the width of the range, because they affect the profitability of exporting or importing gold.

Under the gold standard, all of the currencies of the nations adopting a gold standard were linked together, with their exchange values determined in the manner just described. Just as the mint parities established the exchange rate between the dollar and the pound, they also established the exchange values among the dollar, and the French franc, and the German deutsche mark.

For example, under the gold standard the mint parity of the French franc was Ffr107.008, and the deutsche mark mint parity was DM86.672. The exchange rate between the dollar and the French franc, therefore, was 5.183 Ffr/$ (Ffr107.008/ $20.646). The exchange rate between the dollar and the deutsche mark was 4.198 DM/$ (DM86.672/$20.646). The link to gold determined the cross rates between the various currencies as well. It is in this manner that the adoption of a commodity-backed monetary order by individual nations established the basis of an exchange-rate system.

Fundamental Issue #2: How does a gold standard constitute an exchange-rate system?
A gold standard constitutes an exchange-rate system for an adopting nation because it establishes a domestic and international rate of exchange between the domestic currency and gold. A gold standard also links the exchange-rate systems between all of the nations adopting a gold standard. The exchange value between gold and a nation's currency indirectly establishes rates of exchange among all of the currencies.

Performance of the gold standard

Because the gold standard resulted from the decisions of individual nations made at different times, there is no single starting date for the system. Generally, however, economists consider the gold standard era to have begun in the 1870s. Though the system was temporarily suspended during World War I, and eventually collapsed in the early 1930s, some individuals still argue for a return to a gold standard. During recent U.S. political campaigns, conservatives such as Steve Forbes and Jack Kemp have recommended that a new president should stabilize the dollar value of the nation's gold reserves as a critical first step toward restoring "sound money" to America. What is the record of the gold standard, and why do individuals such as Mr. Forbes and Mr. Kemp long for its return?

Positive and negative aspects of a gold standard

As indicated earlier, an important element of a commodity-backed monetary order is that a nation's quantity of money, or its *money stock*, depends directly on the amount of commodity reserves the nation's monetary authority has. A given amount of commodity reserves may support a multiple number of units of money. As an example, between 1879 and 1913, the U.S. money stock was 8.5 times the amount of the monetary gold stock. Thus, *changes* in a nation's money stock depend only on *changes* in the mining and production of monetary gold.

If the supply of gold is rather constant, this particular aspect of a gold standard, therefore, promotes long-run stability of the nation's money stock and long-run stability of prices and exchange rates. Another important aspect of a commodity-backed monetary order is that it does not require a central bank: An official authority can maintain the ratio of money stock to gold reserves. Canada and the United States, for example, did not have a central bank during the late 1800s and early 1900s.

Nevertheless, a commodity-backed monetary order has some negative aspects. For example, a gold standard has significant resource costs, such as minting and transportation costs. It can be very costly for a nation to maintain and exchange a tangible commodity such as gold. If the supply of gold is not steady, it can result in inflation or a liquidity crisis. A major gold discovery, for example, would generate an increase in the amount of money in circulation and spur inflationary pressure. If the mining of gold fell behind, the amount of money in circulation would contract, potentially leading to a liquidity crisis. Arguably most important is the fact that a gold standard prevents policymakers from pursing discretionary monetary policy. In other words, the commitment to peg the value of the currency to gold prevents policymakers from setting monetary policy to achieve other policy objectives, a subject discussed in Chapter 9.

The economic environment of the gold standard era

Now that you understand these important aspects of a gold standard, let's consider both the conditions that existed in the 1870–1913 period and the contributions of the gold standard to the world economic environment. First, this period was peaceful, with no major wars among the participating nations. Second, there was virtually free capital mobility among nations. Finally, London was the center of the world's money and capital markets.

These latter two characteristics enabled the efficient and smooth functioning of the gold standard. Further, the Bank of England, at the center of the world's financial markets, maintained its gold parity values and established the credibility of the system. The apparent concentration of influence in the London market was so significant that economist J. M. Keynes stated that the Bank of England could almost have claimed to be the "conductor of the international orchestra." We can conclude, therefore, that the early gold standard period had some unique characteristics, at least two of which are not prevalent today.

During this period, most nations did indeed experience stable *long-run* real economic outputs, prices, and exchange rates. It is this long-run stability that proponents of a return to a gold standard praise. Because there were short-run random changes in the demand and supply of gold, however, there were also short-run random changes in the money stock and in the prices of goods and services. The short-run volatility of the money stock, in part, led to periodic financial and banking instability.

Furthermore, the *short-run* volatility of prices was greater under the gold standard than under the exchange-rate systems that followed.

The collapse of the gold standard

In 1914, after the beginning of World War I, many European nations suspended convertibility of their currencies into gold. For all practical purposes, the gold standard was no longer in effect, and exchange values between currencies did fluctuate. Many nations, therefore, restricted the types and amounts of international payments that their residents could make in hopes of maintaining the pre-war values of their currencies.

Early in the twentieth century, policymakers in the leading nations determined there was the need for an international organization to facilitate payments among nations. Following World War I, the **Bank for International Settlements (BIS)** was founded as part of an effort to facilitate German reparations. Located in Basle, Switzerland, this organization assists central banks in the management of their external reserves, conducts economic research, and is a forum for international monetary policy cooperation. (For more on the Bank for International Settlements, see the Online application on page 231.)

World War I formally ended with the signing of the Versailles treaty in 1919. There was a general desire among the leading nations to return to a gold standard. In 1925, the United Kingdom returned to a gold standard at the pre-war parity, but other countries, such as France, returned at much lower values. As a result, many believed that the pre-war parity rate would result in a market value for the pound higher than that predicted by economic models or theories, thereby making the pound an **overvalued currency**. To maintain the parity value, the United Kingdom had to endure high interest rates and high unemployment. The political costs of maintaining the value of the pound became too great, and the United Kingdom abandoned the gold standard in 1931 by suspending the convertibility of the pound to gold. The United States followed suit in 1933. By 1936, most of the industrialized nations had left the gold standard.

What brought about the demise of the gold standard was a return to parity values that led to overvalued currencies, such as the case with the United Kingdom; or to **undervalued currencies**–currencies whose market value is less than that predicted by economic models or theories – such as the case with the French franc. In addition, nations facing a worldwide depression decided to pursue objectives such as higher employment levels and real growth rates, rather than to maintain the exchange value of their currencies.

The collapse of the gold standard, combined with the passage of protectionist trade policies such as the Smoot–Hawley Act in the United States, wreaked havoc on international trade flows. As a result, the volume of international trade in 1933 was less than one-third of its 1929 amount. This, in addition to other prevailing economic factors, contributed to the Great Depression, which began with an industrial depression in the United Kingdom in 1926 and the crash of the stock market in the United States in 1929. The Great Depression continued until the outbreak of World War II. (Even though today there is no longer a gold standard in place, some governments are moving to rebuild their stocks of physical gold; see *Policy Notebook: Germany—and perhaps Texas—wants gold deposits back from the Federal Reserve*.)

Bank for International Settlements (BIS): *An institution based in Basle, Switzerland, which serves as an agent for central banks and a center of economic cooperation among the largest industrialized nations.*

Overvalued currency: *A currency in which the current market-determined value is higher than that predicted by an economic theory or model.*

Undervalued currency: *A currency in which the current market-determined value is lower than that predicted by an economic theory or model.*

POLICY NOTEBOOK

Germany—and perhaps Texas—wants gold deposits back from the Federal Reserve

Recently, Germany's central bank, the Deutsche Bundesbank, announced plans to relocate billions of dollars' worth of gold reserves that it has long held with the Federal Reserve Bank of New York, which in turn stores the gold in a New York facility owned by the British-based bank HSBC. The Bundesbank's plan is to move the gold currently on deposit in New York, as well as gold currently deposited with the Bank of France in Paris, to a German-owned facility in Frankfurt.

On the heels of Germany's announcement, a Texas legislator submitted a bill, supported by the state's governor, to follow Germany's example by moving to Texas about $1 billion worth of gold on deposit with the New York Federal Reserve bank. The bill provides for creating a new "Texas Bullion Depository" to house the state's gold.

Given that there is no longer a gold standard in place, what motivates these governments' desires to incur additional costs of withdrawing gold from Federal Reserve deposits and storing the metal in facilities close to home? The Bundesbank did not comment on its motivations, but a Texas politician remarked, "If you think gold is a hedge or a protection, you always want it as close to the individual and the entity as possible." Observers interpreted this comment as suggesting a lack of confidence in the Federal Reserve's willingness to undertake policies that support the purchasing power of the U.S. dollar. Indeed, another Texas official noted that, today, a dollar can purchase less than 1,600th of an ounce of gold, or 83 percent less gold than it could have purchased in 2000.

Left unstated by both German and Texas officials was another possible rationale noted in media reports: A worry that if, at some future date, the current U.S. monetary order were to collapse, the U.S. federal government might, as it did during the 1930s, freeze deposits of gold held at Federal Reserve banks and elsewhere. Media observers noted that by moving their gold to Frankfurt and Austin, the German and Texas governments would ensure immediate access to the gold that they own, thereby potentially protecting it from any possible efforts by the U.S. federal government to restrict access to the gold.

For critical analysis: What types of expenses would Germany, Texas, and other nations or states have to incur in order to maintain physical stocks of gold within their borders?

The Bretton Woods system

During World War II, the leaders of the United Kingdom and the United States recognized the importance of having a sound monetary order in place when the war ended. The economies of Europe and Japan would be in great need of rebuilding, and would therefore require imports from nations with intact industrial bases, such as the United States. The nations' leaders, therefore, pressed for negotiations on an exchange-rate system that would facilitate international trade and payments.

Although 44 nations participated in the conference that led to the postwar exchange-rate system, the primary architects of the system were Harry Dexter White of the U.S. Treasury and the renowned British economist John Maynard Keynes. Negotiations concluded with the ratification of a new system in 1944 at a small resort in Bretton Woods, New Hampshire, U.S.A. The conference, though officially called the International Monetary and Financial Conference of the United and Associated Nations, became known as the Bretton Woods Conference. Thus, the agreement reached there became known as the Bretton Woods agreement.

The Bretton Woods agreement

One significant outcome of the Bretton Woods agreement was the creation of the **International Monetary Fund (IMF)**. The IMF's principal function was to lend to member nations experiencing a shortage of foreign exchange reserves. Nations could become members of the IMF by subscribing, or paying a quota or fee. The size and economic resources of a nation determined the initial quota, with 25 percent of the quota paid in gold and 75 percent in the nation's currency. Two other important institutions that arose at the end of the war were the International Bank for Reconstruction and Development (IBRD), known as the World Bank, and the General Agreement on Tariffs and Trade (GATT). The **World Bank** initially financed postwar reconstruction. It now focuses on making loans to developing nations to promote long-term development and economic growth. The GATT promoted the reduction of trade barriers and settled trade disputes. The World Trade Organization (WTO) eventually replaced the GATT.

The exchange-rate system that emerged from the agreement was one of pegged, but adjustable, exchange rates. Under a **pegged exchange-rate system**, nations fix the value of their currency to something other than a commodity, such as another nation's currency. As under a gold standard, each nation pegged its exchange rate. In contrast to a gold standard, the U.S. dollar was the anchor of the system. The Bretton Woods system, therefore, was a **dollar-standard exchange-rate system**, which is a system in which nations peg the value of their currency to the dollar and freely exchange their currency for the dollar at the pegged value.

Under the Bretton Woods agreement, each country could choose to state the par value of its currency in terms of gold, or to establish a par value for its currency relative to the U.S. dollar. Every participating country related the value of its currency to the dollar, making the dollar the common unit of value in the system. Each country would then stand ready to buy and sell U.S. dollars in the foreign exchange market to maintain the exchange value of its currency within 1 percent, on either side, of the par value, commonly referred to as the *parity band*.

The United States, by way of contrast, fixed the value of the U.S. dollar to gold at a mint parity of $35 per troy ounce. The United States agreed to buy and sell gold

International Monetary Fund (IMF): *A supranational organization whose major responsibility is to lend reserves to member nations experiencing a shortage.*

World Bank: *A sister institution of the International Monetary Fund that is more narrowly specialized in making loans to about 100 developing nations in an effort to promote their long-term development and growth.*

Pegged exchange-rate system: *An exchange-rate system in which a country pegs the international value of the domestic currency to the currency of another nation.*

Dollar-standard exchange-rate system: *An exchange-rate system in which a country pegs the value of its currency to the U.S. dollar and freely exchanges the domestic currency for the dollar at the pegged rate.*

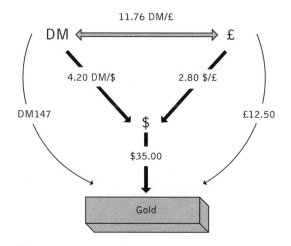

Figure 7.2 *The Bretton Woods exchange-rate system*

In practice, the Bretton Woods system linked all currencies, other than the U.S. dollar, to gold and to each other through the U.S. dollar. The United States pegged the dollar to gold at a parity rate of $35 per troy ounce. Other nations, such as the United Kingdom and West Germany, pegged their currency to the dollar. This indirectly established exchange values among the British pound and the deutsche mark, and among the pound and the deutsche mark and gold.

Devalue: *A situation in which a nation with a pegged exchange-rate arrangement changes the pegged, or parity, value of its currency so that it takes a greater number of domestic currency units to purchase one unit of the foreign currency.*

Revalue: *A situation in which a nation with a pegged exchange-rate system changes the pegged, or parity, value of its currency so that it takes a smaller number of domestic currency units to purchase one unit of the foreign currency.*

with other official monetary agencies in settlement of transactions. Because other countries pegged the value of their currency to the U.S. dollar, and the U.S. maintained the value of the dollar relative to gold, each non-dollar currency was indirectly linked to gold.

Figure 7.2 illustrates the system and the relationships among gold, the U.S. dollar, the British pound, and the German deutsche mark. The figure shows the dollar with a mint parity value of $35 per troy ounce of gold. The British pound was pegged to the dollar at an exchange rate of 2.80 $/£ and the deutsche mark was pegged to the dollar at an exchange rate of 4.20 DM/$. This system established the link between the British pound and gold, the British pound and the deutsche mark, and the deutsche mark and gold.

Although each country pegged its currency, under the Bretton Woods agreement any nation could change the par value with the approval of the IMF. A nation **devalues** its currency when it raises the par value, meaning that a person must offer more units of the currency to purchase a unit of the commodity or foreign currency. A nation **revalues** its currency when it lowers the mint parity value or par value, meaning that one may offer fewer units of the currency to purchase a unit of the commodity or foreign currency. Thus, the Bretton Woods system was an adjustable-peg system, rather than a system of fixed exchange rates. (To contemplate how nations participating in the Bretton Woods system pegged the values of their currencies in relation to the U.S. dollar, see *Visualizing Global Economic Issues: Pegging the pound's dollar value under Bretton Woods*.)

VISUALIZING GLOBAL ECONOMIC ISSUES

Pegging the pound's dollar value under Bretton Woods

To consider how the Bank of England maintained a pegged dollar-per-pound exchange rate of 2.80 $/£, as required by the Bretton Woods agreement, take a look at Figure 7.3. The figure depicts a relatively typical situation in which, during the period in question, the equilibrium exchange rate in the absence of the Bretton Woods agreement would have been higher than 2.80 $/£, such as the 3.00 $/£ exchange rate at which the supply and demand curves cross at the equilibrium quantity of dollars traded, Q_e.

At the Bretton Woods exchange rate of 2.80 $/£, the quantity of British pounds demanded by those seeking to exchange dollars for pounds would equal Q_2. The quantity of British pounds supplied in exchange for dollars, however, would only equal Q_1. Thus, at the 2.80 $/£ exchange rate, there would be an excess quantity of pounds demanded—that is, a shortage of pounds—equal to $Q_2 - Q_1$. In the absence of any actions by the Bank of England, the exchange rate would be bid upward to its market equilibrium level of 3.00 $/£.

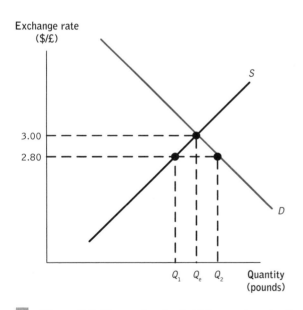

Figure 7.3 *The market for British pounds under Bretton Woods*

This figure depicts a situation in which, during the relevant period, the market dollar-per-pound exchange rate was 3.00 $/£. At the 2.80 $/£ exchange rate established by the Bretton Woods agreement, therefore, there would have been an excess quantity of pounds supplied, or shortage of pounds, equal to $Q_2 - Q_1$ pounds. To eliminate the resulting upward pressure on the exchange rate that otherwise would have caused the pound to appreciate, the Bank of England would have been required to create an additional $Q_2 - Q_1$ pounds to exchange for dollars at the 2.80 $/£ exchange rate.

To keep the dollar-per-pound exchange rate from rising from 2.80 $/£ to 3.00 $/£ and thereby prevent the pound from appreciating relative to the dollar during the period being considered, the Bank of England would have to provide $Q_2 - Q_1$ pounds in exchange for dollars at the 2.80 $/£ Bretton Woods exchange rate. Thus, the Bank of England would, during the period in question, have to create this additional amount of pounds to exchange for dollars. In so doing, the Bank of England would cover the pound shortage and thereby eliminate the pressure for a pound appreciation at the 2.80 $/£ exchange rate established under the Bretton Woods system.

Economists refer to the total quantity of pounds supplied through actions of the Bank of England as the British *money supply*. Other things being equal, when the Bank of England created additional pounds to keep the exchange rate at 2.80 $/£, the British central bank expanded the nation's money supply. In effect, therefore, the Bank of England had to adjust its money supply to ensure compliance with the Bretton Woods system.

For critical analysis: The pound-per-dollar exchange corresponding to the 3.00 $/£ exchange rate depicted in Figure 7.3 would have been 0.3333 £/$, and the pound-per-dollar exchange rate associated with the 2.80 $/£ Bretton Woods exchange rate would have been 0.3571 £/$. At the latter exchange rate, established by the Bretton Woods agreement, would there have been a shortage or surplus of dollars? How would the Bank of England's action discussed above have addressed this situation?

Reserve currency:
The currency commonly used to settle international debts and to express the exchange value of other nations' currencies.

Under the Bretton Woods system, nations used the U.S. dollar to settle international transactions. This made the dollar the primary **reserve currency** of the system, or the currency accepted as a means of settling international transactions.

One problem encountered during the late 1940s and 1950s was that participating nations did not have sufficient U.S. dollar reserves. The Marshall Plan and the European Payments Union alleviated this dollar shortage problem. The purpose of the *Marshall Plan*, officially titled the European Recovery Program, was to help rebuild the European economies by supplying financial capital. The inflow of capital funds yielded dollars that the nations could use to conduct current account transactions.

The *European Payments Union* was a system among European nations to help settle cross-country deficits and surpluses. Under this system, member nations would track their net monthly deficit or surplus balances with each other. At the end of the month, the nations would settle, in U.S. dollars, only the net balance they had with each other.

Fundamental Issue #3: What was the Bretton Woods system of "pegged" exchange rates? The Bretton Woods system was a system of adjustable pegged exchange rates whose parity values could be changed when warranted. Each country established and maintained a parity value of its currency, or peg, relative to gold or the U.S. dollar. All chose the U.S. dollar, making the system a dollar-standard system. Nations could change their parity values, either revaluing or devaluing, with approval of the IMF.

Performance of the Bretton Woods system

Because the United States stated the par value of the dollar in terms of gold, and most other participating countries stated their par values in terms of the U.S. dollar, the system had two sets of rules: One for the United States, and one for all other countries. Accordingly, the United States had to follow an independent and anti-inflationary monetary policy while standing ready to exchange the dollar for gold at the par value. All other nations had to buy or sell U.S. dollar reserves to keep their domestic currency exchange values against the dollar within the 1 percent parity band.

For most of the period between 1945 and 1968, the world economy experienced growth in output and a rapid increase in world trade. Nations did not undergo the type of liquidity crises that were prevalent during the gold standard. Consequently, short-run prices were more stable as well. The Bretton Woods system was not without its shortcomings, however.

Because the United States was the only country committed to converting its domestic currency for gold, the system had an inadvertent weakness. Even if the United States followed an anti-inflationary monetary policy, the possibility of a *run on the dollar*, in which traders and official foreign agencies seek to convert the dollar for gold *en masse*, existed. Because there was a limit to the U.S. gold stock, the dollar would not increase in value relative to gold, but it could always decrease in value. This situation made the dollar the target of foreign exchange speculators, as well as nationalistic politicians who opposed the dollar as the standard of the world's exchange-rate system.

ON THE WEB:

Learn more about the existing Bretton Woods organizations at the Websites of the International Monetary Fund (www.imf.org) and the World Bank (www.worldbank. org).

The gold pool

In 1960, the United States and many of the European economies collectively began to intervene in the gold market. The purpose of these interventions was to maintain the dollar price of gold and to ensure the stability of the exchange-rate system. This coordinated arrangement became known as the *gold pool*.

Beginning in 1964, the U.S. government increased federal spending under heightened military involvement in Vietnam and the social programs termed the Great Society. The United States experienced a considerable economic expansion, accompanied by rising inflation. The United States ran sizable balance-of-payments deficits with Germany and Japan in particular, and as a result, there was a considerable increase in the amount of dollars abroad. What had once been a dollar shortage on the world market was now a dollar glut.

The increase in the volume of dollars on the world market led many traders to believe that the United States would devalue the dollar relative to gold. That is, they anticipated that the dollar's parity value would increase, meaning that they would have to offer more dollars in exchange for a troy ounce of gold. If the parity value of the dollar increased, any individual or government holding dollar reserves would experience a capital loss on those dollar holdings.

In 1967, a devaluation of the British pound, which caused individuals and monetary agencies holding the pound to experience a 14.3 percent capital loss, increased speculation that the United States would devalue the dollar. Because of the speculation that a dollar devaluation was imminent, the demand for gold increased in the London commodities market. To meet the increase in demand and maintain the dollar parity value, the United States had to increase the supply of gold to the market. At one point, U.S. gold sales were so great that the weight of an emergency air shipment from Fort Knox to London collapsed the weighing room floor of the Bank of England.

The participating nations eventually abandoned the gold pool in 1968. Following the end of the gold pool, there was considerable pressure on the central banks of France and Germany to maintain their par values. Eventually, the crisis forced France to devalue the franc relative to the dollar by more than 11 percent. The day after the German elections of September 28, 1969, the German central bank, the Bundesbank, sought to maintain the parity value by purchasing $245 million in dollar reserves in the first hour-and-a-half that the market was open. Eventually, the deutsche mark was revalued by over 9 percent. Although these two nations did change their parity value, other European nations did not, so pressure on the system continued.

In early 1971, the U.S. balance on goods and services (Figure 7.4) swung from a surplus to a surprisingly large deficit, further confirming the perception of an over-valued dollar. In May 1971, as the U.S. trade deficit continued to expand, pressure to maintain the parity values between the European currencies, particularly the deutsche mark, and the U.S. dollar, climaxed. On May 4, 1971, in order to prevent an appreciation of the deutsche mark relative to the dollar, the Bundesbank bought $1 billion on the exchange market. During the first hour of trading on the following

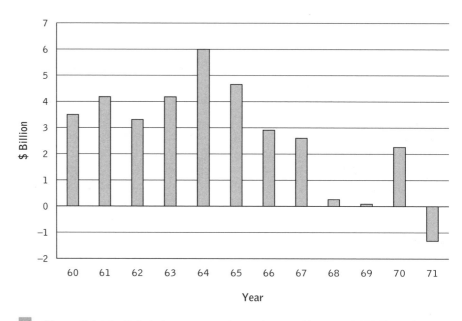

Figure 7.4 *The U.S. balance on goods, services, and income: 1960 through 1971*

The U.S. balance on goods, services, and income changed from a surplus in 1970 to a surprisingly large deficit in 1971. The deficits that emerged early in 1971 reinforced market participants' views that the dollar was overvalued relative to the other major currencies.

Source: Bureau of Economic Analysis, U.S. Department of Commerce.

day, the Bundesbank bought an additional $1 billion. The Bundesbank then announced that it was abandoning official exchange operations to maintain the parity value. Austria, Belgium, the Netherlands, and Switzerland followed suit.

President Nixon closes the gold window

On August 8, 1971, newspapers reported that the French were about to present $191 million of reserves to the United States in exchange for gold, so that the French government could make a loan repayment to the IMF. This amount was far short of being a major concern to the United States. In this regard, economist Peter Kenen said, "No one country was large enough to blackmail Washington by demanding gold for dollars, but each was large enough to fear its actions could undermine the monetary system." Nonetheless, speculation against the dollar increased further, and the media reported gold outflows on a daily basis. Eventually, on August 15, 1971, during a televised address, U.S. President Richard Nixon announced that the United States would temporarily suspend the convertibility of the dollar into gold or other reserve assets.

By abandoning the convertibility of the U.S. dollar into gold for foreign central banks, the United States eliminated the anchor of the Bretton Woods system. The incompatibility of U.S. and European macroeconomic policies, and the unwillingness of the U.S. government to devalue the dollar and of European governments to revalue their currency, brought about the end of the system. Once again, the world's exchange system was in disarray. Consequently, international trade between nations fell into a more chaotic state.

The Smithsonian agreement and the snake in the tunnel

To restore order to the exchange-rate system, the 10 nations with the largest share of reserves of the IMF met on December 16 and 17, 1971, at the Smithsonian Institution in Washington, DC. These 10 nations—Germany, France, Japan, the United Kingdom, the United States, Italy, Canada, Belgium, the Netherlands, and Sweden—which together compose the **Group of Ten (G10)**, negotiated the Smithsonian agreement. It established a new exchange-rate system that was similar in many respects to the Bretton Woods system. The agreement established new par values, most representing a revaluation of European currencies relative to the dollar, but with a wider band of 2.25 percent on either side of the parity value. The U.S. dollar, though devalued relative to gold, would not be convertible into gold. Following the conference, President Nixon characterized the agreement to the media as "the most significant monetary agreement in the history of the world."

Shortly after the Smithsonian agreement, on March 7, 1972, the six member nations of the European Economic Community (EEC)—France, West Germany, Italy, Belgium, the Netherlands, and Luxembourg—announced a plan to move toward greater monetary union. The member countries intended to maintain the exchange values of their currencies relative to each other within 2.25 percent. This system became known as the *snake in the tunnel*. Participating nations would maintain exchange values by selling or buying each other's currencies. Collectively, the EEC

Group of Ten (G10): *The nations France, Germany, Japan, the United Kingdom, the United States, Canada, Italy, Belgium, the Netherlands, and Sweden.*

currencies represented the snake. Whenever the snake would move to the allowable edge of the Smithsonian exchange value—the tunnel—the EEC nations would buy and sell U.S. dollars as needed.

By the middle of 1972, the exchange markets were in turmoil once again. Britain took action first, abandoning the snake in the tunnel in June, only 2 months after joining. Early in 1973, failure of the Smithsonian agreement was on the horizon. Despite enormous diplomatic efforts and a 10 percent devaluation of the dollar against gold by the U.S. Treasury, the European nations participating in the snake announced that they would no longer maintain their parity values relative to outside nations, such as the United States. Thus ended the "most significant monetary agreement in the history of the world," just 15 months after it began.

A FLEXIBLE EXCHANGE-RATE SYSTEM

Flexible exchange-rate system: *An exchange-rate system whereby a nation allows market forces to determine the international value of its currency.*

Although there were attempts to return to some form of an adjustable pegged system, a *de facto* system of flexible exchange rates emerged. A *floating*, or **flexible exchange-rate system**, is one in which the forces of supply and demand determine a currency's exchange value in the private market. Since the early 1950s leading U.S. economists, such as Milton Friedman, had argued in favor of a flexible exchange-rate system.

Economic summits and a new order

Although many countries were operating under a floating-rate system, it could not be called an official system, because the articles of agreement of the IMF did not allow floating rates. In 1975, French President Valéry Giscard d'Estaing decided to host an informal gathering of the leaders of the major industrialized nations—France, the United States, Germany, Japan, Italy, and the United Kingdom.

Discussions on the exchange-rate system continued between the representatives of the United States and France. On the eve on the summit, the two agreed to a system of flexible exchange rates with coordinated interventions in the foreign exchange market whenever they felt such interventions were required to ensure stability of exchange rates. President Giscard d'Estaing announced the breakthrough at the summit and received immediate endorsement for it from the other participating leaders.

Jamaica Accords: *A meeting of the member nations of the IMF, occurring in January 1976, amending the constitution of the IMF to allow, among other things, each member nation to determine its own exchange-rate system.*

With the leaders of the major industrialized countries endorsing the system envisioned in the French–United States negotiations, the members of the IMF rapidly went about completing the details and revising the constitution of the IMF. Member nations completed the negotiations, known as the **Jamaica Accords**, in Jamaica in 1976.

Within 6 months of the first economic summit, U.S. President Gerald Ford decided to host an economic summit of his own. President Ford, to the disapproval of President Giscard d'Estaing, also invited Canada to participate. With this action, President Ford institutionalized the summits, now held during the summer of each year and known as the Economic Summit. In 1997, summit host U.S. President William Clinton invited Russian President Boris Yeltsin to attend the summit from beginning to end, although he was excused from the economic meetings. At the 1998 Birmingham summit, British Prime Minister Tony Blair invited President Yeltsin to participate in all the summit meetings, formally expanding the participating nations to eight, or the **Group of Eight (G8)**.

Performance of the floating-rate system

The flexibility of the current exchange-rate system allowed the major economies to endure some tumultuous economic conditions. Since 1973, which economists recognize as the beginning of the floating exchange-rate period, the major economies have experienced divergent macroeconomic policies, major internal and external economic shocks, and unprecedented fiscal and current account deficits. By allowing its currency's exchange value to be determined by market forces, a floating-rate country is also able to focus monetary policies on domestic objectives. Most nations, however, have experienced periods of dramatic increases and decreases in the exchange values of their currency.

Arguably the greatest challenges to the leading industrialized economies and the exchange-rate system occurred between 1973 and 1974, and in 1979. The outbreak of the Yom Kippur War in the Middle East, and an oil embargo imposed in October 1973, resulted in oil price increases and subsequent inflation in oil-importing countries. In 1979, the Organization of the Petroleum Exporting Countries (OPEC) undertook a series of actions that eventually tripled the price of crude oil on the world market. Already struggling with inflation, the oil-importing economies were hit hard by the increase in oil prices. By the end of the 1970s and early 1980s, Canada, France, Italy, the United Kingdom, and the United States were experiencing double-digit, or near double-digit, rates of inflation.

Also in 1979, U.S. President Jimmy Carter appointed Paul Volcker as chairman of the Federal Reserve. Volcker made it publicly known that the Federal Reserve would pursue a single objective of reducing inflation. The Fed's policy actions resulted in a U.S. recession in 1981 and 1982. More important to our discussion, monetary and fiscal policy actions resulted in very high interest rates and put upward pressure on the value of the dollar relative to other major currencies. (Chapter 8 examines the relationship between interest rates and exchange rates.) As a result, the dollar began an appreciation that continued until early 1985.

Figure 7.5 illustrates the Federal Reserve's nominal effective exchange value of the dollar relative to seven major currencies. The rise of the dollar's value from 1981 through 1985 is one prominent feature of the diagram. The other is the dramatic decline in the dollar's value from 1985 through 1987. We have explained why the dollar appreciated from 1981 through 1985, but why did it peak in 1985 and reverse direction until 1987?

The Plaza Agreement and the Louvre Accord

For some time, the central bankers and finance ministers of a subset of the G10 nations have been meeting to discuss macroeconomic conditions and policies.

Group of Eight (G8): *The nations France, Germany, Japan, the United Kingdom, the United States, Canada, Italy, and Russia.*

ON THE WEB:

Learn more about the annual economic summits from the University of Toronto G8 Research Group at www.g8.utoronto.ca.

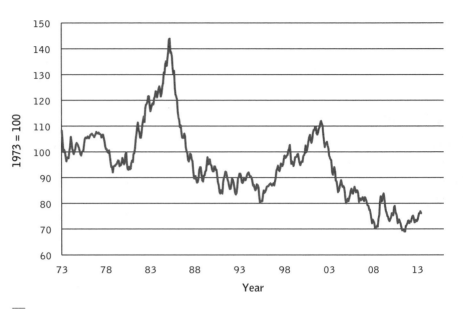

Figure 7.5 *The U.S. nominal effective exchange rate since 1973*

Between 1981 and 1985, the U.S. dollar experienced a considerable appreciation in average value relative to seven major currencies. Within 2 years, the appreciation had been reversed.

Source: U.S. Federal Reserve Bank of St. Louis.

Group of Five (G5): *The nations France, Germany, Japan, the United Kingdom, and the United States.*

Plaza Agreement: *A meeting of the central bankers and finance ministers of the G5 nations that took place at the Plaza Hotel, New York in September 1985. The participants announced that the exchange value of the dollar was too strong, and that the nations would coordinate their intervention actions in order to drive down the value of the dollar.*

Group of Seven (G7): *The nations France, Germany, Japan, the United Kingdom, the United States, Canada, and Italy.*

Louvre Accord: *A meeting of the central bankers and finance ministers of the G7 nations, less Italy, that took place in February 1987. The participants announced that the exchange value of the dollar had fallen to a level consistent with "economic fundamentals," and that the central banks would intervene in the foreign exchange market only to ensure stability of exchange rates.*

This subgroup includes the United States, the United Kingdom, Germany, Japan, and France, and is known as the **Group of Five (G5)**. The content, conclusions, and policy outcomes of these meetings had always been secret. In September 1985, the G5 met at the Plaza Hotel in New York to discuss, primarily, the status of the dollar. In an unprecedented move, the participants issued a statement to the media following the meeting. In what is now known as the **Plaza Agreement**, the G5 announced its belief that the dollar was at a level inconsistent with underlying economic conditions. The G5 said that it would intervene *collectively* to drive down the value of the dollar.

The purpose of the press statement was to convince currency traders that the G5 meant business. The statement and periodic surprise interventions by the G5 appeared to have convinced currency traders. As shown in Figure 7.5, the dollar reversed its prior 4-year appreciation within the subsequent 2 years.

Over the next 2 years, the G5 increased its ranks to include Italy and Canada (becoming consistent with the membership of the annual economic summits at that time). This expanded group is the **Group of Seven (G7)**. In February 1987, the G7 met at the Louvre in France. Once again, the dollar was the focus of discussion. Following the meeting, known as the **Louvre Accord**, the finance ministers and central bankers announced that the dollar had reached a level now consistent with underlying economic conditions. The G7, therefore, would intervene in the foreign exchange market only as needed to ensure stability.

This meeting defined the exchange-rate management approach of the G7 and G10 economies from 1987 through the early 1990s. These nations intervene, usually on a collective and unannounced basis, only when a currency or currencies have reached a critical threshold. What is the critical threshold? This is unknown to traders, who are always trying to anticipate the actions of the finance ministers and central bankers.

Under the Louvre Accord, nations will intervene on behalf of their currency from time to time. Consequently, the system is not a true flexible exchange-rate system. This type of exchange-rate system is a **managed float** (or dirty float), which is a system of flexible exchange rates, but with periodic intervention by official agencies.

Managed or dirty float: *An exchange-rate system in which a nation allows the international value of its currency to be determined primarily by market forces, but intervenes from time to time to stabilize its currency.*

For the international monetary and financial markets, the 1990s proved no less interesting than the previous two decades. In December 1994, a devaluation of the Mexican peso sparked a financial crisis that caused a collapse in the value of the peso and rattled the economies of Latin America. In 1997, financial crisis triggered in Thailand affected several economies in East Asia, including Indonesia, Malaysia, and South Korea. In 1998, financial crises occurred in Russia and in Brazil. Some of these economies rebounded quickly. Others, such as Indonesia, are still suffering the economic consequences.

During 1998, 11 nations of the European Union irrevocably locked their exchange rates, and in January 1999 they created the European Central Bank and launched the euro. They converted banking and financial statements to euros during the next 2.5 years. In January 2002, they began circulating euro notes and coins, and halted the circulation of national currencies.

Fundamental Issue #4: What post-Bretton Woods system of "flexible" exchange rates prevails today? Economists typically characterize the post-Bretton Woods exchange-rate system as one of floating exchange rates. Individual nations, however, have adopted a wide variety of exchange-rate systems, ranging from pegged to fully flexible exchange rates. Furthermore, the leading industrialized nations periodically intervene in the foreign exchange markets to stabilize their currencies, making the system a managed float instead of a truly flexible exchange-rate system.

OTHER FORMS OF EXCHANGE-RATE SYSTEM TODAY

In the previous sections of this chapter, we used an earlier period of the exchange-system to illustrate the workings of a gold standard; the Bretton Woods system to illustrate an adjustable-peg dollar standard; and the post-Bretton Woods system to illustrate a floating-exchange-rate system. Since the breakup of the Bretton Woods system, nations have adopted a wide variety of exchange-rate systems.

Figure 7.6 shows the types of exchange-rate systems that IMF member nations claim to have adopted. The figure shows the share of nations that use the currency of another nation or entity as their legal tender, conventional and non-conventional pegs, limited flexibility systems, and floating systems. The pie chart shows that

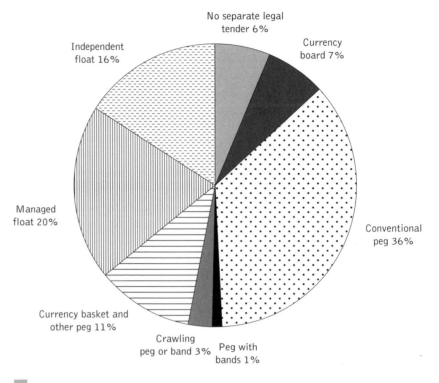

Figure 7.6 *Current foreign exchange-rate system*

Currently, 36 percent of the member nations of the IMF report to have an independent float or managed float exchange-rate system. For those countries that peg their currency in some fashion, the U.S. dollar is the most common currency for a peg; a currency basket is the second most common.

Source: International Monetary Fund.

36 percent of the nations have a managed-float or an independently floating exchange-rate system, while 58 percent peg their currency in some fashion.

Although 16 percent of IMF-member nations claim to have an independently floating exchange-rate system, work by Guillermo Calvo and Carmen Reinhart of the University of Maryland indicates otherwise. Calvo and Reinhart's research shows that the variability of many emerging economies' exchange rates is less than that of "true floaters" such as the United States. These economists conclude that many policymakers in emerging nations still have a fear of floating, and that they continue to intervene in the foreign exchange markets to support their national currency.

Figure 7.6 illustrates that nations have adopted a wide variety of exchange-rate systems. The figure, however, does not provide detail on the operation of these systems. As the currency crises of the late 1990s onward painfully showed, the operation of a nation's currency system is of vital importance. Hence, we shall now consider five additional types of system: pegged with banks, a crawling peg, a currency-basket peg, a currency board (or independent currency authority), and dollarization.

Conventional peg versus pegged with bands

Currently, the IMF considers a pegged-exchange-rate system, described earlier in this chapter, as one in which policymakers peg the value of the domestic currency at a fixed rate of exchange, or *parity rate*, to a foreign currency. The fixed rate of exchange is called the parity rate. The *exchange-rate parity bands* refer to the maximum amounts that the actual exchange rate is allowed to deviate above or below the parity rate. When the parity band allows for a maximum deviation from the parity rate, of plus or minus 1 percent, the exchange-rate arrangement is considered a *conventional pegged arrangement*. When the allowed deviation implied by the parity bands is greater than 1 percent, the exchange-rate arrangement is considered a *pegged-exchange rate within horizontal bands arrangement*. Denmark is an example of a system involving a pegged-exchange rate with horizontal bands. Under a framework called ERMII, Denmark pegs the value of the Danish kroner to the euro at a parity rate of 7.46038 DKr/€ within bands of plus and minus 2.25 percent. Recently, however, Danmarks Nationalbank, the central bank of Denmark, has kept the kroner within a band around the parity rate as narrow as less than plus and minus 1 percent. (From time to time, national governments operating with pegged exchange rates decide to alter their exchange-rate pegs and thereby devalue or revalue their currency; for a recent example, see *Policy Notebook: Venezuela's government makes substantial adjustments to its exchange-rate peg*.)

POLICY NOTEBOOK

Venezuela's government makes substantial adjustments to its exchange-rate peg

Venezuela pegs its currency, officially named the "strong bolivar" but typically called simply the bolivar, to the U.S. dollar. During the past few years, the nation's government has sought to reduce the incentives for residents to import goods and services. At the same time, the government has aimed to boost exports and to decrease the incentives for foreign companies to move funds out of the country.

In 2010, Venezuela's government devalued the bolivar by 50 percent from 2.15 bolivars per dollar to 4.30 bolivars per dollar, and in 2012 it devalued by nearly another 50 percent, to 6.35 bolivars per dollar. Each of these substantial devaluations made imports more expensive for Venezuelans, reduced the prices of the nation's export goods in terms of other nations' currencies, and decreased the foreign currency-denominated values of funds held in Venezuela by foreign firms. Thus, these policy actions were consistent with all three of the government's objectives. Many economists anticipate that the government likely will opt for another significant devaluation in the near future.

For critical analysis: Why do you think that Venezuela's policy actions contributed to short-term boosts in the nation's annual income flow?

Crawling pegs

Even after the collapse of the Bretton Woods system, some nations have decided to peg their currency to the currency of another nation. There are a number of reasons why a nation may choose to do this. The most common argument for pegged exchange rates is that reducing exchange rate volatility and uncertainty may yield gains in economic efficiency. Thus, a nation that has a large volume of trade with another nation, but a less stable currency, may choose to peg its currency. Pegging to another nation's currency and reducing exchange rate volatility, therefore, may promote price stability and greater trade and capital flows between the two nations.

Crawling peg: *An exchange-rate system in which a country pegs its currency to the currency of another nation, but allows the parity value to change at regular time intervals.*

The economic conditions of the two nations, however, may be quite different. When the economic conditions of the two nations differ, it is difficult, if not impossible, to maintain a pegged exchange rate. In this situation, nations that peg the value of their currency to the currency of another nation might allow the parity value to change continuously. This type of exchange-rate system is a **crawling peg**.

Nicaragua's crawling-peg arrangement

Nicaragua's exchange arrangement is a good example of a crawling peg. To promote exchange-rate stability and facilitate exports, Nicaragua pegged the value of its domestic currency, the córdoba, to the U.S. dollar. U.S. and Nicaraguan macroeconomic conditions were very different, however. Inflation in the United States averaged about 2–3 percent, but inflation in Nicaragua remained between 10 and 20 percent a year. Because of this large inflation difference, Nicaraguan officials realized that there would be a general tendency for the córdoba to depreciate against the U.S. dollar. Hence, Nicaragua adopted a crawling peg.

During the late 1990s and early 2000s, Nicaraguan officials reduced the parity value of the córdoba by a small percentage each week. As shown in Figure 7.7, the córdoba depreciated steadily against the U.S. dollar during this period. After cutting inflation substantially by late 1999 and consulting with the IMF, Nicaragua reduced the rate of crawl. As the figure shows, since 2002 the value of the córdoba has depreciated against the dollar at a very steady pace.

Exchange-rate band: *A range of exchange values with an upper and lower limit within which the exchange value of the domestic currency can fluctuate.*

Crawling band: *A range of exchange values that combines features of a crawling peg with the flexibility of an exchange-rate band.*

The parity band

As in the gold standard and the Bretton Woods system, nations that peg their currency usually allow the exchange rate to deviate from the parity value by a certain amount, typically expressed as a percentage, on either side of the parity value. The exchange rate, therefore, is not a fixed value, but can fluctuate within a band, known as an **exchange-rate band**.

Some countries, such as Colombia and Chile, have combined features of a crawling peg with the additional flexibility allowed by an exchange-rate band. This type of arrangement is a **crawling band**. Like an exchange-rate band, a crawling band features an upper and lower parity limit. The central parity, however, is adjusted on a regular basis. The upper and lower parity limits, therefore, change on a regular basis, usually allowing for a steady rate of depreciation.

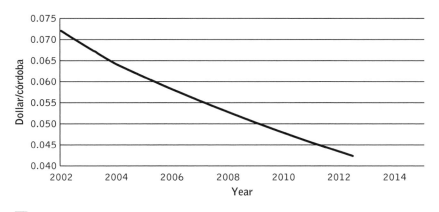

Figure 7.7 *Nicaragua's crawling-peg system since 2002*

Nicaragua's crawling-peg exchange-rate system allows for a small weekly rate of crawl, or depreciation, of the córdoba relative to the U.S. dollar. The crawling peg is illustrated by the negatively sloped plot of weekly downward adjustments of the exchange rate.

Source: Data from International Monetary Fund, *International Financial Statistics.*

Currency baskets

The previous section outlined the most common argument for pegging the value of a nation's currency, which is that reducing exchange-rate volatility and uncertainty may yield gains in economic efficiency. For the same reason, a nation might choose to peg its currency to a weighted average of a number of foreign currencies. This is known as a **currency-basket peg**. The additional motivation for pegging to a currency basket is that the weighted average of a basket of currencies is likely to be less variable than the exchange rate of a single currency.

To better understand what a currency basket is, imagine that you have six different coins in your hand, each from a different country. Next imagine that you place all the coins in a basket. Let's allow the sum of the coins in the basket to equal one unit of your own fictitious currency. The value of the coins in the basket is the value at which you would try to maintain your own currency under a currency-basket system.

Currency-basket peg: *An exchange-rate system in which a country pegs its currency to the weighted average value of a basket, or selected number of currencies.*

Selecting a currency basket

Typically nations, such as Kazakhstan and Kuwait, that adopt a currency-basket peg will include a relatively small number of currencies in the basket, because as the number of currencies to which the nation pegs increases, managing the basket peg becomes more difficult. Most nations using a currency-basket system peg to six or fewer currencies.

The choice of currencies to include in the basket is similar to the choice made in constructing an effective exchange rate (see Chapter 6). A basket typically includes selected currencies most prominent in the nation's international trade, capital flows, or international debt settlement. As in the construction of an effective exchange rate, the basket assigns a weight to each currency. The weights for a currency basket sum to unity, as well. The choice of weights reflects the relative importance of each currency in the nation's international transactions.

Managing the currency basket

Under a pegged exchange-rate system, the nation's monetary authority maintains the exchange rate between the domestic currency and the currency to which the nation pegs its currency. A currency-basket system introduces an interesting wrinkle. The authority must concentrate on the exchange rate between the domestic currency and the currencies included in the currency basket, *and* the cross rates between the currencies in the basket. If these cross rates change, the monetary authorities must take action, either depreciating or appreciating their currency so as to maintain the currency-basket value. The weights determine the amount of appreciation or depreciation.

Other peg arrangements

Recently the IMF introduced a new exchange rate classification of "other peg arrangements." This classification may include the various types of peg arrangement discussed above. This classification includes exchange-rate regimes in which the exchange rate is one of possibly many important targets for monetary policy.

> *Fundamental Issue #5: What are crawling-peg and basket-peg exchange-rate systems?* Crawling-peg and basket-peg exchange-rate systems are types of pegged exchange-rate system. Under a crawling peg, the parity value and the exchange rate bands are allowed to change at regular intervals, providing more flexibility in the system than in a true pegged exchange-rate system. Under a basket-peg system, officials peg the domestic currency to a weighted-average value of a small number of currencies. A weighted-average value of currencies tends to be less volatile than the exchange value of a single currency.

Independent currency authorities

Currency board:
An independent monetary authority that substitutes for a central bank. The currency board pegs the value of the domestic currency, and changes in the foreign reserve holdings of the currency board determine the level of the domestic money stock.

Earlier in this chapter, we explained that a gold standard does not require a central bank. Changes in a nation's official gold reserves govern changes in the nation's money stock. A gold standard requires only an official monetary agency that will increase or decrease the money in circulation as required. Some nations today do not have a central bank. Instead, they have an *independent currency authority* or *currency board*.

A **currency board**, or independent monetary authority, is an independent monetary agency that links the growth of the money stock to the foreign exchange holdings of the currency board. It does this by issuing domestic money in exchange for foreign currency at a fixed exchange rate.

The British Empire established the first currency board in Mauritius in 1849. The currency board was a means of providing Mauritius and other British colonies with a stable and convertible currency. The colony issued its monetary instruments—at a fixed rate of exchange—against the pound sterling assets that the currency board held in London. The colony's money, therefore, was convertible at a fixed rate and was as stable as the pound sterling. The colonies saved considerable resources because they did not need to hold and handle sterling coins and notes. Popularity of the currency-board system peaked in the 1940s, and virtually disappeared during the 1960s.

As practiced today, a currency board pegs the value of its nation's currency to the currency of another nation, and buys or sells foreign-currency reserves as appropriate to maintain the parity value. When the monetary authority buys or sells foreign reserves, it changes the amount of domestic money in circulation. This, and this alone, governs changes in the nation's money stock.

Currency boards have very limited responsibilities. They do not hold notes or bills issued by the domestic government, do not set reserve requirements on the nation's banks, and do not serve as a lender of last resort to the nation's banks, as a central bank typically does.

Because of these limited responsibilities, currency boards cannot engage in discretionary monetary policy and, therefore, are shielded from political influence. For this reason, there has been an increased interest in currency boards during the past few years. Some economists see currency boards as the best means for some nations to establish a credible approach to price stability.

There are several currency boards today, some of which have been established recently. Bulgaria, Estonia, Lithuania, and Hong Kong have currency board systems. Some currency boards have been very successful, while others have failed. Most recently, Argentinean policymakers abandoned the currency board system in favor of a floating exchange rate.

Dollarization

Some nations take an even more dramatic approach to exchange-rate management by allowing the currency of another nation to serve as legal tender. As shown in Figure 7.6 on page 220, 6.3 percent of the member nations of the IMF use the currency of another nation. Additional nations also are considering abandoning their domestic currency altogether. This practice is referred to as **dollarization**, but it actually means the use of any other nation's currency, not just the dollar, as legal tender.

Dollarization: *A system in which the currency of another nation circulates as the sole legal tender.*

Recently Ecuador, El Salvador, and Zimbabwe dollarized their economies. Other Latin American economies already are partially dollarized, and various Central and South American nations, such as Nicaragua and Guatemala, have debated dollarization since the late 1990s.

Proponents of dollarization argue that policymakers of small nations bordering large economies with strong currencies should dollarize their economies so as to achieve economic growth and stability. If policymakers give up the national currency and adopt the currency of another nation, the argument goes, they will no longer be able to mismanage their currency. In turn, interest rates and inflation rates should mirror those of the countries whose currency these nations adopted. After examining

225

the economic record of the small group of dollarized nations, Sebastian Edwards of the National Bureau of Economic Research concluded that dollarized economies have lower rates of inflation than similar non-dollarized economies. A cost of this lower inflation rate appears to be a slower rate of economic growth, however.

Fundamental Issue #6: What is a currency board, and what is dollarization? A currency board (or independent currency authority) supplants a central bank. The responsibilities of a currency board, however, are much more limited than those of a typical central bank. A currency board pegs the value of the domestic currency, and buys and sells foreign reserves in order to maintain the pegged value. Changes in the stock of foreign reserves solely determine the domestic money stock. Currency boards, therefore, better isolate monetary policy from domestic political pressures. Dollarization is the adoption of another nation's currency as the sole legal tender. Recently, policymakers in Ecuador and El Salvador dollarized their economies. Policymakers in other nations, such as Nicaragua and Argentina, continue to debate the benefits and costs of dollarization.

FIXED OR FLOATING EXCHANGE RATES?

Now that we have examined a number of exchange-rate systems, an obvious question is—which one is best? Unfortunately, there is no clear-cut answer to this question, and the debate over the benefits of fixed versus flexible exchange rates is one of the oldest in economics. This is precisely the reason there are so many different types of system in existence today.

On one hand...or the other

On one hand, fixed exchange rates may promote sound macroeconomic policy, helping to reduce inflation and leading to a stable economic environment. This, in turn, can boost an economy's real economic growth. Under a fixed nominal exchange-rate system, however, real exchange rates may appreciate and reduce the competitiveness of the nation's exporters.

Flexible exchange rates, on the other hand, may help a country overcome external shocks, such as an unusual inflow of capital from abroad, or a sudden increase in the price of an imported resource. Nevertheless, flexible exchange rates introduce an additional element of uncertainty and additional volatility. This is the common criticism of flexible rates. In industrialized nations, there is no clear evidence that volatility of nominal exchange rates dampens foreign trade or investment.

What is more important than the type of exchange-rate system is sound economic policymaking. This is perhaps the most overlooked reality in the debate over fixed versus flexible exchange rates. Furthermore, the debate often contrasts the current and imperfect regime with a utopian version of another regime in which governments always conduct policymaking such that it is consistent with the exchange-rate system. As discussed in this chapter, that is not always the case. (A particular threat to a policy of preventing movements in the exchange rate occurs when this policy requires sustained sales of reserves of foreign currencies, because eventually a nation pursuing this policy can run out of foreign currency reserves; see the *Policy Notebook: As the Egyptian pound gets pounded, the nation's foreign exchange reserves disappear.*)

POLICY NOTEBOOK

As the Egyptian pound gets pounded, the nation's foreign exchange reserves disappear

Since 2010, Egypt's political system has experienced considerable disruption. The resulting political unrest and uncertainty has taken a significant toll on the nation's economy. As both foreign and domestic residents responded to the sharp economic downturn by selling off Egyptian pounds, the pound's value dropped from 5.55 pounds per U.S. dollar to nearly 7 pounds per dollar.

Throughout this sustained slide in the pound's value, the Central Bank of Egypt sought to prevent the slide from becoming a crash. The institution traded large volumes of reserves of U.S. dollars and other foreign currencies for Egyptian pounds in the foreign exchange market, in an effort to prop up the pound's relative value. In the process, Egyptian reserves of foreign currencies dropped by more than 75 percent, from nearly $37 billion to below $4 billion. Following the political crisis and coup, newly installed policymakers turned to neighboring countries to borrow needed reserves.

For critical analysis: Why is a nation's government unable to support a desired value of its currency if it has no foreign currency reserves, and the market clearing value of its currency is persistently lower than the government's desired level?

Confronting the "trilemma"

Joshua Aizenman of the University of California at Santa Cruz and Reuven Glick of the Federal Reserve Bank of San Francisco suggest that, when evaluating the appropriate exchange-rate regime, nations must keep in mind an "impossible trinity dilemma," or **trilemma**. This concept refers to the fact that a nation may simultaneously select a combination of any *two*, but *not* all three, of the following: (1) fixed exchange rates; (2) independent, discretionary monetary policy; and (3) open, liberalized markets for financial capital.

Figure 7.8 illustrates the trilemma. As shown in the figure, the three sides of the triangle represent the three potential goals—fixed exchange rates, discretionary monetary policy, and capital market liberalization. The top of the triangle represents the combination of closed capital markets, fixed exchange rates, and discretionary monetary policy. The trilemma indicates that, as a country moves toward liberalized

Trilemma: *The idea that nations may select a combination of two, but not all three, of the following policy options: fixed exchange rates, discretionary monetary policy, and liberalized capital markets.*

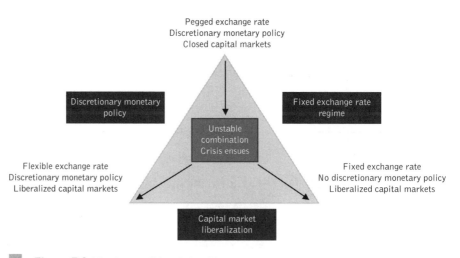

Figure 7.8 *The impossible trinity dilemma*

According to the trilemma, as a nation moves toward more open, liberalized capital markets, a stable policy configuration requires that policymakers forgo either independent, discretionary monetary policy or maintaining fixed exchange rates.

Source: Adapted from Aizenman and Glick (2008a).

capital markets, a stable policy configuration requires that policymakers forgo either discretionary monetary policy or fixed exchange rates. A stable combination is represented by a movement down one side of the triangle or the other. An unstable configuration involves trying to pursue all three goals, represented by a movement through the middle of the triangle.

Aizenman and Glick argue that nations that ignore the limitation imposed by the trilemma typically undergo financial crises. They point to the past experiences of countries such as Mexico and South Korea, which sought to maintain stable exchange rates while simultaneously freeing and opening up their financial markets and independently conducting discretionary monetary policies. The consequences, they contend, were financial crises. In the aftermath of these crises, these nations have permitted their currencies to float. This decision has moved these countries to a combination of exchange rate flexibility, capital market liberalization, and discretionary monetary policy—a movement to the bottom-left corner of the triangle in Figure 7.8.

Fundamental Issue #7: Which is best, a fixed or a flexible exchange-rate system? Whether it is better to peg the value of the domestic currency, or to allow it to be flexible and market-determined, is one of the longest-running debates in economics. There is no clear-cut answer—each system has its own advantages and disadvantages. Sound economic policymaking is more important in creating a stable economic environment than the choice of an exchange-rate system.

CHAPTER SUMMARY

1. **Exchange-rate system:** An exchange-rate system is a nation's set of rules that determine the international exchange value of the domestic currency and link a nation's currency value to the currencies of other nations.

2. **A gold standard as an exchange-rate system:** A gold standard constitutes an exchange-rate system for a nation. With a rule of pegging the value of its currency to gold, a nation establishes the international value of its currency in terms of gold. A gold standard constitutes an exchange-rate system among participating nations. By establishing the value of each currency relative to gold, a gold standard establishes the exchange values among currencies.

3. **The Bretton Woods system of pegged exchange rates:** Under the Bretton Woods system, nations pegged the value of their currency relative to the U.S. dollar, which was linked to gold. Nations could change the parity value, and thus devalue or revalue their currency, with the permission of the IMF. The Bretton Woods system was, therefore, a system of adjustable-pegged exchange rates.

4. **Post-Bretton Woods system of flexible exchange rates:** In today's world economy, a number of exchange-rate systems are in place, ranging from flexible exchange-rate arrangements to fixed- or pegged-exchange-rate arrangements. The leading industrialized nations intervene from time to time in the foreign exchange markets. The overall system, therefore, is primarily one of managed, floating exchange rates.

5. **Crawling-peg and basket-peg exchange-rate systems:** Some nations desire the stability of a fixed exchange rate, but find it difficult to maintain a rigid parity value. As a result, some nations have adopted either a crawling-peg or a basket-peg exchange-rate system. Under a crawling-peg exchange-rate system, a nation pegs the value of its currency, but it adjusts the parity rate at given time intervals. Under a basket-peg exchange-rate system, a nation pegs the value of its currency to the value of a basket of selected currencies.

6. **A currency board (or independent currency authority), and dollarization:** A currency board substitutes for a central bank. The responsibilities of the currency board, however, are much more limited. Under a currency board system, the currency board pegs the value of the nation's currency to another nation's currency. The currency board is responsible for maintaining the pegged value of the domestic currency by conditioning the nation's outstanding stock of money on the amount of foreign reserves that the currency board has. Dollarization is the adoption of another nation's currency as the sole legal tender. Recently, Ecuador and El Salvador dollarized by adopting the U.S. dollar as the sole legal currency. A principal argument for dollarization is that it will reduce inflation and interest rates to mirror those of the nation whose currency is adopted. Although comparative empirical evidence on the economic performance of dollarized economies is limited, this evidence indicates that dollarized economies have lower rates of inflation and economic growth than similar non-dollarized economies.

7. **Fixed versus flexible exchange-rate arrangements:** There is no clear-cut answer regarding whether it is better to peg the value of a nation's currency, or to allow the value of the currency to be determined in the market for foreign exchange. Each type

of exchange-rate system has its benefits and its costs. Sound economic policymaking is actually more important in creating a sound and stable economic environment than is the choice of exchange-rate system.

QUESTIONS AND PROBLEMS

1. List all of the various types of exchange-rate arrangement described in this chapter. (*Hint*: There are eight described in this chapter.) Order the list of exchange-rate arrangements from fixed to most flexible.

2. Following each statement, write the name of the exchange-rate regime you think best describes it.

   (a) The value of the currency is anchored to a given value of another currency, and can only deviate by as little as 0.5 percent above or 0.5 percent below that value.

   (b) The value of the currency is anchored to a given value of another currency, and can only deviate by as little as 1 percent above or 1 percent below that value. That value, however, is increased every trading period.

   (c) Only the forces of supply and demand determine the value of the currency.

   (d) The value of the currency is anchored to the weighted-average value of a selected group of currencies.

   (e) The currency authority anchors the value of the domestic currency one-to-one to the euro. The authority will issue domestic currency notes only when its reserves of the euro rise.

   (f) The domestic currency has been replaced with the euro, and the euro is the sole legal tender, but the domestic country is not part of the European Monetary Union.

   (g) Monetary authorities pretty much let the currency value be determined by market forces, but they will intervene from time to time to move the value in the "right" direction.

3. Describe two primary functions of the International Monetary Fund.

4. Suppose the value of the U.S. dollar is pegged to gold at a rate of $50 per ounce. Next, suppose that the value of the British pound is pegged to the U.S. dollar at a rate of 1.5 dollars per pound, and the value of the Canadian dollar is pegged to the U.S. dollar at a rate of 1.38 Canadian dollars per U.S. dollar. Calculate the value of the Canadian dollar and the British pound relative to gold.

5. Using the information in question 4, calculate the exchange rate between the Canadian dollar and the British pound.

6. Suppose Argentina decides to peg the value of its currency, the peso, to a basket consisting of 0.50 U.S. dollars and 0.50 euros. Further suppose the exchange rate between the U.S. dollar and the euro is 1.35 $/€. If the basket constitutes one peso, what is the appropriate exchange value between the peso and the dollar, and between the peso and the euro?

7. Explain the main difference between the exchange-rate systems of the Smithsonian agreement and the Bretton Woods system. Based on this difference, why do you think the Smithsonian agreement was so short-lived?

8. What is the principal responsibility of a currency board? What are the three main restrictions on a currency board that make it different from a typical central bank?

9. Explain how the Louvre Accord represented a type of exchange-rate system.

10. What factors do you think should be considered when determining the rate of crawl for a crawling-peg exchange-rate system?

11. What, in your opinion, is the chief difference between a currency-board system and dollarization?

ONLINE APPLICATION

Along with the IMF and the World Bank, the Bank for International Settlements is an important international financial institution. The BIS, however, is perhaps the least known and understood of the three institutions.

URL: www.bis.org

Title: The Bank for International Settlements

Navigation: Begin at the home page for the BIS located at the URL provided. Click on the "About BIS" link. Next, under "Related information" on the right-hand side, click on "The BIS – a profile."

Application: After reading the document *The BIS: Supporting Global Monetary and Financial Stability*, answer the following questions.

1. When was the BIS founded, and what is unique about its foundation?

2. What are the four primary functions of the BIS?

3. Approximately how many central banks and financial institutions hold the capital of the BIS?

4. Can private banks use the services of the BIS?

REFERENCES AND RECOMMENDED READINGS

Aizenman, Joshua, and Reuven Glick. "Sterilization, Monetary Policy, and Global Financial Integration." NBER Working Paper W13902, 2008a.

Aizenman, Joshua, and Reuven Glick. "Pegged Exchange Rate Regimes: A Trap?" *Journal of Money, Credit, and Banking* 40(4) (June 2008b): 817–835.

Berck, Peter, and Jonathan Lipow. "Did Monetary Forces Turn the Tide in Iraq?," Working Paper, University of California, Berkeley, and Oberlin College, 2009.

Berg, Andrew, and Eduardo Borensztein. "Full Dollarization: The Pros and Cons." International Monetary Fund, *Economic Issues* No. 24 (December 2000).

Calvo, Guillermo A., and Carmen M. Reinhart. "Fear of Floating." *Quarterly Journal of Economics* 117 (May 2002): 379–408.

Corden, W. Max. *Too Sensational: On the Choice of Exchange Rate Regimes.* Cambridge, MA: MIT Press, 2002.

Craig, Ben, and Christopher Waller. "Dual-Currency Economies as Multiple-Payments Systems." *Federal Reserve Bank of Cleveland Economic Review* 36(1) (Quarter 1, 2000): 2–13.

Daniels, Joseph P., Peter G. Toumanoff, and Marc von der Ruhr. "Optimal Currency Basket Pegs for Developing and Emerging Economies." *Journal of Economic Integration* 16(1) (March 2001): 128–145.

Edwards, Sebastian. "Dollarization and Economic Performance: An Empirical Investigation." NBER Working Paper Number W8274, May 2001.

Ghosh, Atish R., Anne-Marie Gulde, and Holger C. Wolf. *Exchange Rate Regimes, Choices and Consequences*. Cambridge, MA: MIT Press, 2002.

Humpage, Owen F. "Replacing the Dollar with Special Drawing Rights – Will It Work this Time?" Federal Reserve Bank of Cleveland Economic Commentary, March 2009.

International Monetary Fund. *Annual Report on Exchange Arrangements and Exchange Restrictions*. Washington, DC: IMF, 2010.

Jordan, Jerry. "The Evolving Global Monetary Order," Federal Reserve Bank of Cleveland Economic Commentary, January 2000.

Meissner, Christopher, and Nienke Oomes. "Why Do Countries Peg the Way They Peg? The Determinants of Anchor Currency Choice." *Journal of International Money and Finance* 28 (April 2009): 522–547.

Meltzer, Allan, and Jeffrey D. Sachs. "A Blueprint for IMF Reform." *Wall Street Journal* (March 8, 2000): A22.

Rose, Andrew K. "Exchange Rate Regimes in the Modern Era: Fixed, Floating, and Flaky." *Journal of Economic Literature* 49(3): 652–672.

Salvatore, Dominick, James W. Dean, and Thomas Willett, eds. *The Dollarization Debate*. New York: Oxford University Press, 2003.

Steil, Benn. *The Battle of Bretton Woods: John Maynard Keynes, Harry Dexter White, and the Making of a New World Order*. Princeton, NJ: Princeton University Press, 2013.

von Furstenberg, George M. "Can Small Countries Keep Their Own Money and Floating Exchange Rates?" In K. Kaiser, J. Kirton, and J. Daniels, eds., *Shaping a New International Financial System: Challenges of Governance in a Globalizing World*. Aldershot, U.K.: Ashgate Publishing, 2000, pp. 187–202.

Yeyati, Eduardo Levy, and Federico Sturzenegger. *Dollarization: Debates and Policy Alternatives*. Cambridge, MA: MIT Press, 2003.

Chapter 8

The power of arbitrage— purchasing power and interest rate parities

---

FUNDAMENTAL ISSUES

1. What does the concept of absolute purchasing power parity imply about the value of the real exchange rate?
2. What is relative purchasing power parity, and is it useful as a guide to movements in exchange rates?
3. What are the covered and uncovered interest parity conditions?
4. What is the distinction between adaptive and rational expectations?
5. What is foreign exchange market efficiency?
6. Under what conditions does real interest parity hold, and why is it a useful indicator of international integration?

In the spring of 2012, as usual, the German government was able to raise funds by selling bonds to private savers. What was unusual at that time was that the bonds the government sold offered an interest rate of 0 percent. At the time, savers were so nervous about the potential losses that they effectively were willing, in the words of one market analyst, "to park their funds in Germany in exchange for no rate of return whatsoever."

During the same interval when the German government was issuing bonds paying no interest return, the Swiss government also was borrowing funds by issuing bonds— bonds that nervous savers regarded as equally safe instruments in which to "park" their funds. At that time, most market participants anticipated that the Swiss franc would appreciate relative to the euro. Consequently, many observers predicted that the Swiss government would be able to "one-up" the German government. The Swiss government, these observers suggested, would be able to issue bonds at a negative rate of interest. Indeed, at the next auction of Swiss government bonds, savers who bought the bonds agreed to purchase the bonds with more funds than the government would return to the savers at the future maturity date. This arrangement meant, in effect, that buyers of the Swiss bonds paid the Swiss government to hold their funds on their behalf, which implied that savers received a negative rate of return from "parking" their funds with the Swiss government.

How were market observers able to predict, correctly, that if German bonds offered an interest rate of zero, the fact that the Swiss franc was expected to appreciate relative to the euro implied that Swiss bonds should yield a negative market rate of return? Why should the differential between interest rates on bonds that nervous savers regard as equally free of risks be related to anticipated changes in exchange rates? In this chapter, you will learn that to answer these questions, you must develop an understanding of international interest parity relationships. Before tackling this topic, it is helpful first to consider the *law of one price* and a closely related concept known as *purchasing power parity*.

LAW OF ONE PRICE AND ABSOLUTE PURCHASING POWER PARITY

Purchasing power parity (PPP): *A proposition that the price of a good or service in one nation should be the same as the exchange-rate-adjusted price of the same good or service in another nation.*

In its most basic form, the idea of **purchasing power parity (PPP)** presumes the absence of factors such as costs of transportation, cross-country tax differentials, and trade restrictions. Under these conditions, according to the PPP hypothesis, essentially identical goods and services that are traded across national borders should have the same price in two countries after converting their prices into a common currency.

Arbitrage and the law of one price

Economists often refer to the basic concept of PPP as the law of one price. To illustrate the law of one price, suppose that the market price of a high-quality orange is US$0.95 in Seattle, Washington. The market price of the same quality and type of orange in Victoria, British Columbia, is C$1.00. Thus, PPP would imply that the dollar equivalent exchange rate should be US$0.95/C$1.00 = 0.95 U.S. dollar per Canadian dollar. Using this rate, we can convert the Canadian dollar price of the orange in Victoria to a U.S. dollar price of US$0.95 (C$1.00 × 0.95 US$/C$ = US$0.95). Therefore, the orange has the same price in Victoria as it does in Seattle after adjusting for the exchange rate.

Arbitrage: *Buying an item in one market to sell at a higher price in another market.*

If, however, the exchange rate were not 0.95 US$/C$, then there would be an opportunity to engage profitably in **arbitrage**—buying an item in one market to sell at a higher price in another market. Suppose the exchange rate is equal to 0.98 US$/C$. Then the U.S. dollar price of an orange in Victoria would be C$1.00 × 0.98 US$/C$ = US$0.98. A Canadian resident who can buy many oranges in Seattle for US$0.95 per orange and haul them a short distance to Victoria to sell for C$1.00 each will earn a profit of US$0.03 per orange. Thus, if this individual can move 10,000 oranges from Seattle to Victoria to sell in Canada, the profit will be US$300, ignoring the relatively small transportation costs.

If a sufficient number of people engage in these sorts of arbitrage activity, then the result will be a flow of oranges from Seattle to Victoria. Canadian residents must exchange Canadian dollars for U.S. dollars in order to purchase the U.S. oranges. The exchange of the Canadian dollars for U.S. dollars on the foreign exchange market will cause an increase in the demand for U.S. dollars relative to Canadian dollars. The three markets (Seattle orange market, Victoria orange market, and foreign exchange market) will experience adjustments. The outflow of oranges from Seattle will generate an increase in the price of oranges in Seattle. The inflow of oranges to Victoria will cause a decrease in price of oranges in Victoria.

If a number of oranges and other goods and services are arbitraged in response to the misaligned exchange rate, then there will be an increase in the demand for U.S. dollars relative to Canadian dollars. This will cause the value of the U.S. dollar to appreciate relative to the Canadian dollar. All of these adjustments, which result from the arbitrage activity, will tend to equalize the prices of traded goods and services, measured in terms of the same currency, thereby removing any further scope for profiting from cross-border arbitrage.

Absolute purchasing power parity

This analysis of the relationship between prices and exchange rates implies the condition of *absolute purchasing power parity*, which we can formalize in the following manner. Let's define S to be the U.S.-dollar-equivalent exchange rate of the Canadian dollar (US$/C$), P to be the price of oranges in the United States, and $P*$ to be the price of oranges in Canada. Then we can express absolute PPP as

$$P = S \times P*$$

That is, the U.S. price of oranges should equal the Canadian price multiplied by the spot exchange rate. Thus, in our example, if the U.S. dollar–Canadian dollar exchange rate is 0.95 US$/C$, and the Canadian price of oranges is C$1.00 per orange, then the U.S. dollar price of oranges should equal US$0.95.

Applying absolute purchasing power parity to all goods and services: a theory of exchange rates

If *all* goods and services are fully and freely tradable across U.S. and Canadian borders, then absolute PPP will hold for all goods. In this instance, we can interpret P as the overall price level of U.S. goods and services, and $P*$ as the overall price level of Canadian goods and services. Note that, in this instance, we can rearrange the absolute PPP relationship to solve for the spot exchange rate:

$$S = P/P*$$

That is, when absolute PPP holds for all goods and services, the spot exchange rate equals the U.S. price level divided by the Canadian price level.

Thus, absolute PPP is a theory of exchange rates: If absolute PPP holds, then the bilateral spot exchange rate should equal the ratio of the price levels of the two nations. Hence, the demand and supply schedules in foreign exchange markets should move to positions yielding this bilateral exchange rate. Until they do, however, one could say that, based on absolute PPP, one nation's currency is overvalued or undervalued relative to the currency of the other nation.

Problems with absolute purchasing power parity

It is a big jump from oranges to all goods and services, however. To apply the concept of absolute PPP to exchange rates, our simplifying assumptions of no transportation costs, no tax differentials, and no trade restrictions that we used in our orange-exchange example must be met in the real world. This is highly unlikely to be true. After all, loading 10,000 or more oranges into a truck is a costly endeavor, orange sales might be subject to different tax rates in Canada and the United States, or one of the two nations could have legal restraints on orange trade. Certainly, we might expect transportation expenses, different tax treatment, or trade restrictions to apply for a number of other goods, even if they do not have significant effects in the national markets for oranges.

Furthermore, even if transportation costs, tax differences, and trade restrictions are insignificant, we still would anticipate problems in applying absolute PPP to all goods and services of two nations. The reason is that people in two nations may consume different sets of goods and services. As an extreme example, imagine that the typical U.S. consumer buys oranges and apples, but the typical Canadian consumer buys oranges and pears. If these are the only goods people in each nation consume, then using overall price levels for the two nations to make predictions about exchange rates would be a mistake. The price levels for the two nations would be based on the prices of different goods, meaning that the arbitrage argument that lies behind the absolute PPP condition could not apply. Arbitrage could not really relate the prices of both sets of goods, so we would be mistaken to infer an exchange rate from the absolute PPP relationship.

Another way to see why absolute PPP is unlikely to hold in the real world is to recall how we calculate a real exchange rate. As you learned earlier, we multiply the spot exchange rate by the ratio of the price levels for two countries. That is, we multiply the exchange rate S by the price-level ratio P/P^*, which tells us that we can write the real exchange rate as $S \times (P^*/P)$.

If absolute PPP holds, however, then $S = P/P^*$, so that the real exchange rate is equal to

$$S \times (P^*/P) = (P/P^*) \times (P^*/P) = 1$$

When the real exchange rate is equal to 1, this means that one unit of goods and services in a country, such as the United States, always exchanges one-for-one with a unit of goods and services in another country, such as Canada. Thus, absolute PPP implies that the real exchange rate is always equal to 1. If people in different countries consume goods and services in different proportions, however, it is highly unlikely that this will be so.

By the mid-1980s, the PPP doctrine was in such doubt that *The Economist* magazine developed an initially satirical measure of PPP called the "Big Mac index." The idea was that the McDonald's Big Mac sandwich has the same basket of ingredients in all world locations, so if the law of one price holds, the exchange-rate-adjusted price of a Big Mac should be the same everywhere. In fact, from year to year the Big Mac guide to exchange rates does relatively poorly, although its longer-term performance is better. (*Management Notebook: A McCurrency measure of purchasing power parity—the Big Mac index.*)

MANAGEMENT NOTEBOOK

A McCurrency measure of purchasing power parity—the Big Mac index

The Economist magazine publishes its Big Mac index of PPP at least once each year. The 2013 version of the Big Mac index appears in Table 8.1. As you can see, the U.S. price of a Big Mac in this year was $4.56, and the Swiss price was 6.50 Swiss francs (SFr). Using the equation for absolute PPP, $S = P/P^*$, the implied exchange rate is, as shown in the second column of the table, 1.43 SFr/$. The third column reports the actual value of the Swiss franc/dollar exchange rate at the time, which was 0.97 SFr/$. This market-determined value of the Swiss franc relative to the dollar is lower than the value implied by absolute PPP. The value of the Big Mac index, therefore, indicates that the Swiss franc is overvalued in relation to the dollar. We can express this overvaluation as the percentage difference between the implied value of the dollar in terms of Swiss francs according to the Big Mac PPP measure and the market value. This works out to be +55 percent for the Swiss franc, suggesting an overvaluation of the Swiss franc and indicating a likely depreciation of the Swiss franc relative to the dollar.

How does the Big Mac index perform as a guide to exchange rate movements? In the short run, the index certainly is not an accurate predictor of exchange rates. The index performs better in the long run, but most of the adjustment occurs through price changes.

For critical analysis: Studies have found that the Big Mac is a surprisingly good longer-term indicator of PPP valuations of exchange rates. What does the predictive performance of the Big Mac index imply about the likely usefulness of absolute PPP as a shorter-term measure of currency under- or overvaluation?

Fundamental Issue #1: What does the concept of absolute purchasing power parity imply about the value of the real exchange rate? The concept of absolute PPP is based on the law of one price, which indicates that the price of a traded good or service in one nation should equal the exchange-rate-adjusted price of that same good or service in another country. If absolute PPP holds true, then the price level in one country equals the nominal exchange rate multiplied by the price level of another nation. This means that under absolute PPP, the real exchange rate always equals 1, which is rarely likely to be the case.

Table 8.1 *The hamburger standard*

Country	Big Mac prices in local currency	Implied PPP exchange rate	Actual exchange rate	Local currency undervaluation (−)/ overvaluation (+) (percent)
United States	$4.56	–	–	–
Brazil	Real 12.00	2.63 real/$	2.27 real/$	+16
Canada	C$5.53	1.21 C$/$	1.05 C$/$	+15
Sweden	Skr 41.61	9.13 Skr/$	6.76 Skr/$	+35
Switzerland	SFr 6.50	1.43 SFr/$	0.97 SFr/$	+55
Thailand	Baht 89.00	19.53 baht/$	31.28 baht/$	−38

Source: Data from www.economist.com, July 2013.

RELATIVE PURCHASING POWER PARITY

Because real exchange rates often differ from unity, absolute PPP is not a very useful theory of exchange rates. For this reason, economists often use a different benchmark for how exchange rates are determined, known as relative purchasing power parity.

Proportionate price changes and relative purchasing power parity

The problem with absolute PPP is that people in different countries often consume distinctive baskets of goods and services. This means that simply applying the law of one price across prices of goods and services used to calculate measures of the price level such as consumer price indexes is inappropriate. To avoid this pitfall, economists often use the concept of relative PPP, which relates *relative changes* in exchange rates to *relative changes* in countries' price levels.

We can use the expression for absolute PPP to derive the relative version of PPP. Let's denote the percentage change of a variable by placing the characters "%Δ" in front of the variable. Then, for example, %ΔP would represent the proportionate change in a county's price level over a period, which is the nation's inflation rate. By calculating the change of each variable in the equation for absolute PPP, we can express relative PPP as

$$\%\Delta S = \%\Delta P - \%\Delta P*$$

Thus, relative PPP implies that the percentage change in a rate of exchange for two countries' currencies equals the difference between the two nations' inflation rates.

In contrast to absolute PPP, the theory of relative PPP does not require the real exchange rate to equal a value of 1. All that is required for relative PPP to hold true is that the real exchange rate for two countries must be stable over time. This is still a tall order, however, because the purchasing power of goods and services in one country relative to goods and services in another country can shift over time.

How does relative PPP perform as a theoretical predictor of actual exchange-rate changes? Most studies indicate that relative PPP performs better than absolute PPP. Nevertheless, real exchange rates can vary considerably over relatively short-run intervals. Consquently, factors other than relative price levels or inflation rates can have significant effects on exchange rates. Relative PPP, therefore, typically is not a very good theory for predicting exchange-rate movements for periods of less than a few years. Relative PPP often performs better over short-run intervals for countries that experience episodes of very high inflation. This is true because, during such episodes, price changes typically are the dominant influence on the value of the domestic currency.

Purchasing power parity as a long-run determinant of exchange rates

Economists have long recognized the factors that limit their ability to use PPP as a complete theory of exchange rates. Nevertheless, the logic of the law of one price has led most economists to believe that, given sufficient passage of time, exchange rates should *eventually* adjust to values consistent with PPP, at least in its relative form.

In the 1970s and 1980s, however, study after study found that it was difficult to rule out the possibility that real exchange rates follow a *random walk*. This meant that if some factor, such as an abrupt, temporary change in the price level in one nation, were to occur, the real exchange rate would move to a new level. Then the real exchange rate would tend to stay at this new level until the next unexpected, short-lived event took place to "bump" the real exchange rate to another level. As we already noted, absolute PPP implies that the real exchange rate should tend toward the value of 1. Relative PPP is less restrictive, but if relative PPP holds, it turns out that the real exchange rate should tend toward a *constant* value (but not necessarily a value of 1). If the real exchange rate were to move in a random walk, however, then as time passes it would not necessarily settle down to a constant value. Thus, random-walk behavior of real exchange rates was strong evidence against PPP.

During the past 20 years, new rounds of research on real exchange rates have evaluated the possibility that earlier studies were biased because they considered only a few countries or relatively short spans of time. Looking at insufficient observations of the real exchange rate might make short-term variations in the real exchange rate look like random-walk movements, when in fact they were simply movements of real exchange rates toward levels consistent with PPP. One set of studies, therefore, examined large numbers of countries' real exchange rates simultaneously, thereby evaluating PPP with massive amounts of cross-country data. These studies consistently found little evidence of random-walk behavior of exchange rates. Recently, however, a debate has arisen about whether this "cross-country approach" to evaluating PPP suffers from its own special difficulties.

This has led other researchers to concentrate their attention on real-exchange-rate behavior over long time periods, spanning from six decades to as long as nearly seven centuries. The idea is that, if PPP holds, it must hold on average over such long intervals. Indeed, these studies find strong evidence that, if given sufficient time, real exchange rates tend to settle down at constant long-term levels predicted by the PPP doctrine. These studies conclude that there is so little evidence in favor of PPP over shorter-term periods because departures from PPP take so long to disappear. For example, if some temporary factor causes the real exchange rate to move above the level consistent with PPP, these studies of long-run horizons indicate that it typically takes between 3 and 7 years for the real exchange rate to get halfway back to its PPP level. If these more recent studies are correct, PPP is truly a long-run determinant of exchange rates. This may help explain why *The Economist*'s Big Mac index has shown signs of performing better when evaluated over intervals of several years, even though it consistently fails to fit exchange rates on a year-to-year basis.

> *Fundamental Issue #2: What is relative purchasing power parity, and is it useful as a guide to movements in exchange rates?* Relative PPP relates exchange rate appreciation or depreciation to national inflation rates. It states that the proportionate change in the nominal rate of exchange of two nations' currencies should equal the difference between the two countries' inflation rates. Because people in different countries consume differing baskets of goods and services, most economists view relative PPP as superior to absolute PPP when contemplating the relationship between prices and exchange rates. Nevertheless, most evidence indicates that even relative PPP is, at best, a long-run guide to understanding how exchange rates are determined.

INTERNATIONAL INTEREST RATE PARITY

Complications such as transportation costs and trade restrictions limit the extent to which unhindered cross-border arbitrage activities can take place in markets for goods and services, thereby undermining the usefulness of PPP as a theory of exchange rates. By way of contrast, it is much easier to engage in international exchanges of financial assets, such as bonds, shares of stock, and national currencies. There are few costs of transferring shares of ownership across national borders. Indeed, nowadays many parties to exchange of financial assets make ownership transfers electronically. In addition, an increasing number of the world's nations permit nearly unhindered trade of financial assets across their borders.

Consequently, there is considerable scope for arbitrage activities in global financial markets. It turns out that this means that, in today's world, exchange rates and interest rates on financial assets must be related.

The forward exchange market and covered interest parity

The concepts of absolute and relative PPP discussed earlier arise from arbitrage across national markets for goods and services. Arbitrage can also take place across national financial markets, as traders attempt to earn profits by buying and selling bonds issued by individuals, companies, or governments of various nations.

For example, suppose the interest rate on a U.S. bond is 6.6 percent. At the same time, the interest rate on a British bond, with all the same riskiness, liquidity, tax treatment, and term to maturity, is 7.2 percent. Could a U.S. saver profit from shifting funds from the United States to the United Kingdom? The answer to this question depends on whether the realized return on the British bond is greater than the realized return on the U.S. bond. Comparing the realized returns, in turn, requires taking into account how covered interest returns (returns completely hedged against foreign-exchange risk) on the British bond depend on forward and spot exchange rates. Thus, forward exchange rates, spot exchange rates, and national interest rates must ultimately be taken into account by anyone who seeks arbitrage profits from trading bonds internationally.

ON THE WEB:

Where on the Internet can we find euro, yen, and other forward exchange rates relative to the U.S. dollar? One place to check for these forward exchange rates is the Financial Times' Markets Data Research Archive located at http:// markets.ft.com/ft/ markets/ researchArchive.asp.

Covering foreign exchange risk with forward contracts

Now let's suppose that a U.S. resident has two alternatives. One is to purchase a one-period, dollar-denominated bond that has a market interest yield of R_{US}. After one year, the U.S. resident will have accumulated $1 + R_{US}$ dollars for each dollar saved.

The other saving option is to use each dollar to buy British pounds at the spot exchange rate of S dollars per pound, to obtain $1/S$ pounds with each dollar. Then the U.S. resident could use the $1/S$ pounds to buy a 1-year British (U.K.) bond that pays the rate R_{UK}. After a year, the person would have accumulated $(1/S)(1 + R_{UK})$ *pounds*. When the U.S. resident buys the U.K. bond, however, we assume that at the same time the individual sells this quantity of pounds in the forward market at the forward exchange rate of F dollars per pound. This "covers" the individual against risk of exchange-rate changes by insuring that the effective gross return on the U.K. bond will be $(F/S)(1 + R_{UK})$.

Covered interest parity

When no profitable arbitrage opportunities exist, the realized returns on the two bonds will be the same. That is, there is no incentive for U.S. savers to arbitrage across the U.S. and British financial markets if the gross returns are equal:

$$1 + R_{US} = (F/S)(1 + R_{UK})$$

Now we can use the algebraic fact that

$$F/S = (S/S) + (F - S)/S = 1 + (F - S)/S$$

to rewrite the condition as

$$1 + R_{US} = [1 + (F - S)/S](1 + R_{UK})$$

Now we can cross-multiply the right-hand side to get

$$1 + R_{US} = 1 + (F - S)/S + R_{UK} + [R_{UK} \times (F - S)/S]$$

Covered interest parity: *A prediction that the interest rate on one nation's bond should approximately equal the interest rate on a similar bond in another nation plus the forward premium, or the difference between forward exchange rate and the spot exchange rate divided by the spot exchange rate.*

Because R_{UK} and $(F - S)/S$ are both typically small fractions, their product is approximately equal to zero. (For example, if R_{UK} is 0.072 and $(F - S)/S$ is -0.047, then their product is equal to -0.0034, which is very close to zero.) Making this approximation and subtracting 1 from both sides of the equation yields

$$R_{US} = R_{UK} + (F - S)/S$$

This last equation is called the **covered interest parity** condition. (Forces of supply and demand ensure that covered interest parity holds; see *Visualizing Global Economic Issues: Why covered interest parity is often satisfied.*)

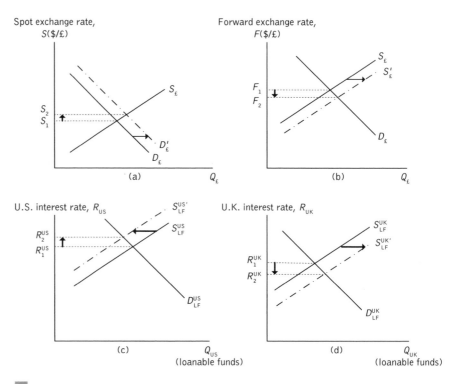

Figure 8.1 *Covered interest arbitrage and interest- and exchange-rate adjustments*

If the interest rate on a U.S. bond is less than the sum of the rate on an equivalent British bond and a forward premium, then the covered interest parity condition does not hold. This induces U.S. savers to move loanable funds into the United Kingdom. Thus, the supply of loanable funds declines in the United States, as shown in panel (c), and the supply of loanable funds in the United Kingdom increases, as depicted in panel (d). To purchase additional British bonds, U.S. savers exchange dollars for pounds in the spot exchange market, which causes a rise in the demand for pounds and a resulting increase in the equilibrium spot exchange rate. If U.S. savers cover their foreign-exchange-risk exposure by contracting for future delivery of dollars in exchange for pounds in the forward exchange market, then there is an increase in the supply of pounds in the forward exchange market, which causes a reduction in the equilibrium forward exchange rate.

VISUALIZING GLOBAL ECONOMIC ISSUES

Why covered interest parity is often satisfied

There is considerable evidence that covered interest parity normally holds true in developed nations with borders that are open to international bond exchanges and to flows of funds in spot and forward exchange markets. To see why this is so, consider what would happened if covered interest parity failed to hold.

In Figure 8.1, panel (a) depicts the spot exchange market for the British pound, and panel (b) shows the forward market for the British pound. Panel (c) illustrates the determination of the U.S. interest rate, which arises where the quantity of *loanable funds* supplied by savers equals the quantity of loanable funds demanded by borrowers within the United States. Likewise, in panel (d), the equilibrium U.K. interest rate arises when the quantity of loanable funds supplied equals the quantity of loanable funds demanded within the United Kingdom.

Suppose that the interest rate on a U.S. bond is less than the sum of the rate on an equivalent British bond and a forward premium. This induces U.S. savers to move loanable funds to the United Kingdom, so the supply of loanable funds in the United States declines, as illustrated by the leftward shift of the supply schedule in panel (c), while the supply of loanable funds in the United Kingdom increases, as depicted by the rightward shift of the supply schedule in panel (d).

To purchase British financial instruments, U.S. savers must exchange dollars for British pounds in the spot exchange market, so the demand for pounds rises in panel (a), causing a rise in the equilibrium spot exchange rate, or a *spot depreciation* of the dollar relative to the pound, shown by the movement from S_1 to S_2. If, as in our example above, U.S. savers cover their exposures to foreign exchange risk, then they also purchase dollars (for future delivery with pounds earned by holding the British financial instruments) using forward currency contracts. As a result, there is an increase in the supply of pounds in the forward exchange market, shown by a rightward shift in the pound supply schedule in panel (b). The increase in the supply of pounds in the forward exchange market results in a *forward depreciation* of the pound relative to the dollar, as shown by the decrease in the equilibrium forward exchange rate from F_1 to F_2.

Thus, market forces tend to push national interest rates toward equilibrium values consistent with covered interest parity. The effort of U.S. savers to earn higher returns in the United Kingdom when the U.S. interest rate is less than the sum of the U.K. rate plus the forward premium tends to push up the equilibrium U.S. interest rate and to push down the equilibrium U.K. interest rate. Their effort to cover their foreign exchange risks also tends to push up the spot exchange rate and to push down the forward exchange rate, thereby reducing the forward premium. Normally, these market adjustments quickly bring about equality between the U.S. interest rate and the sum of the U.K. interest rate and the forward premium. This is why covered interest parity typically holds.

For critical analysis: Under what circumstances could persistent deviations from covered interest parity take place?

As we noted earlier, the quantity $(F - S)/S$ is the forward premium or discount. Thus, the condition of covered interest parity says that the interest rate on a U.S. bond should approximately equal the interest rate on the foreign (U.K.) bond plus the forward premium or discount for the pound.

For instance, suppose that the observed market interest rate on a U.K. bond is 0.052 (5.2 percent), and the forward discount for the U.S. dollar relative to the U.K. pound is 0.008 (0.8 percent). In this instance, the covered interest parity condition indicates that the observed market interest rate on a U.S. bond with the same risk characteristics and the same term to maturity should equal $0.052 + 0.008 = 0.060$ (6.0 percent). (During the global financial crisis following 2007, covered interest parity failed to hold in many nations, but for different reasons in advanced and emerging nations; see the box "Management notebook: Covered interest-parity breakdowns during the financial crisis—developed versus emerging economies.")

MANAGEMENT NOTEBOOK

Covered interest-parity breakdowns during the financial crisis—developed versus emerging economies

There is considerable evidence that the covered interest parity condition typically is satisfied in countries in which residents can engage in virtually unhindered trading of currencies and bonds. Deviations are more commonplace in less developed nations, in which various impediments to such trading tend to arise. Sait Satiroglu and Emrah Sener of Ozyegin University and Yildiray Yildirim of Syracuse University examine deviations of covered interest parity in three developed nations and regions—Japan, the United Kingdom, and Europe's euro area—and three emerging economies—Turkey, South Africa, and Mexico. Consistent with most other studies, these researchers find that, prior to the summer of 2007, deviations from the covered interest parity condition were very nearly equal to zero in the developed group, and to 1 percentage point in the emerging group.

Satiroglu, Sener, and Yildirim find that covered interest-parity deviations jumped well above zero from the middle of 2007 through 2009. Between the fall of 2008 and spring of 2009, these deviations peaked at more than 4 percentage points among the advanced economies that the researchers studied. For the emerging group, the deviations during that period reached nearly 6 percentage points. Thus, deviations from covered interest parity became significantly more pronounced for both sets of countries.

The researchers find evidence suggesting that, during this peak-crisis interval, there was a global drop in trust among banks and other institutions that trade bonds internationally, which caused many institutions in both developed and emerging nations to become unwilling to trade bonds or currencies with each other, even though failure to do so resulted in failing to engage in previously intended covered transactions. Second, during the financial panic, a number of institutions found themselves short of cash to conduct trades consistent with covering their positions. As a consequence of both factors, covered interest parity broke down across both groups of nations. The researchers additionally find, however, that the impediments to financial trade already faced by emerging economies became even more pronounced during the crisis, which explained why covered interest-parity deviations were even more pronounced in these countries.

For critical analysis: Why do you suppose that the decline in deviations from covered interest parity after the autumn of 2008 followed central banks' efforts to stabilize private banks by shoring up the institutions' net worth and extending credit to help them rebuild cash positions?

Uncovered interest arbitrage

As we have discussed, covered interest arbitrage—covering the foreign exchange risk associated with bond transactions across national borders—leads to the covered interest parity condition. Under covered interest parity, the interest rate on a bond in one nation equals the interest rate on the equivalent bond in another country plus the forward premium or discount. What happens, however, if people do not cover foreign exchange risk exposures?

A good reason why someone might choose not to use a forward currency contract to hedge against foreign exchange risks is that the transaction is too small to warrant going to the trouble to set up a forward contract. Indeed, a typical forward currency contract has a denomination of at least $1 million. Hence, the individual might decide to use a different hedging instrument (see Chapter 6), or the individual might choose not to hedge the transaction at all.

Uncovered interest parity

In our example, we considered a U.S. saver with a choice between a U.S. bond and a U.K. bond with equivalent riskiness, tax treatment, liquidity, and term to maturity. Let's consider the same example, but now let's consider a situation in which the U.S. saver does not purchase a forward exchange contract or hedge the foreign exchange risk in any other way, so that the transaction is *uncovered*.

In this case, the U.S. saver again anticipates a *dollar*-denominated interest return of R_{US} by holding a U.S. bond to maturity or a *pound*-denominated interest return of R_{UK} by holding an equivalent British bond to maturity. To the U.S. saver, however, what matters in choosing between the two bonds is the anticipated *dollar* value of the return on the British bond. This is equal to $R_{UK} + \%\Delta S^e$, where $\%\Delta S^e$ is the rate at which people expect the dollar to depreciate (or, if $\%\Delta S^e$ is negative, to appreciate) relative to the pound. If $\%\Delta S^e$ is positive, then the U.S. saver anticipates that the dollar will depreciate in value relative to the pound, and will wish for the U.S. bond's interest rate to be higher than the rate on the British bond to compensate for this expected depreciation of the dollar.

Thus, this U.S. saver will be indifferent between holding U.S. or British bonds only if the anticipated returns are equal. This will be true when

$$R_{US} = R_{UK} + \%\Delta S^e$$

or when the U.S. interest rate equals the U.K. interest rate plus the expected rate of depreciation of the dollar relative to the pound. If the U.S. interest rate is *less than* the U.K. interest rate plus the expected rate of dollar depreciation, then U.S. savers who do not cover their transactions will allocate more savings to *U.K. bonds*. If the U.S. interest rate is *greater than* the U.K. rate plus the anticipated depreciation rate of the dollar, then U.S. savers will allocate more savings to *U.S. bonds*. In theory, shifts of funds in this pursuit of *uncovered arbitrage* profits will tend to push both interest rates to levels consistent with equality between the U.S. interest rate and the sum of the U.K. interest rate and the expected rate of dollar depreciation.

Uncovered interest parity: *A relationship between interest rates on bonds that are similar in all respects other than the fact that they are denominated in different nations' currencies. According to this condition, which applies to a situation in which an individual engages in unhedged currency trades to fund bond purchases abroad, the interest rate on the bond denominated in the currency that holders anticipate will depreciate must exceed the interest rate on the other bond by the rate at which the currency is expected to depreciate.*

The equality between the interest rate in one nation and the sum of the interest rate and expected currency depreciation for another nation is called **uncovered interest parity**. It is called "uncovered" interest parity because it does not arise from foreign-exchange transactions that cover risks. The uncovered interest parity condition is more likely to hold for interest rates of nations that are most open to cross-border flows of funds.

Figure 8.2 plots differences between interest differentials on 3-month Treasury bills and the actual percentage change in the spot rate over the maturity period of the bonds of the United Kingdom and Switzerland relative to the United States. These are *approximate* deviations from the uncovered interest parity, because the true uncovered interest parity condition relates interest rates to *expected*, not actual, percentage changes in the spot rate. Nevertheless, the figure tends to indicate the possibility for persistent deviations from uncovered interest parity, even among the most developed nations. Further, the average absolute value of the deviations shown in Figure 8.2 is about 4.5 percent.

Risk and uncovered interest parity

The uncovered purchase of a foreign bond exposes a U.S. saver to foreign exchange risk. This is so because the saver's expectation about currency depreciation or appreciation during the term to maturity might turn out to be incorrect. In this instance, the realized return on the foreign bond would differ from the anticipated return.

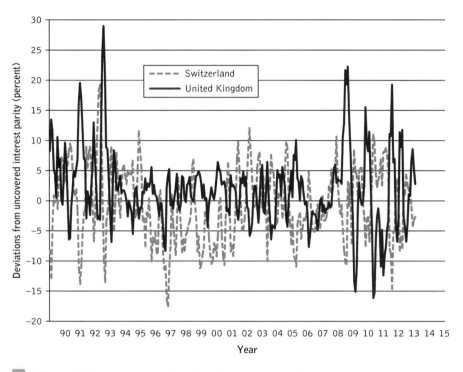

Figure 8.2 *Approximate deviations from uncovered interest parity*

This figure displays the deviations from uncovered interest parity for U.S. and Swiss 3-month treasury bills, and U.S. and U.K. 3-month treasury bills, which are plotted by subtracting the 3-month change in the spot exchange rate from the interest differential. Deviations from uncovered interest parity can persist for extended periods.

Source: International Monetary Fund, *International Financial Statistics.*

If the value of a nation's currency is highly variable, then predicting its future value is difficult. This makes allocating a portion of one's wealth to holdings of a foreign bond a much riskier proposition. Consequently, borrowers located in nations with volatile currency values may have to offer higher interest returns to induce savers to purchase the bonds they issue. In this instance, it may be appropriate to include a risk premium in the uncovered interest parity condition. The risk premium is the increase in the return offered on a bond to compensate individuals for the additional foreign exchange risk they undertake in uncovered transactions.

For instance, if the U.S. dollar's exchange value becomes more volatile and less predictable, then the uncovered interest parity condition may be expressed as

$$R_{US} = R_{UK} + \%\Delta S^e + RP$$

where RP is the risk premium that compensates savers for holding U.S. bonds instead of equivalent U.K. bonds. In this situation, the differential between the U.S. interest rate and the U.K. interest rate should equal the expected depreciation of the dollar relative to the pound plus the risk premium.

If volatility in relative currency values varies over time, then the risk premium can vary from period to period. Thus, the existence of *time-varying risk premiums* could help to account for the existence of deviations from uncovered interest parity indicated in Figure 8.2. Whether foreign exchange markets are efficient depends in part on how one interprets the contribution of risk premiums to deviations from uncovered interest parity (*Management Notebook: Using international bank lending rates to investigate uncovered interest parity.*)

MANAGEMENT NOTEBOOK

Using international bank lending rates to investigate uncovered interest parity

Most studies of uncovered interest parity focus on comparing interest rates on government securities and other money market instruments with arguably the same risks, liquidity features, and tax-treatment characteristics. A recent examination of uncovered interest parity by Muhammad Omer, Jakob de Haan, and Bert Scholtens of the University of Grongingen considers instead the London Interbank Offered Rates (LIBOR) observed on loans extended between international banking institutions. Their study examines bilateral relationships between LIBOR rates for seven currencies—the U.S. dollar, the pound, the euro, the yen, the Swiss franc, the Australian dollar, and the Canadian dollar—and across 14 different loan maturities, ranging from 1 week to 12 months between 2001 and 2008.

Omer, de Haan, and Scholtens find evidence supporting uncovered interest parity for low-maturity international interbank loans. LIBOR rates for country pairings tend to provide successively less support for uncovered interest parity at longer loan maturities. The researchers argue the evidence indicates that, at longer loan maturities, the speed of adjustment to uncovered interest parity is longer, hence uncovered interest parity is less likely to hold at any given point in time.

For critical analysis: Andrea Monticini of Catholic University and Daniel Thornton of the Federal Reserve Bank of St. Louis have provided evidence that, between 2005 and 2008, key banks in the London interbank market systematically underreported LIBOR rates. If all banks equally underreported the interbank loan rates, could uncovered interest parity still hold true?

Fundamental Issue #3: What are the covered and uncovered interest parity conditions? Covered interest parity is a condition that arises if individuals hedge international financial transactions using forward currency contracts. It states that the interest rate in one nation equals the sum of another nation's interest rate plus the forward premium or discount, which is the difference between the forward exchange rate and the spot exchange rate divided by the spot exchange rate. If individuals do not hedge exchange-rate risks associated with purchases of bonds with identical risks, but which are denominated in different currencies, then another interest parity condition—uncovered interest parity—may apply. According to the uncovered interest parity condition, the interest rate for the bond denominated in the currency that is expected to depreciate must be the greater of the two interest rates. The yield of the bond denominated in the currency that is expected to depreciate must exceed the other bond's yield by the rate at which the currency is expected to depreciate.

ARE FOREIGN EXCHANGE MARKETS EFFICIENT?

Those who wish to trade currencies examine past and current market exchange rates in an effort to determine likely future values of exchange rates. They do this using their understanding of how exchange rates are determined. Therefore, *current* exchange rates should reflect how currency traders form their expectations of future exchange rates. This has led economists to develop a theory of the determination of exchange rates that explains how people use current information and forecasts of future exchange rates when they decide how to adjust their holdings of currencies and other financial assets. This theory is called the *efficient-markets hypothesis*. This hypothesis provides an explanation of how expectations about the future relate to current market realities. Consequently, let's first consider alternative ways of looking at how people form expectations of future events.

Adaptive versus rational expectations

Clearly, to make any decisions that have future consequences, you must act on forecasts that you make based on whatever information you currently possess. There are two fundamental theories for how you might go about doing this.

Adaptive expectations

One way to make an inference about a likely future value of an exchange rate, or of a future return on a bond, is to do so "adaptively." The easiest way to understand what this means is to consider an example. Imagine that a friend, or perhaps even a pollster, were to ask you for your forecast of the exchange value of the euro for U.S. dollars a year from now. How would you come up with an answer?

One approach might be to collect data on the euro–dollar exchange rate during recent weeks or months. You then could plot these data on a chart and make a rough drawing of the "trend line" along these points and beyond. The point on your trend line 1 year out from the present date would then give your forecast of the euro–dollar exchange rate a year from now.

If you have completed a statistics course, then you might adopt a more sophisticated approach. You could use statistical techniques to determine the specific equation for the trend line that best fits the euro–dollar exchange rate data that you have collected. This equation would enable you to give a predicted value, or forecast, of the exchange rate for a given time, including a year from now.

Either of these forecasting methods would require you to sacrifice time and effort to collect a considerable amount of data. If you do not wish to incur this opportunity cost to make a sophisticated forecast of the rate of exchange between the euro and the dollar a year from now, then you could choose a simpler method. For instance, you might just guess that next year's exchange rate will turn out to be an average of its value over the past 3 years. Even simpler, you might guess that next year's exchange rate will turn out not to be much different than it has been during the past year.

Adaptive expectations:
Expectations that are based only on information from the past.

Each of these forecasting methods is an example of an **adaptive expectation** process, meaning that each method entails using only *past information*. Drawing a rough trend line, using statistical techniques to calculate an exact trend line, computing a 3-year average, or just extrapolating from the current inflation rate all share the common feature that past data formed the sole basis for the rate-of-return forecast. Relying only on past data makes the forecast an *adaptive forecast*.

Drawbacks of adaptive expectations

One of these examples may relate closely to how you think you make your own forecasts. Nevertheless, many economists reject the idea of adaptive expectations. One reason for this negative judgment is that, if people really were to use adaptive expectations, then they often would make forecasts that they realize in advance should turn out to be wrong.

Suppose for instance, that a person's adaptive method for forecasting next year's rate of exchange of the euro for the dollar is to calculate an average of exchange rates for the past 3 years. If this average exchange rate is equal to, say, 0.769 euros per dollar, then that would be the individual's forecast of the exchange rate for next year. Now suppose the person reads in the newspaper that the European Central Bank is likely to buy or sell large amounts of dollars within the next few days in an effort to influence the euro's market value. A person who stuck with the 3-year-averaging procedure for calculating the exchange rate would consciously ignore this new information, even though the individual reasonably should recognize that actions by the European Central Bank in foreign exchange markets might alter the euro's value relative to the dollar.

This means that an economic theory based on the hypothesis of adaptive expectations would yield forecasts of market exchange rates that consistently ignored information relevant to the actual determination of exchange rates in the future. Thus, any economic theory based on adaptive expectations will be internally inconsistent, because the people whose behavior the model attempts to mimic would behave inconsistently.

Another troublesome aspect of the hypothesis of adaptive expectations is that there is no way to say, in advance, what adaptive expectations process is "best." For example, one individual might draw a chart of 6 months of past exchange rate data to plot a rough trend line to guide her exchange rate forecasts; another person might use the same technique using data from the previous 12 months; and yet another might use 3 years' data. Someone else might calculate a weighted average of exchange rates over the past 5 years. Indeed, there are an infinite number of possible adaptive expectations schemes. Which one should we include in a theory of the determination of exchange rates? There is no good way to answer this question.

Rational expectations

These problems with adaptive expectations led economists to develop an alternative theory of how people make forecasts—the **rational expectations hypothesis**. According to this hypothesis, an individual makes the best possible forecast of a market price or return using all available past *and current* information, *and* drawing on an understanding of what factors affect the price or return. In contrast to an adaptive forecast, which looks only backwards because it is based on past information, a rational forecast looks forward while also taking into account past information.

Consider, for instance, the earlier example, in which someone initially made an exchange rate forecast using an average of exchange rates over the past 3 years, but then learned of imminent central bank actions to influence exchange rates. If that person's goal is to best predict the exchange rate, then sticking with her original, adaptive forecast clearly would not be in her best interest. The *rational* way for her to respond to the new information would be to use her own understanding concerning how central bank actions in foreign exchange markets would likely influence the exchange rate. Then she would update her exchange rate forecast for the coming year accordingly.

Thus, the distinction between adaptive and rational expectations can be summarized in the following manner:

> An *adaptive* expectation is based only on past information. In contrast, a *rational* expectation takes into account both past and current information, plus an understanding of how the economy functions.

Rational expectations hypothesis:
The idea that individuals form expectations based on all available past and current information and on a basic understanding of how markets function.

Advantages of the rational expectations hypothesis

Because the rational expectations hypothesis does not impose artificial constraints on how people use information, it is a more general theory of expectation formation than adaptive expectations. Whereas an adaptive expectations process imposes the use of only past information, the rational expectations hypothesis states that, if an individual can improve on an adaptive forecast, then that is what the individual will do.

This does not deny that a person's rationally formed expectation cannot look like an adaptive expectation from time to time. If a person has only past information, and no special insight into how a market functions, then an adaptive forecast might be the best that person can do. In such a circumstance, an adaptive expectation would be that individual's rational expectation.

It seems most likely, nevertheless, that people would use all available current information plus all conceptions about how markets work when they try to infer market prices and returns. Consequently, a rationally formed expectation should, under most circumstances, differ from a purely adaptive expectation.

It is important to recognize that, even though rational expectations generally will be better than adaptive expectations, forecasts based on all current information and an understanding of how markets operate will not always be correct. For example, the U.S. National Weather Service's adoption of Doppler radar has improved the ability of weather forecasters to predict where tornadoes may form. This means only that tornado forecasts are better than before. It does not mean such forecasts always are on the mark. Indeed, during turbulent weather conditions, very damaging and life-threatening tornadoes can form quickly in locations that Doppler radar previously indicated to be low-probability locales for such storms.

In like manner, rationally formed forecasts of the market prices and returns are better, on average, than adaptive forecasts. *Actual* prices and returns, however, can still turn out to be much higher or lower than people had rationally predicted.

Are there limits on rationality?

The rational expectations hypothesis poses a couple of conceptual problems of its own. One of these is that the hypothesis is very broad—so broad that incorporating it fully into a theory can prove challenging. For instance, each individual has his or her own perspective on how financial markets operate. In addition, at any given instant, each person is informed to a somewhat different extent about current market developments. Does this indicate that economists should try to model every individual's expectations-formation procedure?

A related difficulty is that the rational expectations hypothesis indicates that each person acts on his or her rationally formed expectation of market prices and returns. This means that *realized* market prices and returns will depend on how all individuals form their expectations. If each person realizes that the expectations of others thereby will play a role in affecting actual market prices and returns, does this mean that each person should attempt to forecast others' forecasts?

To get around these problems, economists often use two simplifying assumptions when they construct theories that include rational expectations. The first is the presumption that each person in the marketplace has access to the same information, and has the same conception of how the market works. This assumption gets around the issue of different expectations across individuals in the market. It also dodges the problem of individuals worrying about others' forecasts, because by assumption, each person's forecast is the same.

The second common assumption used in economic models with rational expectations is that people in the marketplace understand how the market functions. That is, an economist using the rational expectations hypothesis typically assumes that the people whose behavior their models try to describe behave *as if* they understand that the economy works according to the economists' own theory. This assumption boils down to presuming that the people in an economic model *know the model*.

Let's think about how we might apply the rational expectations hypothesis to this more realistic view on how exchange rates are determined. Under the rational expectations hypothesis, an optimal forecast reflects all available past *and* current information, as well as an understanding of how the relevant variable is determined. In the case of international interest returns, therefore, the rational expectations hypothesis indicates that exchange rate expectations that can influence market interest rates are rational forecasts of future exchange rates by those who trade foreign currencies.

Fundamental Issue #4: What is the distinction between adaptive and rational expectations? An adaptive expectation is one that is formed using only past information. In contrast, a rationally formed expectation is based on past and current information, and on an understanding of how market prices and returns are determined.

THE EFFICIENT-MARKETS HYPOTHESIS

The reasoning of the rational expectations hypothesis forms the basis for the **efficient-markets hypothesis**. This hypothesis states that prices of, or returns on, financial assets should reflect all available information, including bond traders' understanding of how financial markets determine asset prices.

    More generally, the efficient markets theory says that the return on, or price of, *any* asset should reflect the rational forecast of the asset's returns. Consequently, the rate of exchange for a nation's currency should reflect knowledge of all available information by those who trade the currency. If the market exchange rate were to fail to reflect all such information, then the implication would be that foreign exchange markets function inefficiently, because traders could earn profits if they accounted for such unused information.

Efficient-markets hypothesis: *A theory that stems from application of the rational expectations hypothesis to financial markets, which states that equilibrium prices of and returns on bonds should reflect all past and current information plus traders' understanding of how market prices and returns are determined.*

Foreign exchange market efficiency

The efficient-markets hypothesis has three key implications. First, it indicates that there should be a definite relationship between the market price of, or return on, a bond and traders' expectation of the market price or return. Second, it implies that some factors are likely to cause greater movements in prices or returns than others. Finally, the efficient-markets hypothesis has an important prediction about efforts by traders to earn higher-than-average rates of return.

    If foreign exchange markets are efficient, it follows that returns on internationally traded bonds should reflect all information possessed by those who trade these bonds. To evaluate whether foreign exchange markets are efficient, therefore, we must consider how savers' expectations of future exchange-rate movements influence the returns on internationally traded bonds.

    Note that the two international interest parity conditions discussed above provide two reasons that the interest rate for a U.S. bond might be higher than the interest rate on an otherwise identical British bond. One reason, provided by the *covered* interest parity condition, is the presence of a forward premium in the forward exchange market, so that the differential between the U.S. interest rate and the U.K. interest rate is equal to

$$R_{US} - R_{UK} = (F - S)/S$$

The other reason is the one implied by the *uncovered* interest parity condition:

$$R_{US} - R_{UK} = \%\Delta S^e$$

This condition indicates that, in the absence of a risk premium, the amount by which the U.S. interest rate exceeds the U.K. interest rate should be the expected rate of depreciation of the dollar relative to the pound.

The condition for foreign exchange market efficiency

The only way that both the covered and uncovered interest parity conditions are satisfied is if the right-hand terms in both are equal, or if

$$(F - S)/S = \%\Delta S^e$$

This relationship states that the forward premium (or discount) for the pound relative to the dollar is equal to the rate at which the dollar is expected to depreciate (appreciate) relative to the pound in the spot foreign exchange market. Let's denote the expected future spot exchange rate at the time that a forward currency contract settles as S^e. It follows that the expected rate of dollar depreciation during the term of the contract, $\%\Delta S^e$, is equal to the expected change in the spot exchange rate, $S^e - S$, divided by the current spot exchange rate, S. Thus, $\%\Delta S^e = (S^e - S)/S$. If both covered and uncovered interest parity hold true, then

Foreign exchange market efficiency:

A situation in which the equilibrium spot and forward exchange adjust to reflect all available information, in which case the forward premium is equal to the expected rate of currency depreciation plus any risk premium. This, in turn, implies that the forward exchange rate on average predicts the expected future spot exchange rate.

$$(F - S)/S = (S^e - S)/S$$

or

$$F = S^e$$

If both interest parity conditions are satisfied in the marketplace, the forward exchange rate is equal to the anticipated spot exchange rate at the time of settlement of the forward currency contract.

If this last equality is not satisfied, so that the forward exchange rate differs from the expected future spot exchange rate, then financial market traders perceive an arbitrage opportunity. In an *efficient market*, of course, such opportunities should be very fleeting. Market expectations and prices should adjust speedily to eliminate the potential for arbitrage profits. Thus, **foreign exchange market efficiency** exists when the forward exchange rate is a good predictor—often called an "unbiased predictor"—of the future spot exchange rate, meaning that, on average, the forward exchange rate turns out to equal the future spot exchange rate. When the foreign exchange market is efficient, therefore, forward exchange rates should adjust to the point at which the forward premium is equal to the expected rate of currency depreciation. Under the rational expectations hypothesis, the expected rate of currency depreciation should be the rational forecast of the rate of depreciation, or the forecast of depreciation based on all available information and an understanding of how exchange rates are determined.

Another way of thinking about the foreign exchange market efficiency condition is to relate it back to the efficient market theory. This theory broadly states that the price of a financial asset should reflect all available information. The foreign exchange market efficiency condition is analogous. It states that the forward and spot exchange rates, which are the spot and forward prices of a nation's currency, should take into account rational forecasts of the extent to which the nation's currency will depreciate. As a result, the premium or discount relating the forward and spot exchange rates should reflect all available information.

Evidence on foreign exchange market efficiency

There is considerable evidence that covered interest parity generally holds in the markets for currencies of developed economies. The evidence on uncovered interest parity and, consequently, on foreign exchange market efficiency, is more mixed. For instance, consider Figure 8.3, which plots the percentage difference between 3-month forward exchange rates and the spot exchange rates 3 months later for the U.S. dollar and the British pound. As you can see, the forward exchange rate often underestimates or overestimates the realized spot exchange rate.

Of course, foreign exchange efficiency relates the forward exchange rate to the *expected* future spot exchange rate. If the rational expectations hypothesis is correct, then the expected rate of depreciation should reflect a rational *forecast*. Consequently, studies of foreign exchange market efficiency entail trying to determine if exchange rate *expectations* are formed rationally. Trying to determine statistically whether foreign exchange market efficiency and rational expectations both hold at the same time is a difficult proposition. This is especially true if a risk premium widens the differential between national interest rates. Then economists must disentangle the relative contributions of the risk premium and potential expectational errors as factors causing potential deviations from foreign exchange market efficiency. Most studies indicate that risk premiums are important, but are divided on whether foreign exchange markets are truly efficient.

Fundamental Issue #5: What is foreign exchange market efficiency? According to the efficient-markets hypothesis, the market return on, or price of, a financial asset should reflect all available information in that market. This is so because the demand for, and supply of, an asset (such as a bond or a foreign exchange contract) will take

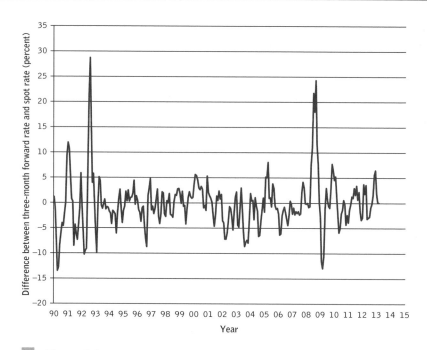

Figure 8.3 *Forward and spot exchange-rate differentials*

This figure plots the difference between the U.S. dollar 3-month forward exchange rate and the actual U.S. dollar spot exchange rate that prevailed 3 months later for the United Kingdom. There are consistently substantial differences between the forward exchange rate and spot exchange rate at the settlement date of forward contracts.

Source: Bank of England.

into account rationally formed expectations of future prices of the asset. Traders form these expectations, in turn, in light of all information in their possession. Foreign exchange markets are efficient if savers cannot persistently earn higher returns by shifting holdings of bonds across national borders. Foreign exchange market efficiency requires that the forward premium, or the difference between the forward and spot exchange rates divided by the spot exchange rate, be equal to the expected rate of currency depreciation. This efficiency condition holds if both the covered and uncovered interest parity conditions are satisfied.

REVISITING GLOBAL INTEGRATION OF THE REAL AND FINANCIAL SECTORS

As we discussed in Chapter 1, most economists believe that international financial markets are becoming more integrated. One reason that the concept of foreign exchange market efficiency is of practical interest is that efficiency of foreign exchange markets indicates that national markets more broadly are integrated.

The covered and uncovered interest parity conditions, however, relate *nominal* interest rate differentials to spot and forward exchange rates and expected spot exchange rates. Over shorter-term horizons, when changes in inflation may be relatively small, the effects of different national inflation rates may have little effect on saving flows. Nevertheless, saving decisions are more likely to respond to overall price changes over longer time horizons. Thus, over longer intervals, savers' decisions about financial-bond allocations are likely to be motivated by *real* interest rate differentials instead of *nominal* differentials.

Real interest rate parity

So far we have discussed interest rates only in *current-dollar* terms. There is a problem with this, however. Inflation can erode the value of interest received when a bond matures. Any individual must take this into account when evaluating how much to save, either domestically or internationally.

The real interest rate

For instance, suppose that a U.S. saver can earn a stated current-dollar or **nominal interest rate** of 4 percent on each dollar that he allocates to a 1-year bond. Suppose, also, that the saver expects that the inflation rate will be $\%\Delta P^e = 2$ percent during the coming year. Such inflation will reduce the amount of goods and services that his interest return will permit him to purchase.

That is, though he earns positive interest on the bond, the saver anticipates that inflation will eat away at that interest at the rate of 2 percent. Hence, the **real interest rate** that this saver anticipates, or his expected inflation-adjusted interest rate, is *approximately* equal to

$$r = R - \%\Delta P^e$$

In this example, therefore, the real interest rate is equal to 4 percent minus 2 percent, i.e. 2 percent. In terms of what the savings can buy, this saver anticipates earning only 2 percent on his 1-year bond.

Combining relative purchasing power parity and uncovered interest parity: real interest parity

If savers anticipate that relative PPP will hold, then it implies that the difference between expected rates of inflation in the two countries should equal the expected rate of depreciation:

$$\%\Delta P^e - \%\Delta P^{*e} = \%\Delta S^e$$

Remember that if uncovered interest parity holds, and if there is no risk premium, then it also will be the case that

$$R - R^* = \%\Delta S^e$$

Nominal interest rate: *A rate of return in current-dollar terms that does not reflect anticipated inflation.*

Real interest rate: *The anticipated rate of return from holding a bond after taking into account the extent to which inflation is expected to reduce the amount of goods and services that this return could be used to buy.*

so that the differential between any two nations' interest rates equals the expected rate of currency depreciation. If we put these two equations together, we get

$$\%\Delta P^e - \%\Delta P^{*e} = R - R^*$$

Finally, we can rearrange this equation to obtain the following relationship:

$$R - \%\Delta P^e = R^* - \%\Delta P^e$$

This says that if both relative PPP and uncovered interest parity hold true, then the real interest rate in one country, $r = R - \%\Delta P^e$, equals the real interest rate in the other country, $r^* = R^* - \%\Delta P^{*e}$.

Real interest parity: *An equality between two nations' real interest rates that arises if both uncovered interest parity and relative PPP are satisfied.*

This is called the **real interest parity** condition, under which real interest returns on equivalent bonds of two nations are equal. Given the way we have obtained it, real interest parity is a condition that requires both relative PPP and uncovered interest parity to hold.

Real interest parity as an indicator of international integration

Remember that uncovered interest parity is more likely to hold if financial markets are more integrated, so that savers can take advantage of opportunities for uncovered

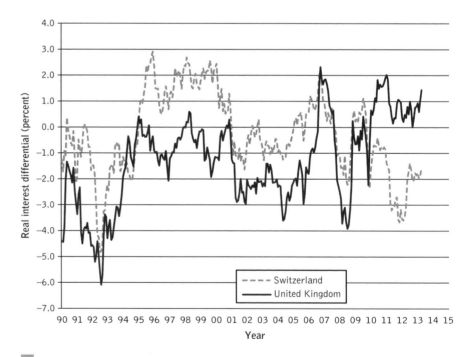

Figure 8.4 *Real interest rate differentials*

Real interest rate differentials often persist, implying that real interest parity typically does not hold.

Source: International Monetary Fund, *International Financial Statistics.*

interest arbitrage. At the same time, relative PPP is more likely to hold if markets for goods and services are also more open to arbitrage.

It follows that, if real interest parity holds true, then international financial and goods markets are likely to be integrated. To get a picture of whether real interest parity is likely to hold for the United States, Switzerland, and the United Kingdom, consider Figure 8.4, which plots differentials in real interest rates for U.S. versus Swiss 3-month treasury bills and for U.S. versus U.K. treasury bills. These differentials use real interest rates, calculated as the nominal treasury bill rate minus the actual inflation rate. Of course, real interest parity is based on real interest rates calculated using *expected* inflation rates, so Figure 8.4 can provide only a rough idea of whether real interest parity may hold for these nations.

Note that there were persistent negative real interest rate differentials in the early 1990s, followed by persistent positive differentials between real interest rates in the late 1990s. These differentials tended to be negative again in the 2000s. These persistent differentials tend to cast doubt on the notion that international markets are fully integrated. In general, more sophisticated statistical tests of real interest parity tend to conclude that real interest differentials exist, even for the most developed, open economies. Nevertheless, work by Richard Marston of the University of Pennsylvania has shown that real interest differentials among these economies tend to be relatively small. This provides some indication that some national markets are fairly highly integrated.

> *Fundamental Issue #6: Under what conditions does real interest parity hold, and why is it a useful indicator of international integration?* If real interest rates in two nations are equal, then real interest parity is satisfied. For real interest parity to hold true, conditions of both uncovered interest parity and relative PPP must be satisfied simultaneously. If this is the case, then there is a high degree of integration of both financial markets and goods markets for the two nations. Hence, economists use real interest parity as an indicator of international integration.

CHAPTER SUMMARY

1. Implications of absolute purchasing power parity for the value of the real exchange rate: The real exchange rate equals the nominal rate of exchange of two nations' currencies multiplied by the ratio of the overall price levels for the two nations. Thus, the real exchange rate adjusts a nominal rate of exchange of national currencies for changes in the nations' price levels, thereby providing a measure of the purchasing power of domestic goods and services in exchange for foreign goods and services. According to the law of one price, the exchange-rate-adjusted price of a tradable good in one nation should equal the price of that good in another nation. Absolute PPP extends the law of one price by relating overall measures of the price levels, such as consumer price indexes, of two countries to the nominal exchange rate. According to

absolute PPP, the nominal exchange rate equals the ratio of two nations' price levels. This implies that, under absolute PPP, the real exchange rate is always equal to 1.

2. **Relative purchasing power parity and its usefulness as a guide to movements in exchange rates:** If relative PPP holds true for two countries, then the proportionate change in the nominal rate of exchange of the two countries' currencies equals the difference between the two countries' inflation rates. Relative PPP allows for the possibility that residents of different countries may consume various baskets of goods and services, so many economists prefer to apply relative PPP, rather than absolute PPP, when evaluating the relationship between national price levels and exchange rates. There is, nonetheless, considerable evidence indicating that even relative PPP is, at best, a long-run guide to understanding how exchange rates are determined.

3. **Covered and uncovered interest parity:** If savers hedge international holdings of bonds by buying forward currency contracts, then they can earn arbitrage profits if the interest rate in one nation is different from the sum of another nation's interest rate and the forward premium. Their efforts to earn covered arbitrage profits by shifting funds between nations result in adjustments of national interest rates and exchange rates toward values consistent with equality of the interest rate in one nation with the other nation's interest rate plus the forward premium, which is the covered interest parity condition. If savers engaged in unhedged currency transactions to finance purchases of bonds that are identical in all respects, other than the fact that they are denominated in different nations' currencies, then the interest rates on these bonds may be related through the uncovered interest parity condition. According to this condition, the difference in interest rates will equal the expected rate of currency depreciation.

4. **The distinction between adaptive and rational expectations:** An expectation that is formed adaptively is based only on past information. A rational expectation is formed using all available past and current information, and relying on an understanding of how markets determine prices.

5. **The efficient-markets hypothesis and foreign exchange market efficiency:** The efficient-markets hypothesis indicates that the market price of a financial asset should reflect all available information in that market. It should also reflect rational expectations about the price of the asset on the part of those who wish to buy and sell the asset. The foreign exchange market efficiency condition stems from combining covered interest parity with uncovered interest parity. It states that the forward premium, which is the difference between the forward and spot exchange rates divided by the spot exchange rate, should be equal to the expected rate of currency depreciation. This implies that the forward exchange rate should, on average, predict the future spot exchange rate in efficient foreign exchange markets. Combining uncovered interest parity with relative PPP also indicates that real interest parity, or equality of national real interest rates, should hold true if international financial and goods markets are integrated.

6. **Conditions for real interest parity, and why it is a useful indicator of international integration:** Real interest parity exists for two nations when their real interest rates are equal. Both the uncovered interest parity and relative PPP conditions must be satisfied simultaneously for real interest parity to hold true, thereby implying a high degree of integration of the nations' markets for financial assets and for goods and services. Consequently, economists regard real interest parity as a key indicator of international integration.

QUESTIONS AND PROBLEMS

1. Suppose the Swiss franc price of a dollar was 1.233 SFr/$ in 2007 and 0.9508 SFr/$ in 2013. The price index for Switzerland (2007 = 100) was 102.82 in 2013, and the price index for the United States (2007 = 100) was 113.77 in 2013. What was the real SFr/$ exchange rate in 2013? Does absolute PPP hold? How can you tell?

2. Using the data provided in question 1, if absolute PPP was assumed to hold, was the dollar overvalued or undervalued, relative to the Swiss franc in 2013? Considering this information, would you expect that the dollar should have appreciated or depreciated? By what percentage?

3. Using the data provided in question 1, was the dollar overvalued or undervalued in 2013 according to relative PPP? Considering this information, would you expect the dollar to appreciate or depreciate, and by how much (in percentage terms)?

4. When economists examine exchange-rate and price-level data available over periods as long as a century, they typically find that real exchange rates can vary considerably from year to year, but can be relatively stable in the long run. What does this imply about relative purchasing power parity over long- versus short-run horizons?

5. Suppose that spot and forward exchange rates are measured in units of domestic currency per unit of foreign currency. There is a positive forward premium for the domestic currency. If covered interest parity holds, what should be true of the difference between the interest rate on a domestic bond and the interest rate on a foreign bond with the same risk and maturity characteristics?

6. What is the difference between covered and uncovered interest arbitrage?

7. Explain how the covered interest parity and uncovered interest parity conditions differ.

8. Could the covered interest parity condition be met if the uncovered interest parity condition is not also satisfied? Why, or why not?

9. Suppose that foreign exchange markets are known to be efficient. The current spot exchange rate is 1.35 dollars per euro, and the current forward exchange rate is 1.38 dollars per euro. Do foreign exchange market traders anticipate that the euro will appreciate or depreciate relative to the dollar in the future?

10. Other things being equal, in a world of highly integrated financial markets but less integrated markets for goods and services, is real interest parity more or less likely to hold true, as compared with covered interest parity? Explain.

ONLINE APPLICATION

URLs: http://stats.oecd.org/Index.aspx?datasetcode=SNA_TABLE4 *and* www.federal reserve.gov/releases/h10/hist/

Titles: Purchasing power parities—Organization for Economic Co-operation and Development *and* Exchange rates—Board of Governors of the Federal Reserve System

Navigation: To obtain data on exchange rates consistent with PPP, go to the above OECD page, and print this document. Next, go to the Federal Reserve Board's home page (www.federalreserve.gov), and click on "Economic Research and Data." Under "Data Releases" in the middle of the Web page, click on "view all." Under "Exchange Rates and International Data," click on "Foreign Exchange Rates (H.10/G.5)."

Application: Use the reports on each Website to apply the PPP doctrine to real-world data.

1. The first set of columns in the OECD table gives the currency-per-U.S.-dollar exchange rates that would be consistent with PPP for various OECD countries. The Federal Reserve's Board of Governors provides data on actual exchange rates for a number of countries. Select a nation in the OECD's PPP table, and compare the exchange rates predicted by PPP for a selected year in the table with its *actual* exchange rates in the Federal Reserve's H.10 release. During the year you selected, did PPP indicate that this nation's currency was overvalued or undervalued?

2. Look over the nation's exchange rates in the Federal Reserve's H.10 release for all 5 years in the OECD table. In your view, were the actual exchange rates for the country you have selected even "roughly" consistent with PPP over this 5-year period?

For group study and analysis: Assign questions 1 and 2 above to several groups, each of which examines the data for a different country. Have each group report its conclusions. Discuss possible reasons that PPP might have been a better approach to understanding exchange-rate determination for some countries, but not for others.

REFERENCES AND RECOMMENDED READINGS

Catão, Loui. "Why Real Exchange Rates?" International Monetary Fund *Finance and Development*, 44 (3, September 2007): 46–47.

Coffey, Niall, Warren Hrung, and Asani Sarkar. "Capital Constraints, Counterparty Risk, and Deviations from Covered Interest Parity." Federal Reserve Bank of New York Staff Report No. 393, September 2009.

Ferreira, Alex Luiz, and Miguel León-Ledesma. "Does the Real Interest Parity Hypothesis Hold? Evidence for Developing and Emerging Markets." *Journal of International Money and Finance* 26(3) (April 2007): 364–382.

Frankel, Jeffrey, and Jumana Poonawala. "The Forward Market in Emerging Currencies: Less Biased Than in Major Currencies." *Journal of International Money and Finance* 29(3) (April 2010): 585–598.

Marstan, Richard. *International Financial Integration: A Study of Interest Differentials between the Major Industrial Countries*, Cambridge University Press: Cambridge, 1995.

Monticini, Andrea, and Daniel Thornton. "The Effect of Underreporting on LIBOR Rates." *Journal of Macroeconomics* 37(1) (September 2013): 345–348.

Omer, Muhammad, Jakob de Haan, and Bert Scholtens. "Testing Uncovered Interest Rate Parity Using LIBOR." CESifo Working Paper No. 3939, June 2012.

Parsley, David, and Shang-Jin Wei. "A Prism into the PPP Puzzles: The Micro-Foundations of Big Mac Real Exchange Rates." *Economic Journal* 117(523) (October 2007): 1336–1356.

Rogoff, Kenneth, Kenneth Froot, and Michael Kim. "The Law of One Price Over 700 Years," International Monetary Fund Working Paper WP/01/174, November 2001.

Satiroglu, Sait, Emrah Sener, and Yildiray Yildirim. "Empirical Investigation of Covered Interest Parity in Developed and Emerging Markets." Working Paper, Oxyegin University and Syracuse University, June 2012.

Sekiuoua, Sofiane. "Real Interest Parity Over the Twentieth Century: New Evidence Based on Confidence Intervals for the Largest Root and Half-Life." *Journal of International Money and Finance* 27(1) (February 2008): 76–101.

Simmons, Walter, and Raj Aggarwal. "Purchasing Power Parity in the Eastern Caribbean Currency Union." *Journal of Developing Areas* 38(2) (Spring 2005): 155–169.

Chapter 9

Global money and banking— where central banks fit into the world economy

---

FUNDAMENTAL ISSUES

1. What are the responsibilities of the world's central banks?
2. What are the primary instruments of monetary policy available to central banks, and how do monetary policy actions affect market interest rates?
3. How do central banks intervene in foreign exchange markets?
4. What is structural interdependence, and how can it lead nations to cooperate or to coordinate their policies?
5. What are the benefits and costs of international policy coordination?
6. Could nations gain from adopting a common currency?

On December 31, 2012, a Federal Reserve program was due to expire. The "dollar swap line" program had been put into place in 2008, during the global financial crisis. As the crisis had spread during that year, foreign banks that had committed to making dollar-denominated loans to their customers experienced difficulties borrowing dollar-denominated funds in interbank markets. Under the dollar swap line program, the Fed would lend dollars to other central banks, which in turn would send back to the Fed an equal amount of funds—in terms of market exchange rates—of their currencies. Those central banks then could stand ready to lend dollar-denominated funds to their nations' banks that desired them for use in making dollar-denominated customer loans.

The Fed had allowed the dollar swap line program to end in February 2010. That timing turned out to be very unfortunate, however, because by May 2010 a new financial crisis in Europe had again placed pressures on foreign banks seeking dollar-denominated funding. Thus, the Fed had been forced to reinstate the program just a few weeks after cancelling it.

On December 12, 2012, the Federal Reserve announced that it planned to extend the dollar swap line program until at least early 2014. Conditions in Europe, Fed officials decided, remained sufficiently unsettled that it seemed premature to halt the program. Indeed, the Fed held out the possibility of extending the program yet again in 2013 if conditions were to warrant such action.

What various roles do national central banks perform alongside their activities in seeking to influence exchange rates via foreign exchange market interventions? What are the effects of these interventions? In this chapter, you will learn the answers to these questions.

THE ROLE OF CENTRAL BANKS

The first central banking institution was established in 1668. It is the Swedish Sveriges Riksbank, which before 1867 was called the Risens Standers Bank. The Swedish Parliament (Riksdag) granted to a special commission the authority to manage the Sveriges Riksbank. Initially, the Riksbank did not issue money, but by 1701 the government had granted the Riksbank the power to issue "transfer notes" that basically functioned as a form of currency. In 1789, the Riksdag established a National Debt Office that formally issued Swedish government currency. Finally, in 1897, the Riksbank Act made this institution the only legal issuer of Swedish currency.

The world's second central bank, which was established in 1694, became better known. It was the Bank of England. The British parliament authorized the Bank of England to issue currency notes redeemable in silver. These notes then circulated alongside notes issued by the government and private companies. The Riksbank and Bank of England were the only central banks until 1800, and the total number of central banks remained a single digit until 1873. As you can see in Figure 9.1, the number of central banks around the globe increased significantly during the latter part of the nineteenth century and the twentieth century. A portion of this growth stemmed from the establishment of central banks by former colonial states that achieved independence and developed their own currencies.

ON THE WEB:

Learn more about the history of the Riksbank at www.riksbank.com.

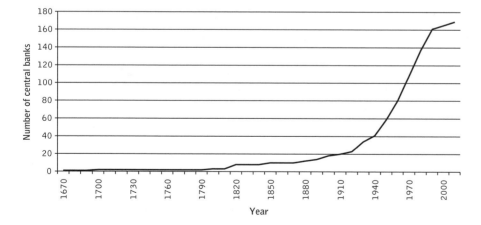

Figure 9.1 *The number of central banking institutions since 1670*

There was considerable growth in the number of central banks during the twentieth century.

Source: Capie et al. (1994).

The most recently established central bank is also one of the most important. In January 1999, the central banks of 11 European nations—Austria, Belgium, Finland, France, Germany, Ireland, Italy, Luxembourg, the Netherlands, Portugal, and Spain—formed the *European System of Central Banks* (ESCB). The six-member executive board for this system is based at the *European Central Bank* (ECB), the hub of the ESCB located in Frankfurt, Germany. All final operating and policy decisions for the system, however, must be approved by a 23-member governing council composed of the six members of the executive board in Frankfurt and the governors of the 17 national central banks (Cyprus, Estonia, Greece, Malta, Slovakia, and Slovenia, are now member nations). Thus, each member nation plays a role in determining the policies of the ECB.

Central banks as government banks

Governments often argue that they "need" central banks. For instance, a primary motivation for the founding of the Bank of England in 1694 was the desire for the bank to raise government funds to finance one of Britain's wars with France. In like manner, a justification that the French government gave for establishing the Banque de France in 1800 was to better manage the nation's public debt that had ballooned as France and Britain continued their military buildups.

Even in countries where providing financial services to governments has not been the key justification for a central bank, central banks typically have become the main governmental banking institutions. For example, in the United States there had been long-standing opposition to central banks, but after the founding of the Federal Reserve System in 1913, the U.S. Treasury quickly began to rely on Federal Reserve banks as providers of depository services.

Central banks as government depositories

National governments may hold unused funds on deposit at a single central bank office or in various regional branch offices of central banks.

For instance, the U.S. Treasury holds deposits at each of the 12 Federal Reserve banks. These regional banks clear checks drawn on those accounts. They also accept deposits of fees and taxes paid by U.S. residents and firms. Furthermore, they make payments at the direction of the U.S. Treasury, just as a private bank makes payments on behalf of a private customer.

Fiscal agent: *A term describing a central bank's role as an agent of its government's finance ministry or treasury department, in which the central bank issues, services, and redeems debts on the government's behalf.*

Central banks as fiscal agents

Central banks typically operate as **fiscal agents** for national governments, meaning that they issue, service, and redeem government debts. Treasury departments or finance ministries issue securities such as bills, notes, and bonds to cover shortfalls between tax receipts and expenditures on goods and services. In nations with highly developed financial markets, such as the United States, Japan, and nations of the European Union (EU), treasury departments or finance ministries issue these securities at auctions. In their role as fiscal agents, central banks often review, tabulate, and summarize bids to purchase the securities, issue securities to successful bidders, and process the purchasers' payments to the government.

In emerging nations with less developed financial markets, central banks may play more direct roles. They may effectively act as investment banks for their governments by lining up private individuals or firms willing to purchase new government security issues. In nations with particularly thin secondary securities markets, central banks even purchase the securities directly from government treasury departments or finance ministries. To help broaden the markets for government securities, central banks in some countries, such as South Korea, have even imposed regulations requiring private banks to purchase government bills, notes, and bonds. Economists say that such rules make private banks *captive buyers* of government debt.

Central banks as bankers' banks

Although the immediate rationale for the 1694 founding of the Bank of England was a government desire to improve its ability to finance wartime expenditures, another justification by the British parliament for creating the Bank was a perceived need for a government-related institution that would stabilize London financial markets and limit periodic fluctuations in the availability of currency and credit throughout England.

Do banks "need" a central bank?

In later years, governments of other nations offered similar rationales for the establishment of central banks. Many proponents of these institutions, in fact, have contended that private banks *need* a central bank. The key rationale for such a "need" is the idea that financial markets are subject to *externalities*, or situations in which transactions among individuals or firms can spill over to affect others.

According to this view, central banking institutions perform socially useful roles in supervising and regulating the processes and systems through which individuals, firms, and banks exchange payments. Hence, private banks "need" a central bank to keep payment systems operating smoothly on a day-to-day basis and to repair any breakdowns in these systems as they may occur.

Lenders of last resort

The most dramatic sort of financial breakdown is a *systemic* failure, in which large numbers of banking institutions fail. The classic example of this type of systemic failure is a *bank run*, in which large numbers of bank customers lose confidence in the ability of banks to maintain their asset values and, hence, anticipate depletion of the banks' net worth. As a result, customers seek to liquidate their deposits. This actually does push large numbers of banks into insolvency.

In principle, a central bank can keep bank runs from occurring by serving as the financial system's **lender of last resort** that stands ready to lend to any temporarily illiquid but otherwise solvent bank. By lending funds when necessary, the central

Lender of last resort: *A central banking function in which the central bank stands willing to lend to any temporarily illiquid, but otherwise solvent, banking institution to prevent its illiquid position from leading to a general loss of confidence in that institution.*

267

bank might prevent such illiquidity from leading to a general loss of confidence that can lead to a system-wide "run on the bank."

Central banks as monetary policymakers

Most central banks devote the bulk of their resources, including the time and effort of their employees, to the tasks of providing services to their nations' governments and banking institutions. Nevertheless, the bulk of media attention on central bankers focuses on deciphering the complex issues involved in their monetary policymaking function.

Central bank balance sheet assets and liabilities

ON THE WEB:

Visit the Bank of Canada at www. bankofcanada.ca.

The best place to begin any examination of the functions of a central bank is its balance sheet, which is a tabulation of the central bank's assets, liabilities, and net worth. Table 9.1 displays consolidated balance sheets of the Bank of Canada. The table displays euro amounts and percentages relative to total assets and to total liabilities and capital (net worth). Because nominal values of the Bank of Canada's assets, liabilities, and net worth change considerably over time, while proportionate allocations tend to remain stable, you should concentrate most attention on the percentages in Table 9.1.

Central bank assets

Examination of Table 9.1 shows that the securities issued by the Canadian government account for 99.2 percent of the assets of the Bank of Canada. Its remaining

Table 9.1 *The consolidated balance sheets of the Bank of Canada (billions of Canadian dollars, as of May 8, 2013)*

Assets			Liabilities and capital		
Asset	Amount	Percent of total assets	Liability	Amount	Percent of total liabilities and capital
Domestic securities and bills	C$83.5	99.2	Currency notes	C$61.5	73.0
			Bank reserve deposits	0.3	0.4
Direct loans to private banks	0.0	0.0	Government deposits	20.2	24.0
Other assets	0.7	0.8	Other liabilities and capital	2.2	2.6
Total assets	C$84.2	100.0	Total liabilities and capital	C$84.2	100.0

Source: Data from Bank of Canada, *Banking and Financial Statistics,* June 2013.

assets include various types of securities, loans, and certificates of ownership. The sum of domestic securities and loans held as assets is called **domestic credit**.

The Bank of Canada maintains holdings of assets denominated in the currencies of other nations. These are foreign currency-denominated securities and deposits. As we have noted in earlier chapters, and later discuss in greater detail, a key reason why central banks hold such securities and deposits is so they can trade the assets when they wish to try to change the value of their nation's currency in foreign exchange markets.

Domestic credit:
Total domestic securities and loans held as assets by a central bank.

Central bank liabilities

More than 70 percent of the Bank of Canada's total liabilities and equity capital is composed of *currency notes*. Accountants designate currency notes as liabilities to indicate that the central banks "owe" holders of the notes something in exchange. For instance, if you had sought to redeem a currency note at the Bank of Canada before the early 1930s, you could have received gold in exchange. Now, however, you would receive a new euro note. So in what sense are these notes really liabilities? The answer is that, if Canada's government were to close down the Bank of Canada, it would be liable to holders of its notes for the Canadian-dollar value of goods and services as at the time of the closures.

Another important liability of the Bank of Canada is bank reserve deposits. Private banks may hold some of these deposits to meet legal requirements established by the central banks. In addition, however, they also hold a portion of these deposits as *excess* reserves to help facilitate check clearing and transactions with the central bank and other private banks, including transfers of funds that they may lend to one another in markets for very short-term loans among banks. These loans have large denominations, and typically have maturities between 1 day and 1 week.

Table 9.1 indicates that an important deposit liability at the Bank of Canada is government deposits. The Canadian government draws on these deposit funds to make payments such as purchases of goods and services, or tax refunds.

Central banks and money

Today, most of us take money for granted. Money performs four key functions: It is a medium of exchange, a store of value, a unit of account, and a standard of deferred payment.

The fundamental function of money is as a *medium of exchange*. This means that people who trade goods, services, or financial assets are willing to accept money in exchange for these items. Money also serves as a *store of value*, meaning that an individual can set money aside today with an intent to purchase items at a later time. Meanwhile, money retains value that the individual can apply to those future purchases. In addition, money functions as a *unit of account*, because people maintain their financial accounts by using money to value goods, services, and financial assets, and they quote prices of goods, services, and financial assets in terms of money. Finally, money serves as a *standard of deferred payment*, which means that people agree to loan contracts that call for future repayments in terms of money.

Monetary aggregate: *A grouping of assets sufficiently liquid to be defined as a measure of money.*

The measures of money that central banks tabulate are sums of various groupings of financial assets. For this reason, central banks refer to them as **monetary aggregates**. Each of these monetary aggregates differs according to the liquidity of the assets that are included or excluded.

The monetary base

To understand how central banks can influence the quantity of money in circulation, we can take a look at their balance sheets. The reason is that the very narrowest measure of money is the **monetary base**, which economists sometimes call *high-powered money*. This is the amount of money produced directly by a central bank, and thereby excludes forms of money created by private banks, such as checkable or debitable accounts.

Monetary base: *Central bank holdings of domestic securities and loans plus foreign exchange reserves, or the sum of currency and bank reserves.*

The monetary base for any nation is the sum of *currency*—paper notes and coins—held outside the government, the central bank, and private banking institutions plus *total reserves* of private banks—funds that private banks hold either as deposits with central banks, or as cash in their vaults. The sources of these funds are the central

Table 9.2 Components of M2

M1	Currency, transactions deposits, and travelers' checks make up the broad category generally known as money.
Savings deposits and *money market deposit accounts* at depository institutions	Savings deposits are interest-bearing deposits without set maturities; money market deposit accounts are savings accounts that permit limited checking privileges.
Small-denomination time deposits at depository institutions	Time deposits have set maturities, meaning that the holder must keep the funds on deposit for a fixed length of time to be guaranteed a negotiated interest return. Small-denomination time deposits have denominations less than $100,000.
Funds held by individuals, brokers, and dealers in *money market mutual funds*	These are mutual funds that specialize in holding money market securities.
Overnight repurchase agreements at depository institutions and *overnight Eurocurrency deposits* held by domestic residents (other than depository institutions) at foreign branches of domestic depository institutions	A repurchase agreement is a contract to sell financial assets, such as government bonds, with a promise to repurchase them at a later time, typically at a slightly higher price, and an *overnight* repurchase agreement permits the original holder to get access to funds for one day. Overnight Eurocurrency deposits are one-day, home currency-denominated deposits in foreign depository institutions and in foreign branches of domestic depository institutions. Despite the name *Eurocurrency*, such deposits might, for instance, be in Japanese or Australian branches of domestic banks.

banks themselves. As you can see in Table 9.1 on p. 268, the sums of currency and reserves that private banks hold with the Bank of Canada make up more than 70 percent of that central bank's total liabilities.

Broader monetary aggregates

A broader definition of money, a monetary aggregate that most central banks call **M1**, is designed to measure funds that are immediately spendable by all individuals and firms within a nation. There are two fundamental components of M1: currency and *transactions deposits* held at depository institutions. These include checking accounts, accounts from which automatic debits can be made, and so on. The currency component of M1 is the same as that used to compute the monetary base.

M1: *Currency plus transactions deposits.*

Another important monetary aggregate is an even broader measure that most central banks refer to as **M2**. Table 9.2 shows how most central banks tabulate this even broader measure of the quantity of money in circulation. As you can see, M2 is equal to M1 plus several other assets that people cannot directly spend, but that are easily convertible to cash. (Many residents of Iran have augmented their "cash" by holding a currency obtainable via the Internet; see *Online Globalization: In Iran, the unofficial quantity of circulating money includes a Web currency*.)

M2: *M1 plus savings and small time deposits, overnight Eurocurrency and repurchase agreements, and balances of individual and broker-dealer money market mutual funds.*

ONLINE GLOBALIZATION

In Iran, the unofficial quantity of circulating money includes a Web currency

Although in recent years the *official* exchange rate for the *rial*, Iran's currency, has been less than 13,000 rials per U.S. dollar, the market-clearing exchange rate in the nation's black markets has sometimes exceeded 36,000 rials per dollar. Because the rial's value, measured both in terms of dollars and in terms of goods and services the currency can buy, has declined considerably, a number of Iranian residents have opted to utilize a different form of circulating currency, called *bitcoins*.

Bitcoins are form of privately traded currency that circulates via Internet transactions. A decentralized global network of thousands of personal computers encrypts and processes bitcoin exchanges. Bitcoins are accepted by a number of online merchants around the globe. In addition, Iranian residents can readily exchange bitcoins for dollars, which legally they are not supposed to hold, on the Web: with little likelihood of detection because there is no central server issuing bitcoins, which instead trade on virtual private networks. Then the Iranian residents can quickly exchange the dollars for items offered for sale at online merchants that do not accept bitcoins for purchases.

There is no way to know how much Iran's effective quantity of money in circulation is expanded via residents' use of bitcoins. What is known with certainty is that

---

271

> many Iranian firms that have a constant Web presence, such as software developers and certain online sellers, will *only* accept payments denominated in bitcoins.
>
> *For critical analysis: Recently, the exchange rate of rials for bitcoins was about 330,000 rials per bitcoin. If the market-clearing rate of exchange of rials for dollars in the black market is 33,000 rials per dollar, what is the approximate rate of exchange of dollars for bitcoins?*

Because a nation's monetary base depends on the size of its central bank's balance sheet, actions of the central bank directly determine the monetary base. Central banks cannot directly control broader monetary aggregates such as M1 and M2, but they can influence them by varying the amounts of their assets and liabilities. In this way, central banks conduct monetary policy.

> *Fundamental Issue #1: What are the responsibilities of the world's central banks?* Central banks are the main depository institutions for national governments, which in many countries are the owners of central banking institutions. Central banks typically serve as fiscal agents operating the systems through which governments issue debt instruments and make interest and principal payments, and by promoting broader markets for government debt instruments. Central banks also provide banking services for private banking institutions, and function as lenders of last resort, providing liquidity in the event of systemic failures such as bank runs. Finally, central banks influence measures of the quantity of money in circulation, such as the monetary base, M1, or M2, by adjusting the size of their own balance sheet. The primary assets of central banks are government securities, loans to private banking institutions, and foreign currency-denominated securities and deposits. Key central bank liabilities are currency notes and reserve deposits of private banking institutions, which constitute a nation's monetary base.

BANKING, MONEY, AND INTEREST RATES

There is good reason that the media often pay close attention to the monetary policy actions of central banks. In a number of economic environments, central banks can considerably affect a nation's level of interest rates. Alterations in interest rates, in turn, influence the exchange value of the nation's currency and the level of economic activity.

Instruments of monetary policy

Central banks, of course, do not set a nation's price level. Nor do they add directly to a nation's real output, aside from the services that they provide to governments and private banks. Nevertheless, they have access to a number of *policy instruments*, which for central banks are financial variables that they can control, either directly or indirectly. By altering available policy instruments, a central bank can bring about variations in market interest rates, thereby changing the volumes of money and credit in its nation's economy, and generating changes in the value of its nation's currency. Such financial-market effects can then, in turn, induce changes in the level of a country's economic activity.

Interest rates on central bank advances

Traditionally, a key central bank policy instrument has been the interest rate charged on *advances*, or loans, to private banks. In the United States, the Federal Reserve's **discount rate** is the interest rate on U.S. central bank advances. In contrast to some other central banks, the discount rate is the *only* rate on advances that the Federal Reserve sets. Since the middle of 2002, the Federal Reserve has set the discount rate 0.25 to 1 percentage point above another market-clearing interest rate, called the *federal funds rate*, which is the market interest rate in the U.S. interbank funds market known as the *federal funds market*.

Discount rate: *The interest rate that the Federal Reserve charges on discount window loans that it extends to depository institutions.*

The ECB establishes *two* interest rates on central bank advances. One of these rates is a discount rate slightly below prevailing interbank funds rates. The ECB established credit quotas for all private banks in the European Monetary Union (EMU). Because the discount rate is lower than market interest rates, banks typically borrow up to these limits. Consequently, the volumes of loans that these central banks make to private banks is relatively larger than in the United States and Japan.

The other interest rate on central bank advances with the EMU is traditionally called the **Lombard rate**, but the ECB formally calls it the *marginal interest rate*. This is an interest rate on advances that these nations' central banks set above current market interest rates. Banks can borrow at this penalty rate whenever they unexpectedly find themselves illiquid. Because EMU banks can finance a known amount of daily funds borrowings at the below-market discount rate, and cover unanticipated credit requirements at the above-market Lombard rate, the market interest rate in the EMU interbank funds market tends to vary between these two central bank rates. Consequently, when it establishes values for the discount and Lombard rates, the ECB essentially places lower and upper limits on daily interest-rate variations.

Lombard rate: *The specific name given to the interest rate on central bank advances that some central banks, such as the European Central Bank, set above current market interest rates.*

The Bank of Japan also advances credit to private banks. The Bank of Japan sets its discount rate below the current interbank funds rate. It does not restrict access to credit at this rate, so the loans it extends to private banks account for a larger portion—about 10 percent—of its assets. In contrast to the ECB, however, the Bank of Japan does not establish fixed credit quotas for private banks. Instead, it engages in discretionary rationing of discount-window credit on a daily basis. The Bank of Japan pursues this policy stance in order to limit the amount of borrowing by private bankers.

Open-market operations

A second fundamental type of monetary policy instrument available to many central banks is **open-market operations**. This term refers to central bank purchases or

Open-market operations: *Central bank purchases or sales of government or private securities.*

273

sales of government or private securities. Most central banking institutions that engage in open-market operations, such as the U.S. Federal Reserve, buy or sell only government securities. Some, such as the Federal Reserve, buy securities in secondary markets, rather than purchasing them directly from the government.

Because the ECB is able to use its discount rate–Lombard rate system for advances to constrain market interest rates from day to day, it does not conduct open-market operations each day. Instead, it offers a set of repurchase agreements at a regular weekly auction. This enables the ECB to maintain a desired level of bank reserves from week to week.

At the Federal Reserve, voting members of the *Federal Open Market Committee* (FOMC)—the seven Federal Reserve Board governors and five Federal Reserve bank presidents—set the overall strategy of open-market operations at meetings that take place every 6–8 weeks. A document called the *FOMC Directive* outlines the FOMC's policy objectives, establishes short-term federal funds rate goals, and lays out specific target ranges for monetary aggregates. The Federal Reserve Bank of New York's *Trading Desk* then implements the Directive from day to day during the weeks between FOMC meetings.

When a central bank purchases a security, it typically makes payment to the prior owner by crediting the owner's deposit account at a banking institution. When the bank receives the funds, its reserves increase. The Trading Desk often uses outright purchases or sales when it wishes to permanently change the aggregate level of bank reserves. In contrast, it typically uses repurchase agreements when its main goal is to keep the current level of reserves from changing for some external reason. Nevertheless, the Trading Desk can substitute repurchase-agreement transactions for outright purchases or sales to change the overall reserve level by continuously mismatching repurchase-agreement transactions as needed.

At the Bank of Japan, most open-market operations involve the purchase or sale of *privately issued* financial instruments, including commercial bills and paper and bank certificates of deposit. In the past, this has allowed the Bank of Japan to try to directly influence a variety of market interest rates. Since the late 1980s, however, the Bank of Japan has aimed its open-market operations primarily at influencing the Japanese interbank funds rate.

Open-market operations are much less common in less developed and emerging economies. The reason for this is simple: These nations do not have well developed markets for government securities and other short-term instruments. This makes it difficult for central banks in these countries to find a critical mass of banks and other institutions that regularly trade securities on a daily or weekly basis.

Reserve requirements:
Central bank regulations requiring private banks to hold specified fractions of transactions and term deposits, either as vault cash or as funds on deposit at the central bank.

Reserve requirements

In years past, an important instrument of monetary policy has been **reserve requirements**. These are rules specifying portions of transactions (checking) and term (time and savings) deposits that private banks must hold either as vault cash, or as funds on deposit at the central bank.

Today, however, reserve requirements are less important instruments of monetary policy. Certainly, central banks rarely change reserve requirements in an effort to exert direct effects on the quantities of money and credit, or on the levels of market interest rates. A key rationale that today's central banks offer for reserve requirements is that they may help ensure that private banks are sufficiently liquid to be able to make rapid, day-to-day reserve adjustments in response to unexpected events. To assist banks in this endeavor, most central banks assess reserve requirements on an *average* basis: Banks must meet their reserve requirements, but they need do so only on average over a period of 1 or 2 weeks.

Interest-rate regulations and direct credit controls

In a number of nations, especially in those with less developed financial markets, central banks traditionally have used more blunt means of influencing the quantities of money and credit. In East Asia, for instance, central banks commonly place restrictions on interest rates that private banks may pay their depositors. They sometimes use these limits as monetary policy instruments. For example, raising the allowable interest rate that banks may pay on deposits potentially can induce individuals and firms to hold more deposits, thereby increasing the amount of deposits, including those that circulate as money.

In nations such as China and Russia, central banks also use *direct credit controls*, which are explicit quantity constraints on how much credit banks and other financial institutions may extend to individuals and firms. If central banks in these nations wish to contract the growth of money and credit, perhaps in an effort to contain inflation, then they tighten credit constraints. If the central banks wish to induce higher growth in money and credit, perhaps to encourage increased near-term economic growth, then they loosen the controls somewhat.

Emergency central bank credit policies

Since the 2007–2009 global financial meltdown, central banks have implemented a new approach to policymaking, centered around **credit policies**, under which they directly extend credit to private banks, other financial institutions, and even non-financial companies. As hundreds of U.S. banks and other financial institutions struggled to avoid severe illiquidity and bankruptcy in 2008, the Federal Reserve introduced a number of emergency programs through which it provided credit directly to these institutions. The Fed auctioned funds to banking institutions, and also bought many debt securities held by a number of these institutions.

When the Federal Reserve initiated this new policy approach in 2008, it indicated that its intention was to make it a temporary undertaking. In reality, the Fed continues to use **credit policy** alongside traditional monetary policy, and appears unlikely to end its direct extensions of credit in the near future. Indeed, today more than $1 trillion, or 40 percent, of the Fed's asset holdings relate to credit policy.

To fund its credit policy, the Fed must induce private banks to maintain substantial reserve deposits with the Federal Reserve banks. Since October 2008, it has done so by paying interest on all reserves that financial institutions hold with Federal Reserve banks. Although the Fed has paid a very low interest rate of about 0.25 percent on

Credit policy:
Central bank policymaking involving direct lending to private financial institutions and non-financial firms.

275

reserve deposits since that date, the market-clearing federal funds rate has been even lower during most weeks since then. Thus, banks have earned more by setting funds aside in reserve deposit accounts at Federal Reserve banks than by lending to other banks in the federal funds market. This means that the Fed essentially has paid banks a per-dollar *subsidy* to keep hundreds of billions of dollars on deposit with the Fed.

All such funds held at Federal Reserve banks do not remain idle, though. Just as private banks can use the deposits of households and firms to fund loans and purchases of securities, the Fed can use the reserve deposits of private banks to fund its own lending and securities-buying activities. Since 2008, reserve deposits at Federal Reserve banks have increased from less than $50 billion to more than $1.5 *trillion*. These funds have financed the Fed's credit policy—lending to domestic and foreign banks, non-financial companies, and central banks and buying risky, longer-term mortgage obligations. Many of the mortgage obligations purchased by the Fed have market values much smaller than the amounts that the Fed has paid for them. Consequently, the Fed faces considerable risk that at least some of the debts will never be fully repaid. This state of affairs is also much different than was true in preceding years, when the bulk of the Fed's assets, about 80 percent of which were U.S. government securities, offered very low risks of loss.

Since 2012, the ECB has also added emergency credit policies to its set of tools. The ECB has provided credit that has enabled banks and other financial institutions to remain afloat in various European trouble spots, such as Greece and Spain. Consequently, the ECB also has added considerably riskier assets to its balance sheet.

Both the Fed and the ECB have indicated that they do not intend to persist in pursuing credit policies that they initiated as temporary emergency measures. Nevertheless, the Fed's utilization of credit policies already has persisted for several years longer than the Fed had initially projected, and as European deficit and debt problems fester, it seems unlikely that the ECB will halt its efforts any time soon. Central bank credit policies appear to be in place for the foreseeable future.

Monetary policy and market interest rates

A key channel through which a central bank's monetary policy actions affect economic activity is by altering market interest rates and thereby influencing the willingness of individuals and firms to borrow and spend at any given price level. Thus, it is important to understand how monetary policy actions influence market interest rates.

The money multiplier

A nation's level of interest rates adjusts to maintain equilibrium in the market for money. Central banks determine the overall supply of money in circulation—measured via a monetary aggregate such as M1 or M2, by varying the size of the monetary base. For instance, in the United States, when the Federal Reserve Bank of New York's trading desk executes a purchase of U.S. government securities, it wires funds to the account of a private bank from which it purchases the securities. This is the means by which the Fed begins the process of new money creation.

It is only the start of this process, however. For instance, if the Trading Desk were to purchase $1 million in government securities from a securities dealer who then has the Fed wire the funds to its checking deposit account in a private bank based in Chicago, the Fed would respond by applying a $1 million credit to that bank's reserve account at the Federal Reserve Bank of Chicago. The private bank then would earmark these funds for the dealer's deposit account with the private bank. The Fed only requires private banks to impose a 10 percent reserve requirement on the bulk of U.S. checking deposits, and so the private Chicago bank would be able to lend $900,000 of the funds that it receives via the security dealer's deposit. If the Chicago bank were to make a loan to a construction company based in Louisville, Kentucky, and if the company were to place the funds in its checking account at a Louisville bank, then this bank would have $900,000 in new cash reserves. Of these, it could lend as much as $810,000, or 90 percent of the $900,000 additional funds now deposited. This ultimately would expand deposits at yet another bank, either in Louisville or elsewhere.

Consequently, the Fed's $1 million security purchase in our example would cause the total quantity of money in circulation to increase by an amount much greater than $1 million. The Chicago security dealer's checking deposits would increase by $1 million, the Louisville construction company's checking deposits would rise by $900,000, and some other loan recipient's checking deposits would rise by $810,000. This process would continue until the Fed's security purchase had an ultimate *multiplier effect* on the total quantity of checking deposits included in the nation's money stock.

To determine the size of the multiplier effect in our example, let's denote the amount of checking deposits at private banks as D, and let's call the total amount of cash reserves of these banks R. Finally, let's denote the Fed's ratio for determining required reserve holdings q. Hence, if banks were to hold no more cash reserves than the Fed required them to hold, total reserves in the banking system would be $R = q \times D$, and any change in reserves owing to a change in checking deposits at banks would be equal to $\Delta R = q \times \Delta D$, where Δ denotes a change in a quantity. We can rearrange this relationship, however, to find a change in checking deposits owing to a change in reserves induced by a Fed purchase of securities. To do so, we simply solve for ΔD by dividing both sides by q, which yields:

$$\Delta D = (1/q) \times \Delta R$$

In our example of a Fed security purchase that causes an initial bank reserve expansion of $1 million with a required reserve ratio of 10 percent, ΔR would equal $1 million, and $1/q$ would equal $1/(0.1) = 10$. Therefore, ΔD would equal $1 million $\times$ 10, or $10 million, and so the Fed's $1 million security purchase ultimately would cause the quantity of money in circulation to rise by a multiple amount of $10 million. The ratio $1/q = 10$ would be a "money multiplier."

Realistically, the final multiplier effect of a Fed security purchase is smaller than this amount. A key reason is that people hold some money in the form of currency. Hence, if the Chicago securities dealer and Louisville construction company in our example had chosen to convert some of the funds they received into currency, rather than depositing all the funds into checking accounts at their bank, then each of their banks would have had fewer funds available to lend. This would have reduced the extent of the deposit multiplier process. Another factor that typically depresses the size of the deposit multiplier effect is bank holdings of reserves over and above those that are required. To the extent that banks might hold such *excess* reserves, they would have fewer reserves available to lend at each stage of the multiplier process.

The supply of money

Of course, monetary aggregates such as M1 and M2 include a number of different types of deposit. They also include currency issued by the central bank. Central banks may also establish different required reserve ratios for separate types of deposits. Nevertheless, a multiplier relationship continues to exist, even when we take into account both currency and various types of deposits.

Specifically, the quantity of money supplied by the central bank must be equal to a money multiplier times the monetary base. As in the simplest case illustrated above, the value of the money multiplier varies inversely with the required reserve ratio. The central bank can then influence the quantity of money by changing the size of its balance sheet, either by varying the quantity of currency it issues or, more likely, varying its policy instruments to alter the quantity of reserves in the banking system.

Money demand, the equilibrium interest rate, and the effects of monetary policy actions

Typically, people hold money to engage in transactions. That is, they desire to have liquidity available to be able to purchase goods and services when they wish to do so. But they also hold money as an alternative to holding other financial assets. There is a relatively low risk to holding money, but most forms of money pay zero or very low interest rates. Hence, by holding money, people incur an opportunity cost equal to the market interest rate that they could have earned by holding a financial asset such as a Treasury security. Consequently, people typically choose to hold less money as the market interest rate increases, or to hold more money as the interest rate declines.

This means that the market interest rate must adjust as necessary to make people willing to hold the quantity of money placed in circulation through actions of a central bank. When people are satisfied to be holding the amount of money outstanding, then the interest rate is at its equilibrium level.

Now consider what happens if the central bank increases the quantity of money, perhaps by engaging in an open-market purchase, or reducing an interest rate on advances to induce banks to increase bank reserves and the monetary base. Through the money multiplier effect, this action raises the overall level of liquidity in the economy. At the previous equilibrium interest rate, people would not desire to hold newly produced money. They would seek to shift funds to interest-bearing assets. This overabundance of liquidity would tend to push the market interest rate downward. (To examine how the market interest rate is determined, and how central bank policy actions influence the interest rate, see *Visualizing Global Economic Issues: Influencing the equilibrium interest rate*.)

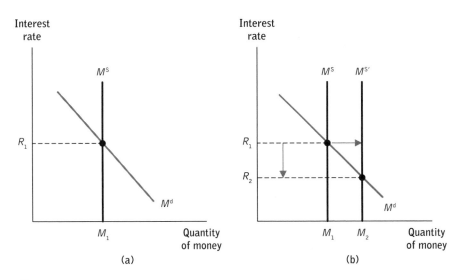

Figure 9.2 *The equilibrium interest rate and monetary policy*

As the interest rate rises, the opportunity cost of holding money increases, inducing peo-
ple to cut back on their money holdings. Hence, the money demand curve slopes down-
ward. The money supply curve is vertical, and the central bank influences the position of
the money supply curve by varying the monetary base or changing the required reserve
ratio. Panel (a) depicts a single point where all individuals in the economy are satisfied
holding the nominal money stock supplied by the central bank at the equilibrium interest
rate R_1. Panel (b) illustrates the adjustment process following an open-market purchase
or reduction in the interest rate on central bank advances. Either action pushes up the
monetary base, thereby increasing the quantity of money in circulation by a multiple
amount and shifting the money supply curve rightward as the quantity of money supplied
increases from M_1 to M_2. There is an excess quantity of money supplied at the initial
equilibrium interest rate R_1, so the interest rate declines to a new equilibrium rate R_2.

VISUALIZING GLOBAL ECONOMIC ISSUES

Influencing the equilibrium interest rate

To evaluate the effects of monetary policy actions on the market interest rate, take
a look at Figure 9.2. In both panels of the figure, the downward-sloping curve
depicts the total *demand for money* in the economy. The money demand curve
slopes downward because, as the interest rate rises, the opportunity cost of holding
money that pays a low, or no, rate of interest increases, inducing people to cut back
on their money holdings. The vertical curve in both panels is the economy's *supply*
of money, which the central bank influences by varying the monetary base or, if it
wishes, by changing the required reserve ratio.

In panel (a), the crossing point of the two schedules depicts a situation in which
all individuals in the economy are satisfied to be holding the nominal money stock
supplied by the central bank. Consequently, at this single point the quantity of money

demanded by the public is equal to the quantity of money supplied via efforts of the central bank. Therefore, the interest adjusts to achieve this equilibrium point, and R_1 is the *equilibrium* interest rate.

Panel (b) shows the adjustment process following a central bank policy action that expands the quantity of money in circulation. An open-market purchase or reduction in the interest rate on central bank advances pushes up the monetary base, thereby increasing the quantity of money in circulation by a multiple amount. Hence, the money supply curve shifts rightward. The quantity of money supplied by the central bank increases from the initial amount M_1 to a larger quantity M_2 at any given interest rate. Thus, there is an excess quantity of money supplied at the initial equilibrium interest rate R_1, and the interest rate must fall to a new equilibrium level, R_2.

For critical analysis: How would a central bank go about trying to push up the equilibrium interest rate?

Fundamental Issue #2: What are the primary instruments of monetary policy available to central banks, and how do monetary policy actions affect market interest rates? By determining values for their policy instruments, which may include interest rates on central bank advances, open-market operations, reserve requirements, and interest-rate and credit restrictions, central banks are able to influence interbank funds rates, and hence bank reserves and the monetary base. The money multiplier determines the size of the effect on the quantity of money caused by a change in the monetary base. The equilibrium interest rate is the rate of interest at which people are satisfied to be holding the quantity of money supplied through policies of the central bank. A central bank action that increases the quantity of money raises the amount of total liquidity in the economy, thereby generating a reduction in the equilibrium interest rate.

FOREIGN EXCHANGE MARKET INTERVENTIONS

Central banks, of course, recognize that variations in exchange rates can influence total desired spending on domestic output and, therefore, equilibrium real GDP and prices. This gives central banks an incentive to engage in foreign exchange interventions in efforts to alter, smooth, or peg exchange rates. They seek to influence exchange rates by purchasing or selling financial assets denominated in foreign currencies.

Mechanics of foreign exchange interventions

Now that you have learned about the balance-sheet compositions, structures, and functions of central banks, and about how their activities can influence national economic performance, we can consider how these institutions conduct foreign exchange market interventions in an effort to influence exchange rates.

Leaning with or against the wind

A central bank intervenes, either on its own account or on behalf of its national government, in an effort to influence the value of its nation's currency in the foreign exchange market. If a central bank intervenes to support, or speed along, the current trend in the value of its nation's currency in the foreign exchange market, then economists say that its interventions **lean with the wind**.

In contrast, economists say that central bank interventions intended to halt or reverse a recent trend in the value of its nation's currency **lean against the wind**. Most often, central banks lean against the wind solely to halt, at least temporarily, sharp swings in market exchange rates. Consequently, a key rationale for many instances of leaning against the wind is simply to reduce volatility in exchange rates. Central banks do not necessarily lean against the wind with an aim of bringing about long-term reversals in the trend value of their currencies, although in some instances this might be an ultimate goal of a central bank or finance ministry upon whose behalf the central bank conducts a policy of leaning against the wind.

Leaning with the wind: *Central bank interventions to support or speed along the current trend in the market exchange value of its nation's currency.*

Leaning against the wind: *Central bank interventions to halt or reverse the current trend in the market exchange value of its nation's currency.*

Financing interventions

If central banks intervene in foreign exchange markets on their own behalf, then they do so using their own reserves of assets denominated in foreign currencies. Many central banks have "war chests" of foreign currency reserves in the event they desire to conduct interventions on their own account. In like manner, governments often maintain reserves of foreign currency-denominated assets.

In the United States, the U.S. Treasury has primary responsibility for initiating foreign exchange interventions. Consequently, the Treasury often determines the timing and extent of U.S. interventions, even though the Federal Reserve conducts these interventions on the Treasury's behalf. The U.S. Treasury's position is that it has the legal authority to order the Federal Reserve to use its own foreign exchange reserves as well as those of the Treasury, and in the past the Federal Reserve has conducted Treasury interventions using its own reserves as well as those of the Treasury. Recently, this has become a source of tension within the Federal Reserve System, as some Federal Reserve officials have openly questioned this "subservience" of the Federal Reserve to the Treasury.

Nonetheless, the U.S. government maintains a separate *exchange stabilization fund* (ESF) that it can use to finance its interventions when Federal Reserve foreign exchange reserves are not involved. If ESF officials intervene in support of the dollar's value by selling assets denominated in foreign currencies, they initially deposit the dollars obtained in the transaction in a Treasury deposit at the Federal Reserve. The Treasury Department then issues a non-marketable security to the ESF, which purchases the Treasury security from its account with the Federal Reserve, which credits the Treasury's deposit account. To ensure that this sequence of transactions has no ultimate effect on the Federal Reserve's balance sheet, and hence on the monetary base, the Treasury then withdraws these funds from its deposit account at the Federal Reserve and redeposits them at private banks.

Sterilization of interventions

Sterilization: *A central bank policy of altering domestic credit in an equal and opposite direction relative to any variation in foreign exchange reserves so as to prevent the monetary base from changing.*

A central bank **sterilizes** foreign exchange interventions when it buys or sells domestic assets in sufficient quantities to prevent the interventions from influencing the domestic money stock. As we noted earlier in this chapter, a key money measure is the *monetary base*, which we can view either as the sum of domestic credit plus foreign exchange reserves, or as the sum of domestic currency and bank reserves. Thus, sterilization of the sale of foreign exchange reserves requires an equal-sized expansion of domestic credit, perhaps via a central bank open-market purchase, that would maintain an unchanged monetary base.

The mechanics of U.S. foreign exchange interventions entail accounting entries that lead to nearly immediate and complete sterilization. The ECB and Bank of Japan also follow policies intended to ensure at least long-term sterilization of interventions.

Many other countries officially espouse a policy of sterilizing foreign exchange interventions, but in practice, most find it difficult fully to offset the effects of the resulting changes in net foreign assets. Thus, many interventions by central banks around the world are at least partly non-sterilized, so that interventions cause changes in relative quantities of national moneys in circulation. It is through this channel, as we shall discuss in more detail in the following chapters, that many economists think interventions actually may influence market exchange rates. As you will learn in the following chapters, non-sterilized interventions can, at least in principle, lead to a number of adjustments in national economies.

Indeed, a number of economists believe that *only* non-sterilized interventions can affect exchange rates. If central banks are able to sterilize interventions, they argue, then interventions really just amount to changes in the currency compositions of domestic and foreign assets that individuals and firms around the world regard as essentially perfect substitutes. Hence, changes in the relative supplies of these assets can have no effects on foreign exchange market equilibrium.

DO INTERVENTIONS MATTER?

If sterilized interventions have no effects, then the implication would be that interventions would be redundant policies. After all, any central bank can vary the amount of money it places in circulation relative to other world currencies, through purely domestic policy actions, such as varying interest rates on advances or engaging in open-market operations, that alter the monetary base. Consequently, an important issue for international monetary economists is whether foreign exchange interventions can, and do, have independent short- and long-term effects on market exchange rates.

Gauging the short-term effects of interventions

Portfolio balance effect: *An exchange rate adjustment resulting from changes in government or central bank holdings of foreign currency-denominated financial instruments that influence the equilibrium prices of the instruments.*

Most economists believe that (at least in theory) sterilized foreign exchange interventions can have, at most, two types of immediate effect on exchange rates. They call one of these the **portfolio balance effect**: If the exchange rate is viewed as the relative price of imperfectly substitutable assets such as bonds, then changes in government or central bank holdings of bonds and other assets denominated in various currencies can influence exchange rates by affecting the equilibrium prices at which traders are willing to hold these assets. For example, if an intervention reduces the supply of domestic assets relative to foreign assets held by individuals and firms, then the expected return on domestic assets must fall to induce individuals and firms to readjust their portfolios. A reduction in the anticipated rate of return on domestic assets, in turn, requires an appreciation of the domestic currency. Hence, a finance ministry or central bank purchase of domestic currency can, through the portfolio balance effect, cause the value of the domestic currency to rise.

The other possible effect is an intervention **announcement effect**, in which foreign exchange interventions may provide traders with previously unknown information that alters their willingness to demand or supply currencies in the foreign exchange markets. The announcement effect can exist, therefore, only if a government or central bank intervention clearly reveals some kind of inside information that traders did not have prior to the intervention. For instance, a central bank that plans to conduct a future anti-inflation policy by contracting its money stock may reveal this intention by leaning against the wind in the face of a recent downward trend in the value of its nation's currency. If currency traders believe this message, provided by the central bank's intervention, then they will expect a future appreciation and will increase their holdings of the currency. This concerted action by currency traders then causes an actual currency appreciation. Thus, the announcement effect of the intervention, like the portfolio balance effect, induces a rise in the value of the domestic currency.

A major study of foreign exchange market interventions during the 1980s and early 1990s by Kathryn Dominguez of Harvard University and Jeffrey Frankel of the University of California at Berkeley found evidence that both effects were at work during that period, especially in the latter part of the 1980s, when many of the world's governments conducted sizable interventions. Dominguez and Frankel found that during this interval, in which central banks coordinated several interventions, the *announcements* of the interventions actually had larger effects on exchange rates than the actual magnitudes of the interventions themselves. This, in their view, provides strong evidence of announcement effects in interventions. Particularly in the case of coordinated interventions during the late 1980s, traders seem to have viewed interventions as signals of government and central bank commitments to future policy changes, and reacted by altering their desired holdings of domestic and foreign assets. The result was changes in market exchange rates, at least in the short run.

Announcement effect: *A change in private market interest rates or exchange rates that results from an anticipation of near-term changes in market conditions signaled by a central bank policy action.*

Can even coordinated interventions work in the long run?

As we discussed in Chapter 7, one of the most significant episodes of coordinated currency interventions took place beginning in 1985. In September of that year, at the Plaza Hotel in New York, the finance ministers and central banks of G5 nations announced that "in view of the present and prospective change in fundamentals, some orderly appreciation of the main non-dollar currencies against the dollar is desirable. We stand ready to cooperate more closely to encourage this when to do so would be helpful." The Plaza Agreement was followed in 1987 by a reaffirmation of the Plaza principles at the Louvre Palace in Paris, called the Louvre Accord. Much official rhetoric since these policy agreements has indicated that the G5 nations believed they largely accomplished their objective of stabilizing exchange rates at "desired" levels.

Some economists, however, believe this is an overstatement. Among these doubters are Michael Bordo of Rutgers University and Anna Schwartz of the National Bureau of Economic Research. In their view, central bank interventions really did not accomplish much, except to distort exchange markets and to subject central banks to excessive risks of loss.

The extent of foreign exchange interventions in the late 1980s

In support of this argument, Bordo and Schwartz conducted a study in which they tabulated data on the foreign exchange interventions coordinated by the United States, Germany, and Japan between early 1985 and late 1989. Figure 9.3 displays their estimates of the combined dollar amounts of interventions by central banks and finance ministries during that period.

Bordo and Schwartz reached two conclusions from their analysis of these interventions. First, the interventions were sporadic and highly variable, which potentially may have *added to*, instead of reducing, foreign exchange market volatility

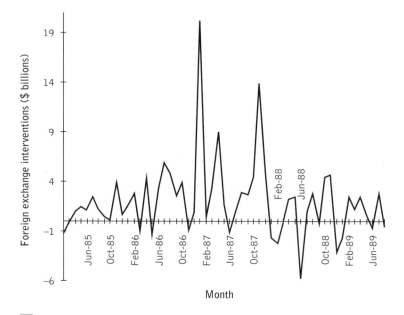

Figure 9.3 *Combined U.S., German, and Japanese interventions, February 1985 to August 1989*

The total dollar amount of the foreign exchange interventions by these nations during the late 1980s varied considerably from month to month.

Source: Bordo and Schwartz (1991).

and uncertainty. These variable—and therefore often unexpected—central bank exchange market interventions likely caused individuals and firms to experience unintended wealth transfers. In addition, the increased risk of such transfers probably induced many traders to undertake more efforts to hedge against the risks of unexpected central bank interventions. This, as we discussed in Chapter 6, can be an effective, yet costly, activity.

Second, interventions during the late 1980s were very small in size relative to total trading in foreign exchange markets. Bordo and Schwartz note, for instance, that in April 1989 total foreign exchange trading amounted to $129 *billion* per day, yet the Fed purchased only $100 *million* in marks and yen in that entire month, on a single day. In fact, Fed purchases of marks and yen for all of 1989 amounted to about $17.7 billion, or the equivalent of less than 14 percent of the amount of an average day's trading in April of that year. Given the meager relative size of foreign exchange trading by even a coalition of the world's largest central banks during the 1985–1989 period, Bordo and Schwartz question the likelihood that central bank exchange market interventions can really have *long-lasting* effects on exchange rates.

Are the direct costs of foreign exchange interventions worth the benefits?

In addition, Bordo and Schwartz argue that efforts by central banks to manipulate exchange rates have significant direct costs. Financing interventions requires expenditures of foreign exchange reserves, which either directly or indirectly (via ownership shares in central banks) are assets of national governments. During the late 1980s, Bordo and Schwartz argue, governments that participated in the coordinated effort to reduce the dollar's value exposed their governments, and hence their taxpaying citizens, to risks of sizable foreign exchange losses.

For instance, they point out that, while the Federal Reserve and Treasury combined for more than $1 billion in realized gains from foreign exchange transactions in 1985 through 1989, the Netherlands lost 600 million Dutch guilders on dollar interventions in 1986 and 1987, and Germany reportedly lost 9 billion deutsche marks in the fourth quarter of 1987 alone. Bordo and Schwartz question the wisdom of central bank and finance ministry gambles with such large stakes, given their limited abilities to achieve exchange rate goals.

Although Bordo and Schwartz make a strong case that the experience of the late 1980s indicates that central banks cannot manipulate exchange rates over long time horizons, many economists join Dominguez and Frankel in arguing that foreign exchange interventions can, and do, influence exchange rates from time to time. They contend that looking at the gains and losses from foreign exchange interventions by any single nation is misleading, because coordinated actions by several central banks are likely to have the most pronounced effects on exchange rates. They also argue that the announced willingness of central banks to influence exchange rates commonly can cause self-fulfilling prophecies: If traders believe that central banks can influence exchange rates, and expect them to do so, then the traders themselves will act on their expectations in ways that push exchange rates in the directions central bankers desire. The coordinated interventions of the late 1980s, they point out, were unambiguously associated with an interval in which the value of the dollar declined. This decline, they note, continued even beyond the active period of interventions, potentially implying longer-term effects.

Efforts to manipulate exchange rates through foreign exchange interventions have been more muted since the 1980s. This may be because nations have less desire to influence exchange rates, or because they have been unable to reach agreement on how to do so. Or it may be, as we shall discuss in Chapter 14, that modern central bankers and finance ministers have recognized the limits on their abilities to lean against the wind in today's foreign exchange markets. Before we reach that point, however, in the intervening chapters that follow you will need to learn much more about how policy actions of government finance ministries and central banks influence economic activity.

Fundamental Issue #3: How do central banks intervene in foreign exchange markets? Central banks typically intervene in the spot market for foreign exchange, using swap transactions primarily to adjust the currency compositions of their portfolios of foreign exchange reserves. If a central bank intervenes to support the current trend in the value of its currency, then it leans with the wind. If it intervenes in an effort to halt or reverse the current trend in the value of its currency, then it leans against the wind. Both central banks and government finance ministries can intervene in foreign exchange markets. Although some nations seek to ensure that their interventions are sterilized, many others do not sterilize interventions fully. Economists are divided about the answer to this question, depending in part on whether one has in mind short-run or long-run effects on interventions. Most economists agree that non-sterilized interventions can have direct, short-run effects on exchange rates by changing relative quantities of currencies in circulation. Some economists also contend that sterilized interventions can alter exchange rates through portfolio balance effects or announcement effects. There is evidence that these latter effects mattered, at least in the short run, during the period of widespread foreign exchange interventions in the 1980s. There also is evidence, however, that even coordinated interventions had relatively small effects, may have added to exchange rate volatility, or may have caused taxpayer losses owing to greater currency risks incurred by governments and central banks.

POLICYMAKING IN AN INTERDEPENDENT WORLD

Globalization causes more countries to share common interests. International transactions in goods, services, and financial assets connect an increasing number of countries, giving their residents a greater incentive to consider jointly determining national economic policy actions.

Structural interdependence and international policy externalities

In today's world, in which countries' citizens trade significant amounts of goods and services, and exchange sizable volumes of financial instruments across national boundaries, national economies are structurally interdependent. This means nations' economic systems—their markets for goods and services, financial markets, and payment systems—are interlinked.

Consequences of structural interdependence

An important consequence of **structural interdependence** is that events that benefit or harm the interests of one country may also have a bearing on the interests of citizens of another nation. That is, the collective actions that a nation's citizens undertake in their own interest may spill over to influence the welfare of other countries' residents. Economists refer to such spillover effects as *externalities*, or costs experienced by one individual or group as a result of actions by another individual or group in a separate location or market.

You will learn in Chapter 12 that an *international externality* may arise if the actions of residents in one nation affect the economic performance of another nation. In some situations, there are negative international externalities, in which events in one country have adverse consequences in another. It is also possible, however, that the collective actions of one nation's residents may improve the economic performance in another country, so that there is a positive international externality.

International policy externalities

A nation's political system typically charges individual leaders, groups of representatives or delegates, or government agencies with conducting economic policies on behalf of the nation's citizens. As we have discussed in the preceding chapters, such policies can alter the choices of private residents and businesses, thereby influencing a country's overall economic performance.

If national economies are structurally interdependent, then **international policy externalities**, or benefits or costs of policy effects that spill over onto other nations, may result. For instance, various trade policies discussed in Chapter 4 cause negative international policy externalities, or *beggar-thy-neighbor effects*. Such policies may accomplish domestic objectives, but bring about worsened economic performance within other nations. Positive international policy externalities can also occur, however. Economists often call these **locomotive effects**, which arise when a policy-induced effect on the domestic economy generates an improvement in economic performance in another country.

National policymakers recognize that their policy actions may affect other countries. They also realize that decisions by foreign policymakers may influence economic performance at home. This gives policymakers an incentive to engage in **strategic policymaking**, meaning that they develop a plan for achieving objectives for their own nation, taking into account the extent to which their nation is structurally linked to others, and courses of action that other nations' policymakers may pursue. Recognition that positive and negative externalities may result from policies that policymakers undertake also may induce them to band together to minimize the negative consequences of their individual policy choices and to enhance the positive spillovers that might result.

Structural interdependence: *A situation in which interconnectedness of national markets for goods, services, and financial assets causes events in one nation to affect the economies of other nations.*

International policy externalities: *Spillover benefits or costs that policy actions within one nation have for the economies of other nations.*

Locomotive effect: *A stimulus to economic activity in one nation generated by an increase in economic activity in another country.*

Strategic policymaking: *The formulation of national policies in light of the structural linkages among nations and the ways in which policymakers in other nations make decisions.*

287

Accounting for interdependence: International policy cooperation and coordination

There are two ways in which nations might try to work together to achieve their economic performance objectives.

International policy cooperation

International policy cooperation: *The development of institutions and procedures through which central banks share data and inform one another about their policy objectives and strategies.*

The first is through **international policy cooperation**. This refers to the formal establishment of institutions and processes through which national policymakers can collaborate on their national goals, provide information about specific approaches they intend to follow in implementing policies, and share information and data about their countries' economic performance.

An example of an institutional arrangement that facilitates international policy cooperation is the *Group of Seven* (G7). This is a collection of seven nations—Canada, France, Germany, Italy, Japan, the United Kingdom, and the United States—whose chief economic policy officials, the finance ministers and central bankers, meet on a regular basis. At these meetings, G7 officials discuss their broad policy objectives and plans, as well as more specific economic issues of concern to the member nations.

Another example is the *Bank for International Settlements* (BIS), based in Basel, Switzerland. This institution functions as a trustee for various international loan agreements, and serves as an agent in miscellaneous foreign exchange markets for many of the world's central banks. Private U.S. banks, including Citibank and J. P. Morgan, participated with governments of the *Group of Ten* (G10) nations—the G7 plus Belgium, the Netherlands, and Sweden—in developing the BIS, beginning in 1930. Indeed, many private banks continue to own shares of ownership in the BIS. Its original task was to supervise the settlement of financial claims among European nations that related to terms of the World War I Armistice. After World War II, the BIS became a central agent for clearing payments among nations participating in the European Recovery Program designed to rebuild the economies of countries recovering from the ravages of that war. Ultimately, the BIS developed into a clearinghouse for information of central banks of the G10 plus the Bank of Switzerland, the Swiss central bank. Economic staff members of the BIS organize periodic briefings for top G10 central banking officials, and coordinate conferences for staff economists of policymaking agencies of the G10 nations.

ON THE WEB:

To access the publications of the G10, go to the BIS/G10 Website at www.bis.org/list/g10publications/index.htm.

International policy coordination

International policy coordination: *The joint determination of monetary policies by a group of central banks for the intended combined benefit of the nations they represent.*

The Bank for International Settlements facilitated one instance of **international policy coordination**, which refers to the joint determination of national economic policies for the mutual benefit of a group of countries. In 1988, central banks and other banking regulators of the G10 nations adopted the *Basel Agreement*, which established common risk-based bank capital adequacy standards—minimum levels of owner backing of banks' assets, adjusted for the riskiness of those assets—for private banking institutions incorporated within those countries.

By coordinating their banking policies, the G10 nations sought to address the international policy externalities that naturally can arise from the widespread competitive interactions of their countries' banks. For instance, if only one of the G10 countries had adopted tough capital standards for its banking system, its banks would have been placed at a competitive disadvantage in international financial markets, because its banks would have needed to back their assets with larger volumes of private capital. Likewise, if one nation had failed to adopt the Basel standards, its nations' banks could have grabbed larger shares of lending around the world. Coordination of the imposition of capital requirements ensured that neither of these policy externalities arose.

Proponents of international policy coordination argue that nations can gain considerably from broad-based policy coordination. Rather than just coordinating their policies from time to time, as in the 1988 Basel Agreement on bank capital standards, these observers contend that nations should make policy coordination a day-to-day process. Indeed, many argue that countries could reap considerable gains from coordinating *all* their economic policies, including those aimed at broad output and inflation objectives.

Fundamental Issue #4: What is structural interdependence, and how can it lead nations to cooperate or to coordinate their policies? When national economies are linked together, they are structurally interdependent. As a result, policy actions in one country can have spillover effects, or international policy externalities, that influence economic performance in other nations. International policy externalities are said to be positive if they improve other countries' economic performances. They are negative if they worsen those nations' prospects. To enhance the potential for positive policy externalities, or to reduce the likelihood of negative externalities, nations may choose to cooperate by sharing information about economic data and policy objectives. They also may choose to coordinate their policymaking by determining policy actions that are in their joint interest.

THE PROS AND CONS OF INTERNATIONAL POLICY COORDINATION

In principle, nations potentially can benefit from working together in pursuit of their national economic goals. Hence, there are several general arguments in favor of international policy coordination. In addition, there are some strong reasons to question whether policy coordination is always beneficial.

Potential benefits of international policy coordination

Proponents of international policy coordination typically offer three fundamental rationales.

Rationale 1: Internalizing international policy externalities

The act of coordinating policies for the mutual benefit of a group of countries effectively requires the nations' policymakers to behave as if their countries were a single entity. Thus, international policy coordination *internalizes* the externalities that individually formulated nation policies otherwise would tend to produce. Imagine, for instance, what would happen if each of the 50 states of the United States were to make all policy decisions without regard to their effects on the other states. By coordinating the entire nation's policies through a federal government, the citizens of the 50 states minimize the potential for negative policy spillovers that would result from non-coordinated policymaking.

Likewise, the Basel Agreement on bank capital regulation reflected a recognition of potential negative competitive consequences for national banking systems of separate national restrictions on bank management. The agreement may have permitted G10 nations to avoid adverse outcomes arising from negative policy externalities.

Rationale 2: Getting the most out of a limited number of policy instruments

It is also possible that international coordination can permit national policymakers to achieve a larger number of goals with the limited policy instruments they possess. As a simple example, suppose that two nations' central banks each have the same two goals: to achieve an increase in equilibrium domestic output, and to minimize exchange rate variability. Each, therefore, has an incentive to increase its money stocks, because doing so pushes up aggregate demand in each nation while preventing one nation's money stock from changing relative to the other's, and thereby preventing an exchange rate change.

This is an intentionally simplified example, but it illustrates the basic point. If national policymakers have few policy instruments but related goals, then by working together to determine the appropriate settings of their policy instruments, the policymakers potentially could come closer to achieving their multiple objectives. Coordination thereby might be mutually beneficial.

Rationale 3: Gaining support from abroad

The third rationale for international policy coordination is that policymakers in various countries might gain additional strength to withstand domestic political pressures by banding together with other policymakers. When faced with internal pressures to enact policies that might provide short-term gains at the expense of long-term social costs, policymakers could use their commitment to international coordination agreements as a justification for holding the line against such actions.

For example, suppose that a Chilean government facing a difficult election were to call upon the Bank of Chile to engage in inflationary policies intended to spur the Chilean economy during the months before the election. If the Bank of Chile could argue that such a policy would violate an accord to coordinate its policies with other central banks, thereby damaging Chile's credibility with those central banks and more broadly in world financial markets, then the Bank of Chile might be able to withstand the government's pressures.

Potential drawbacks of international policy coordination

International policy coordination is not a free lunch. There are at least four possible drawbacks.

Drawback 1: Policy coordination may entail national sacrifice

Ultimately, what defines any nation is its **sovereignty**, or the supremacy of its citizens' own control of the resources within their country's geographic borders. If international policy coordination is to achieve benefits for a nation, its citizens and leaders must be amenable to giving up some degree of sovereignty. They must be willing to pursue *international* objectives along with purely domestic goals.

Sovereignty: *The supremacy of a nation's citizens to control the resources within its geographic borders.*

For instance, suppose that on January 1, 2016, a group of nations were to agree that their relative currency values must be fixed, beginning March 1 of that year. At the end of February, however, one of the nations determines that it could gain by devaluing its currency relative to the currencies of the other countries in the group. Nevertheless, to abide by the policy coordination agreement, the nation's leaders would have to sacrifice the nation's discretion to pursue its own self-interest by devaluing its currency.

Drawback 2: Other countries may not be trustworthy

The latter example illustrates a fundamental problem with international policy coordination, which is that, typically, countries that enter into coordination agreements have incentives to cheat. To see why this is so, consider Figure 9.4. Each cell in the figure gives hypothetical values, in "welfare units," of the citizens of two countries, denoted A and B, when their countries do or do not coordinate their policies. In the upper-left-hand cell of Figure 9.4, we see that if country A and country B conduct independent, non-coordinated policies, each derives a welfare level of 75 units. In contrast, if both nations coordinate their policymaking, then the lower-right-hand cell indicates that they both attain welfare levels of 100 units. Thus, policy coordination is beneficial for both countries.

	Country B does not coordinate	Country B coordinates
Country A does not coordinate	Country A welfare = 75 Country B welfare = 75 Total welfare = 150	Country A welfare = 150 Country B welfare = 25 Total welfare = 175
Country A coordinates	Country A welfare = 25 Country B welfare = 150 Total welfare = 175	Country A welfare = 100 Country B welfare = 100 Total welfare = 200

Figure 9.4 *Hypothetical welfare levels for two nations with and without policy coordination*

If policymakers in two nations fail to coordinate their policies, then their combined welfare is 150 units. If both work together to coordinate policy actions, however, their total welfare is 200 units. The difficulty is that if either nation "cheats" and fails to coordinate as promised, it can raise its own welfare to 150 units, which yields only 25 units of welfare for the other nation that honors the coordination agreement.

Nevertheless, the potential for each country to gain from cheating could still result in a failure to coordinate policies. Country A's policymakers know that country A's welfare can be raised to 150 units if country A fails to follow through on a coordination agreement with country B while country B's policymakers continue to honor the agreement. Consequently, there is an incentive for the policymakers in country A to renege on the deal to achieve higher national welfare. As a result, as indicated in the upper-right-hand cell of Figure 9.4, country B's welfare declines to 25 units. Hence, country A gains, but only at country B's expense. At the same time, country B's policymakers face the same temptation to cheat and pursue a beggar-thy-neighbor policy, as the lower-left-hand cell of the figure shows.

Clearly, in this example the combined welfare of both nations' citizens is highest, at 200 units, if policymakers in the two nations follow through and coordinate their policies. Yet each nation has an incentive to renege in favor of a beggar-thy-neighbor policy that yields a lower welfare level of 175 units. If *both* countries cheat simultaneously, however, then total welfare is at its lowest, at 150 units. Nevertheless, each individual country might feel that it is better off than it would be if it were to stick with the agreement, only to be cheated by the other nation's policymakers.

This example illustrates a key problem of international policy coordination. Agreements to coordinate national policies can work only if all participants trust each other. Hence, each nation's commitment to an international policy coordination arrangement must be *credible* to other participating nations. In the absence of such credibility, each nation would recognize that it is worse off by agreeing to coordinate and exposing its citizens to the adverse effects caused by other nations' cheating.

Drawback 3: Other policymakers could be incompetent

The potential for deception and cheating is not the only factor that can cause individual nations to lose when agreeing to coordinate their policies with those of other countries. Another problem that a nation encounters when it sacrifices some sovereignty in hopes of reaping gains from coordination is the possibility that other nations' policymakers may lack competence to pursue the best common policy. That is, to be willing to cede some of its policymaking sovereignty to another country, a nation must be confident in two things. The nation must have confidence that policymakers in the other country will honor the coordination agreement. The nation also must believe that the other nation's policymakers have the ability to do their jobs effectively.

There is also the possibility that policymakers of coordinating nations may have conflicting outlooks on the appropriate policies for all nations to pursue jointly, even if the policymakers otherwise trust themselves to honor their agreements and to implement policy actions competently. Such conflicts may arise because of different policymaker preferences concerning, say, how much relative weight to place on real output versus inflation objectives. Alternatively, policymakers might not agree about the best way to implement a coordination agreement. For example, if Germany and the United Kingdom were to agree to coordinate their policies, but the Bundesbank's economic staff believed strongly in targeting money growth rates, while the Bank of England economic staff believed just as strongly in targeting nominal interest rates, then such a technical argument concerning policy implementation might still cause a coordination agreement to break down.

Drawback 4: "Successful" coordination can sometimes be counterproductive

Even if nations agree to coordinate, stick to their agreement, and determine their policies taking joint welfare into account, there is still the possibility that in the end their residents could be worse off.

Suppose, for instance, that two nations experience positive international monetary policy externalities. If either nation's central bank increases the quantity of its currency in circulation, there are two effects. One is an increase in home aggregate demand. Another is a locomotive effect as the resulting increase in residents' incomes induces them to purchase goods and services from the other nation's residents, which pushes up their incomes and desired consumption levels, thereby generating an increase in aggregate demand within that nation.

In addition, suppose that the central banks of the two countries both face the problem of time inconsistency and low policy credibility. The residents of their countries know that both policymakers thereby have an incentive to try to raise national output levels by expanding their money stocks and pushing up aggregate demand. In the absence of policy coordination, there will be an increase in aggregate demand in each country following a monetary expansion, and a simultaneous reduction in aggregate production as workers negotiate higher wages in anticipation of higher inflation. The result is an inflation bias in each country.

Now think about what happens if the nations' central banks succeed in coordinating their monetary policies. Each central bank will then take into account not only the incentive it faces to push up output at home, but also the other central bank's incentive to try to boost output in the other nation. As a consequence, each central bank will tend to raise its money stock even more than it would have in the absence of policy coordination. Residents of both nations will realize this, and expect even more inflation, so they will bargain for larger wage boosts when their central banks coordinate their policies. Thus, the inflation bias in each country will be greater with coordinated monetary policies than it would have been if the central banks had chosen not to coordinate. In both nations, residents will have to bear higher inflation costs.

Fundamental Issue #5: What are the benefits and costs of international policy coordination? The most significant gain that might arise from policy coordination is the internalization of international policy externalities, meaning that working together toward joint goals could permit national policymakers to minimize the ill effects of negative externalities or improve the prospect for benefits of positive externalities. It also is possible that policy coordination might increase the number of policy instruments that could be aimed at policymakers' objectives. In addition, the establishment of formal policy coordination agreements or institutions could assist a policymaker's efforts to resist domestic political pressures to enact short-sighted policies with potentially harmful long-term effects. One difficulty with entering into policy coordination agreements is that nations must give up at least some measure of national sovereignty to implement such agreements. In addition, they must trust each other, both to pursue promised policy actions, and to do so in a competent manner. Yet typically there will be an incentive for one nation to cheat on a policy coordination agreement in the pursuit of gains at another country's expense, and there is always the possibility that one nation's policymakers will fail to pursue policies that another nation believes to be appropriate. Finally, international policy coordination can, if policymakers' credibility levels are low within their own countries, lead to higher average inflation rates.

OPTIMAL CURRENCY AREAS AND MONETARY UNIONS

As we have discussed, if a nation chooses to enter into an international policy coordination arrangement, it must give up at least some degree of national sovereignty. Would there be any gain from taking another step and giving up its own currency in favor of a currency common to it and others in a coalition of policy-coordinating nations? That is, should a nation join a formal **monetary union**, a grouping of nation-states that agree to use a single currency? To contemplate this issue, we must consider the theory of optimal currency areas.

Monetary union:
A set of countries that choose to use a common currency.

Optimal currency areas

In 1991, nations of the EU negotiated a treaty in the Netherlands' city of Maastricht. The treaty authorized establishment of a European Central Bank to issue the euro as a circulating currency, beginning in 2002. Initially, 11 nations—Austria, Belgium, Finland, France, Germany, Ireland, Italy, Luxembourg, the Netherlands, Portugal, and Spain—participated in the *European Monetary Union* (EMU) that adopted this new currency.

Throughout the process, many skeptical economists continued to question whether the EMU could last. They based their arguments on an economic theory developed more than 30 years ago by Robert Mundell of Columbia University. This is the **theory of optimal currency areas**, which is an analytical approach to determining the extent of a geographic area whose residents would be better off by fixing their exchange rates or even by using a common currency.

Theory of optimal currency areas: *An approach to determining the size of a geographic area within which residents' welfare is greater if their governments fix exchange rates or adopt a common currency.*

The theory of optimal currency areas

Financial newspapers such as the *Wall Street Journal* or the *Financial Times* publish daily listings of exchange rates for more than 50 national currencies. These are not complete exchange rate listings because these newspapers list only the currencies with large trading volumes in the foreign exchange markets.

Why are there so many different national currencies? Why do residents of all 50 states of the United States use the same currency, even though states such as

California and New York have higher volumes of GDP than most nations of the world? Will all nations within the EU truly benefit from following the example of the 50 U.S. states? Should all of Europe be part of the EMU? The theory of optimal currency areas seeks to address these issues.

The advantage of separate currencies and a floating exchange rate

To understand the essential features of the theory of optimal currency areas, let's consider two hypothetical regions. People in one region, which we shall call region X, specialize in producing pastries. Residents of the other region, denoted region Y, manufacture exercise equipment. In both regions, wages and prices are inflexible in the short run. Initially, both regions experience balanced trade.

Suppose that residents of one region cannot seek employment in the other region, perhaps because of language or cultural barriers, or because governments of one or both of the regions have established restrictions preventing region X residents who are employed in pastry production from moving to region Y to make exercise equipment, and *vice versa*. Nevertheless, residents of the two regions face no restrictions on their ability to purchase both regions' goods.

Finally, let's suppose that each region has its own currency. The exchange rate for these currencies can float in the foreign exchange market, or regional policymakers can fix the exchange rate.

Consider now what happens if residents of both regions become more health conscious. As a result, they cut back on their purchases of high-cholesterol pastries manufactured in region X and increase their demand for the exercise equipment produced in region Y. Region Y begins to run a trade surplus, and its output and employment increases. In contrast, region X begins to experience a trade deficit, and its output and employment decline.

If the rate of exchange between the regions' currencies is fixed, then the assumed short-run stickiness of wage and prices causes unemployment to persist for some time in region X, following the changes in consumers' tastes. In the long run, of course, the price of the exercise equipment manufactured in region Y increases, and the price of the pastries made in region X declines, leading to an ultimate rebalancing of trade between the two regions. Until this long-run adjustment occurs, however, region X can experience a significant unemployment problem.

If the exchange rate is flexible, however, then the trade surplus in region Y and trade deficit in region X induces a speedy depreciation in the value of region X's currency relative to the currency of region Y. This causes an immediate fall in the effective price of pastries from region X as perceived by residents of region Y, and a rapid increase in the effective price of region Y's exercise equipment faced by residents of region X. As a result, trade between the two regions is balanced much more rapidly with a floating exchange rate, and the unemployment problem in region X is much more short-lived.

This example illustrates a situation in which two regions gain from using separate currencies with relative values that adjust freely in the foreign exchange market. Fixing the rate of exchange between the currencies, or taking the further step of adopting a single currency, would prevent the exchange rate from serving as a means of short-run adjustment to changes in relative demands for the regions' goods. This exposes the regions to the potential for chronic payments imbalances and unemployment problems.

Certainly, with separate currencies and a market-determined exchange rate, residents of both nations face foreign exchange risks arising from exchange rate movements and costs of converting one currency to another when they wish to purchase another region's goods. Nonetheless, adopting individual currencies and a floating exchange rate protects the regions from unemployment dangers that arise from language, cultural, or legal barriers to worker migration.

When could nations benefit from using a single currency?

Now suppose that the conditions that have led to past constraints on worker migration break down. As a result, residents of region X can move freely to region Y to work, and *vice versa*. Let's further suppose that, shortly following this development, there is another fall in the demand for the fattening pastries manufactured in region X, and a rise in the demand for region Y's exercise equipment.

The immediate results, again, are a trade surplus, higher output, and higher employment in region Y; and a trade deficit, lower output, and lower employment in region X. Consequently, some residents of region X find themselves without work. Now, however, these unemployed residents of region X can migrate—or perhaps even commute—to newly available jobs in region Y. Thus, region X unemployment is at worst a temporary phenomenon. Indeed, unemployment for both regions together is minimized in the face of such changes in the relative demands for their products.

Optimal currency area: *A geographic area within which labor is sufficiently mobile to permit speedy adjustments to payment imbalances and regional unemployment to permit exchange rates to be fixed and a common currency to be adopted.*

In this example, there is no reason why the rates of exchange between the two regions cannot be fixed, thereby permitting residents of both regions to avoid foreign exchange risks. Indeed, economists would conclude that the two regions together constitute an **optimal currency area**, or a geographic area within which fixed exchange rates may be maintained without slowing regional adjustments to changing regional circumstances. Furthermore, within such an optimal currency area, separate regions find it beneficial to adopt a *common currency* if the cost of converting currencies for regional trade exceeds any perceived gain from having separate currencies.

If, for example, the residents of regions A and B continue to perceive sizable benefits from using separate currencies, even though no barriers otherwise separate their regions, then they might wish to continue to incur currency conversion costs that arise when they trade goods. But if currency conversion costs are sufficiently large, relative to the potential benefits of maintaining separate regional currencies, then the residents of the two regions that constitute an optimal currency area might gain, on net, from adopting a single, common currency.

Are more nearly synchronized economic fluctuations strengthening the case for common currencies?

Various economic factors, such as sudden changes in desired expenditures or asset holds on the part of households and businesses, can affect an individual nation's observed flows of income over time. Furthermore, in countries linked by international trade in goods and services and international flows of financial assets, changes in one nation's income flows, that alter its residents' desired expenditures on exports in another country, also affect the latter country's income flows. That is, nations are structurally interdependent.

The possibility that the economies of many of the world's nations may have become more closely linked suggests that changes in their income flows may have become more synchronized—that is, may move more nearly in tandem—over time. To proponents of currency unions, more synchronized **business cycles**—fluctuations in nations' flows of income derived from spending on goods and services produced by their firms—strengthen the case for countries to utilize a common currency. The reason is that, if the nations' business cycles are synchronized, there will be fewer differences in income flows that generate payments imbalances. Hence, there will be less scope for a floating exchange rate to perform any stabilizing role, implying lower benefits to the countries from having separate currencies.

Business cycle:
Fluctuations over time of a nation's income flows that are derived from spending on goods and services produced by its firms

Recent research has reached mixed conclusions about the degree of business-cycle synchronization across clusters of nations. Michael Bordo of Harvard University and Thomas Helbling of the International Monetary Fund conclude that business cycle synchronization has become more pronounced over the past 30 years among 16 major industrialized nations. Lourdes Montoya of the College of Europe and Jakob de Haan of the University of Groningen find evidence of a greater extent of synchronization of business cycles among the nations that currently utilize the euro. In a study of 125 years of data for 25 industrialized and emerging economies, Michael Artis and George Chouliarakis of the University of Manchester and P.K.G. Harischandra of the Central Bank of Sri Lanka also have concluded, based on a study of 125 years of data for 25 industrialized and emerging economies, that the degree of business-cycle synchronization has become more pronounced for industrialized nations. In the case of emerging nations, however, they find that country-specific factors commonly cause business cycles to diverge from one another. Thus, there is some evidence that real income flows tend to move together for groups of developing nations, but not for less advanced countries. (Some observers have suggested that increased synchronization of business cycles among nations in East Asia might help make them candidates for a future single-currency area; see *Policy Notebook: Could an East Asian monetary union succeed?*)

POLICY NOTEBOOK

Could an East Asian monetary union succeed?

In recent years, suggestions have emerged for a currency union involving nations of East Asia. Proposed nation groupings for a common currency have included countries among the Association of Southeast Asian Nations (ASEAN), such as Indonesia, Malaysia, Philippines, and Thailand, or nations within the set of so-called newly industrialized economies—Hong Kong, Taiwan, Singapore, and South Korea.

Motivating most proponents of a common East Asian currency is an upsurge of trade among nations in this part of the world. Since 1980, intraregional trade has risen from 35 percent of all international trade of East Asian nations to more than 50 percent—a share almost as large as the intraregional trade share within the EU.

Studies by Grace Lee and Sharon Koh of Monash University together with M. Azali of Universiti Putra Malaysia have provided evidence of additional developments that could contribute to a successful East Asian currency union. First, business-cycle fluctuations in East Asian nations increasingly reflect common, instead of country-specific, sources. Hence, relative shifts of economic activity between these countries, that otherwise would create payments imbalances, are less likely than in past years. Second, when such relative shifts of economic activity among East Asian nations occur, adjustments to payments imbalances occur quickly, perhaps reflecting freer mobility of factors of production across national borders of a number of these countries. Thus, the prospects that an East Asian currency union could be beneficial to member nations have improved.

For critical analysis: Why is the observation of continuing immobility of labor resources across most East Asian nations an argument against these nations agreeing to participate in a currency union?

The European common-currency experiment: European Monetary Union

Under the terms of the Maastricht Treaty on European Union, 11 members of the then 15-nation EU adopted a common currency in 1999. This group of countries, which became the EMU, began using the new currency, the euro, in hand-to-hand transactions in 2002. During the following decade, six more EU member nations elected to utilize the euro as well, and had their central banks join the European System of Central Banks and a centralized institution, the ECB, in managing circulation of the euro. The 17 nations that currently participate in the EMU are Austria, Belgium, Cyprus, Estonia, Finland, France, Germany, Greece, Ireland, Italy, Luxembourg, Malta, the Netherlands, Portugal, Slovakia, Slovenia, and Spain.

Is the European Monetary Union an optimal currency area?

The founding EMU nations emphasized the importance of adhering to deficit, debt, and inflation criteria to be considered for membership to the common-currency "club." The Maastricht Treaty requires a country wishing to join the EMU to have a national budget deficit no larger than 3 percent of GDP, total government debt no greater than 60 percent of GDP, an inflation rate no higher than 1.5 percentage points higher than the average of the three best-performing EMU member nations, and long-term interest rates no higher than two points above the same benchmark. Some European nations, such as Denmark and the United Kingdom, that have satisfied these goals have nonetheless passed up on the opportunity to join the EMU.

Undoubtedly, residents of Denmark and the United Kingdom are concerned about losing their currencies, the krona and the pound, which have long been symbols of national sovereignty.

Another reason some Danish and British doubters offer for their hesitancy to join the EMU is uncertainty about whether all the EU nations truly constitute an optimal currency area. Research by Barry Eichengreen of the University of California at Berkeley has compared measures of labor mobility in Western Europe with those of other countries with single currencies. His evidence indicates that, compared with other nations made up of separate states and regions, such as the United States and Canada, labor is much less mobile across the borders of the nations of Western Europe. Follow-up research by other economists has supported Eichengreen's conclusions, with the most recent estimates indicating about five times less labor mobility across borders of European nations compared with U.S. states. The full EU is not necessarily an optimal currency area. Indeed, most studies find that labor immobility between (and even within) the southern and northern tiers of the EU is sufficiently pronounced that the current set of EMU nations does not constitute an optimal currency area, either.

A currency union under stress

In spite of doubts about the underlying economic rationale for the EMU, the currency union appeared to function well during its first decade. By the second decade, however, the currency union was experiencing substantial stresses. Today, even though some economists contend that the EMU will remain intact, and indeed likely will expand once more, other economists have argued that eventually only a few of the initial EMU members are likely to remain euro-utilizing nations. Some economists are even more pessimistic. They predict an eventual cessation of euro circulation and readoption of all European nations' original currencies, although at exchange rates perhaps radically altered from their early 2000s levels.

What has accounted for the sudden turnabout in many economists' perspectives regarding the EMU's ultimate prospects? The answer lies in deficit and debt policies of EMU nations that departed from the original criteria specified by the Maastricht Treaty. Although this treaty established clear limitations on acceptable government deficit and debt levels at the time a nation joined the EMU, it was silent about whether member nations had to continue to adhere to these constraints during subsequent years. Within a few years' time, most EMU governments chose to operate with deficits or debts exceeding the Maastricht Treaty limits. Then, in the wake of the 2007–2009 global financial meltdown, which resulted in lower tax collections as public expenditures continued to grow, EMU governments—particularly those of Portugal, Ireland, Italy, Greece, and Spain (the "PIIGS" nations)—began running substantial public deficits and building up larger public debt levels. Public deficits in the PIIGS nations rose to more than twice the 3 percent Maastricht limit, and these countries' public debt–GDP ratios considerably exceeded the Maastricht Treaty's 60 percent threshold. In fact, by the early 2010s, public debt–GDP ratios exceeded 100 percent in all PIIGS nations except Spain.

As private investors began to form doubts that PIIGS nations' governments would be able to honor these burgeoning debts, they began substituting away from holdings of those nations' governments' debt instruments to those of non-PIIGS countries' governments. Considerable shifts of financial capital from PIIGS nations to other EMU countries contributed to rising balance-of-payments deficits among the former group. Minimal north–south mobility of labor and other productive factors caused unemployment problems to fester across the EMU's southern tier, whereas in Ireland many people responded by moving to other EMU countries to seek employment. Thus, unemployment problems escalated within the southern EMU nations. Incomes in these southern-tier nations decreased further, which caused these countries' governments to experience more reductions in tax revenues, which worsened their deficit and debt positions.

Many economists, such as Carmen Reinhart of the Peterson Institute for International Economics and Kenneth Rogoff of Harvard University, project that the debt problems plaguing the majority of EMU member nations will persist for at least another decade. It remains to be seen how many EMU nations will still be using the euro as their currency by the early 2020s, given the pressures in place for PIIGS nations to abandon the currency in favor of flexible exchange rates that can allow imbalances to adjust—or perhaps for non-PIIGS countries either to ask some of the former nations to leave the EMU, or to give up on the monetary union themselves. (For an example of how uncertainties about the future of the EMU affect firms operating in other currency unions, see *Management Notebook: The European Monetary Union's tribulations create uncertainties for firms operating within African currency unions*.)

MANAGEMENT NOTEBOOK

The European Monetary Union's tribulations create uncertainties for firms operating within African currency unions

Africa is home to two currency unions: the West African Economic and Monetary Union (Benin, Burkina Faso, Ivory Coast, Guinea-Bissau, Mali, Niger, Senegal, and Togo) and the Economic and Monetary Community of Central Africa (Cameroon, Central African Republic, Chad, Republic of the Congo, Equatorial Guinea, and Gabon). Each currency union issues its own "CFA franc" notes. The West African version is the *Communauté Financière d'Afrique* (Financial Community of Africa) franc note issued by the Central Bank of the West African States. The Central African version is the *Coopération Financière Afrique Centrale* (Financial Cooperation in Central Africa) franc note issued by the Bank of the Central African States. Based on currencies originally tied to the French franc, each of these two CFA notes currently is pegged to the EMU's euro at a rate of 655.957 CFA notes per euro.

Because both CFA notes are pegged to the euro at the same rate of exchange, for years companies operating within the two African currency unions regarded the notes as virtually interchangeable in the bulk of their cross-border exchanges. Increasing uncertainties about the longer-term future of the EMU have forced both African currency unions to begin working out contingency plans for their CFA francs, however. In the event of a euro collapse, these plans call for each of the African currency unions to peg their CFA franc notes' values to a broad basket of global currencies. Nevertheless, it is unclear if the two African currency unions would be able to agree on the same currency basket and, if so, an identical pegged value for their CFA franc notes. If not, the days of nearly complete interchangeability of CFA francs across businesses operating within an expanse populated by nearly 125 million people could come to an end.

For critical analysis: In light of the theory of optimal currency areas, why do you suppose that western and central African nations might have chosen to operate separate currency unions instead of one combined currency union?

Fundamental Issue #6: Could nations gain from adopting a common currency? An optimal currency area is a geographic area in which relative shifts of income flows are not common due to business-cycle synchronization. In addition, in an optimal currency area, labor is highly mobile across national boundaries, so that movements of workers among regions alleviate any payments imbalances and related unemployment changes without the need for exchange rate adjustment. In such an environment, nations could save their residents from incurring foreign exchange risks and currency conversion costs by joining a monetary union with a common currency. Most economic studies indicate that European nations fail to satisfy the conditions of an optimal currency area. Initially, this fact failed to hinder the formation and functioning of the EMU, but in recent years problems with public finances in several EMU nations have placed increasing stresses on this currency union.

CHAPTER SUMMARY

1. **Responsibilities of the world's central banks:** Central banks are depositories for funds held by national governments. They act as fiscal agents by operating the systems through which governments issue debt instruments, making interest and principal payments to those who hold government debt, and developing markets for government debt instruments. Central banks perform financial services for private banks and operate as lenders of last resort by providing liquidity to stem bank runs or other systemic banking problems. Furthermore, central banks vary policy instruments, such as interest rates on central bank advances, open-market operations, reserve requirements, and interest-rate and credit restrictions, to affect interbank funds rates and

total bank reserves. This allows them to determine the monetary base. The monetary base is composed of currency notes and reserve deposits of private banks, which are key central bank liabilities. Important central bank assets are government securities, loans to private banks, and reserves of foreign currencies.

2. **Primary central bank instruments of monetary policy, and how monetary policy actions affect market interest rates:** Monetary policy instruments available to central banks include interest rates on central bank advances, open-market operations, reserve requirements, and interest rate and credit restrictions. Central banks can alter these instruments to affect interbank funds rates, bank reserves, the monetary base, and, through the money multiplier, the quantity of money. At the equilibrium interest rate, a nation's residents are satisfied to be holding the quantity of money in circulation. A central bank action that increases the quantity of money raises the amount of total liquidity in the economy, thereby bringing about a decline in the equilibrium interest rate.

3. **How central banks intervene in foreign exchange markets:** Central banks typically intervene by buying or selling currencies in spot foreign exchange markets. Leaning with the wind refers to central bank interventions to support the current trend in the value of its currency, while leaning against the wind refers to interventions intended to halt or reverse the current trend in the value of its currency. Central banks and finance ministries both intervene in foreign exchange markets, though institutional frameworks governing the mechanisms for interventions, and the extent to which they are sterilized, vary from nation to nation. Many economists have concluded that non-sterilized interventions can influence market exchange rates by changing relative quantities of money supplied. Some also argue that sterilized interventions can alter exchange rates via portfolio balance effects or announcement effects. Evidence from the experience with interventions in the 1980s indicates that these latter effects were present, but there is also evidence from these episodes that even coordinated interventions may have had limited exchange-rate effects, or could have contributed to greater exchange-rate variability and taxpayer losses in some nations.

4. **Structural interdependence, and how it can lead nations to cooperate or to coordinate their policies:** National economies are structurally interdependent if one country's economy responds to events affecting the performance of another. In such situations, international policy externalities can exist, meaning that policy actions in one country can have spillover effects on the economies of other nations. Positive international policy externalities exert beneficial spillover effects on other nations' economic performances, whereas negative international policy externalities contribute to a worsening of those nations' economic performances. To enhance positive externalities or mitigate negative externalities, nations may cooperate by establishing institutional structures for sharing data or for collaborating on national goals. They also may decide to coordinate their policies by determining policy actions that are best for their common good.

5. **The benefits and costs of international policy coordination:** A key advantage of international policy coordination is that it can internalize international policy externalities, so that jointly pursuing national objectives might allow economic policymakers to limit the adverse consequences of negative externalities, or to enhance the beneficial

aspects of positive externalities. International policy coordination might increase the number of policy instruments that policymakers can direct toward attainment of their ultimate goals. Furthermore, participating in formal policy-coordination agreements could help domestic policymakers resist domestic pressures to engage in policies that might yield short-term internal political benefits, but undesirable longer-term outcomes. A fundamental drawback associated with international policy coordination is the potential loss of national policymaking sovereignty. National policymakers must also trust that their counterparts will actually pursue promised policy objectives, and that they will do so in a competent manner. Nevertheless, there usually is an incentive for policymakers to cheat on a coordination agreement, and policymakers may disagree about the most appropriate mix of policy actions to implement. In addition, if central banks have imperfect anti-inflation credibility, then coordinating their monetary policies can increase the inflation bias arising from discretionary monetary policymaking.

6. **The possibility that nations could gain from adopting a common currency:** Nations lie inside an optimal currency area if there is sufficient mobility of workers across national boundaries to alleviate unemployment and payments imbalances without the need for exchange rate adjustment. Countries in an optimal currency area could, in principle, eliminate foreign exchange risks and currency conversion costs faced by their residents, if they were to form a monetary union with a common currency. Current evidence indicates that the formation of the European Monetary Union has continued apace even though Europe as a whole probably does not constitute an optimal currency area.

QUESTIONS AND PROBLEMS

1. In your view, what is the single most important role of a central bank? Could a central bank perform this role without performing its other roles?

2. Can a central bank directly "control" the size of the monetary base? Why, or why not?

3. Could a central bank conduct monetary policy solely by varying an interest rate on advances?

4. Under what circumstances does the quantity of money in circulation within a nation change when its central bank conducts foreign exchange interventions?

5. Suppose that a nation's central bank does not use open-market operations to conduct monetary policy. How could the central bank vary the interest rate(s) that it charges on its advances to try to sterilize a foreign exchange intervention intended to raise the value of its nation's currency?

6. True or false? Even though most central banks conduct foreign exchange interventions in the spot market, there is no reason that forward market interventions would not be equally effective. Take a stand, and support your answer.

7. Explain the difference between international policy cooperation and international policy coordination. Which do you believe is most common today?

8. Summarize the potential advantages of coordinating national economic policies. Of these, which do you think is most important? Explain.

9. Discuss the likely disadvantages of international policy coordination. Which do you believe to be the greatest disadvantage? Take a stand, and justify your position.

10. As noted in this chapter, there is not strong evidence that all the nations of Europe constitute an optimal currency area in the conventional sense. Yet many countries outside the EMU continue to express interest in joining it. Can you think of any other arguments that leaders of these nations might give to support their goal of becoming part of the EMU? Explain.

ONLINE APPLICATION

URL: www.ecb.int
Title: About the European Central Bank
Navigation: Begin at the above home page, and click on "The European Central Bank."
Application: Perform the indicated operations, and answer the accompanying questions.

1. Click on "The European Central Bank." On the Web page that follows, click on "ECB, ESCB, and the Eurosystem," and read the article. Which institution has responsibility for monetary policy actions within the set of nations utilizing the euro as its currency: the European System of Central Banks or the ECB? Explain.

2. Click and scan through the links on the left side of the Web page. What aspects of the ESCB's structure promote policy credibility?

For group study and analysis: Divide the class into groups. Assign each group to use the list of euro-area central banks available on the above Website, and the "Central bank hub" available at www.bis.org/cbanks.htm to explore Websites of the central banks that are currently in the ESCB. What are the roles of the individual national central banks within the ESCB? Within their domestic economic and financial systems?

REFERENCES AND RECOMMENDED READINGS

Aizenman, Joshua, and Reuven Glick. "Sterilization, Monetary Policy, and Global Financial Integration." National Bureau of Economic Research, Working Paper 13902, March 2008.

Aizenman, Joshua, and Jaewoo Lee. "International Reserves: Precautionary vs. Mercantilist Views, Theory and Evidence." International Monetary Fund, IMF Working Paper WP/05/198, October 2005.

Artis, Michael, George Chouliarakis, and P.K.G. Harischandra. "Business Cycle Synchronization since 1880." Working Paper, University of Manchester and Central Bank of Sri Lanka, April 2011.

Beine, Michel, Oscar Bernal, Jean-Yves Gnabo, and Christelle Lecourt. "Intervention Policy of the Bank of Japan: A Unified Approach." *Journal of Banking and Finance* 33 (May 2009): 904–913.

Bhalla, Surjit. *Devaluing to Prosperity: Misaligned Currencies and Their Growth Consequences.* Washington, DC: Peterson Institute for International Economics, 2012.

Bordo, Michael. "A Brief History of Central Banks." Federal Reserve Bank of Cleveland Economic Commentary, 2007.

Bordo, Michael, and Thomas Helbling. "International Business Cycle Synchronization in Historical Perspective." *Manchester School* 79(2) (2011): 208–238.

Bordo, Michael, Owen Humpage, and Anna Schwartz. "The Historical Origins of U.S. Exchange Market Intervention Policy." National Bureau of Economic Research, Working Paper 12662, November 2006.

Bordo, Michael, and Anna Schwartz. "What Has Foreign Exchange Market Intervention Since the Plaza Agreement Accomplished?" *Open Economies Review* 2(1) (1991): 39–64.

Brandner, Peter, Harald Grech, and Helmut Stix. "The Effectiveness of Central Bank Intervention in the EMS: The Post 1993 Experience." *Journal of International Money and Finance* 25 (June 2006): 580–597.

Capie, Forrest, Charles Goodhart, and Norbert Schnadt. "The Development of Central Banking." In Capie et al., eds., *The Future of Central Banking: The Tercentenary Symposium of the Bank of England.* Cambridge, U.K.: Cambridge University Press, 1994, pp. 1–231.

De Grauwe, Paul. *Economics of Monetary Union*, 9th edn. Oxford, U.K.: Oxford University Press, 2012.

Dominguez, Kathryn M.E. "When Do Central Bank Interventions Influence Intra-Daily and Longer-Term Exchange Rate Movements?" *Journal of International Money and Finance* 25 (November 2006): 1051–1071.

Dominguez, Kathryn and Jeffry Frankel. "Does Foreign Exchange Intervention Work?" *Institute for International Economics*, Washington DC, 1993.

Eichengreen, Barry. "Is Europe an Optimal Currency Area?" National Bureau of Economic Research Working Paper No. 3579, January 1991.

European Central Bank. "The Accumulation of Foreign Reserves." Occasional Paper Series, Number 43, February 2006.

Fatum, Rasmus, and Michael Hutchison. "Evaluating Foreign Exchange Market Intervention: Self-Selection, Counterfactuals, and Average Treatment Effects." *Journal of International Money and Finance* 29(3) (April 2010): 570–584.

Humpage, Owen. "A New Role for the Exchange Stabilization Fund." Federal Reserve Bank of Cleveland Economic Commentary, August 2008.

Kenen, Peter, and Ellen Meade. *Regional Monetary Integration.* Cambridge, U.K.: Cambridge University Press, 2008.

Kirton, John J., Joseph P. Daniels, and Andreas Freytag. *Guiding Global Order.* Aldershot, U.K.: Ashgate Publishing, 2001.

Lecourt, Christelle, and Helene Raymond. "Central Bank Interventions in Industrialized Countries: A Characterization Based on Survey Results." *International Journal of Economics and Finance* 11 (April 2006): 123–138.

Lee, Grace, and M. Azali. "Is East Asia and Optimum Currency Area?" *Economic Modelling* 29 (2012): 87–95.

Lee, Grace, and Sharon Koh. "The Prospects of a Monetary Union in East Asia." *Economic Modelling* 29 (2012): 96–102.

Montoya, Lourdes, and Jacob de Haan. "Regional Business Cycle Synchronization in Europe?" *International Economics and Economic Policy* 5(1/2) (July 2008): 123–137.

Mundell, Robert. "A Theory of Optimal Currency Areas." *American Economic Review* 51 (1961): 657–665.

Neely, Christopher J. "Central Bank Authorities' Beliefs about Foreign Exchange Intervention." *Journal of International Money and Finance* 27 (2008): 1–25.

Nordvig, Jens. *The Fall of the Euro.* New York: McGraw-Hill, 2014.

Reinhart, Carmen, and Kenneth Rogoff. *A Decade of Debt.* Washington, DC: Peterson Institute for International Economics, September 2011.

Reitz, Stefan, and Mark P. Taylor. "Japanese and Federal Reserve Intervention in the Yen–US Dollar Market: A Coordination Channel of FX Operations?" Department of Economics, Deutsche Bundesbank, and Department of Economics, University of Warwick, April 2008. http://ssrn.com/abstract=1157679

Sarno, Lucio, and Mark P. Taylor. "Official Intervention in the Foreign Exchange Market: Is It Effective and, If So, How Does it Work?" *Journal of Economic Literature* 39(3) (2001): 839–868.

VanHoose, David. "Bank Capital Regulation, Economic Stability, and Monetary Policy: What Does the Academic Literature Tell Us?" *Atlantic Economic Journal* 36 (March 2008): 1–14.

Wonchang, Jang, "How to Intervene in FX Market: Market Microstructure Approach." *Journal of Economic Development* 32(1) (June 2007): 105–128.

Unit IV
Contemporary global economic issues and policies

Chapter 10

Can globalization lift all boats?

FUNDAMENTAL ISSUES

1. What factors influence the demand for a nation's labor resources?
2. How are market wage rates determined, and how can increased international trade affect the wages earned by a nation's workers?
3. What are the implications of the factor proportions approach to international trade for how trade affects workers' earnings?
4. Why do labor and capital resources often flow across national borders?
5. What is international labor outsourcing, and what are its impacts on market wages and equilibrium levels of employment in affected nations?

Since its founding as a nation, the United States has experienced four waves of immigration. The first, which began in the 1820s and peaked during the early 1850s, included many new arrivals from Ireland and the middle portion of Western Europe, particularly Germany. The second wave, which began in the 1870s and peaked during the early 1880s, included a number of people from northern Europe—Denmark, the Netherlands, Norway, Sweden, and Switzerland—and China. The third wave, which started during the 1990s and reached its high point just after the beginning of the twentieth century, involved mainly immigrants from Austro-Hungary, Italy, and Russia. The fourth wave, which began in the early 1990s and peaked during the early part of the twenty-first century, involved people from Asia and Latin America—particularly Mexico.

What factors set in motion these waves of immigration into the United States? Certainly, cultural factors have played important roles. Nevertheless, in each of the waves of immigration that the United States has experienced, the people choosing to start new lives in the United States were able to find employment at higher wages than they had earned in the nation of their birth. Furthermore, the immigration waves tended to dissipate after the differential between available U.S. wages and wages in the immigrants' home countries narrowed significantly. Indeed, by 2012, most demographers—social scientists who study population shifts and trends—agreed that the differential between U.S. wages and wages in Mexico and other origination countries had become sufficiently small that the fourth wave of U.S. immigration likely had concluded.

There are many elements, including ethnic and religious factors, that have influenced movements of people from region to region throughout global history. In this chapter, you will learn how economic incentives can also play an important role in shaping flows of immigration to a nation such as the United States. Among these economic incentives are wage differentials. Thus, you will begin your study of the economic effects of globalization on workers—the subject of this chapter—by learning about the relationship between international trade and wages.

INTERNATIONAL TRADE AND WAGES

A controversial aspect of international trade is its effect on the earnings accruing to the owners of a nation's factors of production, which, as you learned in Chapter 3, are resources used to produce goods and services. A fundamental factor of production in every nation is labor. The return that workers earn from providing their labor services is the wage rate that they earn. A longstanding issue is the extent to which international trade affects the overall level of workers' wages and the distribution of wages across different categories of workers.

The alleged "trade threat" from developing nations

For many U.S. workers, the period between the 1990s and 2008 was a time of higher inflation-adjusted earnings, increased fringe benefits, and (for a time) soaring values of stocks. U.S. residents did not share equally in these gains, however, and since 2008 overall U.S. labor compensation has been stagnant. Some observers have argued that rising international trade with developing nations is the reason.

Rising U.S. earnings inequality

Since the 1970s, the inflation-adjusted pay of male workers among the highest 10 percent of the U.S. income distribution has risen by nearly 10 percent, but the inflation-adjusted compensation received by those among the lowest 10 percent has fallen by more than 20 percent. Female workers 10 percent from the bottom of the U.S. income distribution have done a little better than their male counterparts; their earnings have risen by just under 5 percent. Women in the top 10 percent have done considerably better, however. These high-income women have seen their earnings increase by nearly 30 percent.

Some politicians and union leaders have blamed greater U.S. earnings inequality on international trade. In the early 1970s, they note, only one-sixth of U.S. imports of manufactured goods came from emerging economies. Today the proportion is close to one-half. There must be a simple line of causation, they claim. Extrapolating from these data, they conclude that to keep from losing his job to foreign workers, the pay of an "average Joe" is falling. The "average Jane," they contend, has barely been holding her own in the face of this same competition from abroad.

Is international trade the culprit?

Take a look at Figure 10.1. Panel (a) shows the current shares of U.S. trade with the world's nations. Canada and Mexico are the top U.S. trading partners, followed by China, Japan, the United Kingdom, Germany, the Netherlands, and other developed nations. As you can see, developing and emerging countries other than Mexico currently account for more than a quarter of U.S. trade. Together with China and Mexico, developing and emerging nations as a whole account for about 50 percent of U.S. exports and imports. Panel (b) indicates that, in recent decades, there has been an increase in the share of products that U.S. residents buy from developing nations. Panel (b) also shows that the wages of manufacturing workers residing in other nations, including developing and emerging countries, have increased relative to the earnings of U.S. manufacturing workers.

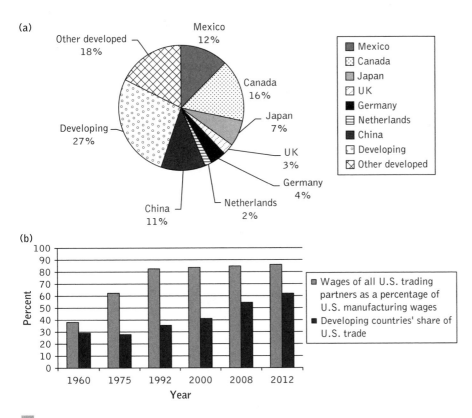

Figure 10.1 *Shares of U.S. trade and wages of manufacturing workers as a percentage of wages of U.S. manufacturing workers*

Panel (a) displays shares of U.S. trade for major trading partners of the United States. Panel (b) shows that in recent years wages earned by workers in manufacturing industries in nations that trade with the United States have increased relative to wages of U.S. manufacturing workers, and at the same time U.S. trade with developing nations has increased.

Sources: International Monetary Fund, *Direction of Trade Statistics;* U.S. Department of Commerce; authors' estimates.

One interpretation of the data displayed in Figure 10.1 is that some politicians and union leaders are correct: By purchasing more goods from developing and emerging nations, U.S. consumers end up reducing the wages of U.S. workers relative to low-wage workers in those countries. Thus, goes the argument, U.S. workers are losing out from freer trade, and the United States should put up barriers against imports from developing and emerging nations.

As you learned in earlier chapters, however, the story is not nearly this simple. The whole point of free trade is that it induces nations to specialize in producing goods for which they have a comparative advantage. Thus, when trade barriers are removed—as many of them were in the United States during the 1970s and 1980s—resources naturally shift into those industries. Resources shift away from industries producing goods for which a nation, such as the United States, does not have a comparative advantage.

How does international trade affect the market wages earned by workers in the United States, or, for that matter, any nation? Does international trade really have anything to do with the changing distribution of earnings in the United States? How does it affect wages and distribution of earnings in other countries, including developing and emerging nations? Let's try to answer each of these questions in turn.

Wages and international trade

Before contemplating how international trade affects wages, it is helpful to look at the extent to which wages differ across countries. In addition, a prerequisite to evaluating the effects of international trade on wage patterns is developing a framework for understanding the fundamental determinants of wage rates.

International wage differences

Figure 10.2 displays index measures of the hourly rates of compensation that manufacturing companies in selected nations have paid their employees since 1975, where a value of 100 is equivalent to the U.S. hourly manufacturing compensation rate. The U.S. Bureau of Labor Statistics tabulates these indexes, which take into account pay for time worked, other indirect pay such as bonuses and holiday compensation, benefits, and labor taxes imposed on companies.

To develop the indexes in Figure 10.2, government statisticians calculate local hourly compensation levels in terms of local currencies. For purposes of comparison with U.S. compensation levels, the statisticians then convert the compensation levels into U.S. dollar amounts using prevailing rates of exchange relative to the dollar. Consequently, these hourly compensation indexes reflect several sources of direct and indirect income that workers receive, and they also take into account changes in the rates at which national currencies exchange.

It is important to recognize that the hourly compensation index values do not take into account price differences across nations. They fail to tell us very much, therefore, about the *purchasing power* of workers' wages. In addition, the indexes apply only to manufacturing workers' compensation. Thus, they are *not* necessarily representative of compensation levels of all workers in the indicated nations relative to all workers in the United States.

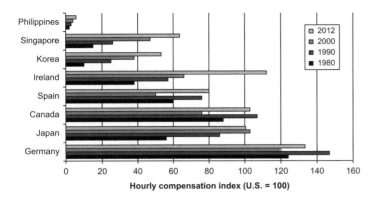

Figure 10.2 *Indexes of hourly compensation costs in manufacturing for selected nations*

This figure shows index measures of the hourly rates of compensation at manufacturers, where a value of 100 is equivalent to the U.S. hourly manufacturing compensation rate. These measures do not take into account price differences across nations, but they indicate significant differences in labor compensation, nonetheless.

Sources: U.S. Bureau of Labor Statistics; authors' estimates.

Nevertheless, the hourly compensation indexes displayed in Figure 10.2 clearly indicate that there have been large differences in hourly wages and benefits paid to manufacturing workers in the nations indicated. Perhaps not surprisingly, Canadian manufacturing workers have earned compensation levels very close to those of workers in U.S. manufacturing. German manufacturing workers' compensation levels have often exceeded U.S. levels in recent years. The hourly compensation of manufacturing workers in the other countries, and in particular the Philippines, has remained well below the compensation received by U.S. manufacturing workers.

Figure 10.2 has two other interesting implications. First, there has been persistence in the compensation differences for the selected countries. Workers' earnings in the Philippines have lagged well behind the levels received by workers in Korea and Singapore, whose earnings have consistently trailed the earnings of workers in Ireland and Spain. Workers in the latter two countries, in turn, have tended to receive lower hourly rates of compensation than those of Canadian and German workers.

Second, since 1990, manufacturing workers in all seven nations, and especially in Germany, have earned noticeably higher hourly rates of compensation relative to the U.S. level. From the perspective of these countries, their manufacturing workers are catching up with U.S. workers. From the perspective of the United States, of course, this implies that, as compared with past years, U.S. manufacturing workers are earning lower rates of compensation relative to workers residing in other nations.

ON THE WEB:

See the latest international wage comparisons at the Website of the Bureau of Labor Statistics: http://stats.bls.gov/fls.

The marginal revenue product of labor

It is a challenge to explain why compensation differences among nations might change even as broad compensation patterns persist. It is, likewise, difficult to determine the role, if any, that international trade plays in influencing the compensation workers receive for their labor.

The main type of compensation is wage payments. Wages are determined in markets for labor. Economists can measure units of labor in one of three ways. One is in terms of hours worked by a given number of people. The second is to measure the number of people employed. The third is to measure units of labor as a combination of these two measures, that economists call "person-hours."

Suppose that you are a manager of a company—say, a firm that provides online travel services—and you are considering how many units of labor (hours, people, or person-hours) to hire. All of the company's other factors of production—land, capital, entrepreneurship, and the like—are fixed. In addition, suppose that your company's goal is to maximize its profits. If you think about this situation for a while, you will probably come up with a fundamental question that you must answer in order to decide how many units of labor to employ: How much revenue will be generated by each unit of labor that the company might hire, and how much will hiring each unit of labor affect the company's overall costs of production? Answering this question, after all, will determine the effect that your hiring decision will have on the company's profits.

Marginal revenue product of labor:
The additional revenue generated by employing an additional unit of labor; also equal to marginal revenue multiplied by the marginal product of labor.

Marginal product of labor: *The additional output generated by employing the next unit of labor.*

Economists call the increase in revenue generated from hiring an additional unit of labor the **marginal revenue product of labor**. Table 10.1 illustrates how economists calculate the marginal revenue product of labor. If you were the manager of the fictitious U.S. company facing the situation illustrated in the table, then reading across the second row of the table indicates that hiring the first unit of labor (column 1) would yield ten units of output of services (column 2). Here, we define a unit of output as the sale of a standard travel package. This would also be the first labor unit's **marginal product of labor**, or the additional output produced by that additional unit of labor (column 3). (Some multinational companies have succeeded in raising the marginal product of labor at their U.S. operations by taking into account lessons learned in other nations; see the box: "Management notebook: Increasing the marginal product of labor at domestic plants by 'twinning' them with foreign counterparts.")

Table 10.1 *Calculating the marginal revenue product of labor*

Quantity of labor (1)	Output (2)	Marginal product (3)	Product price (4) ($)	Total revenue (5) ($)	Marginal revenue (6) ($)	Marginal revenue product (7) ($)
0	0	—	50	0	—	—
1	10	10	50	500	50	500
2	19	9	50	950	50	450
3	27	8	50	1,350	50	400
4	34	7	50	1,700	50	350
5	40	6	50	2,000	50	300
6	45	5	50	2,250	50	250

MANAGEMENT NOTEBOOK

Increasing the marginal product of labor at domestic plants by "twinning" them with foreign counterparts

During the nineteenth century, Andrew Carnegie, the founder of U.S. Steel, pioneered the idea of generating a higher overall marginal product of labor by organizing competitions among his American steel plants. Friendly rivalries were encouraged, in which facilities of similar size that utilized the same production processes sought each month to outdo one another in generating increases in output per worker.

Today, multinational firms are applying Carnegie's idea by "twinning" similar plants located in different countries. In today's global steel industry, for instance, Luxembourg-based ArcelorMittal matches up similar pairs of plants selected from its 112 steelmaking facilities that employ more than 260,000 workers in 20 different nations. Once the company has identified these pairings—such as plants in Germany and Poland, in France and Romania, or in Belgium and Indiana in the United States—it benchmarks production in each facility. Based on observation of input utilizations and outputs within each plant pairing, managers in the facility with lower output per worker adjust their production techniques with an aim to raise per-worker output to the level of the plant with the higher marginal product. For instance, ArcelorMittal learned from its Belgium–Indiana plant pairing that workers in Indiana traditionally relied on phone calls and paper-based calculations to coordinate the movement and processing of iron steel slabs, whereas the Belgian plant had developed a computer model to guide its efforts, which resulted in higher output per worker. The Indiana plant began utilizing a similar computer-based method and quickly boosted its marginal product to match the Belgian plant's level.

In this way, ArcelorMittal and other multinational producers are constantly striving to aim for the highest attainable output per worker. The result is a higher marginal product of labor.

For critical analysis: Why do you suppose that some multinational firms periodically reshuffle pairings of facilities involved in "twinning" efforts intended to raise the marginal productivity of their workers?

If the company can sell each unit of its output at a price of $50 per unit (column 4), then the total revenues forthcoming from selling ten units of output are $500 (column 5). We assume that every company's product is perfectly substitutable with those of others, and that each company's output is sufficiently small relative to total industry production so that no one company can influence the product price. Because each unit sells for the same price, the company's **marginal revenue**—the addition to total revenues from selling an additional unit of output—is $50 per unit (column 6). Finally, the marginal revenue product of labor (column 7) is the additional revenue generated by hiring the first unit of labor. In column 5, total revenues rose from

Marginal revenue:
The additional revenue a firm earns from selling an additional unit of output.

315

$0 to $500, so the marginal revenue product of the first unit of labor is $500 per unit of labor. In addition, however, we can calculate the marginal revenue product in column 7 by multiplying marginal product (column 3) by marginal revenue (column 6). For the first unit of labor, this entails multiplying ten units of output per unit of labor times $50 per unit of output, which yields $500 per unit of labor, shown in column 7. This, again, is the marginal revenue product of labor. Hence, we can always calculate the marginal revenue product of labor by multiplying a company's marginal product of labor by its marginal revenue.

The remaining rows of Table 10.1 (p. 314) provide analogous calculations for the second, third, fourth, fifth, and sixth units of labor that your company might hire. Note that column 2 indicates that, as the company hires each additional unit of labor, its output naturally increases. As column 3 shows, however, the *additional* output per unit of labor hired *declines*. Thus, the marginal product of labor falls as the company hires more workers. This is consistent with a general rule that economists call the **law of diminishing marginal product**: When more and more units of a factor of production such as labor are added to fixed amounts of other productive factors, the additional output for each new unit employed eventually tends to decline. In our example, marginal product rises from zero units of output per unit of labor to ten units of output per unit of labor in column 3. Then the marginal product of labor declines immediately if the company employs additional workers.

Because the product price is the same for each unit of output that the company sells ($50 per unit in column 4) no matter how many units it sells, its marginal revenue is equal to that same amount per unit (column 6). By definition, marginal revenue product is marginal product multiplied by marginal revenue. Marginal revenue is the same no matter how many workers the company hires, but the marginal product of labor declines as the company hires more workers. Consequently, the company's marginal revenue product of labor declines as it hires more workers.

Law of diminishing marginal product: *An economic law stating that, when more and more units of a factor of production such as labor are added to fixed amounts of other productive factors, the additional output for each new unit employed eventually declines.*

The derived demand for labor

Now let's think about the management decision you must make: You must decide how many units of labor to hire. Now you know how your hiring decision will affect your company's revenues. To make your decision, you must also know the wage rate that you must pay to hire each unit of labor.

Let's suppose that units of labor are measured as 1 week of work by each individual you might hire. In addition, let's suppose that the prevailing wage rate paid by all other companies in your industry is $400 per week. Now take a look back at Table 10.1. You might consider hiring four individuals at this wage rate, but the problem is that the fourth person you would hire would generate only an additional $350 in revenues for the company (see the fifth line of column 7). This means that the fourth worker hired would generate a net *loss* of $50, meaning that hiring the fourth worker would reduce your company's profits by $50.

You might, therefore, contemplate hiring only two workers. The second worker would generate $450 additional revenues for your company each week (the fourth line of column 7), and the company would expend only $400 in weekly wages. Thus, it would definitely make sense to hire the second worker, because the company's profits would be increased by $50.

Hence, the company's profits increase with additional hiring, and it makes sense to consider hiring *one more worker beyond the second worker*. Employing a third worker generates $400 in additional revenues (the fifth line of column 7), which just covers the $400 wage expense that the company incurs. At the point where the company hires the third worker, therefore, it has exhausted all possibilities for adding to its profit. This means that hiring the third worker maximizes the company's profits. Thus, we reach the following conclusion:

> **A profit-maximizing firm hires workers up to the point where the marginal revenue product of labor is equal to the wage rate that it pays the next worker hired.**

Suppose that you were just about to offer positions to the first three workers, but then you learn from another manager that the wage rate paid by other companies in your industry has risen to $450 per week. The marginal revenue product of the third worker you would have hired is still only $400, so now you must reconsider your decision. Hiring the third worker would entail losing $50 in profits on net. Indeed, the potential for adding to the company's profits is now used up when you hire the second worker, whose marginal revenue product of $450 per week just covers the $450 weekly wage payment.

A rise in the wage rate that a company must pay to attract workers induces the company to reduce its employment of labor. It decides how much to cut back on hiring by equalizing the new, higher wage with the marginal revenue product of labor. Thus, a company's marginal revenue product is its guide to determining how many workers to hire—that is, it determines the company's demand for labor. (A recent drop in the global price of coal has induced a significant reduction in demand for labor on the part of U.S. coal-mining firms; see *Management Notebook: China's steel industry sneezes, and employment at many U.S. coal mines suffers a near-death experience*.)

MANAGEMENT NOTEBOOK

China's steel industry sneezes, and employment at many U.S. coal mines suffers a near-death experience

Some of the world's richest deposits of high-grade, "metallurgical" coal, utilized in manufacturing steel, are located in the U.S. Appalachian region. During the first decade of this century, an upsurge in worldwide demand for metallurgical coal, fueled in large part by increased demand by China's steel industry, caused the global price of the mineral to rise above $300 per metric ton. This price jump boosted the marginal revenue product of labor services provided by workers in Appalachian coal mines that exported coal, and thereby generated a substantial upswing in the demand for their labor.

Economic activity in China began to stall during the summer of 2011. This downturn induced Chinese steelmakers to cut back their imports of metallurgical coal by more than 40 percent by the end of that year. The demand for coal decreased dramatically, and as a consequence, by the autumn of 2012 the global price of the mineral had dropped by nearly 50 percent. U.S. coal miners' marginal revenue product plummeted. Hence, the demand for their skills plunged. U.S. mining firms responded by laying off thousands of workers in 2012 and 2013.

For critical analysis: Why did the marginal revenue product of miners of metallurgical coal decline?

As Table 10.1 (p. 314) indicates, a company's marginal revenue product of labor depends on its marginal product of labor, and on the price at which it sells its product. The price of its product, in turn, depends on conditions in the marketplace for the good or service that it sells. For this reason, economists say that a company's demand for labor is *derived* from conditions in the market for its product. Hence, labor demand is a derived demand. (It also follows that a graph of the company's marginal revenue product at each quantity of labor must be its labor demand curve; see *Visualizing Global Economic Issues: The labor demand curve.*)

VISUALIZING GLOBAL ECONOMIC ISSUES

The labor demand curve

We can use a graph to examine a firm's demand for labor by graphing the U.S. online travel service company's marginal revenue product at each quantity of labor that it might hire. Figure 10.3 displays the marginal revenue product corresponding to each quantity of labor tabulated in Table 10.1 on page 314. The resulting downward-sloping schedule is the *marginal revenue product curve* for this firm.

As you can see, when the wage rate paid by this company is $400, we can read down from the marginal revenue product curve to see that the profit-maximizing quantity of labor hired by the company is three workers. If the wage rate rises to $450, the company maximizes profits by reducing employment to two workers. Hence, the rise in the wage rate results in an upward movement along the marginal revenue product schedule and a decline in the quantity of labor demanded by the company. This means that the marginal revenue product curve is also the company's *labor demand curve*, which depicts the amount of labor hired at any given wage rate.

For critical analysis: A change in the wage rate results in a movement along a company's labor demand curve. What would happen if an improvement in technology were to raise the marginal product of labor at every given quantity of labor that the company might hire?

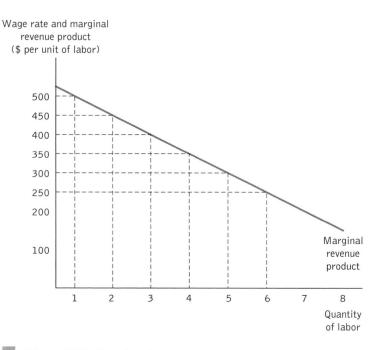

Wage rate and marginal
revenue product
($ per unit of labor)

Figure 10.3 *The labor demand curve*

Plotting the marginal revenue product values in Table 10.1 on page 314 yields a downward-sloping marginal revenue product curve. As the wage rate increases, a profit-maximizing firm reduces employment to the point where the new wage equals a higher marginal revenue product, which induces the firm to cut back on employment of labor. Consequently, the marginal revenue product curve is the firm's labor demand curve.

Fundamental Issue #1: What factors influence the demand for a nation's labor resources? A profit-maximizing firm hires labor to the point at which the marginal revenue product of labor (the additional revenues generated by hiring the next unit of labor) equals the wage rate. The marginal revenue product of labor equals marginal revenue (the additional revenue earned from selling an additional unit of output) multiplied by the marginal product of labor (the additional output that an additional unit of labor can produce). Hence, both the product price and the marginal product of labor determine the quantity of labor that companies wish to hire within a nation's labor market. In addition, so do wage levels in that country.

The market wage rate

The wage rate is the price that companies must pay to hire labor to produce goods and services. It is also the price that sellers of labor—in this case, U.S. workers such as those employed by the U.S. online travel service operator—receive when they

Table 10.2 *Determining the market wage rate*

Weekly wage rate ($)	Quantity of labor demanded by firms	Quantity of labor supplied by workers
550	4,000	13,000
500	6,000	12,000
450	8,000	11,000
400	**10,000**	**10,000**
350	12,000	9,000
300	14,000	8,000
250	16,000	7,000

Market wage rate:

The wage rate at which the quantity of labor supplied by all workers in a labor market is equal to the total quantity of labor demanded by firms in that market.

supply their labor services. The **market wage rate** is the wage rate at which workers are willing to supply the total amount of labor that all companies wish to hire at that particular wage. Hence, at the market wage rate, the quantity of labor supplied by all workers equals the quantity of labor demanded by all companies in the market for labor.

Table 10.2 illustrates the determination of the market wage rate. The first column of the table displays various possible weekly wages. The second column gives the total quantity of labor demanded by all firms in the market at each wage rate. Each of these quantities is simply the sum of the quantity of labor demanded by all companies, including the fictitious online travel service operator we just examined. The third column of Table 10.2 tabulates the quantity of labor that all workers in the market are willing and able to supply at each possible wage rate.

Suppose that, initially, the wage rate is equal to $450 per week. As you saw in Table 10.1, at this wage rate the U.S. online travel service operator is willing to hire two workers. Table 10.2 indicates that this company and others together are willing to hire 8,000 workers. There are 11,000 people, however, who are willing to work at this weekly wage. Thus, 3,000 people are unemployed at this wage. To obtain employment, some of these people will offer to work for a lower wage, so the wage rate will begin to decline toward $400. At this wage rate, the quantity of labor by all firms in the market demanded equals the quantity of labor supplied by all workers. Hence, $400 per week is the market wage rate.

Now let's think about what will happen if there is a decrease in the price of products sold by companies that hire these workers. Recall that the marginal revenue product is equal to marginal product multiplied by marginal revenue. In the case of the online travel service operator, marginal revenue is always equal to the price of the standard travel package it sells. If this price falls below the initial level of $50 (see Table 10.1 on page 314), then marginal revenue product will decrease at every given quantity of labor that the company might hire. Thus, the company's demand for labor will decline: It will now desire to hire fewer workers at any given weekly wage rate. This would be true for all companies in the marketplace as well, following a decrease in the price of the products that they sell.

Table 10.3 Determining the market wage rate following a change in price

Weekly wage rate ($)	Quantity of labor demanded by firms	Quantity of labor supplied by workers
550	1,000	13,000
500	3,000	12,000
450	5,000	11,000
400	7,000	10,000
350	**9,000**	**9,000**
300	11,000	8,000
250	13,000	7,000

Table 10.3 illustrates the effect that a fall in the product price has on the market wage rate. As compared with the second column of Table 10.2, in the second column of Table 10.3 you can see that, following the price decrease, all companies now wish to hire 3,000 fewer workers *at any given wage rate* than they did before. At the previous equilibrium weekly wage rate of $400, therefore, companies will desire to reduce their employment of labor by 3,000 workers. Many workers, however, will choose to work for a lower weekly wage rather than lose their job. As a result, the wage rate will begin to fall in the marketplace, toward a new market wage rate of $350 per hour, at which the total quantity of labor demanded by firms and supplied by workers equals 9,000. Hence, the fall in the price of companies' products causes both a decline in the market wage rate and a decrease in the total quantity of labor employed.

What might cause a decline in the product price received by companies, such as the U.S. online travel service operator, that hire workers in this market for labor? There are several possibilities. Consumers of travel services and related products may have reduced the quantities that they purchase at any price, and this decline in the demand for companies' products may thereby have induced the decline in the price of these products. Alternatively, there may have been an increase in the supply of these products that brought about the price reduction. For instance, new online travel service companies might have entered the market for these products.

Some of these online travel service operators might be based in countries outside the United States. Naturally, U.S. travelers who purchase the services provided by such foreign travel firms import these services. Other things being equal, we can conclude that, by importing the services of foreign online travel service companies, U.S. consumers contribute to a fall in the price of travel services. This price decline, in turn, brings about a decline in the demand for labor services provided by U.S. workers. As a result, both the market wage rate paid to workers, and the number of workers employed in this U.S. labor market, decline. In this way, increased openness to international trade can bring about reduced U.S. wages and lower U.S. employment. (To see a graphical depiction of how these effects take place, see *Visualizing Global Economic Issues: The wage and employment effects of increased competition from abroad*.)

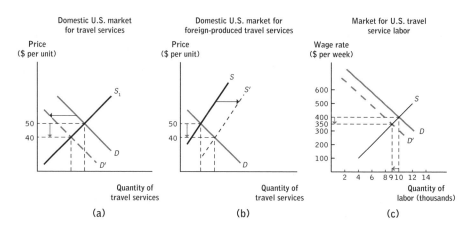

Figure 10.4 *The labor-market effects of a decline in product price induced by increased international trade*

When more foreign travel service companies successfully enter the domestic U.S. market for travel services, there is an increase in the supply of foreign travel services, as shown in panel (b). The price of foreign-provided travel services declines from $50 to $40, so in panel (a) U.S. travelers substitute away from services provided by U.S. travel service companies, and the demand for domestically provided travel services declines. As a result, there is a fall in the U.S. price of a standard travel package, from $50 to $40, so that in panel (c) the marginal revenue product of labor declines at U.S. companies, which implies a fall in the demand for labor in the United States. The U.S. domestic market wage falls to $350 from $400, and employment in the U.S. labor market falls from 10,000 workers to 9,000 workers. Hence, increased international trade in travel services causes a decline in wages and employment in the U.S. travel service industry.

VISUALIZING GLOBAL ECONOMIC ISSUES

The wage and employment effects of increased competition from abroad

In the example illustrated in Table 10.2 (page 320) and Table 10.3 (page 321), increased competition from foreign travel service companies caused a decline in the wage and employment of U.S. workers. To see these effects graphically, take a look at Figure 10.4. Panel (a) displays the demand for, and supply of, domestically provided travel services. The initial price earned by domestic travel service operators is a $50 fee charged for each standard travel package they sell. Panel (b) shows the domestic demand for travel services offered by foreign-based suppliers and the supply of services by these companies, which initially cross at the same $50 price. Finally, panel (c) displays the U.S. market for labor used in the production and sale of U.S. travel services. At the initial product price of $50, the quantity of labor demanded at each possible wage rate is taken from Table 10.2, as is the quantity of labor supplied at each wage rate. Hence, the initial market wage rate is the $400 weekly wage shown in Table 10.2.

If more foreign travel service companies successfully market their products to U.S. consumers, perhaps by establishing online presences that U.S. travelers can access, then the supply of foreign travel services increases in panel (b). This results in a decline in the price of foreign-provided travel services, to $40 per standard travel package. As U.S. travelers who surf the Web for the best travel deals substitute away from services provided by U.S. travel service companies, the demand for domestically provided travel services declines, as shown in panel (b). Hence, the U.S. price of a standard travel package also declines to $40.

As noted earlier, the fall in product price reduces the marginal revenue product of labor for U.S. companies at any given weekly wage. Thus, these companies' total demand for labor declines, as depicted in panel (c). The result is a fall in the market wage rate, from $400 to $350, and a reduction in employment in this U.S. labor market, from 10,000 workers to 9,000 workers. Thus, increased international trade in travel services can reduce wages and employment among workers in the U.S. travel service industry.

For critical analysis: If the U.S. workers who lose their jobs with online travel service companies are successful in offering their services to online retail companies located in the United States, what is likely to happen to the wages of workers in that industry? What is likely to happen to total employment in this online retail industry?

The complicated relationship between international trade and market wages

In the example we just considered, increased international trade led to lower U.S. wages and employment. The reason was that trade took the form of imports that led U.S. residents to substitute away from U.S.-produced products in favor of products from abroad. The resulting decline in the product price reduced the marginal revenue product of labor, causing U.S. companies to reduce their demand for labor.

Of course, greater openness to international trade can also induce more U.S. companies to export goods and services abroad. As more domestic firms enter foreign markets, the demand for U.S. workers rises at any given wage rate. This tends to push the market wage *upward* in labor markets in which these firms compete for labor. In addition, employment *rises* in these labor markets.

Consequently, we can conclude that increased international trade must have conflicting overall effects on U.S. wages and employment. If we imagine that all other things are constant, then greater openness to imports *tends* to depress domestic wages and employment. In contrast, an increased propensity to export goods and services *tends* to raise domestic wages and employment. (Although an increased propensity to import more items tends to reduce the overall demand for domestic labor, contrary effects can occur for specific occupations; see *Online Globalization: A rise in online purchases of imported goods raises employment of motorbike delivery drivers in Nigeria.*)

ONLINE GLOBALIZATION

A rise in online purchases of imported goods raises employment of motorbike delivery drivers in Nigeria

In Nigeria, there has been an upsurge in online purchases of electronics imports from domestic Web retailers. Online credit card fraud is a significant problem in Nigeria. Consequently, the nation's successful online retailers offer delivery of ordered merchandise via couriers, who in turn accept cash payments from customers.

Most online sellers in Nigeria have decided that the most efficient way for the couriers they employ to transport packages containing imported electronics is via motorbikes. Several Nigerian Web retailers have fleets of motorbikes equipped with baskets for carrying foreign-manufactured toasters, microwave ovens, and DVD players. The firms hire couriers, who are charged with darting through the streets of Lagos and other smaller cities to collect cash from customers and to deliver packages containing the purchased items. Thus, in the Nigerian market for the services of couriers possessing the skills to drive motorbikes laden with packages through busy traffic, an increase in desired imports has had the effect of raising the demand for labor. The results in this particular labor market have been a rise in equilibrium employment and an increase in the market clearing wage rate.

For critical analysis: Recently, increased robbery ambushes of couriers and higher injury rates to couriers appear to have generated a decrease in the supply of couriers to Nigerian Web retailers. If this reduction in supply were to persist, what would happen to equilibrium employment and the equilibrium wage rate in this market?

Fundamental Issue #2: How are market wage rates determined, and how can increased international trade affect the wages earned by a nation's workers? At the market wage rate, companies are willing to hire all the workers who are willing and able to work at that wage rate. On one hand, increased openness to foreign imports reduces the product price earned by domestic firms, so the domestic marginal revenue product of labor declines. This results in a reduction in these companies' total demand for labor, which causes the market wage and employment at these firms to fall. On the other hand, when exports of domestic companies rise, the total demand for labor by these firms increases, which pushes up wages and employment at these companies. On net, therefore, if quantities of other factors of production are unchanged, increased international trade can either raise or reduce average wages and employment levels within a country.

LABOR AND CAPITAL MOBILITY

The "other-things-are-constant" assumption plays an important role in leading to the conclusion that importing goods and services tends to depress wages and employment in affected industries, while industries that export goods and services tend to experience higher wages and employment. All other things are not really constant, however. The extent to which labor is mobile, both within a country's borders and across its borders, also affects the wage and employment effects of increased international trade. In addition, the United States is a large country, so adjustments in its product and labor markets can spill back into world markets. Finally, flows of other factors of production, particularly capital, also affect conditions in national labor markets.

Labor mobility within nations, international trade, and the distribution of earnings

Let's consider a situation in which labor does not move across national borders, but is completely mobile among industries within national borders. Nevertheless, for now we shall abstract from spillover effects caused by the large size of the United States. Initially, we shall also assume that factors of production other than labor, including capital, are fixed within each nation that engages in trade.

Factor proportions and trade

Suppose that producers located in two countries—the United States and China—produce two products: computer software and toys. Each country's producers have access to the same technologies for producing these goods, and companies in both nations require two key factors of production to produce the goods: skilled labor and unskilled labor. Because we assume that, within each country, both types of labor are perfectly mobile between the computer software and toy industries, both industries within each country compete in the same marketplaces for skilled and unskilled workers. In each nation, therefore, market wages earned by skilled workers are the same in both industries, and wages earned by unskilled workers are the same in both industries.

Furthermore, we assume that, in both nations, the market wage of skilled workers is higher than the market wage of unskilled workers. In addition, we suppose that, in the absence of trade, U.S. skilled workers earn a higher market wage than Chinese skilled workers. In addition, we assume that U.S. unskilled workers also earn a higher market wage than Chinese unskilled workers.

We also suppose that relative product demands are the same in both countries. That is, residents of both the United States and China desire to consume computer software in the same proportion to their consumption of toys.

In both nations, the best available technology requires using relatively more skilled labor than unskilled labor to produce computer software than to produce toys. Producing toys requires relatively more unskilled labor than skilled labor. Thus, the production of computer software is relatively *skilled-labor-intensive* relative to toy production. This is equivalent to saying that toy production is relatively *unskilled-labor-intensive* relative to the production of computer software.

There are many more workers in China than there are in the United States. This difference between the two nations is not important to the economic argument that follows, however. The crucial respect in which the two nations differ is that, relative to China, a higher proportion of U.S. workers are skilled workers. Consequently, *factor proportions*, which you learned in Chapter 3 are the ratios of quantities of available factors of production, differ in the two nations. What this immediately implies is that the ratio of skilled workers to unskilled workers is higher in the United States, while the ratio of unskilled workers to skilled workers is higher in China. Given the conditions we have imposed on the situation both countries face, this means the United States has a comparative advantage in producing skilled-labor-intensive computer software. China, by way of contrast, has a comparative advantage in producing unskilled-labor-intensive toys.

Thus, in this situation, the United States gains by exporting to China the good in which it has a relative abundance of the factor of production, skilled labor, that must be used more intensively—which is computer software. China gains by exporting toys to the United States, because it has a relative abundance of the unskilled labor required more intensively in the production of toys.

Factor proportions and wages of the skilled and unskilled

Now let's contemplate how opening U.S. and Chinese borders to this flow of trade is likely to affect the wages earned by workers in both nations. As you learned earlier, when U.S. residents import more of a good such as toys, the domestic market price of toys declines. This reduces the marginal revenue product of labor at U.S. toy companies, and toy producers' demand for labor—most of which is unskilled labor—declines. At the same time, when U.S. companies export more of a good such as computer software, their demand for labor increases. In our example, most of the increased labor demand in the U.S. computer software industry is for skilled workers. Thus, the predominant effects within the United States following the opening of a trade flow with China are a net decline in the demand for unskilled U.S. workers and a net increase in the demand for skilled U.S. workers.

In contrast, in China higher imports of U.S.-manufactured computer software reduce the price of computer software in China, which causes the marginal revenue product of labor at Chinese software companies to decline. Thus, there is a fall in the demand for labor—most of which is skilled labor—on the part of Chinese software companies. Chinese toy producers' demand for labor rises, however. Most of this increase in labor demand is for unskilled workers. Hence, the main effects in China after it engages in trade with the United States are a net decline in the demand for skilled Chinese workers and a net increase in the demand for unskilled Chinese workers.

This reasoning leads to three important conclusions that we can draw from a situation in which countries have different factor proportions for skilled and unskilled labor.

■ **International trade will tend to cause the relative wages of U.S. and Chinese workers possessing similar skills to converge**. Because skilled labor is relatively more abundant in the United States than in China, before trade between the two countries took place, the wages of skilled workers in the United States would have been relatively closer to those of unskilled workers. In contrast, in China, where skilled workers are relatively less abundant, the differential between the wage rate for skilled workers and the wage rate for unskilled workers initially would have been relatively higher. Hence, the market wage of skilled workers *relative* to the market wage of unskilled workers would have been lower in the United States than in China before the two nations began to engage in trade. After trade begins, however, there is a net increase in the demand for skilled workers in the United States and a net decrease in the demand for skilled workers in China. At the same time, the advent of trade brings about a net decline in the demand for unskilled workers in the United States and a net increase in the demand for unskilled workers in China. As a result, the market wage earned by skilled U.S. workers will begin to rise relative to the market wage earned by unskilled U.S. workers, and the market wage earned by skilled Chinese workers will start to fall relative to the market wage earned by unskilled Chinese workers. Hence, opening up trade between the nations causes a tendency toward cross-country convergence of the wages of skilled workers relative to unskilled workers.

■ **From the perspective of unskilled workers in China, trade with the United States helps them to "gain ground" relative to skilled Chinese workers**. Exporting toys to the United States and importing U.S.-produced computer software raises the wages of unskilled Chinese workers relative to skilled Chinese workers. Consequently, in China the distribution of earnings among unskilled and skilled workers will tend to even out somewhat after trade with the United States commences.

■ **From the perspective of unskilled workers in the United States, trade with China causes them to "lose ground" relative to skilled U.S. workers**. Exporting computer software to China and importing Chinese-manufactured toys raises the wages of skilled U.S. workers relative to unskilled U.S. workers. In the United States, therefore, the differential between the earnings of skilled workers and unskilled workers will tend to widen following the opening of the two nations' borders to trade.

It is important to keep in mind that these conclusions do not mean that either the United States or China loses, on net, from trade. Because the United States has a comparative advantage in computer software production, while China has a comparative advantage in producing toys, both countries experience overall gains from trade. Nevertheless, relative wages earned by skilled and unskilled workers change *within* both countries. As a result, the distribution of earnings must adjust in each nation. It is only in a *relative* sense that workers in each country might feel that they have "gained" or "lost" ground. Skilled Chinese workers, nonetheless, will rightfully conclude that they do not gain as much as unskilled workers from trade with the United States. Unskilled workers in the United States also will correctly determine that they have not benefited as much as skilled U.S. workers have from trade with China.

Taking into account "big-country" spillover effects

Throughout our discussion of how differing factor proportions can influence the effects of international trade on wages, we maintained the reasonable assumption that workers are immobile between China and the United States. In addition, however, we have assumed that neither China nor the United States is sufficiently large that changes in its wage structure can affect the relative prices of both skilled-labor-intensive goods (such as computer software) and unskilled labor-intensive goods (such as toys). This means we have assumed that the relative demands for both goods in the United States and China are unaffected by changing wages in the two countries.

This, it turns out, is probably not a realistic assumption. U.S. residents make more than a quarter of the world's total expenditures on output. A change in the U.S. wage structure can affect total U.S. spending and thereby alter the relative mix of spending on both types of product. This, in turn, feeds back to influence the wage structures in the two countries. James Harrigan of the University of Virginia has found evidence that this feedback effect is sufficiently important that the net effect of increased U.S. trade with China and other nations on the U.S. earnings distribution has been very small.

Explaining the changing U.S. earnings distribution

As shown in Figure 10.5, the ratio of U.S. college graduates' average wage to the average wage of U.S. high school graduates has increased considerably, from nearly 1.5 in 1980 to more than 1.8 in 2012. Hence, the earnings of a typical college graduate relative to the earnings of a typical high school graduate rose by 20 percent. This means that if a high school graduate at a typical company earned $40,000 in 1980,

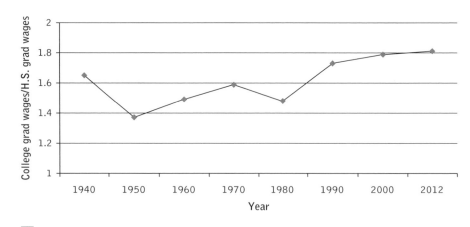

Figure 10.5 *The ratio of the average wage of U.S. college graduates to the average wage of U.S. high school graduates*

The ratio of college graduates' average wages to the average wages of high school graduates declines after World War II before rising over the next two decades and then falling off slightly between 1970 and 1980. Since 1980, however, this ratio has risen noticeably.

Sources: Katz (2000); authors' estimates.

a college graduate at the same company was likely to earn $60,000 that year. If a high school graduate at the same company earned the $40,000 in 2012, however, a college graduate was likely to earn $72,000.

As discussed in Chapter 1, U.S. trade with other nations increased considerably after 1980. Nevertheless, as noted above, the "big-country" effect that the United States has on relative prices of goods and the mix of product consumption tends to reduce the effect that international trade otherwise might have on the U.S. wage structure. If international trade is not the main explanation for a widened differential between the wages of college graduates and high school graduates in the United States, then what factor does account for this change?

So far, most economists have concluded that workers with more skills are earning relatively more simply because the worldwide demand for skilled-labor-intensive products, such as digital devices and apps, has increased. Thus, U.S. industries that specialize in producing skilled-labor-intensive products have benefited, as have their employees, the skilled U.S. workers who manufacture these products. Even if international trade had not increased since 1980, the relative shift in preferences toward skilled-labor-intensive products probably would have widened the differential between the earnings of skilled and unskilled U.S. workers.

If this conclusion is correct, it has an important implication for the United States: U.S. residents undoubtedly have experienced gains from trade as the extent of international trade has risen. Overall, increased U.S. trade with other nations has benefited both skilled and unskilled workers in the United States. It is likely that the earnings of less-skilled workers have not advanced as much as those of higher-skilled workers because higher-skilled workers have been producing many products that people want to buy, and not because U.S. residents engage in more trade with other nations.

Fundamental Issue #3: What are the implications of the factor proportions approach to international trade for how trade affects workers' earnings? The factor proportions approach emphasizes how differences in relative proportions of factors of production can account for comparative advantages and flows of trade between nations. This approach predicts that a nation with a relatively high proportion of skilled workers will tend to export skilled-labor-intensive goods and import unskilled-labor-intensive goods from a country with a relatively high proportion of unskilled workers. In the latter country, with a high proportion of unskilled workers, increased trade tends to narrow the wage difference between skilled and unskilled workers. In the former country, with a high proportion of skilled workers, greater trade tends to widen this wage differential.

International trade and labor and capital flows

Whether they are high-skilled or low-skilled, workers do not produce goods and services in a vacuum. The companies that employ them make use of other factors of production, including entrepreneurship, land, and capital. Taking into account the role of capital is especially important when assessing the effects of international trade.

329

Marginal revenue product of capital: *The additional revenue generated by using an additional unit of capital.*

Marginal product of capital: *The additional output generated by using an additional unit of capital.*

The market for capital

The demand for capital, like the demand for labor, is a *derived demand*. Firms decide how much capital to utilize by equating the price of capital with the **marginal revenue product of capital**, the additional revenue generated by utilizing an additional unit of capital. By definition, the marginal revenue product of capital equals the firm's marginal revenue multiplied by the **marginal product of capital**, which is the additional output forthcoming from utilization of an additional unit of capital. A change in either the price that the firm must pay to obtain capital, or the firm's product price that alters the marginal revenue product of capital, will induce the firm to change the extent to which it utilizes capital as a factor of production.

The price of capital adjusts to bring about equality between the total quantity of capital demanded by firms that utilize capital and the total quantity of capital supplied by capital-producing firms. Just as international trade can affect market wages in domestic labor markets, changes in cross-border flows of trade can influence the market price of capital.

Applying the factor proportions approach to allocations of labor and capital

As a first step toward evaluating how international trade affects conditions in domestic markets for capital, economists often apply the factor proportions approach. Consider again a possible trading relationship between the United States and China. Let's maintain the same assumptions as before: full labor mobility across industries within nations, labor immobility between nations, technology that requires identical factor proportions in both countries, and an absence of big-country effects that might alter fixed and identical relative demands for the products manufactured in each nation.

Now, however, suppose that the two goods that both nations produce are computer servers (the devices that link individual digital devices to communications networks), and textiles (cloth and other materials used to manufacture clothing). In addition, the two factors of production available in each nation are labor and capital. Computer servers are capital-intensive goods, while textiles are labor-intensive goods. Naturally, we shall assume that China has an abundance of labor relative to capital. In contrast, in the United States there is an abundance of capital relative to labor. This means that in the absence of trade, the price of labor—the wage rate—is relatively lower in China than in the United States. The price of capital in China, however, is high relative to the price of capital in the United States.

By the same reasoning we used in our previous example of the factor proportions approach, under these conditions, China has a comparative advantage in producing textiles, and the United States has a comparative advantage in producing computer servers. Now consider what happens, according to the factor proportions approach, when China exports textiles to the United States and the United States exports computer servers to China. The importation of Chinese textiles into the United States tends to push down U.S. textile prices. Hence, the marginal revenue product of labor at U.S. labor-intensive textile firms declines, which tends to reduce the demand for labor in the United States. On net, therefore, the market wage rate earned by U.S. labor declines. As U.S. exports of capital-intensive computer servers to China increase, however, the demand for capital increases in the United States, so the U.S. price of capital rises.

In China, increased imports of U.S.-produced computer servers cause the domestic price of computer servers to decline, which reduces the marginal revenue product of capital at Chinese firms that produce capital-intensive computer servers. On net, the result is a decline in the demand for capital in China, so that the Chinese market price of capital declines.

Exporting capital: Foreign direct investment

What happens if there are barriers to U.S. trade with China? Such barriers might be overt impediments, such as tariffs, quotas, and the like. Distance and associated shipping costs might also discourage trading certain goods and services.

In the face of such trade barriers, it might pay for the companies located in the country with a relative abundance of capital—in this situation, the United States—to export capital to China. By building factories to produce capital-intensive goods such as computer servers in China, the U.S. companies would engage in *foreign direct investment* (see Chapter 1).

By moving capital into China for use in producing capital-intensive goods for sale there, instead of exporting U.S.-produced goods to China, the U.S. companies would circumvent the barriers to direct trade in those goods. Essentially, the U.S. companies would substitute exports of capital for exports of capital-intensive goods.

Exporting labor: Emigration and immigration, legal and illegal

Barriers to trade between the United States and China also could limit Chinese exports of labor-intensive goods such as textiles to the United States. Because this raises the relative wage that workers can earn in the United States, it provides an incentive for the owners of Chinese labor services—Chinese workers themselves— to move to the United States. In the absence of Chinese limitations on emigration and U.S. restraints on immigration from China, therefore, such a movement of labor resources from China to the United States effectively could substitute for exports of labor-intensive Chinese goods to the United States.

As panel (a) of Figure 10.6 shows, the number of U.S. immigrants during the 1991–2000 period surpassed those of the decades with the previous record immigration levels, 1981–1990 and 1901–1910. These figures should be interpreted with some care. After all, there were only about 92 million people in the United States in 1910, so the nearly 9 million immigrants into the United States during the ten preceding years constituted nearly 10 percent of the population at that time. In contrast, the more than 10 million immigrants during the more recent 2001–2012 period make up less than 3 percent of today's U.S. population of more than 300 million people. Yet, the recent flows of U.S. immigration have been significant.

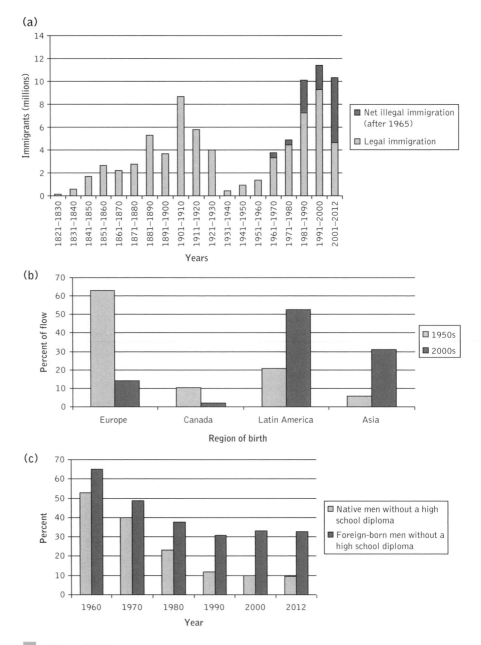

Figure 10.6 *Immigration into the United States*

Panel (a) shows the numbers of immigrants entering the United States during each decade since 1821–1830. The numbers of immigrants have noticeably increased during recent decades. As panel (b) indicates, recently there has been a pronounced shift in the origins of immigrants. In the 1950s, most U.S. immigrants were from Europe and Canada; today most come from Latin America and Asia. Finally, panel (c) shows that, relative to native U.S. residents, U.S. immigrants are increasingly likely not to have graduated from high school.

Sources: Orrenius and Viard (2000); authors' estimates.

Panel (b) indicates that there has been a shift, relative to earlier decades, in U.S. immigrants' points of origin. In the 1950s, most U.S. immigrants arrived from Europe and Canada. In recent years, most have hailed from countries in Asia and Latin America. Undoubtedly, by keeping U.S. wages relatively high, trade barriers that have inhibited U.S. imports of labor-intensive goods have provided one of the many incentives that have motivated people to emigrate from their home country to the United States. As shown in panel (c), an increasing portion of recent U.S. immigrants have been less likely, relative to native U.S. residents, to have attained a high school degree. Hence, many of these U.S. immigrants have sought higher wages for unskilled labor that the United States has in relatively less abundance, as compared with nations in Asia and Latin America.

Limitations of the factor proportions approach

The factor proportions approach helps to explain patterns of trade and cross-country flows of capital and labor. It does a particularly good job of explaining **inter-industry trade**, which is the cross-border exchange of completely different goods and services, such as Chinese purchases of computer software and hardware and U.S. purchases of Chinese toys and textiles. The reason is that the factor proportions approach identifies why comparative advantages in producing dissimilar goods and services might arise from differences in relative factor abundances across nations.

Inter-industry trade: *International trade of completely distinguishable goods and services.*

It is important to recognize, however, that the factor proportions approach has some limitations. The approach is not well suited, for instance, to explaining **intra-industry trade**, which is cross-border trade in similar goods or services, such as U.S. exports of Cadillac autos to Germany and U.S. imports of Mercedes autos from Germany. Explaining intra-industry trade flows and their implications often requires examining situations in which companies have some ability to determine the prices of their products independently from the actions of other producers. The basic factor proportions approach, by way of contrast, relies on the assumption that each company is highly limited by its small relative size, and by the close substitutability of its products for those of other firms. As a result, trying to vary its price from those of its competitors is inconsistent with maximizing its profits. We will revisit this issue in much greater detail in Chapter 12.

Intra-industry trade: *International trade of goods or services that are closely substitutable.*

Fundamental Issue #4: Why do labor and capital resources often flow across national borders? Applying the factor proportions approach to trade in labor-intensive and capital-intensive goods indicates that countries with relatively large proportions of capital resources tend to export capital-intensive goods, and to import labor-intensive goods from countries with relatively large proportions of labor resources. If there are natural or government-erected trade barriers, however, residents of relatively capital-abundant countries tend to export capital by engaging in foreign direct investment. Residents of relatively labor-abundant countries, by way of contrast, may immigrate to capital-intensive countries where they can earn relatively higher wages.

EMPLOYMENT AND WAGE IMPACTS OF INTERNATIONAL LABOR OUTSOURCING

For many people around the globe, computer and telecommunication technologies have simplified the task of working at home. In addition, such technologies have made it possible for a number of companies to hire labor services provided by firms located in other nations. For instance, companies based in Mexico regularly transmit financial records to U.S. accountants so that they can process payrolls and compile income statements. Some European publishers arrange for workers based in India to handle copy-editing and related activities associated with book production. And a number of U.S. financial firms outsource information technology (IT) jobs to Ireland.

International outsourcing (or offshoring): *Employment by a firm of labor outside the nation in which the firm is located.*

A company employing labor based outside the nation in which the company is located engages in international labor **outsourcing** (also called labor *offshoring*). How do international outsourcing activities in the United States and India affect employment and wages in those nations? Who loses and who gains from outsourcing? Let's consider each of these questions in turn.

Wage and employment effects of international labor outsourcing

Equilibrium wages and levels of employment in a country's labor markets are determined by the demands for and supplies of labor in those markets. In today's world, however, demands for and supplies of labor in one nation's markets are increasingly influenced by conditions in other nations' markets, even when workers do not move across national borders. The reason is that, when companies in a domestic nation engage in international outsourcing to firms in a foreign country, this activity alters labor-market conditions in both nations. Likewise, when firms in a foreign country engage in outsourcing in the domestic firm's country, their actions also affect labor-market outcomes in both countries.

Home labor-market effects of international labor outsourcing by domestic firms

It is not difficult to reason out the *immediate* effects of international labor outsourcing. When firms in a nation choose to hire *foreign* labor services that are a close substitute for *domestic* labor services, there are two direct consequences. First, the demand for foreign workers' labor increases. Second, demand for domestic workers' labor decreases. The *net* labor-market effects of international labor outsourcing, however, depend on whether our we view a nation as the "domestic" country or the "foreign" country.

For purposes of illustration, consider the United States to be the home country, and suppose that many U.S. companies decide to hire IT workers in Ireland to perform various services, instead of employing U.S. workers. Thus, the demand for IT labor rises in Ireland. At each possible wage rate in Ireland, there is an increased quantity of Irish labor demanded. As prospective employers bid against one another to attract talented Irish IT employees, the market wage rate for Irish IT workers increases, and the equilibrium quantity of IT labor in Ireland rises.

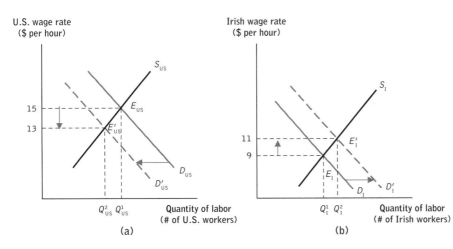

Figure 10.7 *Outsourcing of U.S. IT labor*

Initially, the market wage for U.S. IT workers is $15 per hour at point E_{US} in panel (a), and the initial market wage for Irish workers who provide IT labor is $9 per hour at point E_I in panel (b). Then U.S. firms engage in international outsourcing and substitute away from U.S. workers to Irish workers. The market demand for U.S. labor shifts leftward in panel (a), yielding the new equilibrium point E'_{US}, at which the U.S. market wage and employment level both are lower. The market demand for Irish labor shifts rightward in panel (b), generating higher wages and employment at point E'_I.

Simultaneously, the demand for IT labor provided by U.S. workers falls when U.S. firms shift to employing IT workers in Ireland. At every possible U.S. wage rate, companies desire to purchase fewer services of IT workers in the United States. These individuals seek to obtain employment by offering to work at lower wages, so ultimately the U.S. market wage rate falls. On net, however, fewer U.S. IT workers are hired.

Thus, the immediate effects of U.S. firms' use of international labor outsourcing in Ireland are a rise in employment of Irish IT workers, who receive higher wages. In addition, fewer U.S. IT workers are employed, and those who are earn lower wages. (For a graphical exposition of these wage and employment effects of outsourcing by U.S. firms, see Figure 10.7 *Visualizing Global Economic Issues: Wage and employment effects of U.S. labor outsourcing to Ireland.*)

VISUALIZING GLOBAL ECONOMIC ISSUES

Wage and employment effects of U.S. labor outsourcing to Ireland

To graphically examine the effects of U.S. firms' labor outsourcing to Ireland, take a look at Figure 10.7. Panel (a) depicts demand and supply curves in the U.S. market for IT workers. Before any U.S. firms opt to outsource labor services to Ireland, the initial equilibrium is point E_{US}, at which the market wage rate is

$15 per hour. Panel (b) displays demand and supply curves in a market for labor of Irish IT workers, in which, at the initial equilibrium point E_I, the wage rate in terms of U.S. dollars is $9 per hour.

Now suppose that a number of U.S. firms respond to the lower wage rate for Irish IT labor by boosting the demand for labor services in Ireland and reducing their demand for these services in the United States. In panel (a), the market demand for U.S. IT labor declines, from D_{US} to D'_{US}. At the new equilibrium point E'_{US}, the U.S. market wage is lower, at $13 per hour, and the equilibrium level of employment is higher. In panel (b), the market demand for Irish IT labor rises, from D_I to D'_I. At the new equilibrium point E'_I, the market wage rate for Irish IT employees is $11 per hour, and Irish employment has increased.

For critical analysis: What factors could cause the U.S. market wage rate to IT workers to remain higher than the Irish market wage rate?

Home labor-market effects of international outsourcing by foreign firms

Foreign companies also engage in international labor outsourcing. Let's continue to view the United States as the home country, and contemplate the wage and employment consequences of Mexican firms' employment of U.S. financial accountants.

Suppose that a number of Mexican firms opt to hire financial accountants in the United States instead of employing accountants in Mexico. Thus, the demand for the labor of financial accountants increases in the United States. At every feasible U.S. wage rate, there is a larger amount of U.S. accounting labor demanded. As firms seeking additional labor services bid against one another to hire skilled U.S. financial accountants, the market wage rate for U.S. accountants rises, and the equilibrium quantity of labor provided by U.S. accountants increases.

As these events play out in the United States, the demand for the labor of Mexican financial accountants declines when Mexican firms begin employing U.S. accountants. At each possible Mexican wage rate, firms desire to purchase fewer labor services from Mexican accountants. As Mexican accountants try to obtain jobs by offering to work at lower wages, the Mexican market wage rate decreases. Nevertheless, ultimately the equilibrium employment of Mexican accountants decreases.

In the near term, therefore, international labor outsourcing by Mexican firms who hire U.S. financial accountants results in an increase in U.S. accounting employment, and market wages earned by U.S. financial accountants rise. Furthermore, fewer Mexican accountants are employed, and those who do have jobs earn lower wages. (For a graphical analysis of these effects on wages and employment levels, see Figure 10.8 and *Visualizing Global Economic Issues: Wage and employment effects of Mexican labor outsourcing to the United States.*)

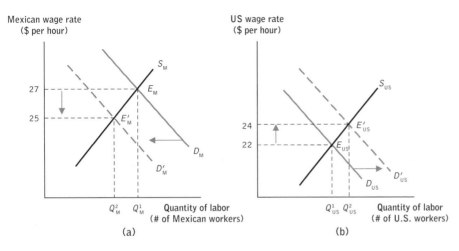

Figure 10.8 *Outsourcing of accounting services by Mexican firms*

The market wage for financial accounting services in Mexico is initially $27 per hour at point E_M in panel (a), but in the United States accountants earn just $22 per hour at point E_{US} in panel (b). When Mexican firms engage in international labor outsourcing of labor services of financial accounts, the market demand for the services of Mexican accountants shifts leftward in panel (a), and at point E'_M fewer Mexican accountants are employed at a lower market wage. The market demand for U.S. accounting services increases in panel (b), which brings about higher wages and employment for U.S. accountants at point E'_{US}.

VISUALIZING GLOBAL ECONOMIC ISSUES

Wage and employment effects of Mexican labor outsourcing to the United States

To determine the effects of Mexican firms' labor outsourcing to the United States, take a look at Figure 10.8, which shows the impacts in the Mexican and U.S. markets for accountants' labor services before and after Mexican firms engage in international labor outsourcing. At point E_M in panel (a), before any international labor outsourcing occurs, the U.S.-dollar-denominated market wage rate for qualified financial accountants in Mexico is $27 per hour. In panel (b), the market wage rate for similarly qualified U.S. accountants is $22 per hour.

When Mexican firms engage in outsourcing of accounting labor services, the demand for labor provided by U.S. financial accountants rises in panel (b), from D_{US} to D'_{US}. Consequently, the market wage rate earned by U.S. accountants rises to $24 per hour at point E'_{US}. Mexican firms substitute away from the services of Mexican accountants, so in panel (a) the demand for their labor services decreases, from D_M to D'_M, and Mexican accountants' wages decline to $25 per hour at point E'_M.

For critical analysis: What would happen to the labor supply curves and market wage rates in Figure 10.8 if some U.S. financial accountants moved across the Mexican border in search of employment at a higher wage rate, and how would these effects alter the incentive for Mexican firms to engage in international labor outsourcing?

EVALUATING THE NET EFFECTS OF INTERNATIONAL LABOR OUTSOURCING

In the situation considered in Figure 10.7 (page 335), the market wage rate and employment level for U.S. IT workers declined as a result of outsourcing by U.S. firms. In contrast, in the situation depicted in Figure 10.8 (page 337), U.S. financial accountants earned a higher wage rate and experienced greater employment as a result of outsourcing by Mexican firms. Together, these examples illustrate a fundamental conclusion concerning the effects of global labor outsourcing in U.S. labor markets:

> **International labor outsourcing by the firms in a home country tends to generate reductions in market wage rates and employment levels in that country. If foreign firms engage in international labor outsourcing in the home country, however, market wage rates and employment levels in the home nation tend to rise.**

Thus, the immediate effects of increased worldwide labor outsourcing are lower wages and employment in some of a nation's labor markets, and higher wages and employment in other labor markets. Some of a nation's workers "lose" from outsourcing, therefore, while others "gain," just as some workers "lose" and others "gain" in other countries.

A longer-term perspective on international labor outsourcing

Increased labor outsourcing has been part of a broader trend toward greater international trade of goods and services. As you learned in Chapter 2, engaging in international trade allows residents of a nation to specialize in producing the goods and services that they can produce most efficiently. The resource saving that results expands the ability of a nation's residents to produce more goods and services than they could have produced in the absence of trade. This generates higher incomes, which the nation's residents can use to consume more items as well.

Long-run cost efficiency gains from outsourcing

It is arguable that international labor outsourcing likewise enables a nation's workers to provide their labor services more efficiently than they could have in the absence of outsourcing. As a consequence, a global resource-saving takes place that expands worldwide production possibilities. Just as gains from trade of goods and services boost incomes and consumption in the long run, so should gains from international trade in labor services. Indeed, recent estimates indicate that every $1.00 that U.S. firms spend on outsourcing yields an overall benefit to the U.S. economy exceeding $1.10.

This longer-term perspective does not deny potentially painful short-run adjustments required of domestic workers displaced by outsourced labor abroad. Nevertheless, realizations of gains from international trade in labor services in the long run tend to make nations' societies better off in the long run. As you learned earlier, the demand for labor is a derived demand determined by each worker's marginal revenue product. In the long run, gains from international labor outsourcing help increase the overall value of the marginal revenue product in industries throughout the U.S. economy. Consequently, the ultimate long-run effect of outsourcing is an increase in the demand for labor in most industries. Increased labor demand, in turn, pushes up wages and raises employment. Labor economists have estimated that, since the early 1990s, labor outsourcing probably created at least 30 million more jobs in the United States than it destroyed. (In the future, countries whose labor markets have experienced the greatest employment and wage gains from outsourcing are likely to experience a leveling off as their populations age; see *Management Notebook: Aging populations may reduce outsourcing gains in some Asian nations while more youthful populations may boost gains in others.*)

MANAGEMENT NOTEBOOK

Aging populations may reduce outsourcing gains in some Asian nations while more youthful populations may boost gains in others

A fundamental incentive for firms in a domestic nation to engage in labor outsourcing in a foreign country is a significant differential between domestic and foreign wages. One key determinant of the level of wages in any nation's labor market, which in turn influences the outsourcing-incentivizing wage differential, is the age distribution of its population.

United Nations population projections indicate that the shares of the populations of China, South Korea, and Japan between the most-working-eligible ages of 15 and 64 are rapidly shrinking—from about 76 percent today to less than 70 percent in 2030 in China; from about 73 percent to 63 percent during the same interval in South Korea; and from 64 percent to 57 percent during the same period in Japan. At the same time, the shares of populations within this most-working-eligible age group in other Asian nations is projected to increase between now and 2030. The result, as indicated in Figure 10.9, will be a considerably higher median age—the age exactly in the middle of a nation's population—in China, South Korea, and Japan than in a number of other Asian countries.

Older workers have accumulated greater experience, and hence tend to offer firms a higher marginal product. Consequently, the wages earned by older workers tend to be higher than those received by their younger counterparts with less experience and an associated lower marginal product. This fact means that, other things being equal, wages tend to be higher in nations with populations more distributed in favor of older workers. In contrast, wages tend to be lower in countries in which younger workers make up a greater population share. The trends summarized above, and by the median-age projections displayed in Figure 10.9, indicate that the future outsourcing-incentivizing wage differential is likely to shrink in the nations—China, South Korea, and Japan—with populations that currently are aging; but is likely to expand in countries—including Myanmar, Indonesia, Malaysia, Cambodia, and the Philippines—with populations that now are trending toward becoming more youthful. A generation from now, the latter Asian nations are more likely to offer wage differentials that will make them the new outsourcing hot spots.

For critical analysis: Why might firms in China and South Korea someday be engaging in labor outsourcing in Cambodia and the Philippines?

Outsourcing versus "insourcing": Attaining a long-term "resourcing" balance

Resourcing: *The acquisition of a firm's full range of inputs for utilization in its production process.*

Gains from trade generated by international labor outsourcing are not limitless. Businesspeople often discuss international outsourcing in the context of a company's **resourcing** choices—decisions whether to (1) incur in-house expenses on development of the factors of production, including labor inputs, via *insourcing* within the company; (2) outsource purchases of those input services from other domestic-company suppliers; or (3) engage in international outsourcing. Any firm's long-term goal, wherever it may be located, is to attain an optimal balance across these alternative resourcing choices.

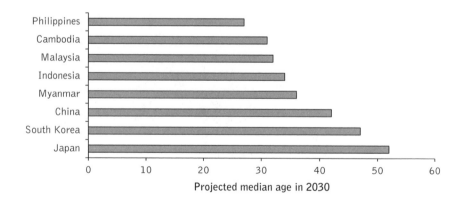

Figure 10.9 *The projected median age in 2030 for selected Asian nations*

Aging workforces in China, South Korea, and Japan are pushing the median age upward toward projected levels above 40 by 2030. In contrast, populations are becoming more youthful in Myanmar, Indonesia, Malaysia, Cambodia, and the Philippines, so that median ages are projected to be 36 or lower in those nations by that year.

Source: United Nations.

Economic theory indicates that a cost-minimizing firm attains a resourcing balance when it hires all of its inputs to the point at which the ratio of the marginal product of each input to that input's overall per-unit price to the firm is equalized across all inputs utilized by the firm. For instance, a firm will utilize particular forms of labor and capital jointly to the point at which the ratio of the marginal product of labor to the wage rate paid the unit of labor equals the ratio of the marginal product of capital to the price of that unit of capital.

Consequently, in the long run, a firm's efficiently balanced choice about the extent to which it insources labor, outsources labor to other domestic firms, or outsources labor abroad equalizes the ratio of marginal product to overall wage rate across each of these three types of labor acquisition. When this condition for cost minimization is satisfied, a company's level of international labor outsourcing is at its optimal level, which is limited by the marginal products and input prices of alternative sources of labor.

Of course, during a short-run interval that can last from several months to a few years, variations in productivity of insourced, domestically outsourced, and foreign-outsourced labor can vary, and so can the overall market clearing wage rates for these alternative sources of labor. As a consequence, firms seek to reconfigure their resourcing choices to maintain the most cost-efficient labor mix. It is during these short-run intervals between re-attainments of long-run resourcing balance that the degree of international labor outsourcing by a nation's firms experiences noticeable ebbs and flows. In recent years, U.S. firms' resourcing choices have flowed more strongly toward utilization of internationally outsourced labor. In future years, such decisions may flow back more in the direction of insourced or domestically outsourced labor.

Fundamental Issue #5: What is international labor outsourcing, and what are its impacts on market wages and equilibrium levels of employment in affected nations? A firm engages in international labor outsourcing when it employs labor outside the country in which the firm is located. In the short run, outsourcing by domestic firms reduces the demand for labor, market wages, and equilibrium employment in domestic labor markets. Outsourcing by foreign firms that hire domestic labor increases the demand for labor, market wages and equilibrium employment in domestic labor markets. Consequently, the net short-run effects on domestic wages and employment are mixed, with some workers "gaining" from outsourcing and others "losing." In the long run, outsourcing enables a nation's firms to operate more efficiently. The resulting gains from international trade in labor services allows resources to be redirected to other revenue-generating activities that bring about overall increases in worldwide wages and employment.

CHAPTER SUMMARY

1. **Factors that influence the demand for a nation's labor resources:** Companies maximize their profits by hiring workers to the point where the marginal revenue product

of the last worker hired, the additional revenues generated by hiring the next worker, equals the wage rate the worker earns. The marginal revenue product of labor equals marginal revenue (the additional revenue earned from selling an additional unit of output) multiplied by the marginal product of labor (the additional output that an additional unit of labor can produce). Consequently, the price that domestic companies earn from selling their product, the marginal product of labor, and wage rates influence how many workers companies hire in a country's labor markets.

2. **How market wage rates are determined, and how greater international trade can affect wages earned by a nation's workers:** The market wage rate is the wage rate at which firms in a labor market are willing to hire all the workers who are willing and able to work at that wage rate. Greater openness to foreign imports reduces the product price earned by domestic firms, which causes the domestic marginal revenue product of labor to fall, thereby reducing the demand for labor. Thus, the market wage and employment at affected firms decline. An increase in exports of domestic companies, however, causes an increase in the total demand for labor by exporting firms. Consequently, wages and employment increase at these companies. On net, therefore, if other factors of production are fixed, increased international trade can either raise or reduce a nation's overall wage and employment levels.

3. **Implications of the factor proportions approach to international trade for how trade affects workers' earnings:** The factor proportions approach emphasizes how differences in relative proportions of factors of production can account for comparative advantages and flows of trade between nations. This approach predicts that a nation with a relatively high proportion of skilled workers will tend to export skilled-labor-intensive goods and import unskilled-labor-intensive goods from a country with a relatively high proportion of unskilled workers. In the latter country, with a high proportion of unskilled workers, increased trade tends to narrow the wage difference between skilled and unskilled workers. In the former country, with a high proportion of skilled workers, greater trade tends to widen this wage differential.

4. **Why labor and capital resources flow across national borders:** The factor proportions approach to trade in labor-intensive and capital-intensive goods predicts that countries with relatively abundant capital resources tend to export capital-intensive goods and to import labor-intensive goods from countries with relatively abundant labor resources. The presence of significant trade barriers tends to induce residents of relatively capital-abundant countries to export capital by engaging in foreign direct investment in relatively labor-abundant nations. In contrast, residents of relatively labor-abundant countries may seek higher relative wages by becoming immigrants of capital-intensive countries.

5. **Wage and employment effects of labor outsourcing:** Firms that engage in international labor outsourcing employ labor located in countries other than their own. The immediate, short-run effects on wages and employment in domestic labor markets are mixed. Outsourcing by domestic firms reduces the demand for labor in domestic labor markets, and thereby pushes down domestic wages and employment. Outsourcing by foreign firms that hire domestic labor, however, raises the demand for labor in domestic labor markets, which boosts wages and employment in those markets. In the long run, outsourcing allows firms to operate more efficiently. The resulting resource savings effectively increase global production and consumption possibilities. The resulting

gains from international trade of labor services ultimately raise incomes and generate overall increases in worldwide labor demand, wages, and employment levels.

QUESTIONS AND PROBLEMS

1. Fill in parts (a–l) in the table below, which applies to a domestic firm's weekly employment and production situation. Draw a rough graph of the labor demand curve for this firm. Suppose that, at the current domestic market price and marginal revenue, the market wage rises from $280 per week to $320 per week. How does the firm's employment change?

Quantity of labor	Output	Marginal product	Product price ($)	Total revenues ($)	Marginal revenue ($)	Marginal revenue product
(1)	(2)	(3)	(4)	(5)	(6)	(7)
0	0	—	40	0	—	—
1	8	(a)	40	320	40	(g)
2	15	(b)	40	600	40	(h)
3	21	(c)	40	840	40	(i)
4	26	(d)	40	1,040	40	(j)
5	30	(e)	40	1,200	40	(k)
6	33	(f)	40	1,320	40	(l)

2. An influx of foreign competition causes the domestic market price and marginal revenue faced by the firm to decline to $30 per unit. On a separate sheet of paper, completely rewrite the table from question 1. Draw a graph of the firm's new labor demand curve. How does increased foreign competition affect the firm's demand for labor?

3. Consider the table below, which applies to a domestic labor market, and answer the questions that follow.

Weekly wage rate ($)	Quantity of labor demanded by firms	Quantity of labor supplied by workers
500	8,000	26,000
450	12,000	24,000
400	16,000	22,000
350	20,000	20,000
300	24,000	18,000
250	28,000	16,000
200	30,000	14,000

(a) What is the current equilibrium quantity of labor? What is the current market wage rate?

(b) Suppose that two events occur: (i) Opportunities to work abroad induce 4,000 domestic residents to move to foreign labor markets, irrespective of domestic wages; and (ii) Increased demand for the products of domestic firms induces them to offer to hire 2,000 more workers each week at any given domestic wage rate. What is the new equilibrium quantity of labor? What is the new market wage rate?

4. Consider the table below, which applies to a domestic labor market, and answer the questions that follow.

Weekly wage rate ($)	Quantity of labor demanded by firms	Quantity of labor supplied by workers
700	4,000	13,000
650	6,000	12,000
600	8,000	11,000
550	10,000	10,000
500	12,000	9,000
450	14,000	8,000
400	16,000	7,000

(a) What is the current equilibrium quantity of labor? What is the current market wage rate?

(b) Suppose that two events occur: (i) An influx of immigration results in an increase in the quantity of labor supplied to the domestic labor market equal to 2,000 units of labor per week; and (ii) Increased foreign rivalry for the products of domestic firms induces a decrease in demand for domestic output, causing domestic firms to cut back on employment by 1,000 per week at any given wage rate. What is the new equilibrium quantity of labor? What is the new market wage rate?

5. Explain, in your own words, why a bilateral agreement with another country that opens a nation's borders to both imports from, and exports to, that country might not necessarily reduce the domestic nation's employment of labor.

6. Northsea and Eastcoast are neighboring countries with border posts that effectively prevent workers from crossing their border. Both have industries that use the same technologies to produce computers and brooms using skilled labor and unskilled labor, and both types of labor are perfectly mobile between the computer and broom industries. Computer production intensively uses skilled workers, and broom production intensively uses unskilled workers. Industries within each nation compete in the same markets for skilled and unskilled workers. Market wages earned by skilled workers are the same in both industries, and wages earned by unskilled workers are the same in both industries. In both nations, the market wage of skilled workers is higher than the market wage of unskilled workers, but in the absence of trade, Northsea's skilled workers earn a higher market wage than skilled workers in Eastcoast. Northsea's unskilled workers also earn a higher market wage than unskilled workers in Eastcoast. Residents of both countries wish to consume computers in the same proportion to their consumption of brooms.

(a) What can you say about relative factor proportions in Northsea and Eastcoast?

(b) Which nation has a comparative advantage in broom production? In computer production? If trade occurs between the two countries, in which directions will trade flow?

    (c) What happens to the demand for skilled workers in each nation? To the demand for unskilled workers in each nation? In which directions do wages of skilled and unskilled workers move in each nation?

7. Reconsider the situation described in question 6, if the first sentence of the question is changed to "Northsea and Eastcoast are neighboring countries that permit workers to cross their border freely." Which type of worker will tend to move (or commute) to Northsea? To Eastcoast? Will Northsea and Eastcoast necessarily desire to engage in trade of computers and brooms? Explain.

8. Southshore is a developed nation with a relative abundance of capital, and Landsend is a neighboring, less developed nation with a relative abundance of labor. Both countries produce capital- and labor-intensive products using the same technologies. Southshore currently prevents immigration from Landsend. Landsend's government prevents inflows of capital and restrains trade with Southshore. Landsend's government is contemplating opening its border with Southshore to flows of capital and trade. Discuss the issues that Landsend's government faces in reaching a decision.

9. Suppose that, in the situation described in question 8, Landsend's government decides to permit free trade, but maintains restraints on capital flows in an effort to protect capital owners. Will this protectionist effort necessarily succeed in preventing lower returns on capital in Landsend? Explain your reasoning.

10. Reconsider the situation described in question 8. Suppose that Landsend's government now decides to permit capital flows, but maintains restraints on trade. At the same time, Southshore decides to allow immigration from Landsend. Assuming that owners of capital and labor can freely relocate their resources, is either group necessarily harmed by Landsend's trade restraints? Explain your reasoning.

11. Top- and mid-level managers of Japanese firms with U.S. offices and plants must travel to the United States several times each month. Most Japanese firms previously employed their own travel staff to arrange these trips, but increasingly they have been outsourcing this work to U.S. travel agents. Assuming this trend becomes widespread, what will happen to wages and employment of Japanese and U.S. workers who provide travel services?

12. Explain why the short-term effects of outsourcing on U.S. wages and employment tend to be more ambiguous than the long-term effects.

ONLINE APPLICATION

URL: http://stat.wto.org/CountryProfile/WSDBCountryPFHome.aspx?Language=E
Title: World Trade Organization Trade Statistics
Navigation: Go to the WTO's home page (www.wto.org). Click on "Documents and Resources." Next, click on "Statistics," and then click on "Trade in Merchandise and Services." Finally, click on "World and Regional Merchandise Exports Profiles."
Application: Perform the indicated operations and answer the accompanying questions.

1. Use the "value" measure of trade to compare regions of the world listed in the pop-up menu. Among the regions you have chosen to compare, which regions have recently

experienced the greatest growth in international trade flows? The least growth? In which regions has growth in international trade been most variable? Least variable?

2.   Using the "volume" measure of trade, which regions of the world have recently experienced the greatest growth in international trade flows? The least growth? In which regions has growth in international trade been most variable? Least variable? Does it matter which measure of trade—value versus volume—is used? If so, why?

For group study and analysis: Separate the class into three groups, and assign each group to compare value and volume measures of trade for selected developing nations within world regions. Which of these developing nations engage in the largest amounts of international trade? Which of these developing nations engage in the smallest amounts of international trade?

REFERENCES AND RECOMMENDED READINGS

Anderson, Kym, and Alan Winters. "The Challenge of Reducing International Trade and Migration Barriers." Centre for Economic Policy Research Working Paper DP6760, May 2008.

Bardhan, Ashok, Dwight Jaffee, and Cynthia Kroll, eds. *The Oxford Handbook of Offshoring and Global Employment.* Oxford, U.K.: Oxford University Press, 2013.

Batra, Ravi, and Hamid Beladi. "Outsourcing and the Heckscher–Ohlin Model." *Review of International Economics* 18 (May 2010): 277–288.

Bhagwati, Jagdish, and Alan Blinder. *Offshoring of American Jobs: What Response from U.S. Economic Policy?* Cambridge, MA: MIT Press, 2009.

Bhagwati, Jagdish, Arvind Panagariya, and T.N. Srinivasan. "The Muddles over Outsourcing." *Journal of Economic Perspectives* 18(4) (Fall 2004): 93–114.

Edwards, Lawrence, and Robert Lawrence. *Rising Tide: Is Growth in Emerging Economies Good for the United States?* Washington, DC: Peterson Institute for International Economics, 2013.

Feenstra, Robert. *Offshoring in the Global Economy: Microeconomic Structure and Macroeconomic Implications.* Cambridge, MA: MIT Press, 2010.

Grossman, Gene, and Esteban Rossi-Hansberg. "The Rise of Offshoring: It's Not Wine for Cloth Anymore." In *The New Economic Geography: Effects and Policy Implications.* Federal Reserve Bank of Kansas City Jackson Hole Conference, Jackson Hole, Wyoming, August 24–26, 2006.

Hoekman, Bernard M., and Marcelo Olarreaga, eds. *Global Trade and Poor Nations: The Poverty Impacts and Policy Implications of Liberalization.* Washington, DC: Brookings Institution Press, 2007.

Jensen, J. Bradford. *Global Trade in Services: Fear, Facts, and Offshoring.* Washington, DC: Peterson Institute of International Economics, 2011.

Katz, Lawrence. "Technological Change, Computerization, and the Wage Structure." In Erik Brynjolfsson and Brian Kahin, eds., *Understanding the Digital Economy.* Cambridge, MA: MIT Press, 2000, pp. 217–246.

Kletzer, Lori. "Trade and Job Loss in U.S. Manufacturing, 1979–1994." In Robert Feenstra, ed., *The Impact of International Trade on Wages*. Chicago, IL: University of Chicago Press, 2000, pp. 349–396.

Krugman, Paul. "Trade and Wages, Reconsidered." *Brookings Panel on Economic Activity* (Spring 2008): 103–137. www.princeton.edu/~pkrugman/pk-bpea-draft.pdf

Leamer, Edward, and Christopher Thornberg. "A New Look at Interindustry Wage Differentials." In Robert Feenstra, ed., *The Impact of International Trade on Wages*. Chicago, IL: University of Chicago Press, 2000, pp. 37–84.

Orrenius, Pia, and Alan Viard. "The Second Great Migration: Economic and Policy Implications." Federal Reserve Bank of Dallas *Southwest Economy* (May/June 2000): 1–8.

Chapter 11

Economic development

FUNDAMENTAL ISSUES

1. What are the fundamental elements of economic development?
2. What are the key indicators and determinants of economic growth?
3. How do the accumulation of human and physical capital, and the activities of entrepreneurs, contribute to economic development?
4. How does greater openness to international trade affect wages and economic growth in developing nations?
5. What are the pros and cons of increased capital flows to developing nations?
6. What organized international efforts are under way to assist residents of developing nations in obtaining credit required to boost utilization of capital resources and increase economic growth?

Since 1981, the World Bank's staff has compiled data on the number of people around the world who subsist on an amount equivalent to $1.25 per day, evaluated in terms of 2005 prices. Year after year thereafter, tabulations of these data—typically completed after a lag of a few years—indicated either that the absolute population of people getting by with such meager resources, or the share of the global population doing so, had increased. For many years, the World Bank's data indicated that both measures had risen simultaneously.

Recently, however, the World Bank's staff delivered a pleasant surprise. In 2008, both the total number of people, and the share of the world's overall population subsisting on less than $1.25 per day, declined. To be sure, it is still the case that more than 380 million people must get by with these meager resources. Nevertheless, for economists who study the development of nations' economies, the absolute and relative declines in this measure of the extent of poverty offered hope that perhaps the global economy had turned a corner—that, over time, persistent reductions in poverty might occur.

Development economics: *The study of factors that contribute to the improvement in a nation's technological capabilities, advancement of the range of products available to its consumers, and growth of the incomes of its residents.*

Economists who specialize in **development economics** study the factors that influence a nation's economic growth and development. In the 1950s, development economists noticed an important byproduct of wage increases experienced by residents of developing nations that observed significant growth: As workers' inflation-adjusted wages rose, so did their productivity. A key reason why this occurred was that, before development took place, many workers in these countries were malnourished. Naturally, earning higher wages enabled these individuals to purchase wider varieties of foods, so that they could eat more balanced meals and build stronger bodies and minds. As a result, they become more productive workers.

DIMENSIONS OF ECONOMIC DEVELOPMENT

Greater worker productivity contributes to technological improvement, to the capability to produce a wider range of products, and to higher inflation-adjusted incomes. Each of these interconnected outcomes represents a fundamental dimension of the process of economic development, which typically contributes to greater well being of a nation's residents.

Technological improvement

The centerpiece of the process of economic development is **technological improvement**, or an enhanced capability to produce goods and services utilizing an unchanged set of resources. Thus, if a nation experiences a technological improvement, it can use the same quantities of labor, capital, and other inputs to produce a larger amount of goods and services.

Technological improvement: *An expanded capability to produce goods and services with the same set of resources.*

How can a larger quantity of any item be produced using an unchanged set of inputs? Consider a simple example. Suppose that an individual sits each day in the same room, at the same desk, with the same desktop computer, producing an online service. Every day during the past week, the individual has been able to produce essentially the same quantity of this service every hour worked. This morning, however, the individual downloaded an update to an office productivity program, and the resulting software reconfiguration has yielded an increase in service production equal to 10 percent per hour. Consequently, this individual has experienced a technological improvement.

Economic development occurs when such improvements take place widely across a nation's economy. One way this might occur is through inventions of new production processes or products. Very few such inventions make an impact, however, because they must survive the winnowing process of **innovation**, or transforming a new process or product into something providing sufficiently tangible benefits to become widely adopted in the marketplace.

Innovation: *A new process or product that yields tangible benefits sufficient for the process or product to be adopted in the marketplace.*

A wider variety of products and markets

Development economist and Nobel Laureate W. Arthur Lewis suggested that "the advantage of economic growth is not that wealth increases happiness, but that it increases the range of human choice." Product innovations yield a wider variety of goods and services for a nation's residents to consume. Innovative products could range from novel means of delivering communications services to disease-combating pharmaceuticals, as well as many other goods and services capable of improving the lives of hundreds of millions of people in developing nations.

For many developing nations, key product innovations include new varieties of foods. Indeed, achieving technological development enhancing the productivity of labor resources, one of the most fundamental inputs, can hinge on product innovations in a nation's food industry. Since the 1950s, development economists have recognized that an important byproduct of economic development was that it enabled previously malnourished workers to purchase wider varieties of foods. Eating more balanced meals and building stronger bodies and minds enabled workers to become more productive.

Product innovation also broadens the range of markets for goods and services. This helps to stimulate private business activity, which in turn expands the number of firms offering to employ a nation's residents in income-generating occupations. As residents' incomes expand, so does their saving and wealth, which in turn feeds back to further expand their range of product choice.

Table 11.1 *Selected low-income, lower-middle-income, and upper-middle-income countries, average annual growth rate of per capita real income, 1990–2013 (percent). This table displays economic growth rates of selected lower- and middle-income nations.*

East Asia		Africa		Central Europe	
China	8.5	Sudan	4.1	Bosnia and Herzegovina	6.4
Vietnam	6.9	Mauritius	3.9	Poland	3.2
Cambodia	4.4	Angola	3.8	Albania	2.7
Malaysia	4.1	Mozambique	3.7	Turkey	2.3
Thailand	3.8	Nigeria	3.2	Hungary	1.6
Indonesia	3.5	Lesotho	3.0	Romania	1.4
Mongolia	2.3	Ethiopia	2.9	Czech Republic	1.3
Papua		Ghana	2.9	Russian Federation	1.0
New Guinea	1.5	Uganda	2.6	Croatia	0.6
		Botswana	2.2		
South Asia/Pacific		South Africa	1.4	*Western Hemisphere*	
		Swaziland	1.4		
Sri Lanka	4.3	Benin	0.7	Venezuela	4.1
India	4.2	Kenya	0.4	Chile	4.0
Bangladesh	3.0	Niger	0.4	Argentina	2.9
Pakistan	2.1	Senegal	0.1	Costa Rica	2.5
Nepal	2.0	Congo Republic	−0.3	Bolivia	1.8
		Central African		Colombia	1.8
Middle East		Republic	−0.3	Ecuador	1.5
		Cameroon	−0.4	Mexico	1.5
Tunisia	2.9	Togo	−0.7	Brazil	1.3
Iran	2.8	Madagascar	−1.2	Haiti	0.4
Egypt	2.7	Burundi	−1.3	Nicaragua	0.3
Oman	1.8	Congo Dem.		Jamaica	0.3
Morocco	1.8	Republic	−3.2	Paraguay	0.3
Algeria	1.1				
Lebanon	1.1				
Jordan	0.2				

Sources: Penn World Tables; International Monetary Fund; World Bank; authors' estimates.

Economic growth

Perhaps the most commonly discussed aspect of economic development is a nation's **economic growth**. Economists measure economic growth as the rate of growth in the *per capita real income* of a nation. **Per capita real income**, in turn, is the aggregate, inflation-adjusted income of the nation divided by the nation's population.

Growth rates of per capita real incomes around the globe

Table 11.1 lists average annual rates of growth of per capita real incomes over two decades for selected low-income, lower-middle-income, and upper-middle-income countries. As you can see, average growth rates of per capita real incomes in these countries range all the way from a high of 8.5 percent per year, experienced by China, down to a low of −3.2 percent per year (that is, an average annual shrinkage) observed in the Democratic Republic of the Congo.

Table 11.2 lists average annual growth rates of per capita real incomes for selected high-income nations. Note that the rates of economic growth experienced by these nations tend to be in the mid-range of growth rates experienced by the countries listed in Table 11.1. They also are uniformly positive—on net, per capita real incomes in all of the high-income countries grew during this two-decade interval.

The importance of economic growth

In any country, a small change in the average rate of growth in per capita real income does not make a significant difference over a span of a few years or less. Over the course of a number of years, however, a small change in the average growth rate of per capita real income makes a substantial difference.

Economic growth: *The rate of change over time in a nation's per capita real income.*

Per capita real income: *The ratio of a nation's aggregate, inflation-adjusted income divided by the country's population.*

Table 11.2 *Selected high-income countries, average annual growth rate of per capita real income, 1990–2013 (percent). This table shows that rates of economic growth tend to be relatively low, but positive, for relatively high-income nations.*

Euro area		Other European		Other	
Ireland	3.5	Norway	2.1	Singapore	4.3
Spain	1.8	Sweden	1.7	South Korea	4.2
Austria	1.6	Denmark	1.3	Australia	2.1
Netherlands	1.5	United Kingdom	1.3	Israel	2.0
Belgium	1.4	Iceland	1.1	New Zealand	1.6
Germany	1.4	Switzerland	0.8	Canada	1.4
Finland	1.3			Kuwait	1.4
Portugal	1.1			United States	1.3
France	0.9			Japan	0.8
Italy	0.9			Saudi Arabia	0.6
Greece	0.9				

Sources: Penn World Tables; International Monetary Fund; authors' estimates.

Table 11.3 *One dollar of per capita real income compounded annual at different rates of growth. Displayed in this table are compounded values of per capita real incomes for various intervals following annual growth at the specified rate in the column heading. If an initial $1 of per capita real income grows at a rate of 1 percent for 50 years, then at the end of that period there is $1.64 in per capita real income. In contrast, if an initial $1 of per capita real income grows at a rate of 8 percent for 50 years, then at the conclusion of that interval there is $46.09 in per capita income.*

Number of years	Percent						
	1	2	3	4	5	6	8
1	1.01	1.02	1.03	1.04	1.05	1.06	1.08
2	1.02	1.04	1.06	1.08	1.10	1.12	1.17
3	1.03	1.06	1.09	1.12	1.16	1.19	1.26
4	1.04	1.08	1.13	1.17	1.22	1.26	1.36
5	1.05	1.10	1.16	1.22	1.28	1.34	1.47
6	1.06	1.13	1.19	1.27	1.34	1.41	1.59
7	1.07	1.15	1.23	1.32	1.41	1.50	1.71
8	1.08	1.17	1.27	1.37	1.48	1.59	1.85
9	1.09	1.20	1.30	1.42	1.55	1.68	2.00
10	1.10	1.22	1.34	1.48	1.63	1.79	2.16
20	1.22	1.49	1.81	2.19	2.65	3.20	4.66
30	1.35	1.81	2.43	3.24	4.32	5.74	10.00
40	1.49	2.21	3.26	4.80	7.04	10.30	21.70
50	1.64	2.69	4.38	7.11	11.50	18.40	46.90

The reason why this is so is the power of growth *compounding*—the fact that small differences in growth over long periods factored through over many years yield multiple effects on *future* real per capita incomes. Table 11.3 shows effects of annual compounding of growth in $1 of real income per capita out to 50 years at various rates of economic growth.

To consider what a difference many years of different growth rates can make, consider how each dollar of per capita real income would grow in China if that nation could maintain an annual rate of economic growth of about 8 percent. At the end of 10 years, each $1 of per capita real income today would correspond to $2.16. After 50 years had passed, each $1 of today's per capita real income would correspond to $46.90.

Of course, it is highly unlikely that China will be able to maintain its currently rapid rate of economic growth. Many years ago, most of the high-income nations listed in Table 11.2 were also able to achieve relatively high rates of economic growth. As time passed, however, their annual growth rates declined to levels near the present averages shown in the table. Nevertheless, if China were able to keep its growth rate at about 8 percent for 50 years, then Table 11.3 indicates that, at the end of that time, the real income of a typical Chinese resident would be nearly 47 times higher than today's level.

The rule of 72

The data in Table 11.3 indicate that the speed at which a country's per capita real income rises depends on the rate of economic growth. A relationship called the **rule of 72** provides a method for calculating the approximate speed of growth. Specifically, the rule of 72 indicates that the number of years required for a country's per capita real income to *double*—that is, to increase by 100 percent—is approximately equal to 72 divided by the average annual rate of economic growth. Thus, at an annual growth rate of 8 percent, per capita real income should double in about 9 years. As you can see in Table 11.3, at an 8 percent growth rate, in 9 years per capita real income will rise by a factor of 2, which corresponds to the doubling predicted by the rule of 72. At an annual growth rate of 4 percent, the rule of 72 predicts that about 18 years—close to 20 in the table—will be required for a nation's per capita real income to double. Table 11.3 verifies this prediction.

The rule of 72 indicates that, at lower rates of economic growth, considerably more time must pass before per capita real income doubles. At a rate of growth of 2 percent per year, about 36 (that is, 72/2) years must pass. At a rate of growth of 1 percent per year, 72 years are required. Clearly, the rule of 72 verifies that, even when differences in year-to-year economic growth are small, over long periods these differences are very important.

Rule of 72:
A relationship indicating that the number of years required for a country's per capita real income to rise by a multiple factor of two is approximately equal to 72 divided by the average annual rate of economic growth.

Fundamental Issue #1: What are the fundamental elements of economic development? The key elements of economic development are technological improvement, a broadening of products and markets, and economic growth. Technological improvement refers to the capability to produce more units of goods and services with the same quantities of inputs, which typically arises from innovation in production processes. Product innovation, or the conceptualization and production of novel forms of goods and services, expands the range of choices available to a nation's residents. Economic growth is the rate of increase in inflation-adjusted per capita income, which via compounding generates cumulative effects on a nation's level of real income. The rule of 72 specifies the approximate number of years required for a nation's real income level to double, which is approximately equal to 72 divided by the nation's rate of economic growth.

Fundamental indicators and determinants of economic growth

Because economists measure a nation's economic growth as the rate of change in its per capita income, a fundamental indicator of a country's development is its level of per capita income. Let's consider current levels of per capita incomes around the globe, as well as factors that determine those income levels.

Per capita incomes

Panel (a) of Figure 11.1 displays both per capita incomes (converted into comparable U.S. dollar units using prevailing exchange rates) and the populations of most of the

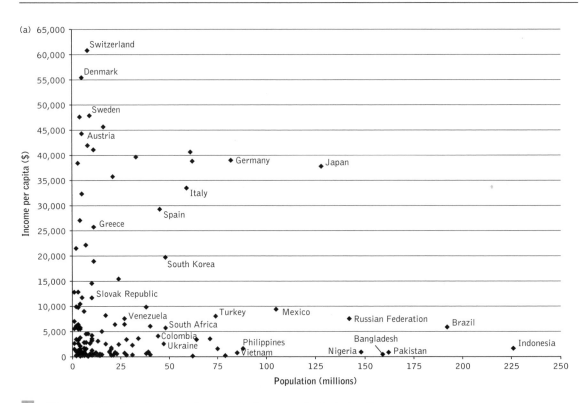

Figure 11.1a *Populations and per capita incomes of selected nations*

Panel (a) displays the populations and inflation-adjusted annual incomes per capita for most of the world's nations. Excluded are three high-population countries: China, 1,318 million people, $2,370 per person per year; India, 1,125 million people, $950 per person per year; and the United States, 313 million people, $46,040 per person per year. Panel (b) displays populations and per capita incomes only for countries with per capita incomes below $5,000 per year.

Source: Penn World Tables.

world's nations (excluding the smallest nations and the three highest-population countries—China, India, and the United States).

Note that in panel (a) there is no clear relationship between income per capita and population. For instance, even though Ukraine, Colombia, South Africa, South Korea, and Spain all have similar populations, their per capita incomes are much dispersed. Spain's per capita income is about 50 percent larger than South Korea's. In turn, South Korea's per capita income is nearly four times larger than South Africa's, more than four times larger than Colombia's, and roughly ten times larger than Ukraine's. Likewise, the populations of Switzerland, Sweden, Greece, and the Slovak Republic are nearly the same, but these nations' incomes also are highly dispersed. Furthermore, Vietnam, Nigeria, and Pakistan have nearly the same levels of per capita income, but very different populations.

A significant portion of the points shown in panel (a) correspond to the nations with the lowest per capita incomes. These points are packed very closely together in panel (a) and consequently are difficult to view. Thus, panel (b) of Figure 11.1 rescales the income

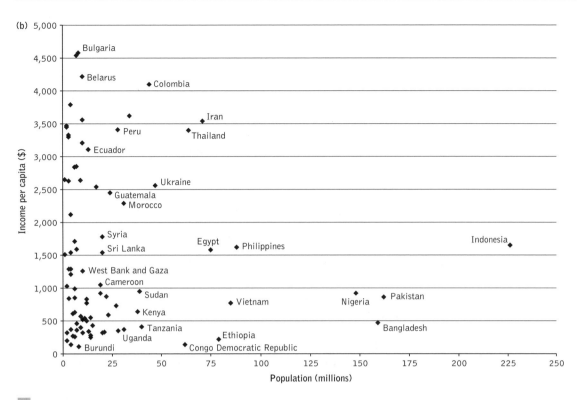

Figure 11.1b *Populations and per capita incomes of selected nations*

axis of panel (a) and displays only countries with per capita incomes of less than $5,000 per year. Even in this panel, a number of points remained clustered near the origin, among which the lowest-income nation of all is the small country of Burundi, which has a per capita income level of only about $110 per year. Nevertheless, the relatively populous Congo Democratic Republic and Ethiopia are also among the world's poorest, with per capita incomes of $140 per year and $220 per year, respectively.

The *World Bank*, an important international institution discussed later in this chapter, classifies the world's nations into four categories according to their per capita incomes. In one category are high-income countries (HIC) with per capita incomes exceeding about $12,000 per year, for several of which average annual growth rates of per capita income over the past two decades are listed in Table 11.2 on page 351. At the other extreme are low-income countries (LIC) with per capita incomes less than about $1,000 per year. Middle-income nations are split into two groupings: upper-middle-income countries (UMC)—many of which are commonly called *emerging economies*—with per capita incomes between about $4,000 per year and just under $12,000 per year; and lower-middle-income countries (LMC) with per capita incomes between about $1,000 per year and just under $4,000 per year. Average annual growth rates of per capita incomes for many of these latter nations are listed in Table 11.1 on page 350. (Although this is the official income classification scheme utilized by the World Bank, such income categories vary with different approaches to

355

converting national incomes to comparable units of measurement; see *Visualizing Global Economic Issues: Should purchasing power parities of incomes be used to classify nations?*)

VISUALIZING GLOBAL ECONOMIC ISSUES

Should purchasing power parities of incomes be used to classify nations?

The per capita dollar income levels displayed in Figure 11.1a and 11.1b on pages 354–355 are based on conversion of each nation's *gross national income*—the total of all incomes of all residents—to dollar values based on prevailing rates of exchange between the nation's currency and the U.S. dollar. Converting all countries' incomes to dollars allows for comparisons such as those shown in Figure 11.1.

Correcting a measurement problem via purchasing-power parity conversions

There is a potentially significant problem associated with the use of exchange rates to convert incomes of different nations into comparable units of measurement. In less developed nations, where wages are considerably lower, prices of non-traded goods tend to be much lower as well. This tends to bias downward exchange rate-converted measures of incomes in these lowest-income nations. In contrast, in higher-income countries, the opposite bias exists. Higher wages in those countries boost prices of non-traded goods, resulting in an upward bias in per capita gross national incomes converted using prevailing exchange rates.

An alternative way to convert countries' gross national incomes to a comparable unit of measurement is to use purchasing power parity units. These are the number of units of a nation's currency required to purchase the identical amount of goods and services within its own borders that $1 would buy in the United States. Using purchasing-power-parity (PPP) conversions of levels of per capita gross national income should reduce the biases associated with wage differentials that cause divergences in prices of non-traded goods in lower- and higher-income countries.

Implications for income classifications

Figure 11.2 (p. 358) displays a number of countries' pairings of exchange rate-converted gross national income per capita versus PPP-converted gross domestic income per capita. Along the line shown in the figure, the two measures of per capita income are identical, so this is an *equal-income line*. The two measures yield the same per capita income levels for the United States, because both measures result in a dollar-for-dollar conversion in terms of the U.S. dollar. *Below and to the right* of the equal-income line in the figure, per capita gross national incomes measured using exchange-rate conversions are *less* than those measured using PPP conversions.

Above and to the left of the equal-income line, per capita incomes measured in exchange rate-converted units *exceed* those measured in PPP-converted units.

As you can see, valuing non-traded goods in terms of PPP does boost the measured per capita gross domestic incomes of lower-income nations. This conversion approach also tends to reduce per capita gross national incomes of higher-income countries — with only two exceptions, Kuwait and Singapore, which have relatively low wages and low-priced non-traded goods, even though they earn high incomes from sales of traded goods. Bosnia is the only lower-income country for which using the PPP conversion of gross domestic income does not lead to a substantial increase in per capita income. Nations at the lower end of the "high-income" range, such as Greece, Italy, New Zealand, and Spain, also have similar per capita incomes using either conversion method.

Figure 11.2 suggests that, if the World Bank were to use PPP conversions of per capita gross national incomes in its classifications of nations into LIC, LMC, UMC, and even HIC categories, its country classifications would change. Some LIC nations would become LMC nations, and a few LMC nations would switch to a UMC classification. A few HIC nations might even end up being placed in the UMC category.

For critical analysis: Could there be any practical effects of reclassifying countries based on per capita incomes computed using PPP conversions? (Hint: An objective of the World Bank is to provide loans aimed at improving growth prospects of countries with lowest per capita incomes.)

Population growth, the rate of growth of labor resources, and economic growth

To measure a nation's per capita real income for given period, economists typically divide an inflation-adjusted, real measure of aggregate income during that interval by the nation's population at that point in time. On one hand, it follows that a higher rate of growth of a nation's aggregate real income, holding its population unchanged, implies a higher rate of growth of per capita real income. On the other hand, it also follows that, holding a nation's aggregate real income unchanged, a higher rate of growth in a nation's population implies a lower rate of growth of per capita real income.

Defining the rate of growth of per capita real income

Indeed, according to the **economic growth definition**, we can express a country's growth rate of per capita real income as:

$$\text{rate of growth of per capita real income} \equiv \text{rate of growth of aggregate real income} - \text{rate of growth of population}$$

For instance, suppose that a nation's aggregate real income grows at a constant pace of 3 percent per year, and that its population has a growth rate of 1 percent per year. Then its per capita real income grows at a rate of 2 percent per year.

Economic growth definition: *An expression defining a country's rate of economic growth as the rate of increase in its aggregate real income minus the rate of increase in its population.*

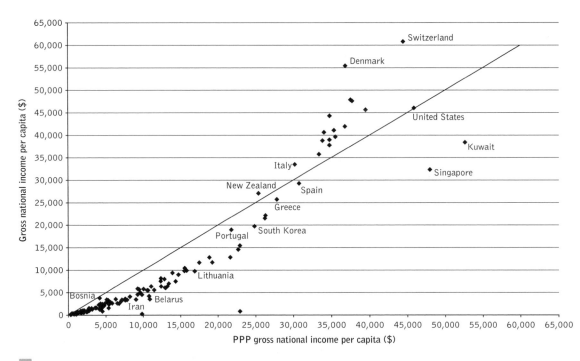

Figure 11.2 *Per capita incomes using exchange rates versus purchasing-power-parity dollar conversions*

Along the solid line, per capita incomes reported in U.S. dollars using exchange rate versus purchasing-power-parity (PPP) conversions would be equal, which holds true by definition for the United States, hence its point is on the line. Wages are relatively low in less developed nations, so prices of non-traded goods tend to be much lower, which produces a downward bias in exchange rate-converted measures of incomes in these low-est-income nations. Purchasing-power-parity conversions help to correct for this bias, which is why points for less developed nations in the figure lie below the line.

Source: Penn World Tables.

Consider how changes in either aggregate real income growth or population growth must affect the rate of growth of per capita real income. If the nation's aggregate real income growth rate falls to 2 percent per year, while its population growth rate remains at 1 percent per year, then its rate of growth of per capita real income drops to 1 percent per year. In contrast, if its aggregate real income growth rate remains steady at 3 percent, but its population growth rate rises to 2 percent per year, then its annual rate of growth of per capita real income declines to 1 percent.

Population growth and economic growth

Currently, the world's population is increasing at a rate exceeding two people per second, which translates into nearly 200,000 people per day, or more than 72 million per year. Does the definitional relationship linking the rate of growth of per capita real income to aggregate real income growth and population growth necessarily imply that higher population growth *must* lead to less economic growth? The answer is no, because a larger population also yields a larger amount of labor resources, which in turn typically boosts the production of goods and services and, hence, aggregate real income. How much the country's aggregate real income increases during any given interval of time is determined by the **growth equation**:

> rate of growth of aggregate real income = rate of growth of growth of productivity of capital and labor resources
>
> + capital's contribution to production × rate of growth of capital resources
>
> + labor's contribution to production × rate of growth of labor resources

Consequently, the observed rate of growth of aggregate real income is the sum of three components. If any one of these increases, holding the other two components unchanged, then so does the rate of growth of aggregate real income. The first component, the rate of growth of productivity of labor and capital resources, captures the effect of technological improvement on production of goods and services. Even if neither the amount of capital resources nor the amount of labor resources grows, greater productivity of labor and capital generated by technological advance nonetheless can boost aggregate real income growth. Of course, if the state of technology and the quantity of labor resources remain unchanged, then an increase in the amount of capital resources can, depending on capital resources' share as an input contributing to production of aggregate real income, bring about growth in aggregate real income. So can an increase in labor resources, given the current state of technology and a fixed quantity of capital resources.

Thus, a rise in a nation's rate of population growth will have two contrasting effects on its rate of growth of per capita real income. On the one hand, we can see from the economic growth rate definition that increased population growth will, given a rate of growth in aggregate real income, reduce the rate of per capita real income. On the other hand, we can also see from the growth equation that an increase in available labor resources, which a rise in population can generate, raises the rate of growth of aggregate real income. Clearly, the net effect of an increased population growth rate depends on which of these two effects predominates.

Population growth does not translate one-for-one into growth in labor resources. In a number of countries, significant numbers of children either die before reaching maturity, or face difficulties in reaching maturity as a consequence of undernourishment. Figure 11.3 shows countries' relative positions in terms of the mortality rate of children under 5 years of age, and the rate at which children under 9 years of age are underweight. There are numerous points clustered near the origin of the figure denoting the positions of high-income countries regarding children's mortality and underweight rates. In these countries, it is more likely that population growth translates into growth of labor resources, which helps to maintain or even raise the rate of

Growth equation: *A relationship indicating that the rate of growth in a country's aggregate real income is equal to the sum of three components: the contribution to aggregate real income of labor resources multiplied by the rate of growth of labor resources; and the contribution to aggregate real income of capital resources multiplied by the rate of growth of capital resources.*

359

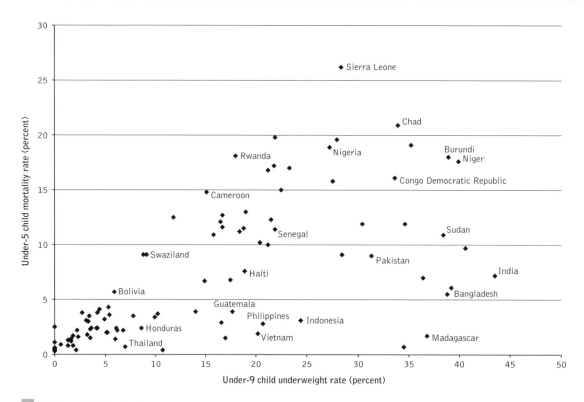

Figure 11.3 *Child mortality and underweight rates across countries*

Many countries experience double-digit mortality rates among children under 5 years old. In addition, a substantial number of nations experience double-digit underweight rates among children below the age of 9. In all these countries, the growth of labor resources and the contribution of a typical unit of labor to production of final goods and services will be lower than in countries with much lower child mortality and underweight rates.

Source: World Bank.

economic growth. Nevertheless, there are also dozens of points clustered well away from the origin, indicating that in many of the world's nations, double-digit rates of child mortality and malnourishment exist. In these nations, many children will fail to mature to productive adulthood, dragging down the rate of growth of labor resources even as the population growth rate remains steady or rises. The economic outcomes for these countries are depressed or even negative rates of growth in per capita real incomes.

Fundamental Issue #2: What are the key indicators and determinants of economic growth? The key indicator of a nation's economic growth is inflation-adjusted per capita income. The most common way to measure this variable is to divide a nation's aggregate real income by the number of people residing within its borders. Comparing per capita real incomes across nations requires converting those incomes into the same currency units, which is commonly done using exchange rates or purchasing power parities (PPP). By definition, a nation's rate of economic growth during a given interval equals its rate of growth in aggregate real income during that period minus the corresponding rate of population growth. The growth equation indicates that the three contributors to aggregate real income growth are growth in productivity of labor and capital resources arising from technological improvements; growth in capital resources; and growth in labor resources. Holding aggregate real income growth unchanged, an increase in population growth reduces a nation's pace of economic growth. But population growth potentially can boost aggregate real income growth by boosting the growth of labor resources and the contribution of these resources to growth in per capita real incomes. Thus, a higher rate of population growth can either add to, or detract from, economic growth.

LABOR PRODUCTIVITY, HUMAN CAPITAL, AND GROWTH

As noted earlier, technological improvements permit the production of a larger amount of goods and services utilizing unchanged quantities of inputs. Because this means that each unit of a given resource can produce more additional units of output than before, technological improvement is synonymous with higher marginal products of labor and capital. Hence, the impact of technological change on economic growth is captured in the growth equation by the rate of growth of the productivity of labor and capital.

One way in which labor resources become more productive is via the accumulation of more skills on the part of labor. As you learned in Chapter 3, *human capital* refers to the knowledge and skills possessed by workers. In today's modern economy, the ability to work with words and symbols—often in the context of sciences, engineering, and management of computer technologies—is particularly important. To develop such abilities, workers usually must able to read words and symbols—that is, they must be literate. Figure 11.4 shows available data on male and female adult literacy rates. Many nations' literacy rates correspond to points at the upper-right end of the line in the figure—approximately 100 percent rates for both male and female adults. For a number of countries, however, male and female adult literacy rates are significantly less than 100 percent, which suggests that many workers in these nations lack the capability to use words and symbols in their work, making them less productive.

Along the upward-sloping line in Figure 11.4, literacy rates of male and female adults are equal. Only a very small handful of countries' points are above and to the left of this line, indicating that in very few countries are women more literate than men. Indeed, the fact that most points are below and to the right of the line implies that it is much more common for women to be less trained in the use of words and symbols. These lower female literacy rates in many of the world's nations translate into lower female labor productivity, depressed wages for women, and reduced

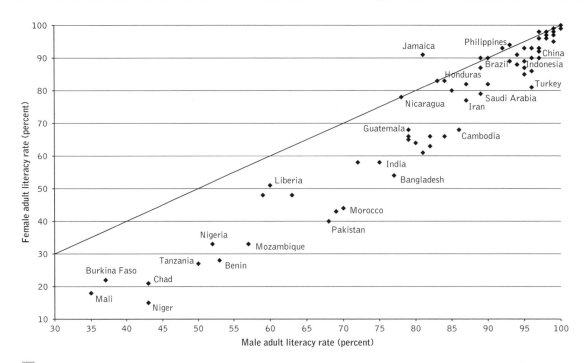

Figure 11.4 *Literacy rates of adult males and females in selected nations*

This figure indicates that literacy rates of both males and females tend to be lowest in the least developed nations. At points along the line, such as points displaying the literacy rates of Nicaragua and Brazil, male and female literacy rates are equal. The fact that points for many nations lie below the line indicates that female literacy rates lag behind those of males in most nations.

Source: World Bank.

per capita incomes. (In some developing countries in Africa, digital devices are giving children online access to reading materials—and potentially providing a path to higher future economic growth; see *Online Globalization: Use of e-readers in African schools promises literacy and productivity gains.*)

ONLINE GLOBALIZATION

Use of e-readers in African schools promises literacy and productivity gains

In past years, poverty and illiteracy in many African nations have been so wide-spread that the people of these countries have often felt trapped in an endless cycle involving both problems. People were impoverished in part because they were illiterate, and consequently lacked a fundamental tool required to become more productive and to boost their income. At the same time, teachers struggled to teach students to read, because books that would stimulate students' enthusiasm for learning to read were unavailable. Schools simply could not afford the books.

Today, availability of relatively inexpensive digital devices and e-reader technologies is bringing about a revolution in many African schools. At the cost of Internet access subscriptions and a few digital devices, schools can now link to globally available online libraries containing all manner of books—dictionaries, encyclopedias, textbooks, and children's illustrated storybooks. The consequence of this development has been an upsurge of youth literacy rates—particularly in nations such as Uganda and Nigeria, in which utilization of such technologies has been most widespread. This development portends future increases in adult literacy rates that undoubtedly will translate into increased labor productivity in these nations.

For critical analysis: Why do you suppose that high literacy rates have become increasingly important for boosting labor productivity as nations have engaged in production and trade of more capital-intensive goods and services?

Capital resources, entrepreneurship, and economic development

Obstacles to the accumulation of human capital and other factors limiting enhancement of labor resources hinder economic development in many nations. So do factors that impede building up a nation's stock of capital resources, such as equipment and facilities, which labor can utilize to generate flows of income by producing goods and services. Only countries that avoid creating substantial disincentives for investment in capital resources typically progress on a path toward higher levels of economic development.

The significance of property rights to capital resources

In addition to productivity growth arising from technological change and additional production generated by growth of labor resources, the rate of economic growth depends on an increment to output of goods and services brought about by accumulation of capital resources. Traditionally, economists point out that important incentives to add to the stock of productive capital include profit anticipations, relatively low inflation-adjusted rates of interest, and low tax rates on capital resources and business profits. Indeed, these factors are crucial elements determining the degree of capital accumulation in both highly developed and developing nations.

Another fundamental element influencing the growth of capital resources, which is often taken for granted in the study of the economies of developed nations, is the establishment and enforcement of property rights to capital goods. Unless entrepreneurs can maintain and transfer ownership of capital resources, they cannot readily trade these resources. Untradeable capital goods, in turn, cannot be readily allocated to their *most efficient* uses, resulting in lower anticipated payoffs to capital investments

363

and, hence, reduced rates of capital accumulation that retard economic growth and development.

Dead capital:

Capital resources for which people fail to possess unambiguous title of ownership, which makes these resources difficult to transfer among entrepreneurs.

Hernando de Soto has applied the term **dead capital** to capital resources lacking clear title of ownership and hence being imperfectly transferrable. In some nations, such as many of those in the Middle East and sub-Saharan Africa, as much as 90 percent of physical structures potentially usable for productive activities have no official title of ownership. In most cases, government regulations in such countries make the process of obtaining formal title so time-consuming and costly that entrepreneurs do not go to the trouble. They simply obtain informal "ownership" of structures—sometimes essentially becoming "squatters" within the buildings—set up equipment within the structures, hire labor resources, and begin producing goods or services. If other entrepreneurs who could utilize the structures to produce goods and services more efficiently would like to obtain the rights to do so, it is not easy for them to do so. This inability to bid for the use of the dead capital hampers efficient production, drives down profitability, reduces incentives to accumulate additional capital, and ultimately depresses the rate of economic growth.

The importance of permitting entrepreneurship to flourish

Entrepreneurs:

People who specialize in organizing labor and capital resources to bring about production of goods and services.

Those organizing the combination of capital and labor resources for the purpose of income-generating production of goods and services are **entrepreneurs**. These individuals seek to earn profits from organizing the production and distribution of goods and services. Thus, in the long run, they will engage in productive activities as long as the maximum feasible revenues generated from sales of goods and services are at least sufficient to cover the minimum feasible costs of producing those goods and services.

To the extent that government rules and regulations governing the formation, operation, and closing of businesses push up the costs experienced by entrepreneurs, such rules and regulations push down entrepreneurs' profits. In a number of the world's nations, the government-created burdens push up entrepreneurs' costs sufficiently to hinder the formation of income-generating businesses. The consequences are decreased production, reduced economic growth, and depressed economic development. (There is evidence of a relationship between the ease of engaging in entrepreneurial activities and per capita incomes across countries; see *Visualizing Global Economic Issues: To boost per capita real income, make doing business easier.*)

VISUALIZING GLOBAL ECONOMIC ISSUES

To boost per capita real income, make doing business easier

The World Bank ranks nations based on the ease of doing business within the countries' borders. To compile its ease of doing business rankings, the World Bank takes into account such factors as the number of procedures, time lags, and costs entrepreneurs face to formally register property, to obtain governmental approval to start or to close a business, and to enforce contracts.

Figure 11.5 plots the World Bank's ease of doing business rankings for a number of countries against the nations' per capita real incomes. There is generally a negative relationship. On one hand, this indicates that, if governments minimize hindrances that entrepreneurs face in setting up and maintaining their businesses, one consequence for a number of countries is higher per capita real incomes. On the other hand, it also implies that per capita real incomes are lower in many nations with governments that establish significant barriers to entrepreneurial activity.

For critical analysis: Who benefits the most from government rules and regulations that deter the formation of new businesses within a nation?

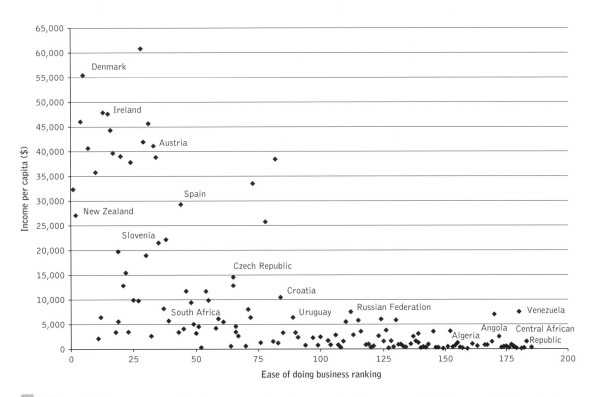

Figure 11.5 *The relationship between nations' per capita incomes and their ease of doing business rankings*

This figure plots pairings of nations' per capita incomes with their rankings by the World Bank on the basis of ease of doing business within their borders. There is a negative relationship. Thus, per capita incomes generally are higher in countries in which there are fewer governmentally imposed hindrances to establishing and operating businesses.

Sources: World Bank, *Doing Business 2013*; Penn World Tables.

Fundamental Issue #3: How do the accumulation of human and physical capital, and the activities of entrepreneurs, contribute to economic development? Improving the amount of education and training that a nation's labor resources receive raises their productivity and thereby constitutes technological improvement that helps to boost the nation's per capita real income. Engaging in capital investment adds to the nation's quantity of capital resources. Not all capital resources are equally usable, however. In many nations, incomplete property rights to ownership of capital contribute to a dead capital problem, in which many capital resources are not tradable and consequently cannot be readily allocated to their most efficient uses. A country's entrepreneurs bring labor and capital resources together to produce goods and services, the sales of which generate incomes, so limiting restraints on the capabilities of entrepreneurs to establish, operate, and close firms helps to boost economic growth, other things being equal.

ON THE WEB:

Learn about how international trade can contribute to economic growth of developing nations at www.wto.org/english/ thewto_e/whatis_e/ 10ben_e/10b07_ e.htm.

INTERNATIONAL TRADE AND ECONOMIC DEVELOPMENT

You learned in Chapter 10 that greater openness to international trade has conflicting effects on workers' wages, but generally bestows gains from trade upon the residents of nations that exchange goods and services. How do gains from trade influence the process of economic development?

Trade and wages in developing nations

To consider how international trade affects the economies of developing nations, we start by examining the extent of trade by these nations. Later, we shall explore whether more open economies tend to experience more growth than economies that are less open.

Developing nations and world trade

Figure 11.6 shows the distribution of the world's population and international trade among six regions of the world. As you can see, the generally most developed regions of North America and Europe together contain only about 13 percent of the world's population, but account for roughly two-thirds of global trade. Asia, which contains a mix of industrialized, emerging, and developing national economies, contains more than half of the world's people. Nevertheless, Asian nations account for only just over a quarter of global trade. Africa has almost one-sixth of the world's population, but accounts for less than 2 percent of total international trade.

The dramatic disparity in trade is also revealed if we divide total trade flows by population to determine per capita trade volumes. In terms of U.S. dollars, the annual per capita trade flow in developing nations is typically less than $75 per year. That is, the average resident of a developing nation exports and imports a total of about $75 in goods and services. In the United States, by way of contrast, the annual per capita trade flow normally exceeds $8,000 a year.

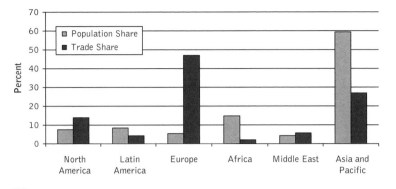

Figure 11.6 *Population and trade shares of selected world regions*

The regions of the world that account for the largest shares of the world's population tend to account for much smaller shares of total world trade.

Source: World Bank, *World Development Indicators,* and International Monetary Fund, *Direction of Trade Statistics.*

These comparisons indicate just how unbalanced international trade is in relation to the distribution of the world's population. You have learned that there are gains from trade, and potentially even wage enhancements that can result from greater openness to trade (depending, of course, on how countervailing wage effects net out). Undoubtedly, residents of the United States, Western Europe, Japan, and other developed nations experience the bulk of these benefits, because they engage in the bulk of the world's trade.

Wages, comparative advantage, and development

Compared with developed nations, developing nations currently have relatively higher factor proportions of resources such as oil and minerals. It is not surprising, therefore, that developing nations account for more than half of the world's exports of fuels and mining products.

In addition, developing countries have relatively abundant labor resources. Developing nations cannot take advantage of this particular relative factor abundance throughout all sectors of their domestic economies, however. To see why, take a look at Table 11.4. It displays estimates of ratios of unit labor costs to value added per employee (relative to the U.S. level) for various industries within selected developing nations. A relatively low value of this ratio within a given industry indicates that a nation is more likely to have a comparative advantage in competing within that industry.

As you can see, possessing a relative abundance of labor does not necessarily give a developing nation a comparative advantage, even within relatively labor-intensive industries such as footwear, textiles, and clothing. Some developing nations naturally will have more success than others in their efforts to transform a relative abundance of labor into a comparative advantage. According to the factor proportions approach, this also means that wages are likely to rise more speedily in some less developed

ON THE WEB:

Track the international trade of all nations and various world regions by going to www. wto.org, clicking on "Documents and resources," and then clicking on "Statistics."

Table 11.4 *Unit labor costs in selected developing countries. (Ratio of wages per employee to value added per employee, divided by the U.S. level.)*

Economy	Footwear	Textiles	Clothing	Metal products	Wood products	Rubber products	Plastic products	Electrical machinery
Egypt	NA	1.50	0.50	0.85	0.48	1.50	1.23	0.93
India	0.99	1.01	0.49	0.97	0.91	0.88	0.88	0.85
Indonesia	0.85	0.47	0.95	0.55	0.53	0.72	0.64	0.76
Kenya	1.13	1.61	1.17	0.91	1.20	0.61	0.63	0.55
Malaysia	1.08	0.73	1.42	0.83	0.85	0.76	0.92	0.97
Mexico	1.62	0.96	1.20	0.76	0.76	0.96	0.83	0.83
Philippines	1.36	0.69	1.12	0.79	0.90	0.71	0.69	0.84
Thailand	1.23	0.87	1.70	0.71	0.57	0.56	0.83	0.65
Turkey	0.69	0.42	0.38	0.46	0.96	0.57	0.34	0.51
Zimbabwe	0.95	0.56	1.26	0.99	0.73	0.74	1.36	1.05

NA, not available.

Source: United Nations, *Trade and Development Report.*

nations than others. To the extent that international trade contributes to the developing world's economic growth, which economists commonly measure using the annual rate of increase in a nation's per capita income, the pace of growth is likely to be unevenly distributed among developing nations.

Stimulating growth: Openness or protectionism?

Should a developing nation that seeks greater growth encourage or discourage trade with other countries? On one hand, promoting such trade could permit a nation to specialize in production of goods and services that its industries can produce most efficiently. On the other hand, inhibiting trade might protect fledgling industries from foreign competition and permit them to grow more quickly.

In years past, and even today, some economists have contended that protectionism promotes economic growth. The basis of this argument is the idea that pure competition might not be the best market structure to promote economic growth. Instead, proponents of protectionism favor the view that the centralization of resources among a few home businesses might permit them to grow more rapidly. In addition, protection for foreign competition can, they argue, keep new home industries from failing prematurely in the face of short-term profit fluctuations that might occur if they were exposed to variations in world prices.

Nevertheless, today most economists who study economic growth tend to believe that greater openness to trade is the best way to promote growth. Developing nations benefit by gaining access to new knowledge and ideas that are diffused around the globe more rapidly when technologies can move across national borders freely, they argue. Furthermore, more developing economies may experience higher rates of economic growth if their own industries have access to a larger market. Home industries that are protected by trade barriers such as tariffs or quotas can become isolated

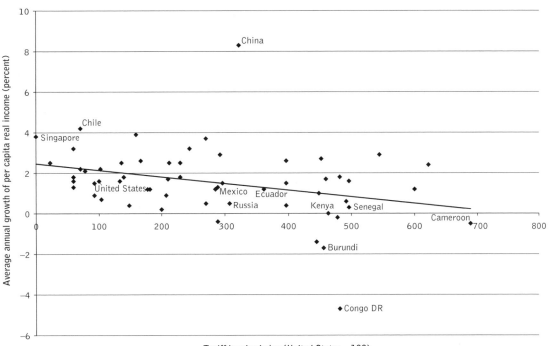

Figure 11.7 *Trade barriers versus economic growth*

Governments of nations with closed economies use trade barriers to prevent imports from entering the country, and sometimes to keep exports from leaving the country. Such protectionism closes off such nations to new technologies and other sources of economic growth. The data appear to favor the view that more nearly closed economies experience lower rates of growth, all other things held constant.

Source: World Bank, *World Development Indicators* and *Competitiveness Indicators*.

from world technological progress. Former communist countries and a number of developing nations in Latin America and elsewhere experienced this problem in years past.

Economists continue to debate this issue. Currently, however, those who promote openness have some strong evidence favoring their view. As Figure 11.7 shows, there seems to be some evidence of an inverse relationship between economic growth and the level of trade barriers in a nation. So far, experience indicates that greater openness is more conducive to higher economic growth.

Fundamental Issue #4: How does greater openness to international trade affect wages and economic growth in developing nations? Developing countries have become increasingly open to international trade, and together these nations now account for about one-third of total global trade flows. Because developing countries tend to be relatively labor-abundant, increased trade with more capital-abundant developed nations is likely to raise the wages of workers in developing countries, thereby pushing up their per capita incomes. Comparative advantages in producing labor-intensive goods vary across developing nations, however, so not all developing countries are likely to share equally in economic growth generated by increased international trade.

Capital flows and developing nations

As just discussed, both labor and capital are fundamental resources required for economic growth. In Chapter 10, you learned that a developing nation with a low proportion of capital relative to labor typically ends up exporting labor-intensive products and importing capital-intensive products. Alternatively, however, residents of such a nation can import capital and manufacture capital-intensive goods on their own. (In hopes of promoting more capital-intensive domestic production, many developing nations actively seek treaties intended to raise foreign direct investment; see *Policy Notebook: Do bilateral treaties succeed in boosting foreign direct investment?*)

POLICY NOTEBOOK

Do bilateral treaties succeed in boosting foreign direct investment?

In the past, developing countries traditionally have relied considerably on labor-intensive production processes. In recent years, however, a growing number of these nations have sought to promote industries relying on more capital-intensive processes, often through the solicitation of foreign direct investment from abroad. Toward this end, governments of developing nations have signed more than 2,000 bilateral treaties intended to provide people abroad with more incentives to engage in direct investment in their countries. For years, economists had wondered if the proliferation of such treaties has really contributed to greater flows of foreign direct investment. Recent studies have cast new light on the answer to this question.

One form of agreement, called a *bilateral investment treaty*, establishes formal rules governing treatment of cross-border funds transfers, legal treatment of investments, and procedures for settlement of any disputes that might arise. Separate studies of the effects of such treaties on foreign direct investment flows have been conducted by Eric Neumayer and Laura Spess of the London School of Economics; and by Peter Egger of the Swiss Federal Institute of Technology and Michael Pfaffermayr of the University of Innsbruck. Both studies conclude that implementation of bilateral investment treaties has unambiguously stimulated foreign direct investment to developing nations. Indeed, Egger and Pfaffermayr find some association between the simple act of signing such treaties—even those never fully implemented—and foreign direct investment, perhaps reflecting that nations that sign such agreements truly seek to, and ultimately do, encourage more foreign direct investment.

Another type of agreement, called a *double taxation treaty*, addresses the disincentives to engage in foreign direct investment that arise if returns on such investment are taxed both by foreign investors' home-country governments and by the government of the country in which the investment is located. A double taxation treaty typically exempts from taxation a specified portion of the return on the investment, or offers tax credits to investors who must pay taxes on the investment in their home nations. Fabian Barthel and Eric Neumayer of the London School of Economics, Matthias Busse of the Institute for Development Research, and Richard Krever of Monash University have conducted a recent analysis of the effects of double taxation treaties on foreign direct investment. They find that, once other factors such as a country's size, per capita income, and inflation rate are taken into account, establishment of this second form of treaty also contributes to greater foreign direct investment.

For critical analysis: Why might we expect that a country's simultaneous implementation of both types of treaty might tend to generate—controlling for other factors—the most significant boost in foreign direct investment?

Are capital inflows "bad" for developing nations?

As we discuss in greater detail in Chapter 14, in recent years a number of developing nations—for instance, Brazil, Indonesia, Mexico, Malaysia, and Thailand in the 1990s, and a wide ranges of Latin American, Eastern European, and South Asian countries in the 2000s—have been "burned" by sudden shifts in international capital flows. During such episodes, many domestic industries that had counted on foreign capital to provide the underpinning for planned expansions have faced sudden halts in capital flows. The consequences have been severe economic shocks and significant contractions in per capita incomes.

Panel (a) of Figure 11.8 on p. 372 shows total net flow of private capital to developing nations, as well as the components of that flow, since 1980. Flows were relatively small and stable until the late 1980s. Then they grew considerably and became more variable by the mid-1990s. Sharp declines occurred in the late 1990s and again during the late 2000s. Recently, capital flows to developing nations have shown signs of some recovery, but remain well below their 2007–2008 peaks.

In panel (b) of Figure 11.8, you can see the consequences of the sharp declines in the flows of private capital to developing nations in the late 1990s and late 2000s. Developing nations experienced significant declines in income growth during these periods.

371

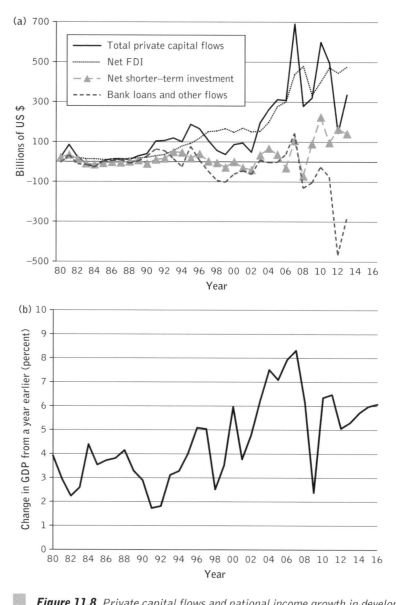

Figure 11.8 *Private capital flows and national income growth in developing nations*

Panel (a) displays total private capital flows to developing nations since 1980 and the sources of these flows. Although foreign direct investment in developing nations increased steadily after the mid-1980s, other sources of private capital flows to these countries have been more variable. As shown in panel (b), the drop-offs in total private capital flows in the late 1990s and late 2000s were associated with volatility in annual aggregate real income growth in the developing world.

Source: International Monetary Fund, *World Economic Outlook Database.*

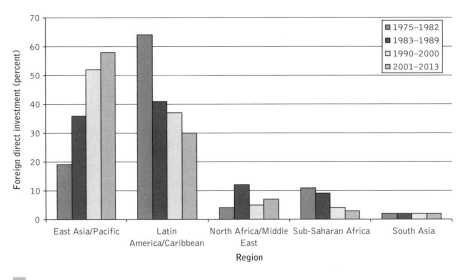

Figure 11.9 *Shares of foreign direct investment in developing regions*

The East Asia/Pacific share of foreign direct investment to developing nations has risen considerably during the past three decades.

Sources: United Nations, *Trade and Development Report*; authors' estimates.

In Figure 11.9 you can see why Asian countries are often hit particularly hard by sudden downturns in international capital flows to developing countries. Decades ago, the main destinations of foreign capital flows were Latin American and Caribbean countries. During the past 20 years, however, East Asian and Pacific nations' share of these flows has risen considerably. This increased reliance on foreign capital exposed Asian countries to the risk of major financial disturbances in the event of sudden disruptions of international capital flows.

During and immediately after the so-called "Asian crisis" of 1997–1998 and the global financial meltdown of the late 2000s, some economists, and even more politicians and policymakers, argued that developing nations would be better off if they were to spurn imports of foreign capital. In the end, most developing nations did not do this. Nevertheless, several tried to find ways to reduce the variability in capital flows depicted in panel (a) of Figure 11.8, often by implementing temporary controls aimed at smoothing capital flows across their borders.

These efforts have typically been little more than band-aids, however. As you have learned in this chapter, only two changes could ultimately counteract the financial crises of the late 1990s and late 2000s: Increased international trade with developing nations mainly exporting labor-intensive goods and importing capital-intensive goods; or a renewed inflow of foreign capital. In fact, both changes took place gradually following the Asian crisis of the late 1990s, which helped to bring about gradual economic recovery in many developing countries. It is too early to judge whether the lesson from this experience will be taken to heart by governments of developing nations seeking to recover from the global financial downturn of the late 2000s.

Developing-nation indebtedness: A burden or a key to growth?

There are two basic ways in which developing nations with an underabundance of capital resources and relatively low national income levels can acquire capital resources from abroad. One is to finance the acquisition of capital by borrowing from abroad. The other is to permit foreign direct investment.

There are three problems with borrowing abroad. One is that interest payments on the debt obligations are transfers from domestic residents to foreign residents who own these obligations. Another is that foreign borrowers may place conditions on loans that effectively transfer some control over resource-allocation decisions away from domestic residents. A third problem, depicted in Figure 11.8 (page 372), is that foreign shorter-term investment and loans can be highly volatile.

Overall, foreign direct investment typically has been a more stable source of capital inflows. Foreign owners of capital resources nonetheless earn all returns on those resources that are not reinvested domestically. In addition, foreign owners typically have considerable say in how capital resources are directed within the domestic economy.

Nevertheless, there is widespread agreement among development economists that sustained capital accumulation is a fundamental prerequisite to achieving and maintaining persistent economic growth within developing countries. For now, most developing nations have cast their lot with the long-term benefits that they perceive will emerge from foreign capital inflows. These nations appear willing to accept the near-term burdens and risks that accompany large but volatile cross-border flows of capital. (Recent research provides some evidence that foreign direct investment performs an important mechanism for developing nations to keep pace with employing the most recent technologies; see *Management Notebook: Foreign direct investment as a route to the latest technologies*.)

MANAGEMENT NOTEBOOK

Foreign direct investment as a route to the latest technologies

Businesspeople usually will risk their funds on investing directly in a foreign venture in a developing country only if they are convinced that the venture will yield a rate of return on their funds consistent with alternative investments elsewhere. Thus, businesspeople typically require assurances that an investment abroad will employ up-to-date technologies that will be used to produce items at lowest feasible expense. As a consequence, for many developing countries, foreign direct investment helps to channel the latest techniques alongside the funds required to engage those techniques in production of goods and services.

In a recent study, Delfim Gomes Neto and Francisco José Veiga of the University of Minho in Portugal examined the role of foreign direct investment in promoting the diffusion of technology and innovation to 139 nations between 1970 and 2009.

They provide evidence that foreign direct investment exerts two distinct effects on this diffusion process. The first is a direct effect in transmitting the most recent technological innovations involving both novel products and new production processes. The second is an indirect effect that involves helping developing countries catch up on implementing *past* innovations that they had missed out on during prior years. Neto and Veiga estimate that a 1-percentage-point increase in foreign direct investment's share of total capital inflows by a developing nation generates a 0.67-percentage-point increase in the country's growth rate over a following 5-year interval.

For critical analysis: Why might the innovation and economic-growth benefits of portfolio investment likely be smaller than those associated with foreign direct investment?

Fundamental Issue #5: What are the pros and cons of increased capital flows to developing nations? Economists have found that capital accumulation contributes to persistent economic growth. Consequently, flows of foreign capital to developing nations, which typically have relatively underabundant capital resources, have contributed to growth of their economies. The downside of reliance on foreign capital inflows is that developing nations must borrow from abroad or permit foreign direct investment. Both methods entail transfers of domestic returns on capital to foreign residents. Borrowing can entail some loss of control over the management of capital projects, and foreign direct investment nearly always does. Although foreign direct investment flows have usually been relatively more stable, flows of capital financed through borrowing can be volatile and thereby can contribute to economic instability.

FIGHTING WORLD POVERTY WITH FINANCE: INSTITUTIONS AND POLICIES

Effective utilization of capital in production of goods and services often requires entrepreneurs to purchase expensive capital resources. Funding such purchases typically requires access to credit. In developing nations, obtaining sufficient funds can be problematic. Traditionally, supranational institutions have supplemented financing efforts by traditional private lenders.

The World Bank

The key supranational institution that provides financial support to developing nations is the **World Bank**. This institution, which was created during the 1944

Bretton Woods conference, makes loans to about 100 developing nations with an aim of reducing poverty and improving living standards. The World Bank estimates that, within its client nations, nearly 3 billion people live on less than $2 per day; about 40,000 die of preventable diseases each day; and more than 100 million never attend school of any type.

Structure and activities of the World Bank

ON THE WEB:

For more information about the various development-finance institutions housed within the World Bank, go to www. worldbank.org.

The World Bank has always specialized in relatively long-term loans used to fund long-run development and growth. Its initial objective was to provide assistance to countries in the post-World War II rebuilding period. In the 1960s, it refocused its mission by broadening its scope to encompass global antipoverty efforts.

Countries typically seek loans from the World Bank to fund specific projects, such as improved irrigation systems, better hospitals, and the like. Nevertheless, in recent years some of the World Bank's programs have overlapped with the International Monetary Fund's efforts to finance longer-term structural adjustments and debt refinancing activities within heavily indebted nations.

The World Bank is composed of five separate institutions, which are listed and described in Table 11.5. These institutions lend to both governments and private firms. They also provide advice and assistance in various aspects of development finance, including resolving disputes that may arise between foreign investors and

Table 11.5 *World Bank institutions*

Institution	Member nations	Role
International Development Association	170	Specializes in funding loans aimed toward poverty reduction in developing nations
International Bank for Reconstruction and Development	188	Provides loans and other forms of development assistance to middle-income countries and the more creditworthy developing nations
International Finance Corporation	184	Promotes private-sector investment in developing countries by committing its own funds, brokering loans from private sources, and offering advice to private firms
Multinational Investment Guarantee Agency	179	Promotes foreign direct investment in developing nations by offering political risk insurance to lenders and investors
International Center for Settlement of Investment Disputes	158	Provides conciliation and arbitration facilities for settling investment disputes arising between foreign investors and developing countries

Source: World Bank.

developing countries. The world's wealthiest countries fund most of its activities, although the World Bank also raises some of its funds in international capital markets.

Rethinking the World Bank's mission

The World Bank currently extends more than $15 billion annually in lending assistance to developing nations. In some nations, particularly Africa, attracting private investment has proved difficult. Consequently, the World Bank has been a key source of credit for these nations. Figure 11.10 displays the recent distribution of the World Bank's loans.

Even though more than $100 billion in private capital flows into developing nations in a typical year, the World Bank continues to make many of its loans to nations that have little trouble attracting private funds. Indeed, the development agency often competes with private investors. In such competitions, the institution typically wins out over private lenders by offering loans at below-market rates. Critics of such loans argue that they distort the market for private capital and encourage inefficient investment.

An important constraint that the World Bank faces is pressure from nations that are net donors to its lending pool to maintain a significant revenue stream of its own, thereby reducing the donors' risks of loss. Projects in developing nations that are most likely to maintain stable and reasonably high returns are also the ones that are most likely to attract the interest of private investors. In contrast, projects in the poorest and most needy countries are least likely to yield steady payoffs for the World Bank.

A key issue is what, if anything, a supranational institution such as the World Bank can do to promote pro-growth institutional improvements within developing nations. From one standpoint, there is little that the World Bank alone can do. After all, the

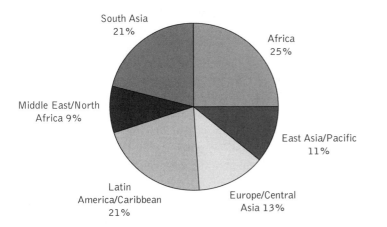

 **Figure 11.10** The distribution of World Bank lending

This figure displays the distribution of recent World Bank loans across global regions.

Source: World Bank.

377

shapes of national institutions are largely political matters for the people of developing nations to decide.

Nevertheless, a number of economists have suggested that the World Bank should adopt strict policies against countries with institutional structures that fail to promote individual property rights, law enforcement, and anticorruption efforts. This would, they argue, give countries an incentive to shape up their institutional structures.

Other economists, in contrast, advocate direct financial assistance to governments attempting to implement such institutional reforms. Funds put to such use, they argue, could compensate those who lose power as a result of reform efforts and could help fund infrastructures required to make reforms work. Those proposing this more active role for supranational lenders contend that the result could be much larger long-term returns for borrower nations and donor nations alike—as compared with the piecemeal payoffs from such projects as dams, power plants, and bridges.

Other supranational institutions

Periodically, governments of developing nations find that that their stocks of international debt have become so large in relation to their capabilities to repay that they can no longer make debt service payments to the World Bank or individual creditor nations such as France, Germany, Japan, or the United States. Such situations arose during the 1980s and 1990s, and appear likely to re-emerge in the 2010s in the wake of the massive financial crisis of the late 2000s.

The Paris Club and the London Club

Supranational organizations involving public or private creditors exist to deal with the prospect of providing debt relief to heavily indebted nations by hammering out rescheduled terms of debt payments. One such organization is the *Paris Club*, which serves as a forum for multinational negotiations between debtor and creditor nations contemplating such debt reschedulings. Currently, the Paris Club consists of financial officials from 19 highly developed nations, who meet about every 6 weeks at the French Ministry of the Economy, Finance, and Industry in Paris. The informal supranational organization was formed when Argentina sought significant debt relief in 1956. Since then, the Paris Club has organized a number of debt reschedulings, including Iraqi debt write-offs in 2004 following the armed conflict affecting that nation, and temporary suspensions of debt obligations of nations affected by the 2004 Indian Ocean earthquake and tsunami.

A private analogue to the Paris Club is the *London Club*, an informal international organization of private creditors first established in 1976 to address repayment problems experienced by Zaire. Recent actions by the London Club to reschedule payments of private loans by less developed nations include a 2002 rescheduling of about $300 million in Indonesian debts, and a 2009 agreement to restructure about $2 billion of debts owed by the West African nation of Ivory Coast.

Internationally organized initiatives to assist heavily indebted nations

In spite of efforts by the Paris Club and the London Club to provide debt relief since the 1950s and 1970s, many of the debt problems of the poorest nations have worsened during the past two decades. In reaction to an upswing of developing-nation debt problems in the 1990s, in 1996 the leaders of the leading seven industrialized countries agreed upon the *Heavily Indebted Poor Countries* (HIPC) *Initiative*. The HIPC Initiative established sets of conditions required for debt relief and put into place means to deliver such relief. Nevertheless, most observers agree that the HIPC Initiative failed to live up to expectations of both debtor and creditor nations.

Consequently, in 1999 a number of developed nations banded together to establish the *Cologne Debt Initiative* (CDI), which was aimed at providing faster, broader, and deeper debt-relief measures. The CDI expanded the number of HIPC nations and aimed to rush debt-rescheduling and debt-forgiveness programs for these countries. Accompanying the CDI was creation of the Millennium Trust Fund for Debt Relief, a trust fund to which private individuals and agencies could make contributions to assist debt-relief efforts. Although the CDI made some headway toward furthering debt-relief measures, a number of developing countries continue to struggle with debt-servicing problems.

Credit, capital, and microlending

Muhammad Yunus of Bangladesh, who received the Nobel Peace Prize in 2006, argues that there is a private solution to financing the accumulation of capital in developing nations. Yunus argues that private lenders are more likely to grant credit to prospective borrowers in poverty-stricken nations if the latter can provide *collateral*, or marketable assets that lenders can obtain if borrowers were to default on repaying loans. In most developed nations, borrowers typically offer as collateral capital assets for which they possess legal title. As noted above, in developing nations many capital resources are informally owned, making it difficult for individuals and families seeking credit to start entrepreneurial businesses to offer acceptable collateral when applying for loans aimed to finance capital purchases. The solution, Yunus decided, was to establish **microlenders**, or banking institutions specializing in making very small loans to entrepreneurs seeking to lift themselves from the lowest rungs of poverty.

Microlenders:
Banking institutions that specialize in extending very small sums of credit to low-income entrepreneurs.

Today, at least 1,000 microlenders extend loans ranging from as low as $100 to as high as $1,500 to about 3 billion borrowers around the world, who offer as collateral items such as water buffalo, hogs, or hand plows. Most microlenders are standalone institutions. Some, however, are owned by multinational banks that regard microlenders as a foreign direct investment. A few microlending institutions even offer ownership shares that are purchased by mutual funds and hedge funds as a form of international portfolio investment. All told, the estimated volume of loans extended globally by commercial microlenders is in excess of $20 billion.

Fundamental Issue #6: What organized international efforts are under way to assist residents of developing nations in obtaining credit required to boost utilization of capital resources and increase economic growth? Developing nations require considerable financial support to fund expenditures on capital resources. The main supranational institution assisting developing nations in this regard is the World Bank. Critics have complained in recent years that although the World Bank directs a significant portion of its financial assistance to the world's poorest countries, it also makes a large amount of loans in countries that receive significant private capital inflows. Informal supranational institutions overseeing efforts to assist heavily indebted developing nations reschedule their debt repayments are the Paris Club, a group of financial officials representing the governments of 19 highly developed nations, and the London Club, an international organization encompassing private lenders. Many private efforts to assist residents of developing nations in obtaining relatively small loans intended to foster entrepreneurial activities have centered around microlending. Multinational banks and other financial institutions have become involved in commercial microlending in recent years. All told, microlenders have extended about $20 billion in private credit to residents of developing nations.

CHAPTER SUMMARY

1. **The fundamental elements of economic development:** The first key element of economic development is technological improvement, or innovation in production processes that expand the capability to produce more units of goods and services with the same quantities of inputs. The second key element of economic development is a broadening of products and markets via product innovation, or the conceptualization and production of new types of goods and services. The third key element is economic growth, measured by the rate of increase in inflation-adjusted per capita income. Compounding economic growth rates brings about cumulative effects on a nation's level of real income, with the approximate number of years being equal to 72 divided by the nation's rate of economic growth.

2. **Key indicators and determinants of economic growth:** The key indicator of a nation's economic growth is inflation-adjusted per capita income, typically measured by dividing a country's aggregate real income by its population. Comparing per capita real incomes across nations requires conversions into the same currency units using exchange rates or PPPs. A country's rate of economic growth during a given period, by definition, is equal to its aggregate real income growth rate minus the population growth rate during the same interval. The growth equation states that the three determinants of aggregate real income growth are growth in productivity of labor and capital resources arising from technological improvements, growth in capital

resources, and growth in labor resources. If aggregate real income growth remains the same, a rise in population growth reduces a nation's economic growth rate. Nevertheless, population growth can contribute to aggregate real income growth by boosting the contribution of labor resources to growth in per capita real incomes. In principle, therefore, a higher population growth rate can either raise or reduce economic growth.

3. **How the accumulation of human and physical capital and the activities of entrepreneurs contribute to economic development:** Increasing the education and training of a nation's labor resources boosts labor productivity, improves technological capabilities, and thereby helps to raise the country's per capita real income. So does accumulating physical capital resources, although not all capital resources are readily usable in many nations. In these countries, failure to completely assign property rights to ownership of capital creates a dead capital problem, in which many capital resources are not tradable and thus cannot be allocated to the most efficient uses. Entrepreneurs organize labor and capital resources for the production of income-generating goods and services. Consequently, constraints on the capabilities of entrepreneurs to establish, operate, and close firms tend to retard economic growth.

4. **How greater openness to international trade affects wages and economic growth in developing nations:** Since the 1980s, the share of global international trade accounted for by developing countries has increased from 10 percent to more than one-third. Developing countries generally have relatively high proportions of labor resources. Hence, increased trade with developed nations that have higher proportions of capital resources is likely to raise the wages of workers in developing countries. As a result, international trade is likely to contribute to higher per capita incomes in developing countries. Nevertheless, because comparative advantages of developing nations differ, increased international trade is likely to make unequal contributions to the economic growth rates of developing countries.

5. **The pros and cons of increased capital flows to developing nations:** There is considerable evidence that capital accumulation contributes to economic growth. Thus, flows of foreign capital to relatively labor-abundant developing nations have helped boost the growth of these nations' economies. Increasing foreign capital inflows requires either borrowing from abroad or attracting foreign direct investment, which has the drawback of transferring domestic returns on capital to foreign residents. Permitting foreign direct investment sacrifices local control over the management of capital resources, and in some instances lenders also have some control over how capital resources are directed. In recent years, flows of foreign direct investment have been relatively stable, but flows of capital financed through borrowing have been much more variable.

6. **Organized international efforts to assist residents of developing nations obtain credit to boost utilization of capital resources and increase economic growth:** The World Bank is the primary supranational institution providing financial support to developing countries for their expenditures on capital resources. Critics suggest that the World Bank directs too much of its financial assistance to nations that are already recipients of private capital inflows instead of to the world's neediest countries. Other more informal supranational institutions are the Paris Club, a set of

government officials from 19 developed nations, and the London Club, an organization of private lenders, which assist in rescheduling, or sometimes even forgiving, debts of developing nations. Private microlenders, which sometimes are associated with multinational banks and other financial institutions, offer relatively small loans that total about $20 billion and are aimed at fostering entrepreneurial activities in less developed countries.

QUESTIONS AND PROBLEMS

1. Per capita real income grows at a constant rate of 2 percent in country A and at a constant rate of 4 percent in country B. Both countries initially have the same level of per capita real income. Use Table 11.3 on page 352 to determine how much higher, in percentage terms, per capita real income will be in country B than in country A after 10 years. How much higher will per capita real income be in country B after 50 years?

2. Per capita real income in country C is currently half as large as per capita real income in country D. Per capita real income grows at a constant rate of 8 percent in country C, however, but only at a constant rate of 1 percent in country D. Based on the data in Table 11.3 on page 352, in about how many years will country C's *level* of per capita real income almost have exactly caught up with the *level* of per capita real income in country D? Explain briefly.

3. According to the rule of 72, if a nation's per capita real income persistently grows at a rate of 2 percent per year, in how many years will its level of per capita real income double? What about if the persistent rate of growth is 4 percent?

4. A nation's aggregate real income is growing at an annual rate of 3.3 percent, and its current rate of growth of per capita real income is 0.4 percent. What is the rate of population growth in this nation?

5. Explain, in your own words, why the rate of population growth exerts theoretically uncertain effects on economic growth.

6. Consider the following World Bank estimates for the following countries.

Country	Number of days required to start a business	Number of legal steps required to start a business	Cost of starting a business (percent of per capita real income)
Cambodia	85	9	138.4
Chad	95	19	176.7
Chile	25	9	6.9
Colombia	26	9	12.8

Rank the nations in order, beginning with the country that you would anticipate to have the highest rate of economic growth, other things being equal. Justify your ranking.

7. Consider the following World Bank estimates for the following countries.

Country	Number of days required to register property	Number of days required to enforce a contract	Recovery rate from closing a business (percent of total amount)
Gambia	371	434	19.4
Georgia	3	255	27.9
Guinea	50	276	22.0
Haiti	405	508	2.7

Rank the nations in order, beginning with the country that you would anticipate to have the highest rate of economic growth, other things being equal. Justify your ranking.

8. Consider the following World Bank estimates for the following countries.

Country	Days required to register property	Cost of registering property (percent of value)
Bangladesh	245	10.2
Belize	60	4.7
Bulgaria	15	2.3
Burundi	69	13.2

Rank the nations in order, beginning with the country that you would anticipate to have the most significant dead capital problem, other things being equal. Justify your ranking.

9. Consider the following World Bank estimates for the following countries.

Country	Strength of legal rights of creditors (lower for lower value)	Depth of credit information index (lower for lower value)
Samoa	6	0
South Africa	9	6
Timor-Leste	1	0
Vietnam	8	4

Rank the nations in order, beginning with the country that you would anticipate to have the highest rate of economic growth, other things being equal. Justify your ranking.

10. Some observers have responded to harsh criticisms of World Bank policies in the 1990s and 2000s by arguing that the World Bank's net-donor members have saddled it with conflicting goals by requiring it to maintain a significant revenue stream of its own. Do you agree that the World Bank confronts conflicting objectives? If not, why not? If so, which of the allegedly conflicting goals do you think should take precedence?

ONLINE APPLICATION

URL: www.doingbusiness.org/EconomyRankings/
Title: World Bank's Doing Business Rankings
Navigation: Go directly to the above Website.
Application: Perform the indicated operations, and answer the questions.

1. In the menu of links along the top of the Web page, click on "Methodology," and then click on "Read about how the methodology was improved this year." How does the World Bank go about trying to standardize its measures of ease in doing business in various nations?
2. Back up to the "Methodology" page, and click on the link to "Common misconceptions about Doing Business." Read this short description. What are some limitations associated with the Doing Business Rankings?

For group study and analysis: Assign groups of students to examine rankings groups of countries by income (low, lower middle, upper middle, and high) and to see where these groups appear to fall on the overall ranking across all nations. Do nations' income classifications appear to be related to the World Bank's overall Doing Business Ranking?

REFERENCES AND RECOMMENDED READINGS

Agénor, Pierre-Richard, and Peter J. Montiel. *Development Macroeconomics*, 3rd edn. Princeton, NJ: Princeton University Press, 2008.

Bardhan, Ashok, Dwight Jaffee, and Cynthia Kroll, eds. *The Oxford Handbook of Offshoring and Global Employment*. Oxford and New York: Oxford University Press, 2011.

Barthel, Fabian, Matthias Busse, Richard Krever, and Eric Neumayer. "The Relationship between Double Taxation Treaties and Foreign Direct Investment." In M. Lang, P. Pistone, J. Schuch, and C. Staringer, eds., *Tax Treaties: Views from the Bridge—Building Bridges between Law and Economics*. Amsterdam: IBFD, 2010.

De Soto, Hernando. *The Mystery of Capital: Why Capitalism Triumphs in the West and Fails Everywhere Else*. New York: Basic Books, 2000.

Egger, Peter, and Michael Pfaffermayr. "The Impact of Bilateral Investment Treaties on Foreign Direct Investment." *Journal of Comparative Economics* 32 (December 2004): 788–804.

Fields, Gary S. *Distribution and Development: A New Look at the Developing World*. New York: MIT Press, 2001.

Hoekman, Bernard, and Marcelo Olarreaga. *Global Trade and Poor Nations: The Poverty Impacts and Policy Implications of Liberalization*. Washington, DC: Brookings Institution Press, 2007.

Lancaster, Carol. *Foreign Aid: Diplomacy, Development, Domestic Politics*. Chicago, IL: University of Chicago Press, 2007.

Lewis, W., Arthur. *The Theory of Economic Growth*, First Published 1955, Routledge Reprint Edition, 2013, p. 420.

Meir, Gerald, and James Rauch. *Leading Issues in Economic Development*, 8th edn. Oxford, U.K.: Oxford University Press, 2004.

Montiel, Peter. *Macroeconomics in Emerging Markets*. Cambridge, U.K.: Cambridge University Press, 2003.

Moreno, Ramon. "What Explains Capital Flows?" Federal Reserve Bank of San Francisco *Economic Letter* No. 22 (July 21, 2000).

Naughton, Barry. *The Chinese Economy: Transitions and Growth*. Cambridge, MA: MIT Press, 2007.

Neto, Delfim Gomes, and Francisco José Veiga. "Financial Globalization, Convergence, and Growth: The Role of Foreign Direct Investment." *Journal of International Money and Finance* 37 (October 2013): 161–186.

Neumayer, Eric, and Laura Spess. "Do Bilateral Investment Treaties Increase Foreign Direct Investment to Developing Countries?" *World Development* 33 (October 2005): 1567–1585.

Oostendorp, Remco. "Globalization and the Gender Wage Gap." *World Bank Economic Review* 23 (1, 2009): 141–161.

Pincus, Jonathan, and Jeffrey Winters, eds. *Reinventing the World Bank*. Ithaca, NY: Cornell University Press, 2002.

Sen, Amartya. *Development as Freedom*. Oxford, U.K.: Oxford University Press, 1999.

Watal, Jayashree. "Developing Countries' Interests in a 'Development Round'." In Jeffrey Schott, ed., *The WTO After Seattle*. Washington, DC: Institute for International Economics, 2000.

Young, Allan, Ivan Teodorovic, and Peter Koveos. *Economies in Transition: Conception, Status, and Prospects*. Hackensack, NJ: World Scientific, 2002.

Yunus, Muhammad. *Creating a World Without Poverty: Social Business and the Future of Capitalism*. New York: Public Affairs, 2007.

Chapter 12

Industrial structure and trade in the global economy— businesses without borders

---

FUNDAMENTAL ISSUES

1. How do economies of scale help to explain a nation's specialization in inter-industry trade?
2. How do economies of scale and product variety provide an explanation for intra-industry trade?
3. In what way can foreign direct investment affect international trading patterns?
4. What are alternative industry structures, and how does industry structure matter in the global economy?
5. Why do companies engage in cross-border mergers and acquisitions, and how do international market linkages complicate measuring the degree to which a few large firms may dominate markets?
6. How do governments regulate international merger and acquisition activities?

Rovio Entertainment Limited has become a business success story in Finland. Rovio's Angry Birds digital videogame has sprouted into a children's entertainment empire involving production and licensing of toys, clothing, soft drinks, playground equipment, activity parks, and even educational literature used in schools. The bulk of the company's entertainment products are exported.

At the same time, Finnish residents continue to import children's entertainment and educational products from abroad. Finnish children still wear Disney-themed merchandise such as T-shirts sporting Minnie Mouse or Donald Duck, and play with Lego building blocks manufactured in Denmark. Finnish parents continue to purchase educational products for their children produced by firms based elsewhere in Europe and in the United States. Finland does not necessarily have a comparative advantage in entertainment or educational products for children, but nonetheless Rovio is a major exporter of such items, even as Finnish residents import many competing products from abroad.

What accounts for cross-border trade in similar but differentiated products in Finland and other nations of the world? In this chapter, you will learn about economic rationales for *intra-industry trade* such as the simultaneous Finnish exports and imports of children's entertainment and educational products. You will learn as well about other issues relating to global industry structure.

INDUSTRIAL ORGANIZATION AND INTERNATIONAL INTEGRATION

Industrial organization is the study of the structures of and interactions among firms and markets. Traditionally, industrial organization economists focused their attention on firm and market structures within nations. Today, however, they must also take into account international issues. Likewise, economists who study international trade increasingly must consider the importance of industry structure as a factor influencing trade flows.

Industrial organization: *The study of the structures of, and interactions among, firms and markets.*

One of several reasons that industrial organization has become an international subject is the significant growth of *intra-industry trade*. The traditional theory of international trade that we first discussed in Chapter 2 and the factor proportions approach to international trade that we examined in Chapter 3 and applied to labor-market issues in Chapter 10 both emphasize *inter-industry trade*, or international trade in different goods and services. Figure 12.1 displays estimates of intra-industry trade shares in different product categories for more than 50 nations compiled by Marius Brülhart of the University of Lausanne.

As you learned in Chapter 10, intra-industry trade often entails the international exchange of goods or services that are close substitutes. Examples include automobiles, computers, beer, financial services, and the like, that flow across a nation's borders as both exports *and* imports. Another aspect of intra-industry trade is the

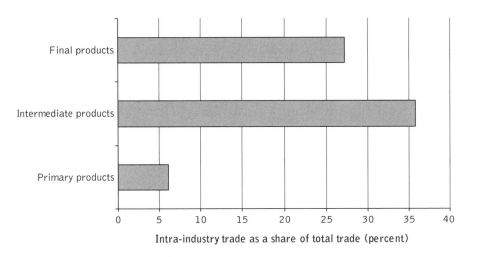

Figure 12.1 *Intra-industry trade as a percentage of international trade for different product groups*

Intra-industry trade accounts for a relatively small percentage of international trade in primary products, but for more significant shares of international trade in intermediate products and final products.

Source: Brülhart (2009).

cross-border exchange of component parts or services at various stages of production prior to completion of a final product, such as when a U.S. auto manufacturer transports parts to an assembly plant based in Mexico and then exports completed vehicles back to the United States.

Economies of scale and international trade

Before we consider the role of industry structure in explaining intra-industry trade, let's take a look at an important way in which industry structure can influence inter-industry trade. In earlier chapters, you learned that inter-industry trade occurs because it allows residents of two countries to take advantage of comparative or absolute advantages that they possess. As a result, they can experience gains from trade. One factor that can help explain the process by which this occurs through the actions of producers is *economies of scale*. As we shall see shortly, this concept is also important in understanding why intra-industry trade occurs.

Long-run average cost: *The ratio of a firm's total production cost to its output when the firm has sufficient time to vary the quantities of all factors of production.*

Economies of scale: *A reduction in long-run average cost induced by an increase in a firm's output.*

Economies of scale

A key factor influencing the optimal size, or *scale*, of a company is its **long-run average cost**, which is the ratio of its total production cost to its output when it is able to adjust quantities of all factors of production, including capital as well as land, labor, and entrepreneurship. Typically, firms are able to adjust their capital over a relatively long period, the *long run*, which stretches from months to years. For most firms, over relatively small ranges of output long-run average cost usually declines as they expand their ability to produce additional units of a product. When this happens, a firm experiences **economies of scale**, which arise any time that an increase in the amount of output that a firm produces leads to a decrease in its long-run average cost.

Economies of scale may arise because of specialization: When a firm's scale of operations increases, its opportunities to specialize in the use of factors of production also increase. For instance, a larger firm may be able to reduce its long-run average cost by dividing its existing work force into separate units that focus on specific aspects of its production process. In addition, a company may be able to take advantage of physical processes that permit it to produce more output with proportionately fewer inputs. For example, consider a company that ships liquids such as chemicals or other fluid products. It can gain from using larger storage containers, because the volume of containers, which helps determine the company's shipping capacity, rises more than proportionately with the surface area of the containers, which helps determine how much steel or plastic must be used in container construction.

Diseconomies of scale: *An increase in long-run average cost caused by an increase in a firm's output.*

Economies of scale normally are not unbounded, however. As a company continues to enlarge the scale of its operations, it encounters factors that can result in **diseconomies of scale**, or increases in long-run average cost generated by increases in its output. This occurs, for instance, when layers of supervision increase as a company's scale of operations increases, so that the costs of compiling information and maintaining communication grow more than proportionately with the size of the firm.

Minimum efficient scale and international trade

A typical company finds that, as it increases its size, initially it experiences economies of scale. As it raises its scale of operations further, however, it eventually begins to experience higher long-run average costs and diseconomies of scale. The scale of operations at which economies of scale end and diseconomies of scale set in is the firm's **minimum efficient scale**. This is the firm size at which the company minimizes its long-run average cost. When all firms in a given industry have achieved their minimum efficient scale, then the industry itself operates at the minimum efficient scale for that industry.

An industry limited to producing and selling only within a single nation's borders may be unable to attain its minimum efficient scale. Taken alone, this can help to reinforce why a nation might gain a comparative advantage in producing a particular good or service. The U.S. aircraft industry, for instance, may be able to achieve its minimum efficient scale at a lower longer-run average cost than aircraft industries in many other countries. Thus, the U.S. aircraft industry can expand output beyond quantities that U.S. residents wish to consume. The industry can export additional jets, turboprop planes, and helicopters to other countries at a lower per-unit cost. Indeed, this is likely to be a reason why the U.S. aircraft industry produces a large portion of the world's aircraft and why a number of nations do not even produce aircraft. (For more details on how this might occur, see *Visualizing Global Economic Issues: International trade and economies of scale*.)

Minimum efficient scale: *The size at which a firm or industry minimizes its long-run average cost over a time frame in which quantities of all factors of production may be adjusted.*

VISUALIZING GLOBAL ECONOMIC ISSUES

International trade and economies of scale

To think about how economies of scale might induce countries to specialize in producing particular goods or services, take a look at Figure 12.2. It depicts a possible *long-run average cost* (LRAC) curve for any given national aircraft industry, under the assumption that all countries have access to the same aircraft-producing technologies.

Let's suppose that, in the absence of trade, two countries, the United States and Israel, have aircraft industries that produce propeller planes, jets, and helicopter craft for domestic consumption. The demand for aircraft within the U.S. aircraft market, however, is much greater than demand within the Israeli market. Hence, in the absence of trade, U.S. aircraft production initially is Q_{US} at point US along the long-run average cost curve. Israeli aircraft production is Q_I at point I, so in the absence of trade, Israeli manufacturers operate at a cost disadvantage relative to U.S. producers, simply because their scale of operations is lower.

Now suppose that the two nations initiate open trade. Even though Israel's aircraft manufacturers have access to the same technology, U.S. producers immediately operate with a cost advantage over Israeli producers. Furthermore, by expanding their production, U.S. companies can reach the minimum efficient scale (MES) for aircraft production at point MES. U.S. aircraft manufacturers then could produce Q_{MES} units. They could continue to sell many of these units domestically, but they could export the remainder to other nations such as Israel. In the end, the United States would develop a specialization in producing aircraft, and Israel ultimately might import most of its aircraft from the United States.

For critical analysis: Who would lose if barriers to trade prevented U.S. companies from exporting aircraft to Israel and other nations? Who would gain? (Hint: In this situation, U.S. and Israeli aircraft production levels would remain at Q_{US} and Q_I in Figure 12.2.)

It turns out that economies of scale can also help to explain why nations with industries producing *similar* but slightly different products may experience international trade involving the products of those industries. This explanation relies on combining the idea of economies of scale with the possibility that competition might exist among firms in different countries that sell closely related, yet slightly different, products. Let's next consider why this is so. (In addition to experiencing economies of scale in aircraft manufacturing, U.S.-based companies gain from cost efficiencies arising from scale economies in the production and sale of other physically large items; see *Management Notebook: Explaining the U.S. predominance as an exporter of large goods.*)

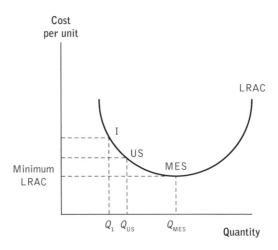

Figure 12.2 *A hypothetical long-run average cost curve for an aircraft industry*

Groups of aircraft manufacturers located in the United States and Israel produce essentially the same products using the same technology. Hence, they face the same long-run average cost (LRAC) curve. Because the demand for the products of firms in the U.S.-based aircraft industry is greater than the demand for products of firms in the Israel-based aircraft industry, however, U.S. output is higher, at point US, than Israeli output, at point I. In the absence of trade, therefore, Israeli aircraft manufacturers operate at a cost disadvantage relative to U.S. firms. Hence, U.S. firms have a cost advantage over Israeli firms if international aircraft trade takes place, and U.S. firms are better positioned to expand toward the minimum efficient scale (MES).

MANAGEMENT NOTEBOOK

Explaining the U.S. predominance as an exporter of large goods

Two firms, U.S.-owned Caterpillar and Japanese-owned Komatsu, account for 85 percent of total global production of large mining trucks, each of which is the size of a two-story house and sells for between $2.5 million and $6 million. Every one of those trucks is produced in the United States. Most of them are exported to other nations, however.

U.S.-based firms account for more than half of all sales in global markets for a number of other physically large merchandise. Examples of such items include other mining and excavating machinery, commercial aircraft, industrial engines, and rail locomotives and freight cars.

Producing, assembling, and primarily exporting the component parts of massive items in large volumes permits these U.S.-located companies to operate at the lowest feasible minimum cost per unit. The resulting gains from scale economies help to ensure that the firms' explicit expenses and opportunity costs are more than covered by revenues from combined domestic and export sales. In this way, the companies are assured of earning sufficient profits to justify continuing their operations into the indefinite future.

For critical analysis: Why do you suppose that firms outside the United States that possess the expertise to produce larger goods, but operate at a lower output scale, have difficulties producing their items at per-unit costs as low as those of U.S. companies operating in these industries?

Fundamental Issue #1: How do economies of scale help to explain a nation's specialization in inter-industry trade? A firm or an industry experiences economies of scale when long-run average cost declines as total output expands through greater usage of all factors of production. At the minimum efficient scale of a firm or industry, long-run average cost is minimized. Any further increase in output would push up long-run average cost and thereby result in diseconomies of scale. Opening national borders to international trade helps give a cost advantage to countries with firms that already have experienced economies of scale. The industry in this nation can use this opportunity more speedily to expand to the minimum efficient scale for output of the good or service produced by that industry.

Product variety, imperfect competition, and intra-industry trade

The previous discussion shows how economies of scale help create a comparative advantage that leads to *inter*-industry trade. Because *intra*-industry trade by definition entails exchanges of similar goods and services, however, gains from trade do not arise from comparative advantage or absolute advantage. Instead, gains from intra-industry trade stem from cost efficiencies that producers experience and from the effects of an expanded *product variety* that intra-industry trade offers to consumers.

Common experience indicates that many industries located in different countries produce goods and services that are easily distinguishable but nonetheless are relatively close substitutes for each other. Examples include German and U.S. beers, Swedish and Japanese automobiles, Swiss and Italian wristwatches, British and Caribbean financial services, and the like. By engaging in intra-industry trade, residents of these and other nations clearly are able to consume a broader variety of products.

A theory of imperfect competition

In addition, the existence of intra-industry trade allows the companies that produce these products to market their goods and services to more consumers. Because the companies sell products that are not identical yet are substitutable, they are said to be *imperfectly competitive* firms. Consumers can distinguish among companies' products, which gives each individual firm the ability to set prices that are different from the average price charged by other firms in the industry. By way of contrast, any single *perfectly competitive* firm that sells products identical to those of other firms has no incentive to set a price that differs from the market price. Setting a price above the market price induces its customers to buy the identical product from other firms, and setting a price below the market price reduces the firm's profits.

Monopolistic competition: *An industry structure with a relatively large number of firms, easy entry or exit, and similar but not identical firm products.*

Economies of scale, and imperfect competition with its variety of similar products, provide an explanation for why nations often experience intra-industry trade. To think about why this is so, consider a situation in which **monopolistic competition** prevails. In this situation, there are many firms, each of which has an output level that is relatively small compared with total industry output. In addition, it is easy for firms to enter or leave the industry. Nevertheless, firms produce similar but not identical products. Because the product of each firm is differentiated from the products offered by its competitors, each firm is able to set the price of its own product taking into account the demand for its product, which depends on the availability of the close substitutes produced by other firms in the industry. (Product differentiation is a central objective of many firms that engage in online marketing of consumer goods intended for sale globally; see *Online Globalization: A global exporter of consumer goods differentiates its product*.)

ONLINE GLOBALIZATION

A global exporter of consumer goods differentiates its product

Etsy is the name of a Web-based firm headquartered in New York. More than 11 million users are registered at its site, which acts as a central marketplace for processing sales of between 2 million and 3 million consumer goods per year, linking sellers and buyers located in 150 different countries.

What sets Etsy apart from other online marketplaces for consumer goods is that it enforces a requirement that every single one of the products sold on its site must be handmade. Whether the item is a glass bead priced at 20 cents or a sculpture that sells for $100,000, that item must have been produced by hand rather than via a large-scale production process.

The managers of Etsy insist on the sale of only handcrafted goods to differentiate Etsy's product from that of other online marketplaces. The managers know that people who purchase items at the site prefer consumer goods that were made by hand. As a consequence, these customers are willing to pay a higher fee for Etsy's services than they otherwise would pay at Websites operated by competitors. That is, requiring the sale only of handcrafted items helps to raise the demand for Etsy's unique marketplace services and thereby to charge a higher price for the services that Etsy provides—currently a commission rate of 3.5 percent on each sale at the firm's online global marketplace.

For critical analysis: Why do you suppose that Etsy is in the midst of expanding the range of languages through which users can offer products or place orders on its Website?

In the short run, a firm in a monopolistically competitive industry can earn a positive economic profit, which means that its total revenue can exceed the opportunity cost of being part of that industry instead of another industry. Positive economic profits, however, encourage other firms to enter the industry. As they enter and capture some of the existing firm's customers, the demand for its product declines, and its economic profit declines toward zero. In the long run, therefore, the total revenue earned by a firm in a monopolistically competitive industry just covers the opportunity cost of remaining in the industry. (To learn how to use graphs to examine the behavior of a monopolistically competitive firm in both the short run and long run, see *Visualizing Global Economic Issues: Monopolistic competition in the short run and in the long run.*)

VISUALIZING GLOBAL ECONOMIC ISSUES

Monopolistic competition in the short run and in the long run

Because a monopolistically competitive firm sells an item that is at least slightly different from the products of all other firms, there is a unique customer demand for its product. In panel (a) of Figure 12.3 (p. 395), the demand curve, which shows the price that the firm's customers are willing and able to pay for each quantity, slopes downward. Thus, if the firm wishes to sell an additional unit of its product, it must reduce the price that it charges. One effect of a price reduction is an increase in the quantity of its product that its customers desire to consume at the lower price, and this effect tends to raise the firm's revenues. Another effect of a price cut, however, is a reduction in revenues on the fewer units it could have sold at a higher price.

Marginal revenue and marginal cost

Together, the two effects of a price reduction imply that at any quantity the firm sells, its *marginal revenue*—the additional revenue it earns from selling an additional unit of its product—is always less than the price it charges. Hence, the firm's *marginal revenue curve*, which shows the marginal revenue it can earn at each quantity it sells, lies below the demand curve.

Panel (a) shows a possible short-run situation that this firm might face when it takes into account its production costs as well as the demand for its product and its implied marginal revenue curve. To simplify a little, we assume that it can always vary all factors of production, so that its long-run average cost curve applies. The other cost curve shown in panel (a) is the firm's *marginal cost curve*. It shows, for each possible rate of output, the additional cost that the firm will incur if it produces one more unit of output, which is its **marginal cost**.

Marginal cost:
The additional cost that the firm incurs from producing an additional unit of output.

Short- and long-run equilibrium under monopolistic competition

To maximize its economic profit—total revenue less all costs, including the opportunity cost of being in this business instead of some other business—the firm produces to the point at which marginal revenue equals marginal cost. This is point S, where the marginal revenue and marginal cost curves cross. Consequently, in the short-run situation shown in panel (b), the firm's profit-maximizing output rate is Q_S. If it were to produce less output, marginal revenue would exceed marginal cost, so the firm could add to its profits by producing more units. If it were to raise its output above Q_S, however, then marginal cost would rise above marginal revenue, and the firm's profit would begin to fall. This is why Q_S is the output rate that maximizes the firm's profit. The firm charges the price P_S that the demand curve indicates its customers are willing to pay for this amount of output. The average cost of producing Q_S units is AC_S. The firm's total profit, therefore, equals ($P_S - AC_S$), which is the height of the shaded rectangle, multiplied by Q_S, which is the base of the rectangle. Thus, the shaded rectangle depicts a positive **economic profit** for the firm.

Economic profit:
Total revenue minus explicit and implicit opportunity costs.

In a monopolistically competitive industry, it is easy for new firms to enter the industry. The fact that the firm depicted in panel (a) earns a positive economic profit is a signal that revenues in this industry are more than sufficient to cover the opportunity cost of being in this industry instead of another one. In the long run, therefore, additional firms will enter the industry. Panel (b) shows what happens at the previously existing firm in panel (a) following the entry of new firms. First, the demand for this firm's product will decline, because some of its customers will buy similar goods from other firms. Thus, the demand curve shifts leftward. Second, because the entry of new firms means that more substitute products are available, the demand for this firm's product becomes more *elastic*. That is, a given proportionate price increase will induce a larger proportionate decrease in the quantity of the firm's product that customers wish to purchase. Because the firm's marginal revenue curve stems from its demand curve, it also shifts leftward and becomes more elastic. The firm's costs are unaffected by entry of new firms, so the result is a decline in the firm's economic profits to zero in the long run. As panel (b) indicates, this occurs when the firm's demand curve shifts to a point of tangency with the long-run average cost curve at point L. At this point, the economic profit of firm falls to zero. It produces a lower rate of output, Q_L, at a lower price, P_L, and the total revenue it earns just covers the opportunity cost of being part of this industry. This removes the incentive for any more firms to enter the industry.

For critical analysis: What would happen if so many new firms initially entered the industry that the firm's demand curve were to "overshoot" point L, so that the firm finds itself operating at a loss (a negative economic profit)?

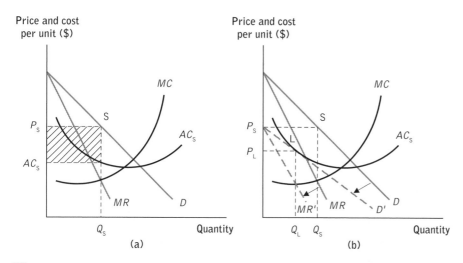

Figure 12.3 *Demand, production, and pricing at a monopolistically competitive firm*

Panel (a) depicts an initial short-run situation faced by a monopolistically competitive firm. Marginal revenue, or the additional revenue earned from selling an additional unit, is always less than the price the firm charges. The firm maximizes its economic profit in the short run by producing to the point where marginal revenue equals marginal cost, at point S, where it produces output Q_S and charges a price P_S, thereby earning maximum profit equal to $(P_S - AC_S) \times Q_S$. In the long run, additional firms enter the industry when this and other firms earn positive economic profits. In panel (b), entry causes the demand for this firm's product to decline, because some of its customers will buy similar goods from other firms, and to become more elastic, so that a given proportionate price increase induces a larger proportionate decrease in the quantity of the firm's product that consumers desire to purchase. In the long run, the firm's economic profits equal zero at point L, where the demand curve is tangent to the firm's long-run average cost curve. The firm's total revenues just cover the opportunity cost of being part of this industry, so there is no incentive for more firms to enter the industry.

Monopolistic competition, economies of scale, and intra-industry trade

Now consider what happens when monopolistically competitive firms in two nations are able to export their products across their nations' borders. In the domestic country, a typical domestic firm experiences an increase in the demand for its product because foreign residents can now purchase it. By itself, this tends to encourage the firm to expand its output.

At the same time, however, foreign firms are able to sell their products to domestic residents, so the demand for the typical domestic firm's product begins to decline somewhat. This induces the domestic firm to cut back slightly on its production, although the net effect of open trade is an increase in its output. In addition, because domestic residents can choose among a wider variety of products, the quantity of the domestic firm's product that they desire to consume becomes more sensitive to changes in the price that the domestic firm charges. This encourages the domestic firm to keep its price low.

In fact, in the long run, the domestic firm responds to open trade by cutting its price somewhat. The reason is that expanding its output allows the domestic firm to experience economies of scale. Its average production cost falls as it increases its output. Because the firm produces more efficiently, keeping its price low to retain its customers in the face of greater competition from abroad is also consistent with its efforts to maximize profit. Nevertheless, in the long run the maximum economic profit that each domestic firm earns remains equal to zero. (To contemplate the theory of intra-industry trade under monopolistic competition, see *Visualizing Global Economic Issues: Intra-industry trade with monopolistically competitive firms.*)

VISUALIZING GLOBAL ECONOMIC ISSUES

Intra-industry trade with monopolistically competitive firms

To see how intra-industry trade tends to affect production and pricing decisions at monopolistically competitive firms, take a look at Figure 12.4. The figure depicts an initial long-run situation, at point N, for a domestic company before any intra-industry trade occurs. To maximize its profit, the firm produces to the point at which marginal revenue cost equals marginal revenue. In this "no-trade" situation, the firm produces Q_N units, charges the price P_N, and earns an economic profit equal to zero. Thus, its total revenue just covers the opportunity cost of being in this industry.

Now think about what happens when intra-industry international trade takes place. When the firm is able to export some of its output for sale to residents of other nations, the demand for its product starts to rise. At the same time, however, companies in other countries are able to sell competing products domestically. This tends to reduce the demand for the domestic firm's product somewhat and, simultaneously, to cause the demand for its product to become more elastic. As a result, the domestic firm ends up in a new long-run, "trade" situation such as the one shown by point T. On net, it produces and sells more output, Q_T. In addition, because there is a downward movement along the firm's long-run average cost curve, the firm experiences economies of scale. Its long-run average cost is lower, so the firm operates more efficiently and thus produces more output to sell at a lower per-unit price, P_T. Thus, the firm's domestic *and* foreign customers gain from intra-industry trade.

For critical analysis: This firm earns an economic profit equal to zero in the long run without or with intra-industry trade, so what is its incentive to export its product? (Hint: What would happen if the firm chooses not to export, but faces increased competition from foreign firms that do choose to engage in intra-industry trade?)

Hence, intra-industry trade broadens the range of products from which consumers can choose. The opportunity to export their products encourages domestic firms to increase their production. They experience economies of scale as they push up their output, which enables them to reduce their prices in the face of competition from foreign imports. On net, therefore, domestic residents are able to consume more industry output from a wider set of firms offering a greater variety of products—at

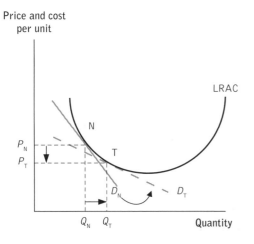

Figure 12.4 *The effects of intra-industry trade under monopolistic competition*

The initial long-run equilibrium for this monopolistically competitive firm in the absence of international trade is at point N, where the firm earns zero economic profits producing Q_N units that it sells at price P_N. When intra-industry international trade takes place, the firm experiences an increase in the demand for its product from foreign residents. At the same time, however, companies located abroad are able to sell their products domestically, which tends to reduce demand somewhat. The availability of more substitute products from abroad also makes the demand for the domestic firm's product more elastic. This results in a new long-run equilibrium with intra-industry trade at point T, at which the firm produces more output, Q_T, at a lower long-run average cost that it sells at a lower price, P_T.

lower prices. So can foreign residents, where these effects are the same. Thus, both domestic and foreign residents experience gains from intra-industry trade.

> *Fundamental Issue #2: How do economies of scale and product variety provide an explanation for intra-industry trade?* Today a significant portion of international trade is intra-industry trade. When consumers can readily distinguish among the products of different firms, and firms can easily enter or leave the industry, then monopolistic competition prevails. In the long run, firms enter or leave the industry until revenue just covers the opportunity cost of being in that industry instead of some other industry. In the presence of international trade, each firm tends to expand its output to reduce its long-run average cost, which permits charging a lower price to help retain customers in the face of greater intra-industry competition from firms in other countries.

FOREIGN DIRECT INVESTMENT AND TRADE PATTERNS

An important factor contributing to the growth of intra-industry trade has been foreign direct investment. Most foreign direct investment occurs through the actions of multinational corporations with operations spanning two or more countries.

Types of foreign direct investment

Horizontal foreign direct investment:
Establishment of a foreign subsidiary of a multinational firm that produces a good or service that is similar to the one the firm produces in its home country.

Vertical foreign direct investment:
Establishment of a foreign subsidiary of a multinational firm that produces components that are assembled elsewhere, or uses components produced elsewhere to assemble the firm's final product.

When engaging in foreign direct investment, multinational firms must decide where to invest, what production techniques to use, what kinds of facilities to establish, whether to buy or lease existing facilities or construct new facilities, and whether to bring in local partners. Most fundamentally for the resulting pattern of trade, they must determine whether to engage in *horizontal* or *vertical* foreign direct investment.

Horizontal investment

A multinational firm may undertake **horizontal foreign direct investment**, in which a foreign subsidiary of the firm produces goods or services similar to those produced in the firm's home country. Horizontal subsidiaries tend to produce for national or regional markets. Generally speaking, it involves multinational firms based in industrialized nations that establish subsidiaries in other industrialized nations.

Vertical investment

A multinational firm may alternatively engage in **vertical foreign direct investment**. In this case, a foreign subsidiary produces components to be assembled elsewhere, or uses components produced elsewhere to complete assembly of a final product. In most circumstances, vertical investment involves multinational firms based in industrialized nations, which establish subsidiaries in less developed countries.

Distributing production facilities across two or more countries allows a firm to take advantage of national differences in the costs of factors of production. For instance, a U.S. multinational company may establish facilities for designing and manufacturing components of its final product in the United States, thereby taking advantage of relatively low costs of capital resources in that relatively capital-abundant country. It then may set up an assembly facility in a relatively labor-abundant nation, such as Mexico, so that it can keep its wage costs relatively low.

Trade effects of foreign direct investment

Horizontal investment provides an inflow of capital to the nation where it occurs. It usually does not, however, contribute substantially to that country's flow of international trade. The reason is that multinational companies tend to create parallel facilities in other nations primarily as a means of avoiding barriers to trade with those nations. Thus, the firms tend to sell most of their horizontal subsidiaries' production within the nations where the goods or services are manufactured.

In contrast, because multinational companies engaging in vertical investment must transfer components from facilities in one nation, such as the United States, to another, such as Mexico, their actions create flows of intra-industry trade. Consequently, recently surging growth in vertical investment has been a major contributor to measured increases in international trade.

Fundamental Issue #3: In what way can foreign direct investment affect international trading patterns? Horizontal foreign direct investment involves a company's establishment of international facilities that produce goods or services similar to those produced in its home country. Although the growth of horizontal foreign direct investment has helped push up worldwide capital flows, it has not had a significant effect on international trade. By way of contrast, vertical foreign direct investment, which entails spreading a company's production processes across different nations, can induce significant increases in measured trade flows when companies transfer components from one nation to another for final assembly. This has helped generate the recent rise in intra-industry trade.

GLOBALIZATION, INDUSTRY STRUCTURE, AND GEOGRAPHY

In a monopolistically competitive industry, consumers gain from intra-industry trade both because they can consume a greater variety of products and because increased international competition induces producers to increase production and cut prices. Thus, imperfect competition can help explain why intra-industry trade takes place. This is not the only way in which imperfect competition plays an important role in the global trading system, however. It has effects in other ways as well.

Barriers to entry

Not every imperfectly competitive industry contains monopolistically competitive firms that can easily enter or leave the industry. Many industries, both within nations and around the globe, contain only a few firms. Within some countries, a nationwide industry comprises a single firm. Let's now consider such industries and their implications for world trade.

Barriers to entry:
Any factors inhibiting entrepreneurs from instantaneously founding a new firm.

Industries with relatively small numbers of firms exist because of **barriers to entry**, which are factors that prevent entrepreneurs from immediately creating a new firm. There are four basic types of entry barrier.

One is the presence of significant economies of scale. If companies in an industry find that increasing the scale of their operations continues to reduce long-run average cost up to relatively large output rates, then it may be that only a few firms can achieve minimum efficient scale within a marketplace.

Another barrier to entry is exclusive ownership of a relatively large portion of a key resource used to produce a good or service. For example, for a number of years a diamond firm called De Beers owned mines containing a large portion of the world's uncut diamonds. This permitted De Beers to dominate the world's diamond market until the 1990s, when other diamond discoveries took place, and new mining firms began to participate actively in the market for uncut diamonds.

First-mover advantage:
A barrier to entry arising from the ability of the initial firm in an industry to develop marketing advantage by identifying its own product as the industry product.

A third barrier to entry can arise from differences among products that help explain monopolistic competition. In some instances, it may be possible that a company has a **first-mover advantage**, meaning that during its time as the only firm in the market, it takes advantage of relatively low marketing costs to establish a long-term entry barrier by identifying its product as the *industry* product. It took a number of years, for example, before later entrants to the copy machine industry were able to overcome the tendency of many people to think of copying pages as "Xeroxing" them.

Fourth, governments can erect barriers to entry by sanctioning government-sponsored firms or by establishing licensing requirements for an industry and then restricting the number of licenses.

Alternative forms of imperfect competition

Under perfect competition, there are many firms and many consumers, firms produce indistinguishable products, and it is easy for firms to enter or leave the industry. Monopolistic competition is a form of imperfect competition that arises because each firm's product can be distinguished from those of other firms. Otherwise, however, a monopolistically competitive industry also has many firms and many consumers, and firms can accomplish industry entry or exit at trivial cost. The existence of barriers to entry makes the entry of new firms difficult in the short run and much more costly in the long run. This naturally tends to limit the number of firms in the industry.

Oligopoly:
An industry structure in which a few firms are the predominant suppliers of the total output of an industry, so that their pricing and production decisions are interdependent.

Oligopoly

Economists use the term **oligopoly** to describe an industry structure in which only a few firms supply the bulk of the industry's output. Most of the world's output of automobiles, for instance, is produced by a handful of companies: General Motors, Ford Motor Company, Daimler, Toyota, and Honda.

In contrast to perfectly competitive or monopolistically competitive firms, firms in an oligopolistic industry practice *strategic pricing*. When they set their prices and quantities, they recognize that their decisions will affect the decisions of their rivals in the marketplace. Economists call this *oligopolistic interdependence*, and there are many theories of the price- and quantity-setting strategies that a few interdependent firms may adopt.

Monopoly

One special case of strategic pricing is cooperative decision making within an oligopolistic industry. In principle, by working together, a few firms can establish a *cartel* and restrain their output, coordinate their pricing decisions, and maximize their joint profit. Essentially, they then act as a **monopoly**, or single producer in a marketplace. True monopoly situations are relatively rare. Nevertheless, traditionally, local telephone, water, and energy services often are provided by government-regulated monopolies. Cartels that mimic a monopoly are perhaps even more rare. The reason is that each cartel member typically has an incentive to cheat on a cartel agreement by expanding its production above limits established by the cartel. Thus, most cartels fail to act as a single monopoly producer for long.

Monopoly:
An industry that consists of a single firm.

The effective operation of a cooperative cartel or of a true monopoly tends to reduce consumer welfare. The reason is that a profit-maximizing monopolist faces the entire demand for the industry's product. By reducing production and pushing up the product price relative to the levels that perfectly competitive firms would choose, a monopoly reduces consumer surplus. (To see how we can use a diagram to illustrate these adverse welfare effects of monopoly, see *Visualizing Global Economic Issues: The welfare effects of monopoly*.)

VISUALIZING GLOBAL ECONOMIC ISSUES

The welfare effects of monopoly

To see why an unregulated monopoly can reduce consumer welfare, take a look at Figure 12.5. It displays a market demand curve that is faced either by a perfectly competitive or monopolistic industry. To simplify, let's assume that, under perfect competition, the market supply curve is perfectly elastic, which is the situation if there are no fixed costs and the marginal cost of each firm in the industry is constant and identical. This automatically implies that marginal cost and average cost are equal. Under perfect competition, the market price, P_{PC}, is equal to marginal cost, and total industry output is equal the quantity demanded at this price, Q_{PC}. Consumer surplus, therefore, is given by the large shaded triangle in the diagram.

If this industry is monopolistic, however, then the single firm faces the market demand curve and the indicated marginal revenue curve. To maximize its profit, the monopoly produces to the point at which marginal revenue equals marginal cost. Hence, the monopoly produces the quantity Q_M. It then charges the price that consumers are willing to pay, which is P_M. Consumer surplus thereby shrinks to the dashed triangle above this monopoly price. Hence, consumer welfare is lower under monopoly.

Monopolistic competition and oligopoly are more common types of industry structure than monopoly. Comparing the welfare implications of these structures directly with perfectly competition is a little more complicated, but under nearly all circumstances, the same basic conclusion follows: Imperfectly competitive industries typically yield lower consumer welfare than perfectly competitive industries.

For critical analysis: Does the monopoly capture the entire amount of the "lost" consumer surplus in the form of profit?

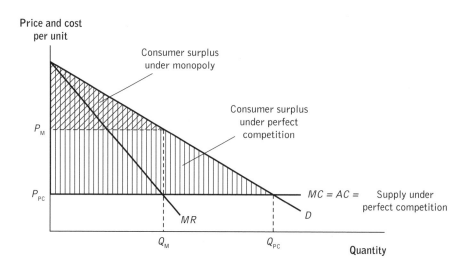

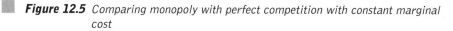

Figure 12.5 *Comparing monopoly with perfect competition with constant marginal cost*

The market demand curve in this diagram applies whether the industry is perfectly competitive or monopolistic. Marginal cost is constant, and hence also equals average cost, and is identical for each firm in the industry. Under perfect competition, therefore, the market supply curve is perfectly elastic. The market price, P_{PC}, is equal to marginal cost. Total industry output equals the quantity demanded at this price, Q_{PC}, and consumer surplus is the large shaded triangle in the diagram. If this industry is monopolistic, then the single firm faces the market demand curve and the corresponding downward-sloping marginal revenue curve. To maximize its profit, the monopoly produces to the point at which marginal revenue equals marginal cost. It produces the quantity Q_M and charges the price P_M, so consumer surplus declines to the dashed triangle above this monopoly price. Thus, consumer welfare is lower under monopoly, as compared with perfect competition.

Market structure and the prices of imports: Dumping revisited

Recall from Chapter 4 that an important type of import penalty that nations impose is antidumping duties. Under international law, a company engages in *dumping* if it sells its product abroad at a price that is either below the price that it charges in its home country, or below its per-unit production cost.

You have learned that under imperfect competition, it is commonplace for firms to charge prices higher than the market price in perfectly competitive industries. Now think about what is likely to happen if a perfectly competitive industry within a domestic nation suddenly confronts import competition from an imperfectly competitive industry located in a foreign country that protects its industries from international competition. Suppose that both industries have the same production costs. Because foreign firms are imperfectly competitive, the price they charge in their home country typically will be higher than the market price charged by perfectly competitive firms in the domestic country. The foreign firms, however, will only be able to sell their products in the domestic market at the lower domestic market price. Once they do, they automatically will engage in dumping as defined by international law, even though increased domestic import competition will benefit domestic consumers. (To learn how to use diagrams to examine why the logic of antidumping rules is problematic, see *Visualizing Global Economic Issues: Foreign monopoly and dumping in a domestic market—who gains, and who loses?*)

VISUALIZING GLOBAL ECONOMIC ISSUES

Foreign monopoly and dumping in a domestic market—who gains, and who loses?

To see why the logic of antidumping rules is problematic, take a look at Figure 12.6 (p. 405). Panel (a) shows a situation in which firms within a domestic industry are perfectly competitive and sell their output at the market price P_D^1. Panel (b) depicts the situation of a relatively large foreign monopoly that is protected from both home and international competition. In the foreign country, therefore, the foreign monopoly charges the price P_F^1 that foreign residents are willing to pay.

Suppose that the domestic market is opened to trade, but the foreign monopoly remains protected from international competition. As long as the domestic price exceeds the foreign firm's average production cost, the foreign firm can expand its profits by producing a higher output rate and selling additional units to domestic residents. Thus, the domestic supply curve shifts rightward in panel (a) by the amount of these foreign exports, which are assumed to be significant relative to total output in the domestic market. This pushes down the domestic price somewhat, to P_D^2. Although total domestic purchases increase to Q_D^2, the amount of output supplied by domestic firms declines to Q_D'. Hence, the foreign firm exports the amount $Q_D^2 - Q_D'$ to the domestic market, so its total production rises from Q_F^1

to $Q_F^2 = Q_F^1 + (Q_D^2 - Q_D')$. As shown in panel (b), the foreign firm continues to sell Q_F^1 units to foreign residents at the price P_F^1. Now, however, it generates additional profit by selling $Q_D^2 - Q_D'$ units to domestic residents at the new domestic market price P_D^2.

Because the foreign firm sells its product in the domestic country at the price P_D^2, which is below the price P_F^1 that it charges foreign residents, thereby earning this additional profit, the foreign firm has engaged in dumping. Domestic firms typically claim to have "lost" revenue equal to the sum of the areas labeled A, B, and C in panel (a). The area A is domestic revenue lost solely because of the market price reduction. The area B is revenue that the foreign firm receives from selling its output in the domestic market at the new market price; and the area C constitutes a transfer of revenue previously earned by domestic firms to the foreign firm. All three of these amounts, however, would normally constitute revenue losses for domestic firms as a result of opening the domestic market to foreign competition. Domestic consumers, of course, gain from the increased competition, because they are able to purchase more units of the good at a lower price.

Nevertheless, under World Trade Organization rules, the domestic country can impose an antidumping penalty on the foreign firm equal to the amount imported times the difference between the foreign market price P_F^1 and the domestic market price P_D^2. This is area E in panel (b). The size of area E, the antidumping penalty, could be as large as, or possibly even larger than, the additional profit that would induce the foreign firm to export additional output to the domestic country in the first place. It is for this reason that most economists regard antidumping rules as protectionist policies aimed primarily at restricting imports and protecting domestic firms from international competition.

For critical analysis: Sometimes companies charge that foreign firms sell some of their output in domestic markets at a price below their average production costs. Are there ever any circumstances in which this could be either a short-run or a long-run profit-maximizing strategy for these foreign firms?

Economic geography, industry structure, and trade

Traditionally, economists studying international trade have tended not to emphasize geographic constraints faced when nations' residents and firms decide whether to exchange goods and services across borders. Once industry structure is taken into account, however, it is difficult to ignore issues relating to the location of firms and their production facilities.

External economies and agglomeration

Most approaches to explaining international trade from an industrial organization perspective, such as the theory of intra-industry trade discussed earlier, emphasize

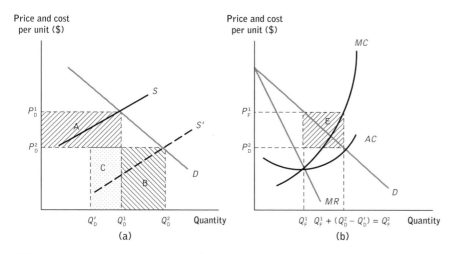

Figure 12.6 *Domestic dumping by a foreign monopoly*

In panel (a), firms in a domestic industry are perfectly competitive and sell their output at the market price P_D^1. In panel (b), a relatively large foreign monopoly that is protected from both home and international competition charges the price P_F^1. If the domestic market is opened to trade, then the foreign firm exports $Q_D^2 - Q_D'$ to the domestic market, so its total production rises from Q_F^1 to $Q_F^2 = Q_F^1 + (Q_D^2 - Q_D')$ in panel (b). The domestic supply curve to shifts to the right in panel (a), which causes the domestic price P_D^2 and total output sold domestically to increase to Q_D^2. The amount of output supplied by domestic firms declines to Q_D'. The foreign price P_F^1 exceeds the domestic price P_D^2, so the foreign firm has engaged in dumping. Area A in panel (a) is domestic revenue lost solely because of the market price reduction; area B is revenue that the foreign firm receives from selling its output in the domestic market at the new market price; and area C is a transfer of revenue previously earned by domestic firms to the foreign firm. Area E in panel (b) equals the amount imported times the difference between the foreign market price P_F^1 and the domestic market price P_D^2, which is the potential antidumping penalty under current world trade rules.

the role of economies of scale within firms, which economists call *internal* scale economies. Nevertheless, the late-nineteenth- and early-twentieth-century economist Alfred Marshall also suggested a possible role for **external economies** arising from locating a firm near important resources, such as skilled workers, capital resources, or required raw materials. Marshall theorized that physical placement of a firm close to key inputs would enable it to reduce its average costs of production.

Of course, if a number of firms were to seek out external economies by locating near the same key inputs, the result would be a cluster of firms and industries utilizing those common factors of production. Economists refer to the formation of clusters of related industries employing common inputs as **agglomeration**. The optimal degree of agglomeration arises from firms balancing gains from external economies relative to costs associated with agglomeration, such as congestion arising from numerous firms operating in close proximity to productive factors.

External economies:
Cost reductions obtained from locating a firm's operations near factors that are external to the firm, such as skilled labor, capital resources, or research and development facilities.

405

Geography and international trade

Economists often apply the concepts of external economies and agglomeration to help explain the existence and structure of cities. After all, if many firms in related industries locate close to common resources such as labor, capital, and raw materials, then people seeking employment with those firms and other businesses will tend to congregate in the same vicinity. The productive activities associated with agglomerated industries, other things being equal, take place in an urban area near the area's center, or *core*. Economic activities associated with exchange among residents of the urban area and its surroundings not driven by external economies will then occur at and beyond the outer edges of the core, or in the *periphery* of the area. Hence, applying the ideas of external economies and agglomeration naturally leads to a *core–periphery model* of economic geography explaining the existence of cities, smaller communities, and rural areas.

By definition, the world's nations confront a geographic environment defined in large part by their political borders, some of which are shared with other nations and others of which are bounded by bodies of water such as seas and oceans. Extending the ideas of external economies and agglomeration to international trade entails considering collections of geographic regions possessing cores and peripheries. Various sets of these regions comprise independent political states, or nations. The portion of the cross-regional exchanges of goods and services that also passes across national borders constitutes international trade.

Distance and trade costs

A key feature of physical geography is distance. Firms in an industry producing a particular item may cluster within a core of a region within one nation, but firms producing a similar item may cluster in the core of a region within another nation located some distance away. If costs of trading over the substantial distance separating the two agglomerations are substantial, then international trade involving products of these agglomerations may not take place. If trading costs over the physical distance separating the agglomerations decline sufficiently, international trade may take place even though the goods are similar. Thus, combining external economies and agglomeration with varying trade costs can help to explain why intra-industry trade may or may not occur, irrespective of traditional economies of scale that are internal to firms.

In principle, external economies and agglomeration can also help to explain the pattern of specializations in production and advantages in trade. A possible geographic explanation for why the entire industry producing a particular item is based in a single country might be that this nation's entire industry realizes external economies by locating within a region in that country. As all firms within that industry move to congregate near a key input, agglomeration occurs. Production of the item becomes centered within the core of a region within that nation, and the nation develops a specialization in trading that item internationally. In this way, political and

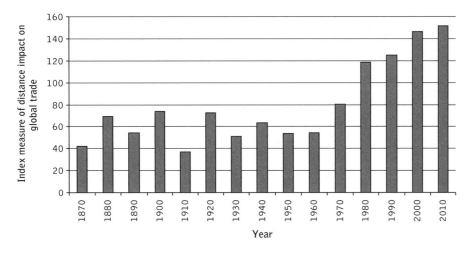

Figure 12.7 *An index measure of the estimated distance effect on international trade*

In spite of major technological developments in transportation and communication, since the mid-twentieth century the estimated magnitude of the distance effect on international trade has increased.

Source: Combes et al. (2008).

physical aspects of the global geographic environment can contribute to understanding inter-industry as well as intra-industry trade.

There has long been considerable evidence that a greater distance for goods and services to traverse reduces international trade. Figure 12.7 provides estimates of the distance effect over several decades as reported by Pierre-Philippe Combes of the University of Aix-Marseilles, Thierry Mayer of Sciences Po Paris, and Jacques-François Thisse of the Catholic University of Louvain. In accordance with results of most other studies, their estimate is that, even as the world's economy has become more interconnected, both offline and online, the size of the distance effect on trade has increased. (Economists have been trying to understand more fully why this distance effect apparently has strengthened even as the world has become more interconnected; see *Management Notebook: The mysteriously growing importance of distance in international trade.*)

MANAGEMENT NOTEBOOK

The mysteriously growing importance of distance in international trade

To understand motions of stars and planets, astronomers must take into account gravity, the fundamental attractive force that varies directly with the masses of two objects and inversely with the distance between the objects. During the past several decades, economists have applied the relationship between gravity, size, and distance to international trade by analyzing the extent to which bilateral international trade flows vary directly with the sizes of two nations, and inversely with the distances between them. Motivations for this idea are that larger nations are more likely to offer wider arrays of goods and services for trade, and engaging in trade is likely to be less costly if the countries are relatively close together. Economists have tested the idea by estimating so-called *gravity equations* hypothesizing a dependence of trade flows on countries' sizes and distances, while taking into account other elements such as comparative advantage, cultural factors, and language barriers. These equations have provided evidence that bilateral trade flows really do vary—other things being equal—positively with country size and negatively with distance between countries.

Based on an analysis of results from more than 100 economic studies, Anne-Célia Disdier of UMR Economie Publique and Keith Head of the University of British Columbia have documented a persistence—and, indeed, potential widening—of the distance effect on international trade flows since the middle of the twentieth century. To many economists, this trend appears perplexing given the growth in interconnectedness of the global economy.

As discussed by Lars Håkanson of the Copenhagen Business School and Douglas Dow of the University of Queensland, there are two competing explanations for the apparently greater role of distance as a determinant of trade flows. One, called the *network view*, suggests that over time a larger portion of international trade has involved goods and services that require more exchanges of information, and hence more personal interactions among buyers and sellers. The other explanation, called the *market view*, suggests that greater availability of information and greater openness of markets has led to increased matching of buyers and sellers who are physically closer to each other. Håkanson and Dow argue that distance effects can be split into two types: a traditional geographic distance effect related to transportation costs, and a "psychic" distance effect arising from information-related transaction costs. Based on a study of bilateral trade involving a set of 25 nations, they find evidence that geographic distance costs have increased over time for some goods and changed only slightly for others. In contrast, psychic distance costs have decreased substantially. Håkanson and Dow suggest that these results support the market view for why the distance effect appears to have become more important. In their view, the distance effect appears to have become more important because markets have become more efficient, leading to more trade with buyers and sellers who reside in nearby locales.

For critical analysis: What would you expect would happen to the magnitude of the trade distance effect if global transportation costs were to decrease substantially during the next decade?

Fundamental Issue #4: What are alternative industry structures, and how does industry structure matter in the global economy? Under perfect competition, many firms produce indistinguishable products and can enter or leave the industry with ease. Monopolistically competitive industries also have many firms and easy entry or exit, but each firm's product is easy to distinguish from the products of other firms. Oligopoly is an imperfectly competitive industry structure characterized by barriers to entry that reduce the number of firms. In the extreme case of monopoly, there is a single firm in the market. As compared with perfect competition, monopoly leads to a reduction in industry output and an increase in the product price, which lead to lower consumer welfare, either within nations or across nations. Differences in market structures across countries complicate evaluating the effects of trade policies such as antidumping penalties. When external economies arising from physical locations of firms are significant, clusters of firms and industries drawing on common key resources called industrial agglomerations can develop within nations. Substantial costs of trade over distances separating agglomerated industries can deter trade, but declines in trade costs can lead to intra-industry trade involving similar products or can contribute to specialization and trading advantage for a nation with an industry agglomeration.

EVALUATING THE COMPETITIVE IMPLICATIONS OF INDUSTRY STRUCTURE

Many companies located in different nations have sought to combine their operations within the past several years. In some cases, the companies involved in these proposed combinations have been very large. Let's think about why such companies might wish to merge, and let's also think about the possible consequences of combining companies across national borders.

Motivations for cross-border mergers and acquisitions

In recent years there has been a burst of cross-border activity in corporate mergers and acquisitions. For instance, Fiat of Italy acquired a majority ownership of Chrysler Corporation of the United States, and the French media giant Vivendi acquired the North American company Seagram, Inc. and then sold it to another French firm. In addition, Deutsche Bank of Germany acquired the U.S. bank Bankers Trust, and the French carmaker Renault acquired portions of the assets of Samsung Motors of Korea.

Traditional justifications for combining companies

Traditionally, there are two essential reasons why companies wish to engage in mergers and acquisitions. One is to combine the resources of firms to assist in achieving economies of scale within a single new company. The resulting cost efficiencies enhance the overall performance of the combined entities.

The other traditional rationale for mergers and acquisitions is that a combined firm may be able to earn higher revenues. Realizing economies of scale from the consolidation of the operations of two or more firms leads to expanded production within the new firm, which may increase total revenue at the combined entity. In addition, consolidating operations through a merger or acquisition may give the newly combined company greater power to push up product prices, thereby enhancing revenue.

Corporate governance in cross-border mergers and acquisitions

Interestingly, in some recent cross-border mergers and acquisitions, another objective appears to have been to alter the nature of *corporate governance*, which is the legal and institutional framework under which companies operate. In some countries, such as the United States, *public companies* are commonplace, and ownership shares are widely distributed among national residents. In others, such as Germany, *private companies* owned by an inside group of partners are more common, and ownership of public companies is often more narrowly distributed among a limited set of wealthy individuals.

In recent years a consensus has emerged among many management experts that publicly owned companies with widely dispersed owners tend to react more flexibly to changes in the marketplace. This conclusion does not rule out the potential for some private companies to outperform public companies. Nevertheless, it has caused many residents of countries where private companies or more narrowly held public companies predominate to contemplate changing the structures of their companies. One speedy way for companies to do this is through mergers with or acquisitions of public companies located in countries where there are numerous shareholders. A number of observers believe that this desire to develop a broader public structure helps explain why Fiat acquired majority ownership of Chrysler, why Deutsche Bank acquired Bankers Trust, and why Deutsche Telecom has sought to acquire U.S. telecommunications companies.

Assessing market concentration and its effects

Do larger firms that compete with fewer rivals necessarily behave in ways that significantly reduce consumer welfare? Unfortunately, there is no consensus about the answer to this question. One fundamental reason is that economists do not agree about just how large firms must be relative to the rest of the market before they can exert effects on market prices. Another reason, however, is that competition from international sources can complicate efforts to define a "market."

Measuring market concentration

Concentration ratio: *The share of total industry sales by the top few firms.*

Traditionally, economists have sought to measure whether a few firms account for a large portion of industry output using **concentration ratios**, which are the portions of total industry sales accounted for by the largest few firms. The most commonly examined concentration ratio is the four-firm concentration ratio, or the percentage of total sales at the top four firms in the market.

An obvious problem with concentration ratios is that they can fail to reflect important differences among structures of different industries. For example, suppose that the top four firms in two different markets each have a 20 percent share within each market, so that the four-firm concentration ratio for each industry is 80 percent. In one of the markets, however, there might be just one more firm, so that rivalry within the market is limited to a total of five firms. In the other market, there might be ten more firms equally sharing the remaining 20 percent of industry sales and attempting to compete actively with the top four companies.

Partly in response to this and to other perceived problems with simple concentration ratios, beginning in the early 1980s the U.S. Department of Justice and Federal Trade Commission began emphasizing a different concentration measure. This measure, called the **Herfindahl–Hirschman index**, is the sum of the squared market shares for all firms in an industry. For the example of a five-firm industry with a 20 percent market share at each firm, this would yield a Herfindahl–Hirschman-index value of 2,000. For the case of the industry in which the top four firms have 20 percent market shares while ten others each have a 2 percent share, the value would be 1,640. The lower index value for the latter industry would thereby reflect its greater potential for more broad-based competition among a relatively large set of producers.

Herfindahl–Hirschman index: *The sum of the squares of the market shares of each firm in an industry.*

Naturally, how high a concentration ratio or Herfindahl–Hirschman-index value must be to indicate that individual firms are likely to have significant power to affect market prices is a judgment call. Even more problematic, however, is that concentration ratios or Herfindahl–Hirschman-index values have meaning only if they are calculated using correctly defined markets. For instance, one might find that the four-firm concentration ratio for the cable-modem Internet-access industry is very high in many areas. Indeed, in most areas where cable-modem service is available there are likely to be fewer than five providers of cable-modem Internet access, so a four-firm concentration ratio of 100 percent is likely to be common. Most economists would agree, however, that this ratio would be meaningless, because the **relevant market**—the true economic marketplace taking into account the availability of all products that directly constrain product prices for individual producers—surely includes other providers of Internet access, such as traditional phone-dial-up providers, providers of Internet direct service lines, and satellite-service providers.

Relevant market: *The true economic marketplace taking into account the availability of all products that directly constrain product prices for individual producers.*

Defining markets: Where does geography fit in?

Because they complicate determining the scope of the relevant market, cross-border mergers and acquisitions add an additional challenge to evaluating the degree of market competition. In nations with borders open to international trade, the availability of close international substitutes for domestically produced goods and services can help restrain the pricing power of domestic sellers. Applying concentration measures only to domestic markets could therefore be misleading.

The presence of significant international competition can complicate government policies regarding mergers. Consider, for instance, the recent experience of the Canadian banking industry. For all its massive geographic size, Canada's population is slightly smaller than California's. The nation has four dominant, Toronto-based banking institutions—the Royal Bank of Canada, the Bank of Montreal, the Toronto-Dominion Bank, and the Canadian Imperial Bank of Commerce—which serve as depositories for two-thirds of all funds in Canadian banks. Recently, these four institutions proposed merging into two, with Royal Bank of Canada set to merge with the Bank of Montreal and the Toronto-Dominion Bank poised to merge with the Canadian Imperial Bank of Commerce. The four institutions wanted to consolidate to assist in fending off competition from big U.S. banks. They also wanted to embark on an effort to compete more successfully in the United States, thereby geographically diversifying their operations.

The Canadian government disallowed both merger requests, however, ruling that the "relevant banking market" was Canada alone. For the banks that had proposed to merge, this was a serious blow to their long-range plans regarding their ability to compete effectively in the *international* banking markets that they felt were most relevant.

Fundamental Issue #5: Why do companies engage in cross-border mergers and acquisitions, and how do international market linkages complicate measuring the degree to which a few large firms may dominate markets? Common justifications for cross-border mergers are that combining the operations of previously independent companies can reduce average costs for the new entity and that a gain in pricing power can allow the merged firm to earn higher revenues than two firms could have earned alone. In some instances, companies have engaged in cross-border mergers in an effort to alter the nature of corporate governance. To gauge the extent to which market concentration may influence the pricing power of firms, economists use concentration ratios (or the portion of sales by the top firms in the market) and the Herfindahl–Hirschman index (or the sum of squares of the market shares of all firms). Interpreting these concentration measures is problematic, especially in light of difficulties in defining the relevant market for calculating either measure.

ANTITRUST IN AN EVOLVING GLOBAL SYSTEM

Antitrust laws: *Statutes designed to achieve benefits of competition for consumers and producers.*

Governments seek to influence the extent of market competition using **antitrust laws**. These legal statutes are aimed at ensuring that consumers and producers experience benefits of market competition within the context of broader national economic policies.

The goals of antitrust laws

In years past, countries have concentrated on enforcing antitrust laws within national borders. As relevant markets have expanded to include foreign firms, however, antitrust policy has increasingly become a global issue.

Traditionally, a fundamental goal of antitrust laws has been to limit the pricing power available to firms. Because cartels have an incentive to enrich participating firms at the expense of consumer welfare and economic efficiency, many antitrust laws explicitly prohibit efforts by combinations of firms to restrain market competition. Indeed, most national antitrust laws make it a crime even to try to form a monopoly.

It is also common for antitrust laws to restrict **price discrimination**. One type of price discrimination entails charging different consumers different prices for identical goods. Another involves charging the same consumer different prices for the same good, depending on the number of units that the consumer purchases. Many nations also prohibit efforts to engage in so-called **predatory pricing**, in which firms are alleged to reduce their prices to drive competitors out of business and dissuade potential rivals from entering the marketplace. Antitrust laws seeking to restrain price discrimination and predatory pricing often generate controversy, because it is not unusual for enforcement of these laws to raise market prices.

In some nations, the balancing act between protecting consumers and promoting the interests of producers is complicated by **industrial policies**. These are government policies that aim actively to promote the development of specific industries. For instance, in 2000 the Japanese government decided that a key national goal was for Japan to have the world's foremost Internet infrastructure by 2005. This obliged the government to establish a regulatory framework consistent with attaining global leadership for its mobile phone and broadband-Internet industries. Industrial policies such as this can become entangled with antitrust enforcement to the benefit of producers, because by pursuing these policies, governments often facilitate interactions among competing firms. This can lay the groundwork for implicit governmental sanctioning of cartel arrangements. (In spite of the potential pitfalls, a growing number of national governments are engaging in industrial policies; see *Policy Notebook: Industrial policies make a comeback*.)

Price discrimination: *Charging different consumers different prices for identical goods or services, or charging the same consumer different prices for the same good or service depending on the number of units that the consumer purchases.*

Predatory pricing: *A situation in which a firm sets artificially low prices intended to induce competitors to leave the industry and to dissuade potential rivals from entering the industry.*

Industrial policies: *Government policies intended to promote the development of specific national industries.*

POLICY NOTEBOOK

Industrial policies make a comeback

During the 1970s and 1980s, industrial policies were very popular around the globe. National governments actively promoted handpicked industries with an aim to make them "national champions" in global marketplaces. Typically, governmental involvement in pressing the agendas of specific home industries in international markets were rationalized as necessary in the face of numerous market imperfections or even failures—problems that allegedly prevented private markets from allowing firms in some countries from competing on an even footing with companies in other nations. The economist Dani Rodrik has summarized what he calls the "strong case for industrial policy (in theory)":

It is if anything too easy to make the case for industrial policy. Few development economists doubt that the market imperfections on which the theoretical arguments for industrial policy *do* exist, and that they are often pervasive. Collateral constraints combined with asymmetric information result in credit market imperfections and incomplete insurance. Problems with monitoring efforts result in labor-market arrangements that are less than efficient. Learning spills over from producers who adopt new processes. Labor can move from employer to employer, taking their on-the-job training with them. Many projects tend to be lumpy relative to the size of the economy, requiring coordination. And so on.

(Rodrik, 2008: p. 5)

Nevertheless, by the end of the 1980s, the governments of a number of nations had concluded that the tools typically utilized to promote the interests of particular national industries, which included domestic subsidies, domestic taxes and tariffs, and sometimes even quotas on imports from abroad, created other forms of market imperfections. Furthermore, government officials often turned out to be no better than private investors at forecasting what industries were more likely to succeed or fail. Many governments ultimately concluded that the pursuit of industrial policies created costs for society that often exceeded those arising from the originally perceived market imperfections that industrial policies were intended to address. Consequently, interest in industrial policies ebbed in the 1990s and 2000s.

During the past few years, the global public-policy pendulum has swung back in toward more interest in pursuing industrial policies. China's government has actively pursued policies aimed at promoting its steel industry, and France's government has provided a range of subsidies intended to support industries ranging from agriculture to finance. Even the U.S. government has joined the industrial policy bandwagon in its efforts to promote firms producing auto batteries and all-electric vehicles. So far, there have been few payoffs, with government-promoted industries in China and France contracting following initially large growth spurts. In the face of weak demand for electric vehicles, U.S. battery firms have failed to reach even half of the required scale to operate at lowest feasible per-unit cost, and most all-electric vehicle manufacturers have been operating at losses of about $10,000 per auto produced. Several U.S. government-supported firms have failed outright and closed their operations. Similarly mixed results or outright failures have resulted in other nations as well. Thus, it remains to be seen how much longer the latest governmental forays into industrial policies will persist.

For critical analysis: When private investors are incorrect in their predictions about what industries will thrive in the future, the funds provided by private individuals for those investments are lost. Whose funds are lost when government officials make bad bets on specific industries?

Antitrust enforcement across national boundaries

How should national antitrust authorities define the relevant market if AT&T decides that it wishes to merge with British Telecommunications, or if Germany's Deutsche Telecom wants to acquire Sprint? How should they have reacted when Time Warner simultaneously attempted to merge with EMI, one of the world's largest recorded-music companies?

These are not just rhetorical questions, as U.S. and EU antitrust authorities learned in the 2000s when all these issues surfaced. The emergence of cross-border markets for many goods and services has increasingly made antitrust policy a global undertaking.

Clashing goals of antitrust enforcement

When U.S. authorities approved the acquisitions of Bankers Trust by Deutsche Bank, and of Chrysler by Fiat, they did so after careful study of relevant markets in automobiles and banking. The relevant market for each industry, U.S. regulators determined, had become sufficiently globally based that these combinations would not have anticompetitive consequences for U.S. consumers.

In 2000, however, EU antitrust authorities ruled against a proposed combination of Time Warner and EMI, which it had appeared the U.S. antitrust authorities were on the way to approving. A year later, EU policymakers decided against approving another planned merger—in this case, one that U.S. regulators had already endorsed—between two large multinational corporations, General Electric and Honeywell International. These cases highlight a significant problem for antitrust enforcement across national borders: conflicting objectives of national antitrust policies.

In the United States, the overriding goal of merger policies is to protect the interests of consumers. This is also a formal objective of EU antitrust efforts. In the EU, however, there is also a requirement that policymakers must reject any merger that "creates or strengthens a dominant position as a result of which effective competition would be significantly impeded." This additional clause currently creates a tension between U.S. and EU policymaking. In the United States, increasing dominance of a market by a single firm raises the concern of antitrust authorities, but U.S. authorities will remain passive if they determine that greater market dominance arises from factors such as exceptional management and greater cost efficiencies that ultimately benefit consumers by reducing prices. By way of contrast, under EU rules antitrust authorities are obliged to block any merger that increases the dominance of any producer, irrespective of what factors motivate its pre-eminence in the marketplace.

ON THE WEB:

To learn more about antitrust policies in various nations, go to www.international antitrust.com.

Will antitrust go global?

The EU's scuttling of the proposed General Electric–Honeywell merger raised concerns in the United States, where during the late 1990s antitrust authorities had given the green light to several mergers between U.S. and EU firms, and to acquisitions of U.S. firms by EU companies. Some U.S. critics argued that the European Union's leadership was using antitrust policy as a weapon of protectionism. The real aim of EU antitrust policies, they claimed, was to prevent U.S. firms from broadening their competitive positions within Europe even as European companies were acquiring U.S. firms.

During the 2000s, EU and U.S. antitrust authorities responded to these criticisms by resolving to strengthen bilateral cooperation in an effort to reduce the risk of future policy disagreements. EU and U.S. policymakers increased the extent of existing interactions among staff lawyers and economists. They also broadened the scope of discussions of methods for harmonizing their approaches to evaluating and enforcing policies governing proposed cross-border mergers and acquisitions.

The initiation of these bilateral efforts encouraged some antitrust experts to propose widening the scope of interactions to a multilateral discussion of appropriate antitrust goals, rules, and enforcement mechanisms. So far, however, multilateral cooperation among the world's antitrust authorities remains a goal rather than a reality.

Fundamental Issue #6: How do governments regulate international merger and acquisition activities? Governments often authorize antitrust authorities with the power to determine whether proposed cross-border mergers and acquisitions will affect the pricing power of firms. Antitrust authorities commonly enforce rules limiting price discrimination or prohibiting predatory pricing. In some nations, antitrust enforcement is complicated by national industrial policies, which aim to promote particular domestic industries. Recently, conflicting objectives of antitrust policies in the United States and the European Union have led to inconsistent decisions about proposed mergers among companies based in those regions of the world. This has led to proposals for coordinated policymaking among U.S. and EU antitrust authorities when firms propose cross-border mergers or acquisitions, but so far, this idea has not advanced beyond the stage of general discussions.

CHAPTER SUMMARY

1. How economies of scale help to explain a nation's specialization in inter-industry trade: Economies of scale arise for a firm or an industry whenever long-run average cost falls as increased usage of all factors of production expands total output. Long-run average cost is minimized at the minimum efficient scale of a firm or industry, beyond which any additional rise in output would increase long-run average cost. Countries containing firms that have already experienced economies of scale will have lower average production costs than firms in other countries when international trade is permitted. Thus, these countries are more readily able to specialize in producing the good or service of that particular industry.

2. **How economies of scale and product variety assist in explaining intra-industry trade:** Under conditions of monopolistic competition, firms produce a variety of easily distinguishable yet similar products, and it is easy for firms to enter or leave the industry whenever revenue rises above or falls below the opportunity cost of being in that industry instead of another. Opening borders to international trade induces a typical monopolistically competitive firm to raise its output. It experiences economies of scale, so it can reduce the price of its product to attract customers in the face of increased intra-industry competition from firms abroad. Horizontal foreign direct investment has contributed to higher global capital flows, but the main way that foreign direct investment has added to intra-industry trade is through vertical investment. Multinational companies that undertake vertical investment transport product components across national borders, and these flows are counted in international trade statistics.

3. **How foreign direct investment affects international trading patterns:** Companies that establish facilities abroad that produce goods or services similar to products of facilities located in their home country engage in horizontal foreign direct investment. In contrast, companies placing facilities that handle products at various stages of production in different nations engage in vertical foreign direct investment. Increased horizontal foreign direct investment has boosted global capital flows but has had relatively small effects on international trade. Greater vertical foreign direct investment can bring about sizable increases in intra-industry trade as firms transfer product components between nations.

4. **Alternative industry structures, and how industry structure matters in the global economy:** Under perfect competition, many firms produce indistinguishable products, and they can enter or leave the industry with ease. Monopolistically competitive industries also have many firms and easy entry or exit, but each firm's product is easy to distinguish from the products of other firms. Oligopoly is an imperfectly competitive industry structure that is characterized by barriers to entry that reduce the number of firms. In the extreme case of monopoly, there is a single firm in the market. As compared with perfect competition, monopoly leads to a reduction in industry output and an increase in the product price, which lead to lower consumer welfare. Differences in national industry structures can complicate evaluating the effects of trade policies such as antidumping penalties. Another factor influencing industry structures across nations is external economies, or reductions in average costs that may occur when firms select common physical locations that enable them to utilize key resources, resulting in industrial agglomerations within geographic regions. Significant trade costs over distances between agglomerated industries can deter trade, but decreases in costs of trade theoretically can foster either intra-industry or inter-industry trade.

5. **Why companies desire to merge across borders, and how international market linkages complicate measuring the market concentration:** One traditional rationale for cross-border mergers is that the new entity may be able to operate at lower average cost than the previously separate companies. Another is that the combination may be able to take advantage of greater pricing power and earn higher revenues than two firms could have earned alone. Companies may also engage in international mergers to take advantage of cross-country differences in the structure of corporate governance.

417

One way in which economists attempt to measure the degree of market concentration is via concentration ratios, which is the percentage of total industry sales by top firms. Another is the Herfindahl–Hirschman index, which is the sum of squares of the market shares of all firms. Using either measure requires subjective judgments, and correctly defining the relevant market for applying the measures can be difficult.

6. **How governments regulate international merger and acquisition activities:** Typically, national governments give antitrust officials the authority to decide if proposed cross-border mergers or acquisitions are appropriate. The effect of mergers and acquisitions on domestic prices is usually the main focus of antitrust policies, but in many nations antitrust authorities also enforce laws restraining price discrimination, forbidding predatory pricing, or enforcing industrial policies that seek to support specific domestic industries. In the early 2000s, differing U.S. and EU antitrust goals caused antitrust authorities for the two regions to reach conflicting conclusions regarding proposed mergers among multinational firms. This has led to preliminary discussions of possible coordination of U.S. and EU antitrust policies.

QUESTIONS AND PROBLEMS

1. Some economists have argued that U.S. e-commerce firms such as eBay.com and Amazon.com have a comparative advantage over Internet-based rivals located abroad, which the U.S. companies derive from their ability to offer differentiated products in relatively greater volumes at relatively lower average cost as they expand the long-run scale of their operations. Without taking a stand on whether this argument may be "correct," use appropriate diagrams to explain why this might be a viable hypothesis for the currently dominant position of many U.S. firms in cross-border Internet-based trade.

2. Suppose that the market for U.S. e-commerce services such as those discussed in question 1 is monopolistically competitive. In addition, however, suppose that experience proves that e-commerce firms located in the United States and elsewhere have essentially identical long-run average costs, which initially decline but eventually increase as firms expand their scale of operations. Assume that short-run and long-run costs at a typical U.S. e-commerce firm are identical, and explain how the demand faced by the firm is likely to be affected if foreign e-commerce firms begin offering products to U.S. consumers even as the U.S. firm broadens its capability to market its products to residents of other nations via the Internet. What are the effects on the U.S. firm's rate of production and on the price it charges for its product?

3. Previously, a domestic market containing monopolistically competitive firms was open to foreign competition. Domestic firms have succeeded, however, in convincing their government to close the nation's borders to foreign competition. As a result, foreign nations have responded by prohibiting the sale of the products of domestic firms within their borders as well. Evaluate the effects of these domestic and foreign policy actions on the production and pricing decisions of a domestic producer.

4. In your own words, distinguish horizontal foreign direct investment from vertical foreign direct investment.

5. A nation has experienced a large increase in foreign direct investment, and measured capital inflows have increased dramatically. So far, however, the country's trade flows have not changed. Provide a possible explanation.

6. Recently, a nation opened its borders to movements of all goods and services, including factors of production. Its government has observed jumps in the rates of growth in measured imports and exports far in excess of increases that could have resulted from greater purchases of final goods and services by consumers at home and abroad. Speculate about other factors that might have contributed to this nation's significant increases in measured imports and exports.

7. In the global market for a good, for a number of years there have been only a few producers, each of which produces an indistinguishable product. What type of market structure is this? What factors could explain this structure?

8. A domestic industry has been able to prove that a foreign producer engaged in dumping. The foreign producer's counterargument is that it has charged higher prices in its home market simply because this is its profit-maximizing strategy in its home market where barriers to entry have given it monopoly pricing power, whereas it faces considerable competition in the domestic market and hence charges a lower price for its product in that market. Explain why this might be a reasonable economic argument, yet might do little to fend off the imposition of antidumping penalties under current international antidumping rules.

9. Consider these fictitious sales data for domestic and foreign firms, and answer the questions that follow.

Domestic sales of domestic firms				Domestic sales of foreign firms			
Firm	Sales	%	%^{2}	Firm	Sales	%	%^{2}
1	750	7.5	56.25	7	4,200	42.0	1764.00
2	50	0.5	0.25	8	2,000	20.0	400.00
3	50	0.5	0.25	9	1,950	19.5	380.25
4	50	0.5	0.25	10	450	4.5	20.25
5	50	0.5	0.25	11	400	4.0	16.00
6	50	0.5	0.25				
Total	1,000			Total	9,000		

Sales are in millions of units of the national currency.

% denotes percentage of domestic and foreign share of total domestic sales, rounded to the nearest tenth of one percentage point.

%^{2} denotes squared percentage of market share of sales.

(a) Domestic producers 1–6 and foreign firms 7–11 produce similar but distinguishable products. Currently, antitrust authorities define the relevant market to include both domestic and foreign firms. Calculate the four-firm concentration ratios and Herfindahl–Hirschman indexes under this definition of the relevant market.

(b) Now suppose that antitrust authorities determine that the relevant market includes only domestic producers. Recalculate the market shares and squared market shares implied by the table under this definition of the relevant market, and use these data to calculate the four-firm concentration ratio and Herfindahl–Hirschman indexes.

(c) What do your answers to (a) and (b) reveal about the importance to antitrust policy of correctly determining the relevant market for a product? Explain.

10. It seems sensible that trade costs should be positively related to the distances between nations. Explain, however, how it might be feasible for costs of trade to decrease for any given distance. In addition, explain how lower trade costs for any given distance could contribute to greater intra- and inter-industry trade.

ONLINE APPLICATION

URL: www.justice.gov/atr/icpac/finalreport.html

Title: Final Report of the International Competition Policy Advisory Committee

Navigation: Go to the home page of the Antitrust Division of the U.S. Department of Justice (www.usdoj.gov/atr). Then click on "Public Documents," and next click on "International Program." Under the heading "Policy Documents, Reports, and Updates," click on "International Competition Policy Advisory Committee (ICPAC)," and finally on "ICPAC Final Report."

Application: Perform the indicated operations, and answer the questions.

1. Click on "Chapter 3—Multijurisdictional Mergers: Rationalizing the Merger Review Process Through Targeted Reform." Take a look at Box 3-A, which gives information about the "merger challenge rate" in selected countries and regions. Suppose that a multinational corporation considering acquiring a firm within these nations regarded the challenge rates of its antitrust authorities as measures of the probability that national policymakers would dispute a proposed acquisition. In which area would the multinational corporation regard its chances of running into difficulties in acquiring a firm to be highest? Lowest?

2. Now consider Box 3-B, which gives approximate dollar values of worldwide sales for a proposed combination of companies that trigger a requirement for firms to provide notification of planned mergers or acquisitions to antitrust authorities within selected countries. How might these notification requirements influence the choice of a foreign firm seeking to expand globally by finding a merger partner or an acquisition target?

For group study and analysis: Assign the above chapter as a reading for the entire class. Then divide the class into three fictitious "countries," denoted A, B, and C. Antitrust goals of each country are as follows: A—maximize consumer welfare; B—minimize the dominance of any one firm; and C—protect domestic industries from foreign competition. Have each group draft a one-paragraph "policy guideline" for judging mergers and acquisitions within its country. Reconvene the class, and compare the guidelines developed by each group. Discuss why differing objectives may help explain significant national differences in antitrust rules and their enforcement.

REFERENCES AND RECOMMENDED READINGS

Broda, Christian, and David Weinstein."Are We Underestimating the Gains from Globalization for the United States?" Federal Reserve Bank of New York *Current Issues in Economics and Finance* 11 (April 2005).

Brülhart, Marius. "An Account of Global Intra-Industry Trade, 1962–2006." *World Economy* 32 (2009): 401–459.

Carlton, Dennis, and Jeffrey Perloff. *Modern Industrial Organization*, 4th edn. Reading, MA: Addison-Wesley-Longman, 2005.

Choi, Jai-Young, and S.H. Yu."External Economies in International Trade Theory: A Survey." *Review of International Economics* 10 (2002): 708–728.

Cimoli, Mario, Giovanni Dosi, and Joseph Stiglitz, eds. *Industrial Policy and Development*. Oxford, U.K.: Oxford University Press, 2009.

Combes, Pierre-Philippe, Thierry Mayer, and Jacques-François Thisse. *Economic Geography: The Integration of Regions and Nations*. Princeton, NJ: Princeton University Press, 2008.

Disdier, Anne-Célia, and Keith Head. "The Puzzling Persistence of the Distance Effect on Bilateral Trade." *Review of Economics and Statistics* 90 (February 2008): 37–48.

Evenett, Simon, Alexander Lehmann, and Benn Steil, eds. *Antitrust Goes Global*. London: Blackwell, 2000.

Feenstra, Robert. *Product Variety and the Gains from International Trade*. Cambridge, MA: MIT Press, 2010.

Grossman, Gene, and Estaban Ross-Hansberg. "External Economies and International Trade Redux." *Quarterly Journal of Economics* 125 (2010): 829–858.

Håkanson, Lars, and Douglas Dow. "Markets and Networks in International Trade: On the Role of Distances in Globalization." *Management International Review* 52 (2012): 761–789.

Krugman, Paul. *Rethinking International Trade*. Cambridge, MA: MIT Press, 2000.

Morici, Peter. *Antitrust in the Global Trading System*. Washington, DC: Economic Strategy Institute, 2000.

Pack, Howard, and Kamal Saggi. "Is There a Case for Industrial Policy? A Critical Survey." *World Bank Research Observer* 21 (Fall 2006): 267–297.

Ramanarayanan, Ananth. "Distance and the Impact of 'Gravity' Help Explain Patterns of International Trade." Federal Reserve Bank of Dallas *Economic Letter* 6 (July 2011).

Rodrik, Dani. "Normalizing Industrial Policy." Working Paper No. 3. Washington, DC: Commission on Growth and Development, 2008.

Utton, Michael. *International Competition Policy: Maintaining Open Markets in the Global Economy*. Cheltenham, U.K.: Edward Elgar, 2006.

Chapter 13

The public sector in the global economy

FUNDAMENTAL ISSUES

1. In what ways do government regulators seek to safeguard the interests of consumers?
2. How do the world's governments protect rights to intellectual property?
3. What are international externalities and global public goods, and what can national governments or multinational institutions do about them?
4. How can the world's nations protect the global environment?
5. How does increased globalization complicate the efforts of governments to finance their activities?

Between 2011 and 2014, the governments of most European nations imposed a variety of increases in tax rates. Italy's government, for instance, imposed a special tax rate on the assessed market value of luxury automobiles. The French and Spanish governments enacted the most substantial increases in tax rates, however. In France, the government raised the top income tax rate by a factor of more than one-half, to 75 percent. The Spanish government instituted a "wealth tax," under which the government applied a tax rate to the outstanding assets—funds in accounts at financial institutions, physical property, and even intellectual property—of its wealthiest residents.

The aim of these tax-rate increases, of course, was to generate more tax revenues for the governments that imposed the rate hikes. In Italy, however, the response of many people who otherwise might have purchased luxury vehicles was to forgo buying automobiles subject to the special tax rate. In France and Spain, a number of the residents with highest incomes and greatest wealth—that is, those hit hardest by the higher French income tax rate and the new Spanish wealth tax rate—responded by moving themselves and their assets to other countries. As a consequence, for all three nations the tax-revenue increases actually observed turned out to be significantly lower than the revenue increases that their governments had predicted.

Why do many increases in tax rates generate fewer new tax revenues than governments anticipate? How does globalization affect the capabilities of governments to collect tax revenues that they desire to generate in order to fund public expenditures?

In this chapter, we consider these specific questions within an analysis of the general role of the public sector in the world economy.

PROTECTING CONSUMER AND PRODUCER INTERESTS IN THE GLOBAL ECONOMY

Traditionally, a fundamental reason why governments have existed has been to provide a coordinated system of safeguarding the interests of their citizens. Thus, for many years governments have protected producer rights to returns on inventions. More recently, governments have also sought to protect consumers from the potentially unscrupulous actions of producers.

Protecting consumers—is there common ground?

"Consumer beware" was once the operative phrase in business-to-consumer exchanges. Today, however, many national governments require companies to meet specified minimal standards in their dealings with customers. For instance, at various times since the turn of the century, the U.S. Federal Trade Commission (FTC) has assessed monetary penalties on several Internet sellers because they failed to ship goods that they had promised to customers in time for Christmas. Such actions would have been unheard of in most nations a few decades ago.

The rationale for consumer protection

Why do governments get involved in consumer protection? The main argument favoring government intervention in business–consumer interactions is the problem of **asymmetric information**, or the possession of information by one party to a transaction that is not possessed by the other party. One way in which asymmetric-information difficulties arise is through **adverse selection**, which refers to the likelihood that businesses that manufacture particularly poor-quality products are the ones that have the greatest incentive to misrepresent their attributes in an effort to sell them. To help generate sales, some businesses also succumb to the temptation to misrepresent the customer services they will provide after a sale takes place. The possibility that a seller may act in such an "immoral" (from a consumer's perspective) manner after a sale occurs is an example of **moral hazard**, which refers to the potential for either a borrower or seller to alter their behavior in an undesirable way following an economic transaction.

These asymmetric-information problems provide a rationale for government agencies such as the FTC to provide consumer protection services. These agencies act both as a "consumer watchdog," in an effort to minimize the adverse selection problem, and as an "industry policeman," with the goal of combating the moral hazard problem.

Differing views about government's role in safeguarding consumers

Governmental interventions aimed at protecting consumers are most common in developed nations in North America, Europe, and, to a lesser extent, Asia. They are

Asymmetric information:
One party's possession of information in an economic transaction that the other party to the transaction does not possess.

Adverse selection:
The tendency for manufacturers of the lowest-quality products to have the greatest incentive to misrepresent the attributes of those products.

Moral hazard:
The potential for a buyer or seller to behave differently after an economic transaction from what was agreed before the transaction.

much less commonplace in other locales. Even within developed countries, there is not complete agreement on the proper scope of consumer protection laws and enforcement.

For example, European regulators commonly require companies to keep all information they have about consumers confidential. Companies can reveal such information to other firms only if consumers explicitly request that they do so. By way of contrast, information sharing among companies has been commonplace in the United States for years. U.S. companies often sell lists of customer names, addresses, phone numbers, and e-mail addresses. Recent legal changes have restricted the ability of U.S. companies to continue some of these practices, but U.S. rules continue to be much less restrictive than those in place in Europe. Undoubtedly, during the coming years consumer protection will emerge as another area of controversy within multilateral trade negotiations.

The advent of international trade conducted via the Internet has further complicated the regulatory landscape. For instance, a few years ago a French judge ruled that the Internet auction firm eBay had violated French laws prohibiting trade of Nazi-related goods when it permitted someone to auction World War II-era Nazi artifacts using the eBay Website. This raised the specter that Web-based firms might eventually have to find a way to design Websites that anyone in any nation can access, while satisfying consumer protection statutes in scores of different countries. Already, some observers are calling for multilateral discussions of minimum global standards for online consumers.

> *Fundamental Issue #1: In what ways do government regulators seek to safeguard the interests of consumers?* Because firms often have more information than consumers about the quality of their products and customer service, there are potential asymmetric-information problems. One problem that can result is adverse selection, or the potential for low-quality products to be offered for sale. Another is moral hazard, or the possibility that one party to an exchange may undertake actions that another party deems undesirable after the exchange has already been arranged or taken place. To address these problems, governments may enact regulations establishing minimal standards for quality or service, and they may establish agencies to enforce those standards.

Safeguarding intellectual property rights

By inventing new products, implementing new production processes, and organizing new ways of marketing, selling, and delivering goods and services, scientists, engineers, and businesspeople contribute to economic development and growth. To encourage the efforts of these individuals, governments often enact systems of **intellectual property rights**, which are legal rules governing the ownership of creative ideas. Today, one of the major issues arising in regional and multilateral trade discussions is concern over how to develop an appropriate framework for the international regulation of intellectual property rights.

Intellectual property rights: *Laws granting ownership of creative ideas, typically in the form of a copyright, trademark, or patent.*

There are three ways in which governments ensure rights to intellectual property. One is by issuing **copyrights**, which grant authors exclusive privileges to reproduce, distribute, perform, or display creative works. Copyrights cover works such as articles, stories and novels, computer programs, audio recordings, and cinematographic films. Governments also protect intellectual property by establishing rules governing **trademarks**. These are words or symbols that companies use to identify their goods or services and distinguish them from the goods or services produced by other firms. **Patents** are legal documents granting an inventor the exclusive right to make, use, and sell an invention for a specified number of years.

Copyright:
An author's legal title to the sole right to reproduce, distribute, perform, or display creative works, including articles, books, software, and audio and video recordings.

Trademark:
A company's legal title to a word or symbol that identifies its product and distinguishes it from the products of other firms.

Patent: *An inventor's legal title to the sole right to manufacture, utilize, and market an invention for a specific period.*

The pros and cons of protecting rights to intellectual property

Currently, many nations abide by international standards for intellectual property rights established by a multilateral agreement called the *Agreement on Trade-Related Aspects of Intellectual Property Rights*, or *TRIPS*. TRIPS establishes a 50-year minimum standard for copyright protection, common rules governing international trademark protections, and a minimum term of patent protection of 20 years.

Society faces a tradeoff in granting intellectual property rights. The rationale for granting international property rights is that, in the absence of such rights, there would be less incentive for inventors and innovators to develop new products and technologies. If people are free to imitate the creative ideas of others, then society gains from the speedy diffusion of products and processes that results. Competition among firms in industries using these ideas, however, leads to zero economic profits. Hence, there is no return beyond covering the opportunity cost of being in the industry to compensate inventors for the time and effort they invested in developing the new product or process. If governments grant patents to an investor, however, then the inventor can charge a monopoly price to those who would like to use the new product or process, which reduces consumer welfare. (To see this tradeoff on a diagram, see *Visualizing Global Economic Issues: The tradeoff in patent protection.*)

VISUALIZING GLOBAL ECONOMIC ISSUES

The tradeoff in patent protection

To see why there is a social tradeoff associated with intellectual property rights, take a look back at Figure 12.5 on page 402. Once a product is available, consumer surplus is greatest if the many perfectly competitive producers have the unhindered right to imitate the product and sell essentially perfect substitutes under their own company name. As a result, the price of the product is equal to marginal cost across the industry, and the quantity produced equals the quantity demanded at this price.

This perfectly competitive result arises, however, only if the product is available for free imitation. The perfectly competitive outcome entails zero economic profit, so there is no inducement for an inventor to incur a potentially sizable up-front cost of developing the product in the first place. As a result, failure to provide intellectual property rights could lead to a complete loss of the large shaded consumer surplus triangle in Figure 12.5.

Granting complete intellectual property rights effectively gives the owner of a patent the power to set a monopoly price for the product. This shrinks consumer surplus to the dashed triangle shown in Figure 12.5. The economic profit earned by the patent's owner is a transfer from society to the inventor. Thus, the tradeoff associated with patent protection is that granting a patent induces an inventor to make a product available but reduces consumer welfare relative to the perfectly competitive welfare level.

For critical analysis: If the inventor who receives a patent lives in another country, then what area in Figure 12.5 constitutes an international resource transfer resulting from granting global patent protection to that inventor?

Who gains and who loses from strengthened intellectual property rights?

In recent years, more nations have agreed to enact protections of intellectual property rights. Figure 13.1 displays significant increases in the number of nations participating in various international conventions for assuring common standards for the protection of international property rights.

Increased protection of intellectual property rights naturally has immediate benefits for current owners of intellectual property. For those who wish to incorporate new ideas and processes into their business, however, strengthening intellectual property rights is likely to push up business expenses by forcing them to make payments to owners of copyrights, trademarks, and patents.

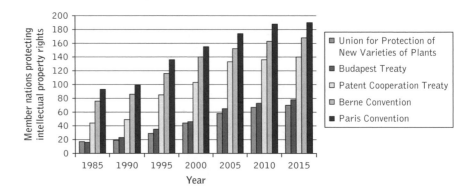

Figure 13.1 *Increased international protection of intellectual property rights*

There has been a significant increase in the number of nations that are members of treaties or conventions protecting intellectual property rights.

Source: World Intellectual Property Organization and authors' estimates.

Currently, most owners of intellectual property reside in the United States and Europe. This means that residents located in these regions are most likely to realize immediate gains from the growing globalization of intellectual property rights. Residents of other regions, most of which are less developed, experience immediate losses.

Nearly all of the recent additions to the memberships of international conventions for protecting intellectual property rights have been developing nations, however. Some of these nations undoubtedly felt pressured by U.S. threats of trade retaliation if they did not join these conventions. Presumably, a number of these nations have also decided that it is in their best interest to incur losses in the present in return for potentially significant gains, in the form of greater development and higher economic growth, in future years. (Since implementation of the TRIPS Agreement and the treaties and conventions summarized in Figure 13.1 on page 426, there has been an upswing in patent applications in both advanced countries and emerging nations; see *Management Notebook: A global upswing in patent applications*.)

ON THE WEB:

What are the various e-commerce programs of the U.S. Patent and Trademark Office? To find out, go to www.uspto.gov, click on "Patents," and in the pop-up list, click on "Electronic Business Center."

MANAGEMENT NOTEBOOK

A global upswing in patent applications

When the TRIPS Agreement was established in January 1995, many of its critics worried that the primary beneficiaries of increased global protection of intellectual property rights would be residents of the most advanced nations, who owned most intellectual property. These TRIPS critics also expressed concern that rights to ownership of intellectual property could continue to be concentrated within the most developed nations.

As shown in Figure 13.2, patent applications did indeed double in the United States and nearly triple in the European Union between 1995 and 2008, the most recent year with comparable international data. Nevertheless, patent applications during the same interval also more than doubled in South Korea and more than tripled in Brazil and India. In China, applications for new patents increased by in excess of 1,300 percent. Since enactment of the TRIPS Agreement, growth of patent applications in emerging nations has considerably exceeded application growth in advanced countries. Although ownership of intellectual property rights remains concentrated in the most developed nations, the distribution of ownership of such rights is steadily becoming more globally distributed.

For critical analysis: How do you suppose that emerging nations' efforts to strengthen the property rights of patent holders have affected the incentive for individuals and firms to apply for patents in these countries?

Circumventing intellectual property rights: Parallel imports

Despite the general trend toward greater worldwide protection of rights to intellectual property, some who engage in international trade continue to find ways to avoid

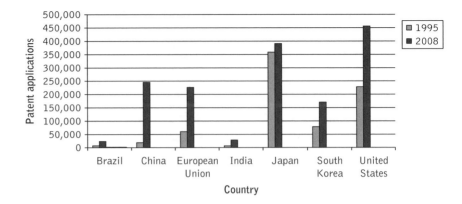

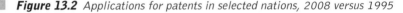

Figure 13.2 *Applications for patents in selected nations, 2008 versus 1995*

The number of patent applications increased substantially both in advanced regions and countries such as the European Union, Japan, and the United States and in emerging nations such as Brazil, China, India, and South Korea.

Source: Maskus (2012).

Parallel imports:

Gray-market imports, or goods and services brought into a country without authorization after initially being permitted to be sold elsewhere.

paying owners of copyrights, trademarks, and patents. One issue that has received particular attention in recent years is **parallel imports**, sometimes known as *gray-market imports*, which are goods or services brought into a country without authorization of the owner of a copyright, trademark, or patent after initially being legitimately placed into circulation in some other locale.

For instance, an authorized Canadian distributor of U.S.-manufactured software might sell software in Canada at a wholesale price below the retail price in Mexico. The Canadian dealer could then profit from transferring the software to Mexico. The Canadian firm thereby would contribute to the flow of parallel imports.

So far, the multilateral TRIPS Agreement leaves addressing the issue of parallel imports to national governments. Some TRIPS member nations have pushed hard for tougher multilateral standards and enforcement mechanisms, and this issue promises to be an important item on the agendas for future multilateral trade negotiations.

Fundamental Issue #2: How do the world's governments protect rights to intellectual property? To encourage the efforts of inventors and innovators, governments typically establish intellectual property rights, or legal rules that determine the ownership of creative ideas. For creative works such as articles, stories and novels, computer programs, audio recordings, and movies, governments grant copyrights, or exclusive privileges to reproduce, distribute, perform, or display such works. Governments establish rules for trademarks, which are words or symbols that companies use to differentiate their products from those of other firms. They also issue patents, that grant an inventor the exclusive right to make, use, and sell an invention for a specified number of years.

DEALING WITH MARKET FAILURES—SHOULD REGULATORS GO GLOBAL?

Even under perfect competition, too few or too many resources can sometimes go to certain economic activities. Such situations are **market failures** that prevent the attainment of economic efficiency, individual freedom, and other potential social goals. Traditionally, many economists argued that addressing market failures requires active intervention by national governments. Today, a growing number of economists contend that market failures have international consequences that may require actions by supranational, *global* authorities.

Are market externalities bounded by borders?

Economic efficiency results only when individuals know the true opportunity costs of their decisions. In some circumstances, the price that someone actually pays for a good or service can be higher or lower than the opportunity cost that society as a whole incurs. In other circumstances, it is possible that private markets will fail to provide goods that would benefit nearly everyone. Such situations can arise domestically. It is possible that they can also span national borders.

Market spillovers and their international consequences

Consider the plight of Hungarian and Slovak fisherman whose livelihood depends on their daily catch from the Tisza River, a tributary of the Danube River. A few years ago, 100,000 tons of cyanide-laden sludge byproducts from Romanian gold-mining operations washed down the river. Within days, more than 100 tons of dead fish floated downstream in both Hungary and Slovakia.

Cyanide is a substance that arises naturally when gold producers separate the shiny metal from other ores. Romanian gold producers must do something with the cyanide, so they normally place it in temporary storage in tanks of water before draining it off for safe disposal. In the meantime, they ship their final product, pure gold, to gold dealers who market the gold to industrial users, jewelry wholesalers, and the like. Fishermen in Hungary and Yugoslavia experienced an **externality**, which is an economic consequence of activity within a market, such as the production of gold, which spills over to affect third parties not directly involved in that market, such as those fishermen.

Most consumers of Romanian gold probably had no idea that cyanide could pollute rivers in Eastern Europe. From their perspective, therefore, the price that they paid in early 2000 had nothing to do with the production of cyanide. The literal spillover effect that Hungarian and Yugoslav fishermen experienced dramatically illustrates how the market price of a product such as gold may fail to reflect the broader social costs relating to its production. Because the market price of Romanian gold was lower than the price that society as a whole had to pay for this metal, production of this good entailed a *negative externality*. From society's perspective, too many resources were allocated to gold production at the private market price of gold. Furthermore,

Market failure:
Inability of unhindered private market processes to produce outcomes that are consistent with economic efficiency, individual freedom, and other broader social goals.

Externality:
A spillover effect influencing the welfare of third parties not involved in transactions within a marketplace.

429

International externality:

A spillover effect arising from market activities in one nation that influences the welfare of third parties in another country.

this was true beyond Romania's borders, so there was an **international externality**, in which spillover effects from market activities within one country affect third parties located in other nations.(Proposals to transport energy-producing coal for shipment from U.S. Pacific ports to China is raising concerns about spillover effects on U.S. farmers; see *Policy Notebook: Could new U.S. exports to China cause mint tea to taste like coal?*)

POLICY NOTEBOOK

Could new U.S. exports to China cause mint tea to taste like coal?

About 40 percent of all coal utilized for production of U.S. electrical power originates in the Powder River Basin of southeastern Montana and northeastern Wyoming. U.S. power plants burn the Powder River Basin coal to fuel turbines that generate electricity. In recent years, however, domestic plants have substituted away from coal-burning turbines in favor of equipment that utilizes lower-priced natural gas. The resulting decline in domestic demand for energy-producing coal has induced producers in the Powder River Basin to seek to satisfy a growing demand for the mineral abroad. A key potential source of foreign demand for the U.S.-produced coal is power plants in China that continue to utilize coal-burning turbines. Indeed, companies operating power plants in China have estimated that at current prices, they likely would be willing each year to import about 150 million tons of U.S. energy-producing coal valued at more than $1 billion.

Shipping coal mined in Montana and Wyoming across the Pacific Ocean to China would require utilizing a new transportation corridor. Most proposals envision rail transport of Powder River Basin coal westward across the middle of Montana, the upper portion of Idaho, the northern tier of Oregon, and then northward through the eastern portion of Washington. Trains would then deliver the coal to specially equipped port facilities in northern Washington. There, the coal would be loaded onto ships for ocean transport to China.

The proposed rail corridor for coal shipments would pass through lands containing farms that grow mints utilized to produce mint oils utilized by manufacturers of chewing gum, toothpaste, candy, and food. One farmers' group opposed to the proposed rail corridor has worried that "if we get coal dust on our mints, we're finished; nobody wants a mint tea with a nice taste of coal in it." From the perspective of these farmers, therefore, establishing a route for China to import U.S. energy-producing coal could be a source of a negative spillover. Thus, increased demand for coal for the production of energy in China has the potential to create an international externality.

For critical analysis: Why do you suppose that some residents of China who already experience considerable air pollution from the burning of coal regard planned U.S. exports of additional coal to China as a likely source of an international externality?

In some situations, private markets can underallocate resources to the production of a good or service. For instance, inoculating the residents of several developing nations with vaccines might prevent the spread of diseases to other developing and developed nations, thereby improving the quality of life for residents of all nations. The private market price of vaccinations in the developing nations may be too low, however, to induce potential producers of such services to offer them in the quantity that would benefit society. Under such circumstances, there is a *positive externality*. Positive externalities may occur either domestically or, as in this example, internationally.

ON THE WEB:

How does the U.S. government use regulations to try to protect the environment? Find out at www.epa.gov/ lawsregs.

A possible role for government: Correcting externalities

Because private market activities do not take externalities into account, it is possible that government action could help to induce producers and consumers in markets that create externalities to take them into account. In the case of a negative externality such as cyanide pollution, a multinational authority might impose and enforce minimum standards for safe storage of cyanide, limitations on cyanide production—and, as a consequence, gold production—or taxation on producers of goods such as gold that yield cyanide as a byproduct.

When there is a positive externality, such as disease-reducing vaccinations, a multinational authority might provide the service directly, subsidize private producers of vaccines and inoculation services, or undertake policies aimed at increasing the demand for the vaccines and inoculation services. (Learn how demand–supply diagrams are used to examine how such policies might help to correct negative and positive externalities—see *Visualizing Global Economic Issues: Correcting international externalities via multilateral interventions*.)

VISUALIZING GLOBAL ECONOMIC ISSUES

Correcting international externalities via multilateral interventions

To think about how a multinational authority developed by coordinated efforts of several nations might address international cyanide pollution by gold producers, consider panel (a) of Figure 13.3. If gold producers and consumers are oblivious to the social costs caused by cyanide byproducts of gold production, then the private market price of gold is P_1, and the quantity of gold produced and consumed is Q_1. If the world's gold producers took into account additional social costs caused by cyanide pollution, however, they would incur these costs and be willing to produce any given quantity of gold, only at a higher price. Thus, the market supply curve would shift upward, from S_1 to S_2. As a result, gold consumers around the world would pay the higher market price P_2, and gold manufacturers would produce Q_2 units of gold.

To bring about this socially preferable outcome, a multinational authority might contemplate policies that limit production of cyanide-producing activities, such as gold production. In principle, one approach might be to place limits on international trade in gold to reduce overall world gold production to the socially preferred level. Most economists, however, doubt that a multinational authority would be able successfully to fine-tune such quantity-focused policies to produce exactly the socially preferred production level. Consequently, economists traditionally have advocated imposing taxes on producers of goods and services that yield negative externalities. If a multinational authority could determine the per-unit amount of the social cost resulting from the polluting effects of gold production, then it might require gold producers to incur these costs. This would have the effect of shifting the market supply curve by exactly the amount shown in panel (a) of Figure 13.3, thereby pushing up the private market price and inducing a cutback in gold production that would reduce cyanide pollution. Alternatively, the authority might induce the same outcome by imposing or requiring national governments to impose a per-unit tax equal to this cost. The authority or national governments could then use the tax revenues to fund pollution cleanup or prevention activities.

Panel (b) shows how a multinational authority might deal with a positive externality. In this situation, only consumers in the locale of this marketplace, who are willing and able to be inoculated against disease, benefit from vaccines, so D_1 is the market demand curve. People elsewhere would also benefit from more widespread inoculations, however, so society as a whole would prefer the demand curve to be D_2. Then the market price would rise from P_1 to P_2, which would induce private producers to supply more vaccines, and the total number of inoculations would increase from Q_1 to Q_2.

For critical analysis: Why do economists tend to prefer price-based approaches to government interventions in markets over efforts to force producers to provide specific quantities?

Are there global public goods?

Public good: *Any good or service that can be consumed by many people at the same time, cannot be consumed by one individual without others also consuming it at no extra cost, and cannot be withheld from a person who has not contributed to funding its production.*

Most goods and services are *private goods* that can be consumed by only one individual at a time. Individuals can consume a number of goods and services simultaneously, such as the entertainment services provided by a band or orchestra concert. Among these goods and services, there are a few that also cannot be provided to some consumers without others being able to derive benefits from them. In addition, some have the property that, once provided, additional people can consume the goods or services at no additional cost. Furthermore, it is difficult, if not impossible, to deny the benefits of these goods or services to an individual who fails to pay for it. A good or service that satisfies these criteria is a **public good**.

Public goods in a global economy

Although most economists agree that there are public goods, it is often difficult to find widespread agreement about specific examples. For instance, one of the most

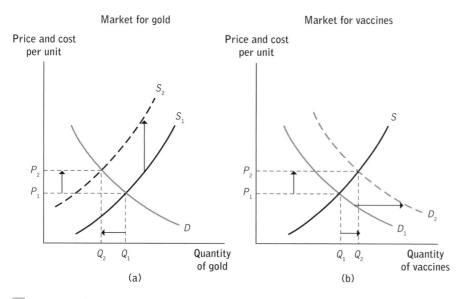

Market for gold   Market for vaccines

(a)   (b)

Figure 13.3 *Policies to correct negative and positive externalities*

Panel (a) shows that if gold producers and consumers ignore the social costs caused by cyanide byproducts of gold production, the private market price of gold is P_1, and the quantity of gold produced and consumed is Q_1. If the gold producers take into account additional social costs caused by cyanide pollution, the market supply curve shifts upward, from S_1 to S_2. As a result, gold consumers around the world pay the higher market price P_2; and gold manufacturers produce Q_2 units of gold. Panel (b) displays a situation in which D_1 is the market demand curve for vaccines when only consumers willing and able to be inoculated against disease benefit from the production and sale of vaccines. Because people elsewhere would also benefit from more widespread inoculations, society prefers for the demand curve to be D_2, so that the market price rises to P_2, producers supply more vaccines, and the total number of inoculations rises to Q_2.

commonly proposed examples of a public good is a lighthouse. Arguably, the services of a lighthouse can be used by several seafarers at the same time, and once a lighthouse is in place, additional ship navigators can use it at no additional cost. In the thirteenth century, however, the French King Louis IX erected a 105-foot tower with a dual purpose. In addition to serving as a lighthouse, it also was a lookout point to spot ships sailing close enough to view its light. Speedy ships of the king's navy would then prevent the masters of these ships from escaping payment for the lighthouse's service. Thus, this French king found a way to try to ensure that everyone paid for the service they received from his lighthouse.

Nevertheless, several goods and services often appear on lists of national or regional public goods. These include national or regional defense, forest fire suppression, groundwater pollution cleanup, flood control, and animal disease control. Some people like to include parks, rivers, waterways, highways, and even the Internet, although most economists classify these as "impure" public goods because it is

Global public good: *A good or service that yields benefits to a number of the world's people simultaneously, cannot provide benefits to one person without others around the world deriving benefits at no additional cost, and cannot be withheld from a person who has failed to contribute to its provision.*

Merit good: *A good or service that residents of a nation determine, typically through a political process, to be socially desirable.*

Free-rider problem: *The potential for an individual to try to avoid contributing funds to pay for provision of a public good because he or she presumes that others will do so.*

possible to prevent people who do not pay from using them. There are also a number of goods and services that often appear on lists of **global public goods** that arguably benefit people worldwide, including ocean pollution cleanup, weather forecasting, protection of the world's ozone layer, and disease eradication. Lists of global public goods also differ from person to person. Some observers include items such as world satellite orbits, continental and oceanic ship and air transport corridors, and allocations of bands of the electromagnetic spectrum, although it is also possible to prevent people from using these goods if they do not pay for them.

It is important to distinguish public goods from the goods and services that government entities sometimes choose to provide. For instance, some observers classify health care as a national, regional, or even global public good. From an economist's standpoint, however, it is incorrect to classify health care as a public good, because it is a simple matter to deny access to health care when people will not or cannot pay for the care. Nevertheless, many national governments around the world fund health care, either partially or fully. Some even provide relatively large amounts of health care services directly. In these countries, health care has been deemed a **merit good** that societies have determined they wish to promote through government intervention in the marketplace. Thus, national governments have chosen to provide health care alongside or instead of privately produced care.

The example of health care illustrates a difficulty that nations experience in determining whether a good or service should be provided directly by government. Economic theory provides a rationale for government provision in the case of items that are public goods. In contrast, economic theory provides no definite rationale for government involvement in the provision of merit goods.

The free-rider problem

Even though what constitutes a true global public good is often in the eye of the beholder, a common feature of any public good is the **free-rider problem**. This problem arises when individuals presume that others will pay for public goods so that, individually, they can escape from paying for their portion without reducing production of the public good.

Naturally, if a sufficiently large number of people attempt to be *free-riders*, it may prove difficult to fund provision of the public good. This is a key reason why most tax systems are compulsory. It is also a reason why taxation is a hotly debated subject everywhere in the world. After all, if a country's citizens disagree about which goods or services to classify as public goods or merit goods, then they are unlikely to agree about how much tax they should contribute to fund the provision of these goods or services.

Fundamental Issue #3: What are international externalities and global public goods, and what can national governments or multinational institutions do about them? International externalities are spillover effects from market activities in one country that affect the well being of third parties in other countries. A global public good can be consumed by many of the world's people simultaneously, cannot be provided to one person without others around the world deriving benefits at no additional cost, and cannot be withheld from a person who has failed to contribute to its provision. To correct negative international externalities such as cross-border environmental pollution, governments or multinational authorities can attempt to limit production or trade of the good or service that generates the externality, require producers to incur the costs of the externality, or tax producers. Although some observers perceive the world's environment to be a public good, there is no consensus concerning appropriate international trade policies to promote preservation of the environment.

PROTECTING THE GLOBAL ENVIRONMENT—A MULTINATIONAL PROBLEM WITH MULTILATERAL SOLUTIONS?

Externalities can affect the world's environment. Some people even view the world's overall environment as a global public good. Certainly, many parts of the world's environment are **common property**, which is a non-exclusive resource that is owned by everyone and thus not by any single individual. For instance, everyone shares the world's atmosphere, but no individual owns any of it. When no-one owns a particular resource, no-one has any incentive (aside from conscience, perhaps) to consider misuse of the resource.

Common property:
A non-exclusive resource owned by everyone and therefore by no single individual.

Public good aspects of the global environment

Even though a significant portion of the Earth's surface is privately owned, individuals or companies may still use these resources in ways that create negative externalities by degrading and polluting the environment. One way of addressing this problem might be for governments to turn many currently private lands into public lands, perhaps by purchasing or even confiscating private property. Under this perspective, the world's resources are a global public good. Hence, there is a need for concerted government efforts to ensure a pristine environment.

Problems with viewing "the" world environment as a public good

Nations' governments have not always proven to be effective managers of their countries' environments. Undoubtedly, those former residents of the defunct Soviet Union who still dwell near the barren and ruined lands around and within the boundaries of the formerly pristine Aral Sea can attest to the potential for governmental failures in environmental protection.

In addition, in most nations the ability to own private property is a fundamental human freedom. Hence, while many governments often purchase and set aside public lands, most do not confiscate lands for the purpose of environmental protection.

Furthermore, many features of the world's environment do not come even close to satisfying the definition of a global public good. Some, arguably, are not even

435

national or regional public goods. For instance, it is relatively easy to exclude people from deriving whatever benefits are available from most tracts of land. In addition, fences and walls can keep out people who refuse to pay for the uses of land. While certain uses of land certainly can create externalities for people in other locations, the world's land does not satisfy the criteria for classification as a global public good.

The world's atmosphere and oceans as global public goods

Other features of the world's environment come closer, however, to satisfying the criteria for categorization as global public goods. The Earth's atmosphere and its bodies of water top the list. In principle, it is possible to exclude certain people from using the air at a certain location on or above the Earth's surface, but from a practical standpoint this would be hard to arrange using a market mechanism.

Likewise, most of the world's oceans and a number of its rivers appear to meet the global public good criteria. It is possible to use police powers to prevent certain individuals from swimming in, boating on, or shipping across a particular region of an ocean, and countries with coastlines often place legal limits on these activities to a certain distance outward from their shores. Any efforts to develop private approaches to excluding these activities on the high seas, however, are likely to prove unfeasible. Naturally, the water within an ocean flows from place to place, so even assigning property rights to portions of an ocean would be a problematic undertaking.

Both the atmosphere and the oceans are classic examples of common property. No single individual "owns" any given portion of the Earth's atmosphere, any more than any other individual "owns" any region of one of the Earth's oceans. This helps to explain why there has been greater success in reaching multilateral agreement concerning efforts to protect the world's air and waters, as compared with its lands.

Alternative approaches to solving the world's environmental problems

Most attempts to improve the global environment have focused on treating misuse of the private property within the global environment as a negative externality, instead of viewing the entire environment as a public good. Thus, most environmental protection efforts focus on regulating the *uses* of private property.

An economic perspective on combating world pollution

Nations have experimented with many approaches to protecting the environment from pollution. For instance, countries may require owners to file *environmental impact statements* before embarking on activities that may destroy wetlands, damage animal habitats, or kill members of endangered species. Many have enacted rules requiring companies to incur significant costs to avoid generating pollution. Some have implemented schemes for taxing polluters.

A significant issue, however, is determining the appropriate goal for national or international environmental protection efforts. Some of the world's citizens and policymakers contend that the goal of reducing pollution, also called *pollution abatement*, should be the eventual elimination of *all* pollution. Most economists argue, however, that the complete elimination of pollution is not *necessarily* best for society. The reason is that society experiences costs as well as benefits from engaging in pollution abatement efforts.

Nearly everyone agrees that efforts to keep the environment clean are beneficial. Every extra bit of additional water cleanliness, for instance, raises overall social welfare. How *much* each additional unit of water cleanliness raises social welfare depends, however, on how polluted the environment already is. Suppose, for instance, that according to a physical standard of measurement, the maximum degree of water cleanliness is 100 percent. If a lake bordering several nations is only 62 percent clean, then an 8-percentage-point increase in water cleanliness is likely to raise welfare by a greater magnitude than will an 8-percentage-point increase in water cleanliness when the water is already 91 percent clean. Water that is only 62 percent clean may be barely drinkable, and an additional 8 percentage points of cleanliness may be improve the water quality sufficiently for people to consume it. By way of contrast, a lake that is already at the 91 percent threshold of cleanliness is already usable in many contexts, so a number of people may not even notice a cleanliness increase of 8 percentage points.

Combating pollution is a costly endeavor. Furthermore, the per-unit cost of reducing pollution tends to vary with the quality of the environment. For example, a lake that is only 62 percent clean may receive pollution from a number of sources, from careless dumping at nearby production facilities to excessive plankton buildup caused by heat emanating from those facilities. Reducing or eliminating careless dumping is likely to be a relatively inexpensive form of pollution abatement that can bring about, say, an 8-percentage-point increase in water quality. When the same lake is already at the 91 percent cleanliness level, however, raising water cleanliness by 8 percentage points may require reducing the transmission of heat. This, in turn, may necessitate considerable reconfiguring of production processes, which is likely to be a very expensive endeavor.

As society brings about additional increases in water cleanliness, therefore, the additional benefit from pollution abatement efforts declines at the same time as the cost of additional pollution abatement rises. This means that attaining perfectly clean water is not likely to be the best outcome for society. It could well be in the best interest of society to aim for, say, 90 percent cleanliness in a lake bordering several nations. (To consider how economists envision the determination of society's optimal level of environment, see *Visualizing Global Economic Issues: Determining how much to reduce pollution*.)

VISUALIZING GLOBAL ECONOMIC ISSUES

Determining how much to reduce pollution

Economists call the additional benefit that society gains from a given increase in water cleanliness the *marginal social benefit of pollution abatement*. The benefit that society derives from raising cleanliness of a body of water by any given amount is lower at a 91 percent cleanliness level than it is at a 62 percent cleanliness level. This implies that the marginal social benefit curve for society depicted in Figure 13.4 slopes downward. As overall water cleanliness increases, the extra benefit that society receives from an additional unit of water cleanliness declines.

In contrast, the additional cost that society incurs to achieve a given increase in cleanliness, which economists call the *marginal social cost of pollution abatement,* increases at higher overall cleanliness levels. Thus, the marginal social cost curve shown in Figure 13.4 is upward sloping.

Now suppose that the degree of overall cleanliness of this body of water is equal to 75 percent. As you can see, at this overall level of water cleanliness the marginal social benefit of pollution abatement is higher than the marginal social cost of pollution abatement. Hence, society experiences a net gain from further efforts to improve water quality. If the overall level of cleanliness of this body of water is equal to 90 percent, however, marginal social cost exceeds marginal social benefit, so society devotes too much effort to pollution abatement. By this line of reasoning, the socially optimal degree of water cleanliness, C^*, is 83 percent, at which the marginal social benefit of pollution abatement is just equal to the marginal social cost of pollution abatement. Note that the optimal extent of water cleanliness is almost never likely to be as high as 100 percent. Social welfare typically is at its highest with at least some amount of water pollution.

For critical analysis: What factors are likely to affect how close C^* is to 100 percent in Figure 13.4?

Multilateral efforts to reduce global pollution

Of course, in many parts of the world the immediate goal of many residents has been simply to find ways to reduce pollution below existing levels that they feel are too high. Only as pollution levels have started to fall have some nations begun the process of determining exactly how low they wish to push pollution levels.

Until recently, the bulk of pollution-abatement efforts have taken place *within* nations. Today, however, a variety of environmentally directed *non-governmental organizations* (NGOs)—private international groups that pursue special interests, including global environmental protection—are pushing for global efforts to coordinate environmental protection efforts.

Some of these efforts have paid dividends for the NGOs. Many of the world's nations have entered into international treaties establishing minimal national pollution standards and worldwide rules for use of shared environmental resources. Current estimates indicate that there are about 500 international agreements relating to environmental regulations. Table 13.1 (p. 440) lists some of the most important multilateral agreements. In some cases, nations signing these treaties have conducted

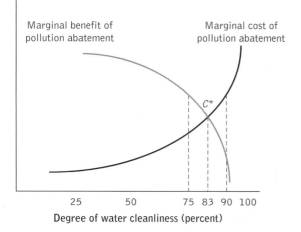

Marginal benefit
and marginal cost

Marginal benefit of
pollution abatement

Marginal cost of
pollution abatement

*C**

25   50   75 83 90 100

Degree of water cleanliness (percent)

Figure 13.4 *Determining the socially optimal degree of water cleanliness*

*The additional benefit that society gains from a given increase in water cleanliness,
or the marginal social benefit of pollution abatement, falls as overall water cleanliness increases, so that the marginal social benefit slopes downward. In contrast, the
additional cost that society incurs to achieve a given increase in cleanliness, or the
marginal social cost of pollution abatement, increases at higher overall cleanliness
levels, so the marginal social cost curve slopes upward. If the degree of overall cleanliness of this body of water is 75 percent, then the marginal social benefit of pollution
abatement exceeds the marginal social cost of pollution abatement, so society experiences a net gain from further efforts to improve water quality. If the overall level of
cleanliness of this body of water is equal to 90 percent, however, marginal social cost
exceeds marginal social benefit, so society allocates too many resources to pollution
abatement. The socially optimal degree of water cleanliness is 83 percent, at which
the marginal social benefit of pollution abatement is just equal to the marginal social
cost of pollution abatement.*

detailed studies of costs and benefits of pollution abatement before agreeing to
national and global targets for antipollution efforts. Nevertheless, many recent
efforts to establish multilateral environmental rules have been focused on the realm
of international trade arrangements.

International trade and the environment

At present, however, beyond agreement that environmental protection is important,
NGOs have failed to reach a consensus in their environmental policy recommendations. Some environmentally focused NGOs, for instance, view international trade as
an environmental threat. The foundation for this view is that foreign direct investment
and other capital flows from developed nations to developing nations will contribute
to degradation of virgin lands that now exist primarily in developing nations.

▓ **Table 13.1** *Key international environmental agreements*

Agreement	Year
Convention for the Regulation of Whaling	1946
Convention on the Prevention of Marine Pollution	1972
Convention on International Trade in Endangered Species	1973
Convention for the Prevention of Pollution from Ships	1973
Convention on Long-Range Transboundary Air Pollution	1979
Vienna Convention for the Protection of the Ozone Layer	1985
Basle Convention on the Control of Transboundary Movements of Hazardous Wastes and Their Disposal	1989
Framework Convention on Climate Change	1992
Convention on Biological Diversity	1992
International Convention to Combat Desertification	1994
Kyoto Climate Change Convention	1997

There are four basic reasons why some NGOs oppose international trade:

■ By increasing the breadth of the world marketplace, international trade worsens the scope for global market failures that harm the environment

■ Greater international trade erodes regulatory standards as governments loosen regulations to assist domestic industries in response to heightened international competition

■ Increased economic growth ultimately is unsustainable, and growth-enhancing international trade only speeds the pace at which the world's resources will be exhausted

■ Multilateral trade agreements and institutions tend to focus on economic aspects of trade without giving due consideration to trade's environmental effects

Thus, those who view international trade as an environmental menace perceive the resulting market failures to be insurmountable, and the economic growth that trade promotes to be counterproductive. Consequently, NGOs continue to lobby and protest against further efforts to expand global trade. A few groups even desire to reverse the recent growth of trade flows.

In contrast, some NGOs view increased international trade as a potential long-term boon to the world's environment. Their position is based on the following arguments:

■ Gains from trade help raise living standards in developing nations, and evidence indicates that environmental protection efforts increase with higher per capita incomes

■ Opening the markets of developing countries encourages industries within these nations to operate in more efficient ways that are less environmentally harmful; in addition, multinational companies that engage in foreign direct investment in developing nations apply the most advanced pollution-control techniques, which help reduce environmental degradation in the developing world

■ Increased international trade and investment will speed the pace of innovation, which will permit sustainable growth of the global economy

■ Multilateral trade agreements and institutions provide forums for facilitating coordinated international efforts to protect the environment

These views, of course, stand in sharp contradiction to the perceptions of those who view international trade as a factor contributing to worldwide environmental peril. Economic arguments can be advanced to support both sets of views. For this reason, the desirable scope for environmental protection within regional and multilateral trade agreements and regulations will have to be sorted out within the political arena.

Nearly everyone agrees that environmental protection is a multinational problem. Given the broad gap in perspectives about how international linkages via foreign trade and investment affect the environment, however, it seems unlikely that multilateral policy solutions will emerge quickly. Nonetheless, discussions about multilateral approaches to environmental protection are likely to dominate the international stage for years to come.

Fundamental Issue #4: How can the world's nations protect the global environment? Most nations engage in unilateral efforts to protect the environment through pollution-abatement policies that attempt to address the negative externalities generated by environmental pollution. To combat environmental externalities that span national borders, governments or multinational authorities can attempt to develop quantitative limits based on perceived marginal benefits and marginal costs of combating the externalities. Currently, multilateral efforts to protect the environment are governed by treaties specifying mutually agreeable environmental goals. Some environmentally focused NGOs contend that trade with developed nations will contribute to degradation of the environments of developing nations, but others argue that trade-induced factors such as increases in living standards or technological improvements will enhance the efforts of developing nations to improve their environment.

FUNDING THE PUBLIC SECTOR—GLOBALIZATION AND INTERNATIONAL TAX COMPETITION

Regulating businesses, providing public goods and merit goods, and attempting to correct externalities are costly activities for national governments and multinational institutions to perform. Hence, they must have sources of funds. Determining how to fund these public-sector activities can be a difficult problem.

The growing international rivalry for tax revenues

To generate the revenues to fund their activities, national governments typically rely on domestic taxes and user fees, tariffs, and other miscellaneous revenue sources. Taxation of domestic residents is the most important source of revenues for the governments of most countries. National governments typically levy taxes on individual and corporate incomes, business sales, and/or household and business consumption.

In the past, domestic considerations have guided governments in structuring their tax systems. Increasingly, however, globalization has caused international considerations to impinge on domestic tax policies.

Determining total tax revenues: The static view

Tax rate: *A fraction of a tax base an individual or company is legally required to transmit to the government.*

Tax base: *The value of goods, services, incomes, or wealth subject to taxation.*

Most tax systems entail a **tax rate**, which is a fraction determining the amount of taxes owed the government, multiplied by a **tax base**, which is an economic quantity such as labor earnings, consumption spending, or capital income subject to taxation. Figure 13.5 displays average tax rates on labor, consumption, and capital in the EU, Japan, and the United States.

In a personal income-tax system, an individual determines total income taxes owed by multiplying the appropriate income tax rate by total income subject to taxation, which is the tax base. In a corporate income-tax system, a firm calculates the total taxes it owes on its net income by multiplying the corporate income tax rate by its total net income, or the tax base for this tax system. In a U.S.-style sales-tax system, a firm determines total sales taxes to transmit to the government by multiplying the sales tax rate by a tax base that equals the firm's total taxable sales.

For many tax systems, therefore, the total tax revenues that a government collects equals the tax rate multiplied by the tax base. A good example is a proportional income-tax system. If the income-tax rate is a fraction t and the tax base B is total income subject to taxation, then the government's total income-tax revenues equal $T = t \times B$. That is, tax collections of the government are a fixed proportion, t, of the tax base. This equation provides the foundation for understanding alternative perspectives about how tax revenues, the tax rate, and the tax base are related.

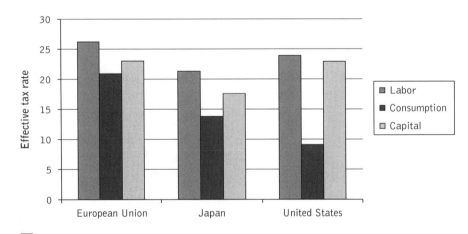

 **Figure 13.5** *Average tax rates in the European Union, Japan, and the United States*

Among these developed regions of the world, tax rates on consumption spending and labor income are highest in the European Union. Tax rates on capital are slightly lower in Japan and are comparable in the United States and the European Union.

Source: Martinez-Mongay (2000).

One of these perspectives is called the *static view*. According to this approach, if a nation's tax base B declines, then maintaining the same amount of tax revenues T requires the nation's government to increase the tax rate t. That is, a nation's government can respond to a fall in the tax base by raising its rate of taxation. This action will keep tax revenues from declining further. (See *Visualizing Global Economic Issues: The static prescription for dealing with a shrinking tax base.*)

VISUALIZING GLOBAL ECONOMIC ISSUES

The static prescription for dealing with a shrinking tax base

To contemplate the static view's tax-policy prescriptions on a diagram, take a look at panel (a) of Figure 13.6, which depicts the equation for a nation's tax revenues, $T = t \times B$, as a straight line extending from the origin. The equation implies that a change in tax revenues, ΔT, which is measured along the vertical axis in the diagram, equals the tax rate t multiplied by a change in the tax base, ΔB, which is measured along the horizontal axis. Hence, $\Delta T = t \times \Delta B$. Rearranging this equation yields $t = \Delta T / \Delta B$. The slope of the *tax schedule* graphed in panel (a), therefore, or the "rise" divided by the "run," is the tax rate t.

Panel (b) of Figure 13.6 illustrates a situation in which a national government desires to collect a total amount of taxes equal to T^*. This tax-revenue goal may be an amount of funding required to build hospitals or provide various social services.

If the tax base is equal to B_1, the government achieves a tax-revenue goal T^* at point A by establishing a tax rate equal to T_1. Setting this tax rate ensures that the tax schedule crosses point A, thereby achieving the desired level of tax collections T^* given the tax base B_1.

Now suppose that the nation's tax base declines, perhaps because residents of this and other nations can earn incomes (in the case of an income tax) or purchase substitute goods (in the case of a sales tax) outside this country at a lower rate of taxation. This implies a lower tax base equal to B_2 at point C, and tax collections fall below the tax-revenue goal T^*, to the quantity T_2.

According to the static view of taxation, the domestic government can respond to this situation by raising the tax rate. As shown in panel (b), a sufficient increase in the tax rate, to t_2, raises the slope of the tax function. At the lower tax base, B_2, this higher tax rate yields tax collections equal to T^*, at point D. Thus, increasing the tax rate can allow the government to attain its tax revenue objective, even though it faces a smaller tax base.

For critical analysis: If a nation experiences considerable economic growth that results in an increase in its income-tax base, what does the static view indicate that its government should do to maintain its tax revenues at a level equal to its tax-revenue goal? Why might a government be tempted to do nothing?

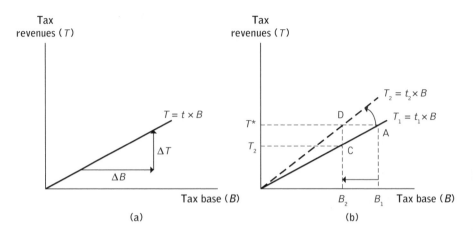

Figure 13.6 *The tax schedule and attaining a national tax-revenue goal by adjusting the tax rate*

Panel (a) shows the tax schedule, which is a graph of the equation $T = t \times B$, where T is the government's tax revenues, B is the tax base, and t is the tax rate. The tax rate is the slope of the tax schedule, which is the "rise," ΔT, divided by the "run," ΔB. Panel (b) displays a situation in which initially the tax base is equal to B_1, and the government can achieve a tax revenue objective T^* at point A by setting a tax rate equal to t_1. If the tax base falls to B_2 at point C because residents of this and other nations shift economic activity to nations with lower rates of taxation, then the government's tax collections fall to T_2. From a static perspective on the relationship between the tax rate and tax revenues, the government can respond to this situation by raising the sales-tax rate t_2, which raises the slope of the tax function and pushes tax collections back up to T^* at point D.

Determining total tax revenues: The dynamic view

There is a problem with the static view of the relationship between the tax rate and actual tax collections. The problem is that it ignores the incentives that taxpayers face to respond to a higher tax rate by finding ways to avoid contributing to the national tax base.

In the case of income-tax systems, for instance, domestic residents could find ways to earn incomes in other nations. Likewise, in a sales-tax system, domestic residents could begin buying more products abroad. The *dynamic view* of the relationship between tax rates and tax revenues takes such incentives into account.

According to the dynamic view, trying to maintain tax revenues at a goal level by raising the tax rate as the tax base declines is likely to be a self-defeating policy. The reason is that an even-higher tax rate will generate an even-smaller tax base. In a highly globalized economy, a nation's residents can find a way to generate incomes, sales, or other taxable activities in other nations, thereby depressing the domestic tax base and domestic tax revenues. Raising tax rates in the face of a declining tax base will only worsen the problem faced by a national government. (See *Visualizing Global Economic Issues: The dynamic view's bad news for efforts to attain a tax-revenue goal with a declining tax base.*)

VISUALIZING GLOBAL ECONOMIC ISSUES

The dynamic view's bad news for efforts to attain a tax-revenue goal with a declining tax base

To understand why those who subscribe to the dynamic view of the relationship between the tax rate, the tax base, and tax revenues are pessimistic about the ability to maintain tax revenues in the face of a declining tax base, consider Figure 13.7. As in Figure 13.6(b) (page 444), Figure 13.7 shows a decline in the tax base, to B_2 at point C, and a resulting fall in tax revenues to T_2, which is below the tax-revenue goal T^*.

The static view prescribes dealing with this situation by raising the tax rate to t_2, thereby increasing and pushing tax revenues back up to T^*, at point D. The problem with this analysis, however, is that it ignores the *dynamic* responses of individuals and firms to the higher tax rate in a globalized economy. Many domestic residents will respond to the new, higher domestic tax rate by moving taxable activities abroad, where lower tax rates exist. This will further lower the domestic tax base, to a level such as B_3 at point E in Figure 13.7. Consequently, the domestic government will still be unable to achieve its tax-revenue goal. Indeed, in the example illustrated in the figure, total tax collections fall even *farther* below the tax-revenue goal.

For critical analysis: Within the context of the dynamic view, is it possible that the domestic government could actually push up its tax collections by reducing its tax rate?

As the tax base declines even more following an increase in the domestic tax rate, the domestic government's tax revenues once again will begin to fall below its tax-revenue goal. If cutting public spending to match the government's lower revenues is not regarded as a feasible option, then if it can only act alone, the domestic government has only three choices, as follows.

■ *Increase the tax rate again.* This action would essentially duplicate the steps recommended by the static view. As the dynamic view makes clear, however, this is likely to lead to a further reduction in the domestic tax base.

■ *Increase tax rates within a different domestic tax system in an effort to raise revenues from a different tax base.* Of course, the same problem of a shrinking tax base in another system may result if lower tax rates apply in other nations. For instance, if the domestic government responds to a fall in domestic income by raising the tax rate on firms' sales, then domestic residents may begin purchasing substitute products in nations with lower sales-tax rates.

■ *Broaden the tax base.* For instance, in an income-tax system, a national government could begin taxing the earnings its residents receive in other nations, thereby

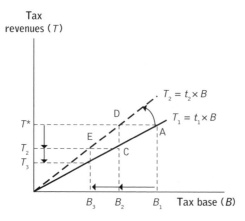

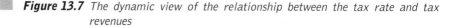

Figure 13.7 *The dynamic view of the relationship between the tax rate and tax revenues*

From a dynamic perspective, the concluding situation in Figure 13.6(b) (page 444) cannot be the conclusion to a government's efforts to maintain its tax revenues after a decline in the tax base. If the government responds to a fall in the tax base to B_2 and a resulting fall in tax revenues to T_2 below the tax-revenue goal T^* by raising the tax rate to t_2, then tax revenues do not necessarily rise back to T^* at point D. The reason is that, in a globalized economy, a number of domestic residents will respond to this increase in the tax rate by moving taxable activities to countries with lower tax rates. This will further reduce the domestic tax base, to a level such as B_3 at point E, and it is possible that total domestic tax collections will fall even farther, to T_3.

removing the incentive to shift earnings abroad. Naturally, this might induce at least some residents to end their residency in the domestic nation as a way to avoid the broadened tax base.

In principle, governments could opt for any or all of these choices. If other nations assess tax rates that are lower than tax rates in the domestic nation, however, these various actions at best will slow the shrinkage of the domestic tax base.

Globalization and tax competition

The dynamic view on the effects of higher domestic tax rates illustrates why nations with relatively high tax rates are likely to observe shrinking tax bases and lower tax revenues. Higher personal income-tax rates, for instance, tend to induce individuals to earn incomes abroad, and higher sales-tax or corporate income-tax rates give firms an incentive to attempt to offer their products for sale in other countries.

Tax competition:
Reducing tax rates below those of other regions in an effort to induce individuals and businesses to engage in taxable activities in that region.

Naturally, the converse is also true: A nation with relatively low tax rates tends to experience a relatively higher tax base. This is one reason why nations' governments sometimes engage in **tax competition**, reducing their tax rates below those prevailing in other countries in an effort to induce individuals and businesses to engage in taxable activities within their borders instead. By reducing their tax rates, a nation actually might be able to broaden its tax base sufficiently to generate a net *increase* in its tax revenue. Alternatively, the decision of a nation's government to hold its own tax rates unchanged as other countries raise their tax rates can also generate higher tax bases and tax revenues. (Indeed, the U.S. government obtained higher tax revenues when the Canadian government assessed higher taxes on airline passengers flying in and out of Canadian airports; see *Management Notebook: U.S. airlines make room for Canadian air travelers—who pay more U.S. taxes and fewer Canadian taxes.*)

MANAGEMENT NOTEBOOK

U.S. airlines make room for Canadian air travelers—who pay more U.S. taxes and fewer Canadian taxes

When Canadians who live within driving distance of U.S. airports compare prices of flying from domestic airports versus the nearby U.S. airports, they typically find that the price of a ticket for a domestic flight is well over $100 higher than for a U.S. flight. Nearly all of that price difference results from higher Canadian taxes on air travel. The Canadian government assesses much higher tax rates on airline tickets than those imposed by the U.S. government.

In light of the significant Canadian–U.S. after-tax price differentials, many Canadians who live near the U.S. border drive or take public transportation to a U.S. airport to catch a cross-continental flight to a Canadian or U.S. destination. U.S. airlines servicing airports in locations close to the Canadian border have responded by increasing flight offerings. On many U.S. airline flights originating from U.S. airports close to Canada, such as in Bellingham, Niagara Falls, and Plattsburgh, New York, Canadians typically account for more than 60 percent of all passengers. The substantial influx of Canadian passengers in recent years has caused traffic at these airports to increase sufficiently that the airports are undergoing expansions to handle even more flights.

Naturally, as more Canadians fly on U.S. airline flights originating from U.S. airports, airline ticket taxes collected by the U.S. government have increased. At the same time, decreasing volumes of passengers flying out of Canadian airports have resulted in much smaller increases in Canadian airline ticket taxes than the Canadian government had predicted when it boosted ticket tax rates.

For critical analysis: How do you suppose private U.S. companies that provide bus transportation between U.S. and Canadian cities have responded to Canadians' increased desire to fly out of U.S. airports to avoid paying higher tax rates on Canadian airline tickets?

Fighting tax competition: International coordination among taxing authorities

There are two basic perspectives on the increased international tax competition that has accompanied globalization. From one point of view, tax competition is harmful.

According to this perspective, national governments realize that their tax base will shrink if they maintain relatively high tax rates, because some portion of residents will attempt to become free-riders by reducing their contribution to their nation's tax base. To avoid inducing a decline in the national tax base, governments will establish lower tax rates than they otherwise would. This, in turn, restrains the ability of national governments to earn revenues high enough to maintain socially desirable spending programs.

Those who view tax competition as harmful typically favor international coordination of tax policies. A number of governments in industrialized nations with well developed tax bases promote tax coordination. Since the formation of the European Monetary Union in 1999, for example, member nations have developed mechanisms for coordinating certain aspects of their tax systems.

Some nations have even coordinated efforts to try to force other countries to join their tax-coordination schemes. The nations of the Organisation for Economic Co-operation and Development (OECD), which include the United States, Japan, Canada, and major European nations, have agreed to abide by a "memorandum of understanding" requiring OECD nations to "blacklist" nations with "harmful tax regimes." Specifically, countries that the OECD determines have set tax rates sufficiently low to "unfairly erode the tax bases of other countries and distort the location of capital and services" can be targeted for various sanctions, such as imposing withholding taxes on payments of residents of harmful tax regimes, denying foreign tax credits for taxes paid to their governments, and perhaps even adopting overt trade sanctions. Interestingly, at various times the tax systems of OECD nations Luxembourg, Switzerland, the United Kingdom, and the United States have qualified as harmful tax regimes under the OECD's definition, but the OECD nations have aimed their coordinated tax sanctions only against non-OECD members.

Tax coordination or tax cartels?

Another perspective views tax competition as a positive side-effect of the process of globalization. Proponents of this contrary view contend that, by depressing tax rates and thereby restraining overall tax revenues, international tax competition induces national governments to be more efficient in their provision of government services and more frugal in their other various types of public expenditure. In addition, they contend, tax competition helps governments resist the temptation to assess high tax rates on growth-promoting activities relating to saving and investment.

According to those who promote this perspective, citizens should resist efforts by their governments to coordinate tax policies. Such activities, they argue, effectively amount to attempts to establish international *tax cartels* among participating national governments intent on establishing uniformly high rates of taxation on the world's residents. Not surprisingly, critics of tax coordination were particularly disapproving of a 2002 UN proposal to move toward worldwide coordination of tax policies and potentially even the creation of a global taxation authority. (Eleven European Union nations have contemplated forming a financial transactions-tax cartel; see *Policy Notebook: Economic realities complicate a European tax cartel effort.*)

POLICY NOTEBOOK

Economic realities complicate a European tax cartel effort

In 1972, the late Nobel laureate James Tobin proposed a tax on currency transactions aimed at reducing private foreign exchange market trading, thereby simplifying efforts by finance ministries and central banks of that time to keep exchange rates fixed. Recently, 11 European nations—Austria, Belgium, Estonia, France, Germany, Greece, Italy, Portugal, Slovakia, Slovenia, and Spain—proposed taxing financial transactions involving stocks, bonds, and derivative securities such as futures and options. The proposed tax rate for stock-and-bond exchanges would be 0.1 percent, and the tax rate for derivatives transactions would be 0.01 percent.

Under the proposed tax scheme, these tax rates would be assessed on trades of any securities issued by entities located in any of these countries. Non-European traders exchanging a security issued by a firm or government within the 11-member group thereby technically would confront the applicable tax rate. In contrast, no taxes would apply to transactions outside of these nations involving bonds issued by firms or governments in other parts of the world. Hence, traders naturally would have a stronger incentive to hold and exchange other nations' securities instead of securities that originated within one of the 11 members of the transactions-tax cartel. To induce traders to hold and exchange their securities instead of those of other nations, therefore, firms and governments within the 11-nation group would have to pay higher rates of return on securities that they would issue.

In addition, the transactions-tax cartel would impose its tax rates on exchanges of any nation's stocks, bonds, or derivative securities on the part of any individuals or companies operating within these 11 nations. For instance, banks located within the 11-nation cartel that borrow more than $300 billion per day from U.S. money market funds by temporarily selling U.S. Treasury securities to those institutions each day would owe daily taxes on the transactions. The result would be a prohibitive increase in European banks' annual borrowing costs, from 0.15 percent per year to nearly *22.00* percent per year. Most financial market specialists predict that, instead of paying this huge tax, European banks would halt their borrowing from the U.S. money market funds. That is, consistent with the dynamic view of taxation, the tax base likely would shrivel, and consequently the 11 European nations' governments would collect much lower revenues from European banks than they were anticipating.

For critical analysis: How did tax competition effects undercut the plans of the proposed financial-transactions-tax cartel? Why do you suppose that the governments of the 11 nations that indicated their plan to participate in the proposed tax scheme have continued to try to convince other governments around the world to join their planned cartel?

Fundamental Issue #5: How does increased globalization complicate the efforts of governments to finance their activities? In a highly globalized economy, residents of a country with a government that imposes relatively high tax rates, assessed on a tax base such as personal income, corporate income, or business sales, can reduce their contribution to the domestic tax base by shifting income-earning or sales-producing activities to nations with relatively lower tax rates. Although a government with relatively high tax rates might be able to maintain its tax collections by further increasing tax rates, another byproduct of these actions is likely to be further erosion of national tax bases. Governments of some nations also may engage in international tax competition by setting relatively low tax rates to encourage residents of other nations to relocate economic activities to their nation. From one perspective, international tax competition harms broader social interests by encouraging free-riders to shift economic activities to lower-tax nations, but another view is that tax competition encourages governments to be more efficient and discourages them from setting high tax rates that can retard economic growth.

CHAPTER SUMMARY

1. **Ways that government regulators seek to safeguard the interests of consumers:** A situation of asymmetric information arises when one party to an exchange has information not possessed by another party to the exchange. This can result in adverse selection, or the potential for sellers to offer low-quality products to customers. In addition, moral hazard, the possibility that one party to an exchange may undertake actions that another party deems undesirable after the exchange has already been arranged or taken place may arise. In an effort to protect consumers from losses that might arise from these asymmetric-information problems, national governments may enact regulations establishing minimal standards for quality or service. Governments also may establish agencies to enforce those standards.

2. **How the world's governments protect rights to intellectual property:** Governments attempt to encourage firms to engage in invention and innovation by establishing intellectual property rights, which are legal rules assigning ownership to creative ideas. Governments award copyrights to creators of works such as articles, stories, novels, computer programs, audio recordings, and movies, giving those individuals or firms exclusive privileges to reproduce, distribute, perform, or display such works. They provide a means for firms to register words or symbols, known as trademarks, which firms use to distinguish their goods or services from those of other firms. Governments also grant patents that give an inventor the exclusive legal right to make, use, and sell an invention for a specified number of years.

3. **International externalities and global public goods, and what national governments or multinational institutions can do about them:** International externalities are welfare spillovers that activities in one nation's marketplace can exert on third parties in other countries. A global public good bestows benefits on many people around the

world at the same time, cannot be provided to one individual without others being able to benefit at zero cost, and cannot be deprived from an individual who has failed to contribute to producing the good. Governments or multinational authorities that wish to correct negative international externalities such as cross-border environmental pollution can attempt to limit production or trade of the good or service that generates the externality, require producers to incur the costs of the externality, or tax producers. Although some observers perceive the world's environment to be a public good, at present there is no consensus concerning appropriate international trade policies to promote preservation of the environment.

4. **How the world's nations seek to protect the global environment:** At present, global efforts to protect the world's environment are coordinated through treaties that commit nations to pursuing pollution-abatement policies aimed at quantitative limits on pollution. National governments or multinational authorities can attempt to develop quantitative limits based on perceived marginal benefits and marginal costs of combating the externalities. Although some NGOs that press environmental issues contend that international trade promotes capital flows that degrade environments of developing nations, others suggest that trade improves living standards, promotes technological improvements and environment-friendly innovations, and provides a forum for making pollution abatement a feature of international trade agreements.

5. **How increased globalization complicates governments' efforts to finance their activities:** Increased globalization makes it easier for residents of a country with relatively high tax rates to shift their taxable economic activities abroad, thereby reducing the domestic tax base. It is possible that a government with relatively high tax rates might be able to maintain its tax collection by further increases in tax rates. Nevertheless, further increases in tax rates are likely to generate additional declines in the nation's tax base. Some nations' governments engage in international tax competition by establishing relatively low tax rates to induce other countries' residents to relocate economic activities within their borders. On one hand, international tax competition can be harmful to society by encouraging free-riders to shift economic activities to lower-tax nations. On the other hand, tax competition encourages governments to be more efficient and to establish lower tax rates that promote economic growth.

QUESTIONS AND PROBLEMS

1. Discuss the key rationales for governmental regulation reviewed in this chapter. Why do you suppose that national governments may disagree about the appropriate scope of consumer-protection regulations?

2. A source of conflict in international trade is a potential tradeoff between free trade and a desire to protect domestic residents from potentially harmful products, such as substandard drugs. Briefly outline one way in which nations might deal with this problem cooperatively within the context of online trade in pharmaceuticals.

3. Under European Union rules, anyone selling goods or services on the Internet is subject to the laws of each of the EU member nations. How might this rule discourage foreign competition, even if it was not intended to be protectionist legislation?

4. At various times since the turn of the century, the U.S. Congress has considered legislation to make it illegal for U.S. residents to import a number of goods, such as perfumes, shampoos, and wristwatches, unless the products had appropriate safety labels. The proposed law immediately drew harsh reaction from online discount retailers, which charged this law was a trade quota in disguise that would damage their businesses. In what way might this law have the same effect as an explicit quota on international trade?

5. If a national government chose to limit itself to issuing only patents, copyrights, or trademarks in the electronic marketplace, which form of intellectual property-right protection do you believe it should choose to enforce? Support your position.

6. What are the advantages and disadvantages for developing nations of enforcing international standards for protecting intellectual property rights?

7. What features of the definition of a global public good make it difficult to identify very many items that everyone can agree are global public goods?

8. The U.S. government has established a pollution-abatement policy in which firms can buy or sell rights to pollute up to a legally mandated pollution limit. Discuss the pros and cons of a multilateral extension of this policy to the rest of the world.

9. Why might some environmentally oriented non-governmental organizations regard a "marginal-benefit-equals-marginal-cost" standard for pollution abatement as undesirable?

10. What nations of the world do you think are most likely to favor fighting "harmful tax competition" by establishing international organizations to coordinate tax policies and pressing efforts to induce all the world's nations to join those organizations? What nations do you suppose are least likely to wish to join such organizations? Why?

ONLINE APPLICATION

URL: www.ciesin.org

Title: Trade Policy and Global Environmental Change

Navigation: Go to the home page of Columbia University's Center for International Earth Science Information Network (www.ciesin.org). In the search box, type in "Trade Policy and Global Environmental Change." Select "Trade Policy and Global Environmental Change Home Page."

Application: Perform the indicated operations, and answer the accompanying questions.

1. Scroll down and click on "Trade and the Environment: Conflicts and Opportunities," and read the article. Why might residents of developing nations be less likely, as compared with residents of developed nations, to be concerned about global externality and public-good aspects of environmental issues? Which of the mechanisms for addressing environmental problems in developing nations that the article discusses do you believe has the greatest potential for success? Why?

2. Back up to the "Trade Policy and Global Environmental Change" page, click on "Harmonization, Trade, and the Environment," and read the article. With respect to environmental issues, what does the author mean by "harmonization?" Of the

advantages and disadvantages of harmonization that the author discusses, which do you regard as most important? On net, do you believe harmonization is a good or bad idea? Use economic arguments based on what you have learned in this chapter to justify your position.

For group study and analysis: Divide the class into two groups, and have each group draft a list of proposed guidelines for determining what activities constitute international environmental externalities; what features of the environment (if any) should be regarded as global public goods; and multinational mechanisms for addressing international environmental problems.

REFERENCES AND RECOMMENDED READINGS

Abrams, David. "Did TRIPS Spur Innovation? An Empirical Analysis of Patent Duration and Incentives to Innovate." University of Pennsylvania Law School Institute for Law and Economics Research Paper No. 09-24, August 2009.

Braithwaite, John, and Peter Drahos. *Global Business Regulation*. Cambridge, U.K.: Cambridge University Press, 2000.

European Policy Forum. *Tax Competition: Broadening the Debate*. June 2000.

Frankel, Jeffrey. "Globalization and the Environment." In Michael Weinstein, ed., *Globalization: What's New*. New York: Columbia University Press, 2005, pp. 129–169.

Gorter, Joeri, and Ashok Parikh. "How Mobile Is Capital within the European Union?" Research Memorandum No. 172. Netherlands Bureau for Economic Policy Analysis, The Hague, November 2000.

Horner, Frances. "The OECD, Tax Competition, and the Future of Tax Reform." Paris: Directorate for Financial, Fiscal, and Enterprise Affairs, OECD, January 2000.

Kaul, Inge, and Pedro Conceição, eds. *The New Public Finance: Responding to Global Challenges*. New York: Oxford University Press, 2006.

Kaul, Inge, Pedro Conceição, Katell Le Goulven, and Ronald Mendoza, eds. *Providing Global Public Goods*. New York: Oxford University Press, 2003.

Martinez-Mongay, Carlos. "ECFIN's Effective Tax Rates: Properties and Comparisons with Other Tax Indicators." Economic Paper No. 146. Directorate for Economic and Financial Affairs, European Commission, October 2000.

Maskus, Keith. *Private Rights and Public Problems: The Global Economics of Intellectual Property Rights in the 21st Century*. Washington, DC: Peterson Institute for International Economics, 2012.

Maskus, Keith, and Jerome Reichman, eds. *International Public Goods and Transfer of Technology under a Globalized Intellectual Property Regime*. Cambridge, U.K.: Cambridge University Press, 2005.

May, Christopher. *The Global Political Economy of Intellectual Property Rights*. London: Routledge, 2010.

Rosen, Harvey, and Ted Gayer. *Public Finance*, 9th edn. New York: McGraw-Hill, 2010.

Chapter 14

Dealing with financial crises—does the world need a new international financial architecture?

FUNDAMENTAL ISSUES

1. How have recent developments in global capital markets differed across regions?
2. What are some of the problems pervasive to financial markets, and what is a financial crisis?
3. What is the difference between portfolio capital flows and foreign direct investment, and what role did these capital flows play in recent financial crises?
4. What type of exchange-rate regime is most appropriate for developing economies?
5. What are the main activities of the International Monetary Fund?
6. What aspects of IMF policymaking have proved controversial in recent years?
7. What changes in the international financial architecture have economists proposed in recent years?

In April 2013, deposit levels at private banks in most of the 17 nations of the eurozone—the set of countries that utilize euros issued by the European Central Bank as their currency—declined noticeably. The largest absolute decrease was in Spain, where private deposits declined by €23 billion. Other significant reductions took place in Greece, in which deposits decreased by nearly €3 billion, and in Cyprus, which recorded a reduction exceeding €3 billion. The deposit drop in Cyprus during the month was proportionately the largest, however, at 7.3 percent, compared with a 1.6 percent decrease in Greece, and a 1.5 percent reduction in Spain.

In Cyprus, the cause of the national deposit reductions was a plan that European officials had floated to impose many of the losses caused by dropping asset values at Cyprus banks onto depositors of those banks. Depositors at the Cyprus banks engaged in rapid deposit withdrawals that halted only after the Cypriot government capped further withdrawals. Worries that European officials might also seek to impose losses on deposits in countries whose banks also had experienced substantial declines in asset values led to the deposit reductions in Greece and Spain, as well as a dozen other eurozone nations judged at that time to have weakened banking systems.

Nevertheless, total private deposits in the eurozone as a whole increased during April 2013. People who withdrew their euro-denominated deposits moved them to banks in a small handful of eurozone nations: Austria, Estonia, France, Germany, and Slovakia. Late that month, the European officials who had proposed the plan to impose Cypriot bank asset losses on depositors began to worry that even the stronger banks in these countries might begin to experience a "deposit run." The officials withdrew their plan, and within just a few weeks' time, deposits had returned to, or exceeded, the levels observed during the preceding March. For the time being, at least, the eurozone as a whole had avoided experiencing a financial crisis.

In recent years, many financial market participants and national governments have worried about the potential for a new international financial crisis on the heels of the global meltdown that took place between 2007 and 2010. In this chapter, you will learn about possible causes of international financial crises, and about efforts by national policymakers to do a better job of predicting and preventing them.

INTERNATIONAL CAPITAL FLOWS

For a number of nations, including the United States, the 2008 financial crisis was the deepest since the Great Depression period of the 1930s. The international spillovers that resulted have induced policymakers and economists around the world to reconsider the **international financial architecture**. This includes the international institutions, national policies and regulatory agencies, and international agreements that govern activity in the international monetary and financial markets. Whether the world's nations should alter the shape of the international financial architecture and, if so, what types of reforms should be adopted, are among the most important global policy issues today.

International financial architecture: *The international institutions, governmental and non-governmental organizations, and policies that govern activity in the international monetary and financial markets.*

Explaining the direction of capital flows

Since the collapse of the Bretton Woods system, the most important feature of the international financial system has been the increased volume of financial flows between nations. As you learned in Chapter 1, in recent years there has been dramatic growth in the volume of transactions in the international capital markets. To understand the nature of this recent upswing, it is important to account for differences between the capital flows experienced by developed countries and emerging economies. It is also crucial to distinguish between foreign direct investment (FDI) and shorter-term capital flows.

Foreign direct investment and developed nations

Growth in FDI is one of the most important developments in the evolution of global capital markets. Foreign direct investment is the acquisition of foreign financial assets that results in an ownership share. Many, but not all, national agencies that measure FDI flows consider an "ownership" share to be an acquisition of 10 percent or more of an entity. Hence, an FDI inflow is an acquisition of domestic financial assets that results in an ownership share of 10 percent or more of a domestic entity by a foreign resident. An FDI outflow is an acquisition of foreign financial assets that results in an ownership share of 10 percent or more of a foreign entity by a domestic resident.

Chapter 1 showed that, despite recent financial crises, between the early and latter part of the first decade of the twenty-first century, growth in world FDI greatly surpassed the growth of world exports. These flows—indeed, much of long-term capital flows—tend to be concentrated among the developed nations, however. Table 14.1 provides the geographic distribution of FDI inflows discussed in Chapter 1. The table shows that, on average, 65 percent of FDI inflows go to the developed nations. In the years immediately following the major emerging-economy financial crises of 1995 and 1998, FDI inflows to the developed economies spiked upward before retreating during the global financial meltdown that began in earnest during 2008. Though FDI flows recovered in 2010 and 2011 for both developed and developing economies, the greatest gains were among the developed nations. There was a significant downturn in 2012 among all three groups of nations, but much more so for the developed nations. The European nations in particular experienced a 41 percent decline in FDI inflows due to uncertainty regarding the sustainability of the European Monetary Union.

Cross-border mergers and acquisitions: *The combining of firms located in different nations, in which one firm absorbs the assets and liabilities of another firm (merger), or purchases the assets and liabilities of another firm (acquisition).*

The concentration of cross-border mergers and acquisitions

As discussed in Chapter 11, cross-border mergers and acquisitions (M&A), which are the combining of firms in different nations, are another prominent feature of the global monetary and financial markets. Cross-border M&A activity is the driving force behind the recent surges and declines in FDI within the developed economies. **Cross-border mergers and acquisitions** are the combining of firms in different

Table 14.1 *Geographical distribution of foreign direct investment, percentage of total inflows (in billions of US dollars). FDI inflows are highly concentrated in the developed nations. On average, more than two-thirds of FDI inflows go to the developed nations. After dropping in the late 1990s, FDI flows to these nations rose early in the first decade of this century before declining again during the financial crisis that occurred later that decade. These flows recovered once again in 2010 and 2011. In 2012, however, there was a precipitous decline in FDI across all country groups. This decline was most pronounced in the developed nations, with a 41 percent decline in FDI inflows to the European Union and a 26 percent decline in the United States. The developing nations fared relatively better with only a 4.5 percent decline in 2012.*

	1990–1995	1996–2000	2001–2005	2006–2010	2011–2012
Developed nations	50.5	67.8	65.4	57.6	46.1
Developing nations	37.1	29.2	31.0	37.1	48.9
Transition economies	3.3	3.0	3.5	5.4	6.0

Source: UNCTAD, *World Investment Report*, various issues.

nations. A *merger* occurs when a firm absorbs the assets and liabilities of another firm. An *acquisition* occurs when a firm purchases the assets and liabilities of another firm. Changes in national tax codes, relaxation of business regulations and labor laws, and a changing shareholder culture spurred a dramatic increase in cross-border M&A deals. As shown in Figure 14.1, after the mid-1990s M&A inflows increased to more than $800 billion annually. M&A inflows also display a pattern of decline during and following periods of economic recession.

Consistent with the geographic pattern of FDI, Figure 14.1 also shows that M&A activity is concentrated among developed nations such as the United States, Japan, and members of the European Union. According to data gathered by the OECD, the United States and the United Kingdom typically attract more M&A deals than all other nations. In 2007, prior to onset of the financial crisis, the United States and the United Kingdom captured approximately a third of global M&A purchases. As with total FDI flows, M&A activity began to recover in 2010 and 2011. In 2012, however, there was a significant drop in the number of M&A deals in both the developed and developing nations.

ON THE WEB:

For data on FDI, M&A, and capital flows, visit the home page of the Organisation for Economic Co-operation and Development (OECD) at www.oecd.org, and the United Nations Conference on Trade and Development (UNCTAD) at www.unctad.org.

Private capital flows to the developing and emerging economies

Chapter 1 detailed another important development in the recent evolution of global capital markets: The growth of private capital flows to the emerging and developing economies. Despite the financial crises faced by various developing nations during

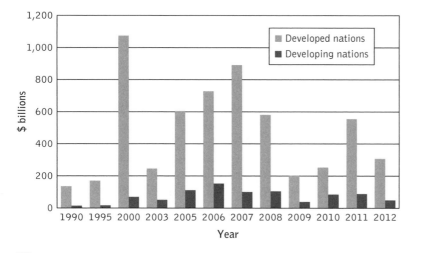

Figure 14.1 *Cross-border merger and acquisition inflows*

Cross-border mergers and acquisitions are the driving force behind recent increases and declines in FDI. During the period shown in the figure, cross-border M&A inflows increased dramatically in 2000, and again in 2005–2007. Cross-border M&A began to rise again in 2010 and 2011, but dropped again in 2012.

Source: United Nations Conference on Trade and Development Cross-border M&A database, www.unctad.org/fdistatistics.

the 1990s and early 2000s, FDI and portfolio investment continued to flow to these countries through 2007. Portfolio investment flows were significantly and negatively affected by the financial crisis and global recession of 2008 and 2009, however. As FDI flows recovered in 2010 and 2011, the developing and emerging economies experienced larger gains than the developed economies.

Many economists contend that large, rapid portfolio capital inflows often lay the foundation for subsequent financial crises. In fact, during recent decades, crisis-stricken nations have relied heavily on portfolio capital and other forms of development aid—that is, short-term capital flows—as opposed to longer-term FDI flows.

Fundamental Issue #1: How have recent developments in global capital markets differed across regions? Two important developments in the global capital markets have been the growth of cross-border M&A and FDI among developed nations, and surging private capital flows to emerging economies. Typically, FDI is concentrated among the United States, Japan, and the European Union, where the rise of cross-border M&A contributed to FDI within these regions. Since the early 1990s, private capital flows to developing economies also increased significantly. These countries experienced dramatic declines in both FDI and portfolio inflows following the financial crisis that began late in the first decade of the twenty-first century. Following the global recession, FDI flows initially rose and then fell again. The gains for the developing and emerging economies, however, were proportionally larger than for the developed economies.

Capital allocations and economic growth

Advocates of *capital-market liberalization*—allowing relatively open issuance and competition in stock and bond markets—argue that unhindered capital movements allow savings to flow to their most productive use, resulting in a more efficient allocation of scarce resources. Those projects that yield high returns reward savers—who are, in fact, financial speculators—for the risk they have assumed. In this way, markets direct resources in the most efficient pattern, resulting in development of real resources and higher productivity. Consequently, savers assume the risks in cross-border financial transactions and provide essential liquidity to a nation's economy.

How capital inflows can smooth domestic business cycles

With access to FDI and portfolio capital provided by foreign savers, domestic households and businesses then might expand their lending and borrowing activities abroad. This allows domestic businesses and consumers to continue to spend and invest during domestic economic downturns. They repay foreign savers during periods of economic growth. In this way, foreign capital inflows can help to offset domestic business cycles, providing greater stability to the domestic economy.

Hence, domestic savers can diversify internationally and reduce their exposure to domestic economic shocks. These positive aspects of foreign capital inflows allow domestic savers to enjoy higher risk-adjusted rates of return, spurring even higher levels of saving and investment activity. In turn, increased saving and investment induce additional economic growth.

How capital inflows can contribute to long-term development

Access to global capital in the form of FDI and portfolio capital inflows considerably reduces the costs to developing nations of financing investment projects. This permits domestic firms and individuals to undertake more investment projects, which contributes to the development of real resources. In the long run, this translates into higher standards of living and higher rates of economic growth. Additionally, private savings from abroad may substitute for uncertain development aid from foreign governments, which often comes with inefficiency costs associated with bureaucratic red tape and constraints.

For emerging economies, **financial-sector development**—the development and strengthening of financial institutions, payment systems, and regulatory agencies—is necessary to attract global capital and promote domestic saving. Economic theory indicates, however, that financial-sector development may either increase or decrease saving. As just discussed, financial-sector development can improve the allocation of domestic and foreign savings flows. Nevertheless, wider availability of the various hedging instruments, such as those described in Chapter 6, potentially reduces precautionary saving. In addition, improvements in household credit markets may allow agents to borrow more than they might otherwise have done, to engage in current consumption or to initiate projects that previously might have been deemed unworthy of financial support. Hence, if financial-sector development induces lower total *net* saving—saving less borrowing—economic growth actually could suffer.

Financial-sector development. *The strengthening and growth of a nation's financial-sector institutions, payments systems, and regulatory agencies.*

In general, economists have two opposing points of view about the contribution of the financial sector to long-run economic development. Some economists argue that the development of real resources, including physical resources such as plant and equipment and the development of technology and human capital are the crucial determinates of long-run economic performance. According to this view, the financial sector does not play an important role in the long run.

An alternative view is that the development of the financial sector induces changes in economic fundamentals. The financial sector can attract foreign capital and affect private agents' long-run saving and borrowing decisions and, therefore, long-run investment strategies. In this way, development of the financial sector influences long-run economic performance.

Why financial development evolves differently across nations is still somewhat unclear. Recent research on the causal relationship between financial development and real-sector growth, however, tends to support the second view above. This research concludes that financial development does indeed affect economic growth by promoting savings and directing funds to the most productive investment projects.

Capital misallocations and their consequences

Despite the arguments for capital-market liberalization, *financial market imperfections* and *policy-created distortions* may cause a nation's financial system to fall short in contributing to its economic development. Let's consider each in turn.

Financial market imperfections

Many economists argue that *asymmetric information*—the fact that one party in a financial transaction, such as a borrower, often possesses information not available to another party, such as a lender—is pervasive to financial markets. Asymmetric information can bring about an inefficient distribution of capital through resulting problems of adverse selection, herding behavior, and moral hazard.

Adverse selection, another type of market imperfection that affects financial markets, is the potential for those who want funds for unworthy projects to be the most likely to want to borrow. Both market imperfections were discussed in Chapter 12. Adverse selection can make savers less willing to lend to or hold instruments, including lending to or holding debt instruments of those seeking to finance high-quality projects. Additionally, poor information may result in herding behavior. *Herding behavior* occurs when savers who lack full information base their decisions on the behavior of others who they think are better informed. In a global context, herding behavior can be a catalyst for *contagion*, the spread of financial instability to regional levels. Herding behavior can also lead to a reduction of asset prices or currency values that greatly exceed what would be warranted.

Another potential problem that may affect financial markets is *moral hazard*, or the potential for a borrower to engage in much riskier behavior after issuing a debt instrument. For instance, moral hazard may arise when a domestic government implicitly or explicitly guarantees that a firm or bank will not be allowed to fail. Knowing that it will not be allowed to fail, the firm may engage in higher-risk projects in search for higher returns. International organizations, such as the International Monetary Fund (IMF), have also been accused of creating moral hazard in much the same way, by standing ready to bail out sovereign nations facing liquidity crises. The argument goes that, if the sovereign government knows the IMF is willing to loan it funds when it runs out of foreign reserves, the government will not conduct its policies in a manner prescribed by its exchange-rate arrangement.

Policy-created distortion: *When a government policy results in a market producing a level of output that is different from the economically efficient level of output, causing a less than optimal allocation of an economy's scarce resources.*

Policy-created distortions

Capital flows may also respond to policy-created distortions, leading to an inefficient and capricious allocation of capital. A **policy-created distortion** results when a government policy leads a market to produce a level of output that is different from the desired level of output, or economically efficient level of output. Microeconomic policies (e.g., tariffs on imports and subsidies to specific industries, such as steel or tires) protect producers in those industries from foreign competition. This type of protection is typically offered to industries that are not competitive in global markets.

Yet, by protecting the industry, these policy measures result in a different level of output and higher economic profits than would be experienced in a competitive environment. In turn, these higher profits attract capital flows into the protected industry and away from other, perhaps more productive, industries. Differential national taxation policies, trade restrictions, and macroeconomic policies are but a few policy-created distortions that can lead to a misallocation of capital.

In addition, differing national regulations of financial transactions may generate *regulatory arbitrage*—that is, domestic institutions may locate abroad, or conduct certain types of operation abroad, in order to avoid domestic regulation and supervision. This diminishes the regulatory abilities of governments and exposes domestic intermediaries to the very types of risk that regulators seek to minimize.

Although these distortions result from domestic economic policies, they should be viewed in an international context as well. In principle, the absence of international cooperation and coordination can bring about a potential "race to the bottom," or a movement toward the regulatory and tax environment of the least stringent nation. The possible role of multinational policy cooperation and coordination in reducing this possibility is discussed later in this chapter.

Financial instability and financial crises

When market imperfections and policy-created distortion are severe, they may result in **financial instability**, a situation in which the financial sector is unable to allocate funds to the most productive projects. Severe financial instability can trigger a **financial crisis**, or complete breakdown in the functioning of financial markets. A financial crisis typically involves a banking crisis, a currency crisis, and a foreign debt crisis. A key policy objective of all nations, therefore, is to reduce the potential for the types of problem described thus far, creating a stable financial environment.

Where do financial intermediaries fit in?

There are several ways in which *financial intermediaries*—the institutions that channel funds from savers to those who ultimately make capital investments—can contribute to financial stability and spur greater economic growth. One key function of financial intermediaries is to funnel savings to borrowers with minimum inefficiencies. The process of intermediation can be costly and, therefore, absorbs a fraction of each dollar of saving being channeled to a borrower. An efficient intermediary absorbs a smaller fraction of each dollar and can channel a greater portion of each dollar of saving on to the borrower. As a result, a greater portion of the nation's saving is invested, spurring greater economic growth. Reducing reserve requirements, a central bank policy instrument discussed in Chapter 9, and unnecessary and costly regulations may improve the efficiency of a nation's financial intermediaries.

Another way in which financial intermediaries reduce inefficiencies is by making it possible for many people to pool their funds together. This increases the amount of total savings managed by a single authority. Such centralization can yield economies of scale that reduce average fund-management costs below the levels savers would

Financial instability: *When a nation's financial sector is no longer able to allocate funds to the most productive projects.*

Financial crisis: *A situation that arises when financial instability becomes so severe that the nation's financial system is unable to function. A financial crisis typically involves a banking crisis, a currency crisis, and a foreign debt crisis.*

incur if they were to manage their savings alone. In this way, intermediaries may increase the amount of savings ultimately invested by reducing unnecessary costs.

An efficient system of financial intermediaries may also reduce the degree of information asymmetries, thereby improving capital allocations and enhancing financial-market stability. By specializing in the assessment of the quality of debt instruments, and continuously monitoring the performance of firms that issue these instruments, financial intermediaries are able to reduce the extent of information imperfections. In addition, if savers are unable to pool risks, they will invest only in the most liquid projects. More productive but less liquid projects are not financed, resulting in lower potential economic growth.

Hence, intermediaries perform a multifaceted role. Relying on their information capabilities, they evaluate investment projects, determine those with the highest potential return, and induce savers to invest in higher-risk but more profitable projects by providing a means of sharing risks at reduced average costs. Because of their important role in allocating capital, the supervision and regulation of financial intermediaries is a key element of various proposals for the reform of the international financial architecture discussed later in this chapter.

Fundamental Issue #2: What are some of the problems pervasive to financial markets, and what is a financial crisis? Several problems are particularly pervasive to financial markets. One type of financial market failure is asymmetric information, or the fact that borrowers and lenders often possess different information. Asymmetric information may result in problems of adverse selection, herding behavior, and moral hazard. Policy distortions, such as differential taxation and regulation, may also result in a less-than-optimal allocation of capital. When financial market imperfections and policy distortions are severe, they may result in financial instability and a financial crisis. A financial crisis is when financial instability becomes so severe that the nation's financial system no longer functions, and usually involves a banking crisis, a currency crisis, and a foreign debt crisis. Efficient financial intermediaries reduce the impact of financial market imperfections, thereby encouraging more saving and financing more investment projects.

CAPITAL FLOWS AND INTERNATIONAL FINANCIAL CRISES

Recent research by economists indicates that capital-market liberalization generally leads to improvements in capital allocations and further development of a nation's financial sector. Nearly every nation that liberalized its capital markets during the past three decades has experienced some type of financial crisis, however. How have international capital flows contributed to recent financial crises?

Are all capital flows equal?

Although capital-market liberalization and access to global capital may reduce the cost of investment projects and spur economic growth, the resulting collective debt obligations may destabilize the economy. The maturity structure of a nation's public and private foreign debt is one important aspect. Attracting both short-term and long-term debt allows for a diversified portfolio of debt instruments, a manageable repayment structure, and, therefore, a more stable portfolio of debt.

Because governments, firms, and households have different borrowing needs, and because investment projects have different time horizons, it is important that a nation's financial sector attracts both short-term investment flows and long-term FDI capital. Economists consider **portfolio investment** as the purchase of financial instruments that results in a less than 10 percent ownership share. Portfolio capital flows tend to have a shorter term to maturity and lower borrowing costs, and typically they are viewed as a means of generating near-term income. On the other hand, FDI is a long-term investment strategy in which the source of funds establishes financial control. Because portfolio capital and FDI represent different investment strategies, and have different maturity structures and different borrowing costs, they are not equivalent in terms of their potential short-run and long-run consequences.

Portfolio investment: *The acquisition of foreign financial assets that results in less than a 10 percent ownership share in the entity.*

Portfolio capital flows

Portfolio capital deals, which are short-term in nature, are easier to arrange, have lower borrowing costs, and do not require a firm to relinquish financial control to a foreign entity. Over time, portfolio capital inflows may improve capital allocations within a nation and help a nation's financial sector to develop. Because portfolio capital is a non-ownership and relatively liquid form of investment, however, portfolio capital flows can reverse direction quickly. Portfolio capital flight out of a developing country can leave its fragile financial sector short of much-needed liquidity, generating financial instability. This can trigger a financial crisis that can threaten both the solvency of a nation's financial intermediaries, and the viability of its exchange-rate regime.

Foreign direct investment

By way of contrast, FDI is a relatively illiquid ownership form of investment that can have a stabilizing effect on a nation's economy. As noted earlier, FDI most often occurs when multinational firms establish foreign affiliates or enter into strategic alliances with foreign firms. In doing so, they seek long-term commitments. As multinational firms become entrenched in foreign nations, they establish valuable relationships and networks with customers and suppliers. One would not, therefore, expect multinational firms engaging in FDI to enter and exit foreign nations with much frequency. It is the potential for long-lasting commitments and corporate entrenchment that makes FDI a stabilizing influence on a nation's economy. These long-term arrangements, however, are more difficult to arrange and result in some degree of foreign ownership of domestic firms.

Hence, portfolio capital and direct investment offer different positive and negative features. Because capital flows are not all equal, it is important for a nation's financial sector to create an environment that attracts both long-term and short-term capital. In this way, capital allocations are improved, spurring real-sector and financial sector development while minimizing financial instability.

The role of capital flows in recent crisis episodes

A key lesson that many developing nations have learned at various times over the past several decades is that excessive reliance on portfolio capital flows can be destabilizing. It is important to note, however, that outflows of foreign portfolio capital have not necessarily been the root cause of financial crises experienced by developing nations over the years. Foreign capital outflows typically have been a symptom, triggered by a loss of confidence in nations' macroeconomic and microeconomic policies, their levels of political stability, and the soundness of their financial markets and real productive and manufacturing sectors.

Foreign direct investment as a stabilizing element

Because FDI is a stabilizing element, many nations strive to create an environment that attracts FDI. Table 14.1 (on page 456) indicates, however, that FDI tends to be concentrated among the developed countries. An important policy issue for developing and emerging economies, therefore, is how to attract FDI and minimize the reliance on portfolio capital flows in financing investment projects.

An important conclusion is that nations should pay attention less to the nationality of multinational corporations and more to the positive impact that the act of locating production or distribution operations of a foreign firm within a country can have on the country's employment and income. Empirical research shows that multinational firms invest in foreign markets because they perceive advantages to doing so: Skilled workforces, good distribution networks, developed supply chains, access to finance, and so on. A country that invests in education, research, training, and infrastructure, therefore, can expect continually to attract FDI, enabling it to maintain high levels of employment and income. In this way, a nation could create a virtuous spiral of growth and investment, whereby domestic investment and FDI continually reinforce one another.

Following the international financial crises of the 1990s and 2000s, academics, private agencies, and international policy groups generated a large body of policy recommendations for nations to improve the mix of capital inflows. A sample of these proposals is provided later in this chapter.

Is there a role for capital controls?

Some economists suggest that countries cannot limit their efforts to attracting FDI. They contend that emerging nations should take steps actively to reduce their level of reliance on portfolio capital flows. Economists favoring greater government intervention often advocate attempting to control short-term portfolio flows in an effort to pace the gradual liberalization of financial markets.

Most economists are skeptical of controls on capital flows, however. Sebastian Edwards of the University of California in Los Angeles studied the effect of Chile's capital controls on the composition of that country's capital flows and its macro-economic stability. One important conclusion that he reaches is that regardless of the type and extent of legislation imposed the private sector eventually finds ways of getting around the restrictions. Edwards argues that controls on capital *outflows* should be avoided, as they are particularly ineffective in this regard.

Controls on capital *inflows* may prove to be effective in the short run and slow the pace of short-term inflows and lengthening the maturity of foreign debt. By lengthening the maturity of debt, they give policymakers an opportunity to liberalize capital markets and allow the financial sector to develop. In the case of Chile, for example, controls on capital inflows resulted in a decline of short-term capital inflows, as a percentage of overall capital inflows, from more than 95 percent in 1988 to less than 3 percent in 1997.

Edwards concludes, however, that capital controls be used as a *temporary stop-gap* measure. He argues that policymakers eventually should remove capital controls as they create additional borrowing costs. As discussed earlier, Chile is removing the last of its capital controls because they have increased the cost of capital significantly. Once the financial sector is developed, complete capital-market liberalization can improve capital allocations, spurring real economic development.

In 2010, large sums of portfolio capital began flowing into many developing and emerging economies. These inflows put upward pressure on the currencies of these countries, and there was concern that another round of capital inflows and sudden stops might occur again. Several countries, including Brazil, South Korea, and Thailand, resorted to capital controls to reduce inflows. The government of South Korea, for example, imposed a 14 percent tax on foreign residents' earnings on South Korean government bonds. (In the European island nation of Cyprus, capital controls have been put into place with the aim of keeping domestic residents from moving funds out of the country; see *Policy Notebook: Euros are all the same everywhere except in Cyprus*.)

POLICY NOTEBOOK

Euros are all the same everywhere except in Cyprus

A fundamental rationale for joining a monetary union, such as the 17-nation group that constitutes the eurozone, is to be able to utilize a common currency in transactions involving goods, services, and financial assets in any participating country. During the first 13 years of the euro's existence, the eurozone operated in this manner. In March 2013, however, in response to a potential banking meltdown, the government of Cyprus imposed capital controls in the form of limitations on the amounts of euros that could be moved out of the country—including to other eurozone member nations. The government's capital-control decree banned all electronic transactions from Cyprus to other nations and prevented any single Cypriot resident from carrying out of the country more than €3,000 in euro notes.

Recently, the Cypriot government has gradually loosened some of its controls on electronic transfers. Nevertheless, since the spring of 2013, the government of Cyprus has prevented a euro held in Cyprus from being equivalent to a euro held in another location around the globe. Cypriot residents cannot readily use euros in other nations, so their euros have less value than the euros held by people outside Cyprus, who naturally have few incentives to move their own euros into Cyprus. In an important sense, therefore, Cyprus has its own, separate version of the euro.

For critical analysis: Why do you suppose that euro-denominated assets in Cyprus that otherwise would be identical in risk and other characteristics to euro-denominated assets held in other nations now commonly have lower market values?

Fundamental Issue #3: What is the difference between portfolio capital flows and foreign direct investment, and what role did these capital flows play in recent financial crises? Because portfolio capital inflows constitute a non-ownership, income-generating form of investment, these flows tend to be shorter-term and more liquid than FDI. An excessive reliance on portfolio capital flows for financing investment projects, therefore, can be destabilizing. By way of contrast, FDI represents a long-term financial control strategy and, hence, may have a stabilizing effect for the economy. An excessive reliance on portfolio capital flows appears to be one of the factors that contributed to the recent financial crises in the emerging economies.

EXCHANGE-RATE REGIMES AND FINANCIAL CRISES

The contribution of exchange-rate policies to the financial crises of the 1990s and 2000s is of particular interest to international economists. From the mid-1990s to the early twenty-first century, for instance, countries that experienced financial crises, such as Mexico, Southeast Asia, Brazil, Russia, Turkey, and Argentina, all had some type of fixed-exchange-rate regime. It appears on the surface, therefore, that pegged exchange-rate regimes can somehow contribute to crises.

Schools of thought on exchange-rate regimes

Two schools of thought on exchange-rate regimes emerged shortly before the financial crises listed above. The first school of thought holds that policymakers should not peg currency values to explicit targets or parity values. According to this view, currency-market participants can closely monitor policymakers' actions by observing differences between the spot exchange rate and the official parity rate. It is possible, therefore, that currency-market participants perceive even small misses from the parity rate, which cause them to determine whether the exchange-rate regime was not credible or trustworthy. If currency-market participants view the exchange-rate peg as non-credible and sell domestic currency-denominated assets in large volumes policymakers might not have sufficient foreign-exchange reserves to maintain the parity rate, and the exchange-rate regime will collapse. Hence, this school of thought suggests that exchange rates should be fully flexible.

Conversely, the second school of thought indicates that an explicit exchange-value target is necessary for policymakers to establish credibility with market participants. By targeting the exchange rate, policymakers make a transparent commitment to their exchange-rate policy. According to this line of thought, an exchange-rate target or parity value constitutes a rule for the conduct of monetary policy. In this way, policymakers are more credible because currency-market participants could closely monitor exchange-rate policy and force policymakers to maintain their commitment to the exchange-rate target. Hence, this school of thought suggests that exchange rates should be fixed or pegged.

The corners hypothesis

Thus, many economists became skeptical of the soundness of *intermediate* or middle-ground exchange-rate regimes—regimes with limited exchange-rate flexibility, such as adjustable pegs, crawling pegs, and basket pegs. During the 1990s and early 2000s, mass selling of currencies by currency-market participants forced many crisis countries—Mexico, Thailand, Korea, Indonesia, Russia, and Brazil, for example—to abandon their intermediate exchange-rate regime.

Hence, a third view on exchange-rate management, the **corners hypothesis**, emerged. This theory suggests that policymakers should make a firm commitment to an exchange-rate regime that lies at one extreme or the other. That is, policymakers should establish a currency board or even dollarize their economy, or allow their currency to float freely in the foreign exchange market and avoid intermediate-exchange-rate regimes.

The corners hypothesis sparked a great deal of research that compared and contrasted exchange-rate regimes and economic and political conditions specific to each of the crisis countries. In the meantime, international organizations such as the IMF and the G7 urged policymakers in developing economies to abandon intermediate-pegged exchange-rate regimes in favor of flexible exchange-rate regimes, or even to dollarize their economies.

Corners hypothesis: *The view that policymakers should choose fully flexible or hard-peg exchange-rate regimes over intermediate regimes such as adjustable-peg, crawling-peg, or basket-peg arrangements.*

Peg, take the middle road, or float?

So what type of exchange-rate regime should developing-economy policymakers choose in hopes of avoiding a financial crisis? Recently, a growing number of economists have rejected the corners hypothesis. The main arguments against the corners hypothesis are that it lacks any theoretical basis and lacks empirical support. Hence, even though many of the crisis-stricken economies employed intermediate exchange-rate regimes, that does not necessarily imply that their exchange-rate regimes have been to blame for the crisis.

Economists who reject the corners hypothesis claim that there is no single type of exchange-rate regime that is right for all countries and, for any given country, no single type of regime may be appropriate at all times. Rather, as discussed in Chapter 3, economic and legal institutions and sound economic policymaking are more important than the choice of an exchange-rate regime in that they determine the viability of a given exchange-rate regime. Consequently, all three categories of exchange-rate regime—hard peg, intermediate peg, and floating regimes—are appropriate for some countries. (Iceland is an example of a nation that has benefited from allowing its exchange rate to float; see *Policy Notebook: A floating exchange rate pays off for Iceland*.)

POLICY NOTEBOOK

A floating exchange rate pays off for Iceland

In 2008, all three of Iceland's banks failed, resulting in the world's largest known banking-system failure in relation to a country's size. In the aftermath of the nation's financial collapse, Iceland's trade surplus evaporated, and the island nation began to experience a substantial trade deficit. In addition, the country's unemployment rate rose from less than 3 percent to over 8 percent by the end of 2010.

In contrast to the 17 nations that had adopted the euro as their currency between 1999 and 2008, and numerous others that kept their currency value pegged to the euro, Iceland retained its own currency, the króna, which floated. The króna proceeded to depreciate by more than 50 percent following in the wake of Iceland's financial meltdown. The resulting drop in the currency's value generated an upswing in the nation's exports and a drop in imports that has led to a return of annual trade surpluses. Although Iceland's residents' wealth levels have not fully recovered from the ill effects of the nation's crisis, their net annual incomes have risen significantly, and the nation's unemployment rate has dropped below 5 percent. Many observers now view Iceland's long-term economic outlook as much stronger than that of many European nations that have opted to utilize the euro, or to peg their own currency's value to the euro.

For critical analysis: Why do you suppose some economists have suggested that the unemployment rates in excess of 20 percent in Greece and Spain likely would drop substantially if those nations were to return to their pre-euro currency and allow its value to float?

Fundamental Issue #4: What type of exchange-rate regime is most appropriate for developing economies? The most appropriate exchange-rate regime for developing economies is a hotly contested and contemporary debate. Some economists argue that policymakers should commit to a hard-peg exchange-rate regime or a fully flexible exchange-rate regime. Others argue that no single regime is appropriate for all developing economies and that intermediate regimes, such as crawling-peg and basket-peg regimes, may be appropriate for some developing economies.

FINANCIAL CRISES AND MULTILATERAL POLICYMAKING

In the past, many nations have sought to develop a stable financial system capable of channeling steady and diversified sources of funds from domestic and foreign savers. Despite these efforts, however, a number of countries have experienced financial crises. Furthermore, crises that have begun in some countries have sometimes cascaded through the global financial system to exert effects on other nations, as was the case in the Asian crisis of 1997 and 1998 and again in the financial crises that have affected the United States and European nations since 2007.

In recognition of the possible inability of individual countries to prevent crises and of the potential for crises to spread internationally, many of the world's nations have developed multinational institutions intended to engender multilateral policy cooperation and coordination. These institutions aim both to limit the likelihood of crises and to contain crises when they occur.

The International Monetary Fund

As discussed in Chapter 7, the IMF is a multinational organization that promotes international monetary cooperation, exchange arrangements, and economic growth and that provides temporary financial assistance to nations experiencing balance-of-payments difficulties. Figure 14.2 charts the growth of IMF membership since the founding of the organization in July 1944. Currently, the IMF has 188 member nations.

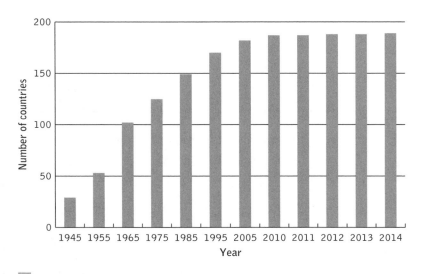

Figure 14.2 *Growth in membership of the International Monetary Fund*

The number of member nations in the IMF is now more than six times larger than it was when the organization was founded.

Source: International Monetary Fund.

Quota subscription: *The pool of funds deposited by IMF member nations that IMF managers can use for loans to member nations experiencing financial difficulties.*

Special drawing right: *A composite currency of the IMF in which the value is based on a weighted average of the currencies of five member nations.*

Conditionality: *The set of limitations on the range of allowable actions of government of a country that is a recipient of IMF loans.*

Structure of the IMF

When a country joins the IMF, it deposits funds to an account, called its **quota subscription**. These funds, which are measured in terms of **special drawing rights**, a composite currency of the IMF, form a pool from which the IMF can draw to lend to members. Figure 14.3 displays current quota subscriptions for selected IMF member nations.

The IMF sets each nation's quota subscription based on its real national income. The quota subscription determines how much a member can borrow from the IMF under the organization's standard credit arrangements. It also determines the member's share of voting power within the IMF. The U.S. quota subscription, for instance, is just over 17 percent of the total funds provided by all member nations, so this is the IMF voting share held by the United States.

When the IMF considers providing financial support to a member country in the way of short-term loans, it normally imposes specific limitations on the actions of that country's government. This IMF policy, called **conditionality**, requires countries to cooperate with the IMF in establishing plans for the nation's financial policies. Sometimes the IMF will not extend assistance to a nation unless it takes certain actions before receiving the loan. As part of broader satisfaction of conditionality requirements, the IMF may request only a general commitment to aim policies in a certain direction, known as *low conditionality*. In this case, the IMF is said to have a *policy understanding* with the nation. Alternatively, the IMF may impose *high conditionality*. Then it requires a nation to aim for specific, quantifiable targets, called *performance criteria*. Failure to meet these targets can lead to suspension of IMF loan disbursements.

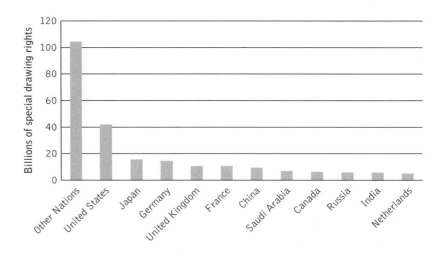

Figure 14.3 *International Monetary Fund quota subscriptions*

The quota subscription of each member nation in the IMF, which is denominated in special drawing rights, depends on the nation's real national income. A country's quota subscription determines its share of voting power within the IMF and how much it is eligible to borrow under standard IMF credit arrangements.

Source: International Monetary Fund.

Table 14.2 lists the main funding programs offered by the IMF. Originally, the IMF's primary function was to provide so-called standby arrangements and short-term credits, and it continues to offer these types of assistance through *non-concessional IMF facilities*. Initially, these facilities were designed to provide temporary funds to countries experiencing balance of payments problems and provide the opportunity to

Table 14.2 IMF financing facilities

Facility	Role
Non-concessional facilities	
Stand-by arrangements (SBA)	The IMF's main instrument for providing assistance to middle-income countries. These funds are intended to address or prevent balance of payment problems and can be provided on a precautionary basis. Disbursements are "conditional" on a country achieving program targets designed to address a balance-of-payments problem. Loans have a maturity of 12–24 months and must be repaid within 3.5–5 years.
Flexible credit line (FCL)	This facility is intended as a crisis-prevention tool for countries with a strong fundamental economic performance, sound policies, and a history of appropriate policy implementation. Countries must meet pre-set qualification criteria. Loans are for 1–2 years, and repayment is the same as for the SBA.
Precautionary credit line (PCL)	This credit line is intended for countries with strong fundamental economic performance, sound policies, and a history of appropriate policy implementation (as under the FCL) and which face "moderate" vulnerabilities and do not qualify large-scale adjustments (as under the SBA). The credit line can be drawn upon if a need arises unexpectedly.
Extended fund facility	This facility was established in 1974 to assist countries in addressing long-term balance-of-payments problems. Loans are typically for 3 years and must be repaid within 4.5–10 years from disbursement.
Concessional facilities	
Extended credit facility (ECF)	The IMF's main instrument for providing medium-term loans to lower-income countries that have "protracted" balance-of-payments problems. These loans have a zero interest rate with a grace period of 5.5 years and a 10-year maturity.
Standby credit facility (SCF)	Provides loans to lower-income countries with short-term balance-of-payments requirements. These loans have a zero interest rate with a grace period of 4 years and an 8-year maturity.
Rapid credit facility (RCF)	Provides rapid financing to lower-income countries with "urgent" balance-of-payments requirements. These loans have a zero interest rate with a grace period of 5.5 years and a 10-year maturity.
Emergency assistance	Emergency assistance is available for countries that experience a natural disaster or are emerging from a conflict. Loans are subject to interest and must be repaid within 3.25–5 years.

Source: International Monetary Fund.

address government deficits and debt problems. The Extended Fund Facility and the Stand-By Arrangements best represent the original funding provided by the IMF.

In 2010, the IMF worked with the European Union to structure a support package for Greece that totaled €110 billion. Of this total, €30 billion was provided through IMF Stand-By Arrangement funds. The financial crises in Europe spread, and by early 2013 the IMF had established funding arrangements with nine European nations totaling over $140 billion through four different funding facilities. Later in 2013, the IMF approved new funding for Cyprus through the Extended Fund Facility in an amount that was in excess of 500 percent of Cyprus' quota with the IMF. Over time, the IMF developed credit lines under the non-concessional facilities to assist any qualifying member experiencing an unusual or unexpected fluctuation in exports or imports, a loss of confidence in its own financial system, or spillover effects from financial crises originating elsewhere. The Flexible Credit Line, for example, was made available for the first time in 2009. The IMF viewed Mexico's macroeconomic conditions as favorable and its balance-of-payments position as "manageable" but was concerned that the global financial crisis and recession in the United States, an important trade partner of Mexico, posed a threat to the Mexican economy. Mexican policymakers stated that they viewed the arrangement as only precautionary and did not intend to draw from it.

After the end of the Bretton Woods system of pegged exchange rates, there was less need for short-term adjustment credit under the regular or non-concessional IMF facilities, and the IMF adapted by expanding other lending programs. These programs fall under *concessional IMF facilities*, which the IMF offers to poor and heavily indebted countries, either as long-term loans intended to support growth-promoting projects or as short- or long-term assistance aimed at helped countries experiencing problems in repaying existing debts. In 2010, for example, the IMF approved a 3-year Extended Credit Facility arrangement for Grenada. The arrangement provided approximately $14 million in loans to help boost the economy of Grenada, which was negatively impacted by a significant drop in tourism following the global financial crisis and recession.

Fundamental Issue #5: What are the main activities of the International Monetary Fund? The IMF and World Bank are multinational economic organizations consisting of more than 180 member nations. One of the IMF's broad objectives is to encourage economic growth by facilitating international monetary cooperation and effective exchange arrangements. Another fundamental IMF goal is to hinder or combat international financial crises by providing temporary and longer-term financial assistance to nations experiencing balance-of-payments difficulties. The World Bank also seeks to promote economic growth, but it does so primarily via longer-term loans to support investment projects within the world's less developed nations.

Ex ante versus ex post conditionality at the IMF

Like any other lender, the IMF encounters two key problems, described earlier in this chapter: adverse selection and moral hazard.

The IMF's policy of imposing conditionality terms on borrowers seeks to address the moral hazard problem. Most observers, however, agree that there are at least two weaknesses in the IMF's approach. First, IMF officials do not publicly announce the terms of the institution's lending agreements with specific nations. This means that it is solely up to the IMF to monitor whether borrower nations are using funds donated by other countries wisely. Often, private investors can discern that a country has failed to abide by its agreement with the IMF only when the IMF undertakes an action such as withholding a scheduled loan installment. Swift adverse market reactions following such IMF moves can place borrower nations in even worse financial straits, making it even more difficult for the borrower to meet the terms of its original agreement with the IMF. Thus, the IMF's policy of keeping loan agreements secret can undermine its efforts to protect members' funds from misuse.

Second, it is common for IMF officials initially to place only very general conditions on the loans they extend. They tend to switch to high conditionality only after a borrower nation has already enacted policies that violate the original low-conditionality arrangement. By that point, of course, the IMF has already failed to avoid the moral hazard problem.

Critics argue that IMF secrecy, and its tendency to impose high conditionality only when pressed to do so, effectively amounts to firm conditionality only on an *ex post*, or after-the-fact, basis. They contend that this after-the-fact, discretionary approach to establishing conditions under which the IMF lends, which they call *ex post* **conditionality**, undermines the IMF's credibility both with actual borrowers and with prospective borrowers. This lack of credibility, they argue, increases the likelihood for moral hazard problems while also widening the scope of the adverse selection problem by attracting borrower nations that are most likely to try to take advantage of vague conditions of a policy of low conditionality.

To reduce the extent of both problems, critics of the IMF have long suggested the use of *ex ante* **conditionality**, or conditions for IMF loans that are publicly known in advance. They have also pushed for imposing a few straightforward conditions, so that it is easy for everyone to monitor whether borrower nations have complied. To date, however, the IMF has maintained its generally secretive and discretionary lending policies.

Ex post **conditionality:**
The imposition of IMF lending conditions after a loan has already been granted.

Ex ante **conditionality:**
The imposition of IMF lending conditions before the IMF grants the loan.

> *Fundamental Issue #6: What aspects of IMF policymaking have proved controversial in recent years?* The IMF has received criticism for failing to publicize conditions it places on loans to member countries. Critics have also questioned the IMF's tendency to make such conditions very general and hard to measure. Both aspects of IMF policymaking, they argue, increase the potential for moral hazard by making it easier for borrowers to commit IMF funds to riskier projects.

DOES THE INTERNATIONAL FINANCIAL ARCHITECTURE NEED A REDESIGN?

Multinational institutions have confronted two types of criticism in recent years. One set of critics believes that these institutions are correctly designed and structured but contends nevertheless that these institutions could do a much better job of heading off financial crises before they occur. Another group, however, criticizes the operations of, and in some cases even the existence of, multinational financial institutions. According to the latter group, at a minimum the international financial architecture requires some retuning, and it may even require a redesign.

Can policymakers predict international financial crises?

To be able to limit, or even prevent, international financial crises, policymakers must have a good idea about their underlying causes. In fact, however, there are differing perspectives concerning the main causes of crises. Let's consider each in turn to discuss what guidance they provide about factors that might help national and supranational authorities determine when they should intervene to try to reduce the likelihood of a crisis.

Economic imbalances and international financial crises

Economic fundamentals: *Basic factors determining a nation's current exchange rate, such as the country's current and likely future economic policies and performance.*

The traditional view of financial crises focuses on **economic fundamentals**, which are underlying factors such as the nation's current and likely future economic prospects and its monetary and fiscal policies. According to this view, an inconsistency between the value of the exchange rate corresponding to a nation's economic fundamentals and an officially targeted exchange-rate value can engender a financial crisis. If foreign exchange traders perceive that the official value of a nation's currency is higher than its true value in private foreign exchange markets based on economic fundamentals, then there naturally will be a tendency for traders to sell their holdings of assets denominated in that currency to avoid losses. By unloading these assets, traders who are averse to risk will reduce their losses if it should happen that the government or central bank runs out of foreign currency reserves used to purchase the currency and maintain the official exchange rate.

Speculative attack: *A concerted effort by financial-market speculators to profit from anticipations of a depletion of official foreign exchange reserves via sales of assets denominated in the nation's currency, intended to induce abandonment of an exchange-rate target that will yield them profits in derivative markets.*

Furthermore, speculators may seek to profit from their anticipations of an imminent exhaustion of official foreign exchange reserves by selling assets denominated in the nation's currency in an effort to push the government or central bank into giving up on supporting the exchange rate at its officially targeted level. At the same time, they can bet on a collapse of the official exchange rate via positions they take in markets for futures, options, and swaps. This type of behavior is called a **speculative attack** on a nation's official exchange rate.

If a speculative attack is successful, then speculators potentially can earn significant profits from taking these positions. They can do this by effectively selling foreign currency-denominated assets at the high official prices via arrangements to buy them in derivatives markets at lower prices more nearly consistent with underlying economic fundamentals. Of course, speculators can, and sometimes do, lose these kinds of bets, so speculative attacks do not necessarily succeed. Nevertheless, if the official exchange rate is sufficiently misaligned with the exchange rate such that it would be consistent with economic fundamentals, the probability increases that a speculative attack will succeed.

Self-fulfilling expectations and contagion effects

A second perspective focuses on the potential role of *self-fulfilling anticipations* and contagion effects, which can bring about an international financial crisis even when underlying economic fundamentals are consistent with an officially pegged exchange rate or when governments and central banks otherwise have sufficient foreign exchange reserves, given a slight misalignment of the government's exchange-rate target. According to this view, all that is needed to induce a speculative attack is a relatively widespread perception by traders that a nation's policymakers face relatively high internal costs, perhaps because of resulting political difficulties, from maintaining the official exchange rate.

Suppose, for instance, that currency speculators perceive a lack of resolve on the part of policymakers. They might then attempt to profit from their anticipation that policymakers will give in and devalue a currency rather than accept higher interest rates or other changes that may have negative economic spillovers. If a sufficient number of speculators develop anticipations that government authorities in a nation lack the will to accept such spillovers, then large sales of assets denominated in the nation's currency can occur. This can induce other risk-averse traders to sell their foreign currency-denominated assets as well in an effort to avoid losses. Essentially, according to this alternative view, a speculative attack takes place simply because of expectations that it will be successful, but not necessarily because of underlying problems with economic fundamentals.

Structural moral hazard problems

Finally, a third perspective focuses on flaws within the structure of a nation's financial system as the major factors that lay the groundwork for a crisis situation. From this view, crisis conditions exist when government policies create a situation of rampant *moral hazard problems*. For instance, a nation's government might require its banks to make loans to specific firms or industries because these firms and industries know that they will receive credit no matter how they use the funds, they commit them to risky undertakings. Many observers of the financial crises in Malaysia and Indonesia during the late 1990s have argued that such moral hazard problems existed in those nations. Ultimately, the risks taken on by those who receive government-directed credit generate actual losses and failures, these observers conclude, which sets off a crisis situation.

Others who emphasize the potential for moral hazard problems to generate financial crises also contend that the policies of multinational institutions such as the IMF and the World Bank can contribute to financial crises. On one hand, they argue, when such institutions provide credit for industries and governments at prices below the market price of credit in the recipient nations, this tends to push down standards of creditworthiness in those countries. The reason, goes this argument, is that in their quest to earn profits, private lenders who are unable to compete for borrowers at the below-market rates charged by the IMF and the World Bank (see Chapter 11) lower their credit standards and make loans to less creditworthy borrowers. On the other hand, because

475

governments know that they can apply for IMF and World Bank assistance if overextension of credit to unworthy borrowers leads to widespread financial failures, they have little incentive to rein in risky lending within their financial systems.

Crisis prediction and early warning systems

Each of these perspectives indicates different factors that might help in predicting financial crises. According to the view that emphasizes the importance of imbalances in economic fundamentals, variables such as exports, imports, foreign exchange reserves, real income, monetary aggregates, exchange rates, and interest rates might all be useful indicators of the potential for a crisis. For instance, if a country's trade balance quickly worsens and its foreign exchange reserves rapidly decline, then a crisis may be in the offing.

The perspective emphasizing moral hazard problems, however, indicates that such changes in economic fundamentals are likely to occur when a crisis is already in progress. Hence, variations in economic fundamentals will not necessarily help predict crises far enough in advance to help prevent them. The view that self-fulfilling expectations can induce crises offers an even more pessimistic view about the usefulness of economic fundamentals as crisis indicators. According to this view, it may be difficult to find a close relationship between fundamentals and crises, because crises may sometimes take place without a previous significant change in fundamentals.

Before considering what factors aid in predicting financial crises, it would be helpful if economists agreed about what constitutes a crisis. There are, however different views on how to determine that a crisis has occurred. Jeffrey Frankel of Harvard University and Andrew Rose of the University of California at Berkeley, for instance, propose that a crisis definitely exists when a nation's currency experiences a nominal depreciation of at least 25 percent within a year, that follows a depreciation of at least 10 percent the previous year. Most economists, however, have considered more flexible index measures of speculative pressures that take into account exchange rate changes and variations in foreign exchange reserves. They consider a crisis to have occurred when such an index exceeds a threshold that depends on the normal, historical pattern of variation that the index has exhibited in prior years.

Financial crisis indicator: *An economic variable that normally moves in a specific direction and by a certain relative amount in advance of a financial crisis, thereby helping to predict a coming crisis.*

In such studies, economists seek to determine whether they can identify any economic variables that serve as **financial crisis indicators,** or factors that typically precede such crises and thereby aid in predicting them. One such study is by Morris Goldstein of the Institute for International Economics, Graciela Kaminsky of George Washington University, and Carmen Reinhart of the University of Maryland. One type of indicator that these authors consider is ratings of the countries' debts, such as credit ratings by Moody's and other credit rating bureaus. These ratings might reflect moral hazard problems. In addition, however, they evaluate a large set of potential "leading indicators" of financial crises, that includes exchange rates, interest rates, national income levels, quantities of money in circulation, and the like. Such variables, naturally, reflect economic fundamentals that the traditional view of financial crises predicts should play important roles, and these variables also provide important information that traders use to form expectations.

These authors find that credit ratings do not help predict financial crises. This could be because moral hazard problems are not a key causal factor in crises, but it is also possible that rating agencies such as Moody's do not have sufficient information to assess accurately the scope of moral hazard and its implications for the true creditworthiness of international borrowers. The authors find that several economic fundamentals together tend to do a better job of predicting financial crises than any single indicator.

The objective of studies searching for financial crisis indicators is to develop an **early warning system**, or a mechanism for monitoring financial and economic data for signals of trouble that might eventually evolve into a crisis. The idea is that if a multinational institution could develop an effective early warning system, it would receive sufficient warning to intervene speedily and head off a crisis before it occurs.

There is some optimism inside and outside the IMF and the World Bank that economists may ultimately develop a reliable early warning system. Many economists remain skeptical, however. Some doubt that any single view of the causes of international financial crises—shifts in economic fundamentals, speculation driven by self-fulfilling expectations, or moral hazard problems caused by inadequate conditions on domestic or multinational loans—can single-handedly "explain" every crisis. Thus, these skeptics doubt that any early warning system based on a limited set of indicators is likely to improve the capability of multinational institutions to react quickly enough to prevent them from occurring.

Early warning system: *A mechanism that multinational institutions might use to track financial crisis indicators to determine that a crisis is on the horizon, thereby permitting a rapid response to head off the crisis.*

Rethinking economic institutions and policies

The strongest critics of multinational institutions contend there is little evidence that these institutions have developed the capability to head off financial crises before they occur. Indeed, a number of critics contend that multinational institutions themselves can contribute to the likelihood of international financial crises. Accordingly, these critics argue, the world's nations should consider making fundamental reforms in the structure of these institutions.

Rethinking long-term development lending

Not all lending by supranational institutions is related to crisis situations. Both the IMF and the World Bank also make longer-term loans intended to foster growing standards of living in many of the world's poorer nations.

Since the early 1990s, one of the main themes of development economics has been that markets work better at promoting growth when a developing nation has more effective institutions, such as basic property rights, well-run legal systems, and uncorrupt government agencies. Considerable evidence indicates that countries where property rights are not well enforced, the rule of law is weak, and governments are corrupt tend to grow more slowly, even if they otherwise permit markets to function without regulatory hindrances.

This implies that a top priority of supranational organizations dedicated to higher standards of living in developing nations should be finding ways to improve those nations' fundamental institutions. At the most basic level, economists emphasize the paramount importance of putting in place basic market foundations, such as property and contract rights. This requires constructing credible legal systems to enforce laws, and setting up the kinds of institutions that are likely to lead to better national policies, perhaps including establishment of independent central banks and transparent budget processes for fiscal authorities.

Furthermore, bringing about structural reforms consistent with achieving a higher long-term growth rate requires nations to develop strategies for making reforms last. This requires building a consensus for reform and sometimes may entail compensating those who lose when reform is enacted.

Alternative institutional structures for limiting financial crises

Most proposals for altering the international financial architecture focus on multinational policymaking related to financial crises. They range from relatively minor changes in existing institutions and procedures to replacement of existing multinational institutions with new institutions.

Several features are common to a number of the proposals, however. These include more frequent and in-depth releases of information by both multinational lenders and national borrowers, improved financial and accounting standards for those receiving funds from multinational lenders, increased use of both high and *ex ante* conditionality for IMF lending; and, in several proposals, increased efforts to induce private lenders to extend credit. Beyond these areas of common ground, however, proposals typically diverge sharply. Some call for more oversight of the IMF, while others suggest a wholesale change in the IMF's management structure. Still other proposals would, if adopted, entail dismantling the IMF and replacing it with new forms of multinational institutions.

So far, few proposals for altering the international financial architecture have led to actual change. The IMF has adopted some minor changes in its procedures for collecting and releasing information, and it has stiffened some of the financial and accounting standards that borrowers must follow to obtain credit. Naturally, the member nations of the IMF would have to agree to the adoption of more dramatic proposals for change. To date there has been little movement in this direction. Nevertheless, debate on the desirability of minor changes in the *status quo* versus potentially significant departures continues. Undoubtedly, consideration of proposals for an altered international financial architecture will continue to generate global debate in the years to come.

Fundamental Issue #7: What changes in the international financial architecture have economists proposed in recent years? Many critics of the IMF and the World Bank have argued that they should develop early warning systems to aid in predicting and perhaps even preventing international financial crises. A fundamental problem that these institutions face in such efforts, however, is that there is little agreement about why crises occur and, hence, about what indicators should be used to try to predict crises. A common theme of existing proposals for altering the international financial architecture is to enforce stronger conditions on the long-term and short-term loans that multinational institutions extend to borrowers. Many proposals also entail more publicity of the internal operations and lending policies of the IMF and the World Bank. Some proposals, however, argue for changing the management structure of the IMF and World Bank, supplementing these institutions with additional multinational institutions, or even replacing them with new multinational institutions that would follow different procedures or pursue different objectives.

CHAPTER SUMMARY

1. **Regional differences in global capital market developments**: The growth of foreign direct investment (FDI) among the developed economies and the growth of private capital flows to the emerging economies, are two of the most important developments taking place in the global capital markets. In spite of remarkable growth in foreign direct investment, much FDI has been concentrated among the triad countries of the United States, Japan, and the European Union. Mergers and acquisitions are the driving force of the recent surge in FDI and are also concentrated in the triad countries.

2. **Problems pervasive to financial markets, and financial crises**: One type of problem pervasive to financial markets is asymmetric information, or when borrowers and lenders possess different information. Asymmetric information may lead to problems of adverse selection, herding behavior, and moral hazard. Policy distortions, such as differential taxation and regulatory policies, are another type of problem. If these problems are severe, they may result in financial instability and a financial crisis. A financial crisis is when financial instability is so severe that a nation's financial system no longer functions. A financial crisis usually involves a banking crisis, a currency crisis, and a foreign debt crisis.

3. **The difference between portfolio capital flows and foreign direct investment, and the role of these capital flows in recent financial crises**: Portfolio capital flows are a non-ownership form of investment and tend to have short-term maturities. Foreign direct investment (FDI) represents an ownership strategy and tends to be long-term in maturity. Recent financial crises demonstrate that an excessive reliance on portfolio capital flows can destabilize an economy FDI, on the other hand, might have a stabilizing influence on an economy.

4. **The appropriate exchange-rate regime for developing economies**: There is considerable debate over the exchange-rate regime best suited for the developing economies. Economists disagree whether policymakers in developing economies should adopt a hard-peg arrangement, a fully flexible arrangement, or an intermediate arrangement such as a crawling-peg or basket-peg arrangement.

5. **The main activities of the International Monetary Fund and the World Bank:** The IMF and World Bank are multinational economic organizations that are owned and operated by more than 180 of the world's nations. The IMF exists to promote global economic growth by encouraging international monetary cooperation and effective exchange arrangements and to limit the scope for international financial crises by providing temporary and longer-term financial assistance to nations experiencing balance-of-payments difficulties.

6. **Aspects of IMF policymaking that have been controversial in recent years:** Although the IMF can place strong and measurable conditions on its loans to member countries, it often fails to do so. The IMF also does not release complete information about the conditions it places on loans. It is arguable that these aspects of IMF policymaking make it easier for borrowers to use IMF funds for unworthy projects, thereby increasing the scope of the moral hazard problem in international financial markets.

7. **Changes in the international financial architecture proposed by economists in recent years:** A number of economists have favored greater IMF and World Bank efforts to head off crises by developing early warning systems that would permit them to predict and respond more rapidly to international financial crises. Nevertheless, skeptics doubt that such efforts will bear fruit in light of general disagreement among economists about why crises occur and, therefore, about what indicators the IMF or World Bank might use to attempt to predict them. A number of proposals for redesigning the international financial architecture include adding and enforcing stricter and more measurable conditions for borrowers to meet before receiving long-term and short-term loans from the IMF and World Bank. Another common feature of many proposals is the release of more public information about the internal operations and lending policies of these institutions. A few proposals suggest more dramatic changes, such as new management structures for the IMF and World Bank, forming additional multinational institutions to supplement their activities, or replacing existing multinational institutions with new institutions that would operate differently or aim to achieve different objectives.

QUESTIONS AND PROBLEMS

1. Suppose you are a policymaker in a developing economy. Explain what types of capital flows you would encourage. What policy actions might you take to encourage these flows?

2. List three benefits of portfolio capital and three benefits of foreign direct investment. Give one negative aspect of each. Explain why it is undesirable to rely on portfolio capital only. Explain why it is undesirable to rely on FDI only.

3. Suppose a nation has a pegged exchange-rate system and you are the nation's chief central banker. Explain what policy actions you would take to maintain the exchange-rate regime under the following circumstances.

   (a) There is an increased inflow of short-term (portfolio) capital that you believe is only temporary in nature.

   (b) There is an increased inflow of long-term (direct investment) capital that you believe will persist for at least a few years.

4. Explain how allowing foreign banks to enter and compete in the domestic financial sector might improve capital market allocations. Explain how, in general, competition among financial intermediaries is important to financial stability.

5. Explain how savers and borrowers might benefit from regulation of a nation's financial intermediaries. Does regulation impose costs? How do these costs affect long-run economic development?

6. In the early 1990s, on the heels of a major political restructuring of central and Eastern European nations, the IMF granted billions of dollars in loans to Russia. Russia ended up partially defaulting on the loans, rescheduling loan payments, and applying for yet more IMF loans. Then, in the late 1990s, in the midst of the fallout from the Asian financial crisis, the IMF granted billions of dollars in additional loans to Russia. Once again, Russia defaulted on loan repayments, postponed many of its payments, and applied for additional IMF funding. Discuss possible reasons for this repetition of IMF–Russian interactions during the 1990s, and offer two proposals for how the IMF and Russia might avoid yet another repetition in the future. Explain why you believe your proposals might be successful in this regard.

7. In 2010, the IMF, along with the European Union, provided assistance to the government of Greece to prevent a default on government debt and allow time for the government to address fiscal problems. The same year, in order to support financial stability, the IMF, along with the European Union, provided assistance to Ireland to prevent Ireland's largest banks from becoming insolvent and collapsing. Explain how the two assistance programs are different, and why the program for Ireland represents a new type of lending for the IMF.

8. Construct a table with three columns. In the first column of the table, list each of the views on the causes of international financial crises. In the second column, list at least one possible financial crisis indicator corresponding to each view, which might be tracked in an IMF early warning system for predicting financial crises. In the third column, propose how to evaluate whether each potential indicator you have proposed actually helps predict a crisis. Does this exercise help explain why economists have a hard time constructing reliable early warning systems?

9. Should multinational institutions lend funds at interest rates below, equivalent to, or above private-market interest rates? Take a stand, and support your position.

ONLINE APPLICATION

URL: www.imf.org

Title: International Monetary Fund

Navigation: Go directly to the above URL for the home page of the IMF. Click on the "About the IMF" tab. Scroll down to "More Resources" and click on "Factsheets." Scroll down to "Where the IMF Gets Its Money" and click on "IMF Quotas."

Application: After reading the Factsheet, answer the following questions.

1. What is the formula for calculating a member country's quota?

2. In what currency are quotas denominated?

3. What are the three key roles of the quota in the IMF?
4. What are the two major changes in the proposed quota review of November 2010?

For group study and analysis: Discuss the changes proposed in the 14th General Review of Quotas. Debate which is more important—the overall increase in the quota system, or the increased quotas of the "dynamic" emerging and developing economies.

REFERENCES AND RECOMMENDED READINGS

Agénor, Pierre-Richard, and Peter J. Montiel. *Development Macroeconomics,* 3rd edn. Princeton, NJ: Princeton University Press, 2008.

Ariyoshi, Akira, Karl Habermeier, Bernard Laurens, Inci Otker-Robe, Jorge Iván Canales-Kriljenko, and Andrei Kirilenko. "Capital Controls: Country Experiences and Their Use and Liberalization." Occasional Paper 190. Washington, DC: International Monetary Fund, May 2000.

Aziz, Jahangir, Francesco Caramazza, and Ranil Salgado. "Currency Crises: In Search of Common Elements." Working Paper 00/67. Washington, DC: International Monetary Fund, 2000.

Corden, Max W. *Too Sensational: On the Choice of Exchange Rate Regimes.* Cambridge, MA: MIT University Press, 2002.

De Grauwe, Paul. *Economics of Monetary Union.* Oxford, U.K.: Oxford University Press, 2012.

Goldstein, Morris, Graciela Kaminsky, and Carmen Reinhart. *Assessing Financial Vulnerability: An Early Warning System for Emerging Markets.* Washington, DC: Institute for International Economics, 2000.

Krugman, Paul, ed. *Currency Crises.* Chicago, IL: University of Chicago Press, 2000.

Montel, Peter J. *Macroeconomic in Emerging Markets.* Cambridge, U.K.: Cambridge University Press, 2003.

Pincus, Jonathan, and Jeffrey Winters. *Reinventing the World Bank.* Ithaca, NY: Cornell University Press, 2002.

Vreeland, James Raymond. *The IMF and Economic Development.* Cambridge, U.K.: Cambridge University Press, 2003.

White, William. "What Have We Learned from Recent Financial Crises and Policy Responses?" Working Paper No. 84. Basel: Bank for International Settlements, January 2000.

Glossary

Absolute advantage: The ability of a nation's residents to produce a good or service at lower cost, measured in resources required to produce the good or service, or, alternatively, the ability to produce more output from given inputs of resources, as compared with other nations.

Absolute quota: A quantitative restriction that limits the amount of a product that can enter a country during a specified time period.

Ad valorem tariff: A tariff calculated as a percentage of the value of the good or service.

Adaptive expectations: Expectations that are based only on information from the past.

Adverse selection: The tendency for manufacturers of the lowest-quality products to have the greatest incentive to misrepresent the attributes of those products.

American option: An option in which the holder may buy or sell an amount of a currency any time before or including the date at which the contract expires.

Announcement effect: A change in private market interest rates or exchange rates that results from an anticipation of near-term changes in market conditions signaled by a central bank policy action.

Antitrust laws: Statutes designed to achieve benefits of competition for consumers and producers.

Arbitrage: Buying an item in one market to sell at a higher price in another market.

Asymmetric information: One party's possession of information in an economic transaction that the other party to the transaction does not possess.

Backward shifted: The amount of a tax that producers pay in the form of lower revenue per unit.

Balance of payments: A system of accounts that measures transaction of goods, services, income, and financial assets between domestic residents, businesses, and governments, and the rest of the world, during a specific time period.

Bank for International Settlements (BIS): An institution based in Basle, Switzerland, which serves as an agent for central banks and a center of economic cooperation among the largest industrialized nations.

Barriers to entry: Any factors inhibiting entrepreneurs from instantaneously founding a new firm.

Beggar-thy-neighbor policy: A policy action that benefits one nation's economy but worsens economic performance in another nation.

Business cycle: Fluctuations over time of a nation's income flows that are derived from spending on goods and services produced by its firms.

Call option: An options contract giving the owner the right to purchase an amount of a currency at a specific rate of exchange.

Capital and financial account: A tabulation of the flows of financial assets between domestic private residents and businesses and foreign private residents and businesses.

Capital: The physical equipment and buildings used to produce goods and services.

Combination tariff: A tariff that combines an *ad valorem* tariff and a specific tariff.

Common market: A trading arrangement under which member nations remove all barriers to trade among their group, erect common barriers to trade with other countries outside the group, and permit unhindered movements of factors of production within the group.

Common property: A non-exclusive resource owned by everyone and therefore by no single individual.

Comparative advantage: The ability of a nation's residents to produce an additional unit of a good or service at a lower opportunity cost relative to other nations.

Concentration ratio: The share of total industry sales by the top few firms.

Conditionality: The set of limitations on the range of allowable actions of government of a country that is a recipient of IMF loans.

Consumer price index (CPI): A weighted sum of prices of goods and services that a typical consumer purchases each year.

Consumer surplus: The benefit that consumers receive from the existence of a market price. Consumer surplus is measured as the difference between what consumers are willing and able to pay for a good or service, and the market price.

Consumption possibilities: All possible combinations of goods and services that a nation's residents can consume.

Convertibility: The ability to freely exchange a currency for a reserve commodity or reserve currency.

Copyright: An author's legal title to the sole right to reproduce, distribute, perform, or display creative works, including articles, books, software, and audio and video recordings.

Corners hypothesis: The view that policymakers should choose fully flexible or hard-peg exchange-rate regimes over intermediate regimes such as adjustable-peg, crawling-peg, or basket-peg arrangements.

Countervailing duty (CVD): A tax on imported goods and services designed to offset the domestic price effect of foreign export policies.

Covered exposure: A foreign exchange risk that has been completely eliminated with a hedging instrument.

Covered interest parity: A prediction that the interest rate on one nation's bond should approximately equal the interest rate on a similar bond in another nation plus the forward premium, or the difference between forward exchange rate and the spot exchange rate divided by the spot exchange rate.

Crawling band: A range of exchange values that combines features of a crawling peg with the flexibility of an exchange-rate band.

Crawling peg: An exchange-rate system in which a country pegs its currency to the currency of another nation, but allows the parity value to change at regular time intervals.

Credit entry: A positive entry in the balance of payments that records a transaction resulting in a payment to a domestic resident from abroad.

Credit policy: Central bank policymaking involving direct lending to private financial institutions and non-financial firms.

Cross-border mergers and acquisitions: The combining of firms located in different nations, in which one firm absorbs the assets and liabilities of another firm (merger), or purchases the assets and liabilities of another firm (acquisition).

Currency board: An independent monetary authority that substitutes for a central bank. The currency board pegs the value of the domestic currency, and changes in the foreign reserve holdings of the currency board determine the level of the domestic money stock.

Currency futures: An agreement to deliver to another party a standardized quantity of a specific nation's currency at a designated future date.

Currency option: A contract granting the right to buy or sell a given amount of a nation's currency at a certain price within a given period or on a specific date.

Currency swap: An exchange of payment flows denominated in different currencies.

Currency-basket peg: An exchange-rate system in which a country pegs its currency to the weighted average value of a basket, or selected number of currencies.

Current account: Measures the flow of goods, services, income, and transfers or gifts between domestic residents, businesses, and governments, and the rest of the world.

Customs union: A trading arrangement that entails eliminating barriers to trade among participating nations and common barriers to trade with other countries outside the group.

Dead capital: Capital resources for which people fail to possess unambiguous title of ownership, which makes these resources difficult to transfer among entrepreneurs.

Deadweight loss: A loss of consumer or producer surplus that is not transferred to any other party and that represents a decline in economy efficiency.

Debit entry: A negative entry in the balance of payments that records a transaction resulting in a payment abroad by a domestic resident.

Demand: The relationship between the prices that consumers are willing and able to pay for various quantities of a good or service for a given time period, all other things being constant.

Devalue: A situation in which a nation with a pegged exchange-rate arrangement changes the pegged, or parity, value of its currency so that it takes a greater number of domestic currency units to purchase one unit of the foreign currency.

Development economics: The study of factors that contribute to the improvement in a nation's technological capabilities, advancement of the range of products available to its consumers, and growth of the incomes of its residents.

Discount rate: The interest rate that the Federal Reserve charges on discount window loans that it extends to depository institutions.

Diseconomies of scale: An increase in long-run average cost caused by an increase in a firm's output.

Dollarization: A system in which the currency of another nation circulates as the sole legal tender.

Dollar-standard exchange-rate system: An exchange-rate system in which a country pegs the value of its currency to the U.S. dollar and freely exchanges the domestic currency for the dollar at the pegged rate.

Domestic credit: Total domestic securities and loans held as assets by a central bank.

Dumping: A situation in which a firm sells its output to foreign consumers at a price less than what the firm charges its domestic consumers, or when a foreign firm prices its exports below their cost of product.

Early warning system: A mechanism that multinational institutions might use to track financial crisis indicators to determine that a crisis is on the horizon, thereby permitting a rapid response to head off the crisis.

Economic efficiency: A condition when scarce resources are allocated in a most productive, least-cost pattern.

Economic exposure: The risk that changes in exchange values might alter today's value of a firm's future income streams.

Economic fundamentals: Basic factors determining a nation's current exchange rate, such as the country's current and likely future economic policies and performance.

Economic growth definition: An expression defining a country's rate of economic growth as the rate of increase in its aggregate real income minus the rate of increase in its population.

Economic growth: Occurs when a nation experiences an increase in available resources or a technological advance and the nation's production possibilities expand. The rate of change over time in a nation's per capita real income.

Economic integration: The extent and strength of real sector and financial sector linkages among national economies.

Economic profit: Total revenue minus explicit and implicit opportunity costs.

Economic union: A trading arrangement that commits participating nations to remove all barriers to trade among their group, to abide by common restrictions on trade with other countries outside the group, to allow unhindered movements of factors of production within the group, and to closely coordinate all economic policies with other participants.

Economies of scale: A reduction in long-run average cost induced by an increase in a firm's output.

Effective exchange rate: A weighted-average measure of the value of a currency relative to two or more currencies.

Efficient-markets hypothesis: A theory that stems from application of the rational expectations hypothesis to financial markets, which states that equilibrium prices of and returns on bonds should reflect all past and current information plus traders' understanding of how market prices and returns are determined.

Entrepreneurs: People who specialize in organizing labor and capital resources to bring about production of goods and services.

Equilibrium market price: The price at which quantity supplied equals quantity demanded. At the equilibrium market price, there is neither an excess quantity demanded nor an excess quantity supplied.

European option: An option in which the holder may buy or sell an amount of a currency only on the day that the contract expires.

Ex ante **conditionality**: The imposition of IMF lending conditions before the IMF grants the loan.

Ex post **conditionality**: The imposition of IMF lending conditions after a loan has already been granted.

Excess quantity demanded: The amount by which quantity demanded exceeds quantity supplied at a given price.

Excess quantity supplied: The amount by which quantity supplied exceeds quantity demanded at a given price.

Exchange rate: Expresses the value of one currency relative to another currency as the number of units of one currency required to purchase one unit of the other currency.

Exchange-rate band: A range of exchange values with an upper and lower limit within which the exchange value of the domestic currency can fluctuate.

Exchange-rate system: A set of rules that determine the international value of a currency.

Exercise price: The price at which the holder of an option has the right to buy or sell a financial instrument; also known as the strike price.

Export subsidy: A payment by a government to a domestic firm for exporting its goods or services.

External economies: Cost reductions obtained from locating a firm's operations near factors that are external to the firm, such as skilled labor, capital resources, or research and development facilities.

Externality: A spillover effect influencing the welfare of third parties not involved in transactions within a marketplace.

Factor price equalization theorem: A theorem indicating that, under the assumptions of the factor proportions model, uninterrupted trade will bring about equalization of goods prices and factor prices across nations.

Factors of production: The resources firms utilize to produce goods and services.

Financial crisis indicator: An economic variable that normally moves in a specific direction and by a certain relative amount in advance of a financial crisis, thereby helping to predict a coming crisis.

Financial crisis: A situation that arises when financial instability becomes so severe that the nation's financial system is unable to function. A financial crisis typically involves a banking crisis, a currency crisis, and a foreign debt crisis.

Financial instability: When a nation's financial sector is no longer able to allocate funds to the most productive projects.

Financial sector development: The strengthening and growth of a nation's financial sector institutions, payments systems, and regulatory agencies.

Financial sector: A designation for the portion of the economy in which people trade financial assets.

First-best trade policy: A trade policy that deals directly with a problem that policymakers seek to remedy.

First-mover advantage: A barrier to entry arising from the ability of the initial firm in an industry to develop marketing advantage by identifying its own product as the industry product.

Fiscal agent: A term describing a central bank's role as an agent of its government's finance ministry or treasury department, in which the central bank issues, services, and redeems debts on the government's behalf.

Flexible exchange-rate system: An exchange-rate system whereby a nation allows market forces to determine the international value of its currency.

Foreign direct investment: The acquisition of assets that involves a long-term relationship and controlling interest of 10 percent or greater in an enterprise located in another economy.

Foreign exchange derivative instruments: Currency instruments with a return that is linked to, or derived from, the returns of other financial instruments.

Foreign exchange market efficiency: A situation in which the equilibrium spot and forward exchange adjust to reflect all available information, in which case the forward premium is equal to the expected rate of currency depreciation plus any risk premium. This, in turn, implies that the forward exchange rate on average predicts the expected future spot exchange rate.

Foreign exchange market: A system of private banks, foreign exchange brokers, and central banks through which households, firms, and governments buy and sell national currencies.

Foreign exchange risk: The risk that the value of a future receipt or obligation will change due to variations in foreign exchange rates.

Foreign currency-denominated financial instrument: A financial asset, such as a bond, a stock, or a bank deposit, whose value is denominated in the currency of another nation.

Forward exchange market: A market for contracts that ensures the future delivery of and payment for a foreign currency at a specified exchange rate.

Forward premium or discount: The difference between the forward exchange rate and the spot exchange rate expressed as a percentage of the spot exchange rate.

Forward shifted: The portion of a tax that consumers pay in the form of a higher price per unit.

Free trade area: A trading arrangement that removes all barriers to trade among participating nations, but that allows each nation to retain its own restrictions on trade with countries outside the free trade area.

Free-rider problem: The potential for an individual to try to avoid contributing funds to pay for provision of a public good because he or she presumes that others will do so.

Gains from trade: Additional goods and services that a nation's residents can consume, over and above the amounts that they could have produced within their own borders, as a consequence of trade with residents of other nations.

General Agreement on Tariffs and Trade (GATT): An international agreement among more than 140 nations about rules governing cross-border trade in goods.

General Agreement on Trade in Services (GATS): An international agreement among more than 130 nations about rules under which services are traded internationally.

Global public good: A good or service that yields benefits to a number of the world's people simultaneously, cannot provide benefits to one person without others around the world deriving benefits at no additional cost, and cannot be withheld from a person who has failed to contribute to its provision.

Globalization: The increasing interconnectedness of peoples and societies and the interdependence of economies, governments, and environments.

Group of Eight (G8): The nations France, Germany, Japan, the United Kingdom, the United States, Canada, Italy, and Russia.

Group of Five (G5): The nations France, Germany, Japan, the United Kingdom, and the United States.

Group of Seven (G7): The nations France, Germany, Japan, the United Kingdom, the United States, Canada, and Italy.

Group of Ten (G10): The nations France, Germany, Japan, the United Kingdom, the United States, Canada, Italy, Belgium, the Netherlands, and Sweden.

Growth equation: A relationship indicating that the rate of growth in a country's aggregate real income is equal to the sum of three components: the rate of growth of productivity of labor and capital; the contribution to aggregate real income of labor resources multiplied by the rate of growth of labor resources; and the contribution to aggregate real income of capital resources multiplied by the rate of growth of capital resources.

Heckscher–Ohlin theorem: A theorem stating that a relatively labor-abundant nation will export a relatively labor-intensive good, while a relatively capital-abundant nation will export a relatively capital-intensive good.

Hedging: The act of offsetting or eliminating risk exposure.

Herfindahl–Hirschman index: The sum of the squares of the market shares of each firm in an industry.

Horizontal foreign direct investment: Establishment of a foreign subsidiary of a multinational firm that produces a good or service that is similar to the one the firm produces in its home country.

Human capital: The knowledge and skills that workers possess.

Import quota: A policy that restricts the quantity of imports.

Industrial organization: The study of the structures of, and interactions among, firms and markets.

Industrial policies: Government policies intended to promote the development of specific national industries.

Innovation: A new process or product that yields tangible benefits sufficient for the process or product to be adopted in the marketplace.

Intellectual property rights: Laws granting ownership of creative ideas, typically in the form of a copyright, trademark, or patent.

Inter-industry trade: International trade of completely distinguishable goods and services.

International externality: A spillover effect arising from market activities in one nation that influences the welfare of third parties in another country.

International financial architecture: The international institutions, governmental and non-governmental organizations, and policies that govern activity in the international monetary and financial markets.

International Monetary Fund (IMF): A supranational organization whose major responsibility is to lend reserves to member nations experiencing a shortage.

International policy cooperation: The development of institutions and procedures through which central banks share data and inform one another about their policy objectives and strategies.

International policy coordination: The joint determination of monetary policies by a group of central banks for the intended combined benefit of the nations they represent.

International policy externalities: Spillover benefits or costs that policy actions within one nation have for the economies of other nations.

Intra-industry trade: International trade of goods or services that are closely substitutable.

Jamaica Accords: A meeting of the member nations of the IMF, occurring in January 1976, amending the constitution of the IMF to allow, among other things, each member nation to determine its own exchange-rate system.

Large country: A large country's market share is sufficiently large that the production and consumption decisions of its residents affect the global prices of goods and services.

Law of demand: An economic law that states that there is an inverse, or negative, relationship between the price that consumers are willing and able to pay and the quantities that they desire to purchase.

Law of diminishing marginal product: An economic law stating that, when more and more units of a factor of production such as labor are added to fixed amounts of other productive factors, the additional output for each new unit employed eventually declines.

Law of supply: An economic law that states that there is a positive or direct relationship between the prices producers receive and the quantities that they are willing to supply to the market.

Leaning against the wind: Central bank interventions to halt or reverse the current trend in the market exchange value of its nation's currency.

Leaning with the wind: Central bank interventions to support or speed along the current trend in the market exchange value of its nation's currency.

Lender of last resort: A central banking function in which the central bank stands willing to lend to any temporarily illiquid, but otherwise solvent, banking institution to prevent its illiquid position from leading to a general loss of confidence in that institution.

Leontief paradox: A finding by Wassily Leontief that contradicted the Heckscher–Ohlin theorem, in that it indicated that imports of the United States, a relatively capital-abundant nation, were relatively more capital intensive than exports of the United States.

Locomotive effect: A stimulus to economic activity in one nation generated by an increase in economic activity in another country.

Lombard rate: The specific name given to the interest rate on central bank advances that some central banks, such as the European Central Bank, set above current market interest rates.

Long-run average cost: The ratio of a firm's total production cost to its output when the firm has sufficient time to vary the quantities of all factors of production.

Louvre Accord: A meeting of the central bankers and finance ministers of the G7 nations, less Italy, that took place in February 1987. The participants announced that the exchange value of the dollar had fallen to a level consistent with "economic fundamentals," and that the central banks would intervene in the foreign exchange market only to ensure stability of exchange rates.

M1: Currency plus transactions deposits.

M2: M1 plus savings and small time deposits, overnight Eurocurrency and repurchase agreements, and balances of individual and broker-dealer money market mutual funds.

Magnification principle: A position of the Stolper–Samuelson theorem which implies that the change in the price of a factor is greater than the change in the price of the good that uses the factor relatively intensively in its production process.

Managed or dirty float: An exchange-rate system in which a nation allows the international value of its currency to be determined primarily by market forces, but intervenes from time to time to stabilize its currency.

Marginal cost: The additional cost that the firm incurs from producing an additional unit of output.

Marginal product of capital: The additional output generated by using an additional unit of capital.

Marginal product of labor: The additional output generated by employing the next unit of labor.

Marginal revenue product of capital: The additional revenue generated by using an additional unit of capital.

Marginal revenue product of labor: The additional revenue generated by employing an additional unit of labor; also equal to marginal revenue multiplied by the marginal product of labor.

Marginal revenue: The additional revenue a firm earns from selling an additional unit of output.

Market demand: A curve illustrating the prices consumers are willing and able to pay for various quantities of a good or service for a given time period, all other things being constant. Because of the negative relationship between price and quantity demanded, the demand curve slopes downward.

Market failure: Inability of unhindered private market processes to produce outcomes that are consistent with economic efficiency, individual freedom, and other broader social goals.

Market price: The price determined by the interactions of all consumers and producers in the marketplace.

Market supply: A curve illustrating the prices producers are willing to accept for various quantities of a good or service they supply to the market for a given time period, all other things being constant. Because of the positive relationship between price and quantity supplied, the supply curve slopes upward.

Market wage rate: The wage rate at which the quantity of labor supplied by all workers in a labor market is equal to the total quantity of labor demanded by firms in that market.

Merit good: A good or service that residents of a nation determine, typically through a political process, to be socially desirable.

Microlenders: Banking institutions that specialize in extending very small sums of credit to low-income entrepreneurs.

Minimum efficient scale: The size at which a firm or industry minimizes its long-run average cost over a time frame in which quantities of all factors of production may be adjusted.

Monetary aggregate: A grouping of assets sufficiently liquid to be defined as a measure of money.

Monetary base: Central bank holdings of domestic securities and loans plus foreign exchange reserves, or the sum of currency and bank reserves.

Monetary order: A set of laws and regulations that establishes the framework within which individuals conduct and settle transactions.

Monetary union: A set of countries that choose to use a common currency.

Monopolistic competition: An industry structure with a relatively large number of firms, easy entry or exit, and similar but not identical firm products.

Monopoly: An industry that consists of a single firm.

Moral hazard: The potential for a buyer or seller to behave differently after an economic transaction from what was agreed before the transaction.

Most favored nation (MFN): A country that receives reductions in trade barriers to promote open international trade.

Multilateralism: An approach to achieving freer international trade via a wide interplay among many of the world's nations, with an aim toward inducing each country to treat others equally in trading arrangements.

Nominal exchange rate: A bilateral exchange rate that is unadjusted for changes in the two nations' price levels.

Nominal interest rate: A rate of return in current-dollar terms that does not reflect anticipated inflation.

Non-tariff barriers: Instruments other than import tariffs that restrict international trade.

Official settlements balance: A balance-of-payments account that tabulates transactions of reserve assets by official government agencies.

Oligopoly: An industry structure in which a few firms are the predominant suppliers of the total output of an industry, so that their pricing and production decisions are interdependent.

Open-market operations: Central bank purchases or sales of government or private securities.

Opportunity cost: The highest-valued, next-best alternative that must be sacrificed to obtain an item.

Optimal currency area: A geographic area within which labor is sufficiently mobile to permit speedy adjustments to payment imbalances and regional unemployment to permit exchange rates to be fixed and a common currency to be adopted.

Outsourcing (or offshoring): Employment by a firm of labor outside the nation in which the firm is located.

Outsourcing: A strategy in which one organization hires another organization to complete a particular stage of the production process.

Overvalued currency: A currency in which the current market-determined value is higher than that predicted by an economic theory or model.

Parallel imports: Gray-market imports, or goods and services brought into a country without authorization after initially being permitted to be sold elsewhere.

Patent: An inventor's legal title to the sole right to manufacture, utilize, and market an invention for a specific period.

Pegged exchange-rate system: An exchange-rate system in which a country pegs the international value of the domestic currency to the currency of another nation.

Per capita real income: The ratio of a nation's aggregate, inflation-adjusted income divided by the country's population.

Plaza Agreement: A meeting of the central bankers and finance ministers of the G5 nations that took place at the Plaza Hotel, New York in September 1985. The participants announced that the exchange value of the dollar was too strong, and that the nations would coordinate their intervention actions in order to drive down the value of the dollar.

Policy-created distortion: When a government policy results in a market producing a level of output that is different from the economically efficient level of output, causing a less than optimal allocation of an economy's scarce resources.

Portfolio balance effect: An exchange rate adjustment resulting from changes in government or central bank holdings of foreign currency-denominated financial instruments that influence the equilibrium prices of the instruments.

Portfolio investment: The acquisition of foreign financial assets that results in less than a 10 percent ownership share in the entity.

Predatory pricing: A situation in which a firm sets artificially low prices intended to induce competitors to leave the industry and to dissuade potential rivals from entering the industry.

Preferential trade arrangement: A trading arrangement in which a nation grants partial trade preferences to one or more trading partners.

Price discrimination: Charging different consumers different prices for identical goods or services, or charging the same consumer different prices for the same good or service depending on the number of units that the consumer purchases.

Producer surplus: The benefit that producers receive from the existence of a market price. Producer surplus is measured as the difference between the price that producers are willing to accept to supply a particular quantity, and the market price.

Production possibilities: All possible combinations of total output of goods and services that residents of a nation can produce, given currently available technology and resources.

Public good: Any good or service that can be consumed by many people at the same time, cannot be consumed by one individual without others also consuming it at no extra cost, and cannot be withheld from a person who has not contributed to funding its production.

Purchasing power parity (PPP): A proposition that the price of a good or service in one nation should be the same as the exchange-rate-adjusted price of the same good or service in another nation.

Put option: An options contract giving the owner the right to sell an amount of a currency at a specific rate of exchange.

Quota rent: A portion of the loss of consumer surplus caused by an import quota that is transferred to the foreign supplier as additional profits.

Quota subscription: The pool of funds deposited by IMF member nations that IMF managers can use for loans to member nations experiencing financial difficulties.

Rational expectations hypothesis: The idea that individuals form expectations based on all available past and current information and on a basic understanding of how markets function.

Real exchange rate: A bilateral exchange rate that has been adjusted for price changes that occurred in the two nations.

Real interest parity: An equality between two nations' real interest rates that arises if both uncovered interest parity and relative PPP are satisfied.

Real interest rate: The anticipated rate of return from holding a bond after taking into account the extent to which inflation is expected to reduce the amount of goods and services that this return could be used to buy.

Real sector: A designation for the portion of the economy engaged in the production and sale of goods and services.

Redistributive effects of trade: Altered allocations of incomes among a nation's residents as a result of changes in international trade flows.

Regionalism: Establishment of trading agreements among geographic groupings of nations.

Relatively capital-abundant nation: In a two-country setting, the nation endowed with more capital units per labor unit than the other nation.

Relatively capital-intensive good: In a two-good setting, the good with a production process requiring more capital per labor unit than the other good.

Relatively labor-abundant nation: In a two-country setting, the nation endowed with more labor units per capital unit than the other nation.

Relatively labor-intensive good: In a two-good setting, the good with a production process requiring more labor per capital unit than the other good.

Relevant market: The true economic marketplace taking into account the availability of all products that directly constrain product prices for individual producers.

Reserve currency: The currency commonly used to settle international debts and to express the exchange value of other nations' currencies.

Reserve requirements: Central bank regulations requiring private banks to hold specified fractions of transactions and term deposits, either as vault cash or as funds on deposit at the central bank.

Resourcing: The acquisition of a firm's full range of inputs for utilization in its production process.

Revalue: A situation in which a nation with a pegged exchange-rate system changes the pegged, or parity, value of its currency so that it takes a smaller number of domestic currency units to purchase one unit of the foreign currency.

Rule of 72: A relationship indicating that the number of years required for a country's per capita real income to rise by a multiple factor of two is approximately equal to 72 divided by the average annual rate of economic growth.

Rules of origin: Regulations governing conditions under which products are eligible for trading preferences under trade agreements.

Rybczynski theorem: The theory that if a nation experiences an increase in the amount of a resource, it will produce more of the good that uses the resource relatively intensively in its production process, and will produce less of the other good.

Second-best trade policy: A trade policy that deals indirectly with a problem that policymakers seek to remedy.

Small country: A country so small its consumption and production decisions do not affect the international price, so that its residents take the international price as a given.

Sovereignty: The supremacy of a nation's citizens to control the resources within its geographic borders.

Special drawing right: A composite currency of the IMF in which the value is based on a weighted average of the currencies of five member nations.

Specific tariff: A tariff specified as an amount of money per unit of the good sold.

Speculative attack: A concerted effort by financial-market speculators to profit from anticipations of a depletion of official foreign exchange reserves via sales of assets denominated in the nation's currency, intended to induce abandonment of an exchange-rate target that will yield them profits in derivative markets.

Spot market: A market for immediate purchase and delivery of currencies.

Sterilization: A central bank policy of altering domestic credit in an equal and opposite direction relative to any variation in foreign exchange reserves so as to prevent the monetary base from changing.

Stolper–Samuelson theorem: Theory that, in the context of the factor proportions model, free trade raises the earnings of the nation's relatively abundant factors and lowers the earnings of the relatively scarce factors.

Strategic policymaking: The formulation of national policies in light of the structural linkages among nations and the ways in which policymakers in other nations make decisions.

Structural interdependence: A situation in which interconnectedness of national markets for goods, services, and financial assets causes events in one nation to affect the economies of other nations.

Supply: The relationship between the prices of a good or service and the quantities supplied to the market by producers within a given time period, all other things being constant.

Tariff: A tax on imported goods and services.

Tariff-rate quota: A quota that allows a specified quantity of a good to enter the country at a reduced tariff rate. Any quantity above that amount is subject to a higher tariff rate.

Tax base: The value of goods, services, incomes, or wealth subject to taxation.

Tax competition: Reducing tax rates below those of other regions in an effort to induce individuals and businesses to engage in taxable activities in that region.

Tax rate: A fraction of a tax base an individual or company is legally required to transmit to the government.

Technological improvement: An expanded capability to produce goods and services with the same set of resources.

Theory of optimal currency areas: An approach to determining the size of a geographic area within which residents' welfare is greater if their governments fix exchange rates or adopt a common currency.

Trade concentration ratio: The sum of bilateral trade shares within a regional trading bloc divided by the region's share of world trade.

Trade creation: An additional amount of international trade resulting from trade preferences that a nation grants to a trading partner.

Trade deflection: The movement of goods or components of goods from a country outside a trading arrangement to one within such an arrangement so that the seller can benefit from trading preferences within the arrangement.

Trade diversion: A shift in international trade caused by one nation giving trade preferences to another, which can cause trade with a third country to decline.

Trade share: One nation's flow of international trade as a percentage of a regional or global trade total.

Trademark: A company's legal title to a word or symbol that identifies its product and distinguishes it from the products of other firms.

Transaction exposure: The risk that the revenues or costs associated with a transaction expressed in terms of the domestic currency may change due to variations in exchange rates.

Translation exposure: Foreign exchange risk resulting from the conversion of a firm's foreign currency-denominated assets and liabilities into the domestic currency value.

Trilemma: The idea that nations may select a combination of two, but not all three, of the following policy options: fixed exchange rates, discretionary monetary policy, and liberalized capital markets.

Uncovered interest parity: A relationship between interest rates on bonds that are similar in all respects other than the fact that they are denominated in different nations' currencies. According to this condition, which applies to a situation in which an individual engages in unhedged currency trades to fund bond purchases abroad, the interest rate on the bond denominated in the currency that holders anticipate will depreciate must exceed the interest rate on the other bond by the rate at which the currency is expected to depreciate.

Undervalued currency: A currency in which the current market-determined value is lower than that predicted by an economic theory or model.

Value added: The revenue received by a producer less the cost of the intermediate good it purchased.

Vertical foreign direct investment: Establishment of a foreign subsidiary of a multinational firm that produces components that are assembled elsewhere, or uses components produced elsewhere to assemble the firm's final product.

Voluntary export restraint (VER): An agreement between policymakers and producers in two nations to restrict the exports at a good from one nation to the other.

World Bank: A sister institution of the International Monetary Fund that is more narrowly specialized in making loans to about 100 developing nations in an effort to promote their long-term development and growth.

World Trade Organization (WTO): The multinational organization that oversees multilateral trade negotiations and adjudicates trade disputes that arise under multilateral trade agreements formed under the GATT and the GATS.

Index